FISMA ar
Risk Management
Framework

FISMA and the Risk Management Framework

The New Practice of Federal Cyber Security

Stephen D. Gantz

Daniel R. Philpott

Darren Windham, Technical Editor

ELSEVIER

AMSTERDAM • BOSTON • HEIDELBERG • LONDON
NEW YORK • OXFORD • PARIS • SAN DIEGO
SAN FRANCISCO • SINGAPORE • SYDNEY • TOKYO

Syngress is an Imprint of Elsevier

Acquiring Editor: Chris Katsaropoulos
Editorial Project Manager: Ben Rearick
Project Manager: Priya Kumaraguruparan
Designer: Matthew Limbert

Syngress is an imprint of Elsevier
225 Wyman Street, Waltham, MA 02451, USA

Notices

Knowledge and best practice in this field are constantly changing. As new research and experience broaden our understanding, changes in research methods or professional practices, may become necessary. Practitioners and researchers must always rely on their own experience and knowledge in evaluating and using any information or methods described herein. In using such information or methods they should be mindful of their own safety and the safety of others, including parties for whom they have a professional responsibility.

To the fullest extent of the law, neither the Publisher nor the authors, contributors, or editors, assume any liability for any injury and/or damage to persons or property as a matter of products liability, negligence or otherwise, or from any use or operation of any methods, products, instructions, or ideas contained in the material herein.

Library of Congress Cataloging-in-Publication Data
FISMA and the risk management framework : the new practice of federal cyber security / edited by Stephen D. Gantz, Daniel R. Philpott—1st ed.
     p. cm.
  Includes bibliographical references and index.
  ISBN: 978-1-59749-641-4
1. Computer security—United States. 2. Computer security—Law and legislation—United States. 3. Information technology—Security measures—United States. 4. Electronic government information—Security measures—United States. 5. Administrative agencies—Information resources management—Security measures—United States. 6. Computer networks—Security measures—United States. 7. United States. Federal Information Security Management Act of 2002. I. Gantz, Stephen D. II. Philpott, Daniel R.
  QA76.9.A25F57   2013
  005.8—dc23

                                            2012039363

British Library Cataloguing-in-Publication Data
A catalogue record for this book is available from the British Library.

Printed in the United States of America
13 14 15   10 9 8 7 6 5 4 3 2 1

Working together to grow
libraries in developing countries

www.elsevier.com | www.bookaid.org | www.sabre.org

ELSEVIER   BOOK AID International   Sabre Foundation

For information on all Syngress publications visit our website at *www.syngress.com*

*This book is dedicated to my father, David A. Gantz,
a gentleman and a scholar.*

Contents

Trademarks

International Council of Electronic Commerce Consultants EC-Council Certified Security Analyst (ECSA)

International Information Systems Security Certification Consortium Certified Accreditation Professional (CAP)

ISACA Certified Information Systems Auditor (CISA)

Microsoft Word and Excel

SANS Institute Global Information Assurance Certification (GIAC)

SANS Institute GIAC Systems and Network Auditor (GSNA)

SecureInfo Risk Management Services (RMS)

Symantec Enterprise Security Manager

Telos Xacta IA Manager

Trusted Integration Trusted Agent FISMA

Acknowledgements

I would like to thank Dan Philpott for conceiving and proposing the book project and for his tireless efforts working to stay abreast of activity and publications coming out of FISMA implementation and other federal security initiatives. I am grateful for the expert support from the Syngress/Elsevier team throughout the long process of bringing this project to fruition, including Angelina Ward, Matt Cater, Steve Elliot, Chris Katsaropoulos, and Meagan White. Thanks also go to Darren Windham for his constructive feedback and technical edits on the book.

I owe a professional debt of gratitude to many of the career civil servants with whom I have worked over the years, particularly including former HHS Deputy CIO John Teeter, HHS Chief Enterprise Architect Mary Forbes, and former HHS and VA CISO Jaren Doherty. I also sincerely appreciate the leadership of Ron Ross and the dedicated team of government and contractor personnel at NIST working on the FISMA Implementation Project and the Joint Task Force Transformation Initiative.

Many friends and co-workers listened attentively and provided a sounding board for ideas incorporated into the book. These patient individuals include colleagues Jim Chen, Davis Foster, Vicki Bowen, Marco Demartin, Tom Howe, Arthur Haubold, and Erik Rolf. This project would not have been possible without the support of my wife Reneé, my son Henry, and my daughters Claire and Gillian. I appreciate their indulgence throughout the writing process.

About the Author

Stephen D. Gantz (CISSP-ISSAP, CEH, CGEIT, CRISC, CIPP/G, C|CISO) is an information security and IT consultant with over 20 years of experience in security and privacy management, enterprise architecture, systems development and integration, and strategic planning. He currently holds an executive position with a health information technology services firm primarily serving federal and state government customers. He is also an Associate Professor of Information Assurance in the Graduate School at University of Maryland University College. He maintains a security-focused website and blog at http://www.securityarchitecture.com.

Steve's security and privacy expertise spans program management, security architecture, policy development and enforcement, risk assessment, and regulatory compliance with major legislation such as FISMA, HIPAA, and the Privacy Act. His industry experience includes health, financial services, higher education, consumer products, and manufacturing, but since 2000 his work has focused on security and other information resources management functions in federal government agencies. His prior work history includes completing projects for government clients including the Departments of Defense, Labor, and Health and Human Services, Office of Management and Budget, Federal Deposit Insurance Corporation, U.S. Postal Service, and U.S. Senate.

Steve holds a master's degree in public policy from the Kennedy School of Government at Harvard University, and also earned his bachelor's degree from Harvard. He is nearing completion of the Doctor of Management program at UMUC, where his dissertation focuses on trust and distrust in networks and inter-organizational relationships. Steve currently resides in Arlington, Virginia with his wife Reneé and children Henry, Claire, and Gillian.

Introduction

The Federal Information Security Management Act (FISMA) provides the framework for securing information systems in federal government agencies and managing risk associated with information resources in those organizations. Within this framework, the National Institute of Standards and Technology (NIST), the Office of Management and Budget (OMB), and many other federal agencies engage in an ongoing collaborative effort to produce the implementation guidance agencies need to successfully implement effective information security management programs and practices. The provisions in FISMA, combined with extensive implementation rules, standards, and guidance issued to agencies under the law's authority, define a comprehensive, consistent, repeatable approach for information security risk management. This book explains the FISMA legislation, identifies the expectations and obligations on federal agencies subject to FISMA and others choosing to follow its provisions, and describes the processes and activities needed to implement effective information security management following FISMA and using the NIST Risk Management Framework.

INTRODUCTION

Contemporary organizations depend on information technology. Both public and private sector organizations rely on information and information systems to enable business operations, enhance productivity, and support the efficient delivery of products and services. Effective use of information technology drives economic performance, spurs innovation, and can even produce competitive advantage for organizations particularly adept at information resources management. In public sector organizations, information technology provides critical support to the execution of mission functions and business processes and when used effectively offers enormous benefits in terms of cost savings, process efficiency, and quality of service to citizens. For over 30 years, federal government agencies have been encouraged and even obligated to automate information collection, improve the efficiency with which they deliver services, and adopt effective uses of information technology, including practices for information technology management. Laws enacted to achieve widespread adoption of information technology explicitly recognize the potential benefits to agencies [1], but the pervasive use of IT and, especially, organizational dependence on information and information systems is not without risk. This fact is recognized in laws, regulations, and policies that require federal agencies to safeguard the privacy and security of their information and information systems, and by doing so to reduce their risk from operating and using information technology [2].

Organizations face a variety of threats due to their use of information technology with the potential to cause loss, damage, harm, or other adverse effects. The often substantial risk represented by these threats and the impact of adverse events that might occur must be balanced against the benefits organizations realize from their use of information technology. Achieving and maintaining the appropriate level of risk—considering both the value of information and information systems to the organization and the potential adverse effects on the organization resulting from their use—is the focus of risk management. The discipline of information security management is a key component of risk management, where the selection, implementation, and effective use of protective measures collectively seek to reduce the risk associated with information systems to a level acceptable to the organization. Risk due to information systems is just one of many types of risk that organizations must manage, but the variety and diversity of threats and vulnerabilities affecting information systems, the complexity of many organizational operating environments, and the differing priorities and levels of risk tolerance among agencies make effective risk management a challenging endeavor.

The primary objective of federal information security management is to provide adequate security, where *adequate* means security commensurate with the risk of adverse impact to the organization resulting from the loss of confidentiality, integrity, or availability of information [3]. Adequate security is both risk-based and cost-effective, taking into account the financial and other resources required to provide security protection and the magnitude of harm that would occur if risk to the organization is realized. FISMA emphasizes the goal of cost-effective reduction of information security risk; in this respect the law and other federal information security management guidance are consistent with the principle of adequate protection, which dictates that an asset should be protected at a level commensurate with its value, and only for as long as the asset has value to the organization [4]. What is important to understand when considering current federal security requirements is that the goal of adequate security is not the same as achieving optimal security, strong security, or even the most effective security. Instead, the purpose of FISMA and associated guidance is to help agencies determine and implement the minimum security controls necessary to protect their information and information systems [5]. Agencies are free to provide additional security beyond the minimum requirements, but decisions to do so should be cost-justified and aligned with organizational risk tolerance. Organizations that focus on compliance in their information security management programs often limit their attention to minimum security requirements without considering the broader risk management context. The difference between *compliant* information security and *effective* information security management lies within risk management—information security is effective when it reduces risk due to information systems to an acceptable level, and supports the maintenance of risk at acceptable levels on an ongoing basis. This book is about effective risk management, not about compliance. The material presented throughout the book approaches information security management requirements and agency expectations from a risk management perspective, to explain how relevant security management practices satisfy the objectives of effective information security and provide essential support to enterprise risk management across all levels of the organization.

Purpose and Rationale

Incorporating risk in information resources management, including information security decision making, is not a novel concept, but the establishment and consistent use of organization-wide risk management practices represents a significant shift in management focus for many organizations. The primary purpose of this book is to help managers at all organizational levels understand and apply effective risk management practices, with particular emphasis on managing risk associated with information systems and the information they contain. To provide this assistance, the material in this book addresses all the processes and activities involved in information security risk management, leveraging relevant official government documentation and incorporating a variety of other standards, industry practices, and sources of guidance where appropriate.

Although FISMA specifies several requirements applicable to agency information security programs, initial implementation of the law's risk management provisions reflected a consistent emphasis on assessing and mitigating risk at the level of individual information systems. This emphasis was evident in key standards and guidance issued by NIST [7] and FISMA reporting requirements specified by OMB [8], which focused on processes and activities associated with certifying and accrediting agency information systems and reporting the results of C&A processes to OMB. Beginning in 2009, NIST led a transformation in emphasis for its information security guidance from a relatively narrow focus on certification and accreditation of individual systems to an enterprise risk management approach considering information security and risk from information system, mission and business, and organization levels, as shown conceptually in Figure 1.1.

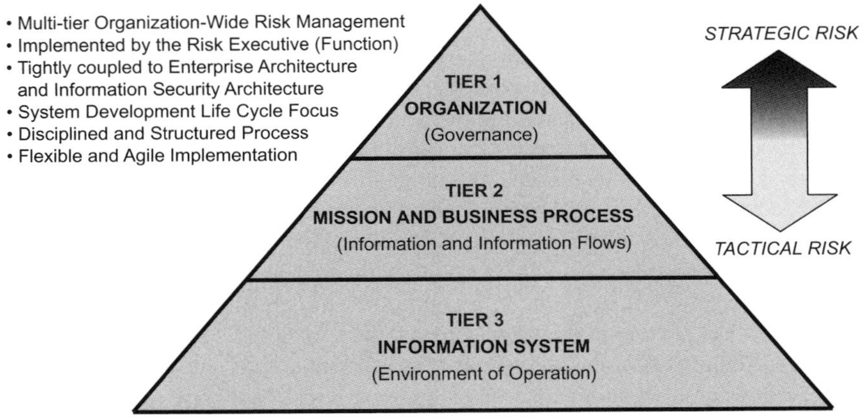

- Multi-tier Organization-Wide Risk Management
- Implemented by the Risk Executive (Function)
- Tightly coupled to Enterprise Architecture and Information Security Architecture
- System Development Life Cycle Focus
- Disciplined and Structured Process
- Flexible and Agile Implementation

STRATEGIC RISK

TIER 1
ORGANIZATION
(Governance)

TIER 2
MISSION AND BUSINESS PROCESS
(Information and Information Flows)

TACTICAL RISK

TIER 3
INFORMATION SYSTEM
(Environment of Operation)

FIGURE 1.1 The Tiered Risk Management Approach Relies on Contributions from all Layers of the Organization to Prioritize and Effectively Address Enterprise Risk [6]

This revised approach positions information security management activities within the Risk Management Framework (RMF) defined in Special Publication 800-37 Revision 1 and illustrated in Figure 1.2, and clarifies the role of information security management as an essential element of organizational risk management [9]. This book describes current expectations and recommended practices for organizational risk management in federal government agencies and other organizations, using the activities and key intended outcomes of the Risk Management Framework as an organizing scheme.

FISMA, enacted in 2002 as Title III of the E-Government Act, recognized a need for more consistent and more effective government-wide management of information security risks, and for the development and adoption of information security standards and guidelines for federal agencies to use to provide appropriate protection to their information and information systems [5]. To facilitate achievement of the FISMA's objectives (many of which reiterated elements of previous legislation including the Computer Security Act of 1987 and the Government Information Security Reform Act of 2000, both of which FISMA superseded), NIST developed or updated many federal information processing standards for information security and a large body of guidance to agencies on information security practices, procedures, and technologies. Despite the relative brevity of the text of the FISMA legislation—comprising only 16 pages as published in the US Statutes at large [11]—subsequent guidance from NIST, OMB, and other official sources on implementing the provisions in the law comprises thousands of pages of documentation. This book provides recommendations to readers conducting risk management activities on effectively utilizing federal standards and guidelines and other applicable sources and identifies relevant sources of guidance for all those activities.

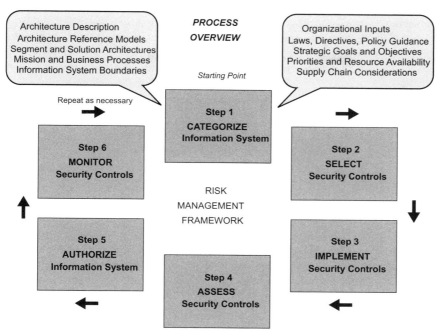

FIGURE 1.2 The NIST Risk Management Framework Defines an Iterative Process Cycle Incorporating Security Planning, System Authorization, and Continuous Monitoring [10]

How to Use This Book

This book is primarily intended to support the performance of effective risk management in organizations subject to FISMA or in other organizations that seek to leverage the extensive information security guidance developed for federal government agencies. The material is organized in a way that facilitates following all the steps in the Risk Management Framework, but should be equally helpful for readers that need to conduct a single activity (such as a risk assessment) or develop a key security artifact (such as a system security plan). In contrast to some other sources available in the marketplace, this book is not a compliance checklist for certification and accreditation, although it does describe in detail all of the tasks required to successfully complete the system authorization process. Finally, because it covers information security and privacy topics and considerations for organizations beyond what FISMA requires, readers should find this book a useful reference on many aspects of information security management.

Key Audience

The requirements in FISMA apply to federal executive agencies, so the primary audience for this book includes system owners, IT managers, security officers, risk managers, and other personnel with responsibility for securing, managing, or overseeing federal information systems and the mission functions and business processes those systems support. This group of stakeholders includes contractors, consultants, and service providers that develop, operate, or support information systems on behalf of the government. Many state and local government agencies voluntarily follow some or all aspects of FISMA and associated standards and guidance, and the broad scope and free availability of federal information security guidance make it attractive for use in the private sector too, so the material in this book is also intended for practitioners and managers in these organizations.

FISMA APPLICABILITY AND IMPLEMENTATION

The applicability of FISMA provisions is based on organization type and on the designation of information systems within each organization. Specifically, FISMA applies only to information systems operated by or on behalf of government organizations in the federal executive branch—the law uses the term agencies to denote these organizations as agencies, where *agency* is defined as "any executive department, military department, Government corporation, Government controlled corporation, or other establishment in the executive branch of the Government (including the Executive Office of the President), or any independent regulatory agency" [12]. This means that systems used by the Senate and the House of Representatives or by the federal courts are not subject to FISMA and its associated regulations. FISMA covers all federal information systems except National Security Systems, a designation indicating a system's use involves intelligence activities, cryptologic activities related to national security, military command and control, weapons systems, or mission-critical military or intelligence functions [13]. As noted in Chapter 2, the exclusion from coverage of National Security Systems reflects an assumption that such systems are already subject to information security and privacy protections that meet or exceed those mandated under FISMA. Beyond the definition in the law, NIST provides additional guidance on identifying National Security Systems in Special Publication 800-59 [14]. For systems subject to FISMA, the law assigns separate oversight responsibility to the Secretary of Defense and Director of National Intelligence for Department of Defense and intelligence systems, respectively, and to the Director of the Office of Management and Budget for systems in all other executive agencies.

Implementation Responsibilities

FISMA delegates the authority to prescribe standards and guidelines for federal information systems to the National Institute of Standards and Technology (NIST) and gives the Secretary of Commerce (NIST is a part of the Department of Commerce) the authority to make such standards mandatory [15]. These provisions reiterate NIST's primary role in developing standards and guidelines for protecting the security and privacy of information in federal information systems, a responsibility first assigned to NIST by the Computer Security Act of 1987 [16]. NIST established the FISMA Implementation Project within its Computer Security Division to support the development of standards and guidelines necessary to implement the law's provisions, and continues to coordinate development, revision, and issuance of associated federal information processing standards and Special Publications. NIST also entered into a collaborative venture with the Department of Defense, Office of the Director for National Intelligence, and the Committee on National Security Systems (CNSS) to harmonize information security standards and guidelines and risk management practices across the federal government. This effort, called the Joint Task Force Transformation Initiative Interagency Working Group, produced Special Publication 800-39—the flagship document in the NIST 800 Series of Special Publications—and completed major updates to other key guidelines including Special Publications 800-37, 800-53, and 800-53A. The executive commitment from leaders in civilian, defense, and intelligence sectors of the government to the Joint Task Force Transformation Initiative suggests that government-wide risk management and information security and privacy protections will converge in the future to a shared approach consistent with the Risk Management Framework defined in Special Publication 800-37 Revision 1.

FISMA Progress to Date

FISMA requires federal agencies to provide annual reports to Congress summarizing their compliance with the law's requirements, and to provide information about their information security programs to OMB to support OMB's oversight of agency information security programs [5]. Annual FISMA reports to Congress provide aggregate and agency-level performance data on different aspects of information security management, with the specific metrics varying from year to year as federal information security priorities and focus areas change. For the first eight years (through fiscal year 2009) following FISMA's enactment, published security metrics emphasized agency compliance in terms of the proportion of systems in agency FISMA inventories with successful certification and accreditation, implemented and tested contingency plans, and implemented and tested security controls, with compliance scores that peaked in 2008 when all three metrics were over 90% [17]. Beginning after the passage of the Government Information Security Reform Act in 2000 and running through 2007, the House Committee on Government Reform also issued annual "report cards" on computer security in federal government agencies. Between 2003 and 2007, when those report cards were based on FISMA requirements, the government-wide average rose from a "D" in 2003 to a "C" in 2007, suggesting that FISMA produced an improvement in overall government performance on information security. More recent FISMA reports note continued high rates of compliance with the law and emphasize results from new security metrics, introduced in fiscal year 2010, including implementation rates for identity management activities, automated configuration management, and vulnerability monitoring capabilities, encryption on portable computing devices, incident response, and security and awareness training [18]. This apparent general trend of continuous improvement in agency information security programs coincides with a dramatic rise in the number of security incidents reported by federal agencies, which increased more than 750% from 2006 to 2010 [19]. Although some of the reported increase in incidents may be attributed to improved monitoring and awareness efforts, the increasing incidence of security events observed by government agencies and the rise and pervasiveness of cyber attacks and other threats to government networks, systems, and infrastructure drive ongoing efforts in Congress to revise FISMA or enact new legislation to enhance information security for government organizations, particularly through the increased use of continuous monitoring of information systems and automated security reporting [20].

FISMA PROVISIONS

The text of the FISMA legislation enumerates six purposes [21], the first four of which appeared previously in the Government Information Security Reform Act of 2000 [22]:

1. Provide a comprehensive framework for ensuring the effectiveness of information security controls over information resources that support federal operations and assets.
2. Recognize the highly networked nature of the current federal computing environment and provide effective government-wide management and oversight of the related information security risks, including coordination of information security efforts throughout the civilian, national security, and law enforcement communities.
3. Provide for development and maintenance of minimum controls required to protect federal information and information systems.
4. Provide a mechanism for improved oversight of federal agency information security programs.
5. Acknowledge that commercially developed information security products offer advanced, dynamic, robust, and effective information security solutions, reflecting market solutions for the protection of critical information infrastructures important to the national defense and economic security of the nation.
6. Recognize that the selection of specific technical hardware and software information security solutions should be left to individual agencies from among commercially developed products.

The law prescribes requirements for all federal agencies, specifying distinct and overlapping responsibilities at the head-of-agency, Chief Information Officer, and agency information security program levels. At the organization level, agencies must protect their information and information systems with security measures commensurate with the risk the agency faces from potential unauthorized access to or use, disclosure, disruption, modification, or destruction of their information assets. Agencies also must comply with the provisions in the law and integrate information security management with strategic and operational planning processes [23]. In the context of these broad requirements, FISMA assigns the responsibility to each agency Chief Information Officer to [23]:

- Designate a senior agency information security officer (a position in many agencies given the title Chief Information Security Officer).
- Establish an agency information security management program.
- Develop and maintain information security policies, procedures, and controls to address all applicable requirements (including existing statutory obligations separate from FISMA provisions).
- Ensure personnel with information security responsibilities are properly trained and overseen.
- Assist other senior agency officials in fulfilling their responsibilities under the law, including reporting annually to the agency head on the effectiveness of the information security management program.

A large proportion of the NIST standards and guidance to agencies issued since FISMA's enactment in 2002 corresponds to agency program requirements in the law. Table 1.1 summarizes FISMA requirements for agency information security programs and identifies the primary sources of implementation guidance available to agencies to help them comply with those requirements.

FISMA also requires annual independent evaluation of each agency information security program, with results reported to OMB; directs agencies to address information security policies, procedures, and practices in reports regarding agency budgets, information resources management, program performance, financial management, and internal accounting and administrative controls; and requires agencies to maintain an inventory of major information systems.

Standards and Guidelines for Federal Information Systems

Separate from requirements directed at federal agencies and their security programs, FISMA establishes standards that apply to federal information systems, which the law defines as information systems "used or operated by an executive agency, by a contractor of an executive agency, or by another organization on behalf of an executive agency" [24]. Within the scope of standards and guidelines FISMA authorizes NIST to prescribe, the law explicitly makes mandatory standards that provide minimum information security requirements and that are needed to improve the security of federal information and information systems [24]. NIST addressed this requirement with FIPS 200, *Minimum Security Requirements for Federal Information and Information Systems*, which directs agencies to select and implement appropriate security controls described in Special Publication 800-53, *Recommended Security Controls for Federal Information*

Table 1.1 FISMA Requirements for Agency Information Security Programs and Corresponding Implementation Guidance

Requirement [23]	Sources of Implementation Guidance
Periodic assessment of risk and magnitude of harm resulting from unauthorized access, use, disclosure, disruption, modification, or destruction of information and information systems	Special Publication 800-30 Revision 1 (draft), *Guide for Conducting Risk Assessments*
Risk-based policies and procedures that cost-effectively reduce information security risk to an acceptable level, address information security throughout the life cycle of each information system, and ensure compliance with FISMA requirements	Special Publication 800-39, *Managing Information Security Risk: Organization, Mission, and Information System View* Special Publication 800-64 Revision 2, *Security Considerations in the System Development Life Cycle*
Plans for providing adequate information security for networks, facilities, and information systems	Special Publication 800-18 Revision 1, *Guide for Developing Security Plans for Federal Information Systems*
Security awareness training for personnel and contractors using agency information systems	Special Publication 800-50, *Building an Information Technology Security Awareness and Training Program*
Periodic testing and evaluation of the effectiveness of information security policies, procedures, and practices	Special Publication 800-53A Revision 1, *Guide for Assessing the Security Controls in Federal Information Systems and Organizations* Special Publication 800-115, *Technical Guide to Information Security Testing and Assessment*
A process for planning, implementing, evaluating, and documenting remedial action to address deficiencies in agency information security policies, procedures, and practices	Special Publication 800-39, *Managing Information Security Risk: Organization, Mission, and Information System View* Special Publication 800-37 Revision 1, *Guide for Applying the Risk Management Framework to Federal Information Systems*
Procedures for detecting, reporting, and responding to security incidents	Special Publication 800-61 Revision 1, *Computer Security Incident Handling Guide*
Plans and procedures to ensure continuity of operations for information systems	Special Publication 800-34 Revision 1, *Contingency Planning Guide for Federal Information Systems*
Annual reporting to OMB and Congress on the adequacy and effectiveness of information security policies, procedures, and practices and compliance with FISMA requirements	Annual OMB Memoranda, *Reporting Instructions for the Federal Information Security Management Act and Agency Privacy Management*

Systems and Organizations. Minimum requirements in FISMA for NIST developed standards and guidelines also include [25]:

- Standards for categorizing information and information systems based on risk and corresponding requirements for information security protection (FIPS 199, *Standards for Security Categorization of Federal Information and Information Systems*).
- Guidelines for types of information and information systems included in each category (Special Publication 800-60 Revision 1, *Guide for Mapping Types of Information and Information Systems to Security Categories*).
- Guidelines concerning detection and handling of information security incidents (Special Publication 800-61 Revision 1, *Computer Security Incident Handling Guide*).
- Guidelines for identifying an information system as a National Security System (Special Publication 800-59, *Guideline for Identifying an Information System as a National Security System*).

Despite the agency requirement to comply with federal information processing standards and obligation to follow guidance in Special Publications, FISMA directs NIST to ensure that its standards and guidelines allow agencies flexibility to choose alternative solutions and approaches to addressing information security risks, permit the use of commercial information security products where applicable, and avoid requiring the use of specific technologies. This flexibility is an essential element of effective risk-based information security management, as it gives agencies the ability to tailor their security programs and implement security controls that satisfy their own security requirements and facilitate compliance with the law.

System Certification and Accreditation

One of the core requirements for federal information systems is certification and accreditation (C&A), a process in which agencies first evaluate the security protections implemented for a system against its security requirements, and then determine if the risk from operating the system is acceptable to the organization. The C&A process, when successfully executed, culminates in *system authorization*—the decision to accept the risk to the organization from operating the system based upon a determination that the system's security protections are adequate. Despite the close association between certification and accreditation activities and FISMA, the requirement for agencies to formally authorize their information systems comes not from FISMA, but from OMB Circular A-130. Appendix III of Circular A-130, *Security of Federal Automated Information Resources*, requires agencies to authorize processing for information systems, taking into account the risk posed to the agency and the security plan and security measures implemented to protect the system [3]. As part of the FISMA Implementation Project, NIST developed new system certification and accreditation guidelines in Special Publication 800-37, replacing a standard developed over 20 years earlier [26]. Certification and accreditation remains a key requirement for newly developed information systems, but C&A processes are now incorporated within the broader set of information security management practices defined in the Risk Management Framework [27].

STRENGTHS AND SHORTCOMINGS OF FISMA

In the years since FISMA went into effect, the implementation guidance to agencies from OMB and NIST has evolved to reflect a greater emphasis on the organization-wide scope of risk management practices and on continuous, ongoing information security management processes, especially with respect to monitoring security controls. Without challenging the validity of the law's explicit purpose and objectives, the requirements in FISMA and the government's approach to implementing the law leave open to debate questions about FISMA's success in improving information security in federal government agencies. Complying with FISMA requirements and implementing the standards and guidelines associated with the law is time and resource intensive, so the government continuously seeks ways to show the effort is worthwhile. Several aspects of security program management and reporting under FISMA present challenges to assessing the law's effectiveness. OMB substantially changed FISMA reporting requirements beginning in 2010 with the introduction of the online Cyber-Scope tool for agency report submission and continues to revise reporting metrics, frequency, and automation [28]. Aside from the specific FISMA compliance information tracked and reported by agencies, both individual agencies and those with oversight for government information security management often seem to struggle to demonstrate the benefits of the law, leaving agency and government-wide programs open to criticism from Congress, industry, and security practitioners.

There are both positive and negative aspects to FISMA and its implementation in federal agencies. Strengths of the government's approach to information security and risk management under the law include its comprehensive scope, risk-based foundation, and flexibility afforded to agencies to tailor their activities to their own risk management priorities and security requirements. The law increased the focus among agencies on information security as a mission-enabling function and critical supporting element of enterprise risk management. It also established formal executive-level agency responsibilities for security management and risk management and raised the visibility of these positions and their relationship to top agency leadership. By tying information security to IT investments and the system development life cycle, FISMA also obligated agencies to more clearly identify and allocate costs associated with security, providing information to support risk-based, cost-effective decisions about security for federal information systems.

The simultaneous improvement in federal information security management measured through FISMA reporting and significant increase in the number, frequency, and variety of security incidents reported by agencies produces conflicting evidence for evaluating the relative effectiveness of the law. One common criticism of the law is its almost exclusive focus on compliance in terms of implementing and configuring controls rather than on measuring the results of those controls once implemented. The government's shift in emphasis to continuous monitoring—and more importantly, continuous monitoring of threats and vulnerabilities and not just of controls [29]—is a step in the right direction towards assessing the effectiveness of information security practices, but not an approach specified in FISMA legislation. The flexibility in FISMA implementation guidance—reflecting an understanding that every organization has different needs, priorities, and risk tolerance levels—also represents a potential weakness, particularly given the subjective nature of many risk management activities. These characteristics not only make it difficult to apply risk evaluation and response analyses across organizations, but in the absence of strong governance also raise the possibility of differing interpretations and inconsistent application of risk management practices within a single organization. FISMA also constrains effective oversight of information security programs and practices by not including penalties for noncompliance, an omission that stands in contrast to other major security and privacy legislation such as the Health Insurance Portability and Accountability Act (HIPAA), Financial Services Modernization Act, and the Privacy Act [30], all of which provide civil and criminal penalties for violations. The only potential action available to OMB, under authority delegated not by FISMA but by the Clinger-Cohen Act [31], is reducing or restricting funding for information resources requested in agency budgets. An agency failing to adhere to FISMA requirements for its information systems could receive less funding for its IT investments, presumably limiting its ability to develop and operate systems funded by those investments, but any such budgetary reduction might also reduce the agency's ability to implement security controls.

This book is designed to help agencies use FISMA and the Risk Management Framework to improve the effectiveness of their security programs, processes, and activities. It does not provide evidence to suggest that FISMA provides an optimal approach to information security management, or that FISMA is better or worse than other approaches. Any shortcomings notwithstanding, FISMA remains the primary federal law governing the security of federal information systems, and agencies are required to comply with the law and implement its provisions in the context of their own information security management programs. This book accepts as given the applicability of the law to federal agencies and other relevant organizations and considers FISMA-related standards and implementation guidance and other sources of information for their value in helping organizations establish and maintain effective risk management practices.

STRUCTURE AND CONTENT

This book cannot hope to provide a substitute for all guidance and information relevant to FISMA and the Risk Management Framework or to obviate the need for system owners, security officers, risk assessors, and others with key roles in information security management to reference official documents. The content presented in this book describes all key processes and activities associated with risk management under FISMA, providing extensive references to source material to help readers navigate the large volume of relevant guidance and requirements. This book is organized in a way that first establishes the appropriate context and offers a foundation for thinking about and executing risk management processes and information security program activities, then describes each of the steps in the Risk Management Framework and provides more detailed explanations of major risk and security management functions, including the preparation of the core deliverables produced in support of system authorization decisions.

Chapters 1 through 5 focus on fundamental aspects of information assurance, risk management, and information systems security as practiced in federal government agencies. This information—reflecting key legislative, regulatory, and policy drivers—provides the background and context for risk management in organizations subject to FISMA, including explanations of government-specific perspectives, points of emphasis, and terminology seen in information security management. Chapters 6 through 9 focus on the NIST Risk Management Framework, as formally defined in Special Publication 800-37 Revision 1 and referenced in current NIST, OMB, and agency standards and guidance used by risk managers, business process owners, system owners, security officers, and other personnel with information security responsibilities. These chapters cover all tasks in the six-step RMF process, presented in the same sequence used in NIST guidance. Chapters 10 through 15 provide detailed guidance on the development of the three primary documents constituting the security authorization package—the system security plan, security assessment report, and plan of action and milestones—and dives deeper into key processes and activities performed across multiple steps of the RMF, including risk management, continuous monitoring, and contingency planning. Chapters 16 and 17 address federal information security management requirements and initiatives beyond the explicit scope of FISMA, to offer readers a more complete view of the set of obligations and expectations applicable to federal agencies of which security management personnel should be aware. A brief summary of each chapter follows.

Chapter 1: Introduction

The introduction (this chapter) presents the purpose and objectives of the book, defines the context of the material, explains the applicability of the material, and identifies the intended audience. The first chapter summarizes FISMA provisions and describes key concepts and processes associated with information security management in federal government organizations. It also explains the structure and content of the book and describes each chapter in brief.

Chapter 2: Federal Information Security Fundamentals

Chapter 2 describes the federal government landscape for information security management, including different types of organizations subject to FISMA and the risk management and information assurance practices those organizations employ. It provides a legislative history of information security management requirements applicable to federal agencies, including the need to authorize federal information systems for processing using formal certification and accreditation processes. The second chapter describes the organizations with primary responsibility for government information security management and the guidance and oversight these organizations provide. It introduces the three-tiered approach to risk management used in NIST guidance and also defines key roles and responsibilities within each agency.

Chapter 3: Thinking About Risk

Chapter 3 covers the discipline of risk management, defining key terms and risk management processes more fully explained in Chapter 13, and positioning information security management as a core component of enterprise risk management. It describes the relationship between risk and other concepts such as trust, distrust, trustworthiness, security, assurance, and uncertainty. It also describes the execution of risk management functions at different levels of the organization and the integration of risk management with security-relevant processes such as system development and system authorization.

Chapter 4: Thinking About Systems

Because FISMA and associated guidance emphasize security of information systems and the information they contain, Chapter 4 defines different types of government systems and presents different perspectives for thinking about and managing systems reflecting emphases on IT investments, enterprise architecture, FISMA requirements, and regulatory compliance. The information in Chapter 4 provides an introduction to key concepts such as major applications, general support systems, and system authorization boundaries that feature prominently in subsequent parts of the book, particularly including Chapters 7 and 10.

Chapter 5: Success Factors

Chapter 5 identifies prerequisites, enablers, and constraints that affect the effectiveness of organizational information security management practices. It highlights necessary resources and organizational and process attributes that, where present, facilitate the consistent, successful execution of Risk Management Framework processes and activities.

Chapter 6: Risk Management Framework Planning and Initiation

Chapter 6 addresses the system-level and organizational activities undertaken to prepare for initiating the six-step RMF process. It emphasizes the importance of careful planning and determining the resources, time, dependencies, and sponsorship or approval involved in an iteration of the Risk Management Framework.

Chapter 7: Risk Management Framework Steps 1 & 2

Chapter 7 describes the tasks and requirements associated with the first two steps of the Risk Management Framework: categorizing the information system and selecting security controls. This material relies heavily on the FIPS 199 standard for security categorization and key NIST guidance including the security control framework and minimum security baselines in Special Publication 800-53.

Chapter 8: Risk Management Framework Steps 3 & 4

Chapter 8 describes the tasks and requirements associated with the third and fourth steps of the Risk Management Framework: implementing security controls and assessing security controls. The requirements in FIPS 199 and FIPS 200 drive these activities, which also extensively leverage the security control framework in Special Publication 800-53 and the security control assessment guidance in Special Publication 800-53A. This chapter introduces several concepts addressed in detail in Chapter 11.

Chapter 9: Risk Management Framework Steps 5 & 6

Chapter 9 describes the tasks and requirements associated with the final two steps of the Risk Management Framework: authorizing information systems and security control monitoring. These steps reference key security documents included in the security authorization package whose development is addressed in detail in Chapters 10–12. Chapter 9 also introduces control monitoring concepts in the RMF context that are the subject of dedicated additional NIST guidance in Special Publication 800-137.

Chapter 10: System Security Plan

Chapter 10 describes the development of the system security plan, the foundational document in the security authorization package and the primary point of reference for security-related information about each federal information system. This chapter includes recommendations on the structure and content expected in system security plans and guidance on security planning contained in Special Publication 800-18.

Chapter 11: Security Assessment Report

Chapter 11 describes the development of the security assessment report, the primary output of the security control assessment process, and a key document in the security authorization package. This chapter incorporates guidance in Special Publication 800-53A on conducting and documenting and analyzing the results of security control assessments, and highlights the use of information in the security assessment report in ongoing information security management.

Chapter 12: Plan of Action and Milestones

Chapter 12 describes the development and maintenance of the plan of action and milestones, a key document in the security authorization package and the location in which system owners and agencies document security weaknesses associated with their information systems and plans for remediating those weaknesses. This chapter explains requirements for and characteristics of plans of action and milestones created at individual information system and at organization-wide levels, and summarizes the internal and external uses of these plans for management, reporting, and oversight.

Chapter 13: Risk Management

Chapter 13 describes the management of risk due to information systems in federal agencies, and highlights the relationship of information security risk to other types of risk relevant for enterprise risk management. This chapter is organized to align with guidance contained in Special Publication 800-39, which defines and overall risk management process comprising risk framing, risk assessment, risk response, and risk monitoring activities. It also describes the key tasks in the risk assessment process, referencing the methodology prescribed in the draft revision of Special Publication 800-30.

Chapter 14: Continuous Monitoring

Chapter 14 describes the process of continuous monitoring, emphasizing system-specific and organizational activities performed as part of ongoing security operations and maintenance for authorized systems. It explains the recent government-wide emphasis on continuous monitoring and incorporates guidance contained in Special Publication 800-137 as well as technical considerations addressed in initial contingency monitoring programs implemented among federal agencies and documented in proposed continuous monitoring reference models.

Chapter 15: Contingency Planning

Chapter 15 describes organizational and system-level contingency planning processes, explains the relationship between contingency planning and related activities such as disaster recovery and incident response, and positions contingency planning within the broader scope of agency and federal continuity of operations. This chapter references contingency planning guidance contained in Special Publication 800-34 and other NIST publications, and federal continuity planning requirements specified in HSPD-20, the Federal Continuity Directives, and other sources of national contingency policy.

Chapter 16: Privacy

Chapter 16 describes the legislative, regulatory, and policy requirements prescribing federal agency obligations for protecting the privacy of information under their stewardship, especially with respect to different types of personally identifiable information that may be stored in federal information systems. The scope of Chapter 16 extends well beyond FISMA, the provisions of which emphasize security safeguards that support privacy protection but do not explicitly address privacy. This chapter summarizes requirements from key legislation such as the Privacy Act, and from numerous regulations and OMB memoranda that mandate specific protective measures for various types of information.

Chapter 17: Federal Initiatives

Recognizing that the scope of federal information security management and risk management activities extends well beyond the provisions in FISMA and associated guidance, Chapter 17 briefly summarizes key federal initiatives with significant ramifications for security management in federal government agencies. It includes government-wide programs and drivers for identity and access management, network security, IT governance, and regulatory compliance, as well as aspects of security management receiving special emphasis in the time since FISMA's enactment.

RELEVANT SOURCE MATERIAL

The primary source for FISMA requirements is the text of the law itself [32]. The full set of NIST Special Publications and Federal Information Processing Standards issued or updated in support of FISMA requirements is extensive. The core guidance documents most relevant to the Risk Management Framework and the processes and activities described in this book include:

- Special Publication 800-39, *Managing Information Security Risk: Organization, Mission, and Information System View* [9].
- Special Publication 800-37 Revision 1, *Guide for Applying the Risk Management Framework to Federal Information Systems* [27].
- Special Publication 800-53 Revision 3, *Recommended Security Controls for Federal Information Systems and Organizations* [33].
- Special Publication 800-53A Revision 1, *Guide for Assessing the Security Controls in Federal Information Systems and Organizations* [34].
- Special Publication 800-18 Revision 1, *Guide for Developing the Security Plans for Federal Information Systems* [35].
- Special Publication 800-137, *Information Security Continuous Monitoring for Federal Information Systems and Organizations* [29].

These and other NIST Special Publications are available from the NIST Computer Security Division Website, at http://csrc.nist.gov/publications/PubsSPs.html.

SUMMARY

This introductory chapter explained the purpose, objectives, and rationale for this book, its intended uses, and the primary audiences for the information it contains. It described the legislative provisions contained in the Federal Information Security Management Act and summarized concepts and processes associated with information security management in federal government contexts. It also explained the structure and content of the book and offered a brief description of each chapter.

REFERENCES

[1] See for example, the Paperwork Reduction Act of 1980, Pub. L. No. 96-511, 94 Stat. 2812; the Paperwork Reduction Act of 1995, Pub. L. No. 104-13, 109 Stat. 1643; the Information Technology Management Reform Act of 1996, Pub. L. No. 104-106, 110 Stat. 679; and the Government Paperwork Elimination Act of 1998, Pub. L. 105-277, 112 Stat. 2681.

[2] See for example the Computer Security Act of 1987, Pub. L. 100-235, 101 Stat. 1724; Paperwork Reduction Act of 1995, Pub. L. No. 104-13, 109 Stat. 1643; the Government Information Security Reform Act of 2000, Pub. L. 106-398, 114 Stat. 1654A; and the E-Government Act of 2002, Pub. L. 107-347, 116 Stat. 2899.

[3] Appendix III, Security of federal automated information resources. Washington, DC: Office of Management and Budget; November 2000. Circular No. A-130, Revised (Transmittal Memorandum No. 4).

[4] Pfleeger CP, Pfleeger SL. Security in computing. 4th ed.. Prentice Hall: Upper Saddle River, (NJ); 2006.

[5] Federal Information Security Management Act of 2002, Pub. L. No. 107-347, 116 Stat. 2946. §301.

[6] Guide for applying the risk management framework to federal information systems. Gaithersburg, MD: National Institute of Standards and Technology, Computer Security Division; February 2010 . Special Publication 800-37 revision 1. p. 5.

[7] FIPS 199 and FIPS 200 as well as the original version of Special Publication 800-37 direct agencies to conduct system-specific activities.

[8] Bolten JB. FY 2004 reporting instructions for the Federal Information Security Management Act. Washington, DC: Office of Management and Budget; August 23, 2004. Memorandum M-04-25.

[9] Managing information security risk: organization, mission, and information system view. Gaithersburg, MD: National Institute of Standards and Technology, Computer Security Division; March 2011. Special Publication 800-39.

[10] Guide for applying the risk management framework to federal information systems. Gaithersburg, MD: National Institute of Standards and Technology, Computer Security Division; February 2010. Special Publication 800-37 revision 1. p. 8.

[11] 116 Stat. 2946-2961.

[12] Definitions. 44 U.S.C. §3502(1).

[13] Definitions. 44 U.S.C. §3542(2)(A).

[14] Barker WC. Guideline for identifying an information system as a national security system. Gaithersburg, MD: National Institute of Standards and Technology, Computer Security Division; August 2003. Special Publication 800-59.

[15] Federal Information Security Management Act of 2002, Pub. L. No. 107-347, 116 Stat. 2946. §302.

[16] Computer Security Act of 1987, Pub. L. 100-235, 101 Stat. 1724; at the time NIST was known as the National Bureau of Standards.

[17] Fiscal year 2009 report to Congress on the implementation of the Federal Information Security Management Act of 2002. Washington, DC: Office of Management and Budget; March 2010. p. 28.

[18] Fiscal year 2010 report to Congress on the implementation of the Federal Information Security Management Act of 2002. Washington, DC: Office of Management and Budget; March 2011. p. 15.

[19] Information security weaknesses continue amid new federal efforts to implement requirements. Washington, DC: Government Accountability Office; October 2011. Report GAO-12-137. p. 4.

[20] Senators Joseph Lieberman, Susan Collins, Tom Carper, and Jay Rockefeller, among others in Congress, have authored or co-sponsored security bills in recent sessions of Congress, including the proposed Cybersecurity and Internet Freedom Act of 2011 (S. 413) and Cybersecurity Act of 2012 (S. 2105).

[21] Federal Information Security Management Act of 2002, Pub. L. No. 107-347, 116 Stat. 2946. §301, codified at 44 U.S.C. §3541.

[22] Government Information Security Reform Act of 2000, Pub. L. 106-398, 114 Stat. 1654A. §1061.

[23] Federal Information Security Management Act of 2002, Pub. L. No. 107-347, 116 Stat. 2946. §301, codified at 44 U.S.C. §3544.

[24] Federal Information Security Management Act of 2002, Pub. L. No. 107-347, 116 Stat. 2946. §302, codified at 40 U.S.C. §11331.

[25] Federal Information Security Management Act of 2002, Pub. L. No. 107-347, 116 Stat. 2946. §303, codified at 15 U.S.C. §278g-3.

[26] Guidelines for computer security certification and accreditation. Gaithersburg, MD: National Bureau of Standards; September 1983. Federal Information Processing Standards Publication 102.

[27] Guide for applying the risk management framework to federal information systems. Gaithersburg, MD: National Institute of Standards and Technology, Computer Security Division; February 2010. Special Publication 800-37 revision 1.

[28] Lew JJ. Reporting instructions for the Federal Information Security Management Act and agency privacy management. Washington, DC: Office of Management and Budget; September 14, 2011. Memorandum M-11-33.

[29] Dempsey K, Chawla N, Johnson A, Johnson R, Jones A, Orebaugh A, et al. Information security continuous monitoring for federal information systems and organizations. Gaithersburg, MD: National Institute of Standards and Technology, Computer Security Division; September 2011.. Special Publication 800-137

[30] Health Insurance Portability and Accountability Act of 1996, Pub. L. No. 104-191, 110 Stat. 1936; Financial Services Modernization Act of 1999, Pub. L. No. 106-102, 113 Stat. 1338; Privacy Act of 1974, Pub. L. No. 93-579, 88 Stat. 1896.

[31] Information Technology Management Reform Act of 1996, Pub. L. No. 104-106, 110 Stat. 679. §5113(b)(5).

[32] Federal Information Security Management Act of 2002, Pub. L. No. 107-347, 116 Stat. 2946.

[33] Recommended security controls for federal information systems and organizations. Gaithersburg, MD: National Institute of Standards and Technology, Computer Security Division; August 2009. Special Publication 800-53 revision 3.

[34] Guide for assessing the security controls in federal information systems and organizations. Gaithersburg, MD: National Institute of Standards and Technology, Computer Security Division; June 2010. Special Publication 800-53A revision 1.

[35] Swanson M, Hash J, Bowen P. Guide for developing security plans for federal information systems. Gaithersburg, MD: National Institute of Standards and Technology, Computer Security Division; February 2006. Special Publication 800-18 revision 1.

Federal Information Security Fundamentals

INFORMATION IN THIS CHAPTER:

- Information Security in the Federal Government
- Government Sector-specific Practices
- History of Information Security Legislation and Other Drivers
- Certification and Accreditation Methodologies
- Organizational Roles and Responsibilities

Organizations implement security to protect assets, where an asset is anything of value owned by or under the control of an organization. Assets comprise both tangible property and intangible items or resources, notably including information; the discipline of information security protects information assets from loss or harm. The practices and protective mechanisms organizations put in place to safeguard their information assets vary depending on asset value, the risk of loss or harm associated with organizational assets, and the objectives that information security is intended to achieve. Information security is often defined in terms of the three key objectives of confidentiality, integrity, and availability—sometimes abbreviated as "CIA," referenced as the "CIA triad," and represented graphically as a triangle or set of interlocking circles. Although interdependencies certainly exist between security objectives, different organizations place different priorities on confidentiality, integrity, availability, and other information attributes addressed by security. To present information security practices associated with FISMA and related guidance and to understand the way government organizations are expected to conduct information security management, confidentiality, integrity, and availability should be considered both separately and in combination, as reflected in Figure 2.1. The official government definition for information security is "the protection of information and information systems from unauthorized access, use, disclosure, disruption, modification, or destruction in order to provide confidentiality, integrity, and availability" where

- *confidentiality* is the preservation of "authorized restrictions on information access and disclosure, including means for protecting personal privacy and proprietary information";

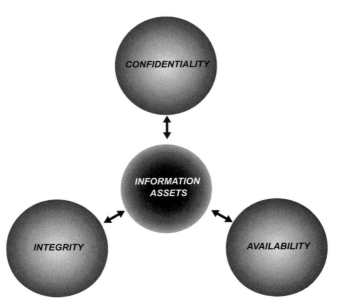

FIGURE 2.1 Information Security Focuses on Protecting the Confidentiality, Integrity, and Availability of Information Assets

- *integrity* is "guarding against improper information modification or destruction, and includes ensuring information nonrepudiation and authenticity"; and
- *availability* ensures "timely and reliable access to and use of information" [1].

In addition to confidentiality, integrity, and availability, information security practices may address other attributes of information assets owned or maintained by an organization, such as information privacy, accuracy, authenticity, utility, value, and possession. Some information security models consider these characteristics distinct from the CIA triad [2], while others (including the Information Assurance Technical Framework [3], the McCumber Cube [4], and other key models developed for use in government domains) describe them as secondary attributes falling within the scope of confidentiality, integrity, or availability. There is no single official definition of privacy used in government contexts, including information security [5], or even in legal and scholarly fields [6], Privacy is sometimes equated with confidentiality, with the connotation that privacy comprises control over the collection, use, and disclosure of information and controlling access to information is within the purview of confidentiality. While confidentiality protection may be required to ensure privacy, maintaining privacy also considers such factors as ownership of information and control of or consent to its use. The substantial attention focused on privacy and wide range of government privacy regulations and requirements—within and distinct from information security management contexts—warrant dedicated treatment of the topic; in this book privacy is addressed in detail in Chapter 16.

Both accuracy and authenticity are often treated as components of integrity, although some definitions of integrity narrower than the one cited above focus only on whether information has been modified without authorization, [7] rather than addressing whether unmodified information is correct, reliable, or comes from a trusted or authoritative source. Utility and value are closely related concepts used to help determine the necessary level of information security protection, where preserving information utility and value is a key outcome sought from security practices. Possession refers to the ability to maintain control of information regardless of the state of other attributes; loss of control may not result in loss of confidentiality, integrity, or availability but is still an outcome organizations want to avoid (for example, the loss or theft of an encrypted backup tape). The security models adopted in civilian, defense, and intelligence domains all represent variations based on the CIA triad, and the material presented in this book reflects the federal government emphasis on confidentiality, integrity, and availability as primary security objectives.

INFORMATION SECURITY IN THE FEDERAL GOVERNMENT

Although information security management practices and legislative drivers like FISMA apply to all federal government agencies, variations in security priorities, policies, areas of emphasis, and even terminology exist among different sectors of the government. FISMA and other information security legislation make a key distinction at the organizational level among federal civilian, defense, and intelligence agencies, and at the information system level between national security systems and all other federal information systems [8]. One notable difference in regulations and guidance issued and practices implemented in military and intelligence domains is the emphasis on *information assurance* as a concept related to but distinct from *information security*. In Department of Defense (DoD) and intelligence community (IC) usage, information security refers to the programs, policies, and processes that protect confidentiality, integrity, and availability, while information assurance refers to the security controls or other measures that provide that protection [9]. DoD issues separate instructions to its component agencies regarding information security program management and implementing information assurance, where information security program guidance is directed at agency-level management and information assurance guidance—including certification and accreditation instructions—applies to information systems [10]. In contrast, NIST uses only the term information security in its standards and guidance to agencies, using *assurance* with a much narrower connotation to refer to the level of confidence agencies and system owners have that implemented system security controls are effective [11]. At the information system level, information security activities prescribed in NIST standards and guidance and information assurance activities in DoD instructions are substantially similar, and distinctions between the two terms may become less important as all government domains move to adopt the common security framework reflected in recent

NIST guidance. This book favors the term *information security*, consistent with its emphasis on FISMA and the Risk Management Framework and the fact that neither the text of the FISMA legislation nor core NIST guidance refers to information assurance in the connotation seen in DoD or IC domains.

Although the CIA triad and related concepts are pervasive in information security management in all types of organizations, information security management in government agencies differs in significant ways from comparable functions in commercial sector organizations. As noted in the introductory chapter, legislative and regulatory requirements for government information security focus on individual information systems and on certifying and accrediting the security of federal information systems before putting them into operation. Information security management standards applicable to all types of organizations—including the International Standards Organization (ISO) 27000 series [12]—have characteristics similar to government standards and guidance in terms of recommended practices, security control frameworks, and grounding in risk management, but do not include formal system authorization. In addition, the historical influence of military requirements for securing classified information resulted in an emphasis on data and system classification or categorization not typically seen in nongovernment contexts. The same influence of military requirements—coupled with the fact that the military sponsored much of the seminal research and development of secure computing models—drives a prioritization in many agencies on protecting confidentiality above all other attributes. Understanding the historical context underlying current agency expectations can help agencies and their system owners identify the drivers for many security requirements and assess the extent to which those drivers align with their own security objectives. In this context, each government agency can more effectively implement information security management practices in ways that are risk-based, cost-effective, and tailored to their organizational requirements.

Brief History of Information Security

Contemporary information security traces its legacy to initial research in computer security conducted during the 1960s, driven by the need to protect classified information in DoD computer systems providing access and shared resources to multiple users. Working from a well-defined context in which users access, store, and process classified information using computer systems, initial research and administrative and technical recommendations focused on robust access control mechanisms and protection against unauthorized disclosure of information [13]. Subsequent information flow control models developed for the military, such as the well-known Bell-LaPadula and Biba multi-level security models, implement mandatory access control policies well suited to environments that use formal classification of information assets, and users. The Bell-LaPadula model [14] assigns classification levels to information objects and the subjects (human or system) that seek access to those objects. Subjects must have a classification level equal to or higher than the objects they view and cannot disclose information to a classification level below their own.

These rules—often expressed simply as "no read up" and "no write down"—are intended to prevent the unauthorized disclosure of information, and thus preserve its confidentiality. The Biba model [15] is structurally similar to Bell-LaPadula but is intended to safeguard the integrity of information, rather than its confidentiality. The Biba model assigns integrity classifications to subjects and objects as an indication of reliability or trustworthiness. Subjects must have an integrity level equal to or lower than the objects they view, and cannot write information to an object at a higher integrity level. The Biba rules—sometimes simplified to "no read down" and "no write up"—guard against the corruption or loss of integrity of relatively more trusted information by preventing exposure to less trusted information. Access control is an essential aspect of security relevant to protecting both confidentiality and integrity, but these models are less applicable to commercial or non-military government organizations that favor role-based access control models or other approaches that emphasize authorization based on what a user wants to do or how information will be used. For transactional systems or technology-enabled business processes that place as much or more importance on protecting information integrity as on maintaining confidentiality, government organizations may find different security models more applicable, including those developed outside military or other government domains [16].

The collective lesson learned from working with different early secure computing approaches is that context matters and theoretical models that attempted to provide uniform methods for protecting confidentiality, integrity, and availability without considering contextual factors could not successfully be applied across the diverse range of government information systems. The National Security Telecommunications and Information Systems Security Committee, responsible for information security policy and guidance for national security systems in the federal government, adopted a multi-dimensional information systems security model developed in 1991 by John McCumber and incorporated in official instructions establishing information security training standards [17]. This model addresses confidentiality, integrity, and availability requirements for information in different states (storage, processing, and transmission) from the perspectives of technology, policy and practice, and education, training, and awareness [4]. The separate consideration of confidentiality, integrity, and availability needs of information systems in specific operational contexts remains a central feature of federal security standards and guidance for identifying system security requirements and determining the appropriate controls to satisfy those requirements.

Current procedures for security categorization, control selection, and certification and accreditation used by federal agencies in all sectors share many common aspects introduced in early secure computing models. One key difference between current information security practices and the original models from which those practices derive is the recent emphasis on risk-based decision making. The number and variety of recommended security controls and level of detail provided in implementation guidance for those controls has grown substantially with the development and enhancement of system certification and accreditation process and the application of those processes to a larger number of federal information systems. Where earlier approaches emphasized the application of entire models to every relevant information system [18], even controls included in recommended baselines for meeting minimum security requirements are subject to tailoring based on system scope, the availability of alternative or compensating controls, and organization-specific parameters, including risk tolerance [19]. Although determinations of security control applicability—at individual information system or organization-wide levels—are at the discretion of each organization, government agencies operating in similar sectors or working with particular types of sensitive information often adopt similar approaches to security control selection.

Civilian, Defense, and Intelligence Sector Practices

Information security management programs operate similarly across different government organizations, but differences exist among agencies in each of three primary sectors: civilian, defense, and intelligence. While all government agencies perform many of the same activities—including security categorization; security control selection, implementation, and assessment; certification and accreditation; and operational security monitoring—the policies, procedures, and guidelines for information security vary among the civilian, defense, and intelligence domains. Under authority delegated by FISMA, oversight of agency information security programs and information systems is different in each sector as well—while the Director of OMB oversees executive agencies in general, the Secretary of Defense and Director of Central Intelligence [20] have authority for systems operated by or on behalf of Department of Defense and the Central Intelligence Agency, respectively [21]. Additional government regulations and policies outside the scope of most FISMA provisions govern national security systems, regardless of the agency that operates them. FISMA directs agencies operating or controlling national security systems to implement the separate standards and guidelines that apply to those systems; the multi-agency Committee on National Security Systems is responsible for

---

NOTE

Despite language in FISMA requiring agencies operating national security systems to provide "information security protections commensurate with the risk and magnitude of the harm" that would result from a loss of confidentiality, integrity, or availability [23], authoritative federal policy on national security systems does not incorporate risk-based security practices. National Security Directive 42, which establishes national policy for these systems, states, "national security systems shall be secured by *such means as are necessary* (emphasis added) to prevent compromise, denial, or exploitation," [24] echoing similar policy language issued several years earlier in National Security Decision Directive 145 for federal systems that process classified information [25]. NSD-42 stresses the importance of maintaining or improving government capabilities to secure national security systems against threats, implying that the primary objective is security, not risk-adjusted security. The policy objectives include effective and efficient use of resources, but there is no consideration of risk anywhere in the directives.

establishing those standards and guidelines [22]. Key differences among the security management practices in each sector include the primary sources of policies, standards, and guidance for each type of agency, approaches to information classification and security categorization, recommended security control frameworks, and procedures for system certification and accreditation.

Sources of Guidance

The civilian, defense, and intelligence sectors each have their own primary sources of policies, standards, and guidance on the protection of federal information systems and the information those systems store, process, and make available to authorized users. The Computer Security Act of 1987 assigned responsibility to the National Institute of Standards and Technology for developing standards and guidance to improve the security and privacy of federal computer systems [26], authority reaffirmed in FISMA that makes NIST a government-wide provider of authoritative guidance and the primary source for civilian agencies. In the federal defense sector, the National Security Agency has long developed substantial security technical guidelines and standards, contributing guidance to government-wide programs in all sectors and supporting the establishment of effective security protective measures for federal information systems in general and national security systems in particular. Under authority in FISMA given to the Secretary of Defense to develop and oversee the implementation of security policy, standards, and guidelines, the Department of Defense Chief Information Officer issues a large number of policy and technical directives, regulations, instructions, and manuals governing information security programs and information assurance activities throughout the defense sector [27]. These DoD materials largely apply to FISMA-covered systems, as a separate set of policies, directives, instructions, and standards apply to national security systems, regardless of the agency that operates them. This special class of systems is addressed in guidance from the Committee on National Security Systems (CNSS), which sets government-wide policy, procedures, and standards for national security systems. CNSS members include many civilian agencies in addition to DoD `components and intelligence agencies, with executive oversight for the Committee provided by the Secretary of Defense and managerial and technical leadership provided by the National Security Agency [22]. All agencies responsible for national security systems follow CNSS guidance, but given the large proportion of intelligence community systems designated as such, the CNSS is the primary source of security guidance for intelligence agencies.

Information Classification and Security Categorization

All federal agencies perform some type of information asset categorization to help determine the appropriate security and privacy safeguards to put in place. The general procedure is specified in the mandatory Federal Information Processing Standards Publication 199 (FIPS 199), which directs agencies to evaluate different types of information and the information systems on which those information types reside [28]. This standard applies low, moderate, or high designations to the three core security objectives of confidentiality, integrity, and availability. Security categorization using FIPS 199 results in three-part ratings for each information type and information system. The overall security categorization is the highest individual rating— so for example an information type categorized as low for availability and low for integrity but high for confidentiality would be assigned an overall rating of high. Similarly, an information system's categorization is always at least as high as the minimum categorization of any of the information types associated with the system. The overall system categorization drives the set of security controls needed to satisfy minimum security requirements.

FIPS 199 applies to federal information systems other than national security systems, but in defense and intelligence sector agencies with information security programs covering both national security systems and less sensitive information systems, agencies and their system owners tend to use the same classification schemes for all systems. In the defense context, system owners assign a mission assurance category (MAC) for each system and a confidentiality level for the information associated with the system. In contrast to the system categorization process in FIPS 199 that considers each security objective first to arrive at the appropriate categorization, defense system owners assign mission assurance categories based on standard definitions, and each MAC level has corresponding integrity and availability levels, listed in Table 2.1. Confidentiality is determined separately, using one of three standard levels: classified, sensitive, or public. The result of using distinct MAC and confidentiality level ratings is nine possible combinations, each of which corresponds to sets of required information assurance controls [29].

Agencies in the intelligence community use formal data classification schemes similar to the ones used by the Department of Defense, in general applying one of three designations to information—top secret, secret, or confidential—specified in Executive Order 12958, [31] where the classification level is based on the harm or

Table 2.1 Mission Assurance Categorization Levels [30]

MAC Level	Definition	Integrity	Availability
I	These systems handle information that is determined to be vital to the operational readiness or mission effectiveness of deployed and contingency forces in terms of both content and timeliness.	High	High
II	These systems handle information that is important to the support of deployed and contingency forces.	High	Medium
III	These systems handle information that is necessary for the conduct of day-to-day business, but does not materially affect support to deployed or contingency forces in the short-term.	Basic	Basic

> **NOTE**
>
> The diversity of information classification approaches used among agencies is not limited to the intelligence community or to highly sensitive information. In a series of executive orders and subsequent guidance the government introduced the standard term *controlled unclassified information* to refer to all information that does not rise to the level of sensitivity requiring national security classification but nonetheless requires protection from unauthorized disclosure or demands other security and privacy safeguards [34].

damage that could occur due to unauthorized information disclosure. Concerns over inconsistent classification procedures among intelligence agencies led to a set of recommendations produced in 2008 to establish a standard classification guide for the intelligence community [32]. These recommendations, coupled with the participation of the Office of the Director of National Intelligence and the Committee on National Security Systems on the Joint Task Force Transformation Initiative Interagency Working Group, resulted in new guidance in 2009 from CNSS on security categorization and control selection that largely adopts FIPS 199 and the security control framework specified in NIST Special Publication 800-53 [33]. The CNSS guidance maintains separate ratings for each information type for confidentiality, integrity, and availability, and assigns each information system the highest categorization for each security objective among all of the information types applicable to the system. Because any given system can be assigned one of three impact ratings for confidentiality, integrity, and availability, there are 27 possible security categorizations for systems covered by CNSS policy.

Security Controls

Information and systems categorized using FIPS 199 are also subject to FIPS 200, which establishes minimum security requirements for systems based on the impact level assigned in the security categorization process. FIPS 200 directs agencies to implement minimum security requirements for their information systems using the security control framework specified in Special Publication 800-53 [35]. Agencies in all government sectors (as well as commercial organizations) use security control frameworks similar in structure to the one NIST maintains, where individual security controls are organized into functional groups. NIST defines 18 security control "families" comprising 198 individual controls [36]. System owners in the Department of Defense select from among 157 controls organized into eight subject areas [29]. Many public and private sector organizations follow the information security management code of practice described in ISO/IEC 27002, which identifies 133 controls across 11 clauses (categories) that collectively define information security practices relevant to a system or an organization [37]. The selection and implementation of controls necessary to satisfy information system security requirements are core activities in the NIST Risk Management Framework and in alternative system authorization methodologies used in the defense and intelligence sectors.

Certification and Accreditation Process

Appendix III of OMB Circular A-130 requires agencies to authorize processing for federal information systems, including general support systems and major applications. System authorization—accomplished through the use of certification and accreditation process—is a formal, written approval that adequate security protection exists for a system before it becomes operational. Not every system is subject to individual certification and accreditation—OMB defines major applications as those requiring "special attention to security due to the risk and magnitude of the harm resulting from the loss, misuse, or unauthorized access to or modification of the information in the application" [38]. Systems not meeting this standard still require some level of protection, but agencies often incorporate non-major applications within the scope of security protection provided by the general support system in which those applications reside. Agencies certifying and accrediting information systems in the civilian, defense, and intelligence sectors follow different processes, each described in more detail in the Certification and Accreditation section later in this chapter. The core tasks and activities in all of these processes are quite similar, and the different sectors are moving towards a common government-wide methodology through the efforts of the Joint Task Force Transformation Initiative. Based

---

WARNING

The terms certification and accreditation are widely used in both public sector and commercial information security management, but their meaning differs between government and non-government contexts, and even varies within government usage. In federal information system certification and accreditation process, including the RMF, DIACAP, and NIACAP, certification refers to the evaluation and affirmation of the extent to which the security controls implemented for a system meet the system's security requirements, in support of an accreditation decision. Accreditation is the formal decision by an authorizing official that a system's implemented security controls and residual risk are acceptable to the organization and that the system is approved to be put into operation. Beyond the scope of authorizing processing for information systems, certification typically indicates compliance, such as with a specific standard or set of requirements, while accreditation refers to the endorsement of an organization as minimally competent to perform a particular function or serve in a particular capacity. For instance, many organizations seek ISO certification to demonstrate conformance with various standards, including those related to information security such as ISO 27001. Such certifications are granted by accredited registrars or other organizations explicitly approved to serve as certification bodies. Both connotations apply to NIST, whose FISMA Implementation Program issues guidance for conducting certification and accreditation of federal information systems, and whose National Voluntary Laboratory Accreditation Program evaluates and approves many types of laboratories as qualified to certify different products for conformance to applicable standards. It is important to clearly specify the context when referring to certification and accreditation activities to avoid potential confusion when using these terms.

on applicable policies and agencies guidance current as of 2012, civilian agencies follow the certification and accreditation process embedded in the NIST Risk Management Framework, [39] defense agencies follow the DoD Information Assurance Certification and Accreditation Process (DIACAP), [40] and intelligence agencies and others operating national security systems are migrating from the National Information Assurance Certification and Accreditation Process (NIACAP) [41] to the RMF.

Legislative History of Information Security Management

Although FISMA receives a lot of attention, current statutory requirements for information security management in federal agencies—including many of the provisions included in FISMA—originated in prior legislation dating back to the earliest days of computing in government. The first laws related to computers—or more precisely, to automatic data processing systems—addressed technical services and federal standards and delegated authority to specific government agencies such as the General Services Administration and the National Bureau of Standards (as NIST was known until 1988), but did not explicitly address security and privacy [42]. The Privacy Act of 1974 established security requirements for federal information systems containing identifying information about individual citizens [43], but it did not cover all systems, or even all those containing sensitive information. The Computer Security Act of 1987 amended several earlier laws and statutory provisions to address standards for federal computer systems, extend the scope of the authority given to the National Bureau of Standards to include computer security and privacy standards and guidelines, and require agencies to develop security plans and administer mandatory training to personnel that manage, use, or operate federal systems containing sensitive information [44]. The FISMA provisions giving NIST the responsibility for developing federal information security standards and guidelines, establishing minimum security requirements, and making standards compulsory where deemed necessary all appeared in the Computer Security Act of 1987. Similarly, much of Appendix III of OMB Circular A-130 (which was first published in 1985 and subsequently reissued three times, most recently in 2000) first appeared in 1978 in OMB Circular A-71, *Security of Federal Automated Information Systems* [45]. Since FISMA's enactment in 2002, changes in requirements for federal information systems and in key agency responsibilities for security management, operations, and oversight have come not from revised legislation or Congressional action but from OMB, particularly including clarifying the responsibilities for agencies such as NSA and NIST with long-standing roles in government-wide information security activities and newer agencies such as those within the Department of Homeland Security [46]. Members of both houses of Congress regularly introduce new draft legislation seeking to strengthen existing federal information security requirements, often by amending or replacing FISMA, but other matters seem to take priority in the legislature, and as of early 2012, no laws significantly altering FISMA or impacting its key provisions have been passed.

CERTIFICATION AND ACCREDITATION

The requirement to formally authorize information systems for processing is unique to the federal government, although standards and processes for certifying the security of information technology products are widely used in public and private sector environments. Research and recommendations on computer security for federal information systems handling classified information long acknowledged the need for security certification as a prerequisite to authorizing systems for operational use and for recertification when significant changes to systems occur [13]. NIST developed the initial federal standard for certification and accreditation in 1983 to help agencies comply with OMB Circular A-71 [47]. Following a 1996 revision to the information security requirements in Appendix III of OMB Circular A-130, [48] the Department of Defense and National Security Telecommunications and Information Systems Security Committee developed new certification and accreditation processes for military and national security systems, respectively. These were the DoD Information Technology Security Certification and Accreditation Process (DITSCAP) [49], released in late 1997 and replaced by the DIACAP in 2007, and the NIACAP, released in 2000. Prompted by FISMA as well as OMB Circular A-130, NIST also developed updated certification and accreditation guidance, released in 2004, to replace FIPS 102 as the recommended process for federal civilian agency systems [50]. As a product of the Joint Task Force Transformation Initiative, the NIST Risk Management Framework is not only a replacement for the C&A process in the original version of Special Publication 800-37, but has the potential to supersede the DIACAP and the NIACAP to provide a single common approach for all federal information systems, including national security systems [51].

All of the certification and accreditation process used by federal government agencies—including the original FIPS 102 standard developed to address computer security in sensitive automated data processing systems—share many of the same key steps and activities. Each process includes an initial planning or preparation phase, followed by separate certification and accreditation phases and a post-accreditation phase during which recertification may be performed when significant changes occur to the system. The individual tasks and activities common across C&A methodologies include:

- Development of a core set of security documentation assembled and prepared as a formal accreditation package to be used in system authorization decisions;
- System description, providing summary functional and technical information about each system, such as its purpose, architecture, operating environment, intended use within the organization, and security requirements;
- System registration, uniquely identifying each system and the organizational units or personnel responsible for system management, operation, authorization, and oversight;
- Security control selection and implementation, at a minimum satisfying security requirements appropriate for each system's sensitivity and sufficient to mitigate information security risk to an acceptable level;

- Security evaluation, verifying the implementation and proper configuration of the system and its security controls, including various types of testing and control assessment procedures;
- Formal statements of certification, attesting to authorizing officials that the security requirements for each system are adequately met;
- Official accreditation decisions, declaring the information security risk associated with each system acceptable to the authorizing official and granting the system authority to operate;
- Ongoing monitoring of the system and its environment, to identify changes that may impact the security posture of the system and, if significant enough, may prompt the need for recertification and accreditation.

The most recent versions of certification and accreditation process and related guidance issued to federal agencies also consistently link C&A and other security management activities to phases of the system development life cycle. Revised versions of C&A processes used in different government sectors make SDLC alignment more explicit, a contrast seen between the Risk Management Framework and the C&A process in the previous version of Special Publication 800-37 [39] and between the DIACAP and the previous DITSCAP methodology it replaced [40]. The following sections present, in chronological order, the C&A processes defined for civilian agency, military, and national security systems prior to the release of the Risk Management Framework in 2010, highlighting similarities and identifying individual areas of emphasis associated with their use in each sector. Although official policy statements and long-term strategies indicate convergence by all agencies on the RMF in the future, for many systems agencies in different sectors continue to follow separate methodologies.

FIPS 102

The process originally prescribed in Federal Information Processing Standards Publication 102 (FIPS 102) centers on just three activities: certification, accreditation, and recertification and reaccreditation at least every three years or whenever changes to a system or its environment occur that impact its security posture [52]. The NIST guidelines in FIPS 102 provided reference information, basic process descriptions, and sample content and templates for federal agencies to use in preparing the necessary documentation to complete certification in support of accreditation decisions. The document breaks the certification step down into subordinate activities—planning, data collection, security evaluation, and reporting findings— and describes four evaluation techniques for use in certification: risk analysis; validation, verification, and testing; security safeguard evaluation; and electronic data processing audit [53]. FIPS 102 also identified potential issues associated with certification and accreditation programs in federal agencies, with the intention that the publication would be used by security staff, system developers, and accrediting officials to determine appropriate protection for sensitive computer systems.

It included guidance intended for agency executives and business and technical managers on establishing C&A programs to ensure consistent, repeatable application of the process throughout each agency. The FIPS publication itself and additional NIST guidance targeted at system personnel responsible for certification and accreditation [54] served an important educational purpose for technical managers and staff, many of whom were new to C&A and the expectations for compliance with requirements in OMB Circular A-71. FIPS 102 aligned key security activities to high-level phases of the system development life cycle, using three phases (initiation, development, and operations and maintenance) in a somewhat simpler model than the typical five-phase sequential SDLC methodology used in more recent NIST guidance, which includes an implementation phase between development and operations and maintenance, and also defines a disposal phase at the end of the life cycle [55].

DITSCAP

The Department of Defense issued its DoD Information Technology Security Certification and Accreditation Process (DITSCAP) instructions in 1997 to implement information security policy, assign responsibilities to system owners and authorizing officials in DoD component agencies, and prescribe procedures to be followed for "any DoD system that collects, stores, transmits, or processes unclassified or classified information" [49]. The DITSCAP defined a four-step process comprising the phases of definition, verification, validation, and post accreditation. DoD instructions issued to component agencies implementing the DITSCAP identified and described key activities and expected outcomes and deliverables produced during each phase, as shown in Figure 2.2. Definition phase activities establish the mission need for the system, describe the system architecture, environment, and corresponding security requirements, and produce an agreement on the approach for implementing necessary security controls. The definition phase culminates in the development of the initial system security authorization agreement (SSAA)—the documented concurrence on the system security requirements and plans to satisfy them by the system owner and the officials responsible for certifying the system and making the accreditation decision. The SSAA is the primary source of security-related information about the system and is used and updated as necessary in each DITSCAP phase. The verification phase focuses on implementing the controls identified in the SSAA and analyzing the security status of the system during the development lifecycle, using an iterative analysis and review cycle that continues until the system is ready for certification. Validation entails a formal evaluation of the system, including conducting testing or other assessment activities needed to provide evidence to support the system's certification. The formal certification of the system is an assertion that the system meets designated security requirements and provides a recommendation to the authorizing official to accredit the system. The decision to accredit is a formal declaration that the system as implemented has sufficient security protection in place to bring the risk associated with the system within acceptable levels and is authorized to operate.

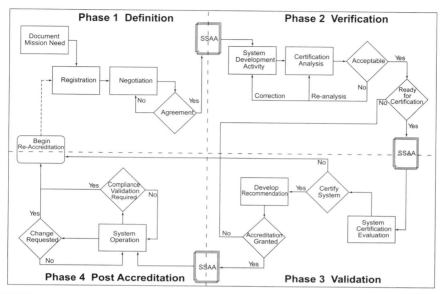

FIGURE 2.2 The DITSCAP Involves a Sequential Set of Activities and Intermediate Checkpoints Linked Through Additions or Updates to the System Security Authorization Agreement (SSAA) Occurring in Each Phase [56]

Post-accreditation activities include routine operations, configuration management, and ongoing compliance to ensure that system operation remains within an acceptable level of risk. Changes to a system or its operating environment that cannot be addressed through normal system operations may trigger a need for recertification and reaccreditation, in which case the process returns to the definition phase for a new C&A iteration.

NIACAP

The National Information Assurance Certification and Accreditation Process (NIACAP) instructions published in 2000 by the National Security Telecommunications and Information Systems Security Committee reflected the same four phases and key intra-phase activities as the DITSCAP and used the same language to describe the phases [41]. As illustrated in Figure 2.3, the system security authorization agreement (SSAA) is the central focus of the NIACAP process from a documentation standpoint, creating a binding agreement between those responsible for the system, those evaluating the system's security and providing certification, and those authorizing the system to operate. The NIACAP documentation provides implementation guidance to comply with government-wide policy requiring all federal government agencies to implement security programs that mandate system certification and accreditation for national security systems [57]. Within a scope covering all national security systems,

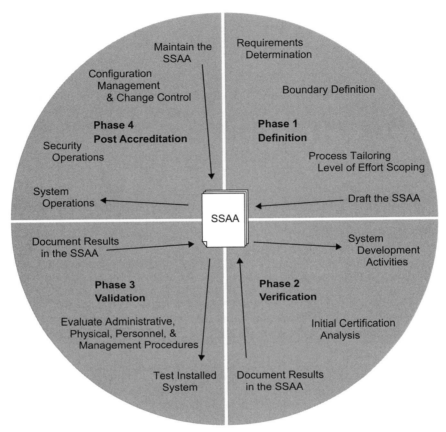

FIGURE 2.3 The Four Phases in the NIACAP Mirror Those in the DITSCAP, with Minor Variations in the Functional Areas of Emphasis Within Each Phase [59]

the NIACAP identifies three different types of accreditation based on the focus of the certification effort: system, site, and type accreditation, the last of which applies to a system that will be deployed to multiple locations. The NIACAP instructions note the expectation that those using the process will integrate C&A activities into their system life cycle processes, but also note that the four C&A phases are independent of life cycle strategies or methodologies agencies may follow [58]. Like the DITSCAP instructions, the NIACAP documentation lists key roles and responsibilities by phase for personnel representing management, security, and user perspectives. Both sets of instructions also provide sample outlines and minimum content requirements for the SSAA, including 18 lettered appendices corresponding to various plans, references, and other documentation typically included with the SSAA in the accreditation package delivered to the authorizing official. The outlines and appendix lists are not identical, but address substantially the same information. The significant extent of process overlap between DITSCAP and NIACAP is understandable given that the Department of Defense occupies the leading management and oversight positions on the Committee on National Security Systems.

NIST Special Publication 800-37

Empowered by the additional authority assigned to NIST by FISMA, updating the certification and accreditation process for federal information systems was one of the initial priorities for the FISMA Implementation Project established at NIST in early 2003. The security C&A process defined in Special Publication 800-37 and shown in Figure 2.4 includes four phases nominally similar to the ones used in the DITSCAP and NIACAP, but with significant differences in the set of activities occurring in each phase. Compared to the steps defined in FIPS 102, the NIST C&A process published in 2004 put much greater emphasis on upfront planning and preparation and on post-accreditation monitoring and status reporting in what NIST termed the initiation phase and continuous monitoring phase, respectively [60]. During the first phase (initiation), the system owner characterizes the system, its sensitivity, and the threats and vulnerabilities associated with the system and documents the set of security controls

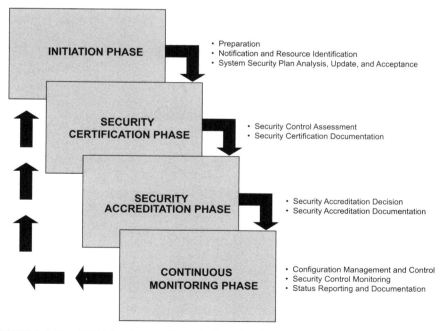

FIGURE 2.4 The NIST C&A Process Expands Upon Previous Government Guidelines with More Prescriptive Information About Effective Planning and Preparation for Subsequent Phases and Activities and About Continuous Monitoring for Operational Systems After Accreditation [61]

and assessed risk in the system security plan. Initiation also includes communicating the need for system C&A to relevant parties within the organization and planning the schedule and resources required to complete the C&A process. The first phase produces the initial system security plan (SSP), analogous in many ways to the SSAA used in the DITSCAP and NIACAP, including its incorporation of many related plans and artifacts as appendices. The second phase (security certification) comprises two major activities: security control assessment and development and assembly of the accreditation package, which comprises the security assessment report and plan of action and milestones in addition to the SSP and required subordinate documentation and appendices. The third phase (security accreditation) focuses almost exclusively on tasks performed by the authorizing official, including determining the information security risk posed to the organization by the system and whether that risk is acceptable. Once the system is authorized to operate, the fourth phase (continuous monitoring) focuses on typical operational processes such as configuration management and security control monitoring, emphasizing the identification of any changes to the system or its environment that may impact the security posture of the system.

DIACAP

The Department of Defense replaced DITSCAP with the DoD Information Assurance Certification and Accreditation Process (DIACAP) in 2007. The most obvious change in the overall C&A process, shown in Figure 2.5, is the addition of a fifth phase (decommission) and the change in phase names for the first four phases compared to the labels used in the DITSCAP. The DIACAP reflects tighter

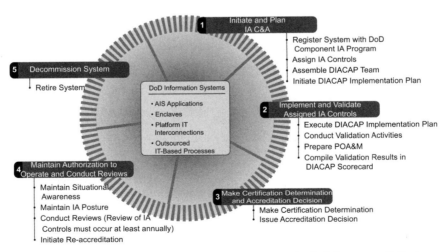

FIGURE 2.5 The DIACAP Revised the Overall Approach to C&A for DoD Systems to Reflect Integration with Standard System Development Life Cycle Phases and to Tailor the Process and Amount and Type of Information Produced to the Type of System Seeking Authorization [63]

integration and more direct alignment with the system development life cycle across all phases of the C&A process, as opposed to the DITSCAP's emphasis on SDLC activities only within the verification phase. Many of the key tasks and activities in the DIACAP parallel the DITSCAP process, although the types of systems to which the process applies differ in the DIACAP, which distinguishes among automated information system applications (stand-alone systems), enclaves, inter-connected systems, and outsourced information technology including systems, services, and processes [62]. The DIACAP instructions also position certification and accreditation and the information assurance controls identified and implemented through C&A activities as department-wide processes to be managed at an enterprise level. The DIACAP assigns responsibilities to a much larger group of organizational roles than the DITSCAP, extending from the DoD Chief Information Officer with the broadest organizational oversight to the individual program managers, system managers, information assurance managers, and user representatives associated with each information system. The DIACAP also moves away from a single overarching set of security documentation (the SSAA) towards a logical aggregation of system information and a summary report—the DIACAP package and DIACAP scorecard, respectively—that can be produced at different levels of detail for different purposes or to communicate security information to different audiences. This shift in information presentation and delivery is consistent with the use of information produced throughout the C&A process to support various system management and oversight functions, in contrast to the prior use of the SSAA for accreditation determinations and other narrowly focused security purposes.

NIST Risk Management Framework

The Risk Management Framework (RMF) released by NIST in 2010 as a product of the Joint Task Force Transformation Initiative represented civilian, defense, and intelligence sector perspectives and recast the certification and accreditation process as an end-to-end security life cycle providing a single common government-wide foundation for security management activities. The RMF replaced the prior NIST process with six steps instead of four, as shown in Figure 2.6, dedicating key steps in the process to security activities such as security control selection, implementation, and assessment that were previously addressed as sub-processes within C&A phases. The revised guidance in Special Publication 800-37 Revision 1 de-emphasizes the use of the terms *certification* and *accreditation*, in both the title and the body of the document, in which the words appear exactly once, and then only to refer to the previous version of the publication [64]. The document refers instead to system authorization, matching usage in Appendix III of OMB Circular A-130 and connoting a departure from the narrower focus on C&A to new areas of emphasis for the RMF. The RMF features explicit integration with the software development life cycle, identifying the relevant SDLC phase for every task described in each step. Special Publication 800-37 Revision 1 continues to apply primarily to individual information systems, but addresses the role of information security risk management at all layers of the

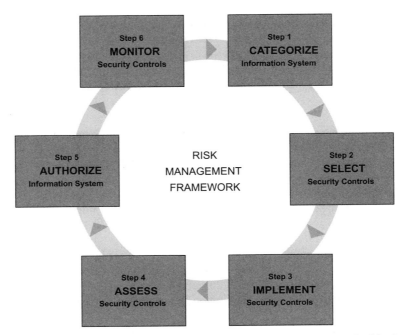

FIGURE 2.6 The RMF Adopts a Life Cycle Approach to Security Management, Positioning Activities Formerly Associated Primarily with Certification and Accreditation in the Broader Context of Information Security Risk Management [65]

organization and emphasizes the goals of more pervasive monitoring of operational systems and timely provision of key security information to organizational leadership with responsibility for managing risk. The six steps and subordinate tasks in the RMF are described in detail in Chapters 7, 8, and 9.

Joint Task Force Transformation Initiative

The Risk Management Framework described in Special Publication 800-37 Revision 1 and key supporting guidance on security controls and security control assessments in the latest revisions to Special Publications 800-53 and 800-53A reflect the input of agencies in all government sectors through the Joint Task Force Transformation Initiative interagency working group. Through this initiative, NIST collaborated with CNSS, the Department of Defense, and Office of the Director of National Intelligence to develop a common information security framework for all government agencies. The long-term vision for the Risk Management Framework is to provide a single approach for all federal information systems, replacing alternative processes such as the DIACAP and NIACAP. With respect to National Security

> **TIP**
>
> Despite stated intentions by senior officials representing all the organizations participating in the Joint Task Force Transformation Initiative, more than two years after the release of Special Publication 800-37 Revision 1 and over four years since the initiative began many federal agencies continue to follow predecessor C&A processes. This is less surprising in DoD component agencies, where the DIACAP remains the standard, but even when official policy declares a change in methodology, system owners in some agencies may continue to follow deprecated processes. If precedent is any guide, for systems in the process of accreditation or operating under authority granted under a previous C&A process, agencies may offer system owners the option to continue under the same approach for ongoing security management, at least until re-authorization is required [69]. The current emphasis on effective continuous monitoring as an alternative to conventional re-authorization for FISMA systems leaves open the question of how agencies should transition their operational systems to the RMF once adopted.

Systems, in early 2012 CNSS announced its intention to replace the NIACAP and related instructions with a new approach to information assurance risk management following NIST guidance produced by the Joint Task Force Transformation Initiative [66]. Specifically, the policy references Special Publications 800-39, 800-37, 800-53, and 800-53A and CNSS Instruction 1253 (on security categorization and control selection) as the implementation guidance for agencies operating national security systems. Under this policy, the same information security risk management approach will apply to national security systems and to systems covered by FISMA, with the exception of security categorization. Security categorization using CNSS Instruction 1253 is conceptually similar to the approach specified in FIPS 199, but CNSS chose not to adopt the "high water mark" approach to consolidating security categories used in FIPS 199, maintaining separate impact ratings for confidentiality, integrity, and availability [67]. For its part, as of early 2012 the Department of Defense was considering revisions to its DIACAP certification and accreditation instructions that would harmonize relevant DoD information assurance processes with the RMF [68].

ORGANIZATIONAL RESPONSIBILITIES

FISMA assigned responsibility for various aspects of information security management, oversight, and implementation guidance to different government agencies. Considering information security management from a government-wide perspective, roles and responsibilities are distributed among many different agencies, at times giving explicit authority to individual agencies but also directing agencies to work cooperatively to achieve common information security objectives. Executive agencies—to which FISMA and its requirements apply—are expected to implement information security programs in compliance with the law and to accept the authority of other agencies to issue implementation guidance or otherwise direct their activities. These obligations include adopting mandatory federal standards and following associated guidance published by NIST, reporting performance metrics and other security-related information to OMB, notifying DHS of security incidents or other events, and adhering to CNSS policies and instructions for any national security systems they operate. Agency leaders, risk managers, security program managers, and system owners need to be aware of key government organizational roles and responsibilities, both to ensure compliance with regulatory requirements and to leverage the expertise offered by these organizations to improve their information security practices and operations.

Office of Management and Budget (OMB)

FISMA gives the Director of OMB responsibility for overseeing the implementation of the law's provisions in federal civilian agencies, monitoring agency progress and compliance with the law, and reporting to Congress on government-wide results from FISMA implementation. OMB prepares and approves information technology sections of the president's budget and performs budgetary oversight of agency investments, including those related to information security. OMB issues annual FISMA reporting instructions to agencies, and coordinates the submission of information security and privacy metrics and other FISMA report information through the online CyberScope tool, available to agencies through OMB's MAX Portal. CyberScope, first launched in 2009 and mandated for agency use beginning in November 2010 [70], is intended to streamline the agency FISMA reporting process by enabling automated data feeds directly from agency security management systems to OMB and offering online forms and document upload capabilities to replace some of the manual document-based submission processes agencies used in the past. OMB also guides agency implementation and compliance with legislative requirements through official circulars and issues memoranda to announce recommended or mandatory actions or provide additional guidance to agencies on satisfying regulatory or policy obligations.

National Institute of Standards and Technology (NIST)

Since the passage of the Computer Security Act of 1987, NIST has primary responsibility for prescribing standards and guidelines for federal information systems (other than national security systems), including standards and guidelines for achieving adequate security protection for those systems. NIST produces Federal Information Processing Standards and Special Publications related to information system security, and leads the Joint Task Force Transformation Initiative interagency working group in the development of a common security framework for all government agencies.

Department of Defense (DoD)

FISMA gives the Secretary of Defense responsibility for implementing the law's provisions for systems (other than national security systems) operated by the DoD or its component agencies. In this context the DoD performs the same oversight role for DoD systems as OMB performs for civilian agency systems. The Department of Defense also occupies a leading role in the oversight of national security systems, as the Secretary of Defense serves as the executive agent of the CNSS and the DoD has authority (shared with the Office of the Director of National Intelligence) over the operations of the National Security Agency.

Office of the Director of National Intelligence (ODNI)

The Director of National Intelligence leads the intelligence community and has important oversight responsibility for both FISMA-covered systems and national security systems operated by intelligence agencies. FISMA assigned responsibility for implementing the law's provisions for central intelligence agency systems (other than national security systems) to the Director of Central Intelligence, but that single position was replaced in 2004 with two roles—the Director of National Intelligence and the Director of the Central Intelligence Agency. The ODNI coordinates activities among many intelligence agencies, including agencies organized under the Departments of Homeland Security and Defense, including the NSA. ODNI is also a member of the CNSS, contributing to the development and implementation of policy and guidance for national security systems.

Department of Homeland Security (DHS)

The Department of Homeland Security, created by an act of Congress just three weeks before FISMA became law, did not have any explicit authority under FISMA other than the responsibilities prescribed for executive agencies. DHS subsequently established and assumed management of US-CERT under its National Cyber Security Division, satisfying the FISMA requirement for a federal information security incident center [71]. DHS leads several government-wide information security initiatives and is a member of CNSS, collaborating with civilian, defense, and intelligence sector agencies on developing policies and guidelines for national security systems. Since 2010, DHS has also had primary responsibility for the operational aspects of information security in federal agencies managing systems subject to FISMA. This responsibility includes overseeing the implementation of security policies, standards, and guidance intended to provide adequate security for federal information systems; monitoring agency compliance with FISMA; overseeing and assisting with agency incident response and other security operations; and conducting annual reviews of agency security programs [46].

National Security Agency (NSA)

The NSA, a component of DoD and a member of the intelligence community overseen by the ODNI, provides technical expertise on information security and critical infrastructure protection to all federal agencies, and works closely with DHS and other agencies to implement key government-wide information security initiatives. The NSA also serves as the CNSS Secretariat, providing administrative support to the Committee, coordinating its working groups and other activities, and issuing CNSS guidance.

General Services Administration (GSA)

The General Services Administration provides a variety of services and types of assistance to other government agencies, including acquisition services related to information technology and security. It manages a range of government-wide contracts through which agencies can procure information technology products, solutions, and services, including a blanket purchase agreement awarded to more than a dozen contractors to provide services to agencies related to the Risk Management Framework. The GSA establishes technical requirements for contractors providing information technology solutions to government agencies, including development, implementation, and operation of federal information systems. The GSA also manages and provides government-wide access to shared services including identity, credential, and access management; public key infrastructure; and security assessment, authorization, and monitoring of cloud computing service providers.

Government Accountability Office (GAO)

The GAO is an independent agency that monitors, investigates, and reports to Congress on federal government operations, assessing the programs and the regulatory compliance of executive agencies. The GAO does not establish policy or set its own requirements, but it does interpret statutory requirements in federal legislation and evaluate agency progress in implementing those requirements. GAO reports often highlight weaknesses or deficiencies in agency programs and initiatives, including achievement of (or failure to achieve) milestones or objectives established for mandatory government-wide initiatives. Individual agency or government-wide GAO investigations and associated reports may identify threats, vulnerabilities, sources of risk, or information useful to agency risk managers, IT program managers, and information security personnel.

Congress

Congress establishes many information security requirements for government agencies through legislative action, and also provides oversight for agency compliance with the law through periodic reviews of information submitted by agencies to OMB and reported to Congressional committees, such as the House Committee on

Oversight and Government Reform and Senate Committee on Homeland Security and Government Affairs. Congress has the primary authority to revise, augment, or replace FISMA and other federal security laws; newly proposed legislation in recent Congressional sessions sought to amend the law to add stronger oversight, security governance, and compliance requirements, but no changes to FISMA have made it through the legislative process.

Executive Office of the President

Aside from overseeing OMB, the president has substantial authority to declare policy and issue mandatory requirements for agencies in many domains related to information security. The scope of this authority ranges from executive orders issued by the president directing agencies to take specific actions to formal policy declarations in the form of National Security Presidential Directives and Homeland Security Presidential Directives. The president's Cybersecurity Coordinator also oversees government-wide security strategy and policy development, working in collaboration with OMB and DHS.

RELEVANT SOURCE MATERIAL

Key concepts and legislative and regulatory requirements for information security in federal government organizations derive primarily from statutory language enacted by Congress and official guidance issued by OMB and other authoritative sources. These sources include:

- Federal Information Security Management Act of 2002 [72].
- Information Technology Management Reform Act of 1996 [73].
- Paperwork Reduction Act of 1995 [74].
- Title 44, Chapter 35 of the US Code, *Coordination of Federal Information Policy* [75].
- Appendix III of OMB Circular A-130, *Security of Federal Automated Information Resources* [38].

Additional useful sources of information, requirements, and instructions related to information security management and operational concepts include the materials provided by the government agencies or multi-agency organizations that specify policy, issue implementation guidance, and oversee compliance in each government sector. Among these sources are:

- FISMA Implementation Project at NIST:
  - http://csrc.nist.gov/groups/SMA/fisma/index.html
- Defense Technical Information Center:
  - http://www.dtic.mil/whs/directives/index.html
- Committee on National Security Systems (CNSS):
  - http://www.cnss.gov/

SUMMARY

This chapter introduced some of the concepts, security objectives, legislative and regulatory requirements, and sources of guidance to agencies performing information assurance and information security management functions. This material provides historical background on current information security practices and establishes the context in which key risk management activities occur in each sector of the government. Recognizing the central role of system certification and accreditation process in government agencies—before and since FISMA's enactment—this chapter also described the evolution of C&A processes in the civilian, defense, and intelligence sectors towards the common government-wide approach envisioned for the Risk Management Framework.

REFERENCES

[1] Definitions. 44 U.S.C. §3542; 2011.

[2] Among the best known alternative model is the six-attribute framework proposed by Donn Parker, which adds authenticity, possession, and utility to the CIA model. See Parker DB. Fighting computer crime: A new framework for protecting information. New York: Wiley; 1998.

[3] Information assurance technical framework (release 3.0). Washington DC: National Security Agency; September 2000.

[4] McCumber J. Assessing and managing security risk in IT systems: a structured methodology. Boca Raton FL: Auerbach; 2005.

[5] The Privacy Act, relevant information security legislation, and US statutory provisions all fail to define privacy and official glossaries from NIST and CNSS also contain no definition for privacy.

[6] The lack of an accepted or standard definition of privacy is a pervasive theme in legal and academic treatments of the subject; see, for example, Solove DJ. Understanding privacy. Cambridge, MA: Harvard University Press; 2008.

[7] The CNSS National Information Assurance Glossary includes one such narrow definition, although it also cites the statutory definition used by NIST in Special Publication 800-53. National information assurance glossary. Fort Meade MD: Committee on National Security Systems; April 2009. CNSS Instruction No. 4009. p. 38.

[8] Federal Information Security Management Act of 2002, Pub. L. No. 107-347, 116 Stat. 2946. §301, codified at 44 U.S.C. §3543.

[9] National information assurance glossary. Fort Meade, MD: Committee on National Security Systems; April 2009. CNSS Instruction No. 4009. p. 35.

[10] See DoD Manual 5200.01, Information Security Program; DoD Instruction 8510.01, Information Assurance Certification and Accreditation Process (DIACAP); and DoD Instruction 8500.02, Information Assurance (IA) Implementation. Washington DC: Department of Defense; February 24, 2012, November 28, 2007, and February 6, 2003, respectively.

[11] Recommended security controls for federal information systems and organizations. Gaithersburg, MD: National Institute of Standards and Technology, Computer Security Division; August 2009 Special Publication 800-53 revision 3. p. 14.

[12] ISO/IEC 27000:2009. Information technology—Security techniques—Information security management systems—Overview and vocabulary.

[13] Ware WH. Security controls for computer systems: Report of defense science board task force on computer security. Santa Monica CA: Rand Corporation; February 1970 [declassified October 1975; reissued October 1979]. RAND Report R-609-1.

[14] Bell DE, LaPadula LJ. Secure computer system: Unifed exposition and multics interpretation. Bedford, MA: The MITRE Corporation; 1976.. MITRE Technical Report 2997.

[15] Biba KJ. Integrity considerations for secure computer systems. Bedford, MA: The MITRE Corporation; 1975. MITRE Report MTR-3153.

[16] See, for example, Clark DD, Wilson DR. A comparison of commercial and military computer security policies. IEEE symposium on security and privacy; April 1987. p. 184–194.

[17] National training standard for information systems security (INFOSEC) professionals. Fort Meade, MD: National Security Telecommunications and Information Systems Security Committee; June 20, 1994. NSTISS Instruction No. 4011.

[18] See for example, the explanation of the intended use of the McCumber cube, which purported to address all aspects of information security in its 27-element framework: National training standard for information systems security (INFOSEC) professionals. Fort Meade, MD: National Security Telecommunications and Information Systems Security Committee; June 20, 1994. NSTISS Instruction No. 4011.

[19] Recommended security controls for federal information systems and organizations. Gaithersburg, MD: National Institute of Standards and Technology, Computer Security Division; August 2009. Special Publication 800-53 revision 3. p. 19.

[20] The explicit title Director of Central Intelligence no longer exists; the role was reestablished in 2004 as the Director of the Central Intelligence Agency, and the responsibility for serving as head of the intelligence community was shifted to the newly created Director of National Intelligence. Intelligence Prevention and Terrorism Reform Act of 2004, Pub. L. No. 108-458, 118 Stat. 3638. §1011.

[21] Federal Information Security Management Act of 2002, Pub. L. No. 107-347, 116 Stat. 2946. §301.

[22] National policy for the security of national security telecommunications and information systems. Washington, DC: The White House; July 5, 1990. National Security Directive 42.

[23] Federal Information Security Management Act of 2002, Pub. L. No. 107-347, 116 Stat. 2946. §301, codified at 44 U.S.C. §3547.

[24] National policy for the security of national security telecommunications and information systems. Washington, DC: The White House; Jul 5, 1990. National Security Directive 42. P. 3.

[25] National policy on telecommunications and automated information systems security. Washington, DC: The White House; September 17, 1984. National Security Decision Directive 145.

[26] Computer Security Act of 1987, Pub. L. 100-235, 101 Stat. 1724. At the time, NIST was known as the National Bureau of Standards.

[27] Department of Defense materials, collectively referred to as "issuances" are available online from the Defense Technical Information Center's Division of Directives: DoD Issuances [Internet]. Fort Belvoir, VA: Defense Technical Information Center; [cited March 27, 2012]. Available from: http://www.dtic.mil/whs/directives/index.html.

[28] Standards for security categorization of federal information and information systems. Gaithersburg, MD: National Institute of Standards and Technology, Computer Security Division; December 2003. Federal Information Processing Standards Publication p. 199.

[29] Security controls applicable to each combination of MAC level and confidentiality level are specified in DoD Instruction 8500.2: Information assurance (IA) implementation. Washington, DC: Department of Defense; February 6, 2003.

[30] Defense acquisition guidebook. Washington, DC: Department of Defense; January 10, 2012. p. 606.

[31] Clinton WJ. Classified national security information. Washington, DC: The White House; April 17, 1995. Executive Order No. 12958.

[32] Intelligence community classification guidance findings and recommendations report. Washington, DC: Office of the Director of National Intelligence; January 2008.

[33] Security categorization and control selection for national security systems. Fort Meade, MD: Committee on National Security Systems; October 2009. CNSS Instruction No. 1253.

[34] The new term replaced the previous designation "sensitive but unclassified" and is subject to decomposition or subcategorization by agencies as needed. Obama B. Controlled unclassified information. Washington, DC: The White House; November 4, 2010. Executive Order 13556.

[35] Minimum security requirements for federal information and information systems. Gaithersburg (MD): National Institute of Standards and Technology, Computer Security Division; March 2006. Federal Information Processing Standards Publication 200. p. 4.

[36] Recommended security controls for federal information systems and organizations. Gaithersburg, MD: National Institute of Standards and Technology, Computer Security Division; August 2009. Special Publication 800-53 revision 3.

[37] ISO/IEC 27002:2005. Information technology—Security techniques—Code of practice for information security management.

[38] Appendix III, Security of federal automated information resources. Washington, DC: Office of Management and Budget; November 2000. Circular No. A-130, Revised [Transmittal Memorandum No. 4].

[39] Guide for applying the risk management framework to federal information systems. Gaithersburg, MD: National Institute of Standards and Technology, Computer Security Division; February 2010. Special Publication 800-37 revision 1.

[40] DoD information assurance certification and accreditation process (DIACAP). Washington, DC: Department of Defense; November 28, 2007. DoD Instruction 8510.01.

[41] National information assurance certification and accreditation process (NIACAP). Fort Meade, MD: National Security Telecommunications and Information Systems Security Committee; April 2000. NSTISS Instruction No. 1000.

[42] See for example the Federal Property and Administrative Services Act of 1949, Pub. L. No. 81-152, 63 Stat. 377, which created the General Services Administration and gave it authority to coordinate purchase and maintenance of automatic data processing equipment for federal agencies, and the Brooks Act of 1965, Pub. L. No. 89-306, 79 Stat. 1127, delegating authority to the Secretary of Commerce to make recommendations establishing automatic data processing standards.

[43] Privacy Act of 1974, Pub. L. No. 93-579, 88 Stat. 1896. §552a(e)(10).

[44] Computer Security Act of 1987, Pub. L. 100-235, 101 Stat. 1724.

[45] Security of federal automated information systems. Washington (DC): Office of Management and Budget; July 27, 1978. Circular No. A-71 (Transmittal Memorandum No. 1).

[46] Orszag PR. Clarifying cybersecurity responsibilities and activities of the Executive Office of the President and the Department of Homeland Security (DHS). Washington, DC: Office of Management and Budget; July 6, 2010. Memorandum M-10-28.

[47] Guideline for computer security certification and accreditation. Gaithersburg, MD: National Bureau of Standards, Institute for Computer Sciences and Technology; September 1983. Federal Information Processing Standards Publication 102.

[48] Appendix III, Security of federal automated information resources. Washington, DC: Office of Management and Budget; February 1996. Circular No. A-130, Revised (Transmittal Memorandum No. 3).

[49] DoD information technology security certification and accreditation process (DITSCAP). Washington, DC: Department of Defense; December 30, 1997. DoD Instruction 5200.40.

[50] Ross R, Swanson M, Stoneburner G, Katzke S, Johnson A. Guide for the security certification and accreditation of federal information systems. Gaithersburg, MD: National Institute of Standards and Technology, Computer Security Division; May 2004. Special Publication 800-37.

[51] CNSS released new policy guidance in early 2012 stating the intention to replace prior policy on certification and accreditation of national security systems and the NIACAP with risk management guidance issued by NIST. Policy on information assurance risk management for national security systems. Fort Meade, MD: Committee on National Security Systems; January 2012. CNSS Policy No. 22.

[52] Guideline for computer security certification and accreditation. Gaithersburg, MD: National Institute of Standards and Technology, Computer Security Division; September 1983. Federal Information Processing Standards Publication 102. p. 52.

[53] Guideline for computer security certification and accreditation. Gaithersburg, MD: National Institute of Standards and Technology, Computer Security Division; September 1983. Federal Information Processing Standards Publication 102. p. 8–10.

[54] Ruthbert ZG, Neugent W. Overview of computer security certification and accreditation. Washington, DC: Government Printing Office; April 1984. Special Publication 500-109

[55] Kissel R, Stine K, Scholl M, Rossman H, Fahlsing J, Gulick J. Security considerations in the system development life cycle. Gaithersburg, MD: National Institute of Standards and Technology, Computer Security Division; October 2008. Special Publication 800-64 revision 2.

[56] DoD information technology security certification and accreditation process (DITSCAP). Washington, DC: Department of Defense; December 30, 1997. DoD Instruction 5200.40. p. 17.

[57] NIACAP instructions reference CNSS Policy No. 6, originally issued in 1994 by NSTSSC and updated in 2005 when the committee had been redesignated as the CNSS. National policy on certification and accreditation of national security systems. Fort Meade, MD: Committee on National Security Systems; October 2005.

[58] National information assurance certification and accreditation process (NIACAP). Fort Meade, MD: National Security Telecommunications and Information Systems Security Committee; April 2000. NSTISS Instruction No. 1000. p. 1.

[59] National information assurance certification and accreditation process (NIACAP). Fort Meade, MD: National Security Telecommunications and Information Systems Security Committee; April 2000. NSTISS Instruction No. 1000. p. 4.

[60] Ross R, Swanson M, Stoneburner G, Katzke S, Johnson A . Guide for the security certification and accreditation of federal information systems. Gaithersburg, MD:

National Institute of Standards and Technology, Computer Security Division; May 2004. Special Publication 800-37.

[61] Ross R, Swanson M, Stoneburner G, Katzke S, Johnson A . Guide for the security certification and accreditation of federal information systems. Gaithersburg, MD: National Institute of Standards and Technology, Computer Security Division; May 2004. Special Publication 800-37. p.25.

[62] DoD information assurance certification and accreditation process (DIACAP). Washington, DC: Department of Defense; November 28, 2007. DoD Instruction 8510.01. p. 23.

[63] DoD information assurance certification and accreditation process (DIACAP). Washington, DC: Department of Defense; November 28, 2007. DoD Instruction 8510.01. p. 13.

[64] Guide for applying the risk management framework to federal information systems. Gaithersburg, MD: National Institute of Standards and Technology, Computer Security Division; February 2010. Special Publication 800-37 revision 1. p. 1.

[65] Guide for applying the risk management framework to federal information systems. Gaithersburg, MD: National Institute of Standards and Technology, Computer Security Division; February 2010. Special Publication 800-37 revision 1. p. 8.

[66] Policy on information assurance risk management for national security systems. Fort Meade, MD: Committee on National Security Systems; January 2012. CNSS Policy No. 22.

[67] Security categorization and control selection for national security systems. Fort Meade, MD: Committee on National Security Systems; October 2009. CNSS Instruction 1253.

[68] The Department of Defense has not issued policy or directives indicating the approach it intends to take or a timeline for migrating to the RMF, but many industry analysts have suggested a new DIARMF process may be released in the near future.

[69] This is the approach used by the DoD for its DITSCAP to DIACAP transition. DoD information assurance certification and accreditation process (DIACAP). Washington, DC: Department of Defense; November 28, 2007. DoD Instruction 8510.01. p. 52–3.

[70] Zients J, Kundra V, Schmidt HA. FY 2010 reporting instructions for the Federal Information Security Management Act and agency privacy management. Washington, DC: Office of Management and Budget; April 21, 2010. Memorandum M-10-15.

[71] NIST established the Federal Computer Incident Response Capability (FedCIRC) in 1996 and the General Services Administration operated it from 1998 until 2003, when its functions were assimilated into US-CERT and placed under the authority of the newly created Department of Homeland Security.

[72] Federal Information Security Management Act of 2002, Pub. L. No. 107-347, 116 Stat. 2946.

[73] Information Technology Management Reform Act of 1996, Pub. L. No. 104-106, 110 Stat. 679.

[74] Paperwork Reduction Act of 1995, Pub. L. No. 104-13, 109 Stat. 1643.

[75] 44 U.S.C. §§35013549.

Thinking About Risk

INFORMATION IN THIS CHAPTER:

- Understanding Risk
- Trust, Assurance, and Security
- Risk Associated with Information Systems
- Risk Management Life Cycle

All organizations have some exposure to risk, defined as the potential for loss, damage, injury, or other undesirable outcome resulting from decisions, actions, or events affecting organizational operations. Risk exists because the future cannot be predicted with certainty; organizational plans or strategies regarding future events reflect assumptions, calculations, or estimates about what will occur, but there is always a chance that events will unfold differently than anticipated, potentially with results less favorable than those for which the organization planned. Theories of risk in organizational management, sociology, economics, political science, and other fields differ in the way they characterize risk, but scholars and practitioners tend to agree on the point that no individual or organizational behavior is free of risk [1]. Contrary to economic and mathematical models that assume decision-makers possess complete information, contemporary theories of organizational behavior propose that organizations operate in environments subject to both anticipated and unexpected changes and that organizational leaders must by necessity make decisions based on incomplete information [2]. The inability to predict future outcomes with precision and the uncertainty inherent in the environments in which organizations operate results in risk. The persistent presence of risk makes it essential for organizations to develop the capabilities and procedures necessary for managing risk. This chapter identifies aspects of risk applicable to all types of organizations and highlights key considerations for risk management from the perspective of federal government organizations. The information presented in this chapter provides an overview of risk and highlights the importance of effective risk management, introducing the core processes used to manage information security-related risk. A more detailed description of information security risk assessment procedures and other risk management practices prescribed in Special Publication 800-39 [3] appears in Chapter 13.

UNDERSTANDING RISK

The primary purposes of information security management include preventing loss or damage to organizational assets and minimizing the extent of adverse impacts when they cannot be prevented; in this respect information security management is a mechanism for managing risk. Similarly, organizational strategic planning, investment decision-making, and operational management all consider potential sources of risk and seek to manage that risk in a manner that consistently maintains risk at or below the level the organization is willing to accept. The Risk Management Framework and risk management processes NIST defines in Special Publication 800-39, provide comprehensive guidance on managing risk associated with information systems and the environments in which those systems operate. This guidance complements other risk management practices and activities that organizations may employ as part of enterprise-wide risk management programs. Although the scope of the RMF and NIST guidance to agencies is explicitly limited to managing information security-related risk, system owners and others responsible for managing or operating information systems should be aware of all types of risk applicable to their organizations and understand how information security-related risk relates to other types of risk. Effective organizational risk management depends on a thorough and accurate understanding of risk, including organizational processes for identifying, measuring, and responding to risk.

Key Concepts

While most basic definitions characterize *risk* as the chance or possibility of loss or other adverse consequences, in management contexts conceptions of risk include dimensions of both frequency and magnitude [4]. The International Organization for Standardization (ISO) defines *risk* simply as "effect of uncertainty on objectives," but notes the common expression of risk in terms of the likelihood of occurrence of event and resulting consequences [5]. In its guidance to federal agencies NIST uses the same concepts, using the terms *likelihood of occurrence* and *impact*, and adopts the definition of risk provided by the Committee on National Security Systems (CNSS):

NOTE

Although risk management strategy in public and private sector organizations often focuses on anticipating and responding to risk resulting in negative consequences, uncertain future outcomes include events with both positive and negative impacts. Financial or investment risk models incorporate the idea of upside risk, in which actual outcomes differ from expectations to the benefit of the organization. The potential for positive outcomes in excess of organizational predictions can represent a strategic or tactical opportunity that helps organizational leaders justify a particular decision or course of action. In the government sector, while the potential for especially favorable outcomes is considered within the scope of enterprise risk management, the emphasis in risk management as practiced in federal agencies is on anticipating and controlling adverse impacts.

"A measure of the extent to which an entity is threatened by a potential circumstance or event," calculated as a function the adverse impacts to an entity and the likelihood of occurrence [6]. Such definitions apply broadly to any type of risk. In practice many organizations and sources of guidance categorize risk into multiple types based on the operational aspects or management objectives to which risk applies or the level of the organization responsible for managing risk. Information technology or information security risk is distinguished from general business risk or other more specific types by the relevant threat sources and the nature of the anticipated impacts, where information security risk reflects impacts to an organization from the loss of confidentiality, integrity, or availability of information or information systems.

Measuring Risk

Organizations typically describe risk magnitude as an estimated value of loss or reduction in operational capability, such as the cost to the organization in dollars, decrease in production of services or other outputs, or time delay in execution of mission functions or business processes. Risk magnitude is not always easy to quantify, so organizations sometimes also assign relative risk values—such as "high," "medium," and "low"—that may not yield precise information about a given risk but enable the comparison of risk from different sources. Similarly, the frequency or likelihood of occurrence associated with risk may be expressed as a quantitative or qualitative probability, reflecting the chance that a threat, adverse event, or undesirable outcome will occur. The choice of quantitative or qualitative forms of risk expression depends in part on the accuracy, completeness, and specificity of the information available for use in risk identification and assessment activities and the reliability of that information [7]. Consistent risk measurement facilitates the evaluation and prioritization of risk at an organization-wide level, so some organizations choose to normalize all risk estimates—whether produced using quantitative or qualitative methods—using a standard rating scale. Given the difficulty associated with performing quantitative risk assessments for some types of risk, many organizations favor qualitative or semi-quantitative risk rating scales, such as those offered by NIST in its guidance on conducting risk assessments [8]. Both of these NIST risk rating approaches include five risk levels, using the same scale as those recommended for measuring likelihood of occurrence and impact—qualitative values are "very low," "low," "moderate," "high," and "very high," each with a corresponding numerical range for semi-quantitative measurement.

Certainty, Uncertainty, and Probability

Risk management decision-making relies on risk determinations produced through the supporting processes of risk identification and assessment. Organizations need to consider the accuracy and confidence level associated with risk determinations as well as the extent to which risk determinations reflect the complete set of outcomes that could occur. Decision-making is the easiest for risk supported by complete information, including a comprehensive understanding of the possible outcomes and the probability associated with each. When operating under certainty, organizational leaders can objectively compare each outcome and alternative courses of action and make a clear risk-based decision about the preferred choice for the organization. Conditions of certainty are rare in risk management, particularly with respect to information security risk sources where the rapid pace of technological change and frequent emergence of new threats and zero-day exploits make it infeasible to identify all possible events and potential adverse outcomes. Even organizations practicing comprehensive risk management need to work under the assumption that the information supporting their determinations of risk is incomplete and that they may not be aware of all potential sources of risk relevant to the organization. Some theories of risk management and organizational behavior distinguish between *risk* and *uncertainty* based on an organization's ability to assign a probability to each possible outcome. From this perspective organizational risk is the set of all outcomes with calculable frequency distributions, while uncertainty exists either when probabilities cannot be determined for different outcomes or when the set of all possible outcomes is unknown [9].

In many established risk management models, including those contained in international standards [10] and in NIST guidance, uncertainty due to incomplete information about the likelihood or impact of an event or its consequences is a contributing factor to risk and, more importantly, to organizational risk management decisions. Organizations need to understand the uncertainty associated with risk determinations to make properly informed risk-based decisions. Organizations may define their risk tolerance—an essential criterion in all risk-based decisions—not just in terms of the relative level of risk they are willing to accept, but also in terms of how much uncertainty they can accommodate in risk determinations. Where risk tolerance is usually expressed in terms of qualitative risk levels, tolerance for uncertainty may be stated in terms of the confidence afforded by the quality, completeness, and integrity of the information used to determine risk. Organizational decision-makers should acknowledge the uncertainty inherent in managing many types of risk and incorporate practices for responding to risk in the face of uncertainty in their risk management strategies.

Assurance

Organizations need to have confidence in the information and processes underlying management of all types of risk. With respect to managing risk associated with operating and maintaining information systems, organizations need to have an appropriate level of confidence that the security measures implemented to protect information systems are effective in achieving their security objectives and in providing adequate security for information assets. In information security management, the level of confidence in the effectiveness of security controls is called *assurance*. Assurance helps organizations determine the level of trustworthiness attributable to information systems and the organizations that operate them and therefore influences the risk determination associated with those systems and organizations, as higher levels of trustworthiness correlate to lower levels of some types of risk [11,12]. Assurance is based on evidence presented to decision-makers, often as the result of assessments, audits, or other types of evaluations conducted on various aspects of organizational operations.

> **NOTE**
>
> In the information security management context assurance evidence often comes in the form of information system or operational testing results, security control assessments, continuous monitoring data, or certifications provided by accredited third parties. The concept of assurance applies in many domains other than information technology and is relevant to risk determinations for types of risk beyond information security risk. Both public and private sector organizations are subject to periodic audits, reviews, or assessments of their financial management and accounting practices, program management performance, safety, regulatory compliance, or other operational characteristics in addition to the effectiveness of the information security and privacy controls. The evidence produced as a result of such evaluations informs risk management decisions made by organizational leaders and external authorities with regulatory oversight or other supervisory responsibilities.

Organizations often perform their own evidence-gathering activities, directly or through the use of independent auditors or assessors. With respect to hardware, software, infrastructure, or services acquired from external vendors, contractors, or service providers, assurance may also be based on evidence produced by organizations that conduct external testing or certification on technology products or service providers. Examples of testing and security certification programs include the Common Criteria Evaluation and Validation Scheme for IT Security (CCEVS) administered by the National Information Assurance Partnership (NIAP) and the third-party assessment of cloud computing service providers under the Federal Risk and Authorization Management Program (FedRAMP). Both of these programs are described in Chapter 17.

Types of Risk

The scope of enterprise risk management covers all organizational aspects for which adverse events have the potential to affect the organization's ability to achieve its objectives. While Risk Management Frameworks often provide risk classification schemes categorizing different types of risk, the fundamental processes used to manage risk tend to be the same regardless of risk type and include risk strategy, risk identification, risk assessment, risk monitoring, and risk response [13]. A key distinction in many models exists between information technology or information system-related risk and various types of business or operational risk, particularly including financial risk. NIST acknowledges many kinds of risk in addition to information security risk and emphasizes the complexity inherent in enterprise risk management [14], but identifies only threat sources relevant to information security risk and does not explicitly correlate information security risk to any of the other types federal government organizations may face. Considering information security risk in isolation may help system owners focus appropriate attention on the most directly relevant sources of risk associated with their information systems, but agencies and their system owners also need to understand how other types of risk can impact information security risk and how information security risks—when realized—affect other types of risk. Figure 3.1 illustrates types of organizational risk subject to enterprise risk management, all of which have some relationship to information security risk.

The federal government has no comprehensive risk management guidance or single enterprise Risk Management Framework applicable to all types of risk. While NIST's Risk Management Framework addresses information security risk and the Government Accountability Office developed a separate Risk Management Framework focused on critical infrastructure protection and homeland security [15], government agencies often look to external sources of guidance on enterprise risk management. Relevant sources include guidance from the International Organization for Standardization (ISO), including ISO/IEC 31000 and related standards on risk management principles, practices, and assessment methods [16] and the enterprise Risk Management Framework produced by the Committee on Sponsoring Organizations of the Treadway Commission (COSO) [17]. In contrast to US government produced alternatives, these frameworks adopt an integrated risk management perspective spanning all types of risk, all levels of an organization, and multiple types of organizational objectives. These models do not enumerate specific types of risk, recognizing that different kinds of organizations or organizations in different sectors may use specific risk categorization schemes and associated risk management

FIGURE 3.1 Although Responsibility for Managing Risk Often Focuses on Just One or a Few Types of Risk, Risk Managers Need Some Understanding of the Many Different Kinds of Risk Their Organizations Face and the Role of Their Risk Management Activities in the Broader Scope of Organizational Risk Management

techniques. Risk management applies to strategic and operational objectives and, for organizations in sectors subject to oversight or regulatory requirements, also supports reporting and compliance objectives. Many sources of guidance identify similar core processes within overall Risk Management Frameworks, including the establishment of risk management context and associated objectives, risk assessment, risk response, risk monitoring, and internal and external communications [18]. Identifying different contexts that enterprise risk management addresses can facilitate the selection of more specific standards and guidance for different types of risk and the effective allocation of risk management resources at each level of the organization.

Information Security Risk

Information security risk comprises the impacts to an organization and its stakeholders that could occur due to the threats and vulnerabilities associated with the operation and use of information systems and the environments in which those systems operate. The primary means of mitigating information security-related risk is through the selection, implementation, maintenance, and continuous monitoring of preventive, detective, and corrective security controls to protect information assets from compromise or to limit the damage to the organization should a compromise occur. Information security risk overlaps with many other types of risk in terms of the kinds of impact that might result from the occurrence of a security-related incident. It is also influenced by factors attributed to other categories of risk, including strategic, budgetary, program management, investment, political, legal, reputation, supply chain, and compliance risk.

Budgetary Risk

Budgetary risk refers both to the risk implicit in organizational budgets and the uncertainty federal agencies face regarding whether budget allocations approved by Congress match the funding they request. The federal government budget planning cycle focuses 12–18 months in the future (for example, the budget formulation process that occurred between March and September 2012 developed funding requests for the 2014 fiscal year beginning October 1, 2013). An agency's ability to execute its plans and implement and operate its programs depends on budget authorization, so when faced with budget shortfalls due to unanticipated reductions in requested funds, continuing resolutions, or other reasons, agencies may need to adjust their priorities based on the resources available. This is true for funding to support security programs and capabilities just as it is for other operational functions. Agencies develop IT security portfolios as part of their budget requests, in which they report prior year and anticipated future costs for security tools in eight different categories as well as costs for Risk Management Framework implementation, required annual FISMA testing, penetration testing, and security awareness and training [19]. Funding sufficient to cover costs expected to be incurred in the budgeted fiscal year is not guaranteed, so agencies should prioritize their security spending and resource allocations and develop potential responses should the funding appropriated fall short of expectations. Funding shortfalls are not the only type of outcome associated with budgetary risk for information security, as the emergence of significant new threats, occurrences of security incidents, or changes in policy may result in additional funding allocations to agencies beyond the levels requested in agency budget requests [20].

Investment Risk

Investment decisions made by organizations typically consider the cost of a given investment and compare the direct or indirect cost with the benefits anticipated or other factors justifying the investment. Organizations use a variety of justification methods to support investment decisions, including strategic alignment, mission criticality, and regulatory compliance or economic calculations such as return on investment, net present value, or cost-benefit analysis. Investment risk stems from the possibility that investments the organization makes do not produce the anticipated results. Because organizations—including government agencies—operate under resource constraints that limit the number and size of investments they can make, investment decisions typically require prioritization or trade-offs among multiple alternatives, so investment risk typically includes the results from investments organizations make as well as the opportunity cost associated with not making other investments. As noted in Chapter 5, agencies may use multiple approaches to justify their security investments, including compliance requirements, economic benefits, and performance improvements. To the extent that agency security investments produce results different from what was anticipated in business cases or other forms of investment justification, security program officials and investment owners may need to provide alternative or more extensive information to justify future investments.

Legal Risk

Legal risk applies to any aspect of an organization subject to legislative or regulatory requirements and includes issues or incidents that result in failure to comply with regulations, breach of contract, statutory penalties, or other forms of legal liability. While FISMA includes no direct penalties for failing to comply with its provisions, the potential impact to agencies from security incidents such as data breaches includes the imposition of civil and even criminal penalties. Legal risk is also related to budgetary, investment, political, and reputation risk, as the occurrence of events associated with legal risk may subject an organization to higher levels of scrutiny and require corrective action to restore confidence in the organization's ability to conduct operations in compliance with legal or regulatory requirements.

Political Risk

Compared to their private sector counterparts, government agencies have relatively little freedom to significantly alter their missions or to commit significant budgetary or other resources without approval from executive and legislative branch authorities. The external authorizing environment for most federal executive agencies includes Congress, which must enact annual legislation to allocate funding for agency programs and operational expenditures. As evidenced by Congressional budget debates in recent years and the repeated need to rely on continuing resolutions to keep the government operating, significant disagreement exists within the legislature regarding the most appropriate use of federal funds and the priorities assigned to government programs. The inability for agencies to accurately predict how Congress will behave, what new legislation will be enacted, or when annual budget appropriations will be determined and made available are all aspects of political risk. Beyond the clear financial implications of political risk, agencies' efforts to plan to satisfy compliance requirements or other obligations are hindered by political uncertainty such as proposed but not-yet-enacted legislation that would impose new requirements. For example, draft cyber security legislation introduced in recent Congressional sessions would, if passed, expand current FISMA provisions in the areas of continuous monitoring and federal oversight of agency security programs [21] and require new levels of information sharing with private sector organizations responsible for managing elements of critical infrastructure [22].

Program Management Risk

Program management risk shares some characteristics with budgetary and investment risk, but with an emphasis on the ability of agency programs to achieve their intended outcomes, and do so in accordance with projected costs and within timelines established as part of initial program funding and implementation and ongoing program planning. Large-scale or high-visibility federal programs are often subject to earned value management (EVM), a formal program performance measurement and tracking approach that requires program managers to establish cost and schedule baselines and to track variance between the projected baseline and actual costs incurred and time required to perform program activities. Since mid-2009 the Office of Management and Budget has published cost and schedule performance data for investments included in federal agency IT portfolios online on the Federal IT Dashboard website [23]. Programs with significant variations in cost or schedule performance may be subject to corrective action or even cancellation, particularly if cost overruns or delays persist.

Reputation Risk

The occurrence of events that occur associated with many types of risk may also result in damage to an organization's reputation, with potential impacts including bad publicity, destruction of public trust, or loss of confidence in the organization's ability to perform its operational functions or successfully execute its mission. Many threats and other kinds of events produce reputation risk, including those applicable to the operation and use of information systems. Individuals and organizations may be less willing to interact with agencies suffering intentional or accidental data breaches, falling victim to cyber attacks, or otherwise failing to demonstrate adequate security and privacy protection for information assets under their management or control. Although no practical alternative exists for many types of government services delivered by government agencies, an agency often must devote additional resources to recover from reputation damage and conduct normal operations in situations where constituents or stakeholders have reduced confidence in the agency.

Safety Risk

Safety risk relates to outcomes from incidents or events that cause injury to people or damage to property and is a central element in many aspects of continuity planning, including contingency planning, disaster recovery, and emergency preparedness and response. Although loss or harm associated with safety risk typically involves financial cost, management of safety risk often emphasizes preventive or reactive measures that seek to limit injury to individuals, loss of life, and destruction of property.

Strategic Risk

Strategic risk results from making the wrong strategic decisions, derived from the uncertainty associated with strategic planning, setting organizational goals and objectives, and efforts aimed at achieving strategic outcomes. Because justifying budget formulation and investment decisions typically requires alignment with strategic goals and objectives, agency strategic planning strongly influences budgetary and investment risk. Strategies based on flawed assumptions or misunderstanding of the internal and external environment in which the organization operates expose agencies to strategic risk. From an information resources management perspective, strategic decisions include choices to establish hardware, software, or infrastructure standards for enterprise-wide adoption, initiatives to modernize or replace major information systems, or changes in system or service operations to the use of external service providers. As with any risk-based decision, agencies mitigate strategic risk by developing as thorough an understanding as possible of the range of positive and negative outcomes that could occur, to provide decision-makers sufficient confidence in the information on which they base strategic decisions.

Supply Chain Risk

Modern organizations rely on an often large and diverse number of suppliers—of products and services, materials, equipment, and information—to support execution of mission functions and business processes and routine operations. Supply chain risk corresponds to the potential disruption or unavailability of necessary resources provided through external sources and the resulting disruption to business operations. Where agency operations depend on specialized resources or minimum service levels, federal agencies often establish detailed contracts or service level agreements prescribing supplier obligations and responsibilities and specifying penalties or other remedies to compensate the government if suppliers cannot meet their obligations. For the provision of critical supporting services such as telecommunications and network services, the federal government emphasizes the use of government-wide acquisition contracts (such as Networx, a program described in Chapter 17) awarded to a small number of vendors selected in part due to the high degree of confidence the government has in the vendors' ability to reliably and consistently provide the relevant services. NIST is developing guidance for federal agencies on the management of supply chain risk in an Interagency Report [24] intended to complement other guidance focused on federal information systems.

Organizational Risk

Because different types of risk can impact operational, tactical, and strategic aspects of individual business units or entire organizations and effective risk management often requires visibility into multiple parts of the organization and coordination of many different resources, risk must be managed at the organizational level. Enterprise risk management comprises all types of risk managed at all levels of the organization, making it an essential strategic management function in both public and private sector organizations [25]. The specific set of functions, personnel, and other resources allocated to enterprise risk management varies depending on the size and complexity of an organization and the maturity of its risk management approach. Organizational components integrated in COSO's framework for enterprise risk management include [17]:

- The internal environment, which comprises the organizational culture and risk management perspective for the organization, influencing both risk management strategy and risk tolerance.
- Strategic goals and objectives, which must be stated clearly in order for organizations to identify potential events affecting their achievement.
- Identification of internal and external events with the potential to positively or negatively impact the achievement of an organization's objectives.
- Assessment of risk, considering likelihood and impact, to support selection of appropriate risk responses or other approaches to managing risk.
- The selection of risk responses—avoidance, acceptance, mitigation, sharing, or transference, alone or in combination—and development of a course of action consistent with the nature of the risk and with the organizational risk tolerance.
- Establishment and implementation of policies and procedures and other control mechanisms sufficient to ensure that risk responses are executed as planned.
- Information sharing and communication at all levels of the organization to enable all risk management stakeholders to carry out their responsibilities.
- Monitoring all relevant types and sources of organizational risk through ongoing operational management activities, purpose-specific evaluations, automated monitoring and reporting capabilities, or other means preferred by the organization.

The importance of managing risk at an organizational level applies equally to managing information security risk and other types of risk, particularly in light of the interdependencies among categories of risk relevant to government organizations. NIST asserts this point explicitly with respect to managing information security risk: "The complex relationships among missions, mission/business processes, and the information systems supporting those missions/processes require an integrated, organization-wide view for managing risk" [26]. Chapter 13 describes the set of organization-level risk management expectations and responsibilities, as well as those applicable to the mission and business process and information systems levels of the organization. This section highlights two essential functions of organizational risk management—establishing the organizational risk strategy and determining and communicating the organization's level of risk tolerance.

Risk Strategy

The risk management strategy reflects the organization's view of how it intends to manage risk—potentially of all types but at least within a discrete category of risk—including policies, procedures, and standards to be used to identify, assess, respond to, monitor, and govern risk. The strategy specifies strategic planning assumptions, constraints, decision-making criteria, and other factors influencing risk management in the organization, including context-specific and overall articulations of organizational risk tolerance. Risk management strategy identifies senior leaders and other stakeholders with significant decision-making authority and, in the context of describing risk governance, should clearly describe the information flows and decision-making processes related to risk management. Following NIST guidance to agencies in Special Publication 800-39, comprehensive organizational strategies for managing the risk associated with agency information systems include clear expression of risk tolerance, preferred or endorsed methodologies for risk assessment, primary risk response alternatives, descriptions of risk-based decision criteria and decision-making processes, and organizational approaches for monitoring risk [27]. The development and implementation of the organizational risk strategy is assumed in NIST guidance to be the responsibility of the risk executive (whether that role corresponds to an individual, a group, or an organizational function).

Risk Tolerance

Risk tolerance is a measure of the level of risk an organization is willing to accept, expressed in either qualitative or quantitative terms and used as a key criterion when making risk-based decisions. Organizations sometimes assign different risk tolerance levels to different types of risk, but if organizations use consistent risk rating or measurement scales, then the same risk tolerance level should apply regardless of the type of risk or its source. Risk tolerance—also sometimes called risk appetite [17] or risk propensity [28]—varies widely among organizations based on many factors, including the relative risk sensitivity of risk managers and other organizational leaders, the organization's mission, and the nature of its assets, resources, and the operational processes they support. In information security or any other risk management domain, risk managers make decisions based not on the total risk potentially faced by the organization, but on the risk that remains after risk mitigation or other measures intended to reduce risk have been put in place. This remaining risk is termed *residual risk* and, as illustrated in Figure 3.2, the organizational risk tolerance determines the acceptable level of residual risk, meaning that two or more organizations with different risk tolerances may respond differently to the same risk determination. When the residual risk relevant to a given decision exceeds the risk tolerance, the organization may choose to take additional action to reduce risk or it may opt not to go forward

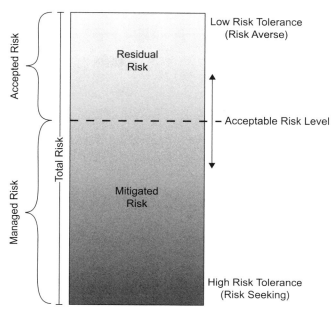

FIGURE 3.2 The Risk Level is Determined by Considering Total Risk and the Risk Mitigation or Other Risk-Reducing Actions Taken By the Organization to Arrive at Residual Risk—the Risk That Remains When All Chosen Mitigating Responses are Implemented

with the risk at the level determined. For organizations seeking consistent risk management, it is essential to both accurately determine risk tolerance and communicate the tolerance level to risk managers and relevant decision-makers throughout the organization.

Risk Executive

NIST envisions the risk executive as a key leadership role established to give organizations an enterprise-wide perspective on risk management. Whether the risk executive function represents an individual or group dedicated to risk management responsibilities or one of many responsibilities shared among agency executives, the risk executive provides a focal point with which risk management stakeholders can communicate and from which they can receive relevant information about the organization's risk management strategy or operational risk management processes. Roles and responsibilities assigned to the risk executive function in the Risk Management Framework and other NIST guidance neither require nor presume a specific or consistent place within the organizational management hierarchy for a risk executive [29]. In many federal organizations, the head of agency has ultimate authority for making decisions regarding organizational risk, but risk-based decision-making occurs at multiple levels throughout an organization and risk management authority

> **TIP**
>
> Establishing the risk executive function as a shared responsibility across multiple organizational leaders can help federal government agencies to ensure that risk-based decisions reflect the appropriate depth and breadth of organizational knowledge and strategic and operational priorities. Enterprise risk management nominally falls under the responsibility of the most senior leaders in an agency, up to and including the head of agency. In cabinet departments and other large agencies, political appointees often occupy the top executive positions, while leaders responsible for core mission or administrative functions may instead be career civil servants [30]. In situations where the executives with the official authority for making decisions about risk do not have the benefit of significant experience working in the organization, agencies may find it more effective to manage risk by sharing risk executive responsibilities among senior management personnel with direct knowledge of the operations potentially impacted by different types of risk.

is often delegated to multiple leaders based on different categories of risk faced by the organization or on which parts of the organization would most likely be affected by adverse impacts. Risk executives expected to manage risk across multiple types need sufficient domain expertise, risk management experience, and knowledge of the organization's strategic goals and objectives, risk tolerance levels, and decision-making criteria to be able to validate the results of risk assessments or other analyses presented in support of risk-based decisions.

TRUST, ASSURANCE, AND SECURITY

Because risk management is largely concerned with mitigating or reducing risk to an acceptable level, organizations have a vested interest in identifying factors that facilitate this aspect of risk management. Trust, assurance, and security are related but distinct concepts that share a common attribute in their potential ability to mitigate risk. Trust is often defined in scholarly and management literature as a willingness to take risk when making decisions that could result in both favorable and unfavorable outcomes [31]. Just as risk is associated with uncertainty rather than certainty, any business decision the results of which are completely and accurately predictable has no need for trust. Trust is a relational attribute that applies between individuals or organizations, although in the case of organizations the decision to trust is also made by individuals, whose authority presumably includes representing the interests of their organizations. For a given situation involving risk, the existence of higher levels of trust serves either to reduce the perceived risk by reducing the likelihood that adverse consequences will occur or raises the risk tolerance to make higher levels of risk acceptable. Similarly, in decisions regarding high levels of risk, organizations may require greater levels of trust or evidence of assurance than for decisions associated with relatively lower levels of risk [32].

> **WARNING**
>
> While a comprehensive theoretical or semantic analysis of trust and associated concepts is beyond the scope of this book, it is important when discussing trust that organizational leaders, risk managers, and information system owners are clear about what it means for the organization to say it trusts an individual, an information system, or an organization, in what context that trust applies, who makes a decision to trust on behalf of the organization, and what information or criteria drive that decision. Information systems do not operate in isolation—they are deployed and managed by individuals and organizations, so any evaluation of the relative trustworthiness of an information system needs to consider the intentions, expectations, and obligations attributed to those responsible for operating it.

Trust and Trustworthiness

In common usage, the term *trust* is often used interchangeably with *trustworthiness*, including when referring to information technology and information security, where many management models and standards address "trusted" computer systems. There is an important distinction regarding trust and trustworthiness in this context, as trust is a cognitive, emotional, or behavioral perspective and trustworthiness similarly embodies behavioral expectations and intentions. From this perspective it is inaccurate to say that an information system can trust, or to denote an information system as trustworthy in the sense of expectations about its intentions. References to trust in or between information systems usually connote confidence, reliability, or predictability, in the sense that different information systems can be evaluated and even certified to demonstrate that they consistently perform as expected for the purpose for which an organization intends to use them. Evidence that organizations have implemented appropriate management, operational, and technical controls for their information systems and that those controls are effective increases the confidence—the level of assurance—associated with the use of those information systems.

Assurance and Confidence

As described previously in this chapter, assurance is a measure of the level of confidence in the effectiveness of controls established or actions taken to mitigate risk, such as security controls implemented to safeguard the confidentiality, integrity, and availability of information systems. While assurance in the information security management context derives from evidence such as security control documentation, testing, and certification, the concept of assurance applies more broadly to the confidence one party has in another's ability to perform as expected. In this respect assurance is similar to the competence-based view of trust that appears in both theoretical and practical research on trust [33,34]. When applied to risk management decisions, organizational risk tolerance may be expressed in a way that specifies the level of assurance required before considering a decision to accept risk. Stronger assurance corresponds to higher levels of trustworthiness attributed to information systems or organizations, which in turn can facilitate the organization's acceptance of risk by reducing the likelihood or lessening the impact of at least some adverse events.

Security

Security is closely related to trust and assurance as well as risk. By preventing or diminishing the impact of adverse events, security reduces many types of risk to which organizations are exposed. Both security and assurance have similar ideal states of surety or certainty that assets under protection are safe from harm. If such an ideal were possible, information security-related risk could be eliminated, organizational decisions would not need to incorporate risk, and organizations would have little need for trust. Because it is sometimes hard to determine the rationale or intent underlying the implementation of security controls and other protective actions taken by organizations, evidence of security is necessary to establish assurance but not sufficient to determine trustworthiness or to substitute for trust in situations involving risk [35]. As clearly outlined in guidance on the Risk Management Framework, the primary value of information security in federal organizations is its role in enabling effective management of the risk associated with operating and using information systems and in establishing cost-effective protection of information assets commensurate with the level of risk faced by the organization [36]. Security controls represent a key risk mitigation mechanism to help organizations operate their information systems in a manner consistent with requirements for assurance and within organizational risk tolerance levels. Security reduces risk directly by mitigating risk through the use of implemented controls and indirectly by providing the evidence needed to help establish the necessary level of assurance or trustworthiness in systems or the organizations that operate them.

Trust Models

The need for organizations to establish internal and external trust relationships is a consistent theme in Special Publication 800-39. NIST recognizes that just as different organizations establish their own governance structures, risk management strategies, risk tolerance levels, and policies and operational procedures, organizations may use different approaches to establish and maintain trust-based relationships. Special Publication 800-39 describes several trust models, including validated trust, direct historical trust, mediated trust, mandated trust, and hybrid trust [37], the last of which represents the simultaneous use of multiple trust models. These models differ in the amount and type of information used to establish the trustworthiness of another organization, the source of that evidence or assertions of trustworthiness, and the level of discretion afforded to decision-makers to determine whether another organization is sufficiently trustworthy for the context under consideration:

- In a *validated trust* approach, one organization relies on evidence provided by another organization to evaluate whether it implements controls and operational practices sufficient to satisfy the assurance requirements of the first organization. Evidence considered for this evaluation may include documentation, direct observation, organizational or independent assessment results, or other information attesting to the scope and effectiveness of the actions taken by another organization.

- A *direct historical trust* approach prioritizes the past experiences and behavioral track record of two or more organizations working together over the course of their relationship, where a history of positive experiences typically produces higher levels of trust between the organizations. Inversely, one or more negative experiences with another organization may engender distrust that constrains the potential for future interaction.

- Where both validated trust and direct historical trust models involve information sharing and interactions between two or more organizations, *mediated trust* relies on a third party to broker trust between organizations that have no direct relationship but that each have an established trust relationship with the third party. Mediated trust models include centralized, distributed, federated, and transitive patterns; the choice of the most appropriate pattern depends on the context, the level of trust that needs to be established, and the nature of the trust relationship between a given organization and the mediating party.

- In a *mandated trust* approach, the trustworthiness of a given organization is asserted by an authoritative source, essentially removing any discretion other organizations have to make their own determinations. Mandated trust is common in federal government environments, where executive orders, new regulations, or government-wide directives often require agencies to disclose information or establish system interconnections to designated organizations. Mandated trust is less commonly applied to relationships between government agencies and non-government organizations.

- Organizations that combine multiple trust models (or incorporate aspects of multiple trust models) implement what NIST terms a *hybrid trust* approach [38]. Federal agencies and other large organizations maintain numerous inter-organizational relationships with different characteristics, so many organizations select their preferred approach to establishing and maintaining trust based on the context, the availability of information about the other organization, the past longevity and expected future duration of the relationship, and other relevant factors.

NOTE

The federal government provides a representative example of a mediated trust model implemented in a distributed pattern in its Federal Public Key Infrastructure, an initiative described in Chapter 17. Due to both technical and political factors, the federal government chose to implement its public key infrastructure in a distributed, explicitly non-hierarchical model in which the Federal Bridge Certification Authority mediates trust relationships among all authorized certificate authorities to facilitate interoperability among the holders of certificates issued by those authorities. In this model the federal government serves as a mutually trusted entity for all issuers of Federal PKI certificates, obviating the need for certificate issuing organizations to establish direct trust relationships.

RISK ASSOCIATED WITH INFORMATION SYSTEMS

With enterprise risk management as a backdrop, the standards and guidance issued by NIST, OMB, DHS, and other government authorities in support of agency FISMA implementation and compliance focus on the management of risk associated with federal information systems. Achieving the goals of adequate security and consistent and effective risk management entails active engagement at all organizational levels—a theme reflected in NIST's overarching risk management guidance in Special Publication 800-39, *Managing Information Security Risk: Organization, Mission, and Information System View*. As shown in Figure 3.3, the approach NIST recommends combines an integrated set of risk management processes and activities performed using the collaborative efforts of risk management stakeholders responsible for individual information systems, the mission functions and business processes those systems support, and the overall management of the organization. Chapter 13 describes in more detail the primary risk management responsibilities associated with each tier of the organization. NIST addresses all organizational levels in its risk management guidance to agencies, but it targets some of that guidance to individual risk management processes and to activities primarily performed at specific tiers of the organization. Table 3.1 identifies key sources of guidance and the risk management aspects on which they focus. The clear implications underlying federal guidance on risk management are that information security risk management is an essential component of organizational management and that managing risk

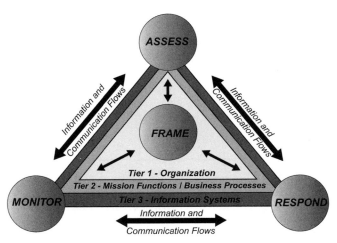

FIGURE 3.3 NIST's Risk Management Process Establishes Core Activities Executed Throughout the Organization to Assess, Respond to, and Monitor Risk in Support of Risk Strategy and Policies, Procedures, and Standards Framed at the Organizational Level [41]

Table 3.1 Key Sources of Federal Guidance on Risk Management

Risk Management Focus	Organizational Level	Source
Risk management process	Organization, mission and business process, and information systems	Special Publication 800-39
Security assurance	Organization	Special Publication 800-23
Risk monitoring	Organization and Information systems	Special Publication 800-137
Risk Management Framework	Information systems	Special Publication 800-37
Risk assessment	Information systems	Special Publication 800-30
Security control assessment	Information systems	Special Publication 800-53A

effectively requires the active engagement of risk management stakeholders through the organization.

Risk Management Framework

The Risk Management Framework applies at an organizational level in the sense that it describes a standard process that federal agencies should follow for all of their information systems and that it includes steps—such as security control monitoring—that may be most efficiently performed using processes and capabilities implemented to support multiple information systems. Special Publication 800-37 reiterates the point that effective information security risk management requires that individuals at each level of an agency understand their roles and responsibilities in providing adequate security and for managing risk associated with information system [39]. NIST proposed the Risk Management Framework as a mechanism to support organizational risk management, but the tasks it prescribes primarily apply to individual information systems. The original guidance NIST offered for conducting risk assessments had a similar focus on information systems, although the revised version of Special Publication 800-30 expands the applicability of the risk assessment processes and techniques it describes to the organization and mission and business process tiers of an organization [8].

With an established focus on managing risk associated with the operation and use of federal information systems, NIST also provides agencies information to facilitate the process of identifying sources of information security risk applicable to government organizations. Special Publication 800-30 offers numerous examples of adversarial and non-adversarial threat sources and threat events, predisposing conditions that may expose agencies to threats or vulnerabilities, and adverse impacts that could result from the occurrence of threat events [40]. Collectively, these inputs can help agencies incorporate an appropriately broad set of risk sources when considering information security risk and identify a range of outcomes and potential impacts that accurately reflect the organizations' information systems and the environments in which they operate.

Risk Management Life Cycle

Risk management is a continuous, iterative process intended to achieve and maintain acceptable levels of all types of risk. The information security risk management life cycle defined in Special Publication 800-39 and recommended for use in federal government agencies is structurally very similar to other Risk Management Frameworks and processes developed to support enterprise risk management in public and private sector organizations. The core processes in the NIST risk management life cycle, as illustrated in Figure 3.3, include risk framing, risk assessment, risk response, and risk monitoring, all supported by information flows and communication across all levels of an organization and among all risk management processes.

Risk Framing

Risk framing establishes the context for risk management, including the aspects of the organization, its assets, and its operating environment that fall within the scope of the risk management process. For enterprise risk management risk framing may need to be more comprehensive than for risk management focused on information security or other types of risk. The risk framing process, typically conducted at the organizational level, produces the risk management strategy that guides the organization's approach to managing risk and the way it will implement the other core processes of assessing, responding to, and monitoring risk. Within the scope of risk framing, organizations define risk management decision-making processes and identify risk executives and other key personnel with decision-making authority. The risk framing process and the strategy it creates specify risk assumptions, risk constraints, risk tolerance levels (including tolerance for uncertainty and organizational assurance requirements where applicable), risk management priorities, and criteria for making risk-based decisions [42].

Risk Assessment

Risk assessment is the process used to identify and evaluate the significance of risk faced by an organization. During risk assessment, organizations identify internal and external threats and vulnerabilities, determine adverse impacts that could occur should those threats materialize, and estimate the likelihood those adverse impacts will occur. The result of the risk assessment process is a qualitative, quantitative, or semi-quantitative calculation of risk to the organization, usually expressed as a function of the magnitude of loss or harm that would result from adverse events and the likelihood of those events occurring. The risk assessment process prescribed in Special Publication 800-30 is described in more detail in Chapter 13.

Risk Response

Organizations determine the appropriate response to risk identified through risk assessment or risk monitoring activities. The process identifies potential courses of action for responding to risk, evaluates alternatives to determine viable responses, considers each alternative in light of organizational priorities and risk tolerance levels established during risk framing, and selects and implements the chosen courses of action. Organizations can facilitate consistent responses to risk in alignment with risk tolerance levels by identifying default or preferred responses and formalizing or standardizing the approaches with which the organization evaluates and selects responses to different types of risk.

Risk Monitoring

Risk monitoring serves multiple purposes in the risk management process, including identifying changes to information systems and their operating environments that could affect the information security risk faced by the organization, verifying that risk response courses of action are implemented as planned, and evaluating the ongoing effectiveness of risk response measures once implemented [43]. Risk monitoring is often closely aligned with information security continuous monitoring strategies and practices, as many of the tools and techniques organizations use for continuous monitoring provide data relevant for risk monitoring.

Other Risk Management Frameworks Used in Government Organizations

The Government Accountability Office (GAO) developed a Risk Management Framework in 2005 that is substantially similar to the NIST life cycle described above. GAO first published its Risk Management Framework as part of a report describing the need for more effective risk assessment in support of homeland security and critical infrastructure protection [44]. In deciding to develop a new framework, GAO noted the unfulfilled responsibility assigned to the Department of Homeland Security in 2003 to establish risk management policies, guidelines, and methodologies for use throughout the homeland security sector [45]. As shown in Figure 3.4, the GAO included five processes in its risk management life cycle, each of which corresponds to a similarly defined process in Special Publication 800-39. Since its development, GAO has applied its Risk Management Framework to agencies and contexts outside the homeland security sector, and updated its guidance to incorporate aspects of the COSO Enterprise Risk Management Framework, including initial evaluation of the internal environment to establish the context for risk management and establishment of information and communication across all levels of the organization [46]. In current usage, the life cycles defined by NIST, GAO, and COSO essentially describe the same risk management processes; Table 3.2 provides a side-by-side comparison of all three models.

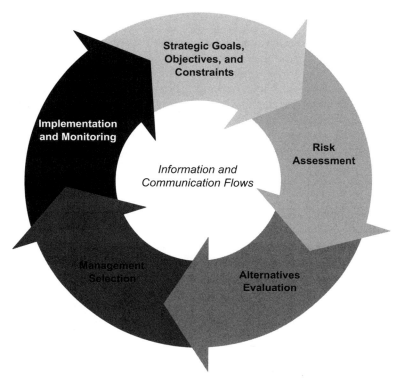

FIGURE 3.4 The Risk Management Framework Recommended by the GAO for Use in Federal Homeland Security and Critical Infrastructure Protection is Structurally Similar to the NIST Risk Management Process, Emphasizing an Iterative Cycle of Assessment, Evaluation and Response, and Monitoring in Support of Organizational Goals and Objectives

The convergence of Risk Management Frameworks developed to address different types of risk in different kinds of organizations suggests that risk management guidance has matured to the point where organizations agree on the set of processes and activities that should be implemented. The commonality between risk management models does not mean that all organizations have achieved similar levels of effectiveness in their risk management practices, for risk management generally or with respect to managing information security-related risk. Subsequent chapters on risk management and risk assessment (Chapter 13), planning for and executing the steps in the Risk Management Framework (Chapters 6–9), and continuous monitoring (Chapter 14) all provide information intended to guide risk management stakeholders at all levels of the organization to understand their roles, responsibilities, and expectations in helping organizations effectively manage risk associated with information systems.

Table 3.2 Life Cycle Processes in Risk Management Frameworks

NIST [3]	GAO [46]	COSO [17]
• Frame	• Internal environment • Strategic goals, objectives, and constraints	• Internal environment • Objective setting
• Assess	• Risk assessment	• Event identification • Risk assessment
• Respond	• Alternatives evaluation • Management selection	• Risk response
• Monitor	• Implementation and monitoring	• Control activities • Monitoring
• Information and communication flows	• Information and communication	• Information and communication

RELEVANT SOURCE MATERIAL

Several NIST Special Publications provide guidance, recommendations, and instructions relevant to understanding and managing risk. The most applicable sources of information include:

- Special Publication 800-39, *Managing Information Security Risk: Organization, Mission, and Information System View* [3].
- Special Publication 800-37 Revision 1, *Guide for Applying the Risk Management Framework to Federal Information Systems* [47].
- Special Publication 800-30 Revision 1, *Guide for Conducting Risk Assessments* [8].
- Special Publication 800-137, *Information Security Continuous Monitoring for Federal Information Systems and Organizations* [48].

These and other NIST Special Publications are available from the NIST Computer Security Division website, at http://csrc.nist.gov/publications/.

SUMMARY

This chapter explained the concept of risk and many of the aspects of risk organizations consider when developing and executing risk management. It identified multiple types of risk to help establish an appropriate context for information security-related risk that is the focus of NIST guidance to federal agencies on managing risk consistent with FISMA and other legislative and regulatory requirements. It also identified relevant standards and risk models developed outside the government that influence the risk management life cycle processes adopted by federal agencies. This chapter also introduced several components of organizational risk management that are described in more detail in later chapters, particularly including the NIST risk management process and risk assessment procedures covered in Chapter 13.

REFERENCES

[1] Luhman N. Risk: a sociological theory. New Brunswick, NJ: Transaction Publishers; 1993. p. 28.

[2] The presumption of "bounded rationality" due to incomplete information is well established in seminal theories of organizational behavior. See for exampleSimon HA. A behavioral model of rational choice. Qtrly J Econ 1955;59:99–118. doi:10.2307/1884852.

[3] Managing information security risk: organization, mission, and information system view. Gaithersburg, MD: National Institute of Standards and Technology, Computer Security Division; March 2011. Special Publication 800-39.

[4] Both the Factor Analysis of Information Risk (FAIR) and ISACA's Risk IT Framework define risk in terms of both frequency and magnitude. SeeJones JA. An introduction to factor analysis of information risk (FAIR). Columbus, OH: Risk Management Insight; 2005. Jones JA. The risk IT framework. Rolling Meadows, IL: ISACA; 2009.

[5] ISO Guide 73:2009. Risk management—vocabulary.

[6] National information assurance glossary. Fort Meade, MD: Committee on National Security Systems; April 2009. CNSS Instruction No. 4009. p. 61.

[7] Managing information security risk: organization, mission, and information system view. Gaithersburg, MD: National Institute of Standards and Technology, Computer Security Division; March 2011. Special Publication 800-39. p. 40.

[8] Guide for conducting risk assessments. Gaithersburg, MD: National Institute of Standards and Technology, Computer Security Division; September 2011. Special Publication 800-30 revision 1. Initial Public Draft.

[9] March J, Simon H. Organizations. 2nd ed. Cambridge, MA: Blackwell; 1993. p. 158

[10] ISO/IEC 31010:2009. Risk management—risk assessment techniques.

[11] Ring PS, Van de Ven AH. Structuring cooperative relationships between organizations. Strat Mgmt J 1992;13:483–98. doi:10.1002/smj.4250130702.

[12] Mayer RC, Davis JH, Schoorman FD. An integrative model of organizational trust. Acad Mgmt Rev 1995;20:709–34. doi:10.2307/258792.

[13] ISO/IEC 31000:2009. Risk management—principles and guidelines.

[14] Managing information security risk: organization, mission, and information system view. Gaithersburg, MD: National Institute of Standards and Technology, Computer Security Division; March 2011. Special Publication 800–39. p. 1.

[15] Wrightson MT, Caldwell SL. Further refinements needed to assess risks and prioritize protective measures at ports and other critical infrastructure. Report to congressional requesters. Washington, DC: Government Accountability Office; December 2005. GAO Report 06-91. Appendix I.

[16] ISO/IEC 31000:2009. Risk management—principles and guidelines; and ISO/IEC 31010:2009. Risk management—risk assessment techniques.

[17] Committee of Sponsoring Organizations of the Treadway Commission. Enterprise risk management—integrated framework. Durham, NC: American Institute of Certified Public Accountants; 2004.

[18] See for example ISO/IEC 31000:2009. Risk management—principles and guidelines. Both NIST and GAO frameworks reflect the same core processes; the COSO ERM framework identifies eight components corresponding to risk management processes and activities, all of which also fall within the scope of the same core processes.

[19] Preparation, submission, and execution of the budget. Washington, DC: Office of Management and Budget. August 2011. Circular No. A-11, revised [Transmittal Memorandum No. 85]. Exhibit 53, p. 19–21.

[20] For example, the Department of Health and Human Services received $50 million under Title VIII of the Recovery Act to improve information technology security: American Recovery and Reinvestment Act of 2009, Pub. L. No. 111-5, 123 Stat. 115.

[21] Federal Information Security Amendments Act of 2012, H.R. 4257, 112th Congress; 2012.

[22] Cybersecurity Act of 2012, S. 2105, 112th Congress; 2012.

[23] Federal IT Dashboard [Internet]. Washington, DC: Office of Management and Budget [cited May 23, 2012]. <http://www.itdashboard.gov/>.

[24] Boyens JM, Paulsen C, Bartol N, Moorthy RS, Shankles SA. National supply chain risk management for federal information systems. Gaithersburg, MD: National Institute of Standards and Technology, Computer Security Division; March 2012. Interagency Report 7622 Second Public Draft.

[25] Association of Insurance and Risk Managers, Public Risk Management Association, Institute of Risk Management. A structured approach to enterprise risk management and the requirements of ISO 31000. London, UK: Institute of Risk Management; 2010.

[26] Managing information security risk: organization, mission, and information system view. Gaithersburg, MD: National Institute of Standards and Technology, Computer Security Division; March 2011. Special Publication 800-39. p. 2.

[27] Managing information security risk: organization, mission, and information system view. Gaithersburg, MD: National Institute of Standards and Technology, Computer Security Division; March 2011. Special Publication 800-39. p. 14.

[28] Sitkin SB, Pablo AL. Reconceptualizing the determinants of risk behavior. Acad Mgmt Rev 1992;17:9–38. doi:10.2307/258646.

[29] Managing information security risk: Organization, mission, and information system view. Gaithersburg, MD: National Institute of Standards and Technology, Computer Security Division; March 2011. Special Publication 800-39. p. 13.

[30] For instance, the role of Chief Information Officer at the Departments of Health and Human Services, Veterans Affairs, Labor, Justice, State, and Treasury is a senior executive position designated at the level of Deputy Assistant Secretary (or equivalent title), reporting to an Assistant Secretary or Under Secretary that is typically a political appointee.

[31] One frequently cited definition comes from:Mayer RC, Davis JH, Schoorman FD. An integrative model of organizational trust. Acad Mgmt Rev 1995;20:709–34. doi:10.2307/25879. p. 712.

[32] Hurley RF. The decision to trust: how leaders create high-trust organizations. San Francisco, CA: Jossey-Bass; 2012.

[33] Barber B. Logic and the limits of trust. New Brunswick, NJ: Rutgers University Press; 1983. p. 14.

[34] Reina DS, Reina ML. Trust and betrayal in the workplace. 2nd ed.. San Francisco, CA: Berrett-Koehler Publishers; 2006. p. 14.

[35] Nissenbaum H. Will security enhance trust online, or supplant it? In: Kramer RM, Cook KS, editors Trust and distrust in organizations. New York, NY: Russell Sage Foundation; 2004. p. 155–88.

[36] Guide for applying the risk management framework to federal information systems. Gaithersburg, MD: National Institute of Standards and Technology, Computer Security Division; February 2010. Special Publication 800-37 revision 1. p. 2.

[37] Managing information security risk: organization, mission, and information system view. Gaithersburg, MD: National Institute of Standards and Technology, Computer Security Division; March 2011. Special Publication 800-39. Appendix G.

[38] While NIST consistently refers to the level or degree of trust that can be achieved between two or more organizations, its models more accurately describe ways to determine trustworthiness.

[39] Guide for applying the risk management framework to federal information systems. Gaithersburg, MD: National Institute of Standards and Technology, Computer Security Division; February 2010. Special Publication 800-37 revision 1. p. 1.

[40] Guide for conducting risk assessments. Gaithersburg, MD: National Institute of Standards and Technology, Computer Security Division; September 2011. Special Publication 800-30 revision 1. Initial Public Draft. Tables listing threat sources, threat events, predisposing conditions, and adverse impacts appear in Appendices D, E, F, and H, respectively.

[41] Managing information security risk: organization, mission, and information system view. Gaithersburg, MD: National Institute of Standards and Technology, Computer Security Division; March 2011. Special Publication 800-39. p. 32.

[42] Managing information security risk: organization, mission, and information system view. Gaithersburg, MD: National Institute of Standards and Technology, Computer Security Division; March 2011. Special Publication 800-39. p. 6.

[43] Managing information security risk: organization, mission, and information system view. Gaithersburg, MD: National Institute of Standards and Technology, Computer Security Division; March 2011. Special Publication 800-39. p. 7.

[44] Wrightson MT, Caldwell SL. Further refinements needed to assess risks and prioritize protective measures at ports and other critical infrastructure. Report to congressional requesters. Washington , DC: Government Accountability Office; December 2005. GAO 06-91. The GAO risk management framework is defined in Appendix A.

[45] Critical infrastructure identification, prioritization, and protection. Washington, DC: Department of Homeland Security; December 2003. Homeland Security Presidential Directive 7.

[46] Kohn LT, Ragland S. Completion of comprehensive risk management program essential to effective oversight. Report to the Ranking Member, Committee on Finance, US Senate. Washington, DC: Government Accountability Office; September 2009. GAO-09-687.

[47] Guide for applying the risk management framework to federal information systems. Gaithersburg, MD: National Institute of Standards and Technology, Computer Security Division; February 2010. Special Publication 800-37 revision 1.

[48] Dempsey K, Chawla N, Johnson A, Johnson R, Jones A, Orebaugh A, Scholl M, Stine K. Information security continuous monitoring for federal information systems and organizations. Gaithersburg, MD: National Institute of Standards and Technology, Computer Security Division; September 2011. Special Publication 800-137.

Thinking About Systems

4

- Defining Systems in Different Contexts
- Perspectives on Information Systems
- Establishing Information System Boundaries
- Maintaining System Inventories

Risk management is an essential function at all levels of an organization. Public and private sector guidance on managing risk agrees on the central tenet that effective risk management must be integrated at an organization-wide level to engage leaders, business owners, and information technology managers and staff in a collaborative approach that promotes understanding of the sources of risk faced by the organization and ways to address that risk. This approach applies to all types of risk, not just to information security risk, but FISMA and associated guidance to federal government agencies on risk management focus explicitly on managing security risk related to the operation and use of information systems [1]. Although FISMA and the Risk Management Framework apply to agencies at an organizational level, agencies execute the RMF process primarily the level of individual information systems, following the guidance provided in Special Publication 800-37, *Guide for Applying the Risk Management Framework to Federal Information Systems* [2]. The statutory definition of *information system* is "A discrete set of information resources organized for the collection, processing, maintenance, use, sharing, dissemination, or disposition of information" [3]. The simplicity of this general concept belies the potential need for organizations to assimilate different interpretations and categorizations of information systems used in different organizational concepts. Developing a clear and consistent understanding of how organizations define information systems is a prerequisite to describing system boundaries and other system attributes in a manner that supports effective application of the RMF. This chapter offers several perspectives on systems generally and information systems in particular that affect how organizations manage their information systems.

DEFINING SYSTEMS IN DIFFERENT CONTEXTS

Although *system* and *information system* are often used interchangeably in information resources management contexts (and in this book), an information system is a specific type of system, where *system* generally refers to "any organized assembly of resources and procedures united and regulated by interaction or interdependence to accomplish a set of specific functions" [4]. Information systems are systems involving information resources, including information technology assets such as hardware, software, and network infrastructure and the data stored, processed, or otherwise used by the organization. Organizations typically define their information systems using factors such as the nature of the information the systems use, the organizational management authority responsible for operating the systems, or the functional purpose the systems and their underlying components are intended to achieve. Information systems range from stand-alone applications running on single computing devices to highly complex "systems of systems" comprising large numbers of components spread across multiple operating environments. From an information security management perspective, fully describing an information system and accurately describing its system boundary are important aspects of step 1 in the RMF process. Individual information systems—also called "IT systems" or "IT capital assets" in some official government guidance [5]—are also identified, organized, and tracked as part of a variety of information resources management functions and to satisfy regulatory and policy requirements for budgeting, investment management, and records management as well as information security and risk management.

Information security personnel executing the RMF process understandably tend to follow the statutory definition of information system referenced in FISMA and NIST documentation, but security management is not performed in isolation and many security stakeholders need to be aware of different conceptions of information systems used in other management activities. This is especially true for information system owners, whose responsibility extends to all aspects of information system development, procurement, integration, modification, operation and maintenance, and disposition. Information system attributes—including those applicable to different information resources management disciplines—drive the expectations and requirements affecting information security activities prior to and following system authorization. Identifying relevant information system attributes during initial planning activities helps information system owners determine the system-specific and organizational resources necessary to support the security management needs of their systems. Key attributes for information systems include the type of system (general support system, major application, or non-major application), the sensitivity of the information the system contains, the impact level assigned as the result of security categorization, whether the scope of information system spans more than one authorization boundary, and whether the system is designated a national security system.

> **NOTE**
>
> The non-technical connotation of the word *system* does appear in IT and information security contexts, highlighting the need for organizations to be specific when defining and describing their systems. For instance, the information security management system (ISMS) defined in ISO/IEC 27001 [6] is not a technical system at all, but an integrated set of management processes and a framework for developing security requirements and selecting security controls to satisfy those requirements. The ISO/IEC 27000 series of standards are used more commonly in the private sector than in government, but NIST acknowledges the overlap between the international standard and Special Publication 800-53 and has suggested that future iterations of NIST's risk management approach will integrate both frameworks [7].

Information Systems in FISMA and the RMF

Key legislation addressing information resources management, including FISMA and the Clinger-Cohen Act, incorporates by reference the statutory definition of *information system* cited above, a definition established in the Paperwork Reduction Act of 1995 [8]. The primary source of government-wide guidance on information resource management is OMB Circular A-130, *Management of Federal Information Resources,* which uses the same information system definition but distinguishes *information* from *information system* and also defines *information resources* to include both the information and the information technology used by government organizations [9]. The explicit distinction between information systems and the information those systems collect, process, maintain, transmit, or disseminate is relevant to many tasks in the RMF, particularly including system categorization, and is reflected in the separately defined roles of information system owner and information owner [10]. Circular A-130 also introduces a definition for *major information system*, denoting "an information system that requires special management attention because of its importance to an agency mission; its high development, operating, or maintenance costs; or its significant role in the administration of agency programs, finances, property, or other resources" [9]. There are other statutory uses of this phrase, dating at least to the Electronic Freedom of Information Act Amendments of 1996 [11], which updated the provisions of the Freedom of Information Act to require agencies to make some records available electronically and required each federal agency to publish an index of its major information systems. OMB's usage of major information system mirrors its definition for *major investment* that appears in Section 53 of Circular A-11 [12], which also notes that systems not categorized as "major" are considered "non-major."

OMB also considers information technology systems to be one of two categories of capital assets (the other is real property), where information technology includes "any equipment or interconnected system or subsystem of equipment, that is used in the automatic acquisition, storage, manipulation, management, movement, control, display, switching, interchange, transmission, or reception of data or information by the executive agency" [13]. Appendix III of Circular A-130, *Security of Federal*

Automated Information Resources, further refines federal information systems, providing definitions for *application, major application, and general support system*, the last of which OMB equates with the more general term *system* [14].

- An "application" means the use of information resources (information and information technology) to satisfy a specific set of user requirements.
- A "major application" means an application that requires special attention to security due to the risk and magnitude of the harm resulting from the loss, misuse, or unauthorized access to or modification of the information in the application.
- A "general support system" or "system" means an interconnected set of information resources under the same direct management control which shares common functionality. A system normally includes hardware, software, information, data, applications, communications, and people.

An information system's designation is one of several factors influencing the security management processes and activities required for the system, including the nature of the security authorization that the information system owner must obtain before putting the system into production.

Information System Attributes

Given the large number of information systems operated by or on behalf of many federal agencies and the diversity of those systems in terms of scale, complexity, and operational characteristics, applying the appropriate management processes and activities to every system can be a challenging undertaking. Identifying key information system attributes and using those attributes to categorize systems often facilitates the development and maintenance of organizational system inventories and the consistent management and oversight of agency information systems. NIST's Risk Management Framework and associated standards and guidance refer frequently to the impact level assigned to each system as a key factor driving information system security requirements and the minimum security controls necessary to achieve adequate security. The security categorization and other attributes described below affect the set of security controls and control enhancements selected for each information system and also help determine which systems agencies include in organizational inventories, the need for system-specific security authorization, requirements to develop certain security artifacts, or whether FISMA applies at all.

Information System Types

Agencies use the general support system and major application security types defined in OMB Circular A-130 to categorize the information systems included in the agency-level inventory of major information systems required under FISMA [15].

The implicit interpretation of FISMA and OMB requirements in NIST guidance is that all major information systems are either general support systems or major applications. The same guidance assumes that agencies do not separately authorize or document the security controls for information systems considered non-major applications because those systems typically operate within the scope of general support systems or major applications [16]. Agencies apply the Risk Management Framework in the same way to both general support systems and major applications; neither Special Publication 800-39 nor Special Publication 800-37 make any distinction between these types of systems. Because general support systems often include within their boundaries one or more major or non-major applications that inherit security controls the general support system implements, the information system owners for general support systems also function in the role of common control providers. Common control providers must not only document their security controls in system security plans, security assessment reports, and plans of action and milestones, but also need to make this documentation available to information system owners responsible for systems that inherit their common controls [17].

Information Sensitivity

The sensitivity of the information that an information system collects, processes, stores, and disseminates provides an indication of the importance the organization assigns to different kinds of information and the nature and extent of protection needed to safeguard information security and privacy. Information sensitivity is a key factor in categorizing the impact level of each information type associated with an information system, influencing the security categorization of the information system and the corresponding minimum security requirements the system must implement [18]. Some information types—such as medical, financial, educational, or legal records—require special protective measures driven by applicable legislative and regulatory requirements. Information systems containing personally identifiable information (PII) require privacy and security documentation and invoke management and oversight processes beyond those associated with standard security authorization practices. Federal agencies must maintain current and accurate inventories of all PII holdings [19], perform privacy impact assessments for information systems containing PII [20], and for information systems using PII to retrieve information about individuals, must also provide public notice about the information systems, the type of information they contain, and how that information is used by the agency [21].

Security Categorization

Federal government agencies categorize all information systems according to the potential impact that could occur due to a loss of confidentiality, integrity, or availability. FISMA mandates security categorization for all federal information systems other than national security systems [22], following the procedures specified in FIPS 199. Agencies operating national security systems also categorize their information systems using an approach very similar to FIPS 199 that adopts the same three categorization levels: low impact, moderate impact, and high impact [23]. The impact level drives the selection and implementation of security controls necessary to provide adequate security for each information system, as described in detail in Chapter 7. Security categorization also influences agency decisions regarding which information systems are considered "major" and subject to security authorization. Although agencies typically include information systems designated as low impact in their system inventories, many agencies do not require system-specific security authorization for low-impact systems, presumably addressing the security needs of these systems within the scope of authorization packages for other information systems. FISMA system inventory data submitted to OMB by federal agencies for fiscal year 2009 indicates that of the nearly 24,000 information systems identified, agencies categorized 36.8% of their systems as low impact, 43.5% as moderate impact, and 11% as high impact, with the remainder not assigned a category [24].

National Security Systems

The designation of an information system as a national security system is extremely significant in federal information resources management, as the majority of the provisions in the Paperwork Reduction Act, Clinger-Cohen Act, FISMA, and other sources of statutory language governing coordination of federal information policy do not apply to national security systems. Under the current official definition, a national security system is "any information system (including any telecommunications system) used or operated by an agency or by a contractor of an agency, or other organization on behalf of an agency the function, operation, or use of which involves intelligence activities; involves cryptologic activities related to national security; involves command and control of military forces; involves equipment that is an integral part of a weapon or weapons system; or is critical to the direct fulfillment of military or intelligence missions provided that this definition does not apply to a system that is used for routine administrative and business applications (including payroll, finance, logistics, and personnel management applications)" [25]. Agencies operating national security systems follow standards and guidelines distinct from those NIST provides for non-national security systems, issued primarily by the Committee on National Security Systems (CNSS). Through the cooperative efforts of the Joint Task Force Transformation Initiative interagency working group, information security and risk management practices for both national security systems and information systems covered under FISMA are converging to a common foundation using NIST guidance including the Risk Management Framework and the security control catalog provided in Special Publication 800-53 [26]. Some information security management procedures differ for national security systems, including the processes for categorizing information and information systems and establishing appropriate security control baselines, so properly identifying national security systems remains important for agencies and their system owners.

NIST provides guidance, developed in collaboration with the Department of Defense, for identifying national security systems [27].

PERSPECTIVES ON INFORMATION SYSTEMS

This book emphasizes the information security management and risk management implications of FISMA on federal government organizations, but FISMA represents just one among many legislative, regulatory, and policy drivers affecting agency information resources management practices. The Information Technology Management Reform Act of 1996, commonly known as the Clinger-Cohen Act, established agency responsibilities for capital planning and investment control, performance management, information technology acquisition, and enterprise architecture in addition to security and privacy management for federal information systems [28]. This legislation also consolidated authority for most information resources management functions under the executive position of Chief Information Officer (CIO), a role to which FISMA assigns the responsibility for ensuring agency compliance with information security requirements in the law [29].

The agency CIO, directly or through the senior agency information security officer, oversees the organizational information security management program to provide appropriate protection to the information and information systems supporting the agency's mission and business operations. Fulfilling this management responsibility depends on the coordinated effort of system owners and other information system stakeholders to address all the information resources management requirements applicable to their information systems. Agencies and their system owners often face a challenge in consistently satisfying the full set of requirements that apply to their information systems due to the different information system perspectives and areas of emphasis that exist within information resources management disciplines. Government-wide guidance to agencies on information system development practices emphasizes the use of integrated project teams to ensure representation from all appropriate functional areas and to provide the necessary skills and roles to help information systems meet all organizational requirements [30, 31]. The following sections summarize the consideration of information systems from the perspectives of information resources management disciplines including information security, capital planning, enterprise architecture, and privacy, leadership for each of which agencies typically assign to a senior management position.

Information Security Management

From an information security and risk management perspective, federal agencies view information systems and the information they contain as key organizational assets enabling successful mission execution and the effective performance of mission-centric and supporting business and administrative functions.

Although this view is consistent with capital planning and enterprise architecture perspectives, the focus on systems within information security risk management emphasizes the provision of adequate security for information systems through the application of the Risk Management Framework process to obtain and maintain authorizations to operate. Performing information security risk management effectively and efficiently requires agencies and their system owners to clearly define the appropriate boundaries for organizational information systems. Information system boundaries help determine the scope of control and agency responsibilities for protecting information systems and identify the organizational resources, operating environments, technical components, and governance applicable to each information system. Information system boundaries correspond to information system management responsibilities at all levels of the organization—and potentially outside the organization in the case of externally provided systems, components, or services—including information owners, information system owners, authorizing officials, and operational security personnel at the individual information system level. Establishing the information system boundary is part of describing the information system in step 1 of the RMF, in which agencies identify the information resources associated with a system and the point of management control or authority over those resources [32]. Agencies need to strike the appropriate balance between defining information system boundaries broadly—potentially adding complexity to risk management processes—and defining boundaries more narrowly, which increases the number of information systems and corresponding operational and management resources allocated to provide adequate security and ensure compliance with FISMA and other applicable regulations. The security management perspective on information systems also focuses on the system as a source of risk to the organization, whether as a target for compromise that exposes the organization to adverse impact or as an essential asset on which mission functions and business processes depend. NIST emphasizes this point explicitly in its risk management guidance to agencies [33] and by focusing the application of the Risk Management Framework on information systems. The language in FISMA and associated NIST guidance to agencies highlights the importance of integrating security management with strategic and operational planning processes at the organizational level [34] and with key activities in all phases of the system development life cycle (SDLC) [35]. To achieve the sort of integrated management envisioned for federal information systems, agencies and their system owners need to address multiple system-based perspectives simultaneously, using explicit information resources management governance processes and the implementation of comprehensive program management or system development life cycle methodologies.

Capital Planning and Investment Control

Capital planning and investment control (CPIC), a core element of the budgeting process in federal government agencies, establishes processes and procedures for selecting, managing, and evaluating the results of agency investments in information technology [36]. From the CPIC perspective, information systems represent a type of capital asset acquired by organizations through explicit funding allocations included in agency budget requests. In contrast to information security and enterprise architecture—which respectively focus on the protection of IT assets such as information systems and define the composition of information systems and the relationships between application components, technologies, information, and the business processes they support—capital planning is concerned with funding the development and operation of information systems. In the CPIC domain, an information system is "a discrete set of information technology, data, and related resources, such as personnel, hardware, software, and associated information technology services organized for the collection, processing, maintenance, use, sharing, dissemination or disposition of information" [37]. Within the CPIC process, agencies develop business cases to justify investments used to fund information system development or acquisition and assess the extent to which those investments produce the outcomes intended by the agency. Under the provisions of the Clinger-Cohen Act, federal agencies also must identify investments in information systems that result in cost savings or other benefits shared among other agencies, measure the benefits and risk associated with proposed investments, and measure the progress or achievements of each investment in terms of cost, timeliness, quality, and capability of the system to meet specified requirements [36]. The CPIC perspective places an emphasis on cost-effectiveness and risk-based decision making similar to that prescribed for security management in FISMA, where CPIC focuses on sound investment decisions rather than adequate security.

Enterprise Architecture

Enterprise architecture (EA) as practiced in federal government agencies distinguishes among enterprise, segment, and solution levels of architectural analysis. The scope of enterprise architecture is the entire organization, which is decomposed functionally into segments representing mission-centric or common business or shared service areas. Agencies identify performance gaps or other organizational needs at the segment architecture level and develop business cases to justify investments (managed through the CPIC process) to support the implementation of solutions that help the organization improve mission performance or enhance delivery of common business or information technology services. All architectural levels include information systems to some degree, but information system development and implementation is ordinarily addressed at the solution architecture level. The scope of a solution architecture is typically limited to a single project, documenting how a system or business solution will be implemented and used by the personnel deploying the system to inform the development, implementation, and operations and maintenance phases of the SDLC [38]. The Federal Enterprise Architecture Framework (FEAF), defined and published in 1999 under the authority of the Federal Chief Information Officers Council, [39] uses the term *application* to represent the concept of a system as defined in federal regulations on information resources management. From the EA perspective, information systems are the focus of solution architectures developed to describe organizational IT assets such as applications or service components that support individual agency business functions. Because solution architecture execution involves the development or acquisition of IT assets, agencies coordinate EA activities with the CPIC process to justify and fund solution architecture implementation.

The organization-wide scope of enterprise architecture comprises business processes, performance metrics, and information resources allocated to support achievement of agency strategic goal and objectives. All four of the layers comprising the Federal Enterprise Architecture Framework—business, data, applications, and technology—relate to the design, development, and operation of federal information systems. Agencies must demonstrate alignment with agency-specific and federal enterprise architecture models in their business cases justifying IT investments to fund information systems [40]. The Department of Defense architecture Framework (DoDAF) provides a similar foundation for EA in DoD agencies, which develop architectural views at the enterprise and solution level, including the "systems viewpoint," one of eight architectural perspectives defined in the current version of the framework. In the DoDAF context, a *system* is "a functionally, physically, and/or behaviorally related group of regularly interacting or interdependent elements" [41] described using some or all of the 10 architecture models summarized in Table 4.1. Documenting systems at this level of detail facilitates the identification of functional and technical characteristics of systems and their interconnections that may have implications for security requirements and the controls implemented to meet those requirements.

In most agencies, enterprise architecture and capital planning are closely coordinated functions, driven in part by requirements imposed by the federal IT budgeting process but also due to the role both functions have in supporting the SDLC, particularly in the initiation and development and acquisition phases.

System Development Life Cycle

Federal government organizations typically manage information systems within the context of specific programs or projects, following processes and procedures prescribed in their system development life cycle (SDLC) methodologies. Although SDLC models vary across agencies—and even among different projects within the same agency—NIST guidance consistently applies a five-phase SDLC, illustrated in Figure 4.1, comprising a sequential process of initiation, development or acquisition, implementation, operations and maintenance, and disposal.

The SDLC integrates EA, CPIC, and information security perspectives on information systems, ideally providing a consistent approach for managing information systems throughout the organization and bringing together the personnel and organizational capabilities necessary to support effective information resources management. Each of the SDLC phases includes tasks and activities relevant to information

Table 4.1 DoDAF Architecture Models in the Systems Viewpoint [42]

Identifier	Model	Description
SV-1	Systems interface description	The identification of systems, system items, and their interconnections
SV-2	Systems resource flow description	A description of resource flows exchanged between systems
SV-3	Systems-systems matrix	The relationships among systems in a given architectural description
SV-4	Systems functionality description	The functions performed by systems and the system data flows among system functions
SV-5a	Operational activity to systems function traceability matrix	A mapping of system functions back to operational activities
SV-5b	Operational activity to systems traceability matrix	A mapping of systems back to capabilities or operational activities
SV-6	System resource flow matrix	Provides details of system resource flow elements being exchanged between systems and the attributes of those exchanges
SV-7	Systems measures matrix	The measures (metrics) of Systems Model elements for the appropriate timeframe(s)
SV-8	Systems evolution description	The planned steps for migrating a suite of systems to a more efficient suite, or toward evolving a current system to a future implementation.
SV-9	Systems technology & skills forecast	The emerging technologies, software/hardware products, and skills that are expected to be available in a given set of timeframes and that will affect future system development
SV-10a	Systems rules model	Identifies constraints imposed on systems functionality due to some aspect of system design or implementation
SV-10b	Systems state transition description	Identifies system responses to events
SV-10c	Systems event-trace description	Identifies system-specific refinements of critical sequences of events described in the Operational Viewpoint.

system security, described in Special Publication 800-64, *Security Considerations in the System Development Life Cycle* and listed in Table 4.2. Many of these activities fall outside the explicit scope of the RMF, but they highlight the intersection of information security management and overall project management for information systems.

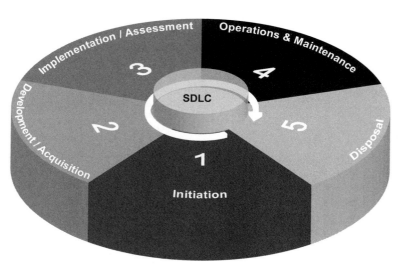

FIGURE 4.1 The System Development Life Cycle (SDLC) Provides a Perspective For Describing and Managing Information Systems in all Phases of Development for as Long as he Organization Uses Each System [43]

System owners, project managers, or other personnel responsible for managing the information system throughout the SDLC have important roles in ensuring that all information system perspectives and corresponding requirements are addressed.

Information Privacy

While all of the information collected, stored, and used by federal information systems presumably has value to the organization and should be protected accordingly, systems containing personal information about individuals are subject to a variety of legislative and regulatory requirements about safeguarding information privacy. Federal agencies must conduct privacy impact assessments before developing or acquiring information systems that collect, store, or provide access to personally identifiable information [20]. When an information system contains personally identifiable information, the system owner also needs to determine if that identifying information is used to retrieve information within the information system. If so, the system must be designated a *system of records*, defined by the Privacy Act of 1974 as "a group of any records under the control of any agency from which information is retrieved by the name of the individual or by some identifying number, symbol, or other identifying particular assigned to the individual" [44]. Agencies must provide public notice regarding their systems of records, identifying for each system its name and location, the type of personal information it contains, the use of personal information, policies and practices for handling that information, and administrative procedures for individuals whose personal information is maintained by the agency [45]. Senior agency

Table 4.2 Security Activities in SDLC Phases [43]

Phase	Activities
Initiation	• Security planning • Information system categorization • Business impact assessment • Privacy impact assessment • Secure information security development processes
Development/ Acquisition	• System risk assessment • Security control selection and documentation • Security architecture design • Security engineering and control development • Security documentation • Developmental, functional, and security testing
Implementation	• Security authorization plan • Environmental and system security integration • System security assessment • Information system authorization
Operations and Maintenance	• Operational readiness review • Configuration management and control • Continuous monitoring
Disposal	• Disposal/Transition planning • Information preservation • Media sanitization • Hardware and software disposal • System closure

officials for privacy provide information about their systems of records as part of the annual FISMA reporting process; for fiscal year 2011, agencies reported 4282 systems containing information in identifiable form, 3366 of which were designated systems of records [46]. As emphasized in Chapter 16, system owners responsible for federal information systems containing personally identifiable information must adhere to an explicit set of practices and procedures in addition to those prescribed in the RMF in order to comply with applicable privacy requirements.

ESTABLISHING INFORMATION SYSTEM BOUNDARIES

Defining the information system boundary is one of the core activities involved in describing an information system. As noted in Chapter 7, the information system description task within step 1 of the RMF often draws on the concept of operations, requirements specifications, and other documentation produced during the initiation phase of the SDLC. The information system boundary definition has implications for subsequent system development, implementation, and operations and maintenance activities, but from an information security perspective, the information system boundary has added significance because it determines the authorization boundary for the information system [32]. The functional and technical components, designated operating environment, and information assets an information system represents help to establish the boundary for the system. Working from the statutory definition of an information system, agencies have broad discretion to define individual information systems and their boundaries. An agency typically characterizes an information system by the common purpose for which the agency allocates the information resources used by the system, where the source of commonality may be shared or integrated functionality, the source of funding, the sphere of management control over the resources, or some combination of factors. To validate the set of information resources identified as belonging to an information system, agencies consider the extent to which the information resources support similar mission objectives and business processes, have similar operational characteristics and technical requirements (including security requirements), and reside in the same or similar operating environments [47].

Where information flows or interfaces exist among discrete operational components, agencies may choose to define information *subsystems*, a term NIST defines as "a major subdivision of an information system consisting of information, information technology, and personnel that perform one or more specific functions" [47]. Subsystems reside within a single information system boundary, although in the case of external subsystems such as those operated by service providers, the inclusion of the subsystem within the agency information system boundary may be logical rather than physical. Agencies may also denote the integration of multiple independent information systems—each potentially under the management control of a different organizational unit within or outside the agency—by defining *systems of systems* related by a common function or purpose. In contrast to information systems with identified subsystems, the individual information systems identified in a system of systems may each have their own separately defined boundaries. Integrating such systems typically requires the development and implementation of formal interconnection agreements executed by the system owners or other parties responsible for the operation of each information system. Systems of systems and information systems comprising multiple subsystems often have system boundaries far more complex than those defined for stand-alone or monolithic systems, but with the advent of service-oriented architectures, cloud computing, and other modular or distributed system deployment patterns, federal information systems more frequently feature complex boundaries.

Subsystems

The selection and implementation of appropriate security controls within a complex information system may require agencies and their system owners to adapt or refine security control baselines to identify which security controls and control enhancements apply to each subsystem or component the information system comprises. Defining subsystem boundaries within the information system boundary, as shown in Figure 4.2, facilitates more targeted security control implementation in which security controls are aligned to the most relevant subsystems. This approach is consistent with guidance in Special Publication 800-37 on security control implementation, which acknowledges that not all security controls apply to every subsystem and that security controls selected for implementation should be allocated to the information system components responsible for providing the capability the security controls are intended to address. Depending on the scale of a complex information system and the functional characteristics of its subsystems, each subsystem within the information system may be categorized separately. In complex information systems with components assigned separate security categorizations, allocating specific security controls to relevant information system components based on their assigned impact level represents a more cost-effective approach to achieving adequate security than applying the same security controls across the entire complex information system. Agencies can choose to perform security control selection, implementation, and assessment and system authorization on a consolidated basis for the entire complex information system or adopt an approach that separately authorizes and manages the risk associated with operating each information system functioning as part of a system of systems.

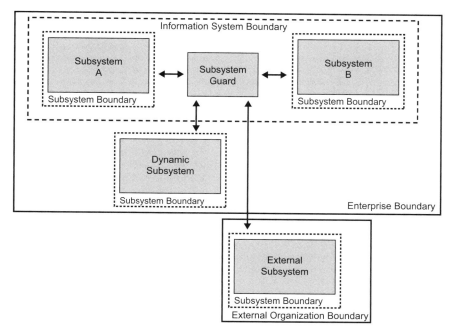

FIGURE 4.2 Agencies Sometimes Represent Large or Complex Systems as "Systems of Systems," Composites of Discretely Defined Subsystems all Operating Within the Same Information System Boundary

Following Risk Management Framework guidance, federal agencies identify subsystems included within their information system boundaries as either persistent or dynamic and specify whether the subsystems are internally or externally provided. The growing use of net-centric architecture patterns increases the likelihood that a federal information system will feature subsystems or service components that are not involved continuously in the operation of the information system, but instead are invoked for particular purposes or to support specific functions on an as-needed basis. System owners document the security requirements and corresponding security controls for such dynamic subsystems in the system security plan, which should also indicate how and under what circumstances the information security boundary may change with the composition of dynamic subsystems. Further complications arise when parties external to the agency operate one or more subsystems associated with an information system. External subsystems are components of an information system managed outside the direct control of the agency responsible for authorizing the information system [48]. Under FISMA, information systems or system components operated by external organizations on behalf of federal agencies are subject to the same security requirements as other federal information systems. Agencies leveraging externally provided subsystems or information systems must either evaluate the security protection afforded by the external entity or rely on the external provider's compliance with applicable legal and regulatory requirements. Agencies that determine the risk associated with externally provided systems or services to be unacceptable need to impose constraints on the way agency information systems leverage external capabilities, agree to accept a greater level of risk, employ compensating controls, or proscribe the use of externally provided systems or services [49].

Government organizations recognize the value offered by external providers for services such as application hosting and cloud computing and also acknowledge the substantial time and effort needed to properly evaluate the security controls implemented by external service providers. Agencies choosing to use external service providers ordinarily must evaluate the security aspects of external operating environments in addition to those within the agency. The Federal Risk and Authorization Management Program (FedRAMP) managed by the General Services Administration (GSA) provides a process through which cloud service providers can attain certification of their compliance with FISMA requirements and receive security authorization [50]. The third-party authorization program for cloud service providers launched in late 2011, and as of July 2012 no providers had been authorized under FedRAMP, but the GSA will publish a list of authorized cloud service providers on its website, giving federal agencies who use those providers some measure of assurance that appropriate security protection is in place. Because the authorizing official has responsibility for assessing and mitigating or otherwise responding to risk to the organization from the use of external service providers, service providers those are already authorized against current FISMA requirements may represent lower risk alternatives to agencies seeking to leverage outsourced information systems, services, or supporting infrastructure.

System Interconnections

Modern information systems rarely operate in isolation and, like other types of organizations, federal agencies frequently integrate two or more systems to exchange data or share information resources. A *system interconnection* is any direct connection between information systems; information system owners must document all system interconnections for their systems in the system security plan and determine appropriate security protections for each interconnection [51]. System owners must document system interconnections between different information systems within the same agency or across agency boundaries, describing for systems at both ends of the interconnection the system name, the organizational unit responsible for the system, the type of interconnection, any agreements in place and their effective dates, the security categorization level, the security authorization status, and the name of the authorizing official [51]. Government-wide guidance to agencies requires the identification and documentation of system interconnections [14], whether those interconnections integrate systems in a single agency, in two different agencies, or between an agency and an external service provider. Figure 4.3 illustrates the variety in system interconnection types. In many agencies, information system owners use alternative approaches to formal interconnections agreements when the connected systems are under the

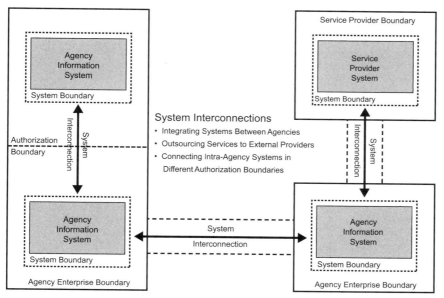

FIGURE 4.3 System Interconnections May Exist Between Systems Within the Same Agency, Between Two or More Agencies, or Between Government Agencies and External Service Providers. Agencies Execute System Interconnection Agreements Between the Organizations or Operating Units Responsible for Managing the Interconnected Systems

supervision of the same authorizing official. Federal guidance on system interconnections applies primarily in situations when each system is owned and operated by a different organization, including different parts of the same agency [52].

Where the information systems at either end of a system interconnection are under different management control, system owners must establish formal agreements governing each system interconnection. These include the interconnection security agreement (ISA), which documents the technical requirements (including security requirements) for establishing and maintaining the interconnection, and the memorandum of understanding (MOU), which provides the terms and conditions under which data will be exchanged or information resources will be shared between the interconnected systems [53]. The MOU documents the purpose of each interconnection and the responsibilities of each party to the agreement, including legal, financial, and governance considerations. The ISA represents the technical specification for the interconnection, identifying connectivity requirements between the systems such as ports, protocols, and transmission mechanisms and often including an architectural diagram describing the points of integration between the systems and the nature and direction of information flows across the connection. NIST provides guidance to agencies on system interconnections in Special Publication 800-47, which defines the four-step process shown in Figure 4.4 and describes the necessary tasks and expected outcomes of planning, establishing, maintaining, and disconnecting system interconnections.

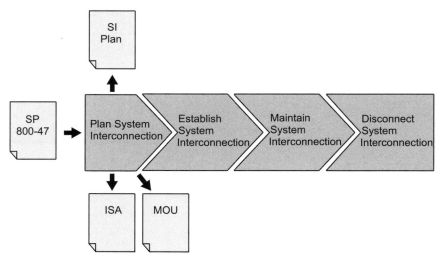

FIGURE 4.4 Agencies Plan, Establish, Maintain, and Disconnect System Interconnections Following a Formal Process That Documents Technical Details and Security Requirements for Each Interconnection in an Interconnection Security Agreement (ISA) and Defines the Responsibilities of Each System Owner in a Memorandum of Understanding (MOU)

> **WARNING**
>
> System interconnections by definition involve two separately managed information systems, each of which is subject to expected or unanticipated changes in their composition, operating environments, or applicable threats and vulnerabilities. Information system owners should not assume that system interconnections and the agreements documenting the security protecting the interconnections will remain the same as they are at the time the interconnections are established. In addition to monitoring their own information systems for changes, system owners using system interconnections must also monitor the factors potentially impacting the security of any interconnected systems.

Where system interconnections involve information systems owned or managed by external organizations, agencies often define the scope of operations, specify resources or services provided by the external information system, or document service level agreements in formal contracts executed in addition to ISAs and MOUs. NIST guidance to federal agencies on the use of external service providers encourages agencies to require the use of the security controls in Special Publication 800-53 [54]. If an agency is unable to negotiate an agency-specific agreement with an external service provider—as may be the case for providers of commodity services or services offered through government-wide acquisition contracts—the agency information system owner whose system is connected to the external service provider must evaluate the adequacy of the security provided by the external entity, documenting any assumptions, responsibilities, or obligations imposed by the external system interconnection that impact the security posture of the agency information system and the risk associated with it.

MAINTAINING SYSTEM INVENTORIES

Federal government agencies maintain several system inventories, driven both by legislative and regulatory requirements and by internally focused information resources management policy and oversight needs. Information system owners are typically responsible for ensuring that their systems are recorded in the appropriate organizational inventories, while the responsibility for establishing and maintaining such inventories rests with the executives with organization-wide authority such as heads of agencies. Key information system inventories include:

- An inventory, required under FISMA, of major information systems (including major national security systems) operated by or under the control of the agency and the interfaces between agency information systems and all other systems or networks, including those not operated by or under the control of the agency [15].
- Reference material or a guide for requesting records or information from the agency, as required under the Electronic Freedom of Information Act

> **TIP**
>
> The need to maintain multiple overlapping system inventories highlights the benefit of assigning unique system identifiers to each information system, both to facilitate reconciliation among inventories and to avoid potential confusion if the same system is referenced using different names in different contexts. Many agencies use the unique investment identifier (UII) assigned to each IT investment, but in cases where the relationship between investments and information systems is anything other than one-to-one, using an investment identifier as a system identifier may introduce inconsistencies or duplicate identifiers in different system inventories.

Amendments of 1996, including an index of all major information systems, a description of major information and record locator systems maintained by the agency, and instructions for obtaining various types and categories of public information from the agency [11].

- A record of the number of information systems operated by the agency or by contractors on behalf of the agency that contain information in identifiable form, required as part of the annual FISMA report information provided by senior agency officials for privacy [55]. Agencies also must report the number systems for which a Privacy Impact Assessment (PIA) is required and for which a PIA has been completed, the number systems for which a system of records notice (SORN) is required for which a current SORN has been published.
- An agency IT investment portfolio including information on all major and non-major IT investments planned by the agency to fund development, modernization, or enhancement of IT assets or operations and maintenance to sustain IT assets at current capability and performance levels [12].

Some agencies also maintain system inventories within their enterprise architectures, to identify the resources allocated to each system and the business processes and strategic goals and objectives each information system supports. System information documented and used by EA and CPIC program personnel contributes to a variety of internal agency information resources management and oversight functions in addition to facilitating compliance with external system inventory reporting requirements.

RELEVANT SOURCE MATERIAL

Several NIST Special Publications and OMB Circulars provide guidance, recommendations, and instructions relevant to defining and working with systems. The most applicable sources of information include:

- Special Publication 800-39, *Managing Information Security Risk: Organization, Mission, and Information System View* [56].

- Special Publication 800-37 Revision 1, *Guide for Applying the Risk Management Framework to Federal Information Systems* [57].
- Special Publication 800-64 Revision 2, *Security Considerations in the System Development Life Cycle* [35].
- Special Publication 800-47, *Security Guide for Interconnecting Information Technology Systems* [52].
- OMB Circular A-11, *Preparation, Submission, and Execution of the Budget.* [5].
- OMB Circular A-130, *Management of Federal Information Resources.* [9]

These and other NIST Special Publications are available from the NIST Computer Security Division Website, at http://csrc.nist.gov/publications/. Current versions of OMB Circulars are available online from OMB at http://www.whitehouse.gov/omb/circulars_default.

SUMMARY

This chapter explained the concept of information systems in the federal government context and offered several distinct yet largely complementary perspectives on considering information systems. While reinforcing the information system-centricity of the Risk Management Framework, the material in this chapter defines information systems and related terms as used in information resources management disciplines other than information security and risk management, including capital planning and investment control, enterprise architecture, privacy, and IT project management using the system development life cycle. Information system owners need to be aware of the different ways in which system information is documented, used, and reported to satisfy internal policies and procedures and comply with legal and regulatory requirements. When working on information security risk management, the clear establishment of the boundary for each information system is an essential prerequisite to selecting, implementing, and monitoring security controls to provide adequate security and to identifying system interconnections or other dependencies between agency information systems operated or managed by different organizations within or outside the agency.

REFERENCES

[1] Managing information security risk: Organization, mission, and information system view. Gaithersburg, MD: National Institute of Standards and Technology, Computer Security Division; March 2011. Special Publication 800-39. p. 2.
[2] Guide for applying the risk management framework to federal information systems. Gaithersburg, MD: National Institute of Standards and Technology, Computer Security Division; February 2010. Special Publication 800-37 revision 1. p. 2.
[3] Definitions. 44 U.S.C. §3502(8).

[4]   National information assurance glossary. Fort Meade, MD: Committee on National Security Systems; April 2009. CNSS Instruction No. 4009. p. 72.

[5]   Preparation, submission, and execution of the budget. Washington, DC: Office of Management and Budget; August 2011. Circular No. A-11, Revised (Transmittal Memorandum No. 85).

[6]   ISO/IEC 27001:2005. Information—Security techniques—Information security management systems—Requirements.

[7]   Recommended security controls for federal information systems and organizations. Gaithersburg, MD: National Institute of Standards and Technology, Computer Security Division; August 2009. Special Publication 800-53 revision 3. p. H-1.

[8]   Paperwork Reduction Act of 1995, Pub. L. No. 104-13, 109 Stat. 1643. §2, codified at 44 U.S.C. §3502(8).

[9]   Management of federal information resources. Washington, DC: Office of Management and Budget; November 2000. Circular No. A-130, Revised (Transmittal Memorandum No. 4).

[10] Guide for applying the risk management framework to federal information systems. Gaithersburg, MD: National Institute of Standards and Technology, Computer Security Division; February 2010. Special Publication 800-37 revision 1. See Appendix D for descriptions of key RMF roles and responsibilities.

[11] Electronic Freedom of Information Act Amendments of 1996, Pub. L. No. 104-231, 110 Stat. 3048. §11, codifed at 5 U.S.C. 552(g).

[12] Preparation, submission, and execution of the budget. Washington, DC: Office of Management and Budget; August 2011. Circular No. A-11, Revised (Transmittal Memorandum No. 85). Exhibit 53, p. 6.

[13] Capital programming guide version 3.0. Supplement to OMB Circular A-11: Preparation, submission, and execution of the budget. Washington, DC: Office of Management and Budget; August 2011. p. 108.

[14] Appendix III, Security of federal automated information resources. Washington, DC: Office of Management and Budget; November 2000. Circular No. A-130, Revised (Transmittal Memorandum No. 4).

[15] Federal Information Security Management Act of 2002, Pub. L. No. 107-347, 116 Stat. 2946. §305, codified at 44 U.S.C. §3505(c).

[16] Swanson M, Hash J, Bowen P. Guide for developing security plans for federal information systems. Gaithersburg, MD: National Institute of Standards and Technology, Computer Security Division; February 2006. Special Publication 800-18 revision 1. p. 2.

[17] Guide for applying the risk management framework to federal information systems. Gaithersburg, MD: National Institute of Standards and Technology, Computer Security Division; February 2010. Special Publication 800-37 revision 1. p. D-5.

[18] Standards for security categorization of federal information and information systems. Gaithersburg, MD: National Institute of Standards and Technology, Computer Security Division; December 2003. Federal Information Processing Standards Publication 199.

[19] Johnson C. Safeguarding against and responding to the breach of personally identifiable information. Washington, DC: Office of Management and Budget; May 22, 2007. Memorandum M-07-16.

[20] E-Government Act of 2002, Pub. L. No. 107-347, 116 Stat. 2899. §208(b).

[21] Privacy Act of 1974, Pub. L. No. 93-579, 88 Stat. 1896. Codified at 5 U.S.C. §552a(e)(4).

[22] Standards for security categorization of federal information and information systems. Gaithersburg, MD: National Institute of Standards and Technology, Computer Security Division; December 2003. Federal Information Processing Standards Publication 199. p. 1.

[23] Security categorization and control selection for national security systems. Fort Meade, MD: Committee on National Security Systems; October 2009. CNSS Instruction 1253. p. 7–8.

[24] Fiscal year 2009 report to Congress on the implementation of the Federal Information Security Management Act of 2002. Washington, DC: Office of Management and Budget; March 2010. p. 28.

[25] Definitions. 44 U.S.C. 3532(b)(2).

[26] Policy on information assurance risk management for national security systems. Fort Meade, MD: Committee on National Security Systems; January 2012. CNSS Policy No. 22.

[27] Barker WC. Guideline for identifying an information system as a national security system. Gaithersburg, MD: National Institute of Standards and Technology, Computer Security Division; August 2003. Special Publication 800-59.

[28] Information Technology Management Reform Act of 1996, Pub. L. No. 104-106, 110 Stat. 679. Title LI, §§5101-5142.

[29] Federal Information Security Management Act of 2002, Pub. L. No. 107-347, 116 Stat. 2946. §301, codified at 44 U.S.C. §3544(a)(3).

[30] Capital programming guide version 3.0. Supplement to OMB Circular A-11: Preparation, submission, and execution of the budget. Washington, DC: Office of Management and Budget; August 2011. p. 9.

[31] Guide for applying the risk management framework to federal information systems. Gaithersburg, MD: National Institute of Standards and Technology, Computer Security Division; February 2010. Special Publication 800-37 revision 1. p. 9.

[32] Guide for applying the risk management framework to federal information systems. Gaithersburg, MD: National Institute of Standards and Technology, Computer Security Division; February 2010. Special Publication 800-37 revision 1. p. 10.

[33] Managing information security risk: Organization, mission, and information system view. Gaithersburg, MD: National Institute of Standards and Technology, Computer Security Division; March 2011. Special Publication 800-39. p.1.

[34] Federal Information Security Management Act of 2002, Pub. L. No. 107-347, 116 Stat. 2946. §301, codified at 44 U.S.C. §3544(a)(1)(C).

[35] Kissel R, Stine K, Scholl M, Rossman H, Fahlsing J, Gulick J. Security considerations in the system development life cycle. Gaithersburg, MD: National Institute of Standards and Technology, Computer Security Division; October 2008. Special Publication 800-64 revision 2.

[36] Information Technology Management Reform Act of 1996, Pub. L. No. 104-106, 110 Stat. 679. Title LI, §5122.

[37] Capital programming guide version 3.0. Supplement to OMB Circular A-11: Preparation, submission, and execution of the budget. Washington, DC: Office of Management and Budget; August 2011. Exhibit 53, p. 6.

[38] FEA practice guidance. Washington, DC: Office of Management and Budget, Federal Enterprise Architecture Program Management Office; November 2007. p. 1–5.

[39] Federal enterprise architecture framework version 1.1. Washington, DC: Chief Information Officers Council; September 1999.

[40] Capital programming guide version 3.0. Supplement to OMB Circular A-11: Preparation, submission, and execution of the budget. Washington, DC: Office of Management and Budget; August 2011. p. 82.

[41] DoD architecture framework version 2.0. Washington, DC: Department of Defense; May 28, 2009. Volume 1, p. B-4.

[42] DoD architecture framework version 2.0. Washington, DC: Department of Defense; May 28, 2009 Volume 1, p. 24–5.

[43] Kissel R, Stine K, Scholl M, Rossman H, Fahlsing J, Gulick J. Security considerations in the system development life cycle. Gaithersburg, MD: National Institute of Standards and Technology, Computer Security Division,october; October 2008. Special Publication 800-64 revision 2. p. 11.

[44] Privacy Act of 1974, Pub. L. No. 93-579, 88 Stat. 1896. §552a(a)(5).

[45] Privacy Act of 1974, Pub. L. No. 93-579, 88 Stat. 1896. §552a(e)(4).

[46] Fiscal year 2011 report to Congress on the implementation of the Federal Information Security Management Act of 2002. Washington, DC: Office of Management and Budget; March 2012. p. 40.

[47] Guide for applying the risk management framework to federal information systems. Gaithersburg, MD: National Institute of Standards and Technology, Computer Security Division; February 2010. Special Publication 800-37 revision 1. p. 11.

[48] Guide for applying the risk management framework to federal information systems. Gaithersburg, MD: National Institute of Standards and Technology, Computer Security Division; February 2010. Special Publication 800-37 revision 1. p. 15.

[49] Guide for applying the risk management framework to federal information systems. Gaithersburg, MD: National Institute of Standards and Technology, Computer Security Division; February 2010. Special Publication 800-37 revision 1. p. 16.

[50] VanRoekel S. Security authorization of information systems in cloud computing environments. Washington, DC: Office of Management and Budget; December 8, 2011.

[51] Swanson M, Hash J, Bowen P. Guide for developing security plans for federal information systems. Gaithersburg, MD: National Institute of Standards and Technology, Computer Security Division; February 2006. Special Publication 800-18 revision 1. p. 23.

[52] Grance T, Hash J, Peck S, Smith J, Korow-Diks K. Security guide for interconnecting information technology systems. Gaithersburg, MD: National Institute of Standards and Technology, Computer Security Division; August 2002. Special Publication 800-47.

[53] Grance T, Hash J, Peck S, Smith J, Korow-Diks K. Security guide for interconnecting information technology systems. Gaithersburg, MD: National Institute of Standards and Technology, Computer Security Division; August 2002. Special Publication 800-47. p. 3-5–6.

[54] Recommended security controls for federal information systems and organizations. Gaithersburg, MD: National Institute of Standards and Technology, Computer Security Division; August 2009. Special Publication 800-53 revision 3. p. 13.

[55] Annual FISMA reporting: Senior Agency Official for Privacy (SAOP) questions, attachment to FY 2009 reporting instructions for the Federal Information Security Management Act and agency privacy management. Washington, DC: Office of Management and Budget; August 20, 2009. Memorandum M-09-29.

[56] Managing information security risk: Organization, mission, and information system view. Gaithersburg, MD: National Institute of Standards and Technology, Computer Security Division; March 2011. Special Publication 800-39.

[57] Guide for applying the risk management framework to federal information systems. Gaithersburg, MD: National Institute of Standards and Technology, Computer Security Division; February 2010. Special Publication 800-37 revision 1.

Success Factors

INFORMATION IN THIS CHAPTER:

- Prerequisites for Organizational Risk Management
- Managing the Information Security Program
- Compliance and Reporting
- Organizational Success Factors
- Measuring Security Effectiveness

Managing risk and conducting effective information security management requires a coordinated effort across all levels of an organization. The Risk Management Framework process emphasizes tasks focused on individual information systems in support of obtaining and maintaining security authorization and providing cost-effective protection for information assets commensurate with risk to the organization from operating their systems. System owners cannot successfully execute the RMF process in isolation, however, as the effective and efficient performance of the RMF relies on several critical success factors. As illustrated in Figure 5.1, these factors include explicit support from management, contributions from the organization-level information security program, the implementation and monitoring of security performance measures, and planning, budgeting, and allocation of resources sufficient to achieve security management objectives. These organizational elements enable consistent use of the RMF for all information systems, provide appropriate protection to the mission functions and business processes those systems support, and facilitate system-specific and agency-level security monitoring, compliance, and reporting activities.

By applying the Risk Management Framework (RMF) to all information systems, organizations can develop an aggregated view of information security risk and security controls implemented to mitigate that risk to a level acceptable to the organization. In addition to establishing agency responsibilities for protecting federal information systems and the information they contain, the Federal Information Security Management Act (FISMA) also requires each federal agency to implement and maintain an organization-wide information security program [1]. Other legislative requirements and government-wide guidance on information resources management emphasize

FIGURE 5.1 Effective Execution of the Risk Management Framework for Information Systems and the Mission and Business Processes Those Systems Support Relies on a Variety of Capabilities and Functions Established upon a Foundation of Organizational Risk Management

the importance of consistent executive oversight, performance measurement, and allocation of agency resources aligned with organizational goals, objectives, and priorities [2,3]. The information security, performance management, and capital planning programs operated by federal agencies provide essential input to organizational risk management and help establish a foundation supporting organizational, mission and business process, and information system security and risk management processes and activities. This chapter highlights key organization-level considerations underlying agency risk management practices and enabling successful application of the Risk Management Framework and related standards and guidance issued to agencies to implement FISMA requirements.

PREREQUISITES FOR ORGANIZATIONAL RISK MANAGEMENT

Risk management is a complex, interdisciplinary set of functions requiring the involvement and coordinated effort of many stakeholders within an organization. To achieve the objectives articulated in FISMA and other federal legislation and guidance, agencies need to address risk management at all levels of the organization, including senior executives developing and implementing agency strategy, program managers and business owners responsible for executing the organizational mission, and system owners and personnel developing and maintaining the information systems supporting all aspects of the organization's operations. In its flagship guidance on managing information security risk, NIST emphasizes the importance of adopting an organization-wide perspective on risk management, integrating the processes and activities conducted at the levels of individual information systems, mission and business processes, and the organization [4]. This guidance encourages agency senior management to recognize the importance of effectively managing information security risk and adopt governance structures that include organizational risk management. Given the extent to which mission execution depends on information systems and the processes they support, agency executives also need to acknowledge the role of risk management as a mission enabler and to mandate risk-based management as a core organizational requirement. Demonstrating executive-level commitment helps agencies helps ensure sufficient allocation of resources to develop and implement effective, organization-wide risk management programs. According to NIST, effective organizational risk management requires agencies to [4]:

- Assign risk management responsibilities to appropriate senior leaders or executives.
- Recognize and understand the information security risks to organizational operations and assets, individuals, other organizations, and the nation arising from the operation and use of information systems.
- Establish the organizational tolerance for risk and communicate the risk tolerance throughout the organization to guide ongoing risk-based decision-making.
- Hold senior leaders accountable for their risk management decisions and for the implementation of effective, organization-wide risk management programs.

Although the importance of securing executive commitment to organizational risk management may be self-evident, many agencies find it challenging to actually achieve the senior management buy-in so frequently touted as essential for success. There is no single best strategy applicable to all agencies for establishing executive commitment, but information security managers and risk management stakeholders often articulate the value of organizational risk management in terms of legal, policy, or regulatory compliance requirements; alignment to and support of strategic goals and objectives and intended mission outcomes; financial benefits; or some combination of these factors.

Justifying Information Security

Performing all the tasks and activities required under FISMA demands a significant commitment of organizational resources, both for agency-level risk management and information security program operations and for implementing security controls and appropriate oversight to achieve adequate security for information systems. All government organizations operate within budget constraints that require agencies to prioritize their programs and activities and allocate investment funding, personnel, and other resources in a manner that aligns with those priorities. In this context, agencies need to be able to demonstrate the value of information security and risk management activities to senior management and justify the allocation of organizational resources needed to achieve risk management objectives. The need to comply with legal and regulatory requirements is one type of justification, but compliance alone is insufficient in many organizations to make information security a high priority, particularly given the lack of meaningful penalties for non-compliance with FISMA and other security requirements. Agencies and their system owners develop business cases to support information security programs and the security resources associated with information systems, using anticipated economic or performance improvement benefits, in addition to compliance objectives, to justify resource allocations.

Federal agencies typically develop business cases for all major IT investments, where *major* denotes a need for special management attention because of the importance of the investment to the agency; significant program or policy implications; high executive visibility; high development, operating, or maintenance costs; or other criteria specified for the agency's capital planning and investment control process [5]. Agency information security programs and significant individual information systems often warrant their own business cases; agencies report information about other systems and overall security spending in the agency's IT investment portfolio and IT security portfolio, respectively. The IT security portfolio includes costs for eight categories of IT security tools—anti-virus, anti-malware, data leakage protection, email filtering software, intrusion detection, intrusion prevention, security information and event management, and Web filtering software—and an aggregate total spending amount [6]. Specific justification information varies to some extent by agency and by the nature of the program or IT investment addressed in the business case, but business cases typically include costs, expected productivity gains or performance improvements, a cost-benefit comparison, and any existing supporting information such as program evaluations or the results of analyses providing the rationale for acquiring or operating information systems or other assets [7]. Federal agencies prepare IT investment business cases following official guidance in the *Capital Programming Guide* provided as part of OMB Circular A-11, which specifies that major investments should [8]:

- Support core or priority mission functions.
- Be undertaken by the agency because no alternative private sector or governmental source can support the function more efficiently.
- Support simplified or otherwise redesigned work processes that reduce costs, improve effectiveness, and make maximum use of commercial, off-the-shelf technology.
- Demonstrate a projected return on the investment equal to or better than alternative uses of available resources, where return may include improved mission performance, reduced cost, increased quality, speed, or flexibility, and increased customer and employee satisfaction.

- Be consistent with federal and agency enterprise architectures.
- Reduce risk.
- Be implemented in phased, successive segments as narrow in scope and brief in duration as practicable.
- Employ an acquisition strategy that appropriately allocates risk between the government and the vendor or contractor, uses competition, ties payments to accomplishments, and takes maximum advantage of commercial technology.

Business cases for IT investments often focus on justifying anticipated or desired budget expenditures in a way that satisfies external requirements for review and oversight, but before a business case is included as part of an agency's IT portfolio it receives review and approval by an investment review board or other IT governance body and by the agency chief information officer, head of agency, and other appropriate executives. The information included in a business case for information security or risk management-related investments typically reflects a combination of agency-specific and government-wide criteria. System owners, business owners, program managers, and others preparing business cases should understand the prioritization criteria used within their agency's capital planning and investment control and IT governance processes to ensure that evidence provided to justify resource allocations satisfies the appropriate criteria. While a business case specifies the costs and benefits expected from information security risk management programs and activities, once those programs are established and activities are underway, measuring and reporting on security is an important way to help justify security spending on an ongoing basis and to justify the allocation of additional resources to take corrective action or otherwise improve security.

Key Upper Management Roles

There are many stakeholders with an interest in organizational risk management. From the perspective of demonstrating value and securing the appropriate level of commitment from the organization's leadership, risk management should involve executives responsible for overseeing information security, information technology, and mission execution. Despite the strong influence of information technology on security, organizational risk management focuses on risk affecting all aspects of agency operations and leaders representing mission functions and business processes have risk management roles just as integral as those of information resources management executives. Like agency strategic planning and many other forms of organizational governance, organizational risk management is considered an inherently governmental function so each of the senior leadership roles involved in information security risk management is assigned only to government personnel [9].

Head of Agency

The senior executive of each federal agency has the visibility and influence to demonstrate the level of priority within the organization for effective information resources management, including risk and information security management. Although in many government organizations the head of the agency is a political appointee, this role—directly or by delegation to other senior executives—establishes the organizational commitment to information security risk management and to allocating resources and taking actions necessary to protect the core mission functions and business processes the agency performs. The head of agency also ensures appropriate accountability for information security through the organizational information security program and through reporting, oversight, and communication relationships established with risk executives, the chief information officer and other senior IT leadership, and senior information officials responsible for security and privacy.

Risk Executive

The role of risk executive—whether filled by an individual, a group, or a functional unit within the organization—provides leadership and oversight of organization-wide risk management, developing and implementing risk management strategy consistent with the strategic goals and objectives of the organization and managing information security risk across the organization in a manner reflecting the organizational risk tolerance. The risk executive coordinates efforts with other senior leaders within the organization to provide a comprehensive risk management strategy, facilitate information sharing and communication among risk management and information security officials and other senior leaders, and oversee all risk management activities across the organization. The risk executive role may be performed by the agency head, another senior leader with appropriate management authority, a risk review board or other leadership group, or some other functional structure that best suits the organization.

Chief Information Officer

The role of chief information officer (CIO) has broad statutory authority assigned by FISMA, the Clinger-Cohen Act, and other key legislation for leading and overseeing many aspects of information resources management, including overall leadership and oversight of the agency information security program. Clinger-Cohen—enacted as the Information Technology Management Reform Act of 1996—formally established the Chief Information Officer role and primary responsibilities in federal executive agencies [10]. FISMA directed agency CIOs to designate a senior information security officer—typically a subordinate reporting to the CIO—and to help ensure that all senior organizational officials with information security authority understand their roles and associated responsibilities. In coordination with the senior information security officer and other senior officials, the CIO acts as the primary liaison between the information resources management programs in the agency and the head of the agency, providing regular status reporting and updates on the overall effectiveness of the organizational information security program and efforts to mitigate or manage risk to the organization. The CIO, risk executive, and senior information security officer work with authorizing officials, common control providers, and information system owners to implement an effective organizational information security program to ensure that organizational information systems are adequately secured and authorized to operate. The CIO also influences planning, budgeting, and resource allocation for security controls and other measures to protect the organization's information assets and the mission functions and business processes those assets support.

Senior Information Security Officer

The senior information security officer (a position often designated chief information security officer (CISO) or senior agency information security officer), in a role established by FISMA [11], carries out the security responsibilities of the chief information officer specified in FISMA and serves as the primary liaison between the CIO and authorizing officials, common control providers, information system owners, and information system security officers. The senior information security officer is also often the official responsible for ensuring agency compliance with FISMA and other applicable information security requirements and for coordinating the collection and reporting of organizational information security program metrics and other information submitted to OMB, DHS, GAO, and other entities overseeing government information security operations. Agencies are expected to provide senior information security officers with the authority and resources necessary to achieve cost-effective, risk-based security for organizational information assets. In some agencies, the senior information security officer may also serve as an authorizing official for information systems providing enterprise-wide functions or services.

Inspector General

Federal government agency inspectors general provide independent review and oversight of agency programs and activities, including information security programs. With respect to FISMA, inspectors general serve in the role of independent auditor, with responsibility for conducting annual evaluations of agency information security programs and reporting the findings of their evaluations as part of annual FISMA reporting requirements. Specifically, each inspector general assesses the agency information security program in 11 functional areas to determine if the program's implementation in each area is consistent with FISMA requirements or needs improvement, based on a set of 96 attributes that information security programs should exhibit [12].

MANAGING THE INFORMATION SECURITY PROGRAM

The organizational information security program provides overarching operational guidance for information system-level security management. This guidance includes policies, procedures, and standards that system owners and common control providers should follow and the definition and implementation of organization-wide management, operational, and technical controls. Many of the activities performed at the organizational information security program-level stem from FISMA requirements specifying responsibilities for each federal agency. These include [13]:

- Performing periodic risk assessments of information security risk associated with agency information and information systems.
- Creating risk-based policies and procedures to cost-effectively reduce information security risk to an acceptable level, address information security throughout the life cycle of each information system, and ensure compliance with FISMA requirements.
- Developing organization-level plans and defining standards or templates for subordinate plans for providing adequate information security for networks, facilities, and information systems.
- Providing security awareness training for personnel and contractors managing or using agency information systems.
- Conducting periodic testing and evaluation of the effectiveness of information security policies, procedures, and practices.
- Developing a process for planning, implementing, evaluating, and documenting remedial action to address deficiencies in agency information security policies, procedures, and practices.
- Developing and implementing procedures for detecting, reporting, and responding to security incidents.
- Developing and implementing plans and procedures to ensure continuity of operations for information systems.

The NIST FISMA Implementation Project issued guidance to federal agencies on each of these requirements (Table 1.1 maps FISMA requirements to corresponding NIST Special Publications) and in 2009 revised Special Publication 800-53 by adding a program management control family with a set of security controls applicable for all information systems and security control baselines but implemented and assessed at the information security program level. These controls, listed in Table 5.1, correspond to key FISMA provisions as well as agency responsibilities and requirements for information resources management detailed in OMB Circular A-130 and other applicable government-wide guidance.

Among the changes to Special Publication 800-53 NIST proposed for Revision 4 is the addition of four more program management controls addressing information security program responsibilities, including implementing an insider threat program, information security workforce development program, operational security program,

> **WARNING**
> System authorization efforts undertaken without close coordination with information security program tend be less cost-effective, requiring more resources or taking longer to execute, and may result in a higher proportion of system-specific controls than the system owner can justify. This is especially true if the system owner and the authorizing official have differing perspectives on the extent to which the information system should follow policies and procedures or leverage other guidance provided by the organizational information security program.

Table 5.1 Program Management Controls Required in Federal Agencies [14]

Number	Control Name	Description
PM-1	Information Security Program Plan	A single document or set of related documents that describe the structure and operation of the organization-wide information security program, including the program requirements and program management controls and organization-level common controls implemented to meet those requirements
PM-2	Senior Information Security Officer	Senior-level organizational official with authority and resources to implement and maintain the organization-wide information security program
PM-3	Information Security Resources	Provides funding, via the capital planning and investment control process, sufficient to provide the resources necessary to implement and operate the information security program
PM-4	Plan of Action and Milestones Process	Organizational-level process prescribing the maintenance of plans of action and milestones for the organization-wide information security program and organizational information systems
PM-5	Information System Inventory	Inventory of all information systems operated or controlled by the organization, maintained to comply with agency system inventory requirement in FISMA
PM-6	Information Security Measures of Performance	Outcome-based performance metrics developed and monitored to assess the implementation, efficiency and effectiveness, and impact of the organization-wide information security program and the controls implemented in support of the program
PM-7	Enterprise Architecture	Organizational information security architecture integrated into the enterprise architecture, incorporating security requirements and associated controls using the Risk Management Framework and supporting standards and guidelines
PM-8	Critical Infrastructure Plan	Document defining and describing the protection of organizational critical infrastructure and key resources, incorporating information security issues and including protection provided by security controls within the set of planning requirements mandated in HSPD-7
PM-9	Risk Management Strategy	Comprehensive strategy developed and implemented to manage organizational information security risk, including clear statement of risk tolerance and specifying approaches for planning, assessing, responding to, and monitoring risk
PM-10	Security Authorization Process	Implementation of the Risk Management Framework process to manage the security of organizational information systems through security authorization as part of organization-wide risk management
PM-11	Mission/Business Process Definition	Formal process descriptions identifying information protection needs and considering information security and risk factors affecting mission and business operations, used to determine necessary security controls for the information systems that support mission and business processes

and a process for overseeing information system level testing, training, and monitoring to ensure consistency and validate adherence to organizational risk management strategy and priorities [15].

Organizational Policies, Procedures, Templates, and Guidance

Agency information security programs are not only mechanisms for monitoring and oversight, they also enable more cost-effective and efficient information security protection for agency information systems. Based on data submitted to OMB and reported to Congress, federal agencies in 2011 devoted more than 10% of their overall IT security spending—roughly $138 million—to activities associated with implementing the Risk Management Framework [16].

System owners and their project teams executing the RMF process produce large volumes of security-related documentation, typically including detailed security control configuration information and operational procedures used to manage their systems on an ongoing basis as well as the artifacts in the system authorization package. NIST provides detailed guidance on the content and recommended structure for much of this documentation, but agencies often find that developing their own templates for the necessary plans and supporting artifacts helps reduce the time required to produce documentation and encourages consistency in the content and level of detail provided for each system. Agency information security programs commonly develop organizational policies and procedures (which correspond to the first control in each of the control families in Special Publication 800-53) prescribing how system owners should address security requirements for their systems. The information security program is also the appropriate level within the organization to develop standard security artifact templates and guidance for system owners, either following the content and structure recommendations in relevant NIST special publications or creating agency-specific templates to satisfy organizational requirements. Agencies may also consider the acquisition and implementation of automated tools to facilitate the collection and maintenance of system security information and the generation of templates and reports to support the development of system security plans, security assessment reports, plans of action and milestones, and other security artifacts. Many of the tools available also provide external reporting capabilities that satisfy FISMA requirements for reporting to DHS and OMB, which emphasize the use of automated data feeds submitted by agencies to the CyberScope online reporting tool [17].

COMPLIANCE AND REPORTING

Providing effective security protection for information systems and other assets is a high priority for most organizations due to the important enabling role of information security in the execution of mission functions and business processes. Where private sector organizations generally have broad latitude to make their own determinations about the level of security and privacy protection to employ, even with respect to safeguarding personally identifiable information and other sensitive data [18], federal government organizations are subject to a wide range of legislative and regulatory requirements regarding security and privacy. For requirements specified in FISMA, agency compliance is mandatory, with the task of ensuring compliance falling within the scope of the agency information security program and ultimate responsibility assigned to the head of each agency [19]. These requirements make compliance—and the collection, management, and submission of agency-wide security information reported to demonstrate compliance—an important part of agency information security program operations. Establishing consistent, repeatable, and reliable compliance and reporting processes supports information security risk management across the entire organization.

Agency Reporting Requirements

FISMA directs each agency to provide annual reports "on the adequacy and effectiveness of information security policies, procedures, and practices" and on compliance with the applicable provisions in the law, and to include similar information in plans and reports developed to satisfy other requirements associated with budget formulation, information resources management, program performance monitoring, financial management, and internal auditing and administrative controls [20]. OMB (and since 2010, DHS) issues annual instructions to federal agencies specifying the set of security program metrics and other information agencies need to submit to satisfy FISMA reporting requirements. The current scope of FISMA reporting activities includes automated monthly data feeds of security information from each agency to CyberScope; written responses to a series of questions to be answered by chief information officers, senior agency officials for privacy, and inspectors general; and participation in "CyberStat" meetings coordinated by DHS intended to help agencies assess existing security posture and develop recommendations and action plans for improving security [21]. While both FISMA and the reporting instructions issued to agencies refer to annual reporting, some security information is reported monthly or quarterly; the shift that began in 2010 towards greater use of automated data feeds for reporting security metrics continues to evolve towards more frequent reporting. Agency officials retrieve current reporting templates and manage document-based submissions through CyberScope. Access to this information is strictly controlled, although summary FISMA report information for each agency is included in annual reports to Congress that are publicly available [22].

Information Security Program Evaluation

In addition to submitting information security metrics and program data for government-wide oversight, FISMA also requires federal agencies to perform annual independent evaluations to assess the effectiveness of their information security programs [23]. These evaluations address established security policies, procedures, and practices as implemented by agency information systems and review the agency's compliance with FISMA requirements and other relevant security and privacy regulations, policies, and guidance. The information security program evaluation is typically performed by the agency inspector general or by an individual or entity external to the organization serving as an independent auditor. Because the agency inspector general is already required to assess the information security program against administration priorities, FISMA metrics, and baseline questions established for FISMA reporting, agencies may find it efficient to use the results of inspector general FISMA reports for internal program evaluation purposes, or to extend the scope of the required FISMA metrics and topic areas to address program characteristics most important to the agency. Under guidance provided by the Department of Homeland Security under its authority to oversee operational security within executive agencies, the questions inspectors general must answer reflect less emphasis on compliance and focus more on demonstrating the effectiveness of security controls and on assessing risk consistent with the guidance provided in Special Publication 800-39 [21]. Agencies can use the results of information security program evaluations and feedback provided to each agency during CyberStat reviews to identify areas of weakness and develop strategies to improve security organization-wide and provide better support to information systems security and risk management activities.

ORGANIZATIONAL SUCCESS FACTORS

In addition to the support provided by the organizational information security program, there are many other factors affecting how effectively and efficiently agencies and their system owners execute the steps in the Risk Management Framework, satisfy the provisions in FISMA and other legal, regulatory, and policy requirements, and manage information security throughout their organizations. When present in an organization, these factors increase the chances for achieving strategic and operational security objectives and help agencies and their system owners balance the requirements necessary to provide adequate security consistent with the mission and business priorities of the organization. The information security management activities and attributes described in this section are not prerequisites—in the sense that agencies can (and often do) implement and maintain compliant security practices without them. Agencies seeking cost-effective information security operations and the willing engagement by all system owners in executing the organization's risk management strategy can, however, engender success by attending to these factors.

Governance

Governance refers to the organizational structure, management authority, and responsibility for decision making within an organization and to the set of practices and processes with which an organization establishes and executes its strategy. Governance determines who makes decisions, the criteria upon which decision-makers act, and the processes by which organizations allocate resources in support of achieving mission goals and objectives. Governance in the context of risk management incorporates risk-based considerations in organizational decisions; establishes the risk management strategy for the organization, including determining how to assess and respond to risk faced by the organization; and specifies who within the organization is authorized to make decisions regarding risk. NIST recognizes three primary types of governance models used in federal government organizations: centralized, decentralized, and hybrid [24]. Regardless of the overall governance model applicable to a given federal agency, the execution of the Risk Management Framework as NIST prescribed presumes a hybrid governance model, in which system owners and common control providers have some degree of authority to accept risk or choose other responses to risk associated with their information systems but make risk-based decisions within the bounds of the risk management strategy, risk tolerance, and related policies and procedures specified at the organizational level. The specific governance model employed by an organization is less important as a factor contributing to the success of agency risk management practices than the strength of governance. Strong risk management governance sets clear expectations about what the organization considers acceptable risk and establishes and applies formal decision-making criteria to allocate resources, approve recommended courses of action, and define roles and responsibilities involved in information security risk management at all levels of the organization. Strong governance is also an indicator of commitment by organizational leaders to manage risk consistently throughout the organization [25].

Planning

The need for effective planning is a consistent theme in FISMA and other legislative sources of information resources management practices and requirements and in NIST standards and guidance on risk management processes. Chapter 6 emphasizes the importance of thorough planning prior to initiating the RMF process for each information system, but comprehensive planning is also essential for organizational information security program activities, organizational risk management strategy development and execution, and successful integration of information security with other key information resources management functions. Federal agencies often structure their risk management and information security program planning activities to produce the formal plans and related security documentation needed to support system authorization, continuous monitoring, and other risk management functions. These planning documents identify and describe organizational and system-specific security requirements derived from mission and business needs and from threats and vulnerabilities identified in risk assessments. Planning also supports efficient resource allocation by identifying organizational priorities and aligning risk-based decisions with those priorities, including provisions for implementing management, operational, and technical controls to satisfy security requirements. The planning process also identifies organizational decision makers and other key risk management roles and responsibilities to facilitate appropriate communication channels and establish accountability for decisions.

Budgeting and Resource Allocation

The tasks specified in the Risk Management Framework cannot be performed effectively without sufficient resources, including the allocation of funding for personnel, tools, training, testing, and monitoring. Federal government agencies report significant investments in information security, with a total of $13.3 billion spent in fiscal year 2011 across all agencies, of which Department of Defense spending alone was more than $10 billion [26]. Spending on information security represented an average of 18% of total IT spending [27], giving many agencies a strong incentive to find ways to control security expenditures while maintaining adequate security protection for their information assets. Personnel costs for government employees and contractors working on security represent the largest proportion of overall information security spending, so opportunities for improving security workforce productivity through more effective training or the introduction of automated technical and operational support tools can help agencies get the most out of their security budget outlays [16]. The federal budgeting process requires agencies to plan anticipated expenditures more than a year in advance [28], presenting a special challenge for information security programs and related activities that need to address dynamic and often unpredictable threats, vulnerabilities, and other factors affecting agency information systems and operating environments. As a component of annual performance plans agencies must submit to OMB, FISMA requires each agency to include the budget, staffing, and training resources necessary to implement the organizational information security program [29]. To ensure adequate resources are allocated for individual information systems, systems owners need to ensure that budget requests and business cases developed in support of individual information systems incorporate funding to satisfy security requirements and that the relevant security tasking and associated resources are included within the scope of contracts issued to acquire, develop, or operate federal information systems.

Communication

Given the array of stakeholders participating in information security and risk management processes, effective communication is essential within and across all layers of the organization to ensure the appropriate information is available to relevant personnel. Members of project teams executing the RMF process and implementing or operating information systems need to establish clear and consistent communication practices to ensure awareness and understanding of requirements and dependencies between the RMF and system development life cycle. Similar interactions also need to happen between personnel working on security and on other key programs such as enterprise architecture, capital planning, budget formulation, and performance monitoring and management. Information security program managers and system owners also need to establish bi-directional communication channels between individuals or organizational units responsible for implementing different parts of the risk management process and between the organizational, mission and business process, and information system tiers NIST references in its risk management guidance [30]. Effective communication in the risk management context includes conveying the results of security monitoring activities through status reports and notifications; providing information about changes to information systems or their operating environments to risk managers, authorizing officials, and other stakeholders potentially affected by the security impact of such changes; and disseminating new or updated strategies, policies, procedures, standards, and guidelines developed at the organizational level to system owners whose security management activities may be predicated on that information.

Standardization, Automation, and Reuse

One approach to making agency information security more cost effective is to encourage or mandate the use of tools, standard technologies and operating procedures, or controls across multiple systems or the entire organization. The provision of common controls is one way to reuse security tools or other capabilities, as the cost of implementing common or hybrid controls for the systems that inherit them is substantially lower than deploying system-specific controls in many cases. In addition to reusing controls, agencies may choose to develop and make available templates or procedural guidance through their information security programs to assist system owners to execute security management activities and produce the documentation necessary to support system authorization. The benefits of reuse accrue for any method or mechanism that minimizes the need for system owners to implement unique security tools and technologies or to develop security documentation from scratch.

Flexibility

All organizations need to strike a balance between their level of standardization or rigid adherence to policies and procedures required at the organizational level and the amount of authority delegated to system owners to adapt security requirements to suit their individual systems. To some degree the flexibility inherent in organizational risk management depends on the governance model adopted by each agency, as decentralized governance presumes greater authority delegated to subordinate

---

NOTE

The increased use of automated security tools is a key factor in moving agencies closer to real-time continuous monitoring and enabling monitoring for a larger proportion of the security controls implemented for each system. Somewhat distinct from automated monitoring tools, automated measurement and reporting tools are becoming essential for FISMA reporting as requirements evolve to require more frequent reporting of a broader set of security metrics and to submit security performance data to CyberScope using automated data feeds.

organizational units to make decisions and determine their own approaches to system implementation and ongoing operations [31]. NIST guidance to agencies emphasizes flexibility in selecting and implementing security controls, assessing risk, and performing continuous monitoring, standard procedures for which system owners tailor to their specific requirements. This flexibility is most explicitly stated in Special Publication 800-53, which acknowledges the mandatory standard in FIPS 200 that requires agencies to use the security control baselines NIST defines but notes, "there is flexibility in how agencies apply the guidance" in consideration of each agency's mission, business functions, and environment of operation [32]. Flexibility in this context means that there may be multiple ways to provide adequate security for different systems that are equally acceptable to authorizing officials and maintain compliance with FISMA and other applicable regulations. NIST, DHS, and OMB all emphasize adherence to the intent underlying guidance in Special Publications when assessing how system owners implement security controls.

MEASURING SECURITY EFFECTIVENESS

Organizations use information security measures to support risk management decision making and identify potential opportunities to improve security posture through the collection, analysis, and reporting of appropriate security performance metrics. Performance measurement is an important aspect of security monitoring, providing information about the status of security controls and security management activities and evidence of weaknesses or deficiencies in operational security that may warrant corrective action. Information security measurement occurs at multiple levels within an organization, with more detailed or frequent measures often collected for information systems, which are then aggregated and communicated to the organizational information security program. Agencies also report both system-level and program-level metrics to senior leaders responsible for information resources management, risk management, and mission and business operations. Performance objectives drive the selection of information security measures. Relevant objectives may stem from agency-level strategic goals and objectives, program or business process objectives and outcomes, and legal, regulatory, or policy requirements. Measurement helps agencies monitor progress towards the achievement of goals and objectives by quantifying the implementation, efficiency and effectiveness, and impact of security controls; analyzing the adequacy of information security program activities; and identifying opportunities for taking action to improve security.

Under provisions enacted in the Government Performance and Results Act (GPRA), all federal agencies are required to address performance requirements for the programs and activities included in agency budgets in annual performance plans that [33]:

- establish performance goals to define the level of performance to be achieved by a program activity;
- express such goals in an objective, quantifiable, and measurable form;

- briefly describe the operational processes, skills and technology, and the human, capital, information, or other resources required to meet the performance goals;
- establish performance indicators to be used in measuring or assessing the relevant outputs, service levels, and outcomes of each program activity;
- provide a basis for comparing actual program results with the established performance goals;
- describe the means to be used to verify and validate measured values.

These requirements drive the selection and implementation of performance measures specified in the context of capital planning and investment control processes and business case development. Guidance to agencies on specifying performance measures for information resources management focuses on measuring inputs, outputs, and outcomes to support program planning and evaluation [34]. NIST provides explicit guidance on information security measurement in Special Publication 800-55 intended to help agencies comply with program performance measurement requirements specified in GPRA, FISMA, and the Clinger-Cohen Act and align performance of information security activities to agency strategic goals and objectives to demonstrate the value of information security in support of achieving program outcomes [35].

A variety of factors influence the development and implementation of information security measures for program-level and information system-level performance management, including the types of measures needed to support information security management reporting and monitoring requirements, the ability to specify quantitative or semi-quantitative metrics to facilitate comparison of measurement values over time, and the availability of the data supporting each measure. Perhaps the most important factors affecting the type and extent of security measures used by an agency are the maturity of the agency information security program and the security controls implemented by its information systems. From a practical standpoint, it is impossible to measure changes in efficiency or effectiveness associated with security controls before those security controls have been implemented, so while agencies and their system owners may specify higher-order measures prior to implementation, the ability to collect measurement data to assess effectiveness and efficiency or impact depends on successful implementation. The feasibility of collecting some types of metrics may also depend on the types of monitoring tools and level of automation they provide, particularly for measures that organizations seek to collect on a frequent basis.

The maturity of an organization's information security program determines the type of measures that can be gathered successfully. NIST defines information security program maturity in terms of the existence and level of institutionalization of security policies, procedures, standards, and guidelines. As the information security program matures, its policies typically become more comprehensive in scope, offer more prescriptive details to facilitate repeatable implementation of security processes, and exhibit greater levels of standardization [36]. Less mature information security programs need to develop goals and objectives and formulate policies and procedures before they can meaningfully measure program performance. As programs mature they typically rely first on implementation measures to evaluate performance, evolving over time and with the benefit of experience to use effectiveness and efficiency and business impact measures to determine the effect of their information security activities on the organization. The information security program depends on senior management support to help define its goals and objectives, typically expressed through information security policies and procedures developed by the information security program and in plans and strategies such as the information security program plan and organizational risk management strategy.

Security Measurement Types

Special Publication 800-55 identifies three primary types of measures: implementation, effectiveness and efficiency, and impact. Implementation measures assess system-level or organizational progress in implementing required security controls, establishing organizational capabilities necessary to support information security risk management, and achieving and maintaining compliance with legal, regulatory, or policy requirements. Similar implementation measures are often used for both system-level and agency-level performance evaluation, where for instance a system owner might measure the percentage of properly configured security controls a system implements and the agency might aggregate such system-level measures to report on the implementation of properly configured controls across all information systems or the percentage of agency information systems that have achieved a target level of control implementation.

Effectiveness and efficiency measures are considered together in NIST guidance, but the terms refer to two different objectives. Effectiveness is a measure of the extent to which a security control or security management activity operates as it should and achieves its intended security outcomes. Efficiency is a measure of security control performance considering the time and resources allocated to its operation, evaluating the timeliness with which a process or activity occurred, or the level of human or technical resources that the process or activity required. Effectiveness and efficiency performance measurement is an important source of evidence demonstrating the relative cost-effectiveness of security controls an agency implements and operates in support of achieving the information resources management goal of adequate security. Agencies may specify both effectiveness and efficiency measures for some controls to gauge different aspects of their performance. For example, an organization might measure how many or what proportion of identified security events it handled with its incident response capability and also measure the average time to respond to or recover from security incidents. The former is an effectiveness measure, the latter an efficiency measure.

Impact measures demonstrate the effects of information security on the organization's mission or other results of information security risk management on the achievement of organizational goals and objectives. Impact measures are often related to effectiveness and efficiency measures, particularly when information security performance is measured in terms of economic impact. For example, cost savings or cost avoidance attributable to the information security program or controls or capabilities implemented by the organization represent one form of economic impact. Government agencies may also be able to tie information security performance to overall program performance measures related to delivering services to citizens or executing mission functions, where information security activities may increase the accessibility of services, demonstrate appropriate protection of personally identifiable information or other sensitive data, or increase the level of trust placed in the agency by citizens, organizations, and other stakeholders.

Security Measurement Process

The security measurement process described in Special Publication 800-55 comprises two separate activities—security measure development and security measure implementation. During security measure development system owners and information security program managers determine relevant measures and select measures appropriate for the state of the security program or the information system. The selection of security measures considers organizational strategic goals and objectives, mission and business priorities, security and information resources requirements, and the operational environments in which information systems are deployed. Agencies also need to ensure that the appropriate technical and functional capabilities are in place before initiating security measurement, including mechanisms for data collection, analysis, and reporting. The process of developing security measures, illustrated in Figure 5.2, first identifies and defines measurement requirements and then selects the set of measures that will satisfy those requirements. Because security measurement and performance management are iterative processes, the type of measures implemented and the specific metrics used to measure performance change over time, as the organization matures its security measurement practices and as it gains new information through the collection of performance data.

The identification of security measurement needs depends in part on ensuring that the process includes all relevant stakeholders and represents their interests. Senior organizational leaders with management or oversight responsibility for information security, information resources management, or risk management are obvious candidates to participate in security measure definition, along with common control providers and information system owners, program managers and business process owners, security officers, and personnel responsible for implementing or operating security controls. Stakeholder interests typically differ depending on the roles and responsibilities stakeholders have, their level within the organization structure, and the employees, users, or program beneficiaries or service consumers they represent. Some stakeholder responsibilities may correspond to needs for particular measures that provide a function—or domain-specific perspective on information security performance. The information security program should encourage stakeholder

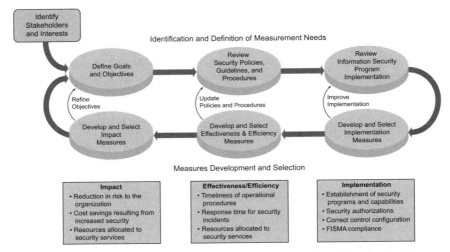

FIGURE 5.2 Security Measurement is an Iterative Process that Aligns Organizational Goals and Objectives to Security Strategy, Policies, and Other Guidance Implemented by Organizational Information Security Programs and Evaluated Using Implementation, Effectiveness and Efficiency, and Impact Metrics [37]

participation throughout the process of security measure development to validate the applicability of the measures selected. The type of measures selected—implementation, effectiveness and efficiency, or impact—also typically vary by stakeholder, as senior leaders may be more interested in impact and efficiency measures while system owners and operational security personnel typically emphasize implementation and effectiveness measures [38]. Agencies identify and document information security goals and objectives and security requirements that guide security control implementation for individual information systems and for the organizational information security program. Sources considered in this part of the process include agency, information technology, and security strategic plans, performance plans, policies, laws, regulations, and associated guidance. With respect to FISMA requirements, FIPS 200 specifies minimum security requirements for information systems categorized at different impact levels [39], corresponding to required security controls selected from Special Publication 800-53. Security controls selected for implementation and documented in information system security plans provide a key source of implementation measures, as system owners and information security program managers have an interest in verifying the proper implementation of selected measures to achieve adequate security protection for their information systems.

Organizational security policies and procedures often include implementation details specifying how different security controls should be implemented based on security control and control enhancement descriptions in Special Publication

> **TIP**
>
> Agencies and their system owners have widely varying experience developing and implementing information security performance measures. NIST lists candidate performance measures in Special Publication 800-55 [40], providing sample measures for each security control family and indicating the type of measure (implementation, effectiveness and efficiency, or impact) and whether the measures apply at the program or system level. Agencies can use these same measures as a guide to developing security measures for their own systems and information security programs to help ensure that the set of measures selected includes all types and addresses all relevant areas of performance.

800-53 and security objectives for each control defined in Special Publication 800-53A. This guidance provides valuable input to the development of security measures and determinations of the most appropriate methods to use to measure security control performance. Agencies should also identify existing metrics and sources of data potentially useful in measuring program-level or system-level security performance, including information in system security plans, risk assessment reports, security assessment reports, plans of action and milestones, inspector general audit reports, and continuous monitoring reports. Selected information security measures may address the security performance of specific security controls, groups of related or interdependent controls, an information system, or security function, service, or program spanning multiple systems. Agencies typically development and implement measures focused on different aspects of security and with different scope to cover all relevant performance objectives, aggregating measures or measurement perspectives to provide and organizational view of information security performance. The set of measures with potential applicability security performance drivers and objectives is typically large and diverse. To overcome the challenges comprehensive measurement would present, agencies need to prioritize performance objectives and implemented measures to ensure that selected measures provide appropriate coverage for security controls and information systems categorized at higher risk levels.

Establishing performance targets is also an important element of defining and implementing information security measures. Performance targets establish a set of objectives against which agencies can measure success. Using initial security measurement results as a baseline for performance, agencies can use initial and current measurement values and performance targets to track progress towards achieving security objectives. Different performance targets typically apply to different types of measures—implementation measure performance targets often reflect full implementation (such as "100%" on a quantitative scale, "implemented" or "complete" on an ordinal scale) while targets for effectiveness and efficiency measures and impact measures are often stated as relative improvements sought at each measurement interval or as the attainment of specific performance levels driven by business objectives.

RELEVANT SOURCE MATERIAL

Several NIST Special Publications and Federal Information Processing Standards provide guidance, recommendations, and instructions relevant to planning RMF activities. The most applicable sources of information include:

- Special Publication 800-39, *Managing Information Security Risk: Organization, Mission, and Information System View* [30].
- Special Publication 800-53 Revision 3, *Recommended Security Controls for Federal Information Systems and Organizations* [41].
- Special Publication 800-53A Revision 1, *Guide for Assessing the Security Controls in Federal Information Systems and Organizations* [42].
- Special Publication 800-55 Revision 1, *Performance Measurement Guide for Information Security* [35].

These and other NIST Special Publications are available from the NIST Computer Security Division Website, at http://csrc.nist.gov/publications/.

SUMMARY

This chapter describes and explains the importance of several organizational factors that influence the success of information security risk management at both organizational and individual information system levels. Specifically, it highlighted the essential role of senior leadership support, the organizational information security program, effective planning and resource allocation, and performance measurement and management in establishing and maintaining compliance with security laws, regulations, and policies; consistently executing the Risk Management Framework for agency information systems, and enabling the achievement of mission objectives and program outcomes. Collectively, these success factors greatly enhance the ability of an organization to manage information security risk and to demonstrate the value and otherwise justify investment in information security programs and associated activities.

REFERENCES

[1] Federal Information Security Management Act of 2002, Pub. L. No. 107-347, 116 Stat. 2946. §301, codified at 44 U.S.C. §3544(b).
[2] Information Technology Management Reform Act of 1996, Pub. L. No. 104-106, 110 Stat. 679. See Subtitle C of Title LI.
[3] Management of federal information resources. Washington, DC: Office of Management and Budget; November 2000. Circular No. A-130, Revised (Transmittal, Memorandum No. 4).
[4] Managing information security risk: organization, mission, and information system view. Gaithersburg, MD: National Institute of Standards and Technology, Computer Security Division; March 2011. Special Publication 800-39. p. 2.

[5] Preparation, submission, and execution of the budget. Washington, DC: Office of Management and Budget; August 2011. Circular No. A-11, Revised (Transmittal Memorandum No. 85). Exhibit 53, p. 6.

[6] Preparation, submission, and execution of the budget. Washington, DC: Office of Management and Budget; August 2011. Circular No. A-11, Revised (Transmittal Memorandum No. 85). Exhibit 53, p. 13.

[7] Preparation, submission, and execution of the budget. Washington, DC: Office of Management and Budget; August 2011. Circular No. A-11, Revised (Transmittal Memorandum No. 85). Section 51.

[8] Preparation, submission, and execution of the budget. Washington, DC: Office of Management and Budget; August 2011. Circular No. A-11, Revised (Transmittal Memorandum No. 85). Capital Programming Guide, p. 102.

[9] Guide for applying the risk management framework to federal information systems. Gaithersburg, MD: National Institute of Standards and Technology, Computer Security Division; February 2010. Special Publication 800-37 revision 1. See Appendix D.

[10] Information Technology Management Reform Act of 1996, Pub. L. No. 104-106, 110 Stat. 679. §5125, codified at 40 U.S.C. §1425 and 44 U.S.C. §3506.

[11] Federal Information Security Management Act of 2002, Pub. L. No. 107-347, 116 Stat. 2946. §301, codified at 44 U.S.C. §3544 (a)(3)(A).

[12] FY 2012 inspector general Federal Information Security Management Act reporting metrics. Washington, DC: Department of Homeland Security, National Cyber Security Division; March 2012.

[13] Federal Information Security Management Act of 2002, Pub. L. No. 107-347, 116 Stat. 2946. §301, codified at §3544(b).

[14] Recommended security controls for federal information systems and organizations. Gaithersburg, MD: National Institute of Standards and Technology, Computer Security Division; August 2009. Special Publication 800-53 revision 3. See Appendix G.

[15] Security and privacy controls for federal information systems and organizations. Gaithersburg, MD: National Institute of Standards and Technology, Computer Security Division; February 2012. Special Publication 800-53 revision 4. Initial Public Draft. See Appendix G.

[16] Fiscal year 2011 report to Congress on the implementation of the Federal Information Security Management Act of 2002. Washington, DC: Office of Management and Budget; March 2012. p. 34.

[17] Lew JJ. Reporting instructions for the Federal Information Security Management Act and agency privacy management. Washington, DC: Office of Management and Budget; September 14, 2011. Memorandum M-11-33.

[18] With the exception of organizations operating in regulated industries such as health care and financial services or handling specific types of data subject to privacy regulations, private sector organizations are not bound by minimum security and privacy requirements comparable to those that apply to federal government organizations.

[19] Federal Information Security Management Act of 2002, Pub. L. No. 107-347, 116 Stat. 2946. §301, codified at §3544(b)(2)(D) and §3544(a)(1)(B), respectively.

[20] Federal Information Security Management Act of 2002, Pub. L. No. 107-347, 116 Stat. 2946. §301, codified at §3544(b)(2)(D) and §3544(a)(1)(B), respectively. §301, codified at §3544(c).

[21] Schaffer G. FY 2012 reporting instructions for the Federal Information Security Management Act and agency privacy management. Arlington, VA: Department of

Homeland Security, National Protection and Programs Directorate; February 2012.. Federal Information Security Memorandum 12-02.

[22] See for example Fiscal year 2011 report to Congress on the implementation of the Federal Information Security Management Act of 2002. Washington, DC: Office of Management and Budget; March 2012.

[23] Federal Information Security Management Act of 2002, Pub. L. No. 107-347, 116 Stat. 2946. §301, codified at §3545(a).

[24] Managing information security risk: organization, mission, and information system view. Gaithersburg, MD: National Institute of Standards and Technology, Computer Security Division; March 2011. Special Publication 800-39. See Appendix F.

[25] Managing information security risk: organization, mission, and information system view. Gaithersburg, MD: National Institute of Standards and Technology, Computer Security Division; March 2011. Special Publication 800-39. p. 12.

[26] Fiscal year 2011 report to Congress on the implementation of the Federal Information Security Management Act of 2002. Washington, DC: Office of Management and Budget; March 2012. p. 31.

[27] Fiscal year 2011 report to Congress on the implementation of the Federal Information Security Management Act of 2002. Washington, DC: Office of Management and Budget; March 2012. p. 33. The security spending proportion reported by individual agencies ranged from 3 to 29 percent.

[28] Budget requests initially developed as early as March and submitted to OMB in September of each year specify funding planned for the federal fiscal year beginning the following October.

[29] Federal Information Security Management Act of 2002, Pub. L. No. 107-347, 116 Stat. 2946. §301, codified at §3544(d)(1)(B).

[30] Managing information security risk: organization, mission, and information system view. Gaithersburg, MD: National Institute of Standards and Technology, Computer Security Division; March 2011. Special Publication 800-39.

[31] Managing information security risk: organization, mission, and information system view. Gaithersburg, MD: National Institute of Standards and Technology, Computer Security Division; March 2011. Special Publication 800-39. See Appendix F.

[32] Recommended security controls for federal information systems and organizations. Gaithersburg, MD: National Institute of Standards and Technology, Computer Security Division; August 2009. Special Publication 800-53 revision 3. p. iv.

[33] Government Performance and Results Act of 1993, Pub. L. 103-62, 107 Stat. 285. §4, codified at 31 U.S.C. §1115(b).

[34] Preparation, submission, and execution of the budget. Washington, DC: Office of Management and Budget; August 2011. Circular No. A-11, Revised (Transmittal Memorandum No. 85). Section 51. p. 5.

[35] Chew E, Swanson M, Stine K, Bartol N, Brown A, Robinson W. Performance measurement guide for information security. Gaithersburg, MD: National Institute of Standards and Technology, Computer Security Division; July 2008. Special Publication 800-55 revision 1.

[36] Chew E, Swanson M, Stine K, Bartol N, Brown A, Robinson W. Performance measurement guide for information security. Gaithersburg, MD: National Institute of Standards and Technology, Computer Security Division; July 2008. Special Publication 800-55 revision 1. p. 11.

[37] Chew E, Swanson M, Stine K, Bartol N, Brown A, Robinson W. Performance measurement guide for information security. Gaithersburg, MD: National Institute of Standards and Technology, Computer Security Division; July 2008. Special Publication 800-55 revision 1. p. 25.

[38] Chew E, Swanson M, Stine K, Bartol N, Brown A, Robinson W. Performance measurement guide for information security. Gaithersburg, MD: National Institute of Standards and Technology, Computer Security Division; July 2008. Special Publication 800-55 revision 1. p. 26.

[39] Minimum security requirements for federal information and information systems. Gaithersburg, MD: National Institute of Standards and Technology, Computer Security Division; March 2006. Federal Information Processing Standards Publication 200.

[40] Chew E, Swanson M, Stine K, Bartol N, Brown A, Robinson W. Performance measurement guide for information security. Gaithersburg, MD: National Institute of Standards and Technology, Computer Security Division; July 2008.. Special Publication 800-55 revision 1. See Appendix A.

[41] Recommended security controls for federal information systems and organizations. Gaithersburg, MD: National Institute of Standards and Technology, Computer Security Division; August 2009. Special Publication 800-53 revision 3.

[42] Guide for assessing the security controls in federal information systems and organizations. Gaithersburg, MD: National Institute of Standards and Technology, Computer Security Division; June 2010. Special Publication 800-53A revision 1.

Risk Management Framework Planning and Initiation

INFORMATION IN THIS CHAPTER:

- Planning for Successful RMF Execution
- Key Prerequisites for RMF Initiation
- Establishing a Project Plan for RMF Iteration
- Organizational Roles and Responsibilities
- Getting the Project Underway

Performing the tasks associated with the Risk Management Framework requires a substantial investment of time and effort and the participation of many different contributors, both within the group of personnel responsible for the system and from other parts of the organization. Information security risk management practices, including the activities prescribed in the RMF, cannot effectively be performed in isolation, as they are integral to the system development life cycle and interdependent with other IT management functions. Federal information systems cannot be put into production until they receive authorization to operate, making the successful completion of the tasks in RMF steps 1 through 5 a prerequisite for a system to finish implementation and move into its operational phase. Effective planning prior to initiating the RMF process helps system owners ensure that sufficient resources are allocated to the effort and that the information needed to start the RMF is available. From an overall information systems management perspective, planning for the RMF both affects and is influenced by tasks, milestones, and dependencies in project plans, work breakdown structures, or integrated master schedules used to manage system development, implementation, and operations and maintenance. This chapter emphasizes the importance of careful planning prior to initiating the RMF, explains the alignment of SDLC phases and RMF steps, identifies key roles and responsibilities at all levels of the organization, and describes the planning process.

PLANNING

Federal government agencies are responsible for integrating information security management with strategic and operational planning processes [1], which in practice means incorporating security within IT strategic planning, enterprise architecture (EA), capital planning and investment control (CPIC), and budget preparation and execution. Statutory regulations on federal information policy and information technology management [2] and key guidance to agencies on the management of federal information resources all emphasize the coordination of information security and risk management with multiple other planning and operational management functions [3]. Integrated management of federal information resources applies at all tiers of the organization, but at the information system-level the point of integration is often the system development life cycle (SDLC), which reflects perspectives from multiple management disciplines, as illustrated in Figure 6.1. Current federal guidance to agencies on information security risk management emphasizes the close alignment between the SDLC and the Risk Management Framework, most clearly indicated in Special Publication 800-37 Revision 1, which identifies the relevant SDLC phases for each task in the RMF [4]. Information systems typically receive funding through one or more agency IT investments, so from a financial management perspective system owners also need to coordinate security planning with CPIC processes and requirements applicable to the investments that provide funding to their systems and security management activities [5].

Planning for any information resources management effort, including information security, involves specifying the set of tasks that need to occur, the personnel and other resources required to complete each task, the schedule for completing each task, and the inputs, outputs, and dependencies for each task. Information resources management planning occurs at strategic, tactical, and operational levels and may address entire organizations, business units or operating divisions, investments, or systems. In government organizations, planning at the information system-level focuses on projects, a term OMB defines as "a temporary endeavor undertaken to accomplish a unique product or service with a defined start and end point and specific objectives that, when attained, signify completion" [9]. Agencies often emphasize planning in the initiation phase of the system development life cycle because the development of a project plan is typically a prerequisite to securing project funding through the budgeting process and proceeding to development or acquisition [9]. To plan effectively for information security risk management activities, system owners need to consider three overlapping perspectives:

1. Organization-level planning for information resources management in general and for information security program management in particular.
2. Investment- or project-level system planning with a scope incorporating all functions and activities included in the system development life cycle.
3. System security planning, either as a set of tasks and activities within a broader project planning effort or as a distinct project.

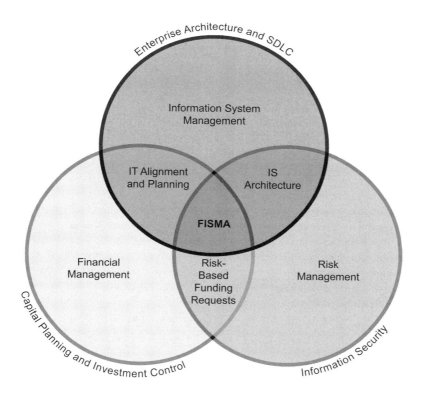

FIGURE 6.1 Information Security Risk Management in Government Organizations is Not an Isolated Function, But Overlaps Substantially with Other Information Resources Management Activities Including Enterprise Architecture, Capital Planning and Investment Control, and the System Development Life Cycle [6]

System owners are actively involved in both overall system planning and system security planning, but depending on the size and complexity of the system and the way the organization manages it, different personnel may be responsible for developing and executing plans for different activities. The degree of integration between planning for security tasks and system-level project plans also depends in part on the way the system owner and the organization choose to acquire or perform key security services such as security control assessment and continuous monitoring. Some organizations explicitly incorporate security functions in system development, implementation, and operations and maintenance projects—whether those projects

> **NOTE**
>
> One of the challenges system owners face is adhering to the different life cycles and phases associated with different information resources management disciplines, both within their agencies and in government-wide guidance. Official guidance to agencies from OMB specifies a performance improvement life cycle for IT management with three phases—architect, invest, implement—that correspond to distinct EA, CPIC, and SLDC processes, respectively [7]. The RMF overlaps to some extent with all of these processes, and NIST offers explicit guidance on integrating security activities with commonly used CPIC and SDLC processes [5,8]. None of this guidance is prescriptive and agencies have the flexibility to define and follow their own methodologies. The most current NIST documentation on the RMF emphasizes integration with the SDLC, so system owners should validate the extent to which the phases referenced in Special Publication 800-37 align with the standard life cycle processes defined in their own organizations.

are staffed by government personnel, contractors, or some combination—while others establish internal security capabilities or services used across multiple systems. No single approach is preferred in all circumstances, but system owners need to consider the relationship between security and other system-related activities in order to plan appropriately for the completion of necessary security tasks. The tasks in the Risk Management Framework apply to major applications and general support systems that may encompass multiple applications within their boundaries, meaning that RMF planning is relevant for both individual systems owners and common control providers.

PLANNING THE RMF PROJECT

The description of the Risk Management Framework in Special Publication 800-37 organizes the process into six steps, with multiple tasks prescribed within each step. This structure facilitates the representation of the RMF process in a formal project plan or work breakdown structure (WBS) that documents the timing, resources, inputs and outputs, milestones, and dependencies for each task. The steps in the RMF align to phases in typical SDLC methodologies, as illustrated in Figure 6.2. System owners may choose to develop a RMF-specific plan or to incorporate RMF tasks into a more comprehensive project plan. In either case tasks in RMF steps should be aligned with relevant SDLC phases and activities, to reflect whether each security-related task precedes, follows, or runs parallel to other project tasks. Decomposing SDLC phases into explicit activities and associated outputs can facilitate planning and ordering security tasks, particularly when RMF tasks rely on information or artifacts produced as the result of SLDC activities. For instance, within the SDLC initiation phase project teams typically develop system descriptions or concepts of operation documents; specify functional and technical requirements; and conduct initial risk assessments and privacy impact assessments. These SDLC work products serve as inputs into tasks in the first two phases of the RMF, and security-focused personnel responsible

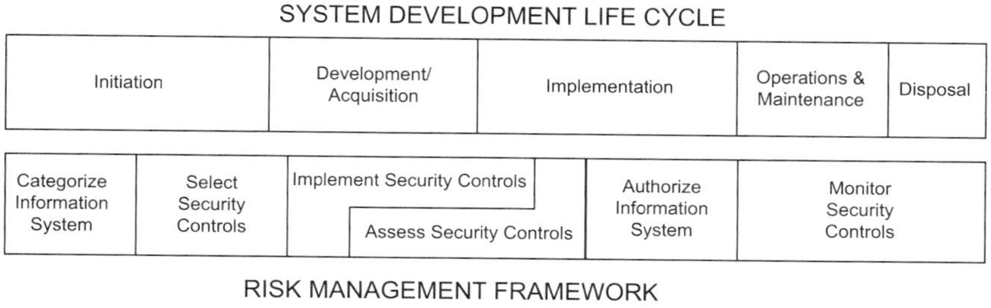

SYSTEM DEVELOPMENT LIFE CYCLE

Initiation	Development/Acquisition	Implementation	Operations & Maintenance	Disposal

Categorize Information System	Select Security Controls	Implement Security Controls / Assess Security Controls	Authorize Information System	Monitor Security Controls

RISK MANAGEMENT FRAMEWORK

FIGURE 6.2 **Aligning the Risk Management Framework to the System Development Life Cycle Helps Identify Timing and Sequence Dependencies Between the Processes and To Coordinate the Shared Use of Information Common to Both Processes**

for executing RMF tasks may contribute to the development of some or all of these within the SDLC before using the information to support the RMF process.

Aligning to the SDLC

Many organizations subdivide their SDLC methodologies into a larger number of phases than the five referenced in NIST guidance, potentially offering closer alignment of SDLC phases and corresponding RMF tasks. Table 6.1 lists some SDLC phase names commonly used in government organizations, arranged by the five general phase names used in NIST documentation and where applicable indicating different terms that may be used to represent the same phase.

The objectives of RMF planning include estimating the time and level of effort required to complete all necessary tasks, adjusting the RMF-specific timeline and milestones for task completion to reflect SDLC dependencies or constraints associated with the project to deploy the system, and beginning the process of assigning the personnel and resources necessary to support the effort. While it is often impossible to accurately predict the time and resources needed for the RMF before completing the system security categorization in step 1, systems owners use planning to evaluate anticipated RMF needs against available resources, including funding, and to determine the best approach for accomplishing the RMF tasks. For systems being developed or implemented by non-government personnel such as contractors, system owners may include appropriate RMF tasks within the scope of work to be performed under the contract. Some key RMF tasks cannot be delegated in this way, notably including security control assessment, which should be performed by an independent assessor, and system authorization, which is an inherently governmental function and therefore can only be performed by government personnel. Organizations may choose to provide or contract for RMF-specific services separate from other aspects of system development and operations, either by establishing internal capabilities to deliver relevant security services and project support or by contracting for such services [11].

Table 6.1 Common SDLC Phases and Outputs

General Phase	Common Phase Names	Relevant RMF Steps
Initiation	Initiation, Definition, Inception Concept, Justification	Categorize Information System
	Planning	Select Security Controls
	Requirements	
Development/Acquisition	Acquisition	Implement Security Controls
	Design, Elaboration	
	Development, Build, Construction	
	Test, Integration, Validation	Assess Security Controls
Implementation	Implementation, Deployment, Transition	Authorize Information System
Operations and Maintenance	Operations and Maintenance Production	Monitor Security Controls
Disposition	Disposition, Retirement	Monitor Security Controls

WARNING

NIST documentation addressing aspects of the system development life cycle typically references Special Publication 800-64, *Security Considerations in the System Development Life Cycle*, the most recent version of which was released in 2008. This guidance describes a representative five-phase SDLC and highlights security activities and considerations in each phase. Special Publication 800-37 aligns each RMF task to one or more SDLC phases, but in some cases positions tasks within different phases than in Special Publication 800-64. For instance, security control selection in step 2 of the RMF is part of the initiation phase Special Publication 800-37 but is presented as part of development in Special Publication 800-64 [10]. System owners should validate that the alignment of RMF tasks to SDLC phases matches the practices and process standards in their own agencies.

Planning the RMF Timeline

Although the structure of the RMF provides a good basis for planning, the wide variation in the type and complexity of federal information systems makes it hard to establish accurate guidelines on how long it should take an agency to progress from initiation to system authorization. System owners should bear in mind that an RMF project's duration is a function not only of the security-related tasks that must be performed, but also the time needed to allow for review and approval of the system security plan and other key artifacts produced throughout the process and for analysis of and response to security control assessments. The approach to review and oversight of system-level RMF activities varies among organizations according to the IT and risk management governance structure and factors such as the proportion of common, hybrid, and system-specific controls implemented and the number of systems for which each authorizing official is responsible. Organizations with established information security programs may provide RMF project plan templates—similar to the document templates many organizations use for system security plans and other authorization package artifacts—for their system owners to use as a basis for system-specific planning. Standard planning templates with initial level of effort and scheduling assumptions help system owners to ensure that the scope of their projects addresses all relevant activities and that system budgets include sufficient resources to complete the tasks necessary to achieve system authorization. Where possible, including anticipated response times for reviews and approval by authorizing officials, senior agency information security officers, or other personnel with management and oversight responsibilities can help system owners allocate sufficient time in the project schedule to complete each task and to transition smoothly from one step to the next.

PREREQUISITES FOR RMF INITIATION

Planning should address all the elements necessary to initiate the RMF process so that the project proceeds as expected once it begins. Key prerequisites include allocation of sufficient funding, personnel, and other resources to support the execution of RMF tasks; identification and availability of organizational and system-specific information used as inputs to the RMF; and completion of SDLC initiation phase activities on which the RMF depends. Successful execution of the tasks in the first five steps of the RMF process typical results in system authorization, where authorizing officials base their decisions on the substantial volume of security-related information produced during RMF tasks and included in the security authorization package. Although system owners rely on information security officers, security control assessors, and other key personnel to assemble security authorization packages, many other functional and technical project personnel contribute significant portions of the content included in those packages. For instance, as noted in Chapter 8, many members of system deployment teams share responsibility for implementing the set of security controls selected for an information system, especially with respect to developing and testing some of the key plans and procedures corresponding to management and operational controls referenced in the system security plan. Many of the initial RMF tasks depend on system-specific and organizational information produced outside the RMF process. As part of planning for RMF initiation, system owners need to identify relevant sources of information used as inputs to the RMF and ensure that information is available to the personnel performing the RMF tasks. In federal government organizations, key sources of information typically include the agency information security program plan and risk management strategy; organizational policies, procedures, standards, and guidelines; common control providers; documentation describing the system's intended use, functional capabilities, operating environment, and technology components; and project management personnel responsible for the system. Before beginning the RMF process, system owners and their project teams need to ensure that the information used as inputs to the initial RMF tasks exists or, if prerequisite processes and artifacts have not been completed, to direct project personnel to develop or gather the necessary information. RMF planning often emphasizes identifying the information needed to support the tasks in the first two steps of the RMF—information system categorization and security control selection.

Inputs to Information System Categorization

The first step in the RMF focuses on categorizing the information system and the information the system uses based on the impact to the organization that would result from a loss of confidentiality, integrity, or availability. As described in more detail in Chapter 7, this step requires system owners to consider each of the different information types relevant to the system and the system overall, the risks to those information assets, and the severity of adverse events that might occur. Information owners have responsibility for identifying and describing the information types relevant for each system. This information is used not only in security categorization but also in risk assessment and privacy impact assessment activities that inform security categorization. System owners and information owners also need to consider any organizational standards regarding information type definitions and security categorization levels, if such standards have been defined. Some agencies specify information types at an organization-wide level and direct system owners to use those specifications in their own security categorization efforts, while other agencies leave information type identification to each system owner [12]. With organizational standards in place, system owners typically have the ability to assign a security categorization equal to or higher than the standard set for each information type. Inventories of information types may be developed as part of the enterprise architecture—where security categorization levels are among the attributes documented in enterprise data models—or by information security or risk management programs. Such standards simplify the security categorization task by identifying all information types used by the organization and evaluating their impact levels, reducing the need for system owners to consult federal guidance on security categorization for generic information types or to define their own information types.

In addition to security categorization, the first step in the RMF also captures descriptive information about the system that is reflected in the system security plan and used in subsequent activities. Functional and technical information about a system may appear in a variety of different documents and SDLC artifacts depending on the methodology being followed, including business cases, functional specifications, system description documents, system design documents, or concepts of operations. Regardless of the terminology used, such documents typically specify the purpose and objectives for the system, the organization deploying it, its intended users, organizational roles and responsibilities, and its operational characteristics.

> **NOTE**
>
> Special Publication 800-53 Revision 3 defines a security concept of operations (CONOPS) as an optional control enhancement to the system security plan (the artifact is proposed as an optional control within the planning family in the draft Special Publication 800-53 Revision 4). This document describes how the organization will operate the system from a security perspective, including the system purpose, its architecture, the schedule for authorizing the system, and the security categorization determined for the system [15]. The security CONOPS explicitly focuses on security, although it may include much of the same descriptive information found in a system's overall concept of operations.

System owners and information security officers use system description documentation throughout the RMF process, both to summarize key information in the system description and purpose section of the system security plan [13] and as a point of reference to validate that selected and implemented security controls satisfy the security objectives for the system and its intended use. System description documentation is especially important for completing the information system description task in step 1 of the RMF, in which system owners document identifying information and operational details about the system, define the system boundary, and formally establish the ownership and other key roles and responsibilities for the system and the information it contains [14]. Documentation produced in the initiation phase of the SDLC also typically provides identifying information about the system used to register it in appropriate system inventories. In many cases, systems will already have unique system or investment identifiers assigned prior to initiating the RMF, but during step 1 system owners need to make sure that the system is accurately reflected in security program documentation such as the FISMA inventory of systems each agency reports to OMB.

Inputs to Security Control Selection

The primary input for the selection of security controls in step 2 of the RMF is the security categorization determined in step 1, a designation often referred to as the system impact level. This categorization corresponds to a security control baseline that serves as the starting point for selecting the appropriate controls to satisfy the security requirements for each system. As described in Chapter 7, security control baselines are subject to tailoring, taking various organizational and system-specific considerations into account. The tailoring process identifies characteristics of the system and its operating environment that warrant a reduction in one or more baseline security controls or that require additional controls to supplement the baseline. System description documentation and requirements specifications developed during the SDLC initiation phase are important inputs to the tailoring process, providing information about security objectives, system components, technology types, physical infrastructure, applicable policies and regulations, operational environments, scalability, and different types of users that will access the system [16]. The set of security requirements that selected security controls must satisfy may span many different functional and technical categories, depending on the way they are organized in requirements specification documents. For example, in the widely used FURPS requirements classification model [17], security requirements appear within functionality and reliability groups, although requirements in other categories may constrain or otherwise influence the selection of security controls. Requirements specifications provide the foundation for requirements traceability analysis that compares the security control documentation produced in step 3 of the RMF with the security-related requirements specified for the system. Risk assessment and privacy impact assessment activities conducted prior to RMF initiation also provide security requirements, often identifying threats to information assets that the selection of supplemental controls can mitigate, as well as highlighting gaps between current security capabilities and the level of protection required for the system.

The security control baselines defined in Special Publication 800-53 apply government wide, but agencies may choose to adapt the baselines to reflect organizational policy, procedures, and standards applicable to information systems [18]. Information security programs in agencies that prescribe their own tailored or enhanced security control baselines should direct system owners to use the agency's minimum security control standards in the security control selection process, substituting for or extending Special Publication 800-53 control documentation as an input to step 2 of the RMF. The scope and availability of common controls and associated documentation also influence security control selection and the level of effort planned to complete control implementation and assessment. System owners performing the common control identification task in RMF step 2 rely on system security plans, security assessment reports, and plans of action and milestones for the common controls their systems will inherit. Figure 6.3 illustrates the relationship between common and system-specific security controls and the documentation used to authorize individual information systems and general support systems or other common control providers. Security documentation produced by common control providers is an input to security control selection and implementation for fully inherited controls and for hybrid controls that have both common and system-specific attributes [19].

Organizational Policies, Procedures, Templates, and Guidance

Federal agencies often establish policies and procedures for security management of the information systems they operate or have operated on their behalf, distinct from or incorporated within standard SDLC processes. These agency-wide policies and procedures may specify entry and exit criteria for SLDC phases and RMF steps, indicate interim checkpoints and final reviews of system-specific activities or the artifacts they produce, and set minimum or maximum timeframes in which activities should be completed or milestones should be achieved. Organization-level guidance for system owners also appears in documentation such as the risk management

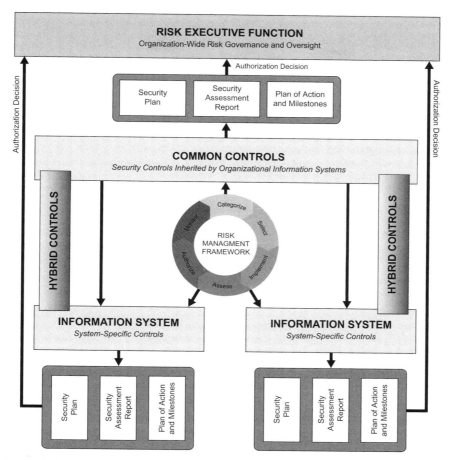

FIGURE 6.3 Security Control Selection Identifies Common Controls Applicable for Fully Inherited or Hybrid Implementation, Relying on System Authorization Package Documentation Produced by Common Control Providers and on Organizational Guidance such as Risk Management Strategy and Security Policies, Standards, and Guidelines [20]

strategy, information security program plan, contingency and continuity of operations plans, and information security continuous monitoring strategy. Many agencies also encapsulate key elements of government-wide security guidance into information security handbooks or other consolidated policy and procedure declarations that govern system-level information security practices, including implementing the RMF. Systems owners use organization-level guidance both to develop their RMF plans and to support the execution of key tasks throughout the RMF process.

The RMF process produces are large volume of security-related documentation, typically including detailed security control configuration information and operational procedures used to manage the system on an ongoing basis as well as the artifacts in the system authorization package. NIST provides detailed guidance on the content and recommended structure for much of this documentation, but agencies often find that developing their own templates for the necessary plans and supporting artifacts helps reduce the time required to produce documentation and encourages consistency in the content and level of detail provided for each system. System owners should consider the availability of templates or other reusable assets when developing RMF plans and should ensure that such assets are readily available to the personnel performing RMF tasks. In agencies that implement automated tools to support security management activities, including generating documentation, this means provisioning user access rights to the tools and providing appropriate training to individuals who will use the tools to complete RMF tasks and other information security activities.

Identifying Responsible Personnel

To assign resources to activities in the RMF plan, system owners need to identify all personnel with relevant roles and responsibilities, recognizing that contributions to RMF tasks often come from many sources within and outside the organization, potentially including contractors, vendors, service providers, or other government agencies [21]. Although the system owner has official responsibility for all aspects of system initiation, development, implementation, operation, maintenance, and disposal of an information system, including security, there are many other key roles involved in the execution of the RMF. Prior to initiating the process, system owners at a minimum should identify the following:

- The information system security officer or other individual who will lead the RMF effort, if the system owner will not have that leadership role.
- Government or contractor personnel who will perform the tasks in the RMF process.
- The project manager or other party responsible for leading each phase of the SDLC for the system.
- Common control providers the system may leverage and the system owners or information system security officers responsible for those common controls.
- The authorizing official who will receive the authorization package and make the determination whether the information security risk associated with the system is acceptable to the organization.
- The senior agency official with oversight responsibility for information resources management.
- The executive sponsor or senior management official with oversight responsibility for the mission functions or business processes the system supports.
- Points of contact for any contractors, vendors, or organizations external to the agency who will contribute information, personnel, or other resources to the RMF effort.

Depending on the scale and complexity of the system, its security categorization level, and the way the organization approaches the RMF, it is possible that some resources needed to complete the RMF will be undetermined at the time of RMF initiation. Systems owners should, however, be able to identify the key roles with responsibility for performing and overseeing system security categorization, security control selection, and security control implementation tasks in the RMF and to finalize resource allocations and assignments of responsible personnel once the process is underway.

ESTABLISHING A PROJECT PLAN

All project planning elements—including tasks, schedules, milestones, dependencies, and staff and other supporting resources—should be documented and reviewed prior to RMF initiation. The level of detail reflected in the project plan varies according to organizational requirements, the scope and complexity of the system, the number of organizational resources involved, and project management policies and procedures applicable to information systems. Information system projects in federal agencies often use graphical project plan representations such as Gantt charts or work breakdown structures to provide a summary view of the work to be performed, the timeline for completion, and the resources responsible for conducting activities, developing work products, or achieving milestones. Project plans should generally decompose tasks to a level of detail sufficient to support accurate cost and schedule estimates. Many government and industry sources of guidance are available on creating project plans and work breakdown structures as standard elements of project management methodologies [22]. System owners typically adopt a project planning approach that uses practices and procedures recommended for project managers in their agency. This includes choosing whether to follow a linear, sequential approach through the steps in the RMF, an iterative model, or some other alternative. Consistent with NIST guidance emphasizing the value of integrated project teams for information system development and implementation [23], plans for RMF activities should be developed in a manner that facilitates alignment to or incorporation in the information system project management plan, including using the same or compatible tools to capture project plan information.

The primary information communicated in planning documentation about the RMF process includes a comprehensive listing of tasks and the order in which they will be performed, the estimated timeframe to complete each task, key resources assigned to each task, and any dependencies with the potential to affect the timely execution of the plan as presented. Figure 6.4 presents a generic RMF project plan with tasks and resources estimated to reflect approximately 1000h of total work effort from initiation through achievement of authorization to operate at the end of step 5. The plan shown here is not intended to be prescriptive, but provides a basic example of the sort of work breakdown structure that might be used to estimate the level of effort and resources required to complete the RMF process, and to communicate that information to system owners and project personnel.

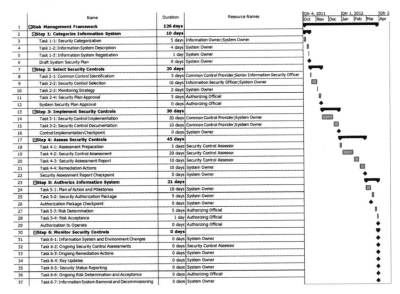

	Name	Duration	Resource Names
1	⊟Risk Management Framework	126 days	
2	⊟Step 1: Categorize Information System	10 days	
3	Task 1-1: Security Categorization	5 days	Information Owner;System Owner
4	Task 1-2: Information System Description	4 days	System Owner
5	Task 1-3: Information System Registration	1 day	System Owner
6	Draft System Security Plan	0 days	System Owner
7	⊟Step 2: Select Security Controls	20 days	
8	Task 2-1: Common Control Identification	3 days	Common Control Provider;Senior Information Security Officer
9	Task 2-2: Security Control Selection	10 days	Information Security Officer;System Owner
10	Task 2-3: Monitoring Strategy	2 days	System Owner
11	Task 2-4: Security Plan Approval	5 days	Authorizing Official
12	System Security Plan Approval	0 days	Authorizing Official
13	⊟Step 3: Implement Security Controls	30 days	
14	Task 3-1: Security Control Implementation	20 days	Common Control Provider;System Owner
15	Task 3-2: Security Control Documentation	10 days	Common Control Provider;System Owner
16	Control Implementation Checkpoint	0 days	System Owner
17	⊟Step 4: Assess Security Controls	45 days	
18	Task 4-1: Assessment Preparation	5 days	Security Control Assessor
19	Task 4-2: Security Control Assessment	20 days	Security Control Assessor
20	Task 4-3: Security Assessment Report	10 days	Security Control Assessor
21	Task 4-4: Remediation Actions	10 days	System Owner
22	Security Assessment Report Checkpoint	0 days	System Owner
23	⊟Step 5: Authorize Information System	21 days	
24	Task 5-1: Plan of Action and Milestones	10 days	System Owner
25	Task 5-2: Security Authorization Package	5 days	System Owner
26	Authorization Package Checkpoint	0 days	System Owner
27	Task 5-3: Risk Determination	5 days	Authorizing Official
28	Task 5-4: Risk Acceptance	1 day	Authorizing Official
29	Authorization to Operate	0 days	Authorizing Official
30	⊟Step 6: Monitor Security Controls	0 days	
31	Task 6-1: Information System and Environment Changes	0 days	System Owner
32	Task 6-2: Ongoing Security Control Assessments	0 days	Security Control Assessor
33	Task 6-3: Ongoing Remediation Actions	0 days	System Owner
34	Task 6-4: Key Updates	0 days	System Owner
35	Task 6-5: Security Status Reporting	0 days	System Owner
36	Task 6-6: Ongoing Risk Determination and Acceptance	0 days	Authorizing Official
37	Task 6-7: Information System Removal and Decommissioning	0 days	System Owner

FIGURE 6.4 **System Owners can Present Risk Management Framework Tasks in a Standalone Project Plan to Support Management and Oversight of the RMF Process. Capturing Task and Resource Information in a Formal Project Planning Tool Facilitates Integrating Security-Specific Tasks with the System Development Life Cycle and Overall System Management Plans**

TIP

The linear "waterfall" approach to both the RMF and SDLC reflected in NIST guidance to agencies is representative, not prescriptive. Although some tasks do need to precede others, Special Publication 800-37 makes clear that agencies may alter the sequential flow as needed to align appropriately to their own SDLC standards or to execute the tasks more efficiently within their own management structures and processes [24]. Similarly, Special Publication 800-64 acknowledges that agency IT projects may follow different kinds of SDLC approaches, including the use of iterative development methodologies and life cycles with a different number or phases or scope of activities within each phase. System owners can take advantage of this flexibility by adapting RMF plans to suit project-specific or agency-level SDLC processes.

ROLES AND RESPONSIBILITIES

The successful completion of the tasks in the RMF requires input and active participation from many individuals and functions across the organization and potentially involves vendors, contractors, or others outside the agency deploying the information system. Special Publication 800-37 identifies several senior management roles with oversight for agency-level information security management programs and ultimate responsibility for ensuring that agency information assets are adequately protected from harm [25]. Senior roles such as the head of agency, risk executive, and chief information officer influence the way the RMF process is executed for information systems in each agency, but they rarely have significant direct involvement the RMF tasks for any given system. Table 6.2 summarizes key RMF roles and responsibilities, indicating the RMF steps in which each role is involved. With the exception of the government positions of information system owner, information owner, authorizing official, and senior information security officer, the roles listed in Table 6.2 may be performed by agency personnel or by contractors or service providers external to the agency.

NIST guidance distinguishes between core security-related roles identified within the scope of the RMF and other information system or organizational roles that contribute to the completion of RMF tasks or use the results of the RMF process to inform their own assigned activities. Table 6.3 summarizes key roles in the system development life cycle that influence or contribute to the security-focused tasks performed within the RMF.

GETTING THE PROJECT UNDERWAY

With RMF planning complete, appropriate personnel identified, and other resources allocated, the system owner is ready to launch the RMF process, assuming the system development life cycle has been initiated. System owners use a kick-off meeting or other initiation milestone to notify participants in the process to begin work on their assigned tasks. The level of formality for such meetings may vary depending on factors such as what system is involved, how many personnel will be engaged to work on the RMF process, and whether the system owner uses a contractor to perform some of the RMF tasks. Although participation in the first step of the RMF may be limited to a small subset of the team that will be involved over the course of the entire process, kick-off meetings often include most or all of the personnel identified in the RMF plan. Having all personnel in attendance gives the system owner an opportunity to describe the plan for executing the RMF process, explain administrative procedures and logistics, and establish points of contact and communication channels for all participants. As with any project, it is important to set expectations up front for all participants so everyone understands what they need to do and when to do it, and to ensure that all personnel involved in the process know where to go for information, guidance, or clarification on roles and responsibilities.

Because many of the RMF roles have counterparts in the overall system development life cycle process, system owners seeking to ensure closely aligned RMF and SDLC efforts can encourage integrated project teams by including representatives from both processes in initial kick-off meetings and in ongoing progress checks or reports on the status of system-related activities. Many RMF tasks occur concurrently with activities in system development life cycle phases, so participants in the RMF should be fully aware of dependencies between their tasks and parallel,

Table 6.2 Key RMF Roles and Responsibilities [26]

Role	Responsibilities	RMF Step 1	2	3	4	5	6
Authorizing Official	Accountable for information security risk to systems under their authority; approves interim system security plans and other artifacts; makes risk acceptance and system authorization decisions	✓	✓		✓	✓	✓
Authorizing Official Designated Representative	Acts on behalf of the authorizing official to perform any AO responsibilities *except* making system authorization decisions	✓	✓		✓	✓	✓
Common Control Provider	Implements, assesses, and monitors common controls inherited by other systems		✓	✓	✓	✓	✓
Information Owner	Official with authority for specified information assets responsible for the ways information is generated, collected, processed, disseminated, and disposed	✓	✓	✓	✓	✓	✓
Information System Owner	Responsible for all aspects and phases of system initiation, development, implementation, maintenance, and disposal, including assembly and submission of the authorization package	✓	✓	✓	✓	✓	✓
Information Security Architect	Verifies that the enterprise and security architectures address all information security requirements necessary to adequately protect systems and the mission functions and business processes they support		✓				
Information System Security Engineer	Ensures security requirements are satisfied through designing, developing, and configuring technical components of the information system		✓	✓	✓		✓
Information System Security Officer	Ensures appropriate security protections are established and maintained for the information system	✓	✓	✓	✓	✓	✓

Table 6.2 Key RMF Roles and Responsibilities [26] (*continued*)

Role	Responsibilities	RMF Step					
		1	2	3	4	5	6
Security Control Assessor	Conducts assessments to evaluate the effectiveness of security controls implemented for the system; identifies weaknesses and deficiencies where present and recommends remediating actions			✓	✓	✓	✓
Senior Information Security Officer	Organizational official responsible for implementing and ensuring agency compliance with FISMA provisions	✓	✓		✓	✓	✓

Table 6.3 SDLC Roles and Responsibilities Involved in the RMF Process [27]

Role	Responsibilities
Program/Project Manager	Represents the system owner and agency interests in the information throughout the system development life cycle, with primary responsibility for managing all aspects of the system
Configuration Manager	Manages changes to the information system, its configuration, or its environment, including changes potentially impacting the security posture of the system
Contracting Officer	Government official with authority to enter into, administer, and terminate contracts and monitor performance of contractors working on behalf of the agency
Privacy Officer	Ensures the system complies with existing privacy laws, regulations, and policies; develops privacy impact assessment
Quality Assurance/ Test Director	Performs system testing and evaluations, including the development and execution of test plans and analysis of test results
Software Developer	Writes program code or installs and configures technical components of the system, including implementing selected security controls
System Administrator	Performs initial and ongoing system installation, configuration, operation, maintenance, and monitoring, including administration of security controls or security-related components of the system
System Architect	Designs the technical architecture of the system and helps to implement the system according to the design

preceding, or subsequent SDLC activities. This type of inter-process coordination helps organizations to successfully integrate information security risk management with system development life cycle processes [24].

RELEVANT SOURCE MATERIAL

Several NIST Special Publications and Federal Information Processing Standards provide guidance, recommendations, and instructions relevant to planning RMF activities. The most applicable sources of information include:

- Special Publication 800-37 Revision 1, *Guide for Applying the Risk Management Framework to Federal Information Systems* [24].
- Special Publication 800-64 Revision 2, *Security Considerations in the System Development Life Cycle* [8].
- Federal Information Processing Standards Publication 199, *Standards for Security Categorization of Federal Information and Information Systems* [28].
- Federal Information Processing Standards Publication 200, *Minimum Security Requirements for Federal Information and Information System* [29].
- Special Publication 800-53 Revision 3, *Recommended Security Controls for Federal Information Systems and Organizations* [30].
- Special Publication 800-53A Revision 1, Guide for Assessing the Security Controls in Federal Information Systems and Organizations [31].
- Special Publication 800-30 Revision 1, *Guide for Conducting Risk Assessments, Initial Public Draft* [32].
- Special Publication 800-18 Revision 1, *Guide for Developing Security Plans for Federal Information Systems* [13].

These and other NIST Special Publications are available from the NIST Computer Security Division Website, at http://csrc.nist.gov/publications/.

SUMMARY

This chapter described the planning process for the Risk Management Framework, and emphasized the importance of effective planning prior to initiating RMF activities. It explained the focus of planning processes and documents, identified key roles and responsibilities involved in RMF steps, and highlighted some of the key information inputs and other prerequisites for initial RMF tasks that should be identified or developed before the process begins. This chapter also described the close alignment between system development life cycle and RMF processes and activities, identifying dependencies that demonstrate the importance of coordination between personnel responsible for executing SDLC activities and RMF tasks.

REFERENCES

[1] Federal Information Security Management Act of 2002, Pub. L. No. 107-347, 116 Stat. 2946. §301, codified at 44 U.S.C. §3544(a)(1)(C).

[2] Primary regulations include Coordination of Federal Information Policy, 44 U.S.C. Chapter 35 and Information Technology Management, 40 U.S.C. Subtitle III.

[3] Management of federal information resources. Washington, DC: Office of Management and Budget; November 2000. Circular No. A-130, Revised (Transmittal Memorandum No. 4).

[4] Guide for applying the risk management framework to federal information systems. Gaithersburg, MD: National Institute of Standards and Technology, Computer Security Division; February2010. Special Publication 800-37 revision 1.

[5] Bowen P, Kissel R, Scholl M, Robinson W, Stansfield J, Voldish L. Recommendations for integrating information security into the capital planning and investment control process. Gaithersburg, MD: National Institute of Standards and Technology, Computer Security Division; July 2009.. Draft Special Publication 800-65 revision 1.

[6] Kissel R, Stine K, Scholl M, Rossman H, Fahlsing J, Gulick J. Security considerations in the system development life cycle. Gaithersburg, MD: National Institute of Standards and Technology, Computer Security Division; October 2008. Special Publication 800-64 revision 2. p. 4.

[7] Preparation, submission, and execution of the budget. Washington, DC: Office of Management and Budget. August 2011. Circular No. A-11, Revised (Transmittal Memorandum No. 85).

[8] Kissel R, Stine K, Scholl M, Rossman H, Fahlsing J, Gulick J. Security considerations in the system development life cycle. Gaithersburg, MD: National Institute of Standards and Technology, Computer Security Division; October 2008. Special Publication 800-64 revision 2.

[9] Preparation, submission, and execution of the budget. Washington, DC: Office of Management and Budget. August 2011. Circular No. A-11, Revised (Transmittal Memorandum No. 85). Exhibit 300. p. 6.

[10] Kissel R, Stine K, Scholl M, Rossman H, Fahlsing J, Gulick J. Security considerations in the system development life cycle. Gaithersburg, MD: National Institute of Standards and Technology, Computer Security Division; October 2008. Special Publication 800-64 revision 2. p. 23.

[11] For example, the General Services Administration maintains a RMF Services blanket purchase agreement available to all government customers. See Risk Management Framework (RMF) Services [Internet]. Washington, DC: General Services Administration [updated April 19, 2012; cited April 24, 2012]. <http://www.gsa.gov/portal/category/102411>.

[12] See, for example, the Center for Medicare and Medicaid Services "System Security and e-Authentication Assurance Levels by Information Type," which identifies 11 information types defined at the organizational level and specifies security categorization levels for CMS systems using those information types. <www.cms.gov/InformationSecurity/downloads/ssl.pdf>.

[13] Swanson M, Hash J, Bowen P. Guide for developing security plans for federal information systems. Gaithersburg, MD: National Institute of Standards and Technology, Computer Security Division; February 2006.. Special Publication 800-18 revision 1.

[14] Guide for applying the risk management framework to federal information systems. Gaithersburg, MD: National Institute of Standards and Technology, Computer Security Division; February 2010. Special Publication 800-37 revision 1. p. 21–2.

[15] Recommended security controls for federal information systems and organizations. Gaithersburg, MD: National Institute of Standards and Technology, Computer Security Division; August 2009. Special Publication 800-53 revision 3. p. F-86.

[16] Recommended security controls for federal information systems and organizations. Gaithersburg, MD: National Institute of Standards and Technology, Computer Security Division; August 2009. Special Publication 800-53 revision 3. p. 20–2.

[17] The acronym FURPS represents functionality, usability, reliability, performance, and sustainability. SeeGrady RB, Caswell DL. Software metrics: Establishing a company-wide program. Upper Saddle River, NJ: Prentice Hall; 1987.

[18] In its draft Revision 4 of Special Publication 800-53, NIST introduces the concept of security control overlays as pre-defined sets of security controls, control enhancements, and guidance to reflect agency-specific contexts, operating environments, security assumptions, or other factors that result in a need to diverge from standard baselines. Security and privacy controls for federal information systems and organizations. Gaithersburg, MD: National Institute of Standards and Technology, Computer Security Division; February 2012. Special Publication 800-53 revision 4. Initial Public Draft. p. 35.

[19] Guide for applying the risk management framework to federal information systems. Gaithersburg, MD: National Institute of Standards and Technology, Computer Security Division; February 2010. Special Publication 800-37 revision 1. p. 24.

[20] Guide for applying the risk management framework to federal information systems. Gaithersburg, MD: National Institute of Standards and Technology, Computer Security Division; February 2010. Special Publication 800-37 revision 1. p. 17.

[21] Guide for applying the risk management framework to federal information systems. Gaithersburg, MD: National Institute of Standards and Technology, Computer Security Division; February 2010. Special Publication 800-37 revision 1. p. 19.

[22] The Project Management Institute's Project Management Body of Knowledge (PMBOK), especially popular among IT contractors providing system development services to the government, is among the sources commonly used in government agencies. See Project Management Institute. A guide to the project management body of knowledge (4th ed.). Newtown Square, PA: Project Management Institute; 2008.

[23] Guide for applying the risk management framework to federal information systems. Gaithersburg, MD: National Institute of Standards and Technology, Computer Security Division; February 2010. Special Publication 800-37 revision 1. p. 9.

[24] Guide for applying the risk management framework to federal information systems. Gaithersburg, MD: National Institute of Standards and Technology, Computer Security Division; February 2010. Special Publication 800-37 revision 1. p. 18.

[25] Guide for applying the risk management framework to federal information systems. Gaithersburg, MD: National Institute of Standards and Technology, Computer Security Division; February 2010. Special Publication 800-37 revision 1. p. D-1–3.

[26] Guide for applying the risk management framework to federal information systems. Gaithersburg, MD: National Institute of Standards and Technology, Computer Security Division; February 2010. Special Publication 800-37 revision 1. See Appendix D.

[27] Kissel R, Stine K, Scholl M, Rossman H, Fahlsing J, Gulick J. Security considerations in the system development life cycle. Gaithersburg, MD: National Institute of Standards

and Technology, Computer Security Division; October 2008. Special Publication 800-64 revision 2. p. 9–10.

[28] Standards for security categorization of federal information and information systems. Gaithersburg, MD: National Institute of Standards and Technology, Computer Security Division; December 2003. Federal Information Processing Standards Publication 199.

[29] Minimum security requirements for federal information and information systems. Gaithersburg, MD: National Institute of Standards and Technology, Computer Security Division; March 2006. Federal Information Processing Standards Publication 200.

[30] Recommended security controls for federal information systems and organizations. Gaithersburg, MD: National Institute of Standards and Technology, Computer Security Division; August 2009. Special Publication 800-53 revision 3.

[31] Guide for assessing the security controls in federal information systems and organizations. Gaithersburg, MD: National Institute of Standards and Technology, Computer Security Division; June 2010. Special Publication 800-53A revision 1.

[32] Guide for conducting risk assessments. Gaithersburg, MD: National Institute of Standards and Technology, Computer Security Division; September 2011. Special Publication 800-30 revision 1. Initial Public Draft.

Risk Management Framework Steps 1 & 2

7

INFORMATION IN THIS CHAPTER:

- Purpose and Objectives for Initial RMF Steps
- Standards and Guidance for Completing RMF Steps 1 & 2
- Tasks in RMF Step 1: Categorize Information System
- Tasks in RMF Step 2: Select Security Controls

Government regulations require all federal agencies to provide adequate security for all information collected, processed, transmitted, stored, or disseminated in federal information systems [1]. Because "adequate" means both risk based and cost effective, the level of security protection implemented for information systems varies across government organizations and, in some cases, within agencies as well. Despite the subjectivity of the adequate security requirement, FISMA mandates standards that provide minimum security requirements for all federal information systems [2]. Specifying the appropriate security provisions for each information system requires system owners to evaluate the characteristics of the system, its intended use, the information it contains, and the need to protect the confidentiality, integrity, and availability of the system and its information. The first two steps of the Risk Management Framework (RMF) focus on this determination of adequate security, incorporating federal standards for security categorization and the selection of minimum security controls. As noted in Chapter 6 on RMF planning, to initiate and successfully complete steps 1 and 2, system owners rely on information and artifacts produced during the initiation phase of the system development life cycle and must identify and ensure the participation of key personnel with knowledge of the system, its operating environment, and the business processes it supports. The security categorization and tailored set of security controls produced as a result of these initial steps establish the foundation for all subsequent RMF activities.

PURPOSE AND OBJECTIVES

Any information resource with value to an organization requires some level of security protection. For federal information systems, the appropriate level of security is commensurate with the value of the system—including the value of the information the system contains—to the organization, the magnitude of harm that would result from a loss of confidentiality, integrity, or availability, and the risk that such a loss could occur. These factors are the focus of the risk assessment process for information systems (described in detail in Chapter 13) and represent important drivers for the security categorization and security control selection activities described in this chapter. The wide variety of federal information systems within and among government organizations results in significantly different security requirements, with the potential for equally different corresponding protective mechanisms to satisfy those requirements. The activities in the Risk Management Framework are intended to assist agencies in approaching information system security in a consistent manner regardless of how varied or unique the systems in their inventories may be. The use of standard methods for categorizing information systems and selecting security controls also helps ensure that authorizing officials have consistent information on which to base system authorization decisions. From an organizational perspective, the RMF and related standards provide the necessary guidance to align information security risk management with agency risk strategies and IT governance. The primary purpose of RMF steps 1 and 2 is to arrive at a tailored set of security controls for each information system that is appropriate for the impact level of the system and reflects any system-specific attributes or requirements, as shown in Figure 7.1.

STANDARDS AND GUIDANCE

The core guidance used in steps 1 and 2 of the RMF corresponds directly to responsibilities assigned to NIST in FISMA that call for standards and guidelines for risk-based categorization of information and information systems, the types of information to be included in each category, and minimum information security requirements applicable to systems in each category [3]. NIST implemented these provisions with FIPS Publication 199, *Standards for Security Categorization of Federal Information and Information Systems*; Special Publication 800-60, *Guide for Mapping Types of Information and Information Systems to Security Categories*; and FIPS Publication 200, *Minimum Security Requirements for Federal Information and Information Systems*; respectively. In addition, FIPS 200 requires federal agencies to meet the minimum security requirements it specifies through the application of security controls in Special Publication 800-53, *Recommended Security Controls for Federal Information Systems and Organizations*.

Collectively, these standards and guidelines support the process flow illustrated in Figure 7.1, establishing the context in which system owners and security officers

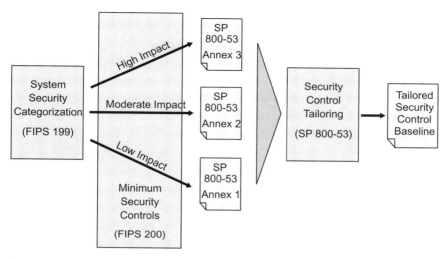

FIGURE 7.1 Following the Procedure Specified in Fips 200, the Impact Level Determined Through Security Categorization Drives the Selection of One of Three Minimum Security Control Baselines Defined in Special Publication 800-53 that System Owners Tailor to Meet the Security Requirements of Each Information System. This Process is Very Similar for National Security Systems Except that the CNSS Guidance on Security Categorization Applied to these Systems may Correspond to One of 27, Rather than Three, Different Baselines

address system security and privacy requirements and begin the development of key authorization package documents such as the system security plan.

The minimum required standards and guidelines referenced in FISMA do not apply to national security systems, although FISMA also directed NIST to work with the Department of Defense to develop guidance for identifying a national security system, resulting in Special Publication 800-59 [4]. CNSS Instruction 1253, *Security Categorization and Control Selection for National Security Systems*, adopted concepts and practices similar to those found in FIPS 199 and FIPS 200, adapted to reflect aspects and considerations associated with protecting national security information [5]. Although CNSSI 1253 substitutes for FIPS 199 and FIPS 200 with respect to national security systems, these instructions use the security control framework defined in Special Publication 800-53, offering a measure of consistency in the security control baselines specified for national security systems and FISMA systems. CNSS also uses the same scale of impact levels found in FIPS 199 and 200 (low, moderate, high), but prescribes a different categorization approach for national security systems, maintaining individual categorizations for confidentiality, integrity, and availability instead of consolidating them at the "high water mark" used in FIPS 200. CNSS explains that the finer level of granularity in security categorization and corresponding control baseline specification reduces the need for tailoring baselines, although it allows risk-based adjustments that consider the effect of physical and personnel security measures often found in national security environments [5].

Special Publication 800-37 includes references to standards and sources of guidance relevant to each task described in the RMF. Table 7.1 summarizes the applicability and primary use of each source in steps 1 and 2 of the RMF. System owners should also refer to organizational risk management strategies and policies, procedures, and standards for information system security management, as these agency-specific perspectives may expand on or constrain the information in government-wide standards and guidelines. In addition to this security-specific reference material, completing the tasks in steps 1 and 2 also depends on the availability and completeness of system-specific information typically produced during the initiation phase of the system development life cycle such as requirements specifications and general functional and technical descriptions of the system.

Table 7.1 Standards and Guidance Used in RMF Steps 1 and 2[6]

Source	Applicability
FIPS Publication 199	Specifies the process of categorizing information and information systems based on impact level; used for all FISMA systems
FIPS Publication 200	Specifies the process of selecting security control baselines based on the impact level established for each system; used for all FISMA systems
CNSS Instruction 1253	Specifies the processes of categorizing information and information systems based on impact level and for selecting corresponding security control baselines; used for national security systems
Special Publication 800-30	Provides guidance for conducting risk assessments, used as an input to security categorization and security control selection
Special Publication 800-39	Defines information security risk management roles, responsibilities, and procedures at all levels of federal government organizations
Special Publication 800-53	Defines a security control framework and specifies security control baselines for low, moderate, and high impact systems; provides tailoring guidance for reducing or supplementing controls based on system-specific considerations
Special Publication 800-53A	Defines security control assessment methods, used in the development of the monitoring strategy for each system
Special Publication 800-59	Provides guidance for identifying an information system as a national security system, which in turn determines the applicable security categorization and security control selection guidance
Special Publication 800-60	Provides recommendations for default confidentiality, integrity, and availability categorizations for government information types

STEP 1: CATEGORIZE INFORMATION SYSTEM

The first step in the RMF establishes the security categorization for the information system, following categorization procedures in FIPS 199 for FISMA systems and in CNSSI 1253 for national security systems. In addition to categorizing each information type contained in the system and the system overall, in step 1 the system owner begins the process of developing the system security plan by documenting security categorization and system description information and executes appropriate procedures to register the system in the agency system inventory. The RMF process begins as early in the system development life cycle as practical, recognizing that the tasks in step 1 rely on system documentation and the results of SDLC processes that must be completed first. As shown in Figure 7.2, key inputs from the SDLC initiation phase include a system concept of operations (CONOPS) or other general descriptive information and functional and technical requirements specified for the system. Some security and privacy artifacts produced outside the RMF process are also useful for security categorization, including privacy impact assessments and initial system risk assessments, particularly to help identify anticipated impacts from threat events and comparing those impacts to the levels defined in FIPS 199. The impact level determined through the security categorization process is the key output of step 1, documented in the draft system security plan along with the system description.

Without diminishing the importance of resource planning that should occur before step 1 of the RMF process begins, the level of effort required to execute subsequent steps depends in part on the results of the security categorization. Because systems with higher impact level designations require a greater number of security controls and control enhancements [9], security control implementation and assessment activities for those systems tend to take longer or require more resources.

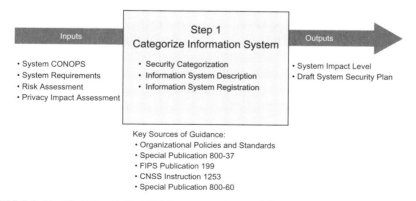

FIGURE 7.2 The First Step in the RMF Focuses on Categorizing the Information System, Capturing Key System Information in the Draft System Security Plan, and Formally Identifying the System and Including it Within the Inventory of Organizational Information Resources

> **NOTE**
>
> The requirement to perform privacy impact assessments comes not from FISMA but from a different part of the E-Government Act of 2002 [7]. These assessments are not explicitly addressed in the RMF, but the privacy impact assessment is a required control in Special Publication 800-53 for information systems at all impact levels [8]. As described in detail in Chapter 16, privacy impact assessments focus on the nature of the information collected, stored, and accessed in information systems and must be completed for systems that use personally identifiable information. Privacy impact assessments do not emphasize protective measures such as security safeguards used to control access to information or otherwise safeguard privacy, so they are not part of security control documentation. They are, however, important sources of system requirements that may be satisfied using security controls.

Security Categorization

Security categorization considers the potential impact to the organization due to the loss of confidentiality, integrity, or availability of any of the information in a federal information system. Although agencies operating national security systems follow different guidance for security categorization and security control selection than agencies with information systems subject to FISMA requirements, government-wide consensus exists on the definitions of confidentiality, integrity, and availability[10] and of the low, moderate, and high impact levels assigned to information types and information systems. Table 7.2 provides the definitions specified in CNSSI 1253 and FIPS 199. Both documents also provide amplification guidance to help clarify the meaning of low, moderate, and high impact, although these explanations use subjective terms such as "minor," "significant," and "severe" that also must be interpreted by agency personnel performing security categorization.

The process prescribed in both FIPS 199 (for FISMA systems) and CNSSI 1253 (for national security systems), shown in Figure 7.3, directs system owners and information owners to first identify each information type residing within an information system and consider separately the potential impact corresponding to confidentiality, integrity, and availability. After assigning impact levels to information types, the categorization of all information types relevant for an information system drives the security categorization of the entire system. Special Publication 800-37 positions security categorization as a collaborative effort among personnel responsible for individual information systems and organizational officials responsible for risk management and for the mission functions and business processes that information systems support [13]. This guidance implies that system owners and information owners should be able to leverage organization-level information on information types and appropriate impact level determinations, rather than making those determinations for their own systems in isolation. CNSSI 1253 assigns responsibility to the head of an organization for determining how security categorization will be conducted for national security systems, giving agencies operating

Table 7.2 Impact Levels Used for Information System Security Categorization [11,12]

Impact Level	Definition
Low	The potential impact is *Low* if the loss of confidentiality, integrity, or availability could be expected to have a *limited* adverse effect on organizational operations, organizational assets, or individuals, other organizations, or the national security interests of the United States.
Moderate	The potential impact is *Moderate* if the loss of confidentiality, integrity, or availability could be expected to have a *serious* adverse effect on organizational operations, organizational assets, individuals, other organizations, or the national security interests of the United States.
High	The potential impact is High if the loss of confidentiality, integrity, or availability could be expected to have a *severe* or *catastrophic* adverse effect on organizational operations, organizational assets, individuals, other organizations, or the national security interests of the United States.

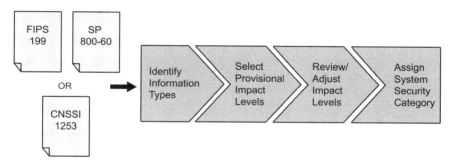

FIGURE 7.3 The Security Categorization Process Emphasizes the Identification of all Relevant Information Types and the Selection and Refinement of Impact Levels for Each Information Type, Either Following Federal Guidance on Information Types and Impact Levels or Using Agency-Defined Information Types

such systems some discretion to apply categorization procedures at the information system level or at the organization level. For FISMA systems, FIPS 200 states explicitly that agencies must perform security categorization from an organization-wide perspective with the involvement of appropriate senior agency officials [14]. When addressed in policies, procedures, and standards developed by organizational information security programs, information system owners can use official interpretations and guidelines for impact levels in multiple security management processes, including risk assessment and security control assessment as well as security categorization.

Identifying Information Types

The first step in the security categorization process is identifying the types of information the system will receive, store, process, or disseminate. This step requires a thorough understanding of the system's purpose and intended use—information typically obtained either by reviewing the concept of operations or other system description documentation developed during the SDLC initiation phase or by discussing the system and its underlying data with the information owners, business sponsor, privacy officer, technology vendor, or others with detailed knowledge of the system and the way it will operate. Information owners and system owners use these descriptions to identify the different types of information residing within the system. Depending on organizational policies and procedures for security categorization, agencies may group information types into agency-defined categories, choose from among the standard types provided in federal guidance to agencies, or create new types. Special Publication 800-60 offers a taxonomy of information types based on the Federal Enterprise Architecture Business Reference Model (BRM), and suggests default security categorizations for each type. The BRM is intended to provide a functional decomposition of the entire federal government—it divides all government operations into 39 lines of business comprising 170 sub-functions [15]. Special Publication 800-60 addresses each of the 170 sub-functions as distinct information types, and adds five additional information types—four to facilitate the identification of information with significant privacy implications, and a "general information" type to accommodate any information not defined in the BRM [16]. Through their enterprise architecture programs, many federal agencies perform analyses to identify which of the BRM lines of business and sub-functions apply to their organizations, and OMB requires agencies to map investments in their IT portfolios to the BRM to help identify government-wide opportunities for collaboration and reuse. If this information is readily available and consistent with the way the information security program approaches system security categorization, system owners and information owners conducting this task may favor the use of pre-defined information types as an alternative to developing their own definitions, either at the organizational level or for individual information systems.

Special Publication 800-60 fulfills a provision in FISMA that directed NIST to develop guidelines identifying types of information used in the federal government and recommending security categorization standards applicable to each information

> **NOTE**
>
> Agencies with closely aligned information security, EA, and CPIC programs may find that using Special Publication 800-60 to assign information types provides a familiar frame of reference for information owners. This federal guidance also includes recommended confidentiality, integrity, and availability impact levels for each information type, but before directing information system owners and information owners to Special Publication 800-60, agencies should determine the extent to which their standards and preferences for security categorization agree with the federal guidance.

type [17]. In this context, NIST explicitly intended Special Publication 800-60 as complementary guidance to FIPS 199. Organizations need to establish and encourage the use of a catalog of information types to achieve consistent information type identification and consistent security categorization determinations for information types across all the information systems an agency operates. Special Publication 800-60 provides one such catalog, but agencies have the ability to define or identify their own information types and to select their own impact levels [18]. Security categorization guidance for national security systems references FIPS 199 but does not refer to Special Publication 800-60 or provide alternate instructions for identifying information types, suggesting that the national security community's routine use of formal data classification schemes, compartmentalization, and transfer of data between secure domains is sufficiently different from non-national security contexts to warrant following a different security categorization process [5]. With the assumption that national security system owners understand the nature and variety of information associated with their systems, the security categorization process described in CNSSI 1253 begins with categorizing information types and does not address information type identification or definition. This is also true for FIPS 199—which NIST published six months before it released the first version of Special Publication 800-60—but FIPS 199 notes the intention to address information type identification in subsequent guidance [19].

Categorizing Information Types

Each information type associated with an information system must be evaluated to determine the potential impact to the organization that could result from a loss of confidentiality, integrity, or availability. The system owner, information owner, and others participating in the security categorization process consider the impact level for each security objective independently, resulting in a three-part categorization for each information type, represented in FIPS 199 and CNSSI 1253 in the general format:

$SC_{\text{information type}}$ = {(**confidentiality**, *impact*), (**integrity**, *impact*), (**availability**, *impact*)}

As noted in Table 7.2, the assigned impact level corresponds to the severity of the adverse effects to the organization that could occur. NIST explains that adverse events could include degradation of mission capability; damage to organizational assets; financial loss; or harm to individuals [20], but these examples are not exhaustive. Agencies can find additional types of adverse impacts in Special Publication 800-30 Revision 1, which provides many examples of types of impacts to operations, assets, individuals, organizations, and the nation [21]. Agencies need to consider many different types of possible adverse effects to accurately determine the appropriate impact level, as the impact level assigned represents the worst case scenario, regardless of the nature of the event. In addition to ensuring that system-specific impact level determinations are consistent with agency standards and guidelines, system owners and information owners can use impact and risk information documented in risk assessments to validate their information type categorizations.

When impact levels are assigned using pre-determined ratings such as those in Special Publication 800-60 or in agency-specific policies, procedures, and standards, system owners and information owners should consider impact levels to be provisional until they can be evaluated in a system-specific context. All systems may be subject to organizational, environmental, operational, or usage factors that might necessitate the adjustment of one or more impact levels. Special Publication 800-60 identifies additional factors applicable to each information type that, when present, may justify increasing or decreasing the default impact level. This guidance tends to emphasize situations in which impact levels should be adjusted upward, but also identifies variations in impact levels at different phases of system development or information production life cycles that may warrant lower categorizations [22]. CNSSI 1253 includes similar provisions for risk-based adjustments to security categorizations, but this activity applies at the information system categorization level, not to individual information types [23].

National Security Information

Like other NIST guidance issued through the FISMA Implementation Project, Special Publication 800-60 does not apply to national security systems, and it repeatedly notes that while the sensitivity of national security information might affect the impact level assigned to an information type, national security systems are outside the scope of the guideline. Some of the lines of business and sub-functions defined in the BRM and referenced in Special Publication 800-60 are often associated with national security systems, including defense and national security, homeland security, and intelligence operations. To the extent information types falling within these lines of business apply to non-national security systems, Special Publication 800-60 recommends high provisional impact levels for most information types, with no recommended level below moderate [24]. Guidance on categorizing national security information in CNSSI 1253 offers no inventory of information types analogous to Special Publication 800-60, noting only that categorization requirements apply to all user information and system information types associated with the information system. CNSS assumes that information types will be defined by each organization or, in some cases, by official policy, directive, regulation, or other executive or legislative requirements. CNSS directs organizations operating national security systems to consider all factors potentially affecting an organization's mission and business processes and systems and associated risks [25]. System owners categorizing national security information should look first to organizational policies or standards for guidance on information types and then develop their own categories if no such guidance exists or their systems use kinds of information beyond the scope of available standards.

Personally Identifiable Information (PII)

Guidance to federal agencies on identifying and categorizing information organizes information types according to their use or the mission or supporting functions they support. Some types of information do not fit neatly within a single functional category, but instead span multiple categories or represent attributes of information rather than ways information is used. NIST recognized this limitation of the BRM when it drafted Special Publication 800-60 when it added four information types to help organizations address privacy considerations that do not correspond to BRM sub-functions. These information types, all of which have provisional impact levels of moderate for confidentiality, integrity, and availability, include: income information, personal identity and authentication, entitlement event information, and representative payee information [26]. These and many other information types have the potential to incorporate personally identifiable information (PII), the protection of which is governed by a wide array of laws, regulations, and official guidance. Although personally identifiable information is not a separately defined information type in Special Publication 800-60, establishing a PII information type and tracking its use can help agencies comply with current government-wide requirements to identify all PII within their organizations, regularly review their holdings of personally identifiable information [27] and perform privacy impact assessments for all information systems containing information in identifiable form about members of the public [28].

In Special Publication 800-122, NIST provides guidance to agencies on identifying PII, assigning confidentiality impact levels to PII, and implementing safeguards to protect PII [29]. In the context of categorizing information types consistent with the procedures described in FIPS 199, NIST recommends that agencies consider PII as a separate factor in assigning confidentiality impact levels, where determining the extent to which the confidentiality of PII needs to be protected supplements the provisional impact levels in Special Publication 800-60 or in agency-specific information type definitions. This approach of first establishing the context in which information is used and then assessing the sensitivity of PII in that context yields a confidentiality impact level for specific instances of PII, rather than for all PII across an organization. Determining confidentiality impact levels for PII within each information type acknowledges the fact that not all PII has the same need for protection and helps organizations avoid implementing protective measures for PII beyond the level commensurate with the risk to the organization if PII is disclosed or modified without authorization or becomes unavailable. Special Publication 800-122 identifies several key factors to use in determining confidentiality impact levels for PII, including how easily PII can be used to identify individuals, the quantity of PII contained in the system, sensitivity of the specific data fields the PII comprises, the context for using PII, obligations to protect PII, and the location and accessibility of the information [30].

Categorizing Information Systems

Once impact levels for all information types have been assigned, system owners determine the security categorization for the information system by analyzing the underlying information types and adjusting the system-level categorization as necessary to reflect system-specific factors. The minimum information system security categorization for each security objective is the highest impact level assigned among any of the system's information types. FIPS 199 refers to this approach as establishing the "high water mark" for confidentiality, integrity, and availability [31], as illustrated in Figure 7.4. FIPS 200 extends the process a step further by assigning a single security categorization value for the entire system equal to the highest impact level among the three security objectives, and using that value to determine the minimum security control baseline. In practice, this means that a high-impact system is one in which at least one security objective is assigned a high impact level, and a low-impact system would be one in which no security objectives are assigned an impact level other than low [32].

The security categorization process prescribed in FIPS 199 concludes with the assignment of a three-part security categorization for the information system. Both Special Publication 800-60 and FIPS 200 extend the procedures in FIPS 199 by providing guidance for consolidating the three-part impact level to a single value (the highest rating among the three security objectives) and using that overall system security categorization as the basis for selecting a security control baseline to satisfy minimum security requirements. Special Publication 800-60 also addresses the possibility that the appropriate impact level for an information system may be higher than the level produced through examination of the information types alone. Factors affecting the decision of whether to raise the impact level for the system include [33]:

- The aggregation of large volumes of information of a single type or combination of multiple types of information may increase the sensitivity of

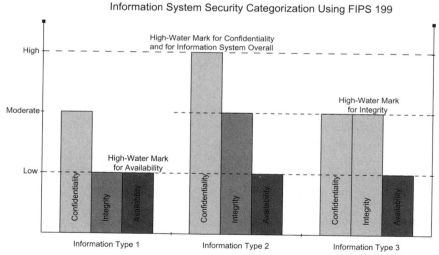

FIGURE 7.4 The Security Categorization Process Defined in FIPS 199 Applies the "High Water Mark" Concept to Determine the Impact Level for Each Security Objective and for the Information System as a Whole. The Security Categorization for a System with Information Type Impact Levels as Shown would be High, Representing the Maximum Impact Level Assigned: SC information system = {(confidentiality, *High*), (integrity, *Moderate*), (availability, *Low*)} = *High*

the information and increase the information security risk for the system to a degree that warrants a higher impact level.

- The impact level assigned for a system to which other systems connect or on which other systems rely may be higher when considering the broader context of system interconnections and dependencies than when evaluating the system in isolation.
- Many factors beyond the information a system contains may influence the potential impact to the organization if loss, damage, or compromise occurs, including extenuating circumstances such as the system's role in supporting a critical process or capability, visibility within the organization or to the public, extent of interconnections to other dependent systems, or cost of replacement.

In presenting these factors, NIST implicitly acknowledges the potential limitations of a security categorization process that evaluates the system in isolation without considering the organizational and environmental context for the system and the information it contains. Agencies and their system owners should categorize their systems and underlying information types based not only on the systems' intrinsic value and sensitivity of their information types but also on the impact to other systems or operational functions indirectly supported by the system.

CNSSI 1253 adopts the high water mark approach when aggregating information type impact levels to categorize information systems, but does not consolidate system-level confidentiality, integrity, and availability ratings to a single impact designation. Instead, national security systems maintain their three-part categorization ratings for the security control selection process. CNSS adapts the security control baselines in Special Publication 800-53 to indicate control applicability at each impact level and each security objective [34]. Much like the guidance applicable to FISMA systems, CNSSI 1253 includes guidelines for making risk adjustments that might justify a different system security categorization than the worst-case impact level derived from the levels assigned to underlying information types. Where Special Publication 800-60 highlights factors that would lead an organization to assign a higher impact level to an information system than the high water mark from its information types, CNSSI 1253 permits national security system owners, with proper justification, to select security control baselines corresponding to lower or higher impact levels than the level assigned using information type categorizations. Risk adjustment factors applicable to national security systems include information aggregation and system criticality, both of which might result in the assignment of a higher impact level. The physical, personnel, and organizational security protections often afforded to systems operating in agencies processing classified information may serve to mitigate the risk of the system in isolation and may therefore justify reducing the impact level [35]. CNSSI 1253 instructs national security system owners to perform risk assessments on the information types and operating environment associated with a system to determine whether to apply a risk adjustment to the assigned security categorization.

Information System Description

The information system description task in step 1 of the RMF gathers functional and technical details about the system and documents the information in the system security plan. Because the system security plan is a core document in the security authorization package and represents a comprehensive source of security requirements and corresponding controls for an information system, the system description should be accurate, current, and provided in sufficient detail to identify the characteristics of the system relevant to specifying security measures commensurate with the risk associated with operating the system. Each organization determines the amount of information and level of detail needed in its information system descriptions, which may vary according to the system's security categorization, the scope or type of system described, and the extent of existing system documentation produced through the system development life cycle. Special Publication 800-37 suggests the following information be included in the system description [36]:

- Full descriptive name of the information system including any associated acronym;
- Unique information system identifier;
- Name and contact information for the information system owner and authorizing official;
- Parent or governing organization that manages, owns, and/or controls the information system;
- Location of the information system and environment in which it operates;
- Version or release number of the information system;
- Purpose, functions, and capabilities of the information system and missions and business processes supported;
- How the information system is integrated into the enterprise architecture and information security architecture;
- Status of the information system with respect to its phase in the system development life cycle;
- Results of the security categorization process for the information and information system;
- Types of information processed, stored, and transmitted by the information system;
- Boundary of the information system for risk management and security authorization purposes;
- Applicable laws, directives, policies, regulations, or standards affecting the security of the information system;
- Architectural description of the information system including network topology;
- Hardware and firmware devices included within the information system;
- System and application software resident on the information system;
- Hardware, software, and internal and external system interfaces;
- Subsystems (static and dynamic) associated with the information system;

- Information flows and paths (including inputs and outputs) within the information system;
- Cross domain devices/requirements;
- Network connection rules for communicating with external information systems;
- Interconnected information systems and identifiers for those systems;
- Encryption techniques used for information processing, transmission, and storage;
- Cryptographic key management information, if applicable;
- Information system users (including organizational affiliations, access rights, privileges, and citizenship, if applicable);
- Ownership and operation of the information system (e.g. government-owned, government-operated; government-owned, contractor-operated; contractor-owned, contractor-operated; nonfederal);
- Security authorization date and authorization termination date;
- Incident response points of contact;
- Other information as required by the organization.

Although some of the details in the system description may be gathered or provided by personnel executing the RMF for the system, at the time the RMF process is initiated much of this information should already have been captured in system documentation. When incorporating system description information, the system owner, information system security officer, and others contributing to developing the system security plan should validate any information drawn from existing documentation to ensure it is up to date and accurately reflects the information system. System description information, like many other components of the system security plan, often changes as the system progresses through the SDLC and the steps in the RMF, so while this information is first documented in step 1, tasks in subsequent steps of the RMF resulting in additions or updates to the system security plan represent opportunities to augment or revise the information system description.

Information System Registration

The task of registering the information system uniquely identifies each information system, records the system in relevant agency inventories, and indicates the organization responsible for the system and its management and supervision. The formal identification of federal information systems often occurs during the initiation phase of the system development life cycle, so in many cases the information system registration task within the RMF is not the first or only such activity performed for a given information system. If the information system has already been registered in appropriate agency inventories, the task for system owners becomes one of validation and of ensuring that the system is correctly represented with all relevant security management attributes. FISMA requires each federal agency to develop, maintain, and update at least annually an inventory of its major information systems and to use its system inventory to support information resources management functions including information technology planning, budgeting, and information security [37]. The FISMA system inventory is only one among many agency-level listings or indices agencies are required to provide; others include a publicly available index of systems mandated under amendments to the Freedom of Information Act [38] and portfolios of IT investment and IT security information submitted to OMB as part of the federal budget preparation process [39]. In the RMF context, information system registration is intended to inform the organization and its information security program of the system's existence, its key characteristics, and the security implications for the organization associated with operating the system [40]. From an information resources management perspective, registering the information system supports planning and resource allocation, system owner and business sponsor accountability, and effective management and oversight for the system, including complying with FISMA and other government-wide reporting requirements.

STEP 2: SELECT SECURITY CONTROLS

The second step in the RMF identifies all the security controls needed to satisfy an information system's security requirements and documents those controls in the system security plan. The results of the system security categorization completed in step 1 drive the selection of security controls, as the impact level assigned to the information system corresponds to a baseline set of security controls, defined in Special Publication 800-53, that collectively represent the minimum security necessary to protect systems categorized at each impact level. System owners and other personnel with responsibility for establishing the security posture of the system use security requirements and risk assessment information developed for the system in conjunction with the system security categorization to identify the appropriate security control baseline and modify that baseline to address the needs of the system. The primary outputs of the security control selection process, as indicated in Figure 7.5, are a tailored security control baseline, system monitoring strategy, and an approved initial version of the system security plan. Security control selection identifies all the controls relevant to each information system regardless of who is responsible for providing them. Federal information systems typically include a mix of system-specific, common, and hybrid security controls. Security control baselines documented in system security plans indicate the type for each control and, in the case of common or hybrid controls, may incorporate or refer to control information in other system security plans. At the completion of step 2, system owners not only receive independent review and approval of their system security plans from agency officials, but also have the information necessary to finalize the resource allocation and timeline in the RMF project plan. The tailored security control baseline defined during step 2 of the RMF is the basis for security control implementation and assessment activities conducted in steps 3 and 4, respectively, so the effectiveness of subsequent parts of the process depends on the accuracy and thoroughness of security control selection.

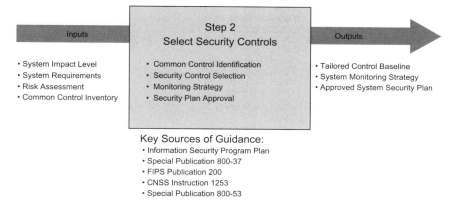

FIGURE 7.5 The Second Step in the RMF Identifies all the Controls Needed to Provide Adequate Security for the Information System, Tailoring the Appropriate Security Control Baseline to Reflect the Requirements of Each System and Documenting the Selected Set of Controls in the System Security Plan

System owners first identify relevant controls using federal standards and guidelines and system-specific considerations, and then determine how those controls will be provided and monitored once the system is operational.

The security control framework described in Special Publication 800-53 provides a common reference for federal government agencies when selecting security controls. Although the system categorization and control baseline selection procedures differ for FISMA systems and national security systems, FIPS 200 and CNSSI 1253 both use Special Publication 800-53 as the source of security controls. Special Publication 800-53 organizes security controls into 18 families spanning three categories of controls—management, operational, and technical—as seen in Table 7.3. Management controls address risk management and information security management for systems; operational controls correspond to security processes and procedures primarily executed by people rather than systems; and technical controls are security measures implemented and executed by the information system using hardware, software, or infrastructure mechanisms [41]. Of the 18 families, 17 correspond to the security-related areas identified in FIPS 200; NIST added the program management family as part of the changes to its guidance in Revision 3 of Special Publication 800-53.

FIPS 200 also specifies minimum security requirements for each security-related area that the individual controls in each family address, presented in Table 7.4. NIST does not provide definitions or general descriptions for its security control families; instead, the specifications in FIPS 200 provide the context for each set of security controls that collectively meet or exceed minimum security requirements. The close alignment between security-related areas and security control families resulted from NIST's parallel development of Special Publication 800-53 and FIPS 200 (the first

Table 7.3 Security Control Identifiers, Families, and Classes [42]

Identifier	Family	Class
AC	Access Control	Technical
AT	Awareness and Training	Operational
AU	Audit and Accountability	Technical
CA	Security Assessment and Authorization	Management
CM	Configuration Management	Operational
CP	Contingency Planning	Operational
IA	Identification and Authentication	Technical
IR	Incident Response	Operational
MA	Maintenance	Operational
MP	Media Protection	Operational
PE	Physical and Environmental Protection	Operational
PL	Planning	Management
PS	Personnel Security	Operational
RA	Risk Assessment	Management
SA	System and Services Acquisition	Management
SC	System and Communications Protection	Technical
SI	System and Information Integrity	Operational
PM	Program Management	Management

NOTE

Federal guidance bases the association of each family with its corresponding security control class on the nature of the majority of the controls in each family, although individual controls may be more closely aligned to a different class. For instance, the first control in each family is policy and procedures for the security topic addressed by the family. Documented policies and procedures are examples of management controls, even when they apply to a set of operational or technical controls.

release of Special Publication 800-53 predated FIPS 200 by more than a year). NIST drew on a variety of existing government and industry sources of security requirements and security control specifications to provide a sufficiently broad and deep catalog of security controls to satisfy applicable requirements and help agencies demonstrate compliance with legal, regulatory, and policy requirements, including those in FISMA [43].

FIPS 200 requirements notwithstanding, each agency is responsible for selecting, implementing, and effectively using the appropriate set of security controls for each

Table 7.4 Specifications for Minimum Security Requirements [44]

Security-Related Area	Specification
Access Control	Organizations must limit information system access to authorized users, processes acting on behalf of authorized users, or devices (including other information systems) and to the types of transactions and functions that authorized users are permitted to exercise.
Awareness and Training	Organizations must: (i) ensure that managers and users of organizational information systems are made aware of the security risks associated with their activities and of the applicable laws, Executive Orders, directives, policies, standards, instructions, regulations, or procedures related to the security of organizational information systems; and (ii) ensure that organizational personnel are adequately trained to carry out their assigned information security-related duties and responsibilities.
Audit and Accountability	Organizations must: (i) create, protect, and retain information system audit records to the extent needed to enable the monitoring, analysis, investigation, and reporting of unlawful, unauthorized, or inappropriate information system activity; and (ii) ensure that the actions of individual information system users can be uniquely traced to those users so they can be held accountable for their actions.
Certification, Accreditation, and Security Assessment	Organizations must: (i) periodically assess the security controls in organizational information systems to determine if the controls are effective in their application; (ii) develop and implement plans of action designed to correct deficiencies and reduce or eliminate vulnerabilities in organizational information systems; (iii) authorize the operation of organizational information systems and any associated information system connections; and (iv) monitor information system security controls on an ongoing basis to ensure the continued effectiveness of the controls.
Configuration Management	Organizations must: (i) establish and maintain baseline configurations and inventories of organizational information systems (including hardware, software, firmware, and documentation) throughout the respective system development life cycles; and (ii) establish and enforce security configuration settings for information technology products employed in organizational information systems.
Contingency Planning	Organizations must establish, maintain, and effectively implement plans for emergency response, backup operations, and post-disaster recovery for organizational information systems to ensure the availability of critical information resources and continuity of operations in emergency situations.
Identification and Authentication	Organizations must identify information system users, processes acting on behalf of users, or devices and authenticate (or verify) the identities of those users, processes, or devices, as a prerequisite to allowing access to organizational information systems.

Table 7.4 Specifications for Minimum Security Requirements [44] (*continued*)

Security-Related Area	Specification
Incident Response	Organizations must: (i) establish an operational incident handling capability for organizational information systems that includes adequate preparation, detection, analysis, containment, recovery, and user response activities; and (ii) track, document, and report incidents to appropriate organizational officials and/or authorities.
Maintenance	Organizations must: (i) perform periodic and timely maintenance on organizational information systems; and (ii) provide effective controls on the tools, techniques, mechanisms, and personnel used to conduct information system maintenance.
Media Protection	Organizations must: (i) protect information system media, both paper and digital; (ii) limit access to information on information system media to authorized users; and (iii) sanitize or destroy information system media before disposal or release for reuse.
Physical and Environmental Protection	Organizations must: (i) limit physical access to information systems, equipment, and the respective operating environments to authorized individuals; (ii) protect the physical plant and support infrastructure for information systems; (iii) provide supporting utilities for information systems; (iv) protect information systems against environmental hazards; and (v) provide appropriate environmental controls in facilities containing information systems.
Planning	Organizations must develop, document, periodically update, and implement security plans for organizational information systems that describe the security controls in place or planned for the information systems and the rules of behavior for individuals accessing the information systems.
Personnel Security	Organizations must: (i) ensure that individuals occupying positions of responsibility within organizations (including third-party service providers) are trustworthy and meet established security criteria for those positions; (ii) ensure that organizational information and information systems are protected during and after personnel actions such as terminations and transfers; and (iii) employ formal sanctions for personnel failing to comply with organizational security policies and procedures.
Risk Assessment	Organizations must periodically assess the risk to organizational operations (including mission, functions, image, or reputation), organizational assets, and individuals, resulting from the operation of organizational information systems and the associated processing, storage, or transmission of organizational information.

Table 7.4 Specifications for Minimum Security Requirements [44] (*continued*)

Security-Related Area	Specification
System and Services Acquisition	Organizations must: (i) allocate sufficient resources to adequately protect organizational information systems; (ii) employ system development life cycle processes that incorporate information security considerations; (iii) employ software usage and installation restrictions; and (iv) ensure that third-party providers employ adequate security measures to protect information, applications, and/or services outsourced from the organization.
System and Communications Protection	Organizations must: (i) monitor, control, and protect organizational communications (i.e. information transmitted or received by organizational information systems) at the external boundaries and key internal boundaries of the information systems; and (ii) employ architectural designs, software development techniques, and systems engineering principles that promote effective information security within organizational information systems.
System and Information Integrity	Organizations must: (i) identify, report, and correct information and information system flaws in a timely manner; (ii) provide protection from malicious code at appropriate locations within organizational information systems; and (iii) monitor information system security alerts and advisories and take appropriate actions in response.

information system, where compliance with applicable requirements is necessary but not sufficient to demonstrate effective security. The level of confidence—what NIST refers to as "minimum assurance"—organizations require that system security controls are in place, implemented correctly, functioning properly, and producing the intended security outcome varies according to organizational risk tolerance and the

NOTE

System owners, information system security officers, common control providers, and others participating in security control selection, implementation, and assessment should develop a thorough understanding of the NIST-defined security control families and security controls and enhancements applicable to their systems. The number of controls and control enhancements and the volume of descriptive information about them make it infeasible to provide descriptions of these controls within this book. NIST publishes low-impact, moderate-impact, and high-impact security control baselines as annexes to Special Publication 800-53, offering a more concise reference to support security control selection. System owners considering the selection of additional controls beyond the minimum specified in each baseline still need to reference the full security control documentation in Special Publication 800-53, as the annexes include only the required controls and control enhancements for each baseline.

impact level assigned to the system. For low-impact systems, agencies may be satisfied with demonstrations of successful implementation and compliance with baseline requirements but for moderate- or high-impact systems NIST guidance recommends initial and ongoing analysis and testing of security controls to provide additional evidence demonstrating control effectiveness [45].

Common Control Identification

The full set of security controls selected for an information system typically includes both system-specific controls provided by the system or the operational and management resources dedicated to the system and common controls provided by other systems or parts of the organization (or external organizations) that protect multiple systems. Few federal information systems have sufficient scope or allocated resources to provide all necessary security controls at a system-specific level, even if organizational governance permitted such an approach. Instead, federal agencies specify common controls that their information systems inherit, either exactly as implemented by common control providers or with some system-specific modification or extension to create hybrid controls. Prior to selecting security controls, system owners need to identify common control providers and the security controls available for their information systems to use, and understand common controls in sufficient detail to determine if they meet the system's requirements. When available common controls do not fully satisfy information system security requirements, system owners must determine whether to implement a system-specific alternative or if the common control can be partially utilized in a hybrid control implementation [46].

The agency-level information security program is one source of common controls, but government organizations often have multiple common control providers potentially applicable to a given information system. Information security programs develop organizational strategies, plans, and policies and procedures that correspond to management controls that all information systems are expected to inherit. Typical examples of operational and technical common controls include those provided by data centers, local and wide area networks, security and network operations centers, incident response centers, and centralized security monitoring capabilities. The identification of common controls can be performed at an organizational level, with a directory or inventory of controls made available to information system owners. The existence of pre-identified sources of common controls simplifies the control identification process for personnel executing the RMF, obviating the need to search for common control providers and allowing attention to be focused on assessing the suitability of available controls. Many sources of common controls are subject to authorization as general support systems, so the common control provider's system security plan and other contents of the security authorization package represent key sources of control information used in information system-level security control selection. System owners reflect this relationship, illustrated in the previous chapter in Figure 6.3, in their system security plans by clearly identifying common controls inherited by their systems and reproducing or incorporating by reference common

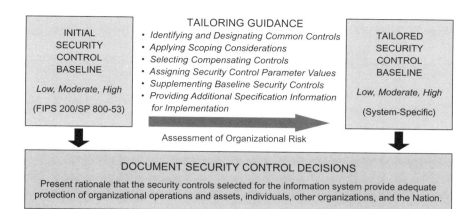

FIGURE 7.6 Security Control Tailoring Considers the Potential Need to Add Optional Controls or Control Enhancements to the Baseline as Well as Identifying and Removing Controls that Do Not Apply to a Given Information System [58]

control documentation maintained by common control providers [47]. Personnel performing common control identification should also be aware of the potential that more than one provider exists for some controls, as is often the case when more than one operating environment is available for information system deployment.

Common and Hybrid Control Candidates

Depending on the scope and complexity of an information system, many security controls may be good candidates for inheritance from common control providers. Organizations with well-established information security programs often emphasize the common provision of management controls such as family-specific policies and procedures, risk management strategies, contingency plans, and continuous monitoring strategies. Security control families representing security requirements that many systems share also may be more efficiently provided as common controls, such as those associated with security awareness and training, personnel security, and incident response. Systems residing within agency data centers or hosted by external organizations typically identify as common the controls providing physical and environmental protection, maintenance, media protection, and configuration management, although high-impact systems or those processing PII or other sensitive information may require system-specific parameters or service level agreements to satisfy requirements.

There are also controls for which some level of system-specific implementation is expected or required, including management controls such as the system security plan, security assessments, plan of action and milestones, and privacy impact assessment. If organizational policy dictates that system owners identify system-specific requirements as part of their control implementation—perhaps following procedures, standards, or guidelines developed at the agency level—then a hybrid model may be most appropriate. For instance, as part of the monitoring strategy developed within step 2 of the RMF, system owners may leverage monitoring capabilities provided at the organization level, but determine the monitoring frequency and controls to be monitored on a system-specific basis. Hybrid controls also include document templates and automated information collection and reporting tools that organizations provide to system owners for use in developing plans and executing processes required by various security controls [48].

Security Control Selection

Organizations following current federal standards and guidelines begin security control selection by identifying the baseline security controls corresponding to the impact level assigned to the information system during security categorization. For FISMA systems NIST facilitates the process of selecting relevant security controls from the full set defined in Special Publication 800-53 by publishing three excerpts—one each for low-impact, moderate-impact, and high-impact systems—that identify the subset of controls and control enhancements applicable to systems in each security category [49]. These baselines represent the starting point for security control selection, serving as the basis for the reduction or supplementation of security controls in the tailoring process. Because the security control baselines include *only* the security controls and control enhancements corresponding to minimum security requirements for systems at each impact level, information security architects, information system security officers, and system owners need to refer to the full set of controls in Special Publication 800-53 to identify and evaluate optional controls or enhancements they might select for their systems.

Identifying baseline controls for national security systems is somewhat less straightforward than for FISMA systems. Due to the use of three-part system security categorizations rather than single overall impact levels assigned to systems following FIPS 200, there are 27 possible security categorizations under CNSS guidance. Rather than subdividing controls into 27 different baselines, CNSSI 1253 provides a single matrix listing all controls and control enhancements in Special Publication 800-53 and indicating their applicability to each confidentiality, integrity, and availability impact level [50]. Personnel selecting controls for national security systems also refer to the full control definitions in Special Publication 800-53 to help identify appropriate security measures in addition to the baseline.

Security Control Descriptions

The security control catalog (Appendix F of Special Publication 800-53) identifies each control by name and unique identifier, specifies possible security control enhancements, provides security objectives—statements describing the behavior, mechanisms, or indications of implementation—for each control and control enhancement, and offers supplemental guidance and references to other relevant documentation. The supplemental guidance provided for each control describes the context to which the control applies, suggests factors or circumstances organizations should

> **NOTE**
>
> The current security control catalog represents the result of a process of continuous expansion and refinement in the years since the Special Publication 800-53 was first released in early 2005. The most significant changes—in terms of the number of controls and control enhancements added to the catalog—have occurred since NIST incorporated input of the defense and intelligence communities through the Joint Task Force Transformation Initiative. Revision 3 added 23 system-level controls (in addition to the 11 organization-level controls in the program management family), with an additional 26 security controls proposed in the initial public draft of Special Publication 800-53 Revision 4. The system and communications protection family shows the most extensive changes, expanding from 19 controls to 41 over the five versions of the catalog.

consider when selecting and implementing the control, and identifies related controls that may address similar objectives or intended outcomes or are interdependent with the control. The catalog also indicates the baseline or baselines to which each control is allocated, if any, and the recommended implementation priority established for each control using a scale of P0 to P3, where controls with priority code P1 have a higher priority than P2 and P3 (P0 indicates no priority has been assigned). Regardless of priority, all security controls specified in each baseline need to be implemented to achieve adequate security for the system, but the priority and associated sequencing recommendations can help agencies ensure that controls on which other controls depend are implemented first [51].

The security control catalog in Special Publication 800-53 Revision 3 describes 198 controls, 187 of which are relevant for individual information systems; the other 11 belong to the program management family and are therefore deployed at an organizational level supporting all information systems [52]. Not all controls and control enhancements are assigned to baselines—the low-impact, moderate-impact, and high-impact baselines include 115, 159, and 167 required controls of the total 187, respectively. Security control enhancements add a significant proportion of security requirements for moderate- and high-impact systems, as those baselines include 93 and 161 required control enhancements, respectively, in addition to baseline security controls. While the number of required controls and enhancements does not necessarily correspond to a linear increase in the level of effort to implement them, the fact that Special Publication 800-53 prescribes more than twice as many requirements for moderate-impact systems as it does for low-impact systems provides some indication of the effect the security categorization has on the scope and resource requirements of the RMF effort.

Tailoring Baseline Controls

Security control baselines defined using Special Publication 800-53 satisfy minimum security requirements developed broadly to apply across the entire federal government. It is infeasible for these baselines to align exactly to the agency needs, operational environments, and specific circumstances relevant to every federal information system. Guidance on security control selection gives agencies and their system owners the flexibility to adjust baselines to reflect the security requirements of each system and achieve appropriate levels of protection. As shown in Figure 7.6, the process of modifying the security control baseline to address organizational and system-specific considerations includes:

- Applying scoping guidance to determine the applicability of baseline controls;
- Selecting compensating security controls, if needed, as more cost-effective or more feasible alternatives to required baseline controls;
- Determining system-specific or organization-defined values for security control parameters;
- Supplementing baselines with additional security controls and control enhancements, if needed;
- Documenting decisions to deviate from security control baseline requirements, the rationale for such decisions, and relevant control information needed to support implementation.

Agencies may choose to tailor security control baselines at the organizational level, the information system level, or some combination of both. Tailoring performed within an organization's information security program produces agency-specific versions of baselines to be used in the RMF process for each information system.

System owners apply scoping guidance to identify organizational conditions or characteristics of their systems or the environments in which they operate that affect the relevance or applicability of baseline security controls and control enhancements. Scoping considerations can address common, hybrid, and system-specific controls, although system owners should recognize that decisions not to select baseline controls identified as common are the responsibility of the common control provider. Many of the scoping considerations NIST identifies in Special Publication 800-53 emphasize the importance of analyzing precisely which aspects of the system security controls target. In some cases security controls apply to specific components, technologies, infrastructure elements, and operating environment characteristics assumed to be present in federal information systems; if general assumptions do

---

NOTE

In previous versions of Special Publication 800-53, up to and including Revision 3 currently in effect, NIST used the term *tailoring* to denote risk-based decisions not to select security controls allocated to the appropriate baseline and distinguishes tailoring from *supplementing* baselines with controls or enhancements in addition to those specified in the baseline. In the description of the security control selection process in the initial public draft of Special Publication 800-53 Revision 4, however, *tailoring* refers to all baseline adjustment activities, including those resulting in reductions or additions of controls [53]. This chapter follows the most recent NIST usage, but to avoid semantic confusion also substitutes terms such as "adjustment" or "modification" when referring to the broader process of adapting NIST security control baselines to the requirements of specific systems and their operating environments.

not hold true for a given system, the controls specified based on those assumptions may not be applicable. For instance, controls addressing wireless technology, remote access, mobile code, or public key infrastructure certificates are irrelevant for systems that do not employ such technologies. NIST guidance also permits "downgrading" some security controls to a lower level baseline, if the controls support a security objective categorized at a level lower than the overall impact level for the system [54]. This approach is logically consistent with the system categorization procedures in CNSSI 1253, which consider separately the impact levels for confidentiality, integrity, and availability when establishing security control baselines.

Organizations sometimes find that a baseline security control applies for a system, but implementing the control specified in the baseline is beyond the organization's capability or cannot be cost justified. Before determining whether to accept, avoid, or otherwise respond to the risk posed to the organization by failing to implement a required control, agencies may consider the selection of compensating controls as an alternative that satisfies the same security objectives. NIST defines compensating controls as those "employed by an organization in lieu of a recommended security control in the low, moderate, or high baselines that provide an equivalent or comparable level of protection for an information system and the information processed, stored, or transmitted by that system" [55]. Compensating controls should only be used when they can be drawn from Special Publication 800-53 or another acceptable source and when the organization agrees to accept the risk associated with substituting the compensating controls for those specified in the security control baseline. As with other tailoring decisions, agencies and their system owners need to document the selection of compensating controls and explain the rationale for choosing alternative controls instead of the ones in the baseline [56].

System-specific considerations may also lead system owners to select supplemental security controls beyond the minimum requirements specified in the appropriate baseline for the system. Special Publication 800-53 provides the primary source of information for supplemental controls and control enhancements, which system owners may choose from the requirements in a higher level baseline or from among the many optional controls and enhancements in the security control catalog that are not allocated to any baseline. Agencies and their system owners determine the need for supplemental controls by comparing the security requirements specified for each

---

WARNING

It is possible for a system owner to try to deploy an information system or information technology service that is beyond the organization's capacity to adequately protect, either due to resource constraints or because no level of selected security controls is sufficient to reduce risk to an acceptable level. These circumstances may arise with systems that implement emerging or unproven technology or that involve components outside the control of the organization. Faced with unacceptable information security risk, organizations may need to restrict the use of such technologies, either by limiting access to the system and the information it contains or by reducing the functionality of the deployed system.

system with current capabilities and the expected effect of implementing baseline controls; any requirements not fully satisfied by baseline controls may indicate a need for supplementation. System owners should document their decisions to add security controls or enhancements and provide supporting rationale or cost justification so that risk managers, authorizing officials, and other agency officials understand the basis for and will approve the implementation of supplemental controls.

Part of the process of documenting security controls—including reductions or additions to the applicable security control baseline—is assigning system-specific values to parameters in controls selected for implementation. This information not only satisfies expectations for the contents of security control documentation in the system security plan, but also provides guidance to system developers, information system security officers, or other personnel with responsibility for implementing and configuring security controls to satisfy the system's security requirements. Many management, operational, and technical controls include parameterized statements of policy, acceptable use, time periods, frequency of execution, or other attributes that vary among information systems. Selection of these controls is not complete until values for these variables have been determined and documented in sufficient detail to support the proper implementation and configuration of each control [57].

Monitoring Strategy

Although monitoring for a system's security controls does not begin until the system is authorized to operate and transitions to its operational phase, Special Publication 800-37 emphasizes the importance of developing the monitoring strategy for the system early in the RMF process so that the strategy can inform system design or technology acquisition and help ensure that existing or planned information security continuous monitoring capabilities are sufficient to satisfy the system's requirements. Monitoring activities span a variety of administrative processes and operations and maintenance functions, including configuration management and control, security impact analyses of changes to the system or its operating environment, ongoing security control assessments, and security status reporting [59]. System owners and common control providers determine which of their controls will be monitored and specify the frequency of monitoring, and approach to be used for security control assessments. Not all controls require monitoring and those that do often vary in terms of how often monitoring should be performed. The monitoring strategy should consider threats and vulnerabilities faced by the system, resource constraints, types of monitoring available, and the level of automation available to support system-specific or organizational monitoring activities.

The current emphasis by OMB, DHS, and NIST on continuous monitoring as a means to provide agencies with real-time or near real-time situational awareness of the security posture of their systems results in an expectation that agencies will define organization-wide continuous monitoring strategies and establish and implement continuous monitoring programs [60]. The monitoring strategy developed during step 2 of the RMF and documented in the system security plan should incorporate relevant aspects of the organizational information security continuous monitoring strategy and identify any system-specific requirements in terms of the controls selected for monitoring, the monitoring frequency, and the nature, level of detail, and intended audience for status reports and other outputs of the monitoring process.

Security Plan Approval

For the final task in step 2 of the RMF, system owners document the results of all the key activities performed during steps 1 and 2 in the system security plan and submit the plan to the authorizing official for review and approval. This interim approval evaluates the system security plan for completeness; verifies compliance with agency requirements in terms of content, structure, and level of detail; and assesses the extent to which the tailored set of security controls selected for implementation are consistent with the impact level assigned to the system and will satisfy the system's security requirements. Consistent with NIST guidelines on developing system security plans, the version of the plan submitted for approval at this stage of the RMF should include a declaration of the system security categorization, the system description, a listing of security controls selected for the system including common, hybrid, and system-specific designations, and details of the monitoring strategy planned for the system. NIST guidance positions security plan approval as a necessary prerequisite for a system to advance to the next step in the RMF and for the system owner to determine the level of effort needed to complete the RMF process [61]. Acceptance of the system security plan by the authorizing official is also an important milestone in the SDLC process, as the agreed-upon set of selected security controls is a key input to system development or acquisition.

RELEVANT SOURCE MATERIAL

Several NIST Special Publications and Federal Information Processing Standards provide guidance, recommendations, and instructions relevant to performing security categorization and security control selection. The most applicable sources of information include:

- Special Publication 800-37 Revision 1, *Guide for Applying the Risk Management Framework to Federal Information Systems* [61].
- Federal Information Processing Standards Publication 199, *Standards for Security Categorization of Federal Information and Information Systems* [62].
- Federal Information Processing Standards Publication 200, *Minimum Security Requirements for Federal Information and Information Systems* [63].
- Committee on National Security Systems Instruction 1253, *Security Categorization and Control Selection for National Security Systems* [64].
- Special Publication 800-53 Revision 3, *Recommended Security Controls for Federal Information Systems and Organizations* [65].

- Special Publication 800-60 Revision 1, *Guide for Mapping Types of Information and Information Systems to Security Categories* [66].
- Special Publication 800-18 Revision 1, *Guide for Developing Security Plans for Federal Information Systems* [67].

These and other NIST Special Publications are available from the NIST Computer Security Division website, at http://csrc.nist.gov/publications/. CNSS publications are available at http://www.cnss.gov/.

SUMMARY

This chapter described the tasks performed in the first two steps of the Risk Management Framework, categorize information system and select security controls. It identified and summarized key sources of guidance to system owners and RMF project teams on completing these initial steps in the process and described the foundational role security categorization and security control selection have in the overall process. The material in this chapter emphasized the incorporation of federal guidance applicable to all agencies and information systems in organizational and system-specific decision making regarding security controls. It also described key aspects of the security control catalog and associated baselines defined in Special Publication 800-53 that are just as relevant to security control implementation and assessment (the next two steps in the RMF process and the subject of Chapter 8) as they are to security control selection.

REFERENCES

[1] Appendix III, Security of federal automated information resources. Washington, DC: Office of Management and Budget; November 2000. Circular No. A-130, Revised (Transmittal Memorandum No. 4).

[2] Federal Information Security Management Act of 2002, Pub. L. No. 107-347, 116 Stat. 2946. §302, codified at 40 U.S.C. §11331(b)(2).

[3] Federal Information Security Management Act of 2002, Pub. L. No. 107-347, 116 Stat. 2946. §303, codified at 15 U.S.C. §278g-3.

[4] Barker WC. Guideline for identifying an information system as a national security system. Gaithersburg, MD: National Institute of Standards and Technology, Computer Security Division; August 2003. Special Publication 800-59.

[5] Security categorization and control selection for national security systems. Fort Meade, MD: Committee on National Security Systems; October 2009. CNSS Instruction 1253. p. 5.

[6] Guide for applying the risk management framework to federal information systems. Gaithersburg, MD: National Institute of Standards and Technology, Computer Security Division; 2010 Feb. Special Publication 800-37 Revision 1.

[7] E-Government Act of 2002, Pub. L. No. 107-347, 116 Stat. 2899. See §208.

[8] Recommended security controls for federal information systems and organizations. Gaithersburg, MD: National Institute of Standards and Technology, Computer Security Division; 2009 Aug. Special Publication 800-53 Revision 3. p. F-87.

[9] The total number of required controls and enhancements in the Special Publication 800-53 Revision 3 baselines for low, moderate, and high impact systems is 115, 252, and 328, respectively. The baselines do not include program management family controls, as these are deployed organization-wide.

[10] Both FIPS 199 and CNSSI 1253 cite the statutory definitions of confidentiality, integrity, and availability used in FISMA and codified at 44 U.S.C. §3542.

[11] Security categorization and control selection for national security systems. Fort Meade, MD: Committee on National Security Systems; 2009 Oct. CNSS Instruction 1253. p. 7–8.

[12] Standards for security categorization of federal information and information systems. Gaithersburg, MD: National Institute of Standards and Technology, Computer Security Division; December 2003. Federal Information Processing Standards Publication 199. p. 2–3.

[13] Guide for applying the risk management framework to federal information systems. Gaithersburg, MD: National Institute of Standards and Technology, Computer Security Division; February 2010. Special Publication 800-37 Revision 1. p. 21.

[14] Minimum security requirements for federal information and information systems. Gaithersburg, MD: National Institute of Standards and Technology, Computer Security Division; March 2006. Federal Information Processing Standards Publication 200. p. 4, Footnote 7.

[15] FEA consolidated reference model version 2.3. Washington, DC: Office of Management and Budget; October 2007.

[16] Stine K, Kissel R, Barker W, Fahlsing J, Gulick J. Volume I: Guide for mapping types of information and information systems to security categories. Gaithersburg, MD: National Institute of Standards and Technology, Computer Security Division; August 2008. Special Publication 800-60 Revision 1. p. 17.

[17] Federal Information Security Management Act of 2002, Pub. L. No. 107-347, 116 Stat. 2946. §303, codified at 15 U.S.C. §287g-3(b)(1)(B).

[18] Stine K, Kissel R, Barker W, Fahlsing J, Gulick J. Volume I: Guide for mapping types of information and information systems to security categories. Gaithersburg, MD: National Institute of Standards and Technology Computer Security Division; August 2008. Special Publication 800-60 Revision 1. p. 18.

[19] Standards for security categorization of federal information and information systems. Gaithersburg, MD: National Institute of Standards and Technology, Computer Security Division; December 2003. Federal Information Processing Standards Publication 199. p. 1.

[20] Standards for security categorization of federal information and information systems. Gaithersburg, MD: National Institute of Standards and Technology, Computer Security Division; December 2003. Federal Information Processing Standards Publication 199. p. 2–3.

[21] Guide for conducting risk assessments. Gaithersburg, MD: National Institute of Standards and Technology, Computer Security Division; September 2011. Special Publication 800-30 Revision 1. Initial Public Draft. See Appendix H.

[22] Stine K, Kissel R, Barker W, Fahlsing J, Gulick J. Volume I: Guide for mapping types of information and information systems to security categories. Gaithersburg, MD: National Institute of Standards and Technology, Computer Security Division; August 2008. Special Publication 800-60 Revision 1. p. 23.

[23] Security categorization and control selection for national security systems. Fort Meade, MD: Committee on National Security Systems; October 2009. CNSS Instruction 1253. p. 9.

[24] Stine K, Kissel R, Barker W, Fahlsing J, Gulick J. Volume I: Guide for mapping types of information and information systems to security categories. Gaithersburg, MD: National Institute of Standards and Technology, Computer Security Division; August 2008. Special Publication 800-60 Revision 1. p. 104.

[25] Security categorization and control selection for national security systems. Fort Meade, MD: Committee on National Security Systems; October 2009. CNSS Instruction 1253. p. 8–9.

[26] Stine K, Kissel R, Barker W, Fahlsing J, Gulick J. Volume I: Guide for mapping types of information and information systems to security categories. Gaithersburg, MD: National Institute of Standards and Technology, Computer Security Division; August 2008. Special Publication 800-60 Revision 1. p. 5.

[27] Johnson C. Safeguarding against and responding to the breach of personally identifiable information. Washington, DC: Office of Management and Budget; 2007. May 22. Memorandum M-07-16.

[28] Bolten JB. OMB Guidance for implementing the privacy provisions of the E-Government Act of 2002. Washington, DC: Office of Management and Budget; 2003. September 26. Memorandum M-03-22.

[29] McCallister E, Grance T, Scarfone K. Guide to protecting the confidentiality of personally identifiable information (PII). Gaithersburg, MD: National Institute of Standards and Technology, Computer Security Division; April 2010. Special Publication 800-122.

[30] McCallister E, Grance T, Scarfone K. Guide to protecting the confidentiality of personally identifiable information (PII). Gaithersburg, MD: National Institute of Standards and Technology, Computer Security Division; April 2010. Special Publication 800-122. p. 3-3–3-5.

[31] Standards for security categorization of federal information and information systems. Gaithersburg, MD: National Institute of Standards and Technology, Computer Security Division; December 2003. Federal Information Processing Standards Publication 199. p. 4.

[32] Stine K, Kissel R, Barker W, Fahlsing J, Gulick J. Volume I: Guide for mapping types of information and information systems to security categories. Gaithersburg, MD: National Institute of Standards and Technology, Computer Security Division; August 2008. Special Publication 800-60 Revision 1. p. 31.

[33] Stine K, Kissel R, Barker W, Fahlsing J, Gulick J. Volume I: Guide for mapping types of information and information systems to security categories. Gaithersburg, MD: National Institute of Standards and Technology, Computer Security Division; August 2008. Special Publication 800-60 Revision 1.p. 27–28.

[34] Security categorization and control selection for national security systems. Fort Meade, MD: Committee on National Security Systems; 2009 Oct. CNSS Instruction 1253. p. 5. For security control baselines, see Appendix D.

[35] Security categorization and control selection for national security systems. Fort Meade, MD: Committee on National Security Systems; 2009 Oct. CNSS Instruction 1253. p. 10. For security control baselines, see Appendix D.

[36] Guide for applying the risk management framework to federal information systems. Gaithersburg, MD: National Institute of Standards and Technology, Computer Security Division; February 2010. Special Publication 800-37 Revision 1. p. 21–22.

[37] Federal Information Security Management Act of 2002, Pub. L. No. 107-347, 116 Stat. 2946. §305, codified at 44 U.S.C. §3505.

[38] Electronic Freedom of Information Act Amendments of 1996, Pub. L. No. 104-231, 110 Stat. 3048. §11, codifed at 5 U.S.C. §552(g).

[39] Preparation, submission, and execution of the budget. Washington (DC): Office of Management and Budget. 2011 Aug. Circular No. A-11, Revised (Transmittal Memorandum No. 85). Exhibit 53.

[40] Guide for applying the risk management framework to federal information systems. Gaithersburg, MD: National Institute of Standards and Technology, Computer Security Division; February 2010. Special Publication 800-37 Revision 1. p. 22.

[41] These terms are defined in FIPS 200. See Minimum security requirements for federal information and information systems. Gaithersburg, MD: National Institute of Standards and Technology, Computer Security Division; March 2006. Federal Information Processing Standards Publication 200. Appendix A.

[42] Recommended security controls for federal information systems and organizations. Gaithersburg, MD: National Institute of Standards and Technology, Computer Security Division; August 2009. Special Publication 800-53 Revision 3. p. 6.

[43] Ross R, Katzke S, Johnson A, Swanson M, Stoneburner G, Rogers G, Lee A. Recommended security controls for federal information systems. Gaithersburg, MD: National Institute of Standards and Technology, Computer Security Division; February 2005. Special Publication 800-53. p. 3.

[44] Minimum security requirements for federal information and information systems. Gaithersburg, MD: National Institute of Standards and Technology, Computer Security Division; March 2006. Federal Information Processing Standards Publication 200. p. 2–4.

[45] Recommended security controls for federal information systems and organizations. Gaithersburg, MD: National Institute of Standards and Technology, Computer Security Division; August 2009. Special Publication 800-53 Revision 3. Appendix E.

[46] Guide for applying the risk management framework to federal information systems. Gaithersburg, MD: National Institute of Standards and Technology, Computer Security Division; February 2010. Special Publication 800-37 Revision 1. p. 24.

[47] Swanson M, Hash J, Bowen P. Guide for developing security plans for federal information systems. Gaithersburg, MD: National Institute of Standards and Technology, Computer Security Division; February 2006. Special Publication 800-18 Revision 1. p. 16.

[48] Recommended security controls for federal information systems and organizations. Gaithersburg, MD: National Institute of Standards and Technology, Computer Security Division; August 2009. Special Publication 800-53 Revision 3. p. 11.

[49] Annex 1, Annex 2, and Annex 3 represent low-impact, moderate-impact, and high-impact security control baselines, respectively.

[50] Security categorization and control selection for national security systems. Fort Meade, MD: Committee on National Security Systems; October 2009. CNSS Instruction 1253. p. 22–33.

[51] Recommended security controls for federal information systems and organizations. Gaithersburg, MD: National Institute of Standards and Technology, Computer Security Division; August 2009. Special Publication 800-53 Revision 3. p. D-1.

[52] Recommended security controls for federal information systems and organizations. Gaithersburg, MD: National Institute of Standards and Technology, Computer Security Division; August 2009. Special Publication 800-53 Revision 3. p. D-1. Appendix F.

[53] Security and privacy controls for federal information systems and organizations. Gaithersburg, MD: National Institute of Standards and Technology, Computer Security Division; February 2012. Special Publication 800-53 Revision 4. Initial Public Draft. p. 25.

[54] Recommended security controls for federal information systems and organizations. Gaithersburg, MD: National Institute of Standards and Technology, Computer Security Division; August 2009. Special Publication 800-53 Revision 3. p. 20.

[55] Recommended security controls for federal information systems and organizations. Gaithersburg, MD: National Institute of Standards and Technology, Computer Security Division; August 2009. Special Publication 800-53 Revision 3. p. 22.

[56] Recommended security controls for federal information systems and organizations. Gaithersburg, MD: National Institute of Standards and Technology, Computer Security Division; August 2009. Special Publication 800-53 Revision 3. p. 23.

[57] Guide for applying the risk management framework to federal information systems. Gaithersburg, MD: National Institute of Standards and Technology, Computer Security Division; February 2010. Special Publication 800-37 Revision 1. p. 25.

[58] Security and privacy controls for federal information systems and organizations. Gaithersburg, MD: National Institute of Standards and Technology, Computer Security Division; February 2012. Special Publication 800-53 Revision 4. Initial Public Draft. p. 37.

[59] Guide for applying the risk management framework to federal information systems. Gaithersburg, MD: National Institute of Standards and Technology, Computer Security Division; February 2010. Special Publication 800-37 Revision 1. p. 26.

[60] Dempsey K, Chawla N, Johnson A, Johnson R, Jones A, Orebaugh A, Scholl M, Stine K. Information security continuous monitoring for federal information systems and organizations. Gaithersburg, MD: National Institute of Standards and Technology, Computer Security Division; September 2011. Special Publication 800-137.

[61] Guide for applying the risk management framework to federal information systems. Gaithersburg, MD: National Institute of Standards and Technology, Computer Security Division; February 2010. Special Publication 800-37 Revision 1. p. 27.

[62] Standards for security categorization of federal information and information systems. Gaithersburg, MD: National Institute of Standards and Technology, Computer Security Division; December 2003. Federal Information Processing Standards Publication 199.

[63] Minimum security requirements for federal information and information systems. Gaithersburg, MD: National Institute of Standards and Technology, Computer Security Division; March 2006. Federal Information Processing Standards Publication 200.

[64] Security categorization and control selection for national security systems. Fort Meade, MD: Committee on National Security Systems; October 2009. CNSS Instruction 1253.

[65] Recommended security controls for federal information systems and organizations. Gaithersburg, MD: National Institute of Standards and Technology, Computer Security Division; August 2009. Special Publication 800-53 Revision 3.

[66] Stine K, Kissel R, Barker W, Fahlsing J, Gulick J. Volume I: Guide for mapping types of information and information systems to security categories. Gaithersburg, MD: National Institute of Standards and Technology, Computer Security Division; August 2008. Special Publication 800-60 revision 1.

[67] Swanson M, Hash J, Bowen P. Guide for developing security plans for federal information systems. Gaithersburg, MD: National Institute of Standards and Technology, Computer Security Division; February 2006. Special Publication 800-18 revision 1.

Risk Management Framework Steps 3 & 4

8

INFORMATION IN THIS CHAPTER:

- Working with Security Control Baselines
- Key Roles and Responsibilities
- Tasks in RMF Step 3: Implement Security Controls
- Tasks in RMF Step 4: Assess Security Controls

Security control selection culminates in the specification of a tailored set of security controls—documented in the system security plan and approved by the system's authorizing official—that the system owner and the organization agree will satisfy the minimum security requirements for the system. Having reached agreement on what security controls the system needs, the focus of the Risk Management Framework process shifts to implementing the selected security controls and ensuring that the controls are implemented correctly and will achieve their intended security objectives. Step 3 of the RMF addresses security control implementation and the provision of detailed security control documentation to support the assessment process in step 4. Together, the tasks completed in these steps make tangible the controls planned for the system and produce most of the documentation and supporting information needed for the security authorization package that system owners assemble and submit for approval in step 5. Depending on the nature of the system, its security requirements, and its functional and technical capabilities, security control implementation may involve developing or acquiring new controls for the system, configuring existing controls, leveraging common controls provided elsewhere in the organization, or some combination of these alternatives. System owners and common control providers coordinate the efforts of security-focused personnel executing RMF tasks and system development or deployment teams conducting software development life cycle (SDLC) activities to ensure that all selected controls are implemented and configured properly. These teams perform various forms of testing as security controls are implemented and document technical specifications, secure configurations, and other implementation details for each control; all of this information is used in security control assessments. The tasks in steps 3 and 4 rely—more than any other parts of the RMF—on activities conducted and information produced within the scope of the SDLC; tight integration between the RMF and the SDLC is essential for efficient and effective completion of security control implementation and assessment.

WORKING WITH SECURITY CONTROL BASELINES

As described in Chapter 7, the security control catalog in Special Publication 800-53 establishes the control allocation for the security control baselines selected by each system owner on the basis of the system security categorization. Special Publication 800-53 is also a preferred source of information about controls removed from or added to security control baselines during the tailoring process and provides the primary point of reference for security control implementation and assessment. Special Publication 800-53A specifies security objectives and assessment procedures for each control in Special Publication 800-53, so these documents together offer important information to developers and other security control implementers about what the selected controls should do and how their implementation will be evaluated. In this way control descriptions and assessment procedures become key inputs to security design, engineering, testing, and documentation activities in the development and acquisition phase of the SDLC, as depicted in Figure 8.1. The tailored security control baselines documented in the system security plan also establish the scope for the security control assessment performed after implementation is complete. Personnel responsible for implementing security controls use the baseline—in

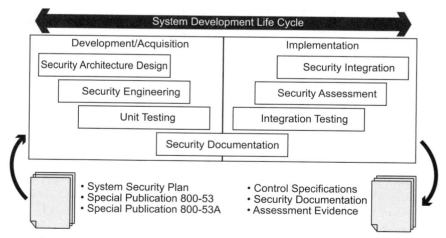

FIGURE 8.1 The Tasks in Steps 3 and 4 of the RMF Depend Heavily on Security Design, Engineering, Integration, Testing, and Documentation Activities Performed Within the Development/Acquisition and Implementation Phases of the SDLC

> **NOTE**
>
> As the description of security control implementation and assessment in this chapter makes clear, guidance to federal agencies on selecting security controls and assessing those controls once implemented share a common frame of reference in the security control framework defined in Special Publication 800-53. Special Publication 800-53A Revision 1 prescribes assessment objectives, methods, and objects for every security control in Special Publication 800-53 Revision 3. NIST typically issues revisions to the security control catalog before corresponding revisions to security control assessment procedures [2]. Many agencies wait to adopt new versions of Special Publication 800-53 until the associated assessment guidance is ready, so deciding which security control catalog version to follow is constrained by the availability of up-to-date assessment procedures. There are other practical considerations affecting agency migration from one version of Special Publication 800-53 to another, including the need to update internal policies, procedures, and guidelines based on previous versions and to evaluate the extent of changes required to comply with new versions of security control baselines.

conjunction with applicable organizational policies, procedures, and standards and assurance requirements for the system—to help determine expectations for how controls should be implemented and what level of detail should be provided in control specifications and other supporting documentation used as evidence in security control assessments.

The tasks in steps 3 and 4 of the RMF both span the development and acquisition and implementation phases of the SDLC; Special Publication 800-64 distinguishes implementation and assessment activities within each phase by their focus [1]. During the development phase security controls are designed, created, and integrated into the system, tested for functionality, and documented. In the implementation phase the focus shifts from the system in isolation to the system as it will be deployed in its operating environment, with a corresponding emphasis on developing, integrating, configuring, and testing common controls and system-specific controls associated with the deployment environment. Although the description of security control implementation and assessment in Special Publication 800-37 implies that each task is completed before the next begins, in practice implementation and assessment are often performed iteratively or even in parallel as project teams work to ensure that they address all security requirements and deploy systems with controls that satisfy minimum assurance requirements.

Assurance Requirements

NIST defines *assurance* as "the grounds for confidence that the security controls implemented within an information system are effective in their application" [3] and in Special Publication 800-53 establishes minimum assurance requirements for federal information systems based on their assigned impact levels. A system's assurance level corresponds to guidance directed at security control implementers that specifies the nature and extent of control implementation evidence required for low-impact, moderate-impact, and high-impact systems. These requirements, which apply to all security controls implemented for the system, are included in Table 8.1.

Agencies typically establish policies and procedures for security control implementation and documentation reflecting these assurance levels, either as part of standard SDLC processes and guidelines or as standalone guidance for achieving adequate security. Security control assessors use minimum assurance requirements to adjust their expectations about the types and amount of evidence they need in order to complete their assessments, so communicating the correct assurance level to security control implementers increases the likelihood that the activities they perform will satisfy assessment requirements.

Sources of Guidance on Security Controls

While NIST provides extensive guidance in Special Publication 800-53 on what security controls to implement and the objectives each is intended to achieve, federal guidance is far less prescriptive in terms of how controls should be implemented. The lack of comprehensive guidance on control implementation is understandable given the wide variety of security controls included in baselines among the management, operational, and technical classes into which NIST categorizes its controls. Conventional development and acquisition activities often focus on technical controls in the form of hardware, software, and infrastructure components deployed as part of the system and the documentation that describes their implementation. In contrast, many management controls are implemented as written documents or other artifacts used to govern the system once it is authorized, while operational controls are often implemented as processes and procedures captured in system documentation and executed by designated personnel during the system's operations and maintenance phase. NIST does offer narrowly focused guidance and recommendations on developing and implementing many kinds of controls; Table 8.2 lists Special Publications relevant to security control implementation and assessment, grouped by control class and indicating the core subject matter of each publication and the control families the guidance addresses. In addition to management, operational, and technical controls the table identifies broader scope guidance on controls and indicates technical controls typically implemented within general support systems or other common control providing contexts rather than by individual information systems.

Much of the guidance listed in Table 8.2 is intended to offer recommendations and accepted government or industry practices to agencies implementing security controls. Agencies typically use this guidance as along with many other sources potentially incorporated in system development and implementation plans. Many agencies maintain their own standards and practices or use those provided by the system integrators, vendors, or other contractors often responsible for building, deploying, and operating information systems for federal agencies.

Table 8.1 Minimum Assurance Requirements for Information Systems [4]

Requirement	Applies to Systems at:
Evidence that the security control is in place and functioning as intended	All impact levels
Documentation that provides, in sufficient detail to support control evaluation and testing, information including:	
• A functional description of the control	Moderate-impact level
• Design and implementation details of the control	High-impact level
Responsibilities and actions assigned to each control that increase confidence that the control when implemented will:	
• Meet its required function or intended purpose	Low-impact level
• Continuously and consistently satisfy functional requirements and objectives	Moderate-impact level
• Support improvements in control effectiveness	High-impact level
Evidence from control development and implementation that the control as implemented is complete, consistent, and correct	Moderate-and high-impact levels

Table 8.2 Guidance on Control Development, Implementation, Testing, and Operation [5]

Number (date)	Subject	Relevant 800-53 Control Families
Broadly Applicable Guidance on Controls		
800-23 (2000)	Assurance and use of tested products	Most operational and technical controls
800-27A (2004)	Security engineering principles	All controls
800-36 (2003)	Selecting security products	Most operational and technical controls
800-47 (2002)	Securing system interconnections	Access Control; Security Assessment and Authorization; System and Communications Protection
800-122 (2010)	Protecting personally identifiable information (PII)	Access Control; System and Information Integrity
Management and Operational Controls		
800-16 (1998)	Security training	Awareness and Training
800-18 (2006)	Developing security plans	Security Assessment and Authorization; Planning

Table 8.2 Guidance on Control Development, Implementation, Testing, and Operation [5] (*continued*)

Number (date)	Subject	Relevant 800-53 Control Families
800-30 (2012)	Risk assessment	Risk Assessment; System Assessment and Authorization
800-34 (2010)	Contingency planning	Contingency Planning
800-50 (2003)	Security awareness and training	Awareness and Training
800-61 (2008)	Security incident handling	Incident Response
800-84 (2006)	Testing, training, and exercises	Contingency Planning; Incident Response; Risk Assessment
800-88 (2006)	Media sanitization	Media Protection
800-92 (2006)	Log management	Audit and Accountability
800-115 (2008)	Security testing and assessment	Risk Assessment; System Assessment and Authorization; System and Information Integrity
800-117 (2010)	Security content automation protocol (SCAP)	Configuration Management; System and Information Integrity
800-128 (2011)	Security-focused configuration management	Configuration Management
800-137 (2011)	Continuous monitoring	System Assessment and Authorization; System and Information Integrity
Technical Controls		
800-19 (1999)	Mobile agent security	Access Control; System and Communications Protection
800-21 (2005)	Implementing cryptography	Access Control; Identification and Authentication; Media Protection; System and Communications Protection
800-25 (2000)	Public-key technology	Access Control; Identification and Authentication
800-28 (2008)	Active content and mobile code	System and Communications Protection
800-41 (2009)	Firewalls*	Access Control; System and Communications Protection; System and Information Integrity
800-44 (2007)	Securing public Web servers*	System and Communications Protection; System and Information Integrity
800-45 (2007)	E-mail security*	System and Communications Protection; System and Information Integrity
800-46 (2009)	Telework and remote access security*	Access Control; Identification and Authentication; System and Information Integrity
800-52 (2005)	Transport layer security (TLS)	Access Control; System and Communications Protection

Table 8.2 Guidance on Control Development, Implementation, Testing, and Operation[5] (*continued*)

Number (date)	Subject	Relevant 800-53 Control Families
800-57 (2007)	Key management	Access Control; System and Communications Protection
800-63 (2011)	Electronic authentication	Access Control; Identification and Authentication
800-77 (2005)	IPsec virtual private networks*	Access Control; System and Communications Protection
800-81 (2010)	Secure domain name system (DNS)*	System and Communications Protection
800-83 (2005)	Malware prevention and handling*	Incident Response; System and Information Integrity
800-94 (2007)	Intrusion detection and prevention*	Incident Response; System and Communications Protection; System and Information Integrity
800-95 (2007)	Secure Web services	System and Communications Protection; System and Information Integrity
800-97 (2007)	Wireless network security*	Access Control; System and Communications Protection; System and Information Integrity
800-98 (2007)	Radio frequency identification (RFID)*	Access Control; Physical and Environmental Protection
800-107 (2009)	Approved hash algorithms	System and Information Integrity
800-113 (2008)	SSL virtual private networks*	Access Control; System and Communications Protection
800-119 (2010)	Secure deployment of IPv6*	System and Communications Protection
800-120 (2009)	Wireless network authentication*	Access Control; Identification and Authentication
800-121 (2008)	Bluetooth security	Access Control
800-123 (2008)	Server security	Configuration Management; System and Information Integrity
800-125 (2011)	Securing virtualization technologies	System and Communications Protection
800-127 (2010)	Securing WiMAX*	Access Control; System and Communications Protection
800-144 (2011)	Public cloud computing*	System and Communications Protection
800-153 (2012)	Securing wireless local area networks (WLANs)	Access Control; System and Communications Protection

* Indicates guidance targeted at controls typically implemented by common control providers and inherited by information systems.

ROLES AND RESPONSIBILITIES

Many individuals working on security and overall system development share responsibility for implementing and assessing security controls in federal information systems. Guidance to federal agencies emphasizes the value of integrated project teams that bring together the knowledge and skills necessary to develop and implement information systems that satisfy all organizational requirements, not just those focused on security [6]. Compared to the other steps in the RMF, security control implementation involves the largest number of individuals with contributing roles from outside the core security team, because security engineers, architects, and system security officers typically have responsibility for developing only a subset of the controls needed for their information systems. Security control assessment also relies on personnel in non-security-focused roles and information they produced to furnish the evidence needed to support accurate and complete assessments. In most cases the role of security control assessor, who has primary responsibility for performing the tasks in step 4, should also be assigned to an individual or group of individuals outside the development, operational, or management chain for the system to ensure assessor independence [7]. System owners and common control providers are ultimately responsible for ensuring the effective implementation of the controls specified in their system security plans, but actual development, acquisition, implementation, configuration, and testing of those controls is accomplished by many different individuals working under their direction.

Management Controls

Management controls in Special Publication 800-53 largely consist of plans, written policies and procedures, and other information in document form. Even in agencies providing document templates and detailed instructions to system owners on completing these artifacts, the skill set and experience required to develop security plans and other documentation differs substantially from the skills associated with implementing technical controls. Organization-level information security programs often produce the policies and procedures identified as the first control in each family in Special Publication 800-53. Where system-specific requirements fall outside the scope covered by organizational policies and procedures these controls may more appropriately be implemented as hybrid controls, requiring system owners and information security officers to provide documentation to augment or explain deviations from organizational standards. System owners also need to take or delegate responsibility for developing the plans documenting management processes applicable to various controls, such as plans for configuration management, incident response, contingency operations, technology and services acquisition, risk assessment, testing, and monitoring, in addition to the system security plan and plan of action and milestones needed for security authorization.

Operational Controls

Implementing and assessing operational controls often requires explicit system-specific or organizational capabilities to be funded, established, staffed, and managed on an ongoing basis. Many operational controls have formally documented processes and procedures to explain their intended function and guide the execution of the services, functions, or activities they provide, but assessment procedures for these controls often require evidence of operational capabilities, including the results of tests or exercises. Security control assessors may choose to interview personnel with responsibility for performing processes and activities specified in operational controls [8], so the key role involved in implementing and assessing these controls includes the individuals who operate or administer the relevant capabilities for the system (or for the organization in the case of common controls). The breadth of controls within the operational family demands a wide range of implementation skills and abilities, particularly when requirements warrant operational control resources dedicated to the information system. Agencies often implement certain types of operational controls at the organizational level, including security awareness and training, contingency planning, incident response, and continuous monitoring. Other operational controls may be prescribed by the organization's information security program but implemented at an information system level, such as configuration management, system maintenance, personnel security, and many aspects of system and information integrity.

Technical Controls

The implementation and assessment of technical controls includes developing system functionality related to protecting confidentiality, integrity, or availability; acquiring, installing, and configuring security-specific tools or components to provide capabilities beyond those delivered in the system; and leveraging common controls available for use with the system. System developers and other control implementers use the tailored security control baseline produced in step 2 of the RMF and the security control objectives and assessment procedures specified in Special Publication 800-53A to guide the implementation of technical controls in a manner that satisfies system and organizational requirements and meets assessment objectives and assurance requirements. Security officers and security engineers work closely with system developers and system architects to incorporate selected security controls into the design of the system and ensure that the necessary capabilities are developed or acquired before the system moves into the SDLC implementation phase. The RMF emphasizes the need for thorough documentation describing how security controls are implemented to support assessment and provide traceability to system requirements and implementation decisions made for the system [9]. The potential exists for wide variation in the way different organizations—and systems within an organization—implement technical security controls, especially considering the large number of optional controls and control enhancements in the technical control families of system and communications protection, access control, identification and authentication, and audit and accountability. Some controls categorized as operational also have supporting technologies associated with them, such as the scanning, data gathering, and notification tools used in continuous monitoring.

Program Management, Infrastructure, and Other Common Controls

Beginning with Revision 3 of Special Publication 800-53, released in 2009, NIST added a program management family to the security control catalog with 11 management controls applicable to organization-level information security programs. While system owners and common control providers within an agency are rarely directly responsible for the implementation of these controls, the controls are required for all federal agencies and are intended to support all security control baselines [10]. Special Publication 800-53A also includes detailed assessment procedures for program management controls so depending on organizational policy and requirements driving security control assessments, the scope of an information system security assessment may include program management controls, either directly assessed with the system or using the results of existing assessments as would be the case with any common controls inherited by the system. Other types of security controls—notably including those related to physical and environmental security, network and communications infrastructure, and incident response and other types of continuous monitoring—are frequently provided as common controls. System owners are not responsible for implementing or assessing common controls used by their systems unless there is some shared responsibility between the common control provider and the system owner (as with hybrid controls) or the system security plans and security assessment reports addressing the common controls are insufficient to satisfy the assurance requirements for the system [11].

STEP 3: IMPLEMENT SECURITY CONTROLS

In step 3 of the RMF, the system owner incorporates the controls listed in the approved system security plan within the functional and technical requirements specified for the system and its overall design. The two tasks in step 3—security control implementation and security control documentation—are executed within the scope of the development (or acquisition) and implementation phases of the SDLC through a series of activities in which the information system security officer, security engineer, and other personnel responsible for executing the RMF collaborate with system architects and system developers working to deliver the system. Ideally, coordinated interaction between security-focused personnel and the functional and technical members of the system development team begins early in the system development life cycle so that roles and expected contributions from all team members are well understood by the time the system enters the development phase. As shown in Figure 8.2, existing documentation in the form of system requirements

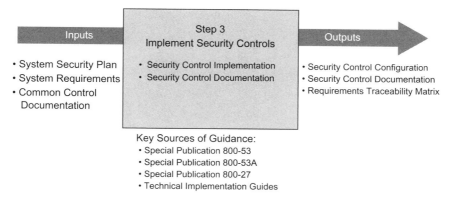

Key Sources of Guidance:
- Special Publication 800-53
- Special Publication 800-53A
- Special Publication 800-27
- Technical Implementation Guides

FIGURE 8.2 In Step 3 of the RMF, System Development, Implementation, and Security Teams Implement the Agreed-Upon Set of Controls Selected for the System and Documented in the Approved System Security Plan and Describe the Controls in Sufficient Detail to Enable Security Control Assessors to Verify Their Implementation Satisfies the System Security Requirements and is Consistent with Applicable Standards and Guidelines

---

WARNING

System owners need to make candid assessments regarding the maturity of their organization's system development life cycle processes, especially with respect executing the SDLC for their information systems. It is important to set realistic expectations about the timely availability, completeness, and quality of system documentation, plans, and other information needed in association with security control implementation so the security-focused personnel performing RMF tasks understand where their assistance may be required or what management and operational controls need to be produced. Inaccurate assumptions about the ability of the development team to implement and document all relevant controls for the system will likely result in delays in both security control implementation and assessment if the evidence needed to perform the security control assessment is not complete or readily available.

---

and descriptions of system-specific and common controls drives security control implementation activities. These activities, performed as part of the SDLC development phase, include architectural design, system engineering, testing, and writing documentation [1]. The details underlying these activities vary depending on the type of controls to be implemented and their source, as different controls may potentially be custom developed, enabled through deployment or configuration of capabilities already designed into the system, delivered using commercially available or open-source tools, or inherited from common control providers. The outputs resulting from this step include a set of implemented, correctly configured controls documented at a level of detail sufficient to support security control assessment and other system authorization tasks and to allow functional and technical validation against the requirements specified for the system.

Security Architecture Design

Following security control selection, the system security plan describes what controls and control enhancements will be implemented for the system. During security control implementation, system owners and functional and technical members of the project team determine how each control should be implemented and assign responsibility for all controls to personnel with appropriate skills and system knowledge to implement them. As noted above in the Roles and Responsibilities section, the nature of the work required to implement a control varies considerably across management, operational, and technical controls. Part of the process of designing the security architecture for the system is distinguishing among different types of controls and identifying the resources available within the organization to provide them. Architectural design considers the system and the functions and services it will perform in the context of the organization's enterprise architecture. This perspective helps identify existing business processes, services, technologies, and capabilities the system may be able to reuse and ensures that the system does not conflict with or duplicate functions or services already deployed in the organization [12]. Architecture design also typically produces detailed diagrams showing the different components making up the system and its operating environment, points of interconnection to other systems or environments, and the placement or integration of security controls. Any diagrams created during security control implementation may be added to the system description section of the system security plan. The security architecture indicates which security controls apply to different components of the system (recognizing that not all controls apply to all parts of each system) and clearly identifies common or hybrid controls allocated to the system [13]. With respect to the common controls identified in the system security plan, the security architecture design process analyzes the descriptions in common control documentation to either validate that the common controls satisfy relevant requirements for the information system or to determine if any of the controls are better suited to hybrid or system-specific implementation.

Security Engineering and Control Implementation

Security engineering is the process of incorporating security controls into the information system so that they become an integral part of the system's operational capabilities. Current legislation and guidance to agencies on effective information resources management emphasizes the integration of security in all phases of the system development life cycle, an idea that is sometimes easier to accept in principle than to put into practice. Security engineering principles and practices apply most directly to the design, development, and implementation of technical controls, although NIST guidance consistently highlights the importance of considering management and operational controls such as policies and procedures when designing and implementing system security [15]. Security engineering within the software development life cycle comprises security-focused design, software development, coding, and configuration, some or all of which may be relevant for a given information system. System development teams performing security engineering activities may choose to follow applicable guidance from NIST or other government sources, industry standards and practices, internal agency procedures, or methods recommended by vendors, contractors, or other third-party sources. Potentially relevant sources include:

*   NIST Special Publication 800-27 Revision A, *Engineering Principles for Information Technology Security* [15].
*   DHS Software Assurance Workgroup, *Software Assurance: A Curriculum Guide to the Common Body of Knowledge to Produce, Acquire and Sustain Secure Software* [16].
*   DoD Information Assurance Technology Analysis Center, *Software Security Assurance: A State of the Art Report* [17].
*   ISO/IEC 15026, *Systems and Software Engineering—Systems and Software Assurance* [18].

These sources provide general guidance on secure systems engineering and recommended practices for software assurance; the decision to use any particular source within an agency depends on applicable organizational policy, requirements, or constraints for system development projects. Special Publication 800-27 presents a set of 33 security engineering principles organizations should consider in the design, development, and operation of their information systems. These principles are organized into six categories representing the ideas that security provides a foundation for information systems, is risk based, should be easy to use, increases system and organizational resilience, reduces vulnerabilities, and is designed with the network in mind [19]. Special Publication 800-27 aligns security engineering principles to the same five SDLC phases used in Special Publication 800-64 and other NIST guidance; it identifies all 33 principles as applicable to the SDLC development phase. Guidance from DHS' Software Assurance Workgroup and DoD's Information Assurance Technology Analysis Center (IATAC) is educational in nature, intended primarily to help train system developers in secure engineering and software assurance practices—incorporating standards such as ISO/IEC 15026—so that the systems they produce will be more secure by design.

Secure Development, Implementation, and Configuration

Security engineering principles offer general guidance or rules governing security control design and development, but developers and other personnel tasked with implementing information system security controls often require more explicit development and implementation instructions. While many available industry sources address secure coding and associated security-related development techniques applicable to information systems using custom-developed software [20], NIST and most other federal sources of guidance do not prescribe development practices at a level of granularity that would inform custom development using specific technologies or programming languages. Instead, guidance to agencies focuses on implementing and validating secure configuration for different types of system components and IT products. Representative examples of this type of guidance includes technology-specific guidelines such as many of the documents listed in Table 8.1 and security technical implementation guides (STIGs) or other types of security configuration checklists [21]. The potential for a single information system to implement controls subject to different standard configuration specifications, development and implementation practices, and general sources of secure engineering guidance makes it essential for security control implementers to provide detailed documentation describing the implementation and configuration of each security control.

Commercially Available Security Tools

Many security controls implemented in federal information systems are acquired rather than developed. FISMA explicitly recognizes "that commercially developed information security products offer advanced, dynamic, robust, and effective information security solutions [22]." With the vast array of products available and the rapid pace of market evolution in security solutions, guidance on IT product selection and acquisition typically stops short of recommending specific hardware or software but does emphasize the benefits of choosing tested or certified products when possible. Special Publication 800-23 offers guidance to agencies on acquiring and using technology products that have been tested to demonstrate various levels of security assurance [23]. Government agencies determine the assurance level of a tool or technology used in a system through a variety of methods—including conventional security testing and assessment and through the application of secure development practices—but NIST gives special attention to formal evaluation of products by approved or accredited testing and certification organizations such as those accredited through its National Voluntary Laboratory Accreditation Program (NVLAP). When controls come from acquired tools or technology, tested and certified technologies may be favored under organizational or government-wide policy, but policies and standards vary among organizations. Agencies with strong adherence to tested or certified product standards may constrain the acquisition process and even foreclose technical options such as open-source technology, which tends not to be certified except in specific deployment contexts or configurations.

Various security testing programs exist to evaluate commercially available hardware and software products, including evaluations conducted by NIST and other government agencies and those performed by government-approved or endorsed testing and certification providers outside the government. The Common Criteria for Information Technology Security Evaluation is an international standard used to evaluate, assert, and certify the relative security assurance levels of hardware and software products [24]. NIST and the NSA maintain the National Information Assurance Partnership (NIAP) to evaluate IT products for conformance to Common

> **NOTE**
>
> The meaning of the terms *certified* or *certification* in the context of acquiring and implementing IT products is different than in the context of system authorization. The certification of a product is typically an attestation by an approved certifying agent that the product has specific properties or meets explicit functional objectives. This is similar to but distinct from the certification of a system in support of an authorization decision, which assesses the proper implementation and operational effectiveness of security controls against the security requirements established for the system. Because third-party certifications are awarded without consideration for the operational environment into which certified products are deployed or any system-specific attributes, product certifications cannot substitute for required control examination and testing conducted in the course of security control assessments.

Criteria. Under the Common Criteria Evaluation and Validation Scheme for IT Security (CCEVS), NIAP oversees independent testing organizations and manages research and development efforts to specify protection profiles for various types of technologies and security functions [25]. Once certified, products evaluated against Common Criteria standards are listed on a publicly available Website, providing the assurance level achieved, date of certification, and full security report details for each product [26]. System owners, security officers, IT managers, acquisition officials, and other agency personnel involved in the selection of information technology use certification information to confirm that the products they implement satisfy applicable security requirements, standards, and policies.

Security Control Documentation

During step 3 of the RMF, system owners update the system security plan to describe the implementation details for system-specific, hybrid, and common controls (working in collaboration with common control providers where appropriate), developing supplemental control configurations, technical specifications, and other documentation as needed to support ongoing management of the system once it is operational and to provide evidence for the security control assessment. In addition to control descriptions reflected in the system security plan, the implementation of management and operational controls results in the production of many other documents that either directly represent required security controls or describe security controls as implemented. These documents typically include plans for configuration management, contingency operations, incident response, system maintenance and administration, continuous monitoring, and security awareness and training. For technical controls, Special Publication 800-37 calls for documentation to include not only technical implementation details but also functional descriptions of expected control behavior and the inputs and outputs anticipated for each component in the information system [9]. Organizations determine the amount of information and level of detail required for each implemented control, considering factors such as the

> **TIP**
>
> Security control documentation is an essential form of evidence for security control assessments, used to support both examine and test assessment methods. Conventional SDLC development and implementation phase activities include component, system, and integration testing that give security control implementers the opportunity to test controls—refining their implementation or configuration as necessary—in advance of testing within the scope of security control assessments. Such preliminary testing supports the security requirements traceability sought during the SDLC development and implementation phases and can help avoid delays in system deployment incurred when security control assessments identify weaknesses that must be remediated prior to system authorization.

complexity and impact level of the system while also balancing the effort required to produce documentation with other system development and RMF tasks potentially competing for the same resources.

NIST encourages agencies to leverage existing sources of technical information where feasible when producing security control documentation, including functional and technical specifications from vendors responsible for IT products incorporated into the system, policies, procedures, and plans for management and operational controls from the organizational entities that implement them, and similar documentation from common control providers. System owners can refer to applicable control assessment procedures in Special Publication 800-53A to determine the evidence requirements anticipated for the assessment process and ensure that the documentation produced during security control implementation is sufficient to meet those requirements.

STEP 4: ASSESS SECURITY CONTROLS

The security control assessment and associated tasks performed in step 4 of the RMF gather and evaluate security control information and evidence produced by the information security program, common control providers, and personnel responsible for developing and deploying the information system. The security assessment process and the security control assessors who execute it typically have no responsibility for developing or enhancing any security controls—assessment considers what has already been implemented or accomplished and produces a series of findings as to whether the security controls implemented for the system satisfy their intended objectives. As shown in Figure 8.3, the security control assessment process relies on documentation and other evidence developed during the tasks in the prior steps in the RMF and produces a separate set of documentation recording the assessment results, identifying any findings differing from expectations, and making recommendations for corrective actions to address any weaknesses or deficiencies found in the security posture of the information system.

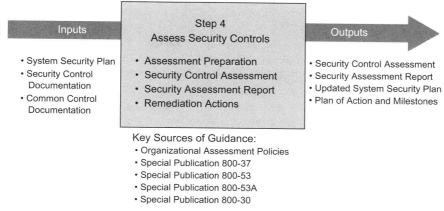

FIGURE 8.3 A Security Control Assessment Evaluates System Documentation, the System Itself, and Other Relevant Evidence to Assess the Extent to Which Implemented Security Controls Satisfy System Security Requirements and Meet Explicit Security Objectives, Identifying Security Control Gaps or Weaknesses and Making Recommendations for Corrective Action

The security control assessment and the security assessment report produced during the process provide essential information used by authorizing officials to make system authorization decisions, but assessments support many other security, risk, and information resources management processes executed at a broader level than the RMF. Organizations can use the information resulting from security control assessments to [27]:

- Identify issues or shortcomings in the organization's implementation of the RMF.
- Identify and document information system weaknesses and deficiencies.
- Prioritize corrective actions, deficiency mediation, or other responses to risks associated with assessment findings.
- Confirm through re-assessment of relevant controls that identified information system weaknesses and deficiencies have been addressed.
- Support continuous monitoring activities and information security situational awareness.
- Inform IT investment business cases and budgetary decisions.

Within the scope of the RMF process, security control assessment is both the focus of step 4 and a key element in continuous monitoring and other operational security management functions addressed in step 6. Security assessments may be performed at multiple stages of the system development life cycle, where control developers and implementers can leverage specific assessment procedures to support activities in the SDLC development and implementation phases such as design and code reviews, vulnerability scanning, functional validation, and unit, integration, and regression testing [28]. Because one primary purpose of security control assessment is the identification of weaknesses or deficiencies in implemented controls, the early identification of such problems may afford opportunities to take corrective action with fewer resources than would be required if the problems were discovered after implementation. System owners and common control providers also conduct security control assessments during the operations and maintenance phase of the SDLC to confirm the proper function and configuration of controls provisioned for their information systems. Periodic control assessments for operational systems help satisfy requirements for federal agencies specified in FISMA [29] and comply with agency and system-specific continuous monitoring strategies developed during the RMF process. Agencies often conduct security assessments during the disposal phase of the SDLC as well, to help ensure that sensitive information or other assets are removed from the information system and its storage media prior to disposal [28].

Security Control Assessment Components

Security control assessment guidance in Special Publication 800-53A provides detailed assessment procedures for each control in Special Publication 800-53, presented in a standard format. Each assessment procedure includes one or more assessment *objectives* that state precisely what the assessor is trying to determine to evaluate the effectiveness of each assessed control. Each assessment objective is associated with assessment *methods* and assessment *objects* that prescribe how assessors should evaluate the control and what the focus of evaluations using each method should be. Assessment methods include examine, interview, and test [30]:

- The *examine* method is the process of reviewing, inspecting, observing, studying, or analyzing assessment objects that may include specifications, mechanisms, or activities.
- The *interview* method is the process of holding discussions with individuals or groups of individuals (the assessment objects) within an organization to facilitate assessor understanding, achieve clarification, or obtain evidence regarding implemented security controls.
- The *test* method is the process of exercising one or more assessment objects, such as mechanisms or activities, under specified conditions to compare actual with expected or intended behavior.

Assessors work with system owners during the security control assessment planning process to choose the appropriate methods and objects for each control and to determine the *depth* and *coverage* associated with each assessment method. Values for both of these attributes include basic, focused, and comprehensive, corresponding to a hierarchical set of requirements for performing examination, interviewing, and testing with a scope and level of detail commensurate with the minimum assurance requirements for the system. Special Publication 800-53A describes expectations for basic, focused, and comprehensive examinations, interviews, and tests [31]. Security control assessors and system owners use this guidance to plan the level of effort and amount and nature of evidence needed to perform the assessment of each control and to guide the level of detail needed for assessment information documented by assessors in security assessment reports.

Organizations have substantial flexibility to adapt security control assessment procedures to suit their information systems and the environments in which those systems operate. Much as the security control selection process allows agencies to tailor minimum security baselines to reflect the requirements of each system, system owners and security control assessors can tailor the recommended assessment procedures in Special Publication 800-53A. Some agencies prefer to use standardized, explicit instructions on assessing security controls at specific levels of assurance; for these agencies NIST offers a set of security control assessment cases—one for each control in Special Publication 800-53 Revision 3—produced in collaboration with several federal agencies under the Assessment Case Development Project [32]. The assessment cases explain specific steps assessors should follow to gather evidence and evaluate controls and control enhancements using each of the relevant assessment methods. Assessment cases are developed from a government-wide perspective, so agencies following procedures prescribed in assessment cases may still need to adjust them for organizational or system-specific requirements. Where available assessment cases align well with agency or system-level needs, their use can reduce the time and level of effort required to develop security assessment plans.

Special Publication 800-37 divides the security control assessment step of the RMF into four sequential tasks: preparing for assessment, performing the security control assessment, developing the security assessment report, and conducting remediation actions to address findings in the security assessment report. The task descriptions in the RMF also direct system owners and security control assessors to Special Publication 800-53A, *Guide for Assessing the Security Controls in Federal Information Systems and Organizations*, as the primary source of guidance for all assessment-related activities. The assessment process recommended in Special Publication 800-53A also has four steps, shown in Figure 8.4, which differ slightly in scope from corresponding RMF tasks and which offer detailed descriptions of the activities, prerequisites, expected outcomes, and key considerations applicable to each part of the assessment process.

Assessment Preparation

The assessment preparation task within step 4 of the RMF comprises activities described in Special Publication 800-53A associated with preparing for assessments and developing security assessment plans. Security control assessors develop security assessment plans for each information system, but some assessment-supporting activities may be performed at the organization level in addition to system-specific preparations. Many agencies develop assessment procedures tailored to

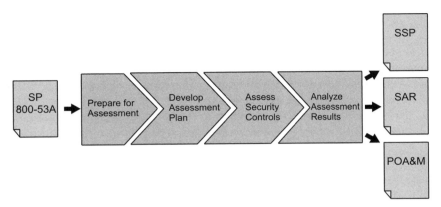

FIGURE 8.4 The Security Control Assessment Process Includes Detailed Preparation and Planning Activities Prior to the Assessment Itself, as Well as the Analysis of Findings Produced from the Assessment and the Development of Recommendations for Taking Corrective Action to Remediate Any Identified Weaknesses or Deficiencies

their organizational requirements, operating environments, and risk tolerance levels and make these procedures available (on an optional or mandatory basis) for use in information system assessments. Similarly, organizational information security programs may develop document templates for recording control assessment results and producing security assessment reports or deploy automated assessment tools or other mechanisms to facilitate the consistent execution of assessments across the organization.

The security control assessment process begins with information gathering, the identification of assessors and supporting resources, and other activities to confirm that the system, its operating environment, and its supporting resources are ready for the assessment. NIST identifies assessment preparation activities conducted by the organization, system owner, and security control assessors; Table 8.3 summarizes these activities.

Scoping the Assessment

The level of effort required to properly prepare for a security control assessment is—like the assessment itself—driven by the scope of the assessment, in terms of the number and types of security controls to be assessed, the assessment procedures chosen, and the amount and variety of evidence needed to support the efficient application of those procedures. NIST identifies three factors influencing the selection of assessment procedures and the extent of the assessment: the system security categorization, the level of assurance the organization needs to satisfy to determine the effectiveness of implemented security controls, and the set of security controls selected for the system that fall within the scope of the assessment [34]. Special Publication 800-53A provides assessment procedures for every control and control enhancement

Table 8.3 Security Control Assessment Preparation Activities [33]

Level	Activities
Organizational Preparation	<ul><li>Ensure that appropriate policies covering security control assessments are in place and understood by system owners and others within the organization to whom they apply</li><li>Ensure that the steps in the RMF preceding the security control assessment have been successfully completed</li><li>Ensure that appropriate organizational responsibility is assigned for development and implementation of common controls</li></ul>
System Owner Preparation	<ul><li>Establish the objectives and scope of the security control assessment</li><li>Notify appropriate organizational officials of the pending assessment and allocating necessary resources to carry it out</li><li>Establish appropriate communication channels among personnel and organizational entities with an interest in or affected by the assessment</li><li>Establish time frames for completing the security control assessment and associated milestones and decision points</li><li>Identify and select a competent and appropriately independent assessor or assessment team that will be responsible for conducting the security control assessment</li><li>Collect documentation and other evidentiary artifacts to provide to assessors</li><li>Establish an understanding between the organization and the assessor to minimize ambiguities or misunderstandings about security control implementation and any security control weaknesses or deficiencies identified during the assessment</li></ul>

Table 8.3 Security Control Assessment Preparation Activities [33] (*continued*)

Level	Activities
Assessor Preparation	• Obtain a general understanding of the organization's operations and how the information system to be assessed supports those operations • Obtain an understanding of the functional characteristics and technical architecture of the system • Obtain a thorough understanding of the security controls being assessed, including system-specific, hybrid, and common controls • Identify the organizational entities responsible for the development, implementation, and assessment and documentation of common controls • Establish appropriate organizational points of contact needed to carry out the security control assessment • Obtain documentation, control implementation specifications, and other artifacts needed for the security control assessment • Obtain any previous assessment results that may be appropriately reused for the security control assessment • Meet with appropriate organizational officials to ensure common understanding for assessment objectives and the proposed rigor and scope of the assessment • Develop a security assessment plan

in the security control catalog in Special Publication 800-53, so the starting point for planning and preparing for assessment is identifying the exact set of controls to be assessed and the assessment approach to be employed for those controls. There is no expectation that an agency use all the methods and objects provided in Special Publication 800-53A to assess its information systems. Instead, agencies and their system

> **NOTE**
>
> Although they share some similarities, agencies and security control assessors must recognize that *assessment cases* and *assurance cases* are different things. The scope of an assessment case is limited to a single security control; in contrast, assurance cases typically apply to entire information systems. Both types of cases describe the evidence required to support a determination or assessment finding, but for assessment cases those determinations are whether controls satisfy explicit security objectives, while assurance cases seek to demonstrate the validity of a claim about a system's security.

owners adapt assessment procedures to achieve the intended assessment objectives, taking into consideration factors such as the impact level of the system and assurance requirements that must be satisfied. One approach to security control assessment scoping recommended in guidance to federal agencies is the development and use of explicit *assurance cases* that specify the evidence necessary to demonstrate the validity of a claim about an information system such as the assertion that a system is adequately secure [35]. Organizations use assurance cases when an assessment needs to show a system exhibits a specific property or characteristic, such as reliability, resilience, or stability. In the case of security control assessments as defined within the RMF, the security assessment report documents the assurance case for the system by describing all the evidence used by the assessor to determine the effectiveness of implemented security controls. Determining the scope of the assessment and the timeline in which it needs to be performed also helps system owners allocate sufficient resources to the assessment, including the decision to assign more than one assessor to the task. Given the subjective nature of security control effectiveness determinations, agencies dividing assessment activities among multiple assessors need to ensure that each assessor has sufficient expertise to evaluate their assigned controls and that all assessors have a common understanding of the criteria for making a "satisfied" finding.

Assessor Qualifications

Whether the security control assessment is performed by a single assessor or an assessment team, agencies and their system owners need to evaluate assessment provider qualifications to ensure that assessors have sufficient expertise and capabilities to carry out the assessment of all security controls. Given the variety of management, operational, and technical controls an assessor needs to evaluate, assessment providers need a broad knowledge base and the technical expertise to determine the effectiveness of many different types of controls and understand the information systems they protect. For technical controls the necessary skills may include penetration testing or other hands-on approaches to verifying control implementations and validating specifications or configurations. For management and operational controls, assessors must have the knowledge and experience to assess the content quality and completeness of plans and procedures and other document-based evidence and the proper execution of security processes. Prior to the release of the RMF, NIST

> **NOTE**
>
> Security control assessment procedures focus assessor attention on determination statements used to evaluate the extent to which each control meets specific security objectives. Current guidance specifies just two possible findings for each determination statement—satisfied or other than satisfied—that require assessors to apply expert judgment to evaluate the effectiveness of each implemented control. This approach represents a stark contrast to the security self-assessment guidance that many agencies followed before NIST first published Special Publication 800-53A in 2008. That guidance, withdrawn when Special Publication 800-53A superceded it, used a five-level effectiveness rating scale emphasizing the presence of required controls and their level of integration within an organization's information security program [37]. Security control assessments using the procedures prescribed in Special Publication 800-53A are intended to provide a thorough evaluation of security control effectiveness, but agencies and system owners choosing assessors need to be aware that deeper or more rigorous levels of analysis often require more experienced assessors.

developed a draft interagency report describing requirements for security control assessment providers that identifies relevant knowledge, skills, and abilities assessors should possess and includes a checklist for agencies to use to validate assessment providers against organizational requirements [36]. Agencies also need to consider the objectivity of their assessors—characterized in NIST guidance as the level of *assessor independence*—to help ensure that assessment findings are impartial and that assessments are free of inappropriate influence from system owners or others with a vested stake in the outcome. The precise level of independence required for a particular security control assessment varies according to organizational policy, the impact level of the system, or extenuating circumstances that might require assessments to be performed by individuals subject to managerial oversight of the system owner despite the potential conflict of interest. NIST assigns the responsibility for specifying the required level of assessor independence to authorizing officials, who rely on the reliability, credibility, and objectivity of security assessment results to arrive at accurate determinations of risk and make appropriate system authorization decisions [7].

Security Assessment Plan

The security assessment plan documents the controls and control enhancements to be assessed, based on the purpose of the assessment and the implemented controls identified and described in the system security plan. The security assessment plan defines the scope of the assessment, in particular indicating whether a complete or partial assessment will be performed and if the assessment is intended to support initial pre-authorization activities associated with a new or significantly changed system or ongoing assessment used for operational systems. The security assessment plan also describes the procedures to be used for each control—typically drawn from Special Publication 800-53A or from available assessment cases and tailored as necessary to satisfy organizational or system-specific requirements—including the selection of assessment methods and objects and assigned depth and coverage attributes. The process of developing a security assessment plan includes the following actions [38]:

- Determine the set of security controls and control enhancements to be included in the scope of the assessment.
- Select the appropriate assessment procedures to be used based on the set of controls and control enhancements within scope and on organizational factors such as minimum assurance levels.
- Tailor the assessment methods and objects to agency or system-specific requirements and assign depth and coverage attribute values to each selected method.
- Develop additional assessment procedures to address any security requirements or controls implemented that fall outside the scope of the security control catalog in Special Publication 800-53.
- Document the resource requirements and anticipated time to complete the assessment, considering opportunities to sequence or consolidate procedures to reduce duplication of effort.
- Finalize the assessment plan and obtain the necessary approvals to execute the security control assessment according to the plan.

The security control assessor submits the assessment plan for approval—by system owners, authorizing officials, or other designated organizational officials—prior to initiating the assessment. The assessment plan should include sufficient detail to clearly indicate the scope of the assessment, the schedule for completing it, the individual or individuals responsible, and the assessment procedures planned for assessing each control. System owners rely on the information in the assessment plan to allocate appropriate resources to the assessment, including personnel who will provide documentation, participate in interviews, or facilitate access to the system as well as those performing the assessment.

Security Control Assessment

With an approved, complete security assessment plan in place, the security control assessment should proceed according to the schedule and approach specified in the plan. The security control assessment verifies the implementation of security controls documented in the system security plan by examining evidence produced by control implementers, interviewing personnel with knowledge of the system, and testing relevant controls to determine whether they function as expected. The assessment follows procedures specified for each control in the security assessment plan, examining, interviewing, or testing relevant assessment objects and reviewing available evidence to make a determination for each assessment objective. For each determination statement included in selected assessment procedures, the evaluation of evidence by the assessor results in a finding of "satisfied" or "other than satisfied [39]". Assessors achieve assessment objectives for each control by performing the selected assessment methods on appropriate assessment objects and documenting the evidence used to evaluate each determination statement. Assessors reach a finding of satisfied if the evidence associated with each determination statement supports a conclusion that the control meets the assessment objective. A finding of other than satisfied indicates that the evidence associated with the determination statement is insufficient to meet the assessment objective. While the discovery of weaknesses or deficiencies in a control's implementation results in an other-than-satisfied finding, the same finding may be warranted in other circumstances, such as cases where the assessor cannot obtain sufficient information to evaluate the determination statement for a control.

Security control assessment findings should be objective, evidence-based indications of the way the organization implements each security control. Because assessors use documentation and observation as sources of evidence for many assessed controls and must judge the completeness, correctness, and quality of this evidence, complete objectivity is not always feasible. The assessment cases NIST provides [32] to encourage more efficient and consistent security control assessments offer recommendations to assessors in terms of what actions to take and what sequence of steps to follow, but they do not define standard or reference implementations that reflect satisfactory achievement of assessment objectives. For each other-than-satisfied finding, assessors document what aspects of the security control were deemed unsatisfactory or were unable to be assessed and describe how the control as implemented differs from what was planned or expected. Assessors should document security control assessment results at a level of detail appropriate for the type of assessment being performed and in accordance with organizational policy and any requirements or expectations specified by the authorizing officials who will review the assessment results as part of the risk determination underlying authorization decisions.

Security Assessment Report

The primary result of the security control assessment process is the security assessment report, which documents the assurance case for the information system and is one of three key documents (with the system security plan and plan of action and milestones) in the security authorization package prepared by information system owners and common control providers and submitted to authorizing officials. The security assessment report documents assessment findings and indicates the effectiveness determined for each security control implemented for the information system. The development of the security assessment report is described in detail in Chapter 11, but the general format and content of security assessment reports often follows recommendations provided by NIST in Special Publication 800-53A [40]. The security assessment report documents assessment findings and recommendations for correcting any weaknesses, deficiencies, or other-than-satisfied determinations made during the assessment. The content provided in security assessment reports includes:

- The information system name and agency-assigned identifier.
- The impact level assigned to the system based on the security categorization process.

- Where and when the assessment occurred.
- The name, contact information, and credentials of the security control assessor or assessment team.
- Results of previous assessments or other documentation used in the assessment.
- The identifier of each control or control enhancement assessed.
- The assessment methods and objects used and level of depth and coverage for each control or enhancement.
- A summary of assessment findings.
- Assessor comments or recommendations, particularly for other-than-satisfied findings.

Just as Special Publication 800-53 provides control assessment procedures in a consistent structure, the security assessment report presents the result of assessing each control with a listing of determination statements, the assessment finding for each determination statement, and comments and recommendations from the assessor.

Information system owners and common control providers rely on the technical knowledge and expert judgment of security control assessors to accurately assess the controls implemented for information systems and to provide recommendations on how to correct weaknesses or deficiencies identified during assessments. Assessors may provide their assessment results in an initial security assessment report, to offer system owners the opportunity to supply missing evidence or correct identified control weaknesses or deficiencies before the security assessment report is finalized. The assessor reevaluates any security controls added or revised during this process and includes the updated assessment findings in the final security assessment report.

Remediation Actions

Designation of assessment findings as satisfied and other than satisfied in the security assessment report provides visibility for system owners and other organizational officials into specific weaknesses and deficiencies in security controls implemented for an information system and supports a consistent, structured approach for mitigating or otherwise responding to risk associated with assessment findings. Although NIST allocates the task of developing the plan of action and milestones (POA&M) to step 5 of the RMF, many of the items included in the POA&M trace back to weaknesses and deficiencies identified during security control assessment. The results of the security control assessment directly influence the contents of both the system security plan and the plan of action and milestones as system owners finalize them for delivery in the security authorization package. In the case of weaknesses or deficiencies identified in information systems and the information security risk those issues represent, system owners often try to address some other-than-satisfied assessment findings before the point at which the authorization decision needs to be made. System owners and common control providers review the security assessment report and consider recommendations for corrective action provided in the report, in many cases applying the same sort of formal methodology to individual weaknesses that they use for information system-level risk assessments. The process of assessing the risk to the organization represented by system weaknesses or deficiencies is described in more detail in Chapters 12 and 13; the focus of the analysis of other-than-satisfied findings within step 4 of the RMF is identifying remediating actions that can or should be taken before preparing the system for authorization in step 5. Of particular concern to system owners are findings with potential adverse impacts serious enough to threaten the authorization of the system or with risks determined to be too great to defer corrective action [41]. Depending on the security policies or security control priorities established by an organization, such findings might result when implementing commercially available software that was not designed to satisfy federal requirements for audit logging, encryption, input validation, separation of duties, or other functions. In situations in which the software cannot be configured to satisfy these requirements, agencies may have to develop custom modifications or implement compensating controls.

Depending on the severity of adverse impacts that could result from weaknesses or deficiencies identified in an information system, system owners may need to involve senior management or organizational risk managers in deciding on the most appropriate risk response, to ensure that resources allocated to remediation efforts are commensurate with the risk and need for mitigation and consistent with organizational priorities [42]. System owners document the decision to remediate weaknesses or deficiencies and describe the intended approach for remediation in the system security plan and the security assessment report. This information may also be included in the system's plan of action and milestones, even if the schedule for implementing corrective actions and achieving milestones precedes the anticipated date of system authorization.

RELEVANT SOURCE MATERIAL

Several NIST Special Publications provide guidance, recommendations, and instructions relevant to performing security categorization and security control selection. The most applicable sources of information include:

- Special Publication 800-37 Revision 1, *Guide for Applying the Risk Management Framework to Federal Information Systems* [43].
- Special Publication 800-53 Revision 3, *Recommended Security Controls for Federal Information Systems and Organizations* [44].
- Special Publication 800-53A Revision 1, *Guide for Assessing the Security Controls in Federal Information Systems and Organizations* [27].
- Special Publication 800-64 Revision 2, *Security Considerations in the System Development Life Cycle* [1].

These and other NIST Special Publications are available from the NIST Computer Security Division Website, at http://csrc.nist.gov/publications/.

SUMMARY

This chapter described the Risk Management Framework tasks and system development activities associated with implementing security controls from the tailored baseline produced as an output of step 2 and documented in the system security plan and formally assessing those controls once implemented. Given the nature and variety of management, operational, and technical controls included in tailored baselines, control implementation comprises a wide range of activities performed by security-focused personnel and members of system development teams with both technical and functional roles. This chapter identified relevant sources of guidance on effective control implementation, including secure software engineering principles and government, industry, and vendor guidelines applicable to different types of technologies. It also described the security control assessment process, incorporating procedural guidance from NIST in Special Publication 800-53A, and highlighted the essential role of security control assessment in achieving initial system authorization and maintaining system security through continuous monitoring.

REFERENCES

[1] Kissel R, Stine K, Scholl M, Rossman H, Fahlsing J, Gulick J. Security considerations in the system development life cycle. Gaithersburg, MD: National Institute of Standards and Technology, Computer Security Division; October 2008. Special Publication 800-64 revision 2.

[2] The release of Special Publication 800-53A followed Special Publication 800-53 Revision 2 by eight months; NIST released Special Publication 800-53A Revision 1 ten months after Special Publication 800-53 Revision 3.

[3] Recommended security controls for federal information systems and organizations. Gaithersburg, MD: National Institute of Standards and Technology, Computer Security Division; August 2009. Special Publication 800-53 revision 3. p. 14.

[4] Recommended security controls for federal information systems and organizations. Gaithersburg, MD: National Institute of Standards and Technology, Computer Security Division; August 2009. Special Publication 800-53 revision 3. Appendix E.

[5] Special Publications [Internet]. Gaithersburg, MD: National Institute of Standards and Technology; [created July 3, 2007. updated February 28, 2012. cited April 24, 2012]. <http://csrc.nist.gov/publications/PubsSPs.html>.

[6] Guide for applying the risk management framework to federal information systems. Gaithersburg, MD: National Institute of Standards and Technology, Computer Security Division; February 2010 . Special Publication 800-37 revision 1. p. 9.

[7] Guide for assessing the security controls in federal information systems and organizations. Gaithersburg, MD: National Institute of Standards and Technology, Computer Security Division; June 2010. Special Publication 800-53A revision 1. p. 15.

[8] Guide for assessing the security controls in federal information systems and organizations. Gaithersburg, MD: National Institute of Standards and Technology, Computer Security Division; June 2010. Special Publication 800-53A revision 1. p. D-4.

[9] Guide for applying the risk management framework to federal information systems. Gaithersburg, MD: National Institute of Standards and Technology, Computer Security Division; February 2010. Special Publication 800-37 revision 1. p. 29.

[10] Guide for assessing the security controls in federal information systems and organizations. Gaithersburg, MD: National Institute of Standards and Technology, Computer Security Division; June 2010. Special Publication 800-53A revision 1. p. D-7.

[11] Guide for assessing the security controls in federal information systems and organizations. Gaithersburg, MD: National Institute of Standards and Technology, Computer Security Division; June 2010. Special Publication 800-53A revision 1. p. 18.

[12] Kissel R, Stine K, Scholl M, Rossman H, Fahlsing J, Gulick J. Security considerations in the system development life cycle. Gaithersburg, MD: National Institute of Standards and Technology, Computer Security Division; October 2008.. Special Publication 800-64 revision 2.p. 24.

[13] Guide for applying the risk management framework to federal information systems. Gaithersburg, MD: National Institute of Standards and Technology, Computer Security Division; February 2010. Special Publication 800-37 revision 1. p. 28.

[14] Stoneburner G, Hayden C, Feringa A. Engineering principles for information technology security. Gaithersburg, MD: National Institute of Standards and Technology, Computer Security Division; June 2004.. Special Publication 800-27 revision A. p. 5.

[15] Redwine ST, editor. Software assurance: a curriculum guide to the common body of knowledge to produce, acquire and sustain secure software. Washington, DC: Department of Homeland Security, Software Assurance Workforce Education and Training Working Group; October 2007.

[16] Goertezl KM, Winograd T, McKinley HL, Oh L, Colon M, McGibbon . Software security assurance: A state-of-the-art report. Herndon, VA: Information Assurance Technology Analysis Center; July 2007.

[17] ISO/IEC 15026:2011. systems and software engineering – Systems and software assurance.

[18] Stoneburner G, Hayden C, Feringa A. Engineering principles for information technology security. Gaithersburg, MD: National Institute of Standards and Technology, Computer Security Division; June 2004.. Special Publication 800-27 revision A. p. 6.

[19] . Examples includeGrembi J. Secure software development: a security programmer's guide. Boston, MA: Cengage Learning; 2008 and McGraw G. Software security: Building security in. Upper Saddle River, NJ: Addison-Wesley; 2006.

[20] Quinn S, Souppaya M, Cook M, Scarfone K. National checklist program for IT products – guidelines for checklist users and developers. Gaithersburg, MD: National Institute of Standards and Technology, Computer Security Division; February 2011.. Special Publication 800-70 revision 2.

[21] Federal Information Security Management Act of 2002, Pub. L. No. 107-347, 116 Stat. 2946. §301, codified at 44 U.S.C. §3541.

[22] Roback EA. Guidelines to federal organizations on security assurance and acquisition/use of tested/evaluated products. Gaithersburg, MD: National Institute of Standards and Technology, Computer Security Division; August 2000.. Special Publication 800-23.

[23] ISO/IEC 15408:2009. Information technology — Security techniques — Evaluation criteria for IT security.

[24] US Government Approved Protection Profiles [Internet]. Ft. Meade, MD: National Information Assurance Partnership [cited March 24, 2012].<http://www.niap-ccevs.org/pp/>.

[25] Certified Products: The Common Criteria Portal [Internet]. Cheltenham, UK: Communications-Electronics Security Group [cited March 24, 2012]. <http://www.commoncriteriaportal.org/products/>.

[26] Guide for assessing the security controls in federal information systems and organizations. Gaithersburg, MD: National Institute of Standards and Technology, Computer Security Division; June 2010. Special Publication 800-53A revision 1.

[27] Guide for assessing the security controls in federal information systems and organizations. Gaithersburg, MD: National Institute of Standards and Technology, Computer Security Division; June 2010. Special Publication 800-53A revision 1. p. 6.

[28] Federal Information Security Management Act of 2002, Pub. L. No. 107-347, 116 Stat. 2946. §301, codified at 44 U.S.C. §3544(a)(2)(D).

[29] Guide for assessing the security controls in federal information systems and organizations. Gaithersburg, MD: National Institute of Standards and Technology, Computer Security Division; June 2010. Special Publication 800-53A revision 1. p. 9.

[30] Guide for assessing the security controls in federal information systems and organizations. Gaithersburg, MD: National Institute of Standards and Technology, Computer Security Division; June 2010. Special Publication 800-53A revision 1. See Appendix D.

[31] Assessment Cases Download Page [Internet]. Gaithersburg, MD: National Institute of Standards and Technology, Computer Security Division [created August 7, 2008; updated February 12, 2012; cited May 11, 2012]. <http://csrc.nist.gov/groups/SMA/fisma/assessment-cases.html>.

[32] Guide for assessing the security controls in federal information systems and organizations. Gaithersburg, MD: National Institute of Standards and Technology, Computer Security Division; June 2010. Special Publication 800-53A revision 1. p. 13–4.

[33] Guide for assessing the security controls in federal information systems and organizations. Gaithersburg, MD: National Institute of Standards and Technology, Computer Security Division; June 2010. Special Publication 800-53A revision 1. p. 2–3.

[34] Arguing Security – Creating Security Assurance Cases [Internet]. Washington, DC: Department of Homeland Security, National Cyber Security Division [created January 4, 2007. updated October 9, 2008. cited May 11, 2012]. <https://buildsecurityin.us-cert.gov/bsi/articles/knowledge/assurance/643-BSI.html>.

[35] Despite the length of time since NIST released the initial public draft in 2007, the report has never been finalized. Johnson A, Toth P. Security assessment provider requirements and customer responsibilities: building a security assessment credentialing program for federal information systems. Gaithersburg, MD: National Institute of Standards and Technology, Computer Security Division; September 2007. Interagency Report 7328 Initial Public Draft.

[36] Swanson M. Security self-assessment guide for information technology systems. Gaithersburg, MD: National Institute of Standards and Technology, Computer Security Division; 2001.. Special Publication 800-26.

[37] Guide for assessing the security controls in federal information systems and organizations. Gaithersburg, MD: National Institute of Standards and Technology, Computer Security Division; June 2010. Special Publication 800-53A revision 1. p. 16.

[38] Guide for assessing the security controls in federal information systems and organizations. Gaithersburg, MD: National Institute of Standards and Technology, Computer Security Division; June 2010. Special Publication 800-53A revision 1. p. 22.

[39] Guide for assessing the security controls in federal information systems and organizations. Gaithersburg, MD: National Institute of Standards and Technology, Computer Security Division; June 2010. Special Publication 800-53A revision 1. Appendix G.

[40] Guide for applying the risk management framework to federal information systems. Gaithersburg, MD: National Institute of Standards and Technology, Computer Security Division; February 2010. Special Publication 800-37 revision 1. p. 32.

[41] Guide for assessing the security controls in federal information systems and organizations. Gaithersburg, MD: National Institute of Standards and Technology, Computer Security Division; June 2010. Special Publication 800-53A revision 1. p. 24.

[42] Guide for applying the risk management framework to federal information systems. Gaithersburg, MD: National Institute of Standards and Technology, Computer Security Division; February 2010. Special Publication 800-37 revision 1.

[43] Recommended security controls for federal information systems and organizations. Gaithersburg, MD: National Institute of Standards and Technology, Computer Security Division; August 2009. Special Publication 800-53 revision 3.

CHAPTER

Risk Management Framework Steps 5 & 6

9

INFORMATION IN THIS CHAPTER:

- Preparing for System Authorization
- Tasks in RMF Step 5: Authorize Information System
- Tasks in RMF Step 6: Monitor Security Controls

The decision to authorize a system to operate is an indication that the security controls documented in the system security plan are adequate to satisfy the system's requirements, supported by the results of security control assessments that validate the successful implementation and effectiveness of security controls. Authorizing officials consider security documentation and other information provided by system owners and common control providers that offer evidence regarding the security of their systems and the risk to the organization associated with operating them. Authorizing officials do not directly assess the security of information systems under their oversight; instead, they use the information in the system authorization package as evidence to support system owners' assertions regarding implemented security controls, evaluate the information security risk that remains despite the implementation of controls, and decide whether that risk is acceptable to the organization. An authorization decision is an evaluation of information security risk at a specific point in time—potentially a point in the future—so the risk management process prescribes a series of tasks to be performed after authorization to ensure that security remains adequate and the risk associated with the information system continues to be managed within acceptable levels.

Step 5 in the RMF finalizes security control implementation and configuration and identifies any corrective actions that still need to be accomplished, prior to or after the authorization decision. The system owner then assembles the security authorization package and delivers it to the authorizing official for evaluation and approval. The decision to accept the risk associated with the system and authorize it to operate represents a key prerequisite for the system to transition out of the implementation phase and into operations and maintenance. For the system owner, system authorization is both the end of the system deployment process and the beginning of ongoing security management, a milestone coinciding with the shift in the RMF from a primarily linear, sequential process to an iterative set of recurring tasks in step 6 that provide continuous monitoring, maintain an appropriate security posture for the system, and keep current all security controls and associated documentation. The information included in the system authorization package addresses not only how the system has been implemented to prepare for production operation, but also how the organization and the system owner will manage its security over time, including specifying any activities planned to enhance security and reduce residual risk.

PREPARING FOR SYSTEM AUTHORIZATION

Preparing for and achieving system authorization is a central objective for step 5 of the RMF and for the implementation phase of the system development lifecycle. System owners coordinate the efforts of developers, security control implementers, and security control assessors during the implementation phase to complete security testing, evaluate and respond to the results produced by testing and assessment activities, and determine the level of effort associated with any corrective actions documented in the plan of action and milestones (POA&M) [1]. System owners also need to look beyond the scope of their own systems to consider the organizational policies, procedures, and standards that prescribe or constrain the way the system will be managed during the SDLC operations and maintenance phase. The security authorization package replicates or incorporates by reference information from the organizational risk management strategy, continuous monitoring strategy, and ongoing security management policies and procedures to demonstrate the compliance of system-specific activities with organizational requirements and identify any organizational security management capabilities and services used by the system. The combined information from the organizational information security program, common control providers, and system owners offers a complete picture of the system's security posture to the authorizing official, to enable consideration of all applicable risk factors underlying the authorization decision.

By the time a system reaches step 5 in the RMF, all security controls necessary to satisfy the system's requirements should be documented in the system security plan and formally evaluated for effectiveness using security control assessment procedures. If the security control assessment identifies no weaknesses or deficiencies, then the system security plan should accurately reflect the current state of the system and its security, validated with the evidence documented in the security assessment report. More commonly, the security control assessment does find weaknesses or deficiencies in implemented controls that must be corrected to bring information security risk within acceptable levels. In these cases, security control assessors describe all identified weaknesses and deficiencies and recommendations for corrective action in the security assessment report, and the system owner documents all corrective actions that will be taken in the plan of action and milestones. The authorizing official considers the set of actions and the schedule for their completion to which the system owner commits in the plan of action and milestones when determining the risk associated with the system. Authorizing a system with known weaknesses and deficiencies is essentially a conditional decision—the authorizing official agrees to temporarily accept what might otherwise be an unacceptable risk to the organization if actions to mitigate the risk will be taken within a specified timeframe. Depending on organizational policies regarding system authorization and the magnitude of risk due to system weaknesses and deficiencies to be addressed by the POA&M, authorizing officials may choose to authorize systems for periods of variable duration, although the maximum generally does not exceed the standard established in government-wide guidance [2]. The decision to grant a limited or interim authorization to operate may be justified by the mission criticality of the system to the organization or other extenuating circumstances, after which the system authorization decision is revisited with the expectation that enhancements made to system security controls should reduce risk to acceptable levels [3]. Current NIST guidance on system authorization de-emphasizes the alternative of granting an interim authorization to operate, identifying just two possible outcomes for an authorization decision: authorized or not authorized [4], although the authorizing official may attach terms and conditions to the authorization.

The set of activities needed to prepare for system authorization depends in part of what type of authorization will be requested and the anticipated duration of the authorization period in addition to system-specific factors such as the security categorization, the part of the organization responsible for operating or managing the system, and whether the system is a major application or general support system. The primary types of authorization are initial and ongoing—the first five steps of the RMF, and step 5 in particular, support the objective of receiving initial authorization for a new system while step 6 addresses the need to periodically reauthorize an operational system. The application of the Risk Management Framework described in Special Publication 800-37 emphasizes tasks necessary to achieve initial system authorization for newly developed or implemented systems, although the steps also apply to legacy systems [5], where *legacy system* is an operational system that was either authorized on a basis other than the criteria currently in use under FISMA or one that was never formally authorized. While the ongoing risk determination and acceptance task in step 6 remains applicable to operational information systems, in practice much of the procedural guidance in RMF step 6 now more accurately falls within the scope of continuous monitoring, expectations and guidance for which NIST provides in Special Publication 800-137 [6].

The maximum authorization period for a system is typically constrained by federal and organizational policy to no longer than 3 years, reflecting the requirement in Appendix III of OMB Circular A-130 that all federal systems be reauthorized at least that often. The use of a three-year authorization window presumes that sufficient operational controls are in place to ensure that at least a subset of each system's security controls are periodically reassessed; in the absence of such procedures, organizations may choose to shorten the authorization period to require system owners to formally reassess their security controls and validate that the level of protection afforded their systems remains adequate. Federal agencies that establish sufficiently robust continuous monitoring programs may choose to eliminate authorization termination dates, effectively replacing periodic reauthorization requirements with ongoing maintenance and updates to authorized systems [7]. OMB reiterated this point in its FISMA reporting instructions to agencies, stating its intention to stop enforcing the three-year reauthorization requirement and instead directing agencies to implement continuous monitoring programs and report the results of ongoing authorizations for their information systems [8].

STEP 5: AUTHORIZE INFORMATION SYSTEM

The primary focus of step 5 in the RMF process is completing the planning, decision making, and documentation necessary for the system owner to assemble the security authorization package and deliver it to the authorizing official for evaluation in support of the system authorization decision. The system owner uses the security assessment report and updated system security plan produced in step 4 to develop the plan of action and milestones, which when complete is included with the other documents as the third major element of the security authorization package. While the security assessment report documents *all* weaknesses and deficiencies found in the information system, the appropriate response to the risk associated with some of those findings may be to accept or avoid the risk rather than taking action to mitigate it. The possible risk responses considered by a system owner or organization may be described in risk assessment reports or similar documentation, and decisions to response in ways other than mitigating risk are typically documented in the system security plan to provide the authorizing official with information relevant to making a risk determination for the information system. The plan of action and milestones includes the corrective actions planned to address the risk from system weaknesses and deficiencies that the system owner determines—in consultation with the authorizing official, senior information security officer, security engineers, information owners, and other relevant personnel—must be mitigated through remediation [9]. Corrective actions recommended in the security assessment report that are completed before finalizing the security authorization package need not be reflected in the plan of action and milestones, although any changes in implemented controls should be documented in the updated system security plan.

Developing the plan of action and milestones is the final task needed to assemble the security authorization package and submit the package to the authorizing official for approval. As shown in Figure 9.1, the plan of action and milestones and the rest of the security authorization package are the primary outputs from step 5 in the RMF, while the authorization decision is the key prerequisite for a system to move on to step 6. All of the tasks in step 5 occur within the implementation phase of the system development life cycle, in parallel with other key system activities such as finalizing system documentation, performing end-to-end functional, security, and integration testing, and conducting operational readiness reviews [10]. Depending on the specific SDLC methodology an organization follows, the security authorization decision may represent the final criterion that must be met to put the system into production and transition to the SDLC operations and maintenance phase.

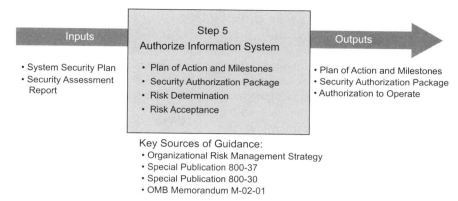

FIGURE 9.1 In Step 5 of The RMF, the Security Assessment Results and Artifacts Produced During Security Control Implementation Drive Updates to and Finalization of the Core Documents Making Up the Security Authorization Package So That Authorizing Officials Can Determine If the Risk Associated with the System is Acceptable and, If So, Authorize the System to Operate

Plan of Action and Milestones

The plan of action and milestones (POA&M) identifies the tasks to be accomplished to correct weaknesses or deficiencies in the system, either before or after system deployment, the resources required to accomplish the tasks, milestones associated with the tasks, and the schedule for achieving each of the milestones. The POA&M also describes actions planned to address vulnerabilities in the system, whether discovered through security control assessments, vulnerability scanning or other forms of monitoring, or advisories from government or industry sources. The requirement for agencies to develop plans of action and milestones for their systems predates FISMA; the authoritative source of guidance to agencies on preparing security-related POA&Ms is a memorandum issued by OMB in 2001 [11] to elaborate on reporting requirements associated with the Government Information Security Reform Act of 2000. NIST's definition of the security authorization package integrates OMB guidance on POA&Ms with Circular A-130 instructions requiring agencies to develop system security plans and periodically review their security controls. In the context of the Risk Management Framework, the POA&M is used not only in the authorization decision, but also as part of ongoing security management to monitor progress in correcting weaknesses or deficiencies identified during the security control assessment. Chapter 12 provides detailed guidance on developing system-specific and agency-wide plans of action and milestones, including the process of assessing the risk posed by identified weaknesses and deficiencies. The information presented below focuses on system-level POA&M requirements because security authorization considers the set of corrective actions planned for each system.

Determining Actions to Include in the POA&M

The decision to take corrective action to address an identified weakness or deficiency and include that action and associated milestones in the POA&M is the result of a type of risk assessment. Security assessors document all weaknesses and deficiencies— findings that security objectives are "other than satisfied"—in the security assessment report, typically with recommendations for how to remedy such findings. System owners consider each weakness or deficiency to assess the risk it presents to the organization and determine the appropriate risk response. If the chosen response is to accept the risk or act to mitigate it before finalizing the security authorization package, those decisions are documented in the system security plan and the final security assessment report. All unremediated weaknesses or deficiencies must be documented in the plan of action and milestones with the course of action planned for addressing each issue, the resources required to perform each action, and a timeframe for completion [11].

System owners and common control providers should adhere to organizational policies and procedures for developing plans of action and milestones to help ensure consistent assessment of and responses to risk and to align corrective actions and the resources they require with organizational priorities. System-level POA&Ms should reflect organizational policy about managing risk for systems at each security categorization level, adapting POA&M items to the nature and significance of identified control weaknesses, prioritizing responses based on the potential adverse impact to the organization, and any standard or preferred approaches to risk mitigation [9]. Weaknesses or deficiencies discovered in common controls often receive higher priority for remediation than system-specific issues due to the potential impact to multiple systems that inherit those controls. When organizations identify common control weaknesses or deficiencies, system owners whose systems use those controls may be required to document the problem in their own POA&Ms to maintain an accurate representation of the security posture of the information system. Similarly, if a newly discovered vulnerability affects multiple systems, organizations may direct each system owner to create a separate system-specific POA&M item to enable the organization to track corrective actions implemented for each system. For example, the government-wide transition in early 2011 to the use of stronger hash algorithms for encryption used to generate digital signatures [12] required many agencies to modify their existing systems to accommodate the stronger encryption requirements. Until system owners updated the identification and authentication controls implemented in their systems the

---

NOTE

In principle, it is possible for a security control assessment to produce no findings significant enough to warrant corrective action or for a system owner to accept all risk (subject to agreement with organizational policy) associated with any weaknesses and deficiencies, resulting in no actions to be documented in a plan of action and milestones. Given the constantly changing set of threats organizations face and the frequent discovery of vulnerabilities in products or technologies already deployed, any POA&M-free status for a system is likely to be temporary.

use of weaker encryption algorithms represented a weakness, but the corrective action required had to be performed for each system and agencies could only demonstrate compliance with the new requirements after all their affected systems were updated.

POA&M Content

OMB specifies minimum information requirements for POA&Ms developed at the organizational level in its annual FISMA reporting instructions [13]. Because agencies produce organizational POA&Ms using information documented in system-level documentation, these content requirements—originally prescribed in 2004 and summarized in Table 9.1—are the same for system-level POA&M items.

Plans of action and milestones represent active efforts to correct weaknesses and deficiencies and mitigate risk associated with each system. The POA&M submitted as part of the security authorization package needs to be complete and up to date, but POA&Ms in place for operational systems are subject to frequent updates

Table 9.1 Required Data Elements for Agency-Level and System-Level POA&Ms [14]

Data Element	Description
Severity and brief description of the weakness	• Severity values are: "significant deficiency," "reportable condition," or "other weakness" • Description must provide sufficient data to permit oversight and tracking
Point of contact	• Identity of the individual or office within the organization responsible for resolving the weakness
Resources required	• Estimated amount and source of funding needed to resolve the weakness
Scheduled completion date	• Target completion date for all corrective actions
Key milestones with completion dates	• Milestones are associated with specific requirements to correct each weakness
Changes to milestones	• Includes new completion dates for milestones, if originally targeted date is changed
Source	• Identifies the source of the weakness (e.g. security assessment, continuous monitoring, program review, internal or external audit)
Status	• Current status of corrective actions; acceptable values are "ongoing" or "completed" • "Completed" indicates that a weakness has been fully resolved and corrective action has been tested; date of completion should be provided

> **TIP**
>
> The RMF emphasizes the development and management of system-specific POA&Ms, but each federal agency is also required to maintain an organization-level POA&M representing an aggregation of corrective actions across all systems. Agencies that use automated tools to capture and track POA&M details at the system level typically find it easier to produce aggregated plans to support federal reporting and compliance requirements. Agencies are increasingly expected to employ such tools to manage their system security information and facilitate the submission of automated data feeds to OMB to satisfy FISMA reporting requirements [15]. Providing an aggregated view of weaknesses and deficiencies across all agency systems can also help identify problems that may be shared by multiple systems, potentially enabling a resolution through corrective action taken at the organizational level.

as corrective actions are completed, milestones are achieved, and new weaknesses, deficiencies, or system vulnerabilities are discovered that must be addressed through newly defined corrective actions.

Using the POA&M to Support Security Management

For authorized systems, the plan of action and milestones has an important role in operational security management, providing a basis for system owners, senior information security officers, risk management program managers, and other organizational officials to monitor progress in implementing corrective actions and achieving milestones specified in the POA&M. At an organizational level, POA&Ms provide management visibility into current and planned allocation of security resources and risk mitigation activities. This information helps organizations ensure that system operations teams implement corrective actions as planned and therefore continue to manage information security risk within acceptable levels. In addition, when continuous monitoring activities identify new threats or vulnerabilities that impact the security of operational systems, organizations aware of existing and scheduled security enhancement activities will be better able to re-prioritize the allocation of available resources as needed to respond to the most significant sources of risk. As with other forms of security monitoring, organizations can facilitate the ability of their authorizing officials and risk managers to track the completion of POA&M items if they develop and implement tools or standard templates for capturing and reporting on corrective actions documented in POA&Ms.

Security Authorization Package

The security authorization package contains three core documents—the system security plan, security assessment report, and plan of action and milestones—and any additional supporting information required by the authorizing official. Each system owner or common control provider assembles these documents and other necessary information into the security authorization package and submits it to the appropriate authorizing official, a task depicted in Figure 9.2. The information in the security authorization package provides the basis for the system authorization decision, so the

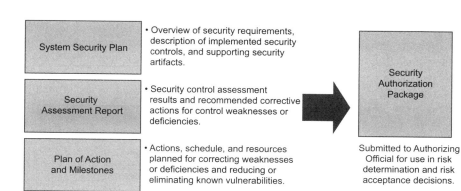

FIGURE 9.2 The Core Components of the Security Authorization Package Include the System Security Plan, Security Assessment Report, and Plan of Action and Milestones, All of Which are Carefully Evaluated by the Authorizing Official to Help Reach a Decision About the Level of Risk Associated with Operating the System [16]

primary consideration for system owners or common control providers submitting authorization packages is ensuring the accuracy and completeness of the information provided to authorizing officials. For systems leveraging common controls or security controls implemented or provided by organizations external to the agency, the system owner must ensure that all common control providers or external providers furnish the security documentation needed by authorizing officials. The documents

---

NOTE

NIST guidance to agencies recommends the use of automated system authorization support tools to manage the information included in the security authorization package, provide an efficient mechanism for security information dissemination and oversight, and facilitate maintenance and updates of that information. There are many tools available to agencies that support system security management, authorization, and FISMA compliance and reporting activities, including government-furnished services, commercial off-the-shelf products, and open-source software. Examples include:

- Cyber Security Assessment and Management (CSAM), a tool managed by the Department of Justice and available to other government agencies.
- Trusted Integration Trusted Agent FISMA.
- Telos Xacta IA Manager.
- SecureInfo Risk Management Services.
- Symantec Enterprise Security Manager for FISMA.
- OpenFISMA, sponsored by Endeavor Systems and available in open-source and commercial versions.When deployed for agency-wide use, tools such as these help ensure consistent execution of Risk Management Framework tasks and other security management activities and typically offer integrated monitoring and reporting capabilities to allow authorizing officials, risk managers, and security management personnel to track compliance with agency policies and federal requirements at individual information system and organizational levels.

in the security authorization package represent the formal assertion by the system owner or common control provider that the security controls implemented for the system (including those planned for implementation within explicit timeframes as indicated in the plan of action and milestones) are effective and sufficient to provide adequate security. The authorizing official relies on the information in the security authorization package to validate the assertion of adequate security, determine the risk to the organization associated with operating the system, and decide if that risk is acceptable.

Risk Determination

Security authorization is a risk-based decision, balancing the benefits of operating an information system against the potential adverse impacts to the organization if the system or the information it contains suffers a loss of confidentiality, integrity, or availability. The authorizing official uses the information provided in the security authorization package to determine the magnitude of the information security risk posed by the system, taking into account all security controls currently implemented or planned for implementation. The authorizing official, often in collaboration with the senior information security officer, assesses the information provided by the system owner or common control provider characterizing the security posture of the system and the recommendations for addressing any residual risk. System-level risk assessment is a required security control for information systems at all security categorization levels [17], so a risk assessment report or other risk assessment documentation is typically included in the security authorization package. Depending on the scope of the risk assessment and when it was performed, the authorizing official may choose to conduct additional formal or informal risk assessments to identify current threats, vulnerabilities, and potential adverse impacts or to evaluate the risk mitigation recommendations developed for the system. Alternatively, the authorizing official may rely on the results of previously conducted risk assessments, considered in the context of risk-related factors such as the criticality of mission functions or business processes the system supports and the risk management strategy for the organization.

As described in Chapter 13, the organizational risk management strategy describes how risk is identified and assessed within the organization; how risks are evaluated with regard to severity or criticality; approaches to risk mitigation or other types of risk response; and the organizational level of risk tolerance. When making the final risk determination, the authorizing official considers organizational risk management guidance, input from senior information security and risk management officials, and the information provided in the security authorization package. Consistent with NIST guidance for conducting risk assessments, the risk determination in support of security authorization can be expressed quantitatively, qualitatively, or semi-quantitatively depending on the preferences of the organization and the nature and level of detail in information the organization has available to support its risk assessments [18]. Agencies that adopt the impact and risk rating guidelines NIST proposes may assign qualitative values (very high, high, moderate, low, very low) or semi-quantitative numerical equivalents to system risk determinations. The intent should be to ensure that authorizing officials assign risk ratings in a way that supports direct comparison of risk levels among systems and prioritization of risk responses in alignment with the organizational risk management strategy [19]. The type of risk rating scale or measurement used when assigning risk determinations should also be consistent with the way in which organizational risk tolerance is stated in the risk management strategy, to facilitate comparison of the risk associated with the system and the risk tolerance level declared for the organization.

Risk Acceptance

Organizations may choose to respond to risk in different ways, typically by choosing among acceptance, avoidance, mitigation, sharing, or transference [20]. Some or all of these alternatives may be available to organizations and authorizing officials when determining the appropriate response to information security risk. In the context of security authorization decisions, however, authorizing officials focus on the suitability of a single response: acceptance. NIST guidance assigns responsibility for the risk acceptance decision to the authorizing official, explicitly prohibiting the delegation of that decision to any other organizational officials [21]. The decision to accept the risk associated with the information system equates to authorizing the system to operate at its present level of security, or at the level of security that will be achieved when the items in the plan of action and milestones are completed. Any other response results in a denial of authorization to operate, potentially accompanied by instructions to the system owner or common control provider to implement risk mitigation or other recommended course of action, after which the authorization decision may be reconsidered. Risk acceptance is the appropriate risk response when the identified risk is within the organization's level of risk tolerance.

There is no standard for evaluating the level of risk that will be deemed acceptable for each organization, especially in light of the fact that federal agencies and many other organizations have the authority to make their own system authorization decisions, based on their own determinations of risk and risk tolerance levels. An authorizing official may choose to accept even high levels of risk for an information system if the system supports essential mission and business needs or operational requirements. Authorizing officials consider both the level of risk and the type of risk presented by the system when determining whether the risk is acceptable to the organization, striving to balance organizational interests and mission, business, and operational requirements with the potential adverse impact to organizational assets.

The authorizing official provides the result of the risk acceptance decision in an authorization decision document that conveys the final security authorization decision, any terms and conditions placed on the authorization of the system, and the authorization termination date. The authorization decision has two possible values: "authorized to operate" or "not authorized to operate" [7]. At their discretion, authorizing officials may specify terms and conditions for the authorization and describe any specific limitations or restrictions placed on the operation of the information system. System owners and common control providers are expected to acknowledge and implement the terms and conditions of the authorization and notify the authorizing official when the terms and conditions have been satisfied. The ability authorizing officials have to attach terms and conditions to authorization decisions enables a wider range of risk to be accepted, by providing multiple types of conditional authorization decisions. Where system owners create their own conditions in the form of plans of action and milestones, authorizing officials can reiterate the importance of correcting weaknesses and deficiencies already identified for the system or specify additional terms and conditions issued with authorization decisions. The authorization termination date, established by the authorizing official in alignment with organizational policy, indicates when the security authorization expires or—if the information in the security authorization package indicates continuous monitoring procedures are implemented effectively for the system—authorization to operate may be granted without a specified expiration date. Authorizing officials therefore need to consider the maturity and effectiveness of the organization's continuous monitoring program and the plans for the information system to leverage organizational and system-specific monitoring capabilities before agreeing to waive a formal expiration date for the system authorization.

STEP 6: MONITOR SECURITY CONTROLS

Once a system receives authorization to operate, the focus for tasks prescribed in the Risk Management Framework shifts from attaining adequate security to maintaining effective security on an ongoing basis, monitoring the system for any changes potentially impacting its security posture and adjusting the implemented security controls as necessary to keep information security risk within acceptable levels. The change in step 6 of the RMF from preparing for implementation to managing the security of authorized systems mirrors the transition in the software development lifecycle from the implementation phase to the operations and maintenance phase [22]. Security monitoring is one of several operational and administrative functions implemented for federal information systems; other related processes include change management and configuration control, system maintenance, and system, environment, and network performance monitoring. Ongoing system security management is driven in part by the activities and timelines in the plan of action and milestones, but also incorporates routine administrative and maintenance activities in addition to monitoring the system, its operating environment, and the organization for the occurrence of events or the emergence of new threats or vulnerabilities that introduce new sources of risk.

The security documentation developed during the first five steps of the RMF process provides the foundation for ongoing security management activities, in conjunction with organizational risk management and continuous monitoring strategies and processes or services that help system owners identify threats and vulnerabilities or other factors impacting system security. During security monitoring, system owners perform many of the same tasks completed during earlier steps in the RMF, including security control assessments, risk assessments, and updates to system security information in plans and other documentation, as shown in Figure 9.3. System owners also ensure the completion of security testing, training, and exercises associated with implemented operational controls and provide regular security status reports to authorizing officials, risk managers, senior information security officers, and designated executives. Collectively, this information represents key outputs of security monitoring processes that enable ongoing management of information security risk and help determine when more detailed reviews of system security are warranted, including the potential need to reauthorize an operational system.

With the exception of information system removal and decommissioning, which only occurs after the operational phase when a system will no longer be used in an organization, the tasks in step 6 of the RMF all fall within the context of continuous monitoring, as illustrated in Figure 9.4. NIST prescribes the processes and requirements for information security continuous monitoring of federal information systems in Special Publication 800-137. The current emphasis placed on continuous monitoring by NIST, OMB, and legislators proposing updates to the statutory requirements in FISMA [23] makes the topic important enough to warrant consideration beyond its role in the RMF; Chapter 14 provides a detailed description of organizational and system-specific continuous monitoring expectations.

Within the RMF process and the certification and accreditation guidance that preceded it, the use of the term *continuous monitoring* to denote the post-authorization phase for information systems comprises the key tasks of configuration management,

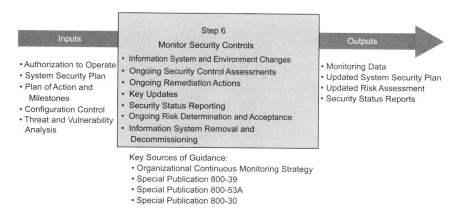

FIGURE 9.3 Step 6 of the RMF Incorporates Versions of Many Tasks Conducted in Previous Steps to Ensure the Effectiveness of Approved Security Controls Implemented for the System and Identify any Changes to the System or its Operating Environment that Might Require Adjustments to the System's Security Posture

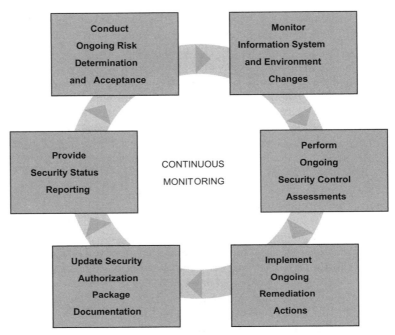

FIGURE 9.4 Execution of the RMF for an Operational System is an Iterative Process Performed Within the Scope of Continuous Monitoring Activities, with Security Control Assessments and Risk Analyses Repeated on a Periodic Basis or Whenever Warranted by Changes to the System, its Operating Environment, or the Threats and Vulnerabilities Faced by the Organization

security control monitoring, and status reporting and updates to core system security documentation [24]. These activities focus primarily on known or anticipated changes to information systems and their operating environments and on periodic reviews and reassessments of selected security controls to validate their effectiveness and identify any weaknesses or deficiencies that may have arisen since the time the previous assessment was completed. In some cases new assessment objectives, control implementation recommendations, or technical standards apply at the time of reassessment that did not exist during prior assessments, so weaknesses or deficiencies discovered in during reassessments may help system owners identify missing controls or control enhancements that need to be implemented to maintain compliance with current guidance or requirements. In the past, many agencies mandated ongoing security assessments on no more than an annual basis—a frequency that complies with FISMA requirements and avoids the need to commit additional resources for more frequent evaluations given the significant resources already required to perform annual assessments. As agencies expand their continuous monitoring programs and acquire technologies to support monitoring activities, the ability to perform many

> **WARNING**
>
> Security control assessments are only as reliable as the assessors who perform them. The purpose of ongoing security control assessments is typically to assess a subset of implemented security controls on a regular basis to give the organization confidence that implemented controls continue to function as intended and reflect proper configuration and that authorized systems remain adequately secure. Ongoing assessments often leverage results from previous assessment activities, at least to the extent that the objectives assessed and the methods and objects used in prior assessments are still valid. Some organizations discover—particularly when using a different assessor for ongoing assessments than the one who produced the security assessment report used in system authorization—that the procedures followed or judgment applied to available evidence by a new assessor calls into question the validity of the prior assessment findings. Agencies can mitigate the risk of insufficiently rigorous assessments by requiring highly experienced assessors with verified credentials and experience and by ensuring appropriate levels of assessor independence.

kinds of security control monitoring with automated tools should enable ongoing monitoring and assessment that really is continuous.

Information System and Environment Changes

The system authorization decision reflects the security posture of an information system in an explicitly defined environment operating at a determined level of risk at a specific point in time. Systems and their information security risk are dynamic, subject to changes to system components and operating environments as well as internal or external changes in the threats and vulnerabilities those systems face. Step 6 of the Risk Management Framework emphasizes the importance of implementing a consistent, structured approach for identifying, managing, documenting, and responding to changes that may impact the security of operational information systems. Continuous monitoring supports this process by identifying changes to systems and their operating environments and providing information that can be used in ongoing security control assessments.

Agencies implement formal configuration management and control processes to manage the process of making necessary changes to systems and their environments, using continuous monitoring to help identify internally or externally driven factors that require such changes. Configuration management establishes baseline system configuration information using details provided in system design documentation, technology specifications, system security plans, operational procedure manuals, and other sources. System owners or their operations teams should provide detailed information about system components identified as configuration items, including hardware specifications, software versions, configuration settings, and security control implementation descriptions [25]. Along with similar details about the environment in which the system operates, this information provides the basis for considering planned or unanticipated changes and assessing the potential security impact of those changes. Ideally, organizations do not make changes to information systems without assessing the security impact in advance but not all changes are intentional or planned, so the automated tools increasingly used by agencies to support continuous monitoring provide an important means of detecting and reporting on and system changes.

Agencies conduct security impact analyses to determine the extent to which planned or already-occurred changes to the information system or its operating environment affect the security posture of the system or the risk is operation poses to the organization. The range of possible changes affecting an information system include how controls are implementation or configured, new threats or vulnerabilities that existing controls may not adequately address, and new legal, regulatory, or policy requirements that correspond to a need to implement new security controls or control enhancements. Security impact analysis identifies factors affecting system security that require corrective action, potentially necessitating the creation of new items in the plan of action and milestones and updates to the system security plan as well as the need to assess modified or newly implemented controls [26].

Ongoing Security Control Assessments

The security control assessment performed during step 4 of the RMF addresses all security controls implemented for an information system, assessing the effectiveness of controls as implemented and identifying weaknesses or deficiencies that can be addresses by correcting control configuration or augmenting the implemented baseline with additional controls or control enhancements. Organizations cannot assume that the effectiveness of security controls at the time of system authorization will persist over time given the dynamic internal and external environments in which their systems operate. New vulnerabilities regularly emerge in operating systems, software applications, infrastructure components, and service providers, all of which may present new sources of risk and require reevaluation of the extent to which the set of implement security controls adequately protect operational systems. Ongoing security assessments enable organizations and their system owners to confirm the continued effectiveness of their security controls or evaluate the achievement of security objectives for changed or newly implemented controls, such as those implemented as corrective actions specified in the plan of action and milestones or in response to information system or environment changes identified through continuous monitoring. System owners typically assess a subset of their security controls on a periodic basis to satisfy FISMA requirements and adhere to the monitoring strategy developed during security control selection. Depending on the monitoring tools agencies have in place, some types of ongoing assessment procedures may be performed automatically, particularly for technical controls with configurations specified as checklists using the Security Content Automation Protocol (SCAP) [27]. These predefined configuration profiles help organizations validate control configuration for initial implementation and during ongoing monitoring.

Agencies may specify the set of security controls subject to ongoing assessment—using continuous monitoring or following assessment procedures described in Special Publication 800-53A—at the organization, environment, or information system level. The selection of security controls and the frequency with which reassessment or monitoring occurs are based on the monitoring strategy developed by the information system and applicable provisions in the organizational information security continuous monitoring strategy. With respect to automated monitoring capabilities provided for multiple systems, system owners need to verify that the monitoring tools or processes implemented by their agencies satisfy the system's monitoring requirements and that monitoring tools have the functional and technical capability to perform the desired type of monitoring on the system's security controls. For assessor-administered security control assessments, system owners need to verify the assessor's knowledge, skills, and abilities and degree of assessor independence—the same considerations used to select assessors for initial security control assessments [28]. Assessor independence is particularly important if the agency intends to use the results of ongoing security control assessments to comply with the FISMA provision requiring an annual *independent* evaluation including testing the effectiveness of implemented security controls.

Federal government organizations often use the results of ongoing assessments to satisfy the requirement in FISMA mandating periodic "testing and evaluation" of implemented security controls [29]. Agencies may use assessment results from multiple assessment activities, aggregated as needed to support internal or external security status reporting. Potential sources of assessment information include the results of formal security control assessment procedures conducted in support of system authorization, data produced by continuous monitoring activities, security-related findings in internal or external system audits, or security testing and evaluation of the system performed as part of the system development life cycle. Reusing available sources of control assessment data can greatly improve the cost-effectiveness and efficiency of complying with ongoing monitoring requirements, although system owners need to ensure that results from prior assessments are reused only if they remain valid [28].

Ongoing Remediation Actions

FISMA not only requires periodic testing of security controls implemented for each federal information system, but requires that agencies also must have in place processes for determining appropriate remedial action necessary to correct weaknesses and deficiencies discovered in ongoing assessments and documenting the actions taken [30]. System owners, information system security officers, authorizing officials, and other key personnel may receive the results of continuous monitoring activities and ongoing control assessments through routine security status reports, monitoring dashboards or other summary representations, or updated security assessment report documentation. System owners use this information to review recommendations for correcting weaknesses or deficiencies in their system security controls and to assess the risk associated with these issues and with newly identified threats or vulnerabilities. Where the appropriate response is risk mitigation, system owners plan and initiate remediation actions, adding the details regarding corrective actions and the schedule for their completion to the plan of action and milestones. Any security controls added, modified, or enhanced during the continuous monitoring process or as a result of ongoing security control assessments should be reassessed to ensure that the actions taken satisfactorily address the identified weaknesses or deficiencies.

Key Updates

To achieve the continuous monitoring objectives of maintaining situational awareness of all operational information systems and enabling real-time risk management [31], organizations need to establish the technical and procedural capabilities to collect and communicate accurate security status information to system owners, authorizing officials, and other designated information resources management decision makers. One way to provide this information is to implement automated monitoring tools and aggregate the monitoring data they produce in a format and level of detail that facilitates reporting and active risk management. Because the system security plan, security assessment report, and plan of action and milestones collectively represent the authoritative source of security information about an information system, system owners also need to keep the information in these documents current, updating them as necessary to reflect changes effected as a result of continuous monitoring activities, ongoing assessments, or responses to risk associated with new threats or vulnerabilities [32].

System security plan updates include control specifications and any modifications to security control configuration implemented to mitigate risk, including changes corresponding to completed corrective actions described in the plan of action and milestones. Security control assessors update the security assessment report and supporting assessment documentation whenever ongoing assessments are performed. Even when subsequent assessments confirm the findings of previous evaluations and identify no new weaknesses or deficiencies, the security assessment report should be updated to indicate the most recent date of assessment. Conversely, when agencies identify weaknesses and deficiencies—through ongoing assessments or manual or automated monitoring activities—system owners update the plan of action and milestones to include new corrective actions to be taken. The POA&M should also be updated as corrective actions are completed and milestones are achieved to record progress made against outstanding items listed in the plan. Keeping system security documentation current helps ensure that authorizing officials, senior information security officers, and other organizational officials who rely on documentation to support effective risk-based decision-making act on accurate information.

Given the volume of information contained in key system security documentation, organizations that maintain this information in document-based form may not find it practical to update and release new versions of major documents after each and every change. Many automated security management and reporting tools store control implementation and assessment information and POA&M details in a structured repository or database and have the capability to generate security plans and other artifacts on-demand. Such tools facilitate the implementation of configuration control processes on system security information, provide version control and audit trails for changes in assessment and implementation details, and allow system owners and authorizing officials to view the most current system information.

Security Status Reporting

Security status reporting summarizes system security information collected through continuous monitoring and other ongoing operational security activities and delivers or makes available the report information to system owners, authorizing officials, senior information security officers, and other appropriate organizational officials. Reporting occurs on an ongoing basis at a frequency and level of detail specified in organizational and system-specific monitoring strategies or as needed to comply with applicable regulatory requirements, including those for reporting POA&M information and other security metrics required to support agency-level FISMA reporting.

The results of all ongoing security management and monitoring activities should be documented to provide visibility into operational systems security, establish tracking and individual accountability for the completion of corrective actions and security-related administration and maintenance functions, and facilitate the identification of trends in the organizational information security program. Depending on organizational policy and the monitoring and reporting capabilities an organization implements, security status reporting may be event-driven, time-driven; or both [32]. Security status reports provide current information regarding the security state of each information system, including the effectiveness of deployed security controls where this information can be collected through automated monitoring. Security status reports also describe the ongoing monitoring activities applicable to each system, identifying the types of controls or specific controls subject to various types of monitoring and indicating the monitoring frequency (or referring to this information in the system monitoring strategy). Security status reports also enumerate weaknesses, deficiencies, or vulnerabilities identified through security control assessments or control monitoring and report progress on addressing those issues.

With the exception of system-level information needed to support aggregated agency security reporting to satisfy FISMA requirements, federal agencies have substantial flexibility to specify the level of security reporting that best suits organizational monitoring and risk management needs. This flexibility extends to the breadth and depth of security information reported and the frequency with which status reports are provided to organizational officials, allowing agencies to determine the most cost-effective or efficient approach to reporting consistent with achieving reporting objectives [32]. Many agencies emphasize reporting security status when changes occur to systems and their system security plans, security assessment reports, and plans of action and milestones. For some organizations, reports indicating no change in status are also considered important to provide evidence to suggest that currently implemented security controls are operating as intended.

Ongoing Risk Determination and Acceptance

The authorizing official regularly reviews the security status reports and updated system security documentation to determine the current information security risk to the organization. When the risk associated with an information system changes, the authorizing official determines—with input from the senior information security officer, risk managers, and other personnel as appropriate—whether the current risk is acceptable to the organization. The use of automated continuous monitoring and security reporting tools can facilitate process of reassessing information security risk, although given the subjective nature of risk level assignment and agency articulations of risk tolerance, risk determination and acceptance generally cannot be completely automated. Risk is dynamic; the sources and magnitude of risk faced by the organization change over time due to factors identified through continuous monitoring and ongoing security assessments and provided in security status reports [33]. Authorizing officials and organizational risk managers must evaluate how changing circumstances affect the information security risk to mission or business needs to determine the level of protection required to maintain adequate security. The process of ongoing risk determination and risk acceptance is particularly important for maintaining system security authorization in organizations that have waived fixed authorization periods in favor of continuous monitoring.

Information System Removal and Decommissioning

When a federal information system reaches the end of its useful life and is withdrawn from operation, the system owner's primary security-related is ensuring that all assets of value to the organization are retained and that all agency information is removed from the system and its storage media. The RMF directs agencies to establish a format information system decommissioning strategy, comprising several processes corresponding to operational security controls that system owners execute when removing a system from operation [33]. Key system removal and decommissioning procedures include those specified in security control implementation guidance for configuration management planning, controlled maintenance, and media sanitization [34]. While agencies and their system owners are justifiably concerned about preventing the exposure of sensitive information, media sanitization procedures applicable to information systems at all security categorization levels require agencies to remove all information from all types of media intended for disposal or reuse [35]. Requirements associated with system removal also apply when agencies modify systems by replacing or removing subsystems or system components and the associated hardware, software, and storage media.

Agencies perform security-related activities for information system removal and decommissioning within the broader SDLC context of system disposal. System owner responsibilities include updating system inventories and IT asset tracking systems to reflect the removal of the system and its components and indicating the change in phase for the system in security and other status reports [36].

> **NOTE**
>
> Not all federal information systems have clearly defined ends to their operation. It is common in federal agencies for systems to undergo significant development, modification, and enhancement throughout the operations and maintenance phase of the SDLC, so a single system with the same name and unique identifier may evolve over time to bear little resemblance to the system as originally deployed. Periodic upgrades to systems or replacement of underlying technologies may trigger a need for reauthorization of the modified system rather than disposal. Individual system components may be retired or replaced as functional requirements change and technologies evolves, but in such cases system owners often continue to maintain the system under the same name and IT investment, updating their system security plans and other documentation to reflect the changes. Organizations may specify their own policies regarding the extent of changes to a system that requires decommissioning rather than revision.

System disposal activities emphasize the continued protection of government resources and information assets associated with the system, including preserving any information about the system that could inform future deployment of the same or similar systems. Information owners responsible for data stored or processed by the system need to evaluate the value of the data to the organization, the need for the agency to continue to use or access the data, and applicable policy or regulations about data preservation such as records management requirements. System owners oversee archiving of any information the organization needs to retain, media sanitization, and disposal of physical IT assets such as hardware, whether by destruction or by approved repurposing or reuse where authorized.

RELEVANT SOURCE MATERIAL

Several NIST Special Publications and Federal Information Processing Standards provide guidance, recommendations, and instructions relevant to performing security categorization and security control selection. The most applicable sources of information include:

- Special Publication 800-37 Revision 1, *Guide for Applying the Risk Management Framework to Federal Information Systems* [37].
- Special Publication 800-53 Revision 3, *Recommended Security Controls for Federal Information Systems and Organizations* [34].
- Special Publication 800-53A Revision 1, *Guide for Assessing the Security Controls in Federal Information Systems and Organizations* [38].
- Special Publication 800-137, Information Security Continuous Monitoring for Federal Information Systems and Organizations [6].

These and other NIST Special Publications are available from the NIST Computer Security Division Website, at http://csrc.nist.gov/publications/.

SUMMARY

This chapter described the RMF tasks leading up to the decision to authorize an information system to operate and the ongoing monitoring and security management activities performed for operational systems once authorized. It identified some of the key factors organizations and their authorizing officials consider when determining information security risk and evaluating systems to ensure that the security controls implemented and assessed for each system provide adequate security to bring risk within levels acceptable to the organization. The chapter also described the iterative set of tasks executed to support ongoing risk management for information systems, which collectively help system owners ensure that the security posture of their systems continues to satisfy security requirements, even if those requirements change to reflect new threats and vulnerabilities, added or removed functional and technical capabilities, or modifications to the environment in which the systems operate.

REFERENCES

[1] Kissel R, Stine K, Scholl M, Rossman H, Fahlsing J, Gulick J. Security considerations in the system development life cycle. Gaithersburg, MD: National Institute of Standards and Technology, Computer Security Division; October 2008. Special Publication 800-64 revision 2. p. 31.

[2] OMB specifies a maximum three-year period in Appendix III, Security of federal automated information resources. Washington, DC: Office of Management and Budget; November 2000. Circular No. A-130, Revised (Transmittal Memorandum No. 4).

[3] Guide for applying the risk management framework to federal information systems. Gaithersburg, MD: National Institute of Standards and Technology, Computer Security Division; February 2010. Special Publication 800-37 revision 1. p. F-4.

[4] Guide for applying the risk management framework to federal information systems. Gaithersburg, MD: National Institute of Standards and Technology, Computer Security Division; February 2010. Special Publication 800-37 revision 1. p. 36. In contrast, the previous version of Special Publication 800-37 explicitly identified three decision alternatives: authorization to operate, interim authorization to operate, or denial of authorization.

[5] Guide for applying the risk management framework to federal information systems. Gaithersburg, MD: National Institute of Standards and Technology, Computer Security Division; February 2010. Special Publication 800-37 revision 1. p. 19.

[6] Dempsey K, Chawla N, Johnson A, Johnson R, Jones A, Orebaugh A, et al. Information security continuous monitoring for federal information systems and organizations. Gaithersburg, MD: National Institute of Standards and Technology, Computer Security Division; September 2011.. Special Publication 800-137.

[7] Guide for applying the risk management framework to federal information systems. Gaithersburg, MD: National Institute of Standards and Technology, Computer Security Division; February 2010. Special Publication 800-37 revision 1. p. 36.

[8] Lew JJ. Reporting instructions for the Federal Information Security Management Act and agency privacy management. Washington, DC: Office of Management and Budget;

September 14, 2011. Memorandum M-11-33. Response to question 28 in "Frequently Asked Questions on Reporting for FISMA." p. 10–1.

[9] Guide for applying the risk management framework to federal information systems. Gaithersburg, MD: National Institute of Standards and Technology, Computer Security Division; February 2010. Special Publication 800-37 revision 1. p. 34.

[10] Kissel R, Stine K, Scholl M, Rossman H, Fahlsing J, Gulick J. Security considerations in the system development life cycle. Gaithersburg, MD: National Institute of Standards and Technology, Computer Security Division; October 2008. Special Publication 800-64 revision 2. p. 28.

[11] Daniels ME. Guidance for preparing and submitting security plans of action and milestones. Washington, DC: Office of Management and Budget; October 17, 2001. Memorandum M-02-01.

[12] Barker E, Roginsky A. Transitions: recommendation for transitioning the use of cryptographic algorithms and key lengths. Gaithersburg, MD: National Institute of Standards and Technology, Computer Security Division; January 2011. Special Publication 800-131A. pp. 13–4.

[13] . See for exampleLew JJ. Reporting instructions for the Federal Information Security Management Act and agency privacy management. Washington, DC: Office of Management and Budget; September 14, 2011. Memorandum M-11-33.

[14] Bolten JB. FY 2004 reporting instructions for the Federal Information Security Management Act. Washington, DC: Office of Management and Budget; August 23, 2004.. Memorandum M-04-25. p. 15–6.

[15] OMB mandated automated security reporting through the CyberScope online tool beginning in late 2010. See Zients J, Kundra V, Schmidt HA. FY 2010 reporting instructions for the Federal Information Security Management Act and agency privacy management. Washington, DC: Office of Management and Budget; April 21, 2010. Memorandum M-10-15.

[16] Adapted from Guide for applying the risk management framework to federal information systems. Gaithersburg, MD: National Institute of Standards and Technology, Computer Security Division; February 2010. Special Publication 800-37 revision 1. p. F-3.

[17] Recommended security controls for federal information systems and organizations. Gaithersburg, MD: National Institute of Standards and Technology, Computer Security Division; August 2009. Special Publication 800-53 revision 3. p. F-93.

[18] Guide for conducting risk assessments. Gaithersburg, MD: National Institute of Standards and Technology, Computer Security Division; September 2011. Special Publication 800-30 revision 1. Initial Public Draft. p. 11.

[19] Managing information security risk: organization, mission, and information system view. Gaithersburg, MD: National Institute of Standards and Technology, Computer Security Division; March 2011. Special Publication 800-39. p. 7.

[20] Managing information security risk: organization, mission, and information system view. Gaithersburg, MD: National Institute of Standards and Technology, Computer Security Division; March 2011. Special Publication 800-39. p. 42.

[21] Guide for applying the risk management framework to federal information systems. Gaithersburg, MD: National Institute of Standards and Technology, Computer Security Division; February 2010. Special Publication 800-37 revision 1. p. 35.

[22] Kissel R, Stine K, Scholl M, Rossman H, Fahlsing J, Gulick J. Security considerations in the system development life cycle. Gaithersburg, MD: National Institute of Standards and Technology, Computer Security Division; October 2008.. Special Publication 800-64 revision 2. p. 32.

[23] Multiple pieces of draft legislation introduced in both the House of Representatives and the Senate during the 112th Congress emphasize continuous monitoring of agency information system security. See for example the Federal Information Security Amendments Act of 2012 (H.R. 4257), the Cybersecurity Act of 2012 (S. 2105), and the Strengthening and Enhancing Cybersecurity by Using Research, Education, Information, and Technology Act of 2012 (H.R. 4263 and S.2151).

[24] Ross R, Swanson M, Stoneburner G, Katzke S, Johnson A. Guide for the security certification and accreditation of federal information systems. Gaithersburg, MD: National Institute of Standards and Technology, Computer Security Division; May 2004. Special Publication 800-37.

[25] Kissel R, Stine K, Scholl M, Rossman H, Fahlsing J, Gulick J. Security considerations in the system development life cycle. Gaithersburg, MD: National Institute of Standards and Technology, Computer Security Division; October 2008.. Special Publication 800-64 revision 2. p. 33.

[26] Guide for applying the risk management framework to federal information systems. Gaithersburg, MD: National Institute of Standards and Technology, Computer Security Division; February 2010. Special Publication 800-37 revision 1. p. 38.

[27] Many commercial vendors of security monitoring, vulnerability scanning, and event management tools support the SCAP protocol in their products. See Security Content Automation Protocol Validated Products [Internet]. Washington, DC: Department of Homeland Security, National Cyber Security Division [cited May 17, 2012]. <http://nvd.nist.gov/scapproducts.cfm>.

[28] Guide for applying the risk management framework to federal information systems. Gaithersburg, MD: National Institute of Standards and Technology, Computer Security Division; February 2010. Special Publication 800-37 revision 1. p. 39.

[29] Federal Information Security Management Act of 2002, Pub. L. No. 107-347, 116 Stat. 2946. §301, codified at 44 U.S.C. §3544(b)(5).

[30] Federal Information Security Management Act of 2002, Pub. L. No. 107-347, 116 Stat. 2946. §301, codified at 44 U.S.C. §3544(b)(6).

[31] Dempsey K, Chawla N, Johnson A, Johnson R, Jones A, Orebaugh A, et al. Information security continuous monitoring for federal information systems and organizations. Gaithersburg, MD: National Institute of Standards and Technology, Computer Security Division; September 2011.. Special Publication 800-137. p. 1.

[32] Guide for applying the risk management framework to federal information systems. Gaithersburg, MD: National Institute of Standards and Technology, Computer Security Division; February 2010. Special Publication 800-37 revision 1. p. 40.

[33] Guide for applying the risk management framework to federal information systems. Gaithersburg, MD: National Institute of Standards and Technology, Computer Security Division; February 2010. Special Publication 800-37 revision 1. p. 41.

[34] Recommended security controls for federal information systems and organizations. Gaithersburg, MD: National Institute of Standards and Technology, Computer Security Division; August 2009. Special Publication 800-53 revision 3.

[35] Recommended security controls for federal information systems and organizations. Gaithersburg, MD: National Institute of Standards and Technology, Computer Security Division; August 2009. Special Publication 800-53 revision 3. p. F-75.

[36] Kissel R, Stine K, Scholl M, Rossman H, Fahlsing J, Gulick J. Security considerations in the system development life cycle. Gaithersburg, MD: National Institute of Standards

and Technology, Computer Security Division; October 2008.. Special Publication 800-64 revision 2. p. 36.

[37] Guide for applying the risk management framework to federal information systems. Gaithersburg, MD: National Institute of Standards and Technology, Computer Security Division; February 2010. Special Publication 800-37 revision 1.

[38] Guide for assessing the security controls in federal information systems and organizations. Gaithersburg, MD: National Institute of Standards and Technology, Computer Security Division; June 2010. Special Publication 800-53A revision 1.

System Security Plan

10

INFORMATION IN THIS CHAPTER:

- Purpose and Role of the System Security Plan
- Contents of the System Security Plan
- Processes and Activities for Developing the SSP
- Finalizing and Delivering the SSP
- Using and Maintaining the System Security Plan

Information security is an essential part of the development, deployment, and operation of any system that establishes and maintains appropriate measures to protect the confidentiality, integrity, and availability of the system and the data accessed via the system. Implementing and managing effective information security for information systems requires careful thought and analysis about what level of protection is needed and the best way to provide that protection. Key inputs to information system security include risk assessments, security categorization of systems and the information they contain, and functional and technical requirements that systems must satisfy to serve their intended purpose. Security planning is the process by which organizations consider their information systems, determine system security requirements, and select security controls or other protective measures to adequately safeguard their systems and the environment in which they operate. These system-level and organizational considerations are formally documented in a system security plan (SSP). The system security plan describes the general functional and technical characteristics of the information system, its security requirements, and the set of controls implemented or planned for implementation to satisfy those requirements [1]. The SSP is the primary piece of security documentation for an information system, providing a foundational element of the certification and accreditation package used to support system authorization to operate, and serving as the master guide for managing the operational security of a system once authorized [2]. Beyond its practical purpose, the SSP is also required for each information system under the provisions of OMB Circular A-130 [3] and the Federal Information Security Management Act (FISMA) [4] and is included as a required Special Publication 800-53 security control (PL-2) for systems at all impact levels [5]. This chapter describes the purpose and scope of the system security plan, its central position within the Risk Management Framework, the structure and typical content of a SSP, and the process of developing, finalizing, and delivering the SSP to authorizing officials and other key stakeholders. It also explains the use and periodic review and update of the SSP in support of operational security management practices such as continuous monitoring.

PURPOSE AND ROLE OF THE SYSTEM SECURITY PLAN

The main purpose of the system security plan is to fully describe the security posture of an information system, including providing a comprehensive listing of all controls selected for the system. This detailed documentation offers readers of the SSP a single authoritative source of security information about an information system and provides a primary point of reference to other plans and artifacts referenced in the SSP. The information contained in the SSP is used by numerous other RMF processes and activities and serves as an input to many other security-related plans, such as those for configuration management, business continuity, incident response. The SSP also constitutes one of the most influential documents—along with the security assessment report and plan of action and milestones—used by authorizing officials to make decisions about whether to authorize an information system. The SSP is often among the first security documents to be developed, at least in draft form, but is also one of the last to be finalized, since in its final form it includes updates and summary information drawn from other artifacts. The security planning process parallels conventional system development life cycle (SLDC) processes, with activities or steps related to system security plans occurring in every major SDLC phase from initiation through disposal [6]. The SSP informs and is informed by non-security related system development decisions and, given the critical role of the SSP in obtaining authorization to operate, completing the SSP represents a key milestone in the process of successfully deploying a new information system.

System Security Plan Scope

The scope of a system security plan is, as the name implies, a single system. While the NIST Risk Management Framework and much of the recent guidance offered in NIST Special Publications addresses security from an enterprise perspective, system-specific security plans are required for each information system. The general term *information system* has a very specific meaning in the federal information security context, comprising three categories: major applications, minor applications, and general support systems [7]. The official definitions for *major application* (MA) and *general support system* (GSS) come from OMB Circular A-130, Appendix III, in which a major application is one "that requires special attention to security due to the risk and magnitude of the harm resulting from the loss, misuse, or unauthorized access to or modification of the information in the application" and a general support system is "an interconnected set of information resources under the same direct management control which shares common functionality" [3]. Minor (sometimes called "non-major") applications are those that constitute neither major applications nor general support systems. The distinction between major and minor applications is somewhat subjective, but federal guidance suggests that applications deemed to require explicit management attention or special oversight and should be treated as major [7]. In addition, Special Publication 800-18 notes that major applications are expected to have security categorizations of moderate or high, with low-impact applications typically not classified as major [8]. Minor applications certainly require protective measures, but the security controls for such applications are captured in the security plans of the general support systems or major applications whose boundaries include the minor applications. This means the single "system" described in a system security plan may encompass multiple minor applications, but reflects at most one major application or general support system.

Defining the System Boundary

Whether for a major application or a general support system, the system boundary establishes the explicit scope of a system security plan for an information system. Both logical and physical perspectives inform the system boundary definition, so system owners need to consider not only the set of components, technologies, or information resources that belong to the system, but also the environment in which the system operates and the management responsibility for the system and its operating environment. In general, the set of assets and resources identified as part of a system and addressed in a single system security plan should be under the same management control [9]. For a general support system (GSS) this means that subsystems or minor applications operating within the GSS ordinarily fall under the same management control, just as their authorization to operate is under the authority of the same authorizing official. The official definition of system is sufficiently vague that agencies typically have some latitude in defining their information systems. NIST suggests that when determining whether to define multiple components or resources as part of the same information system, agencies should consider the extent to which they serve the same purpose, have similar operating characteristics and security requirements, and physically reside in the same or similar operating environments [10]. The system boundary establishes the scope not only of the system security plan, but also of the certification and accreditation boundary to which system authorization decision applies. Agencies and their system owners need to carefully consider the business, technical, and practical implications for system boundary definition, particularly when multiple applications or subsystems are involved. Given the potential for such complex systems to reflect more than one security categorization level, system owners should exercise particular caution when defining system boundaries comprising more than one security impact level. With the FIPS 200 requirement that the highest categorization for any application or subsystem sets the categorization for the entire system [11], system security plans for non-national security systems should include the security impact level for all information types, system components and subsystems, to ensure that the overall system security categorization reflects the high-water mark. Similarly, the security categorization for a general support system must be equal to or higher than the categorization for any major or non-major applications that reside within the GSS boundary. The security categorization guidance applicable to national security systems does not use the high-water mark approach found in FIPS 200, but the security categorizations established for confidentiality, integrity, and availability still determine the minimum security control baselines for such systems [12].

From an enterprise perspective, the set of system boundaries defined for different major applications and general support systems often produces a hierarchical or nested structure, as illustrated in Figure 10.1. Depending on the system's characteristics, system security plans may need to refer to the system-specific boundary, a general support system boundary such as that defined for a data center that hosts the system, and an enterprise system boundary reflecting organization-wide policies, standards, resources, funding, or oversight. Many agencies engage third parties such as contractors or infrastructure, platform, and application service providers to host, operate, or manage their systems. In such cases the system boundary includes operating environments and information resources external to the agency.

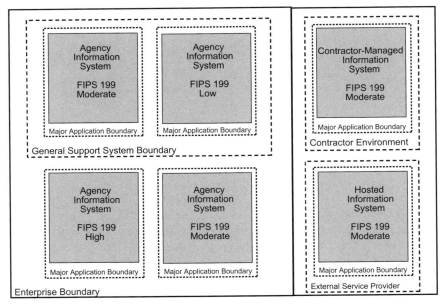

FIGURE 10.1 System boundaries reflect system resources and any relevant subsystems as well as the environment in which the system operates, whether that environment is internal or external to the organization

The system boundary describes the operating environment, the set of assets and resources belonging or assigned to the system, the minor applications (if any) operating within the system boundary, and relevant security controls. Although the security categorization level drives the baseline set of minimum security controls for a system, most federal information systems incorporate at least some agency-level or non-system-specific common controls, which the system security plan includes along with the system-specific controls. Common controls at the agency level—such as the policies and procedures associated with each of the security control families in Special Publication 800-53 [13]—are often provided and managed outside the system boundary. These controls and any resources used by the system but outside its sphere of management control are identified in the system security plan and incorporated by reference, rather than described in detail within the SSP.

Key Roles and Responsibilities

The primary responsibility for the system security plan rests with the system owner, but developing a SSP is not a one-person job, and delivering a complete SSP typically requires input and active participation from many different sources and individuals. Table 10.1 summarizes the responsibilities associated with key roles in the system security planning process. For federal information systems, the system owner, information owner, information system security officer, and authorizing official are all roles filled by agency personnel [1]; common control providers and information security architect roles may be performed by agency personnel or by non-government personnel where system development or operations and maintenance are provided under contract or other arrangements.

The Role of the SSP within the RMF

The system security plan is one of three core documents—along with the security assessment report and plan of action and milestones—on which authorizing officials rely to make decisions about granting or denying authority to operate for federal information systems. Because the SSP includes functional and technical information about the system, the security requirements needed to ensure the confidentiality, integrity, and availability of the system, and a complete listing of controls selected and implement for the system, the SSP typically serves as the primary authoritative source of information about securing the system and managing its safeguards. The SSP is the first of the core RMF documents to be developed, beginning with the information produced in step 1 (categorize information system) and step 2 (select security controls) [2]. Subsequent steps of the risk management framework rely on information captured in the system security plan during these initial phases, particularly including the implementation and assessment of security controls (RMF steps 3 and 4, respectively) specified in the SSP. The results of key activities such as the security control assessment serve as inputs back to the SSP, which is updated to reflect control remediation and other recommendations in the security assessment report.

Table 10.1 Roles and Responsibilities for System Security Planning [10,14]

Participant	Roles
Common Control Provider	Documents security controls provided to systems
Information Owner	Establishes rules of behavior for information used by the system; provides input on security requirements and security controls for the system(s) where the information resides; determines access requirements and privileges; helps identify and assess the common security controls
Information Security Architect	Helps the information system owner select the controls for the system and document those controls in the SSP
Information System Owner	Develops the SSP in coordination with information owners, the system administrator, the information system security officer, the senior agency information security officer, and system development or deployment personnel; maintains the SSP and ensures the system is deployed and operated according to the agreed-upon security requirements; updates the SSP whenever a significant change occurs; and helps identify and assess the common security controls
Information System Security Officer	Assists the senior agency information security officer to identify, implement, and assess common security controls; actively contributes to developing and updating the SSP as well as coordinating with the information system owner
Authorizing Official	Reviews and approves the SSP; authorizes (or rejects the authorization of) the information system to operate

NOTE

Federal guidance clearly places the responsibility for system security plan development with the information system owner, defined in Special Publication 800-37 as "an *organizational* official responsible for the procurement, development, integration, modification, operation, maintenance, and disposal of an information system" (emphasis added) [15]. This assignment means that even when agencies rely on contractors or other entities to develop, implement, or operate their systems, responsibility for the system security plan and rests with government personnel. In early 2012, the General Services Administration (GSA) published a final rule requiring contractors working under GSA acquisition rules to submit an IT security plan within 30 days of contract award "that describes the processes and procedures that will be followed to ensure appropriate security of IT resources that are developed, processed, or used under the contract" [16]. The GSA rule refers to an "IT security plan" rather than system security plan, but requires plans prepared by contractors to comply with FISMA and other applicable laws and to meet government-wide and GSA requirements for IT security. Given the compliance requirements in the final rule, GSA contractors (notably including those working under government-wide acquisition contracts administered by GSA) are subject to substantially the same security planning requirements that apply to government agency system owners.

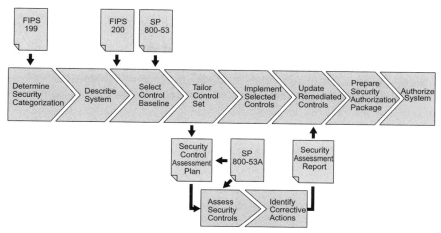

FIGURE 10.2 The System Security Plan Occupies a Foundational Position within the RMF, Providing an Essential Input to Key Processes Such As the Security Control Assessment

Figure 10.2 depicts the relationship between system security plan development activities and the security control assessment process.

The system security plan is so important to the system certification and accreditation process that the RMF includes a task for security plan approval by the authorizing official [17] separate from the risk acceptance and security authorization package approval associated with authorizing the information system. This approval, falling within step 2 of the RMF, provides an opportunity to evaluate the system security plan for its completeness and extent to which it satisfies the security requirements of the system, and to determine whether the SSP accurately identifies risk associated with the system and the residual risk faced by the agency if the system is authorized to operate with the specified security controls.

STRUCTURE AND CONTENT OF THE SYSTEM SECURITY PLAN

As the master source of information about the system from a security standpoint, the system security plan typically includes a large quantity of information. To make this information readily accessible and useful to authorized audiences, it is helpful to organize the content in the SSP in a logical manner and structure the plan itself in a way that makes it easy for readers to find the information they are seeking. To the extent that agencies have the governance in place to implement and enforce security documentation standards, using the same SSP structure and content requirements for all information systems across an agency facilitates the review and assessment of the plans by authorizing officials and others who manage, evaluate, or oversee multiple systems in the same agency. While the SSP contains a great deal of detailed information about an information system, it also provides links or references to related documents, subordinate plans and security artifacts, policies and procedures, and information about the implementation details of specific security controls. The fact that the SSP lists all the selected security controls for an information system means that system security plans are often long documents, adding a further incentive to structure the SSP in a way that makes it possible to navigate efficiently to find specific information when needed.

System Security Plan Format

Special Publication 800-18, *Guide for Developing Security Plans for Federal Information Systems*, specifies the minimum content requirements for a system security plan, and provides a basic template and instructions for completing the SSP following the content outline [1]. There is no specific format required for the SSP, although the conventional presentation of the SSP as a document-based artifact leads most agencies to develop their plans using common word processing and print or online publication formats. System owners in agencies using computer-assisted certification and accreditation processes may be able to enter the relevant SSP information into online forms or databases and use the computer program to generate the SSP artifact using the information captured and stored in the program. Following NIST guidance, system security plans are often organized into two major sections, with the first presenting descriptive information about the system and the second provided a detailed listing of all security controls selected for the system. The following subsections describe the key content elements for system security plans prescribed by Special Publication 800-18, highlighting the nature of the information expected to be included in the plan, likely sources for this information, and the roles or individuals responsible for providing it.

TIP

Most federal agencies develop their own system security plan templates and require system owners to use those templates to ensure consistency for all systems across an agency or at least within the management purview of the authorizing official. Many agency-specific templates are publicly available, so in cases where a system owner is faced with developing a new SSP from scratch there are examples to follow. Agency templates typically include at least the content items specified in Special Publication 800-18, and may include additional information requirements based on the needs of the agency producing the template. Representative examples of agency SSP templates include those from the National Aeronautics and Space Administration (NASA) [18], Department of Housing and Urban Development (HUD) [19], Federal Deposit Insurance Corporation (FDIC) [20], and Centers for Disease Control and Prevention (CDC) [21], the last of which is offered as an explicit example by NIST on its website.[22] The SSP template from the Centers for Medicare and Medicaid Services (CMS) [23] offers an example of a plan extending beyond NIST guidance to reflect cross-references to risk assessment and risk management activities as well as integration with system development life cycle (SDLC) processes.

System Identification

Every system security plan documents a different system, so the first item the SSP describes is the name of the system and its identifier. NIST guidance assumes that agencies assign unique identifiers to all systems (whether or not the system name is unique), to enable effective tracking and consistent references to the system across the agency [24]. Agencies report different types of information about systems to OMB, GAO, and other oversight bodies using different processes, forms, and methods, so the use of unique system identifiers facilitates tracking and correlation of system-level information communicated at different times through different mechanisms. Agencies are free to use any naming and identification standards they wish, but the use of unique identifiers falls under agency-wide IT governance, to ensure that system owners select identifiers that are actually unique within the agency. Various security information about systems is included in the agency FISMA inventory, incident reports, and other communications to audiences outside the agency, so is also a good idea to use system identifiers that uniquely identify the agency responsible for the system. One approach familiar to many system owners is the construction of the unique project identifier (UPI) used to identify each IT investment in the agency's IT portfolio as part of the capital planning and investment control (CPIC) process. Although in 2011 OMB simplified the requirements for unique investment identifiers, guidance to agencies on reporting IT investments still provides a detailed numeric coding scheme that captures descriptive aspects about the nature, purpose, and ownership of each investment [25]. Agencies that choose to adopt meaningful coding standards for unique system identifiers need to make system owners aware of the proper procedure for developing an identifier. Information system owners typically have responsibility for assigning unique system identifiers and registering the system or otherwise officially recording the name and any other identification attributes [26]. Determining an appropriate identifier may require coordination with or input from the investment owner or owners responsible for funding the system (if the investment owner is different from the system owner), the senior agency

---

WARNING

Because major applications and general support systems often involve substantial capital investments for the agencies that develop and operate them, many agencies use unique investment identifiers as reported on their IT investment portfolios (or the corresponding unique project identifier used prior to the fiscal year 2013 budget cycle) to identify information systems. OMB Circular A-11 requires each agency IT investment to be uniquely identified, using a coding standard that also identifies the agency to which the investment belongs [27]. Nothing in federal CPIC guidance, however, requires a one-to-one mapping between IT investments and the systems whose development or sustainment those investments fund. This means it is possible for a single IT investment to fund more than one information system in an agency, or for a single system to be partially funded by multiple investments. Unless IT investment identifiers correspond to only one system each, agencies should use system-specific unique identifiers instead of or in addition to investment identifiers.

information security officer or others responsible for the agency's FISMA inventory, or designated other IT governance personnel. Support for system identifier selection can also be provided to system owners as part of the information system registration task in step 1 of the RMF.

System Categorization

The system security plan documents the results of the security categorization task carried out at the beginning of step 1 in the RMF. As described in detail in Chapter 7, every federal information system must be categorized following guidance in FIPS 199 [28] that instruct agencies and their information system owners and information owners to assess the potential impact associated with a loss of confidentiality, integrity, or availability of the information system or the information it contains. Using the security categorization process, system owners determine the overall impact level for each information system, with three possible categorizations: low, moderate, or high (Table 7.2 lists the standard definitions for these impact levels). The security impact level for an information system determines the minimum security requirements needed to safeguard its confidentiality, integrity, and availability, and corresponds to one of three security control baselines in Special Publication 800-53 [13]. The baselines represent starting points for information system owners to select the appropriate set of security controls for their systems, so completing the security categorization is a prerequisite to beginning the security control selection process. Agencies operating national security systems follow similar procedures for system security categorization, but assign separate impact levels for confidentiality, integrity, and availability, resulting in 27 possible combinations and corresponding baselines [29].

Federal guidance directs each system owner to follow the same security categorization process, first assessing the information types used by the system and then considering the system itself. The overall security categorization reflects the highest level determined for confidentiality, integrity, or availability for the system or any of its information types. This high-water mark approach [30] means that the minimum security requirements for an information system are whatever is needed to protect the most sensitive or highest impact information the system stores, processes, or accesses. Information owners and system owners are expected to adopt an organization-wide perspective when conducting security categorizations, to ensure that impact levels accurately reflect mission and business objectives [31]. Security categorization under the RMF is usually documented separately using a FIPS 199-based template or worksheet, with the system security plan typically containing only the results of the security categorization process. Information system owners in agencies requiring more detailed explanations or justification for the categorization sometimes include separate confidentiality, integrity, and availability categorizations for the system, or a list of information types used by the system and their associated impact levels.

Security categorization is inherently a subjective process. Information owners and system owners use their knowledge of the organization, the information system, and the way the system will be used and apply their best judgment regarding the severity of a loss of confidentiality, integrity, or availability. The definitions in FIPS 199 for low-, moderate-, and high-impact levels are also subjective, corresponding to "limited," "serious," or "severe or catastrophic" adverse effects [32]. The fact that each system owner follows the same security categorization process cannot ensure that information types are accurately or consistently identified across systems, or that impact levels are consistently assigned. Agencies that leave security categorization entirely up to personnel associated with each system run the risk of information systems with similar information types and potential impacts being categorized differently. In such situations the potential exists for agencies to under- or over-allocate resources to safeguard inaccurately categorized systems—either by implementing unnecessary controls for a system mis-categorized at a higher impact level or by failing to implement appropriate controls for a system mis-categorized at a lower impact level. One way to mitigate this risk is for agencies to develop standard categorizations for information types and impact levels and to provide explicit guidance to system owners on evaluating their systems. NIST offers guidance to agencies on default categorizations by information type in Special Publication 800-60 [33], but many agencies may find that their use of certain information types raises security concerns that do not apply to every agency. In contrast, issuing agency-specific (or bureau- or operating division-specific) guidance to system owners on accurately identifying and categorizing information types in their systems can both simplify the security categorization process for system owners and ensure more consistent impact level determinations across the agency [34].

Designation of Key Roles

The system security plan identifies key individual associated with the system and their roles, providing contact information for each individual. There is no minimum or maximum number of roles that might be included in an SSP, although Special Publication 800-18 lists the system owner, authorizing official, individual responsible for system security, and "other designated contacts" [35]. Depending on the scope of the system, the environment in which it is deployed, and the parties responsible for developing, maintaining, or managing it, the SSP might also designate roles and individuals responsible for providing common controls, operating and supporting the system, and responding to incidents or maintaining business continuity for the system. For federal information systems developed or managed on behalf of the government by third parties, such as contractors or hosting service providers, the SSP might also include roles and contact information for the project manager, information system security officer, data center or managed service provider, and contract officer or other government personnel responsible for managing the relationship between the agency and the third party.

Operational Status

System security plans are required for newly developed systems as well as those already in operation. System owners indicate the status of the information system documented in the SSP using one of three values: operational, under development, or undergoing a major modification [36]. Prior to receiving authorization to operate, new systems are designated "under development," with the status updated to "operational" once authority to operate has been approved and the system has been put into production. Systems "undergoing a major modification" may remain in production while the modification occurs, but this designation provides an indication that the functional and technical characteristics of the system will change, invoking a need to update system certification and accreditation documentation and, potentially, to re-authorize the system once modifications are complete.

System Type

As noted previous in the section System Security Plan Scope, information systems documented in system security plans are one of two types: major applications or general support systems. The SSP explicitly indicates the system type, referencing the system boundary and general system description information where relevant. The SSP describes the relationship between the system that is the subject of the SSP and any subordinate systems such as minor applications incorporated within the same system boundary. System security plans for general support systems should identify all applications operating within the general support system boundary. Systems designated as major applications may still rely on general support systems (such as data centers or local area networks), so the SSP also describes any dependencies, connections, or interrelationships between the major application and general support systems. System owners responsible for major applications with such dependencies must be aware of the security controls implemented for the general support system—whether or not the information system inherits them as common controls—and accept the risk associated with the general support system's security posture. In addition to documenting the system type and documenting any relationships with general support systems, Special Publication 800-18 directs major application system owners to notify the general support system owner of security requirements for the major application; furnish a copy of the major application's SSP to the general support system owner; request a copy of and review the SSP for the general support system; and include references to the general support system security plan where applicable, such as when the general support system provides a common control inherited by the major application [37].

NOTE

OMB and NIST guidance suggests that moderate or high security categorizations are expected for major applications. In contrast, general support systems may appropriately be categorized as low impact, as long as all of the applications supported by the general support system are also designated as low impact according to FIPS 199. The security categorization for a general support system must be equal to or higher than the applications operating within it. System owners developing system security plans for major applications intended to be deployed within a general support system must ensure, once the system type and security categorization have been established, that the security categorization for the general support system is high enough to accommodate the major application.

A minor application does not have its own system security plans, but instead is documented as part of the system security plan for the major application or general support system in which it operates. In practice, this means that the security of the minor application is the responsibility of the major application or general support system that encompasses it, and from a security planning standpoint the system owner for the major application or general support system is considered to be the system owner for the minor application [38]. Common examples of minor applications include administrative, project management, or content or document management tools that do not store or process sensitive information.

System Description

While the primary purpose of the system security plan is to document the security requirements and corresponding controls for the system, the SSP also includes a general description of the function, purpose, and intended use of the information system. The system description for a general support system should also list all the major and minor applications residing within the general support system. Providing descriptive information about system and the mission and business functions it supports helps the authorizing official and other SSP readers to better understand the system, its value to the agency, and the risk to the agency applicable to the system. Documenting the system functionality and the information collected, processed, or made available to users of the system also provides some insight into the drivers behind the security requirements for the system. The system description should also include any designated primary mission essential functions the system supports, as systems serving such a role are subject to specific continuity of operations requirements that affect many security controls implemented for the system, particularly those associated with continuity planning [39]. The content for the system description information in the SSP can often be drawn from other documentation, potentially including business cases written to justify capital investments to fund the system, system design documents for developed systems, or vendor-provided materials for systems that implement commercial off-the-shelf technologies. System descriptions in the SSP documents should be brief [36], as the intent is not to exhaustively document the system functionality, but instead to characterize its general purpose, its functional and technical characteristics, and the types of internal or external users the system supports.

System Environment

The system security plan also provides a brief technical description of the system, addressing its major technical components and the nature of the environment in which the system operates. Special Publication 800-18 defines three common environment types: standalone, managed or enterprise, and custom [40]. Stand-alone environments typically refer to small system installations such as those that might be associated with a home office or telecommuting location. Managed or enterprise environments are characterized by well-defined network, hardware, and software components and configurations operated by IT personnel. The custom categorization is used when neither standalone nor managed or enterprise types apply, due to the unusual nature of the system or specialized requirements associated with its operating environment. As with the general system description, the system environment description in the SSP is intended to give basic technical information and highlight any special security issues or requirements. It is not intended to provide the sort of comprehensive or highly detailed information that might be expected to appear in other technical system documentation. Where feasible, including a logical or physical system architecture diagram—such as those commonly prepared during the design phase of the system development life cycle—is one way to concisely present this type of technical information.

System Interconnection and Information Sharing

Modern information systems rarely operate in isolation; more often, information systems are integrated or otherwise connected with other systems to enable data or resource sharing. Any direct connection from one information system to another represents a potential security concern, particularly when the interconnected system is owned or managed by an organization outside the agency. In such circumstances, it is essential for the system owner to understand the nature of system-to-system connections, the vulnerabilities associated with system interconnections, and the security controls other organizations put in place to safeguard their systems and points of interconnection. The system interconnection section of the SSP provides a list of, and key details about, all systems interconnected with the information system that is the subject of the SSP. More complete information about these interconnections is documented separately in the interconnection security agreements or memoranda of understanding developed and executed by the system owners; the use of these formal documents is required (as Special Publication 800-53 control CA-3) for all federal information systems [13], with the exception of intra-agency interconnections between systems subject to the same security requirements or under the supervision of the same authorizing official. Special Publication 800-47 provides guidance to agencies on using and securing system interconnections and on properly documenting all information sharing connections between systems [41]. Within the SSP, system owners should identify and provide basic descriptive information about each interconnected system, including its name, owning organization, interconnection type, interconnection authorization and date, security categorization, certification and accreditation status, and authorizing official [42]. System owners typically need to work with their counterparts responsible for interconnected systems to gather and accurately document the necessary details.

Laws, Regulations, and Policies

A wide array of laws, regulations, and policies include security and privacy requirements that may apply to a particular information system. All federal agency information systems are subject to general information security requirements in laws such as FISMA [43] and the Clinger-Cohen Act [44] and in memoranda and other guidance from OMB on implementing the provisions in these laws. Other legislation addresses uses of information and necessary safeguards specific to certain types of information, purposes for use, or segments of the population that apply to some agencies and systems but not others. The system security plan should list laws, regulations, or policies relevant to the security requirements of the system in question. Special Publication 800-18 emphasizes the inclusion of system- or agency-specific drivers of security requirements, suggesting that broadly applicable laws such as FISMA need not be cited in security plans [45]. Many agencies choose to include these laws, prepopulating their SSP templates with universally applicable laws, to which system owners can add system- or domain-specific sources of security requirements. For information systems that store or process records subject to the Privacy Act [46], the SSP should include not only a reference to the Privacy Act but also the system of record number and an indication of whether the system is used for computer matching activities [45]. This information is typically captured separately in the privacy impact assessment for the information system, so system owners can refer to that documentation when including the information in the SSP.

Security Control Selection

The heart of the system security plan is the selection of security controls needed to satisfy the system's security requirements. The process of selecting appropriate security controls—as described in detail in Chapter 8 and referenced again in Chapter 11—begins with the identification of the minimum necessary security controls. The security categorization drives this identification, where the impact level assigned to the system determines the appropriate starting point for the system security controls, in the form of one of the three security control baselines—specified for systems categorized as high-impact, moderate-impact, or low-impact—associated with Special Publication 800-53 [47]. There is no expectation that each system directly provides all the security controls in the designated baseline, but the SSP documents the full set of controls applicable to the system, including common controls provided at a general support system or agency-wide level, hybrid controls (those partially inherited and partially system-specific), and controls implemented specifically for the system. The security control selection section of the SSP documents the planned or actual implementation of all selected security controls, providing (in addition to the name of each control) a brief description of how each control is implemented and who is responsible for implementing it.

The security control baseline represents only a starting point because each system owner has the flexibility—subject to agency security policies, procedures, standards, and guidelines—to tailor the security control set to meet the needs of the system. Tailoring may include adding security controls beyond those specified in the baseline, substituting alternative or comparable compensating controls that differ from those in the baseline, specifying of system-level parameters for applicable controls, and applying one or more scoping factors that may affect the applicability of some controls in the baseline to the system [48]. All security control tailoring should be documented in the system security plan, as such documentation explains any deviations from the baseline controls that would be expected for a system at a designated security categorization level. Scoping considerations influence decisions to augment security control baselines, such as by implementing optional controls or control enhancements from Special Publication 800-53, or to choose not to implement specific controls due to their inapplicability to the system. Special Publication 800-18 identifies six categories of considerations that fall under the application of scoping guidance [49]:

- *Technology-related considerations* apply to security controls that address specific technologies, where such controls do not apply to systems that do not use the relevant technologies, or specific components of the system that provide security capabilities. Such considerations also apply where the mechanisms needed to deliver the security functionality required for the control are not readily available or technically feasible for the system, in which case the use of compensating controls may instead be used to meet minimum security requirements.
- *Common security control-related considerations* apply when agency-wide, group, or operating environment common controls are in place, particularly when the potential exists to implement system-specific controls to meet the same security requirements. Common controls are typically managed outside the responsibility of the system owner, so the use of common controls where feasible represents not only a source of cost efficiency but also a reduction in security management and oversight for the system owner. System owners need, however, to ensure that the capabilities of available common controls adequately meet the requirements of the system; if this is not the case, the control may need to be addressed as a hybrid or system-specific control instead.
- *Public access information systems-related considerations* apply for systems whose intended use includes public access, as some of the minimum security controls specified in security control baselines may not be applicable to use by the public or other non-agency users. Conversely, security controls intended to protect systems from threat sources using public interfaces may not apply to systems that restrict access to internal agency users.
- *Infrastructure-related considerations* apply in particular to physical and environmental controls associated with agency facilities that are likely to be provided as common controls for individual information systems and, even for general support systems such as data centers, apply only to the aspects of the physical, technical, or network infrastructure that protect, support, or otherwise relate to the information systems operating within the general support system environment. In many cases system owners have little ability to affect, alter, or even choose the infrastructure-related services and controls on which their systems depend, although it is important for system owners to recognize when the common infrastructure controls available to them may be insufficient to satisfy their system security requirements. In such cases, compensating controls may be necessary.
- *Scalability-related considerations* refer to the potential variability in some security controls—common or system-specific—depending on the size and

complexity of the agency implementing the controls, the mission-criticality or security categorization of the information system, and the scope of the controls within the agency. Consistent with principles of risk-based, cost-effective security management, security controls implemented should be commensurate with the functional scope defined in the relevant security control baseline, and with the environmental and operational needs of the agency and its information systems.

- *Risk-related considerations* apply to the extent that the system owner, authorizing official, or other agency risk executive decided to downgrade one or more security controls to the level specified in a lower baseline than indicated for the security categorization of the information system. The high-water mark rule in FIPS 199 means that a high-impact categorization for a single information type or security aspect of the system can result in an obligation to implement high-impact baseline controls across the board, potentially at a cost or level of effort not otherwise supported by risk assessments. Choosing to implement controls at a lower baseline level than the overall system security categorization is generally permitted only when the lower level implementation for the control is consistent with the security categorization before applying the high-water mark and when the lower level implementation satisfies the agency risk tolerance and the assessment of risk for the system.

Security control selection and tailoring address all security controls needed to satisfy the security requirements of the information system, regardless of the source providing each control. To fully understand and document the implementation of selected security controls, system owners must identify the common controls to be used by their systems, working in collaboration with their senior agency information security officers and general support system owners or other common control providers [51]. There are practical advantages to using common controls where feasible, and agencies may specify by policy preferences for or explicit requirements that information systems use the common controls available to them. The simple

> **NOTE**
>
> The use of Special Publication 800-53 baselines to set the scope for security controls documented in the system security plan and the flexibility afforded to system owners to tailor their security controls raises the question of whether *all* controls in the relevant baseline should be listed in the SSP, or only those controls actually implemented. Special Publication 800-18 indicates that the set security controls described in the SSP should reflect the results of selection, tailoring, and common control identification processes, suggesting that baseline controls deemed not applicable for the system are omitted from the SSP [50]. Agencies that prescribe the use of a standard security control template for all information systems may prefer, however, to include applicable, inherited, and not applicable controls in order to maintain consistency among SSP documents developed for different systems. Regardless of the inclusion of these controls in the SSP security control listing, any determination that a baseline security control does not apply to a system should be documented with appropriate explanation in the tailoring section of the SSP.

fact that a common control exists within the agency and is available to the information system does not necessarily mean that it is appropriate for the system owner to choose to inherit the common control rather than providing a system-specific or hybrid implementation. System owners must evaluate the available common controls against their system security requirements and, in cases where the common control is deemed insufficient, determine a hybrid implementation or select a compensating control that will satisfy the system need. To assist in this evaluation, common control providers typically make available to system owners their security control assessments, general support system security plans, or other relevant documentation.

Security Control Listing

The system security plan provides a complete listing of security control implemented for the system, including common controls implemented by other systems or providers. The volume of information and level of detail included in the SSP for each control may vary according to agency policy or SSP standards, or requirements set by the authorizing official who approves the completed plan. The minimum content expected for each control description, following guidance in Special Publication 800-18 [52], is the security control title; how the control is or is planned to be implemented; any scoping guidance applied to the control, indicating type of consideration; and the control's designation as system-specific, hybrid, or common, specifying the common control provider where applicable. Even with succinct descriptions, the security control listing occupies a large proportion of the system security plan, as the baseline for a moderate-impact level system includes 160 controls and 95 required control enhancements [51]. The security control baselines published with Special Publication 800-53 group security controls into 17 families organized into three classes—management, operational, and technical—offering a consistent structure for security control listings. The security control listing in agency system security plans may be presented in alphabetical order by control family (the order used in the security control catalog in Special Publication 800-53), grouped by control class, or arranged in some other manner according to agency preferences. For consistency, it is helpful for system security plans to use the same structure at least within the agency, and a preferred or required organizing scheme may be provided in the SSP templates used by system owners. Similarly, using the standard security control identifiers and titles from Special Publication 800-53 ensures internal and cross-agency consistency in the way security plans refer to security controls.

Common controls selected for an information system are reflected in the SSP along with system-specific and hybrid controls, although common control implementation descriptions may be less detailed than for other categories of controls, depending on the expectations of authorizing officials or other readers of the system security plan. Because common controls are usually implemented, managed, and documented separately from the information systems that inherit them, system security plans for inheriting systems may incorporate common control descriptions by reference or by copying the control documentation from the provider's documentation into the SSP. The maintenance and update process for system security plans can be simplified by using references to separate common control documentation, as any changes in the implementation details for the common controls will only need to be updated in the common control provider's documentation, not in each SSP that inherits them.

Completion and Approval Dates

As noted throughout the RMF task descriptions in Special Publication 800-37, the process of developing a system security plan involves many intermediate steps and incremental updates before finalizing the SSP and submitting it for approval. All system security plans should include both the completion date and approval date for the SSP. The completion date offers an important point of reference for system owners and SSP readers regarding how current the information in the plan is and when the next periodic review and potential update of the plan is due. System owners should update the completion date whenever a relevant change occurs to the SSP, recognizing that system security plan updates may be required in response to system or environmental changes distinct from routine SSP maintenance. Special Publication 800-18 also recommends the use of a version number for system security plans [13], incremented with each update, to provide a readily apparent indication when the plan has changed.

While the system security plan is a core element in the certification and accreditation package submitted for approval in support of system authorization, the SSP on its own must be reviewed and approved by the authorizing official or designated representative; this approval represents the final task in step 2 of the RMF [55]. The independent review of the SSP is intended to confirm the completeness of the plan, its consistency with agency standards and expectations, and the sufficiency of the controls it includes to satisfy the security requirements of the system [17]. The system security plan, when finalized, should include the approval date and accompanying evidence of approval such as a signature page or separate letter or approval memorandum included with the SSP as an attachment [56].

TIP

Although NIST guidance does not specify or prescribe a formal numbering standard agencies may find it useful use a simple version numbering scheme reflecting major releases and incremental updates of the SSP or other security documents. One common numbering scheme—implemented for major and minor version designation in document management systems such as Documentum [53] and Microsoft Sharepoint [54]—is to use whole numbers to represent major releases and tenths to represent minor updates. The first complete and approved SSP might be designated version 1.0 with subsequent annual updates designated version 2.0, 3.0, and so forth. Any other updates to the plan would be reflected through increments to the tenths digit—for example, following this type of pattern, a SSP designated "version 1.2" would indicate the second incremental update of the first major release of the plan.

Ongoing Maintenance Plan

The system security plan supports both initial system authorization and ongoing operation and security management activities for the system once deployed into production. The completed system security plan describes the process by which the security plan itself will be assessed and updated as necessary, including the schedule for routine periodic reviews and events or circumstances that would trigger review and might result in changes to the SSP. NIST guidance, consistent with provisions in FISMA, directs system owners to review and update their system security plans at least annually [53]. Special Publication 800-18 lists a series of potential changes to systems or their management and oversight that should prompt review of the SSP, including changes in information system owner, information security officer, or authorizing official; changes in system architecture or system interconnections; and changes in system scope, operating status, or certification and accreditation status [17].

The ongoing maintenance description in the system security plan should also reference the continuous monitoring strategy developed for the system, or organizational unit, environment, or agency continuous monitoring strategies if a broader scope approach is used instead of a system-specific strategy. The monitoring strategy can be included in the system security plan, inherited and incorporated by reference from a general support system or other common control provider, or developed and documented separately from the SSP. Current NIST guidance to agencies on continuous monitoring [57] provides much more explicit direction to agencies than what is included in Special Publication 800-37 on the process to be followed and content to be included in information security continuous monitoring strategies, and Special Publication 800-18 does not explicitly reference continuous monitoring at all. The monitoring strategy task in the RMF emphasizes ongoing monitoring of system-specific security controls [17], but agencies increasingly specify monitoring requirements in organization-wide policies and procedures. Special Publication 800-137 directs agencies to define continuous monitoring strategies and implement monitoring programs at an organization-wide scope that also address mission and business and system-specific monitoring practices and procedures [57]. With the increased attention focused on continuous monitoring activities and the broad perspective continuous monitoring strategies must reflect, system owners are generally less likely to develop their own system-specific approaches. Even where system-specific continuous monitoring strategies are needed, such strategies will need to reference and incorporate agency-wide strategies and risk management information typically beyond the scope of the SSP. For these reasons, agencies and their system owners should find it more practical and efficient to develop continuous monitoring documentation separate from system security plans, and provide references to continuous monitoring strategies and procedures from the SSP.

SSP Linkage to Other Key Artifacts

The system security plan is a key input to many risk management framework tasks, and influences the development of several other artifacts produced during the certification and accreditation process. As depicted in Figure 10.2, the set of security controls specified for implementation in the SSP drives the scope of the security control assessment process; the control list is reflected in both the security control assessment plan and in the security assessment report produced as a result of the control assessment. Depending on the remediating action or other response to weaknesses or deficiencies identified in the security assessment report, the system security plan may need to be updated after the security control assessment to reflect changes to control implementation details. In some cases, changes needed to remediate weaknesses or deficiencies may be planned to occur after system authorization occurs. Such changes will be reflected in the plan of action and milestones (POA&M) along with the dates by which changes will be made. Control descriptions in the SSP should indicate any such anticipated changes to the way the system will implement its controls, and may include references to POA&M action items or milestones where applicable.

As the foundational security document provided to authorizing officials, the system security plan typically includes references to a large number of other security artifacts. In many agencies these artifacts are designated system security plan appendices, referenced by appendix letter within the SSP, and packaged with the SSP for delivery to the authorizing official. Figure 10.3 presents an example SSP appendix listing from the Cyber Security Assessment and Management (CSAM) tool used

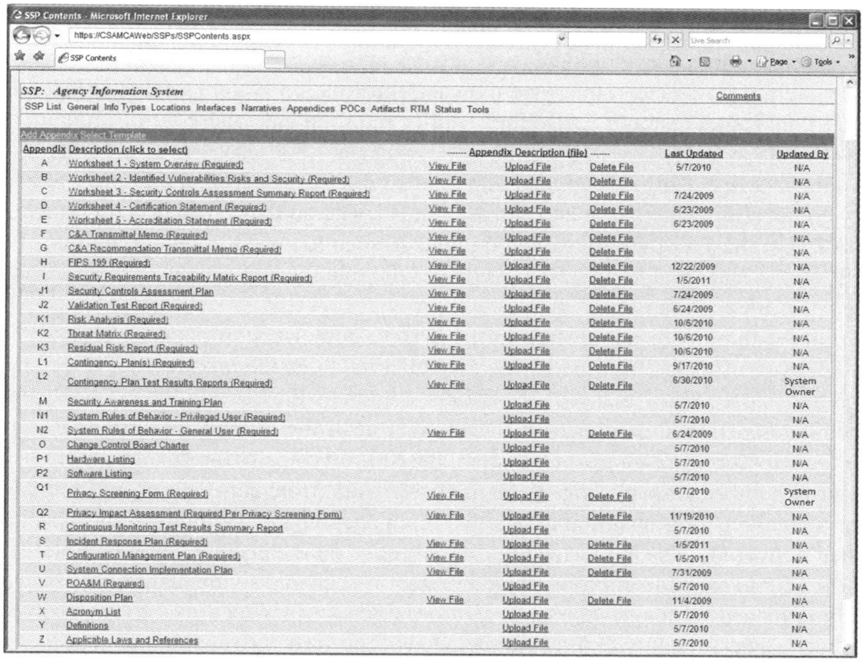

FIGURE 10.3 Numerous Security Documents and Associated Artifacts are Designated System Security Plan Appendices and Associated with the SSP for a Given System Managed in CSAM [58]

by some federal agencies to support their certification and accreditation and system security management activities. Many of these artifacts represent the implementation of documentation-based security controls required in Special Publication 800-53 baselines, such as the contingency plan (required by control CP-2), incident response plan (required by control IR-8), and plan of action and milestones (required by control CA-5) [13]. The interrelated nature of these documents and the need to insert and maintain accurate cross-references between the SSP and associated security artifacts means system owners must reflect accurate identifying details and current information for all documents referenced by the system security plan.

DEVELOPING THE SYSTEM SECURITY PLAN

The system security plan is referenced in every step of the risk management framework [2]. Whether or not agencies formally integrate security planning activities with their system development life cycles, system owners should begin developing the SSP during the initiation or equivalent phase in the process of developing or deploying a new system. Using information gathered about the business purpose and intended uses of the system, system owners categorize the impact level of the system, develop its security requirements, and identify appropriate security controls. All of this information is documented in the system security plan. As the system undergoes design, development, and testing and the operational characteristics of the system become clear, the system owner, information system security officer, and other contributors should revise the security requirements and control implementation details as necessary in the SSP. Following the RMF process, a full draft of the system security plan is developed and approved by the end of step 2, prior to security control implementation and assessment [2]. The guidance in Special Publication 800-18 emphasizes the activities and inputs needed to produce the initial draft of the SSP, and as shown in Figure 10.4, describes the relationship of key security management processes to the SSP.

Of the three core documents in the system authorization package prepared for authorizing officials, the system security plan includes the broadest set of information and incorporates many of the salient details of the security assessment report and plan of action and milestones. Due to its role as the primary authoritative source for security information about a system, the SSP is typically the last document in the security authorization package to be finalized (aside from certification and accreditation statements or transmittal letters that often accompany the authorization package when delivered). The authorization official relies on the accuracy and completeness of the SSP to make an appropriate authorization decision, so the plan should be carefully reviewed by the system owner, information system security officer, and other authorized personnel with direct knowledge of the system to ensure that it accurately reflects the security controls as actually implemented for the system.

The SSP provides an overview of the system security requirements and corresponding security controls, describing control information in sufficient detail to

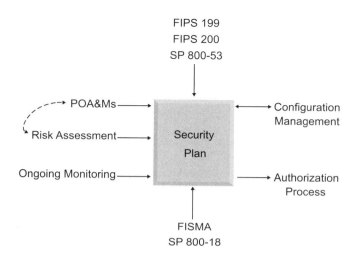

FIPS 199
FIPS 200
SP 800-53

POA&Ms
Risk Assessment
Ongoing Monitoring

Security
Plan

Configuration
Management

Authorization
Process

FISMA
SP 800-18

FIGURE 10.4 The System Security Plan Occupies a Central Position in All System Security Management Processes, Providing Key Descriptive Information about the System that Supports Initial System Authorization and Ongoing Operational Activities [59]

provide an understanding of the planned or actual implementation of each security control, including security configuration details. The SSP also includes supporting appendices and references to appropriate additional sources documenting enterprise and system risk assessment, privacy impact assessment, system interconnection agreements, contingency plans, configuration management plan, incident response plan, and continuous monitoring strategy. Due to the sensitivity of security control implementation details and other information in the SSP, access to the document associated artifacts in the authorization package should be strictly controlled, consistent with agency and federal policies [2]. Beyond the authorizing official, potential legitimate access needs for the SSP include requests by system owners or authorized representatives responsible for interconnected systems, common control providers whose controls are inherited by the system, or in the case of general support systems, system owners whose systems will operate within or depend on the general support system.

Rules of Behavior

Federal requirements contained in OMB Circular A-130 require formal rules of behavior to be developed for all major applications and general support systems [3], with system users required to acknowledge receipt and agree to the terms of use in the rule of behavior prior to receiving access to the system. Special Publication 800-53 includes rules of behavior as a required control (PL-4) in the security control baselines for all systems, regardless of security categorization [60]. System owners typically maintain records of signed user rules of behavior separate from system authorization documentation, with a copy of the rules of behavior typically included in the authorization package as an appendix to the SSP. Special Publication 800-18 explains the need for rules of behavior to be developed for each system and typical topics that should be addressed, including [61]:

- Defining and describing user roles, responsibilities, and expected use of the system.
- Describing limits on interconnections permitted to the system, including means of access.
- Defining service provisions and restoration priorities.
- Delineating acceptable and unacceptable user behavior and the consequences for violation of the rules of behavior.
- Explaining policies applicable to the system to which users must adhere.

In addition to complying with security control requirements, the process of developing rules of behavior can help identify functional aspects of the system and its intended operation that drive security requirements. For instance, rules of behavior typically address topics such as user permissions or restrictions related to remote access, user monitoring and individual accountability, and disclosure of information available through the system. Decisions about such expected and acceptable uses of the system translate into functional and technical capabilities the system offers and corresponding security and privacy controls the system must implement.

MANAGING SYSTEM SECURITY USING THE SSP

Once a system has successfully achieved authorization to operate, the primary use of the system security plan shifts to support ongoing operation and maintenance of the system and managing its security posture, including monitoring implemented security controls. Ongoing security management corresponds to the sixth and final step in the RMF, and aligns with the operations and maintenance phase in a typical system development life cycle [2]. The system security plan is intended to reflect accurate and up to date information about implemented security controls, including processes and schedules for reviewing and assessing the SSP, often in conjunction with validating the effectiveness of its security controls through annual security control assessments. As agencies move to implement more robust continuous monitoring practices and capabilities, including those supported by automated security tools, the assessments of security control effectiveness are becoming more frequent, with a corresponding increase in the likelihood that changes to system security controls will be recommended or required. To the extent that system owners can ensure that control descriptions accurately reflect implementation details, the SSP can serve as a point of reference for identifying configuration errors or other potential sources of vulnerabilities. As described in more detail in Chapter 15 on continuous monitoring, automated scanning tools can often identify system configuration settings that fail to comply with agency or federal standards or that expose unpatched or unmitigated vulnerabilities. Automated scanning cannot, however, identify all deviations from specified configurations, practices, or standards, so a thorough validation of security control implementation details in the SSP should be included as part of periodic security control assessments, SSP reviews, and continuous monitoring strategies.

RELEVANT SOURCE MATERIAL

Several NIST Special Publications and Federal Information Processing Standards provide guidance, recommendations, and instructions relevant to the development of system security plans and their use in support of system authorization and in post-authorization operational security management. The most applicable sources of information include:

- Special Publication 800-18 Revision 1, *Guide for Developing Security Plans for Federal Information Systems* [1].
- Special Publication 800-37 Revision 1, *Guide for Applying the Risk Management Framework to Federal Information Systems* [2].
- Special Publication 800-53 Revision 3, *Recommended Security Controls for Federal Information Systems and Organizations* [13].
- Special Publication 800-39, *Managing Information Security Risk Management: Organization, mission, and information system viewt* [62].
- Federal Information Processing Standard Publication 199, *Standards for Security Categorization of Federal Information and Information Systems* [28].
- Federal Information Processing Standard Publication 200, *Minimum Security Requirements for Federal Information and Information Systems* [63].

These and other NIST Special Publications and FIPS Publications are available from the NIST Computer Security Division website, at http://csrc.nist.gov/publications/.

SUMMARY

The system security plan is the single most comprehensive source of security information related to an information system. It serves as the basis of system authorization decisions by authorizing officials and provides detailed information to support many processes and activities in the system development life cycle. This chapter described the process of developing a system security plan and the contents expected to be included in the plan, and the ways in which the system security plan supports key security management activities before and after system authorization. This chapter also explained the ways in which system security plans are affected by and used to support other activities in the system authorization process described in NIST's Risk Management Framework.

REFERENCES

[1] Guide for developing security plans for federal information systems. Gaithersburg, MD: National Institute of Standards and Technology, Computer Security Division; February 2006. Special Publication 800–18 revision 1.

[2] Guide for applying the risk management framework to federal information systems. Gaithersburg, MD: National Institute of Standards and Technology, Computer Security Division; February 2010. Special Publication 800–37 revision 1.

[3] Appendix III, Security of federal automated information resources. Washington, DC: Office of Management and Budget; November 2000. Circular No. A-130, Revised (Transmittal, Memorandum No. 4).

[4] Federal Information Security Management Act of 2002, Pub. L. No. 107–347, 44 U.S.C. §3541 (December 17, 2002).

[5] Recommended security controls for federal information systems and organizations. Gaithersburg, MD: National Institute of Standards and Technology, Computer Security Division; August 2009. Special Publication 800–53 revision 3. p. F-85.

[6] Kissel R, Stine K, Scholl M, Rossman H, Fahlsing J, Gulick J. Security considerations in the system development life cycle. Gaithersburg, MD: National Institute of Standards and Technology, Computer Security Division; October 2008. Special Publication 800–64 revision 2.

[7] Guide for developing security plans for federal information systems. Gaithersburg, MD: National Institute of Standards and Technology, Computer Security Division; February 2006. Special Publication 800–18 revision 1. p. 2.

[8] Guide for developing security plans for federal information systems. Gaithersburg, MD: National Institute of Standards and Technology, Computer Security Division; February 2006. Special Publication 800–18 revision 1. p. 11.

[9] Guide for developing security plans for federal information systems. Gaithersburg, MD: National Institute of Standards and Technology, Computer Security Division; February 2006. Special Publication 800–18 revision 1. p. 9.

[10] Guide for developing security plans for federal information systems. Gaithersburg, MD: National Institute of Standards and Technology, Computer Security Division; February 2006. Special Publication 800–18 revision 1. p. 9–10.

[11] Minimum security requirements for federal information and information systems. Gaithersburg, MD: National Institute of Standards and Technology, Computer Security Division; March 2006. Federal Information Processing Standards Publication 200.

[12] Security categorization and control selection for national security systems. Fort Meade, MD: Committee on National Security Systems; October 2009. CNSS Instruction 1253.

[13] Recommended security controls for federal information systems and organizations. Gaithersburg, MD: National Institute of Standards and Technology, Computer Security Division; August 2009. Special Publication 800–53 revision 3.

[14] Guide for applying the risk management framework to federal information systems. Gaithersburg, MD: National Institute of Standards and Technology, Computer Security Division; February 2010. Special Publication 800–37 revision 1. Appendix D.

[15] Guide for applying the risk management framework to federal information systems. Gaithersburg, MD: National Institute of Standards and Technology, Computer Security Division; February 2010. Special Publication 800–37 revision 1. Appendix D. p. D-5.

[16] General Services Administration Acquisition Regulation; implementation of information technology security provision; final rule. 77 Fed. Reg. 749 (2012).

[17] Guide for applying the risk management framework to federal information systems. Gaithersburg, MD: National Institute of Standards and Technology, Computer Security Division; February 2010. Special Publication 800–37 revision 1. p. 26.

[18] Information technology security plan template, requirements, guidance, and examples. Washington, DC: National Aeronautics and Space Administration; April 2008. Available from <http://www.nasa.gov/pdf/322695main_ITS-SOP-0016-C-IT-Security-Plan-Template-Requirements-Guidance-Examples.pdf>.

[19] Department of Housing and Urban Development system security plan (SSP) template. Washington, DC: Department of Housing and Urban Development. Available from: <http://portal.hud.gov/hudportal/documents/huddoc?id=DOC_15139.doc>.

[20] FDIC system security plan template. Washington, DC: Federal Deposit Insurance Corporation; Available from: <http://www.fdic.gov/buying/goods/acquisition/ITSecurityPlanTemplate.doc>.

[21] Centers for Disease Control and Prevention draft system security plan. Atlanta, GA: Centers for Disease Control and Prevention; 2007 Jan. Available from: <http://csrc.nist.gov/groups/SMA/fasp/documents/system_security/System_Security_Plan_Template_01102007.doc>.

[22] Computer security resource center: FASP areas [Internet]. Gaithersburg, MD: National Institute of Standards and Technology, Computer Security Division [updated October 24 2010; cited December 9 2011]. Available from: <http://csrc.nist.gov/groups/SMA/fasp/areas.html>.

[23] System security plan (SSP) template. Baltimore, MD: Centers for Medicare and Medicaid Services; May 2009. Available from: <http://www.cms.gov/informationsecurity/downloads/ssp_template.zip>.

[24] Guide for developing security plans for federal information systems. Gaithersburg, MD: National Institute of Standards and Technology, Computer Security Division; February 2006. Special Publication 800–18 revision 1. p. 19.

[25] Exhibit 53, Information technology and e-government. In: Preparation, submission, and execution of the budget. Washington, DC: Office of Management and Budget. August 2011. Circular No. A-11, Revised (Transmittal Memorandum No. 85). p. 13–4.

[26] Guide for applying the risk management framework to federal information systems. Gaithersburg, MD: National Institute of Standards and Technology, Computer Security Division; February 2010. Special Publication 800–37 revision 1. p. 22.

[27] Exhibit 53, Information technology and e-government. In: Preparation, submission, and execution of the budget. Washington, DC: Office of Management and Budget. August 2011. Circular No. A-11, Revised (Transmittal Memorandum No. 85). p. 8.

[28] Standards for security categorization of federal information and information systems. Gaithersburg, MD: National Institute of Standards and Technology, Computer Security Division; December 2003. Federal Information Processing Standards Publication 199.

[29] Security categorization and control selection for national security systems. Fort Meade, MD: Committee on National Security Systems; October 2009. CNSS Instruction 1253. p. 5.

[30] Standards for security categorization of federal information and information systems. Gaithersburg, MD: National Institute of Standards and Technology, Computer Security Division; December 2003. Federal Information Processing Standards, Publication 199. p. 4.

[31] Guide for applying the risk management framework to federal information systems. Gaithersburg, MD: National Institute of Standards and Technology, Computer Security Division; February 2010. Special Publication 800–37 revision 1. p. 21.

[32] Standards for security categorization of federal information and information systems. Gaithersburg, MD: National Institute of Standards and Technology, Computer Security Division; December 2003. Federal Information Processing Standards, Publication 199. p. 6.

[33] For a representative example of such guidance, seeStine K, Kissel R, Barker W, Fahlsing J, Gulick J. Guide for mapping types of information and information systems to security sategories. Gaithersburg, MD: National Institute of Standards and Technology, Computer Security Division; August 2008.. Special Publication 800–60 revision 1.

[34] CMS system security and e-authentication assurance levels by information type. Baltimore, MD: Centers for Medicare and Medicaid Services; March 2011. Available from: <https://www.cms.gov/informationsecurity/downloads/ssl.pdf>.

[35] Guide for developing security plans for federal information systems. Gaithersburg, MD: National Institute of Standards and Technology, Computer Security Division; February 2006. Special Publication 800–18 revision 1. p. 19–21.

[36] Guide for developing security plans for federal information systems. Gaithersburg, MD: National Institute of Standards and Technology, Computer Security Division; February 2006. Special Publication 800–18 revision 1. p. 21.

[37] Guide for developing security plans for federal information systems. Gaithersburg, MD: National Institute of Standards and Technology, Computer Security Division; February 2006. Special Publication 800–18 revision 1. p. 11–2.

[38] Guide for developing security plans for federal information systems. Gaithersburg, MD: National Institute of Standards and Technology, Computer Security Division; February 2006. Special Publication 800–18 revision 1. p. 12.

[39] Swanson M, Bowen P, Philips A, Gallup D, Lynes D. Contingency planning guide for federal information systems. Gaithersburg, MD: National Institute of Standards and Technology, Computer Security Division; May 2010. Special Publication 800–34 revision 1.

[40] Guide for developing security plans for federal information systems. Gaithersburg, MD: National Institute of Standards and Technology, Computer Security Division; February 2006. Special Publication 800–18 revision 1. p. 22.

[41] Grance T, Hash J, Peck S, Smith J, Korow-Diks K. Security guide for interconnecting information technology systems. Gaithersburg, MD: National Institute of Standards and Technology, Computer Security Division; August 2002. Special Publication 800–47.

[42] Guide for developing security plans for federal information systems. Gaithersburg, MD: National Institute of Standards and Technology, Computer Security Division; February 2006. Special Publication 800–18 revision 1. p. 23.

[43] Federal Information Security Management Act of 2002, Pub. L. No. 107–347, 116 Stat. 2946 (December. 17, 2002).

[44] Information Technology Management Reform Act of 1996, Pub. L. No. 104–106, 110 Stat. 679 (February. 10, 1996).

[45] Guide for developing security plans for federal information systems. Gaithersburg, MD: National Institute of Standards and Technology, Computer Security Division; February 2006. Special Publication 800–18 revision 1. p. 24.

[46] Privacy Act of 1974, Pub. L. No. 93–579, 5 U.S.C. §522a (December. 31, 1974).

[47] Minimum security requirements for federal information and information systems. Gaithersburg, MD: National Institute of Standards and Technology, Computer Security Division; March 2006. Federal Information Processing Standards, Publication 200. p. 4.

[48] Guide for developing security plans for federal information systems. Gaithersburg, MD: National Institute of Standards and Technology, Computer Security Division; February 2006. Special Publication 800–18 revision 1. p. 13.

[49] Guide for developing security plans for federal information systems. Gaithersburg, MD: National Institute of Standards and Technology, Computer Security Division; February 2006. Special Publication 800–18 revision 1. p. 13–5.

[50] Guide for developing security plans for federal information systems. Gaithersburg, MD: National Institute of Standards and Technology, Computer Security Division; February 2006. Special Publication 800–18 revision 1. p. 15.

[51] Guide for developing security plans for federal information systems. Gaithersburg, MD: National Institute of Standards and Technology, Computer Security Division; February 2006. Special Publication 800–18 revision 1. p. 24–5.

[52] Guide for applying the risk management framework to federal information systems. Gaithersburg, MD: National Institute of Standards and Technology, Computer Security Division; February 2010. Special Publication 800–37 revision 1. p. 24.

[53] Guide for developing security plans for federal information systems. Gaithersburg, MD: National Institute of Standards and Technology, Computer Security Division; February 2006. Special Publication 800–18 revision 1. p. 26.

[54] Kumar P. Documentum 6.5 content management foundations. Birmingham, UK: Packt Publishing; 2010. p. 51.

[55] Curry B. Microsoft SharePoint 2010 administrator's pocket consultant. Redmond, WA: Microsoft Press; 2010. p. 373.

[56] Guide for applying the risk management framework to federal information systems. Gaithersburg, MD: National Institute of Standards and Technology, Computer Security Division; February 2010. Special Publication 800–37 revision 1. p. 27.

[57] Dempsey K, Chawla N, Johnson A, Johnson R, Jones A, Orebaugh A, Scholl M, Stine K. Information security continuous monitoring for federal information systems and organizations. Gaithersburg, MD: National Institute of Standards and Technology, Computer Security Division; September 2011. Special Publication 800–137.

[58] Cyber Security Assessment & Management (CSAM) [computer program]. Version 2.1.5.2. Washington, DC: Department of Justice; 2010.

[59] Guide for developing security plans for federal information systems. Gaithersburg, MD: National Institute of Standards and Technology, Computer Security Division; February 2006. Special Publication 800–18 revision 1. p. 4.

[60] Recommended security controls for federal information systems and organizations. Gaithersburg, MD: National Institute of Standards and Technology, Computer Security Division; August 2009. Special Publication 800–53 revision 3. p. F-87.

[61] Guide for developing security plans for federal information systems. Gaithersburg, MD: National Institute of Standards and Technology, Computer Security Division; February 2006. Special Publication 800–18 revision 1. p. 7–8.

[62] Managing information security risk: Organization, mission, and information system view. Gaithersburg, MD: National Institute of Standards and Technology, Computer Security Division; March 2011. Special, Publication 800–39.

[63] Minimum security requirements for federal information and information systems. Gaithersburg, MD: National Institute of Standards and Technology, Computer Security Division; March 2006. Federal Information Processing Standards Publication 200.

Security Assessment Report

INFORMATION IN THIS CHAPTER:

- Security Assessment Fundamentals
- Performing Security Control Assessments
- The Security Assessment Report in Context
- Relevant Source Material

The *security assessment report* is the primary documented result of the security control assessment initially performed in step 4 of the Risk Management Framework, and repeated as part of the operational monitoring phase described in step 6 of the RMF. Along with the system security plan and the plan of action and milestones, the security assessment report is one of the three documents, authorizing officials use to make the decision to authorize a given information system for production operation. Among all the artifacts produced in a system certification and accreditation package, the security assessment report provides the most comprehensive information about the security controls selected, whether those controls are implemented appropriately and weaknesses or deficiencies in the security posture of the information system found as a result of the security control assessment. The security assessment report serves as the mechanism with which the security control assessor (or assessment team) delivers the findings from the security control assessment to the information system owner and other parties responsible for the assessed controls. The information presented in the security assessment report is essential not only for determining the risk associated with an information system taking all its controls into account, but also as a key source of information for the development of the plan of action and milestones (a detailed description of the plan of action and milestones (POA&M) appears in Chapter 12).

This chapter describes the process of producing a security assessment report, the content contained within such a report, and key considerations for establishing the scope of the report based on the intended use of the assessment information it provides. The information presented here reflects relevant guidance found in Special Publication 800-53A, *Guide for Assessing the Security Controls in Federal Information Systems and Organizations* [1], and in Special Publication 800-37, *Guide for Applying the Risk Management Framework to Federal Information Systems* [2].

The generation of the security assessment report depends in many ways on the planning and performance of the security control assessment, so this chapter addresses several aspects of that process (first introduced in Chapter 8) that influence the production of the security assessment report. These aspects include determining the set of controls to be assessed, choosing the procedures, methods, and evidentiary requirements for the assessment, and selecting the appropriate resources to conduct the security control assessment and produce the security assessment report. It also describes the relationship between the security assessment report and other activities, processes, and artifacts (as illustrated in Figure 11.1), putting the report in the proper context within the Risk Management Framework.

SECURITY ASSESSMENT FUNDAMENTALS

Given the central role of the security assessment report as a decision-support document used by authorizing officials and other information system stakeholders, it is important to understand the security control assessment process that produces the findings contained in the security assessment report. The following sections describe key characteristics of security control assessments that should be considered in order to produce security assessment reports that are accurate, actionable, and reflect the appropriate level of detail. Understanding the elements that go into a security control assessment and the assessment report will also help participants in the system authorization process adapt the assessment process to their own specific needs and intended outcomes.

Security Control Assessors and Supporting Roles

The security control assessor has the primary functional responsibility for conducting security control assessments and for preparing the security assessment report with the assessment results. Depending on the nature of the system under evaluation and the scope, complexity, and logistics involved for the security control assessment, the role of security control assessor may be assigned to one individual, a team or group, or an organization (the latter case often applies where system owners use contracted assessment services). The responsibility of the security control assessor is to perform an assessment of all security controls implemented by an information system to determine whether the controls satisfy the assessment objectives specified in Special Publication 800-53A, and whether they comply with organizational security policies and procedures, standards, and security requirements applicable to the system [4]. In this role the security control assessor is tasked with evaluating the effectiveness of information system security, in accordance with FISMA requirements and related federal guidance. In addition to conducting assessments and preparing security assessment reports, the security control assessor performs an analysis of the selected security controls in the system security plan, and contributes to the development of the plan of action and milestones by identifying weaknesses

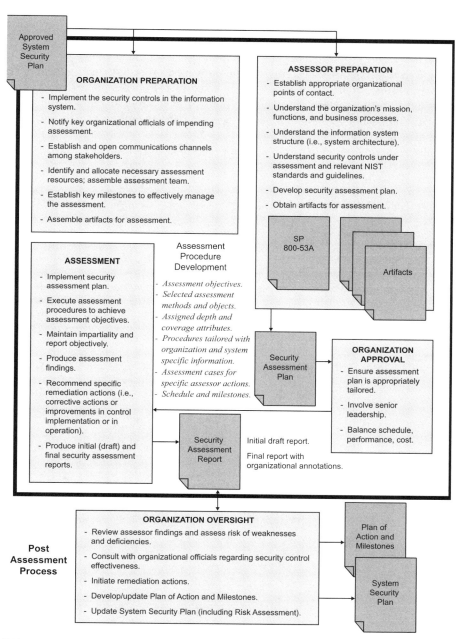

Approved System Security Plan

ORGANIZATION PREPARATION

- Implement the security controls in the information system.
- Notify key organizational officials of impending assessment.
- Establish and open communications channels among stakeholders.
- Identify and allocate necessary assessment resources; assemble assessment team.
- Establish key milestones to effectively manage the assessment.
- Assemble artifacts for assessment.

ASSESSOR PREPARATION

- Establish appropriate organizational points of contact.
- Understand the organization's mission, functions, and business processes.
- Understand the information system structure (i.e., system architecture).
- Understand security controls under assessment and relevant NIST standards and guidelines.
- Develop security assessment plan.
- Obtain artifacts for assessment.

SP 800-53A

Artifacts

ASSESSMENT

- Implement security assessment plan.
- Execute assessment procedures to achieve assessment objectives.
- Maintain impartiality and report objectively.
- Produce assessment findings.
- Recommend specific remediation actions (i.e., corrective actions or improvements in control implementation or in operation).
- Produce initial (draft) and final security assessment reports.

Assessment Procedure Development

- *Assessment objectives.*
- *Selected assessment methods and objects.*
- *Assigned depth and coverage attributes.*
- *Procedures tailored with organization and system specific information.*
- *Assessment cases for specific assessor actions.*
- *Schedule and milestones.*

Security Assessment Plan

ORGANIZATION APPROVAL

- Ensure assessment plan is appropriately tailored.
- Involve senior leadership.
- Balance schedule, performance, cost.

Security Assessment Report

Initial draft report.

Final report with organizational annotations.

Post Assessment Process

ORGANIZATION OVERSIGHT

- Review assessor findings and assess risk of weaknesses and deficiencies.
- Consult with organizational officials regarding security control effectiveness.
- Initiate remediation actions.
- Develop/update Plan of Action and Milestones.
- Update System Security Plan (including Risk Assessment).

Plan of Action and Milestones

System Security Plan

FIGURE 11.1 The Security Control Assessment Process Integrates Organizational and system-Specific Planning, Preparation, Assessment Procedures, and Oversight [3]

or deficiencies in the security posture of the information system and recommending corrective action to address any issues raised during the assessment [5].

While security control assessors are expected to have broad knowledge of information security controls and corresponding assessment procedures, the assessor relies on several supporting roles (summarized in Table 11.1) to be able to perform assessments and prepare security assessment reports in an efficient and effective manner. Information system owners, information owners (to the extent these are distinct from system owners) common control providers, and information system security officers are all important sources of information for security control assessors. Individuals in

Table 11.1 Roles and Responsibilities for Security Control Assessment Participants [6]

Participant	Roles
Security Control Assessor	Conducts assessments of all security controls implemented by the system to determine their overall effectiveness; documents assessment results in the security assessment report; identifies weaknesses and corrective actions that may be addressed through POA&M items
Common Control Provider	Conducts security control assessments for common security controls inherited by the system; makes assessment results available to system owners and security control assessors evaluating systems that use the common controls
Information Owner/Steward	Serves as the authority for rules, policies, and procedures on collecting, processing, disseminating, and disposing of specific information used, accessed, or protected by the information system; provides guidance to security control assessors regarding legal or policy requirements for data protection
Information System Owner	Provides access to information system, security control documentation, personnel, and other relevant sources of evidence about the security controls being assessed
Information System Security Officer	Works in close collaboration with the system owner to establish and maintain an appropriate security posture for an information system; provides information and expertise to security control assessors about the specific administrative, operational, and technical controls implemented for or used by the system

each of these supporting roles may furnish documentation or other evidence needed by the assessor in order to accurately evaluate security controls and make well-supported determinations of control effectiveness. The information system owner plays a particularly important role in facilitating the performance of the security control assessment, with responsibility for providing system-specific information relevant to the assessment as well as granting necessary levels of information system access to the assessor. Common control providers are responsible for assessing their controls, producing corresponding security assessment reports, and making such information available to information system owners whose systems inherit those common controls. Information system security officers have responsibility for providing appropriate security measures for their information systems, and work in cooperation with system owners to ensure that necessary and appropriate security controls are implemented, maintained, and monitored.

Assessor Independence

Security control assessments are intended to be objective evaluations of an information system's security posture, and security assessment reports are similarly expected to be accurate and impartial representations of assessment findings. One way to try to ensure objective assessments is to use an independent assessor, where *independent* means that the assessor has no vested stake in the outcome of the assessment that might produce a conflict of interest. Questions of bias can arise when security control assessments are performed by members of program or project teams tasked with developing, implementing, or operating the information system being assessed, or when the terms agreed for contracted assessments offer implicit or explicit incentives to complete the assessment expediently or with a favorable outcome. Ensuring assessor independence can help maximize the credibility of the security assessment report and increase the confidence with which authorizing officials can rely on assessment results to make decisions [7]. Requirements for assessor independence are typically established by authorizing officials at either a system-specific or an organizational level. These requirements may vary based on the nature of the assessment, the criticality of the system (as indicated by its security categorization), the operational status of the system, or other factors. For instance, different levels of assessor independence may apply for to an assessment of a new system seeking initial authorization to operate than for a reassessment of an operational system that has already been authorized [8].

Faced with resource constraints that limit their ability to obtain independent assessment services from internal capabilities or external service providers, many organizations do allow security control assessments to be performed by assessors that fall within the contractual or managerial purview of the information system owner. In such situations where assessors are less than fully independent, organizations can mitigate the potential for bias by subjecting security assessment reports and other assessment outputs to careful review, analysis, and oversight by individuals or groups with appropriate security expertise [8]. Many federal agencies employ this type of oversight function as part of their information security program management activities, at the same level of the organization where responsibility rests for FISMA compliance and reporting.

Assessment Resources and Assessor Skills

Another important factor in ensuring the quality of security control assessments is the technical expertise of the assessors evaluating security control effectiveness. To accurately determine the effectiveness of security controls as implemented for a specific system, it is necessary but not sufficient for assessors to be well-versed in relevant NIST guidance and applicable federal regulations. Organizations and system owners also need to enlist security control assessors that understand the characteristics of the system being assessed, that have knowledge of the way system-specific and hybrid controls are implemented for the system, and that are familiar with the common controls inherited by the system [8]. The need for system-specific knowledge does not diminish the importance for assessors to have detailed knowledge of applicable organizational security policies and procedures and of current versions of NIST guidelines in use by the organization. Not all organizations find it practical or feasible to quickly adopt the latest releases of Special Publications and other guidance—in addition to educating system owners, security officers, and other personnel on the changes, organizations may also be dependent on FISMA reporting tool vendors or other external parties to revise or update the systems used to capture system security information such as assessment data.

Federal guidelines do not specify minimum experience requirements for assessors, but conducting effective security control assessments using current assessment guidance and procedures requires a level of expertise typically associated with security specialists. Prior to the first release of Special Publication 800-53A in 2008, many system security assessments took the form of self-assessments following procedures and an assessment questionnaire provided in Special Publication 800-26, *Security Self-Assessment Guide for Information Technology Systems* [9]. The federal information technology assessment framework described in Special Publication 800-26 used a five-level rating scale for security controls, reflecting a sort of maturity model ranging from "documented policy" at level 1 to "fully integrated procedures and controls" at level 5 [10]. Each of the rating levels was defined with prescriptive guidance and assessment criteria that assessors could use to evaluate controls. Special Publication 800-26 was withdrawn by NIST in 2007 and replaced by Special Publication 800-53A. In contrast to the five-level rating scale previously used for self-assessments, controls assessed using Special Publication 800-53A are evaluated against specific assessment objectives, with objectives for each control found to be "satisfied" or "other than satisfied [11]." Security control assessments are subjective, relying on the knowledge and expertise of security control assessors, as well as their ability to effectively perform appropriate assessment procedures for each control. Assessors are empowered to make determinations about the effectiveness of security controls, so organizations and system owners should enlist the services of individuals with sufficient experience (and an appropriate level of independence) to instill confidence in the results documented in the security assessment report.

> **NOTE**
>
> To perform security control assessments effectively, assessors must have a thorough understanding of information security control objectives and associated procedures and technologies. An assessor working alone must have broad security knowledge across all the security control families in Special Publication 800-53 and enough experience with examining security controls in practice to be able to make accurate evaluations of the effectiveness of specific security control implementations. Recognizing the need for system owners to be able to choose appropriately qualified assessors, NIST developed Interagency Report 7328 [12], which includes a validation checklist that can be used to evaluate the capabilities of candidate security control assessors. When choosing an assessor, professional security certifications can also give some indication of qualifications. Although there is no certification specific to conducting security control assessments for government information systems, there are certifications focused on general information systems security control effectiveness [13–15], and on the federal certification and accreditation process [16]. Organizations seeking to enlist the services of an assessor should not rely on certifications alone, but instead should evaluate the knowledge and experience of the assessor to make sure that experience applies to the type of system and operational environment being assessed.

Security control assessors must be mindful of the guidance in force for a given system, and be aware of any potential changes planned by the organization that may affect the security controls selected for the system and the scope of the assessment and corresponding security assessment report. As an example, the set of security controls listed in Special Publication 800-53 changed when Revision 3 of the document was released in final form in August 2009. The corresponding security control assessment guidance in Special Publication 800-53A Revision 1 was not finalized until June 2010, so few agencies (or the tool vendors some of those agencies use) updated their adopted control baselines until more than a year after they were available, continuing instead to use Special Publication 800-53 Revision 2 (which was released in December 2007). For a moderate-impact system, the move from Revision 2 to Revision 3 of Special Publication 800-53 resulted in 21 changes in required controls (seven new controls, eight revised or otherwise modified, and six deprecated [17]), so while assessors may not be too concerned with which control set should be applied to a system, it is helpful to avoid switching from one version to another during the time between when the security assessment report is produced and when it is evaluated. The breadth of security controls to be evaluated also influences the choice of assessor, particularly including whether to use multiple assessors or just one. A complete security control assessment for a moderate-impact system can require evaluation of as many as 250 discrete controls and enhancements (depending on the number of inherited and not applicable controls), so where comprehensive breadth or coverage are specified, it can be difficult to find individual assessors with sufficient knowledge to address all the assessment objectives in scope.

Assessment Timing and Frequency

Security control assessments are conducted both as part of initial certification and accreditation activities in support of system authorization decisions, and on an ongoing basis as an element of continuous monitoring and to comply with periodic evaluations of security control effectiveness required under FISMA [18]. Once a system has been authorized, system owners are typically required to reassess all of the system's security controls on an annual basis, and subsets of controls may be reassessed more frequently as part of continuous monitoring activities, in accordance with monitoring policies or procedures applicable to the system [19,20]. Security assessment reports are intended to present the results from security control assessments, so a new security assessment report is typically produced whenever a new assessment is performed, to keep the security assessment report accurate and current. The process of re-generating security assessment reports is greatly facilitated by the use of automated tools to support security assessments. Where manual procedures are followed, organizations can simplify the process of revising and reproducing security assessment reports by establishing and tracking due dates for reassessments, both of the full set of controls selected for the system and of subsets or individual controls subject to more frequent evaluation. The presentation of controls in Special Publication 800-53, which organizes controls into 18 categories (called families), offers one approach for subdividing control assessment reports. Where security assessment reports are structured in a way that follows Special Publication 800-53, individual sections of the report can be updated separately when necessary, facilitating a reassessment approach that covers one control family at a time. It is often not feasible to isolate individual controls or control families for assessment, as many controls have preceding or succeeding dependencies on other controls that may not be part of the same control family. For example, the media protection controls MP-4 (Media Storage) and MP-5 (Media Transport) are both related to control AC-19 (Access Control for Portable and Media Devices), so it may not be possible to fully assess MP-4 and MP-5 without having assessed AC-19 as well [21].

Assessing New Systems Prior to Authorization

Organizations conduct security control assessments of all controls used by an information system (both inherited controls and those provided by the system) as part of the initial system authorization process in step 4 of the Risk Management Framework [22], as described in Chapter 8. The results of the security control assessment are documented first in an initial or draft security assessment report, which is reviewed by the information system owner, information system security officer, and other officials as needed to review any weaknesses and deficiencies identified in the initial report and choose which issues need to be remedied and what corrective actions to take. Once appropriate actions are taken, relevant controls are reassessed and the initial security assessment report is updated to produce a final version, which is delivered to the authorizing official along with the rest of the system accreditation package documentation. Depending on the type of system being developed or implemented and the project plan or system development life cycle being followed, initial security control assessments may be conducted incrementally or all at once. Guidance to agencies provided in Special Publication 800-37 recommends that security control assessments be performed as early in the development life cycle as possible [4], bearing in mind that some selected controls may not be implemented or fully documented until the system nears implementation. Planning for such developmental testing and evaluation assessments should take into account the fact that prior assessment information does not exist (as it often does for ongoing assessments of operational systems), although information should be available about any common controls to be employed by the system. In situations where new systems implement commercial off-the-shelf (COTS) software, some vendors offer documentation to federal customers to support security assessments of their products. Security assessment reports produced for these systems may rely on a variety of sources of potentially reusable security assessment results, which can reduce the total time required to conduct security control assessments and produce security assessment reports.

Assessing (and Reassessing) Operational Systems

While the core assessment process is much the same for operational systems as it is for newly authorized systems, there are several factors that influence the way in which ongoing security assessments are performed. Perhaps most significant of these is the simple fact that since at least one assessment has already been conducted in support of initial authorization, subsequent assessments can draw on the results of previous assessments to streamline the process. Special Publication 800-37 identifies several potential sources of previous assessment results that can be used for reassessment, assuming the underlying controls are still the same and that the environmental characteristics of the controls are still accurate. These sources include [4]:

i. security control assessments conducted as part of an information system authorization, ongoing authorization, or formal reauthorization;
ii. continuous monitoring activities;

iii. testing and evaluation of the information system as part of the system development life cycle process or audit.

Special Publication 800-53A also emphasizes the concept of reuse when conducting security control assessments, in the sense both of reusing evidence corresponding to specific controls, and of reusing the results of previously performed assessments. This guidance emphasizes several considerations that should be taken into account when determining whether previous assessment results should be reused, including the extent to which conditions may have changed with respect to security controls under evaluation; the amount of time elapsed between the previous and current assessments; and the level of independence associated with the previous assessments [23]. These factors can help system owners and common control providers determine whether previously conducted analysis satisfies current control assessment objectives and whether evidence used to support previous assessment findings is still accurate and applicable. Security assessment reports produced as a result of reassessments can in many cases take the form of edited or revised versions of previously delivered reports, as the implementation specifics for many security controls do not change during the year (or less) between assessments. Even where a given control has not changed and the evidence consulted is the same, assessment results for each control should be updated to reflect the most recent date of assessment, and complete security assessment reports should include the current date of delivery, a revision history listing previous versions of the report, and summary information explaining what previous assessment results were reused, if any.

Scope and Level of Detail

The security assessment report provides assessment details, findings, and recommendations for each control that is evaluated. This means that the scope of the security assessment report is typically a reflection of the scope of the security control assessment, but different organizations may have different interpretations about what should be included in both the assessment and the assessment report. There are two primary schools of thought on this topic: the first focuses on the set of assessed controls that are specific to the information system, and excludes information on common controls. The assessment for common controls—such as backup power generation, fire suppression, or security guards provided by a data center where a system is hosted—is typically the responsibility of the common control owner, not the assessor or the owner of the system undergoing authorization, so to include common control assessment information in the security assessment report the assessor needs to gain access to the assessment details for the common controls. The second approach includes all controls relevant for the system, whether system-specific, common, or hybrid. This alternative approach results in a security assessment report that addresses all the controls and enhancements implemented for the system, regardless of whether the controls fall within the system boundary or are inherited or otherwise provided outside the system boundary. The most appropriate approach to take depends on the expectations of the authorizing official that will use the security assessment report in support of authorization decisions, or on the requirements dictated by organizational security policies.

In organizations where authorizing officials or other reviewers of security assessment reports compare security assessment report contents to security control baselines, the report should be structured in a way that identifies the status of all controls, to avoid any potential confusion as to whether an anticipated control might have been overlooked in the assessment. During the process of security control selection (within step 2 of the RMF), information system owners identify common controls used by their systems and tailor and supplement the security control baseline as appropriate for each system [24]. This process results in a categorization of security controls—documented in the system security plan—as either "applicable," "not applicable," or "inherited." Security control assessments typically do not cover inherited (common) or not applicable controls, but if corresponding security assessment reports do not provide details on inherited or not applicable controls, then the reports should explain that fact and provide a reference to sources of information on controls that are not addressed in the report. Organizations using automated tools supporting certification and accreditation activities may be able to generate a report indicating which controls are applicable, not applicable, or inherited (for example, in the Cyber Security

Assessment and Management (CSAM) application, such a listing is provided in the Security Requirements Traceability Matrix Report, an excerpt of which is shown in Figure 11.2).

In addition to the set of controls covered in the security assessment report, it is important to understand the level of detail expected for the report so that appropriate instructions can be given to security control assessors, and to ensure that assessors use the right methods and objects and assessments are conducted with the necessary levels of depth and coverage. The intent is to make sure that security assessment reports include the right amount of detail to meet organizational expectations, and to comply with applicable organizational or federal policies. Security assessment reports typically provide only summary information about the assessment procedures used for each control and the evidence consulted to arrive at the assessment findings, with references given to more detailed assessment tasks and specific sources of evidence [26]. The security assessment report places greater emphasis on weaknesses or deficiencies noted by the assessor, and recommendations for remediating, correcting, or compensating for any controls failing to satisfy the stated assessment objectives. The key factor determining the level of detail to include for each control in the security assessment report is the need expressed by authorizing officials, risk managers, system owners, and others who use the report for decision making purposes. Providing too little detail will result in additional information requests and corresponding delays in decision making processes that rely on the security

Security RTM Report:

	Applicable	Inherited	Not Applicable	Control Requirement	Explanations
IR-02(1)	☐	☐	☒	Incident Response Training (1) - The organization incorporates simulated events into incident response training to facilitate effective response by personnel in crisis situations.	Not Required by RTM (based on applied factor values)
IR-02(2)	☐	☐	☒	Incident Response Training (2) - The organization employs automated mechanisms to provide a more thorough and realistic training environment.	Not Required by RTM (based on applied factor values)
IR-03	☒	☐	☐	Incident Response Testing and Exercises - The organization tests and/or exercises the incident response capability for the information system no less than annually using scenario based exercises to determine the incident response effectiveness and documents the results.	
IR-03(1)	☐	☐	☒	Incident Response Testing and Exercises (1) - The organization employs automated mechanisms to more thoroughly and effectively test/exercise the incident response capability.	Not Required by RTM (based on applied factor values)
IR-04	☒	☐	☐	Incident Handling - The organization implements an incident handling capability for security incidents that includes preparation, detection and analysis, containment, eradication, and recovery.	
IR-04(1)	☒	☐	☐	Incident Handling (1) - The organization employs automated mechanisms to support the incident handling process.	
IR-05	☒	☐	☐	Incident Monitoring - The organization tracks and documents information system security incidents on an ongoing basis.	
IR-05(1)	☐	☐	☒	Incident Monitoring (1) - The organization employs automated mechanisms to assist in the tracking of security incidents and in the collection and analysis of incident information.	Not Required by RTM (based on applied factor values)
IR-06	☒	☐	☐	Incident Reporting - The organization promptly reports incident information to appropriate authorities.	
IR-06(1)	☐	☒	☐	Incident Reporting (1) - The organization employs automated mechanisms to assist in the reporting of security incidents.	Inherited from Incident Response
IR-07	☐	☒	☐	Incidence Response Assistance - The organization provides an incident support resource that offers advice and assistance to users of the information system for the handling and reporting of security incidents. The support resource is an integral part of the organization's incident response capability.	Inherited from Incident Response

FIGURE 11.2 The Security RTM Report Generated by CSAM Shows the Key Elements Included in a Security Control Requirements Traceability Matrix, Including the Applicability of Each Baseline Control for the System and Whether the Control is Inherited or System-Specific [25]

assessment report, while too much detail runs the risk of over-burdening users of the report, especially considering that a security assessment report for a moderate-impact system may cover more than 250 controls and enhancements. The intended level of detail should be specified, along with assessment objectives and other expectations for security control assessments, in the security assessment plan [7].

Security Control Baselines

Information security controls for federal information systems are specified in Special Publication 800-53. The applicability of the controls in Special Publication 800-53 is based on the security categorization of the information system, with a security control baseline (a subset of the 198 controls in Special Publication 800-53 Revision 3 [17]) for each of the three impact levels defined in Federal Information Processing Standards Publication 199 (FIPS 199) [27]. The low-impact, moderate-impact, and high-impact baselines are published separately as excerpts of Special Publication 800-53, to provide impact-level-specific references for required security controls and control enhancements. These baselines are intended to provide the set of controls necessary to satisfy the *minimum* security requirements for an information system categorized at each impact level [28]. Organizations are encouraged and expected to augment the baseline security controls as necessary to provide adequate protection of confidentiality, integrity, and availability of information and information systems. As explained in Chapter 7, during the security control selection process in step 2 of the RMF system owners can make the decision to deviate from the security control baseline—either to tailor the baseline by exempting a system from certain controls (with proper justification), or to supplement the baseline by implementing optional controls or enhancements from Special Publication 800-53 [17] or by adding additional controls from sources beyond standard guidance.

Comparisons among the different security control baselines often focus on the number of required controls at each impact level. When considering security control assessments, it is just as important to consider required control enhancements, which for moderate- and high-impact systems represent a significant proportion of the total items to be evaluated in a security control assessment and described in a security assessment report, as summarized in Table 11.2. Depending on organizational preferences,

Table 11.2 Baseline Controls and Control Enhancements [17]

	Baseline		
	Low	Moderate	High
Required controls	112	160	167
Required enhancements	3	95	163
Total required assessment items	115	255	330

optional control enhancements may also be a factor; Revision 3 of Special Publication 800-53 includes 252 optional enhancements that are not required under any of the security control baselines [17], but which may be deemed appropriate for a particular system.

Controls, Enhancements, and Objectives

Each control and control enhancement corresponds to at least one assessment objective in Special Publication 800-53A that assessors must evaluate in order to determine if the requirements for the control or enhancement are satisfied [1]. The findings for each assessment objective are included in the security assessment report, so the decision to include a particular enhancement translates directly into evaluation tasks for the assessor, and to content that will be included in the security assessment report. There is wide variation in the number of optional control enhancements specified for security controls across Special Publication 800-53; of the 187 system-level controls (11 others apply at the information security program level), 92 have no optional enhancements, while 95 have at least one optional enhancement [17]. The availability of optional control enhancements gives organizations and system owners great flexibility in augmenting their security control baselines with additional security measures where desired. The presence of a large number of available enhancements for some controls also gives some indication of the level of variation seen among organizations in the implementation of those controls. For example, the System and Integrity Protection control for Information System Monitoring (SI-4), required for both moderate- and high-impact systems, offers a total of 17 control enhancements—four required and 13 optional [29]. Similarly, the System and Communications Protection control for Boundary Protection (SC-7), a required part of the control baseline for systems at all impact levels, offers a total of 18 control enhancements, 10 of which are optional even for high-impact systems [30]. The potential applicability of these optional enhancements depends on the information system and the characteristics of its operating environment, as well as organizational policies, procedures, standards, and guidelines.

TIP

At 237 pages, Special Publication 800-53 can be somewhat overwhelming to work with, as it provides detailed descriptions for nearly 200 security controls and over 400 control enhancements, many of which are not applicable to a given system. NIST publishes three annexes to Special Publication 800-53 based on the security categorization assigned to a system: one each for low-impact, moderate-impact, and high-impact systems [31]. By choosing the appropriate security control baseline, system owners, security officers, and security assessors can focus just on the subset of controls applicable to the system in question, making the process of selecting and tailoring controls more efficient.

Security Assessment Report Structure and Contents

There is no single standard format used for security assessment reports. Following NIST guidance in the Risk Management Framework, the choice of format should consider the purpose and type of security control assessment for which results are being reported, and the way in which the report will be used [2]. At a minimum, security assessment reports should include assessment findings and related information for all controls and control enhancements that were assessed. Organizations may add report elements such as finding summaries, references to sources of evidence or additional assessment detail, and other details that facilitate the review of the report by authorizing officials or other audiences. Security assessment reports can be produced as a separate output from the security control assessment process, or documented incrementally as the assessment progresses. Agencies using automated tools to support security control assessments—such as the Cyber Security Assessment and Management (CSAM) system offered by the Department of Justice for use by federal agencies—can typically produce security assessment report documents in a variety of electronic file formats. These electronically generated reports tend to follow the sample structure and content provided in Appendix G of Special Publication 800-53A [1], which organizes report detail by security control objective. This sample structure reproduces the objective statements from Special Publication 800-53A for each assessed control or control enhancement, followed by the assessor's findings, rationale, and any comments and recommendations that might have been included as part of the security control assessment. Where an automated tool is not available or direct data entry of assessment information is not feasible, assessment findings can be recorded using a document template or other standard format, such as the example shown in Figure 11.3, which would be used to record the results of the control assessment for user identification and authorization (IA-2).

Report Contents

While the security assessment report is often delivered with other system certification and accreditation documents, it is helpful to readers of the report if system owners or assessors include descriptive information about the system described in the report and the security control assessment that produced the results included in the report. Appendix G of Special Publication 800-53A provides guidance for documenting security control assessments findings, and lists several key elements to be included in security assessment reports [1]:

- Information system name.
- Security categorization.
- Site(s) assessed and assessment date(s).
- Assessor's name/identification.
- Previous assessment results (if reused).
- Security control or control enhancement designator.
- Selected assessment methods and objects.
- Depth and coverage attributes values.

Control No: IA-02 - User Identification and Authentication

Test Preparation: The assessment procedures for this control are selected from the following and documented in the Assessment Results section(s) below.

   IA-2.1:

     Examine: [SELECT FROM: Identification and authentication policy; NIST Special Publication 800-63; procedures addressing user identification and authentication; information system design documentation; e-authentication risk assessment results; information system configuration settings and associated documentation; information system audit records; other relevant documents or records]. (L) (M) (H)

Test: [SELECT FROM: Automated mechanisms implementing identification and authentication capability for the information system]. (M) (H)

Assessment Objective: IA-2.1 Determine if:

(i)

the information system uniquely identifies and authenticates users (or processes acting on behalf of users); and

(ii)

authentication levels for users (or processes acting on behalf of users) are consistent with NIST Special Publication 800-63 and e-authentication risk assessment results.

Determine If:

IA-02.01-01 - The information system uniquely identifies and authenticates users (or processes acting on behalf of users).

Assessment Results   **Assessed By:** _____   **Assessment Date:** _____

_____

	NA	Satisfied	Other than Satisfied (POAM Req'd)	RBD
	☐	☐	☐	☐

_____

_____

IA-02.01-02 - Authentication levels for users (or processes acting on behalf of users) are consistent with NIST Special Publication 800-63 and e-authentication risk assessment results.

Assessment Results   **Assessed By:** _____   **Assessment Date:** _____

_____

	NA	Satisfied	Other than Satisfied (POAM Req'd)	RBD
	☐	☐	☐	☐

_____

_____

FIGURE 11.3 A Standard Form Such as this Example for Control IA-2 can be used to Record Assessment Results that will be Included in the Security Assessment Report [25]

- Assessment finding summary (indicating satisfied or other than satisfied).
- Assessor comments (weaknesses or deficiencies noted).
- Assessor recommendations (priorities, remediation, corrective actions, or improvements).

The first two of these elements (information system name and security categorization) apply across the scope of the security control assessment and help establish expectations about which controls and enhancements will be included in the scope of the assessment report. The other nine elements apply to each of the assessed controls or enhancements described in the report, as the specific assessment procedures followed typically vary from control to control. Conducting a full security control assessment is a significant undertaking that generally requires days or weeks to perform and may involve the use of multiple assessors, so the assessment date and assessor's name should be recorded for each control or enhancement in the report. The other recommended elements are intended to provide a formal structure both for documenting assessment findings and for providing information to support decisions made in response to the findings, including implementing corrective actions. The guidance in Special Publication 800-53A makes clear that security assessment reports are not expected to include all the information produced or evidence consulted during the course of the assessment. System owners and organizations do however have a vested interest in tracking and maintaining access to assessment evidence, to support auditability of assessment results, to help ensure the reliability of the assessment process, and to encourage evidence reuse, where appropriate.

Assessment Methods and Objects

Security control assessment guidance offered in Appendix D of Special Publication 800-53A identifies three assessment methods that can be used, individually or together, to perform assessments of all security controls. These methods are *examine*, *interview*, and *test*. For each method, the guidance also specifies assessment objects to which the methods can be applied [32]; the assessment objects applicable to each method are listed in Table 11.3. Security control assessors, working in collaboration with system owners and other organizational personnel, are responsible for selecting the appropriate methods to be used to assess each control, and for documenting the methods used in the information presented about each control in the security assessment report. By choosing assessment methods as part of the security assessment planning process in advance of the actual assessment, information owners, system owners, and others in supporting roles can identify and facilitate

Table 11.3 Security Control Assessment Methods and Objects [32]

Method	Objects
Examine	• Specifications (e.g. policies, plans, procedures, system requirements, designs) • Mechanisms (e.g. functionality implemented in hardware, software, firmware) • Activities (e.g. system operations, administration, management, exercises)
Interview	• Individuals • Groups
Test	• Mechanisms (e.g. hardware, software, firmware) • Activities (e.g. system operations, administration, management, exercises)

access to relevant artifacts, processes, and personnel that can provide evidence for the assessor during the assessment. Documenting the assessment methods and objects in the security assessment report, along with assigned depth and coverage attributes, allows authorizing officials and others reading the report to consider the methodology employed to produce the findings, and therefore to make a determination whether the methods used were appropriate and convey a sufficient level of confidence that the assessed controls are implemented effectively [32]. Appendix F of Special Publication 800-53A includes a list of assessment methods and objects potentially applicable for evaluating the assessment objectives associated with every control and control enhancement identified in Special Publication 800-53. These suggested assessment methods offer helpful guidance to security control assessors and system owners during both the planning and execution of security assessments.

Depth and Coverage

For each assessment method described in Appendix D of Special Publication 800-53A (examine, interview, and test), the level of detail sought in the control assessment and scope of the assessment process is indicated using attributes for *depth* and *coverage*. The possible values for depth and coverage attributes are the same: "basic," "focused," or "comprehensive." Appendix D of Special Publication 800-53A describes the implications of each depth and coverage attribute value, as summarized in Table 11.4, giving system owners and security control assessors explicit guidance how to conduct assessment activities at a level of assurance appropriate for the information system's assigned impact level. Minimum assurance requirements for low-, medium-, and high-impact systems are specified in Appendix E of Special Publication 800-53 [33], while Special Publication 800-53A applies those requirements to each assessment method [1].

As with assessment methods and objects, security assessment report detail should include the depth and coverage attributes corresponding to each assessed control, to give some indication to readers of the report as to the rigor and scope of the assessment procedures that were followed.

Penetration Testing

Penetration testing is a specialized form of security control assessment in which the security assessor assumes the role of an attacker and attempts to overcome the security measures in place intended to safeguard the information system. Penetration testing can be employed for new information systems prior to authorization, or for operational systems as part of routine security testing or when significant changes have occurred in the system's operating environment or in the set of potential threats faced by the system [34]. Penetration testing is not applicable to every security control, but it can be used to assess a variety of administrative, operational, and technical controls, using attack scenarios including simulated hacking by outside attackers, social engineering attempts, or insider threats that might try

Table 11.4 Assessment Guidance by Depth and Coverage Attribute [32]

Level	Depth	Coverage
Basic	Consists of high-level reviews, checks, observations, or inspections of the assessment objects, discussions with individuals, or tests assuming no knowledge of internal control implementation details. This type of assessment is conducted using a limited body of evidence, generalized questions, or functional control specifications. Basic assessments provide a level of understanding of the security control necessary for determining whether the control is implemented and free of obvious errors	Uses a representative sample of assessment objects to provide a level of coverage necessary for determining whether the security control is implemented and free of obvious errors
Focused	Adds more in-depth studies/analyses of the assessment object. This type of assessment is conducted using a substantial body of evidence or documentation, in-depth questions, or high-level design and process descriptions for controls. Focused assessments provide a level of understanding of the security control necessary for determining whether the control is implemented and free of obvious errors and whether there are increased grounds for confidence that the control is implemented correctly and operating as intended	Uses a representative sample of assessment objects and other specific assessment objects deemed particularly important to achieving the assessment objective to provide a level of coverage necessary for determining whether the security control is implemented and free of obvious errors and whether there are increased grounds for confidence that the control is implemented correctly and operating as intended
Comprehensive	Consists of activities from basic and focused levels and more in depth, detailed, and thorough studies/analyses of the assessment object. This type of assessment is conducted using an extensive body of evidence or documentation, probing and in-depth questions, or detailed technical control specifications. Comprehensive assessments provide a level of understanding of the security control necessary for determining whether the control is implemented and free of obvious errors and whether there are further increased grounds for confidence that the control is implemented correctly and operating as intended on an ongoing and consistent basis, and that there is support for continuous improvement in the effectiveness of the control	Uses a sufficiently large sample of assessment objects and other specific assessment objects deemed particularly important to achieving the assessment objective to provide a level of coverage necessary for determining whether the security control is implemented and free of obvious errors and whether there are further increased grounds for confidence that the control is implemented correctly and operating as intended on an ongoing and consistent basis, and that there is support for continuous improvement in the effectiveness of the control

to circumvent security controls. Penetration tests often involve the simultaneous assessment of multiple controls, since attack scenarios and tools used for penetration testing seek to compromise the information system security in any way that might be attempted by an actual attacker. Penetration testing may require skill sets beyond those possessed by conventional security control assessors, due to the complexity of the tests and extensive set of tools and techniques that might be employed to simulate an attack. Special Publication 800-53A gives special emphasis to penetration testing in Appendix E, but cautions that such assessment methods should not be viewed as a way to verify an information system's security posture, but instead to identify weaknesses in current controls and to provide information to the organization about the system, its security controls, and the level of effort that might be needed to defeat or circumvent the security controls that are implemented [35].

PERFORMING SECURITY CONTROL ASSESSMENTS

The security control assessment process applies the selected assessment methods to the appropriate objects in order to produce evidence that the assessor needs to reach a conclusion whether the assessment objectives for the control have been met. Specific procedures followed by security control assessors vary depending on the nature of the system under evaluation, organizational policies and requirements, and the type of control or enhancement being assessed. Appendix F of Special Publication 800-53A provides a detailed set of example assessment procedures that may be used for every security control and control enhancement. The methods and objects provided in Appendix F are not intended to be prescriptive, and organizations have the flexibility to tailor, supplement, or substitute assessment procedures as needed to satisfy organizational or system-specific assessment requirements [36]. The assessment procedures selected for each control should be sufficient to enable the assessor to make a determination as to whether the assessment objectives are satisfied. Choosing insufficient or inappropriate assessment procedures will likely prevent the assessor from making such a determination, leading to a need for additional evidence, assessment activities, or corrective actions. Selecting multiple assessment procedures that produce evidence beyond what is needed to demonstrate that the assessment objectives have been met may extend the time required to conduct the assessment and incur additional resource costs that deliver no additional value.

Assessment Determinations

The primary finding reported for each assessment objective is a determination that the objective is either *satisfied* or *other-than-satisfied*. In order to declare a control objective satisfied, the evidence evaluated by the assessor must be sufficient to conclude that all the characteristics or criteria used by the assessor have been met.

All other situations result in a finding of other than satisfied, so the assessor's comments must be examined to learn whether an other-than-satisfied finding is due to a control weakness or deficiency or due to insufficient evidence available for the assessor to be able to fully evaluate the assessment objectives [37]. Assessor comments for other-than-satisfied findings should indicate exactly what assessment criteria were not met, and should explain how the control as assessed differed from what the assessor expected or needed to find in order to make a finding of satisfied. When such findings are presented in the initial version of the security assessment report, this information helps system owners identify appropriate responses and take any corrective actions that can be completed before the final assessment report is delivered to authorizing officials.

When assessment results are first delivered in the initial security assessment report, system owners, working in cooperation with information system security officers and others, examine the findings and recommendations produced by the assessor to understand any weaknesses, deficiencies, or other issues identified during the assessment. System owners and common control providers may act on the assessor's recommendations in order to correct weaknesses or deficiencies before the security assessment report is finalized, choose instead to establish a future plan for making such corrections, or make risk-based determinations that making the corrections is not necessary or that the associated risks do not justify corrective action [38]. Controls that are changed in some way in to correct assessment findings are reassessed before the final security assessment report is produced. Corrective actions that are deferred to a future date are captured in the plan of action and milestones so that authorizing officials can consider other-than-satisfied assessment findings together with formal plans for satisfying assessment objectives within specified timeframes. Other-than-satisfied findings for which no corrective action will be taken require a formal decision by the system owner to accept the risk associated with leaving weaknesses or deficiencies unmitigated. Security assessment report detail for these controls should indicate that a risk-based decision has been made not to take corrective action.

Recommendations and Responses

Recommendations for correcting other-than-satisfied assessment findings should be carefully evaluated by system owners and other stakeholders. Where a large number of findings are produced or where there is significant variation in the types of weaknesses and deficiencies identified and their potential impact to the organization, Special Publication 800-53A recommends that findings be categorized based on their severity or criticality to the organization [39]. Using categories for assessment findings can help organizations and system owners identify issues that can be addressed quickly or with minimal resource expenditures, and to prioritize corrective actions based on the level of risk faced by the organization and the potential to mitigate that risk. Establishing a repeatable approach to categorizing findings and associated risks can also help system owners to prepare plans of action and milestones in a consistent manner, which helps authorizing officials and executives with risk management responsibility to manage risk effectively and to oversee ongoing corrective actions across the organization.

Not every weakness or deficiency can be corrected, and not every possible risk mitigation can be justified against the cost required. Almost all federal agencies are self-accrediting, which gives authorizing officials a great deal of latitude in terms of what constitutes acceptable risk. This flexibility means that the risk-based response to a weaknesses or deficiency by a system owner in one organization may not be the same as the response in a different organization. It is important for system owners to clearly indicate their response to risks identified through the security control assessment process. Every other-than-satisfied finding presented in final security assessment reports should include an indication of the chosen response. Conventional risk management methodologies, including the process described in Special Publication 800-39, include at least five possible responses to risk: accept, avoid, mitigate, share, or transfer [40]. In the context of a security assessment report, a decision to avoid risk usually translates into changing the way in which a system is deployed or the set of functionality delivered for the system, and may result in the removal of specific controls from the set selected for the system. Decisions to mitigate, share, or transfer risks related to control weaknesses or deficiencies can all be documented as items in the plan of action and milestones (POA&M), so any of these responses to other-than-satisfied assessment findings should include an indication that a POA&M item has been created. A decision to accept risk (essentially, a decision to take no action) does not result in the creation of a POA&M item, but also does nothing to change the other-than-satisfied finding, so these findings should be accompanied in the security assessment report by an indication of the decision to accept the risk.

Assessment Cases

Organizations are given broad latitude to conduct security control assessments in a manner appropriate for the organization, its operating environments, and its information systems. Most of the guidance offered to federal agencies in Special Publication 800-53A can be tailored to suit specific organizational needs and the guidelines contain recommendations, not requirements. Recognizing that some organizations

---

WARNING

Corrective actions are often specified in a POA&M because an other-than-satisfied finding resulted from a security control assessment. The creation of a POA&M is a statement of intent by the system owner to take corrective action by a future point in time, but until corrections are made, the security control objective remains other than satisfied. Some system owners mistakenly revise the assessment finding to "satisfied" once the POA&M has been declared, but this practice can give an inaccurate portrayal of the security posture of the system. No changes should be made to the security control assessment findings until the corrective action in the POA&M has been taken and the control has been reassessed [41].

prefer a more prescriptive approach to security control assessment, NIST makes available a set of security control assessment cases that interested organizations can download and use [42]. These assessment cases follow a standard template format described in Appendix H of Special Publication 800-53A [1], with a separate assessment case document produced for each control contained in Special Publication 800-53. Compared to the assessment procedures provided in Appendix F, the assessment cases describe specific evidence gathering actions assessors can take for each assessment method relevant to the controls and control enhancements being evaluated. Assessors should still expect some organizational or system-specific variations to be needed when following assessment cases, but the detailed steps provided in the assessment cases gives specific instructions that, if followed, are intended to produce sufficient evidence to allow an assessor to make a determination for each of the required assessment objectives.

Producing the Security Assessment Report

The process of producing the security assessment report is conceptually very simple. The report reproduces, aggregates, and summarizes information created by security control assessors during the assessment process, and typically provides basic identifying information about the system, system owner, and control assessor, as well as details about the timing and scope of the assessment and the procedures used to conduct it. Many organizations provide document templates that assessors can use to produce security assessment reports in a manner consistent with organizational requirements and the expectations of authorizing officials or other readers of the reports. The use of an automated tool to support security control assessments can significantly reduce the effort needed to produce security assessment reports, as new system-generated reports can be run whenever needed, a function illustrated in Figure 11.4. Depending on organizational preferences, security assessment reports may provide executive summaries or other introductory information that explain overall assessment results and highlight findings that deserve particular attention. A security assessment report typically refers to both the system security plan and the plan of action and milestones, so the report is often delivered together with these other key documents to ensure that authorization officials have all the necessary decision-making information available at the same time.

THE SECURITY ASSESSMENT REPORT IN CONTEXT

The security assessment report contains the assessor's findings for each of the assessment objectives considered during the security control assessment. Perhaps obviously, the security assessment report is dependent on the security control assessment, but the scope and content of the report is also driven by many other factors and RMF activities that precede the security control assessment. The relationship between the RMF activities and outputs influencing the scope of the security control assessment is shown in Figure 11.5.

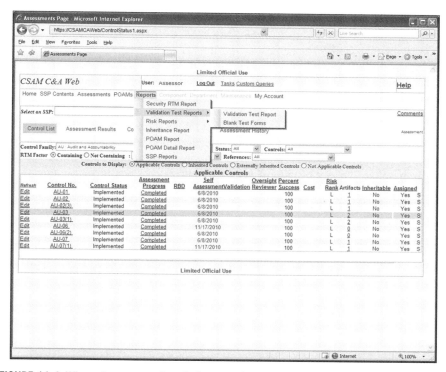

FIGURE 11.4 Where Assessment Data is Captured in a Tool Such as CSAM, a Current Security Assessment Report can be Generated Automatically when Needed, Facilitating the Process of Keeping Assessment Information Current and Accurately Reflecting the Results of Ongoing Assessment Activities [25]

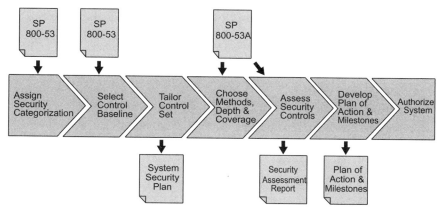

FIGURE 11.5 The Scope of the Security Control Assessment is Influenced by the Outcome of Several Activities in Earlier Steps of the RMF, Particularly Including the Security Categorization and Selection and Tailoring of the Security Control Baseline

As described in detail in Chapter 7, the security categorization of an information system performed during step 1 of the RMF process drives the selection of security controls for that system. Specifically, the impact level determined for the system determines the baseline set of security controls from Special Publication 800-53 that must be implemented for the system [43,44]. Starting from the appropriate security control baseline, the information system owner, working with technical experts such as information system architects and in consultation with security officers and engineers [24], tailors the set of security controls to reflect the protective needs of the system, taking into account the organization's security policies, applicable regulations, and other influences that might lead to exceptions from or additions to the security control baseline. The set of tailored security controls are documented in the system security plan and provide a key input to the development of the security assessment plan. The security assessment plan identifies the controls and relevant enhancements that should be assessed, based on the selections documented in the system security plan and the purpose (and therefore the scope) of the assessment that will be conducted. The security assessment plan also specifies the appropriate procedures to be used to evaluate the controls and enhancements against the assessment objectives in Special Publication 800-53A. The security assessment report typically includes the assessment method or methods employed to assess each control, so to the extent these methods are determined in advance, they can be incorporated in the control assessment guidance, instructions, or templates given to each assessor.

Once the security control assessment is complete and the security assessment report is documented (or generated, in the case where an organization uses an automated assessment system), the system owner, system security officer, security control assessor, and other agency personnel analyze the report findings to determine what corrective actions are required for the system, if any, and to translate other-than-satisfied findings into items included in the plan of action and milestones. When evaluating an initial security assessment report, there may be no expectation that a POA&M item will be created for every other-than-satisfied finding, but when the security assessment report is finalized and delivered to authorizing officials, there should be an explicit response to every other-than-satisfied finding, either in the form of a POA&M item or a documented decision by the system owner to accept the risk corresponding to the weakness or deficiency.

The Purpose and Role of the Security Assessment Report

The security assessment report includes the full set of controls and control enhancements selected for the information system, the assessment objectives corresponding to those controls and enhancements, and the assessor's findings for each assessment objective along with the rationale for the assessor's findings. Where other-than-satisfied findings are indicated, the security assessment report also includes a description of weaknesses or deficiencies found or other reasons why the objective was not satisfied, and recommendations for corrective action needed to achieve a satisfied result for each objective. The security assessment report indicates the methods used to assess each control and includes references to artifacts or sources of evidence used by the assessor, but copies of the actual evidence consulted by the assessor are typically not included with the report. Given the size and level of detail associated with security assessment reports, some organizations choose to incorporate summary findings that highlight overall assessment results and call attention to areas of weakness or deficiency that need to be addressed. The specific format and structure of the security assessment report should reflect the requirements and preferences of the organization and the personnel who will be using the information in the report.

Risk Assessment Report

The security assessment report includes detailed findings from the security control assessment, but it does not contain information on threats to the system or its operating environment or on the likelihood of those threats occurring or the impact to the organization should they occur. These risk determinations are typically addressed instead in a risk assessment report, produced as the result of a formal risk assessment process such as that described in Special Publication 800-30, *Guide for Conducting Risk Assessments* [45]. Risk assessments may be conducted prior to or after the security control assessment is performed with the results documented in a risk assessment report that informs the process of determining what action to take (if any) to remediate weaknesses or deficiencies identified in the security assessment report. (More detailed information on conducting risk assessments appears in Chapter 13.)

Security Test and Evaluation

While security control assessors may utilize multiple types of testing as one of several applicable assessment methods, the assessment of many security controls involves the examination of documents or other evidence of control implementation, interviews with appropriate organizational personnel, and other manual methods. Security control assessors may or may not be fully independent actors separate from the system owner and development, implementation, or operations teams. In contrast, security test and evaluation (ST&E) activities include direct testing of the information system following a specified test plan, with test procedures that may or may not focus on individual security controls. Testers performing ST&E activities against production systems are almost always—by policy and by practice—independent from the system team to ensure the objectivity of the test results. The ST&E is often performed as a part of the process of authorizing a newly accredited system, or as part of continuous monitoring activities for operational systems.

NOTE

Many processes and activities within the RMF involve "assessment" of one sort or another, so it is often helpful to distinguish between the security control assessment and security assessment report and other processes and artifacts that sound similar but are intended to address other aspects of the system authorization process.

Independent Evaluation

Under FISMA, federal agencies are required to undergo annual independent evaluations of their information security practices, including "testing of the effectiveness of information security policies, procedures, and practices of a representative subset of the agency's information systems" [46]. These evaluations must be performed either by the agency's Inspector General or by an external auditor, as they are intended to provide an independent opinion on the extent to which the agency is complying with FISMA requirements, based in part on an assessment of the security posture of at least some of the systems in the agency's FISMA system inventory. FISMA also requires agencies to test, no less than annually, the effectiveness of their security controls for *every* system in the FISMA inventory, but this periodic testing is distinct from the annual independent evaluation. The requirement for periodic testing and evaluation of system security controls can be met using security control assessments within the monitoring phase of the RMF; the annual independent evaluation may consider the results of continuous monitoring processes and security assessment reports but does not rely solely on these sources.

Using the Security Assessment Report

Ultimately, the format, content, and method of delivery for the security assessment report should be optimized to make the document effective for its intended purposes. This includes making sure that the security assessment report is accessible and understandable to system owners, risk managers, authorizing officials, and others who need to use the information in the report to make decisions. The security assessment report is used in its initial or draft form by system owners, both in order to understand the current security posture of the information system from the perspective of the assessor, and to evaluate findings and recommended corrective actions to see if control weaknesses or deficiencies can be resolved before the final report is produced [39]. Both the initial and final versions of the security assessment report provide information that is important for the development of items in the plan of action and milestones. When finalized, the security assessment report also serves as the most comprehensive source of information for authorizing officials, system owners, and other system stakeholders about the security controls implemented to safeguard each information system.

RELEVANT SOURCE MATERIAL

Several NIST Special Publications provide guidance, recommendations, and instructions relevant to the performance of security control assessments and the production of security assessment reports. The most applicable sources of information include:

- Special Publication 800-53 Revision 3, *Recommended Security Controls for Federal Information Systems and Organizations* [17].

- Special Publication 800-53A Revision 1, *Guide for Assessing the Security Controls in Federal Information Systems and Organizations* [1].
- Special Publication 800-37 Revision 1, *Guide for Applying the Risk Management Framework to Federal Information* Systems [2].

These and other NIST Special Publications are available from the NIST Computer Security Division website, at http://csrc.nist.gov/publications/PubsSPs.html.

SUMMARY

The security assessment report presents the findings from security control assessments conducted as part of the initial system authorization process for newly deployed systems or for periodic assessment of operational systems as required under FISMA. In addition to assessment results and recommendations to address any system weaknesses or deficiencies identified during security control assessments, the security assessment report describes the purpose and scope of the assessment and procedures employed by assessors to arrive at their determinations. The results provided in the security assessment report, in conjunction with the system security plan and plan of assessment and milestones, enable authorizing officials to thoroughly evaluate the effectiveness of security controls implemented for an information system, and to make informed decisions about whether an information system should be authorized to operate. This chapter described the process of producing a security assessment report, and explained many aspects of planning and conducting security control assessments that influence the contents and usability of the report. This chapter also summarized key information about security control assessments contained in federal guidance available to system owners and security assessors, and highlighted the ways in which security assessment reports are affected by and used to support other activities in the system authorization process described in NIST's Risk Management Framework.

REFERENCES

[1] Guide for assessing the security controls in federal information systems and organizations. Gaithersburg, MD: National Institute of Standards and Technology, Computer Security Division; June 2010. Special Publication 800-53A revision 1.

[2] Guide for applying the risk management framework to federal information systems. Gaithersburg, MD: National Institute of Standards and Technology, Computer Security Division; February 2010. Special Publication 800-37 revision 1.

[3] Guide for assessing the security controls in federal information systems and organizations. Gaithersburg, MD: National Institute of Standards and Technology, Computer Security Division; June 2010. Special Publication 800-53A revision 1. p. 25.

[4] Guide for applying the risk management framework to federal information systems. Gaithersburg, MD: National Institute of Standards and Technology, Computer Security Division; February 2010. Special Publication 800-37 revision 1. p. 31.

[5] Guide for applying the risk management framework to federal information systems. Gaithersburg, MD: National Institute of Standards and Technology, Computer Security Division; February 2010. Special Publication 800-37 revision 1. p. D-7.

[6] Guide for applying the risk management framework to federal information systems. Gaithersburg, MD: National Institute of Standards and Technology, Computer Security Division; February 2010. Special Publication 800-37 revision 1. See Appendix D.

[7] Guide for applying the risk management framework to federal information systems. Gaithersburg, MD: National Institute of Standards and Technology, Computer Security Division; February 2010. Special Publication 800-37 revision 1. p. 30.

[8] Guide for assessing the security controls in federal information systems and organizations. Gaithersburg, MD: National Institute of Standards and Technology, Computer Security Division; June 2010. Special Publication 800-53A revision 1. p. 15.

[9] Swanson M. Security self-assessment guide for information technology systems. Gaithersburg, MD: National Institute of Standards and Technology, Computer Security Division; November 2001. Special Publication 800-26.

[10] Swanson M. Security self-assessment guide for information technology systems. Gaithersburg, MD: National Institute of Standards and Technology, Computer Security Division; November 2001. Special Publication 800-26. p. 10.

[11] Guide for assessing the security controls in federal information systems and organizations. Gaithersburg, MD: National Institute of Standards and Technology, Computer Security Division; June 2010. Special Publication 800-53A revision 1. p. 22.

[12] Johnson A, Toth P. Security assessment provider requirements and customer responsibilities: building a security assessment credentialing program for federal information systems. Gaithersburg, MD: National Institute of Standards and Technology, Computer Security Division; September 2007. Interagency Report 7328 Initial Public Draft. p. 43–5.

[13] Information Systems Audit and Control Association. CISA: Certified Information Systems Auditor [cited January 13, 2012]. <http://www.isaca.org/Certification/CISA-Certified-Information-Systems-Auditor/Pages/default.aspx>.

[14] International Council of Electronic Commerce Consultants. EC-Council Certified Security Analyst (ECSA) [cited January 13, 2012]. <https://cert.eccouncil.org/certification/certificate-categories/ec-council-certified-security-analyst-ecsa>.

[15] SysAdmin, Audit, Network, Security (SANS) Institute. Global Information Assurance Certification Systems and Network Auditor (GSNA) [cited January 13, 2012]. <http://www.giac.org/certification/systems-network-auditor-gsna>.

[16] See for example the Certified Authorization Professional (CAP) certification offered by the International Information Systems Security Certification Consortium [updated January 4, 2011; cited January 13, 2012]. <https://www.isc2.org/cap/default.aspx>.

[17] Recommended security controls for federal information systems and organizations. Gaithersburg, MD: National Institute of Standards and Technology, Computer Security Division; August 2009. Special Publication 800-53 revision 3.

[18] Federal Information Security Management Act of 2002, Pub. L. No. 107-347, 116 Stat. 2949. §301, codified at 44 U.S.C. §3544(b)(5).

[19] Guide for assessing the security controls in federal information systems and organizations. Gaithersburg, MD: National Institute of Standards and Technology, Computer Security Division; June 2010. Special Publication 800-53A revision 1. p. 16.

[20] Guide for applying the risk management framework to federal information systems. Gaithersburg, MD: National Institute of Standards and Technology, Computer Security Division; February 2010. Special Publication 800-37 revision 1. p. 39.

[21] Guide for assessing the security controls in federal information systems and organizations. Gaithersburg, MD: National Institute of Standards and Technology, Computer Security Division; June 2010. Special Publication 800-53A revision 1. p. 21.

[22] Guide for applying the risk management framework to federal information systems. Gaithersburg, MD: National Institute of Standards and Technology, Computer Security Division; February 2010. Special Publication 800-37 revision 1. p. 30–3.

[23] Guide for assessing the security controls in federal information systems and organizations. Gaithersburg, MD: National Institute of Standards and Technology, Computer Security Division; June 2010. Special Publication 800-53A revision 1. p. 19–20.

[24] Guide for applying the risk management framework to federal information systems. Gaithersburg, MD: National Institute of Standards and Technology, Computer Security Division; February 2010. Special Publication 800-37 revision 1. p. 25.

[25] Cyber Security Assessment & Management (CSAM) [computer program]. Version 2.1.5.2. Washington, DC: Department of Justice; 2010.

[26] Guide for assessing the security controls in federal information systems and organizations. Gaithersburg, MD: National Institute of Standards and Technology, Computer Security Division; June 2010. Special Publication 800-53A revision 1. p. G-1.

[27] Standards for security categorization of federal information and information systems. Gaithersburg, MD: National Institute of Standards and Technology, Computer Security Division; December 2003. Federal Information Processing Standards Publication 199.

[28] Minimum security requirements for federal information and information systems. Gaithersburg, MD: National Institute of Standards and Technology, Computer Security Division; March 2006. Federal Information Processing Standards Publication 200.

[29] Recommended security controls for federal information systems and organizations. Gaithersburg, MD: National Institute of Standards and Technology, Computer Security Division; August 2009. Special Publication 800-53 revision 3. p. F-127.

[30] Recommended security controls for federal information systems and organizations. Gaithersburg, MD: National Institute of Standards and Technology, Computer Security Division; August 2009. Special Publication 800-53 revision 3. p. F-109.

[31] Annex 1: Low-impact baseline; Annex 2: Moderate-impact baseline; and Annex 3: High-impact baseline. Recommended security controls for federal information systems and organizations. Gaithersburg, MD: National Institute of Standards and Technology, Computer Security Division; August 2009. Special Publication 800-53 revision 3 excerpts.

[32] Guide for assessing the security controls in federal information systems and organizations. Gaithersburg, MD: National Institute of Standards and Technology, Computer Security Division; June 2010. Special Publication 800-53A revision 1. See Appendix D.

[33] Recommended security controls for federal information systems and organizations. Gaithersburg, MD: National Institute of Standards and Technology, Computer Security Division; August 2009. Special Publication 800-53 revision 3. See Appendix E.

[34] Guide for assessing the security controls in federal information systems and organizations. Gaithersburg, MD: National Institute of Standards and Technology, Computer Security Division; June 2010. Special Publication 800-53A revision 1. See Appendix E.

[35] Guide for assessing the security controls in federal information systems and organizations. Gaithersburg, MD: National Institute of Standards and Technology, Computer Security Division; June 2010. Special Publication 800-53A revision 1. p. E-1.

[36] Guide for assessing the security controls in federal information systems and organizations. Gaithersburg, MD: National Institute of Standards and Technology, Computer Security Division; June 2010. Special Publication 800-53A revision 1. p. F-2.

[37] Guide for assessing the security controls in federal information systems and organizations. Gaithersburg, MD: National Institute of Standards and Technology, Computer Security Division; June 2010. Special Publication 800-53A revision 1. p. 22–3.

[38] Guide for assessing the security controls in federal information systems and organizations. Gaithersburg, MD: National Institute of Standards and Technology, Computer Security Division; June 2010. Special Publication 800-53A revision 1. p. 24.

[39] Guide for assessing the security controls in federal information systems and organizations. Gaithersburg, MD: National Institute of Standards and Technology, Computer Security Division; June 2010. Special Publication 800-53A revision 1. p. 23.

[40] Managing information security risk: organization, mission, and information system view. Gaithersburg, MD: National Institute of Standards and Technology, Computer Security Division; March 2011. Special Publication 800-39. p. 26.

[41] Guide for applying the risk management framework to federal information systems. Gaithersburg, MD: National Institute of Standards and Technology, Computer Security Division; February 2010. Special Publication 800-37 revision 1. p. 33.

[42] Assessment Cases Download Page [Internet]. Gaithersburg, MD: National Institute of Standards and Technology, Computer Security Division [created August 7, 2008; updated August 17, 2010; cited December 27, 2010]. <http://csrc.nist.gov/groups/SMA/fisma/assessment-cases.html>.

[43] Recommended security controls for federal information systems and organizations. Gaithersburg, MD: National Institute of Standards and Technology, Computer Security Division; August 2009. Special Publication 800-53 revision 3. p. 4.

[44] Minimum security requirements for federal information and information systems. Gaithersburg, MD: National Institute of Standards and Technology, Computer Security Division; March 2006. Federal Information Processing Standards Publication 200. p. 4.

[45] Guide for conducting risk assessments. Gaithersburg, MD: National Institute of Standards and Technology, Computer Security Division; September 2011. Special Publication 800-30 revision 1. Initial Public Draft.

[46] Federal Information Security Management Act of 2002, Pub. L. No. 107-347, 116 Stat. 2952. §301, codified at 44 U.S.C. §3545.

Plan of Action and Milestones

INFORMATION IN THIS CHAPTER:

- Regulatory Background
- Structure and Content of the Plan of Action and Milestones
- Weaknesses and Deficiencies
- Producing the Plan of Action and Milestones
- Maintaining and Monitoring the Plan of Action and Milestones
- Relevant Source Material

No system is perfectly secure, and a system deemed to have adequate protective measures in place still presents some risk that the system will be compromised in a way that results in loss or damage to the organization. Information security also is not static, as the set of threats and vulnerabilities that might affect a system can and do change over time. For both of these reasons, system owners and organizational information security programs must monitor and evaluate security control effectiveness on an ongoing basis. Where risks exist due to weaknesses or deficiencies, those responsible for information systems security must decide on, plan for, and implement appropriate actions to address weaknesses and deficiencies to improve system security and bring risk to a level acceptable to the organization. Security control assessments are one primary way to identify weaknesses and deficiencies in implemented security controls, and the security assessment report includes both information about weaknesses and deficiencies and recommendations for addressing those issues. System owners and common control providers use the results in the security assessment report to determine the most appropriate risk-based response to weaknesses and deficiencies—those responses are documented in the plan of action and milestones (POA&M). A plan of action and milestones is defined in federal guidance simply as a document "that identifies tasks that need to be accomplished" to correct security weaknesses in systems and programs [1]. Together with the system security plan and the security assessment report, the plan of action and milestones provides the essential documentation authorizing officials rely on to decide whether the risk associated with operating a given system is acceptable to the organization.

Security control assessments provide information about the security posture of a system at a specific point in time. Decisions to authorize (or continue) operation of a system consider the risk stemming from operating the information system. If the risk associated with a system exceeds the risk tolerance level of the organization, the authorizing official will not grant the system an authority to operate [2]. By establishing a plan and explicit timeframe for reducing the risk to the organization, the plan of action and milestones enables authorizing officials to accept certain risks on a temporary basis, on the condition that the activities in the POA&M are completed according to the schedule provided in the plan. This makes the plan of action and milestones an important document for ongoing management and monitoring of the information system, in addition to its role in the system authorization decision making process. The plan of action and milestones is updated not only when new security assessments are conducted, but whenever new weaknesses or deficiencies are discovered, and whenever actions in the POA&M are completed.

This chapter describes the development and use of the plan of action and milestones, both in support of system authorization and in continuous monitoring. This description includes using the findings in the security assessment report and other potential sources of system weaknesses, analyzing those weaknesses in order to determine appropriate corrective action or other responses, creating individual entries in the plan, and producing the POA&M document. The information presented here reflects relevant guidance found in OMB Memorandum M-02-01, *Guidance for Preparing and Submitting Security Plans of Action and Milestones* [1], NIST Special Publication 800-37, *Guide for Applying the Risk Management Framework to Federal Information Systems*[3], and OMB instructions to agencies on FISMA reporting [4,5]. The security assessment report, detailed in the previous chapter, is often the single most significant source of information leading to the addition of items to the POA&M, so this chapter incorporates many of the topics and information presented in Chapter 11.

One point about terminology is in order: the term "plan of action and milestones" (typically abbreviated as "POA&M" or "POAM") can apply to a single weakness or deficiency, the set of weaknesses and deficiencies for a single system, or to the collective weaknesses and deficiencies associated with information systems operated by an organization. These multiple usages are all correct, but still have the potential to cause confusion. From the perspective of the NIST Risk Management Framework, the plan of action and milestones is a document (or equivalent electronic artifact) detailing the tasks that are planned to address weaknesses or deficiencies in an information system [6]. The term "POAM item" is sometimes used to refer to the set of activities and planned completion dates associated with a single weakness or deficiency. For example, there are many security controls that require the development of specific types of policies, procedures, and plans, such as access control policies, system maintenance procedures, contingency plans, incident response plans, and other types of documentation [7]. Operating without one of these required documents is a weakness, and a POA&M to address such a weakness would describe the activities and expected completion dates for developing, approving, and implementing the missing documentation.

REGULATORY BACKGROUND

Federal agencies prepare plans of action and milestones—and submit them to OMB upon request—to satisfy reporting requirements associated with provisions of the Federal Information Security Management Act (FISMA) [8]. These requirements predate FISMA, as language in the Government Information Security Reform Act of 2000 directed agencies to "examine the adequacy and effectiveness of information security policies, procedures, and practices" and report any significant deficiency to OMB as a material weakness [9]. To assist agencies in complying with this requirement, OMB issued a series of memoranda in 2001 to explain expectations for agency reporting of material weaknesses [10], describe the content and format requirements for summary information to be included by each agency along with materials about their information security programs [11], and provide more explicit instructions on the specific information that agencies should include for each system in their plans of action and milestones [1]. While the Government Information Security Reform Act was superseded by FISMA, the last of these OMB Memoranda, M-02-01, is cited in Special Publication 800-37 as the reference for agencies on developing plans of action and milestones to satisfy federal reporting requirements [6]. Similarly, beginning in 2004 [4], detailed instructions issued annually to agencies on FISMA reporting requirements recommend the same standard format and content items originally published in M-02-01. While agencies do not have to use the exact format specified, they are required to include all the data elements enumerated by OMB for the POA&M entries they create [12]. The POA&M documents prepared and submitted to OMB or other external audiences may not provide the same level of detail as that necessary for internal use by the agencies that create the plans, but OMB's instructions serve as a minimum set of requirements about what information should be captured about each weakness and the agency's plans for remediation.

Plans of action and milestones are unique among information system security documents in that some item-level detail is required to be reported outside the agency to satisfy FISMA reporting requirements. In contrast, agencies report only summary information about the security categorization, authorization status, and periodic assessment of the systems included on their FISMA inventories, as the emphasis in security reporting metrics is on information security and privacy program effectiveness, not on characteristics of individual systems. Agency-level POA&Ms are intended to reflect consolidated security weaknesses identified through any review, assessment, or audit, whether conducted internally or externally [12]. Where system-level POA&M documents are intended primarily for use by system owners, common control providers, and authorizing officials [6], agency POA&Ms are expected to be furnished to agency inspectors general as well as OMB, to provide independent oversight at an organizational level and to monitor the completion of corrective actions against the milestones committed to in the POA&M timeline [13]. While full POA&Ms must be submitted to OMB only upon request, summary information on agency-level POA&Ms is required to be reported on a quarterly basis—such information includes the total number of weaknesses and the number of weaknesses for which corrective action has been completed, is in progress on schedule, or has been delayed [14].

STRUCTURE AND CONTENT OF THE PLAN OF ACTION AND MILESTONES

The structure of POA&M documents emphasizes the explanation of weaknesses and the specific activities planned to address those weaknesses, with a simplicity that often belies the significant analysis that goes into producing the information contained in the POA&M. This structure reflects the primary purpose of the POA&M as a management tool used to monitor the achievement of specific objectives on an ongoing basis and is in stark contrast to related artifacts such as the security assessment report that are intended to provide comprehensive descriptions of system security at a specific point in time. The format used to produce the POA&M can vary from organization to organization depending on agency-specific requirements, but for a given organization, the structure tends to be the same regardless of the reason the POA&M is produced. Information system owners and common control providers—who have primary responsibility for preparing POA&Ms [6]—can therefore typically use the same POA&M reporting format whether the document is provided as part of an accreditation package, as a report of remediation progress for an operational system, or as updated in response to new weaknesses found through security assessments, audits, or other reviews. There is also some variation in POA&Ms prepared for individual systems and in agency-level POA&M documents, as agency-level POA&Ms must comply with external reporting requirements specified by OMB in addition to satisfying any agency-specific needs.

Agency-Level POA&M

At the agency-wide level, plans of action and milestones must be prepared not just for information systems, but also for programs with identified security weaknesses [10]. Recognizing that the agency-level POA&M provides an aggregation of information drawn from multiple system-level POA&Ms, official guidance to agencies recommends a tabular format for POA&M reporting, with spreadsheets originally envisioned as the reporting format [15]. Since 2004, FISMA reporting instructions from OMB have offered examples to agencies of POA&M tables for both programs and systems, although agencies are no longer required to follow the example format as long as the necessary data elements are included [12]. The use of spreadsheets as a POA&M submission format is also being replaced with online submission through OMB's CyberScope electronic FISMA reporting application. Agency use of Cyber-Scope became mandatory beginning in November 2010. The preferred submission method is to use data feeds directly to OMB from agency security management tools; an alternative mechanism uses an Extensible Markup Language (XML) to upload template for Microsoft Excel [16].

Agency-wide POA&Ms include much of the same detail as system-level POA&Ms about individual weaknesses and plans for correcting them, but some information included in reports for OMB reporting purposes—like weakness descriptions—is typically less detailed than the same type of information appearing in system-level POA&Ms. There is also some additional information required by OMB that may not always be found in system-level POA&Ms. For instance, agency-level POA&Ms reported to OMB must be linked to the agency budget, using the unique investment identifier (UII) for the system to which each weakness applies. The UII (previously known as the unique project identifier or UPI) is a data element assigned to all investments appearing in agency IT portfolios as part of the capital planning and investment control process. The "unique" in unique investment identifier refers to the investment (as reported on the Agency's IT Investment Portfolio, also known as Exhibit 53A of the agency budget submission), not to the system, as a single investment may fund more than one information system [17]. To facilitate the generation of complete agency-level POA&M reports, system owners and common control providers either need to make sure that UPI information is captured in POA&M detail or cross-reference information systems in the FISMA inventory to UIIs in the IT Investment Portfolio.

Agency-wide POA&Ms are also intended to include security weaknesses identified through any type of review or from any source, to produce an authoritative list of all weaknesses across the organization [13,12]. This scope in general should apply to system-level POA&Ms too, so organizations should take care when identifying weaknesses reflected on the POA&M not to put too great an emphasis on security control assessments at the expense of other equally important sources beyond the security assessment report.

POA&M Detail for Agency-Level Reports

In annual instructions on FISMA reporting requirements [12], agencies are referred to a set of eight attributes that must be described for each weakness included in the POA&M. These attributes are summarized in Table 12.1.

System-Level POA&M Information

For systems seeking authorization to operate via procedures defined in the NIST Risk Management Framework (RMF), the plan of action and milestones is created to describe the corrective actions that system owners or common control providers intend to take to address weaknesses or deficiencies identified during security control assessments [6]. Once prepared, the POA&M is also used to monitor the progress made by the system owner or other parties responsible for performing the actions specified in the POA&M. By documenting "all security weaknesses or deficiencies identified during the security control assessment," the POA&M establishes an audit trail of actions to which system owners have committed and a timeline within which those actions will be completed [6]. The POA&M is updated as milestones are reached and corrective actions are completed, and is also revised as necessary to reflect the addition

Table 12.1 Required Data Elements for Agency-Level POA&Ms [4]

Element	Description
Severity and brief description	• Severity values are: "significant deficiency," "reportable condition," or "other weakness" • Description must provide sufficient data to permit oversight and tracking
Party responsible for resolution	• Identity of the office or organization that the agency head will hold responsible for resolving the weakness
Resources required for resolution	• Estimate cost to complete corrective actions • Includes the anticipated source of funding and whether a request for new funding is anticipated • Also identify other, non-funding, obstacles and challenges to resolving the weakness
Scheduled completion date	• Provide target completion date for all corrective actions • Once entered, initial scheduled completion date should not be changed
Key milestones and completion dates	• One or more milestones should be included for each weakness in the POA&M, with targeted completion dates for each milestone
Changes to milestones	• Includes new completion dates for milestones, if originally specified date is changed
Source	• Identify the source of the weakness (e.g. security assessment, program review, internal or external audit, etc.)
Status	• Status values are: "ongoing" or "completed" • "Completed" should be used only when a weakness has been fully resolved and the corrective action has been tested • When completed, include the date of completion

of POA&M items for newly identified weaknesses, or a change in the nature of the response planned by the system owner, such as a decision to accept the risk associated with a given weakness, rather than expend the resources necessary to remediate it.

The core information reported for individual POA&M items has much in common with the POA&M details included in agency-level POA&M documents. System-level POA&M information tends to provide more detail on the nature of weaknesses and deficiencies and the corresponding risk faced by the organization, and may include security control cross-references such as the control identifier and specific assessment objectives (from Special Publication 800-53A) that were found to be deficient during security control assessments. While POA&M items always include dates by which milestones will be completed, there are several other dates that may be tracked, depending on organizational needs for POA&M management, to support monitoring, or for other purposes. Typical examples of relevant dates include the date corrective actions are assigned to parties responsible for completing them, when they are scheduled to start, when the weakness was identified, or when the POA&M item was created. The declaration and reporting of planned and actual start and completion dates for milestones is a practice familiar to many system owners from capital planning and investment control processes, as the Exhibit 300 business cases agencies submit for their major investments require reporting of planned and actual start and completion dates for cost and schedule performance milestones [18]. While POA&M reports submitted to external audiences like OMB only summarize information about corrective actions that are underway or completed, system-level POA&Ms may also provide status indications corresponding to internal process steps, such as POA&M reviews, evaluation of evidence, and approvals. The sample POA&M entries in Figures 12.1–12.3 show attributes available in the Cyber Security

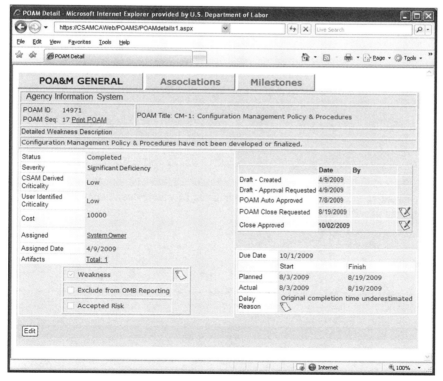

FIGURE 12.1 Failure to Implement a Required Control, such as the Missing Configuration Management Policies and Procedures Identified Here, Typically Represents a Significant Deficiency [19]

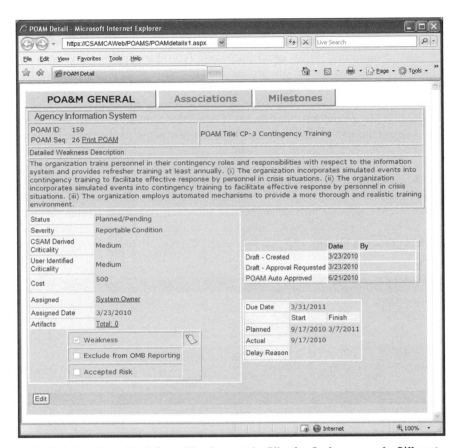

FIGURE 12.2 One Control Deficiency May Prevent the Effective Performance of a Different Control, such as a Lack of Training For Planning and Executing Operational Controls like Contingency Operations [19]

WARNING

The estimated cost and other resources associated with POA&M corrective actions should be based on sound analysis to support accurate risk-based decision making about which weaknesses to remediate. In some organizations, there may be a temptation to overstate cost estimates to help justify a decision to accept the risk associated with a weakness or deficiency rather than allocate resources to correct the problem. Cost and other resource estimates should be calculated based on the actual effort required to remediate the weakness; system owners can make the decision whether to incur those costs by comparing them to the risk faced by the organization if the weakness is left uncorrected.

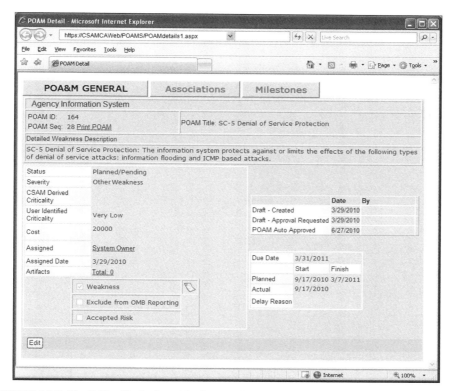

FIGURE 12.3 The Criticality Assigned By System Owners to Weaknesses Identified in Vulnerability Scanning or Other System Testing Should Give an Indication of the Perceived Exposure of the System [19]

Assessment and Management (CSAM) application used by many federal agencies; other commercial certification and accreditation support and FISMA reporting tools offer similar data elements.

A summary of information typically contained for each weakness in system-level POA&M items appears in Table 12.2. The elements described in the table are representative and do not constitute an exhaustive list; actual POA&M information required or recommended for system owners varies according to organizational policy, standards, and reporting requirements.

Creating POA&M Items

Once weaknesses have been identified for which corrective action will be taken, system owners need to develop a POA&M for each weakness, with input sought as necessary from security officers, security assessors, or others with relevant knowledge. System owners—or others authorized to create POA&Ms for their systems—should

Table 12.2 Required Data Elements for Agency-Level POA&Ms[*]

Element	Description
POA&M Identifier	• System- or agency-unique value assigned to each POA&M • Facilitates communication about POA&M items as well as tracking and reporting
POA&M label Description	• Name or descriptive label of the POA&M, characterizing the nature of the weakness • Details may include the control or assessment objectives to which the weakness corresponds, the specific deficiency, if known, and any other information that might be useful to support corrective actions
Status	• Current status of the POA&M • "Completed" should be used only when all underlying milestones have been achieved and corrective actions for the weakness have been tested • May include dates when status changes occur
Severity and criticality	• Severity is an indicator of the relative importance of the weakness, typically based in the impact that might result if the weakness is exploited • Criticality is an indicator of the relative priority placed on correcting the weakness • Depending on organizational practices, values for these attributes may be pre-determined based on the type of weakness or assigned by system owners or security officers based on their own judgment about the significance of the weakness
Responsibility	• Person or organization component assigned ownership of corrective actions • Depending on the extent of the POA&M, responsible parties may be identified for each milestone as well completion of the POA&M
Resources required	• Estimated resources needed to complete the actions listed in the POA&M • Often expressed as a dollar cost estimate, resource needs can also be expressed qualitatively based on relative level of effort (e.g. low, medium, high)
Milestones	• One or more milestones should be included for each weakness in the POA&M, reflecting specific objectives to be achieved

Table 12.2 Required Data Elements for Agency-Level POA&Ms [*] (continued)

Element	Description

POA&M dates	• In addition to target and actual completion dates, additional dates can be included as necessary to support POA&M management and oversight
	  ○ Date created
	  ○ Date assigned
	  ○ Planned start date
	  ○ Actual start date
	  ○ Date of last update/change in status
	  ○ Planned and actual milestone completion dates
	  ○ Dates associated with POA&M workflow

Changes to plan	• Changes to milestone or overall POA&M completion dates or deviations in actual corrective action progress compared to plan should include explanatory information about why the change occurred
Supporting information	• Can include any additional explanatory detail, assessment evidence, risk analysis, or other artifacts supporting completion of corrective actions

[*]Items in the table reflect information appearing in sample POA&M templates from NIST, POA&M fields in the Cyber Security Assessment and Management tool, and guidance and templates used by multiple federal agencies.

be aware of the documentation and level of detail needed to create a POA&M that satisfies organizational requirements, and gather the necessary information. The use of standard paper-based or electronic POA&M templates can help organizations ensure that POA&Ms are created consistently with all required information included. Online tools may be particularly helpful in this regard (see Figure 12.4), both by enforcing minimum information requirements during POA&M data entry and by automating the linkage of new POA&Ms to the system security controls where weaknesses were identified. The completion of corrective actions described in a POA&M does not resolve the weakness until the control or other deficient aspect of the system has been reassessed and found to satisfy all relevant objectives. POA&M creators should provide sufficient information to let action item owners and other reviewers understand the expectations for each system security control, the deviation found from those expectations, and the action or evidence that would bring the control objective to a satisfied status.

Planning for Remediation

Creating a POA&M requires system owners to develop estimates for the level of effort, type and number of resources, and funding needed to remediate weaknesses, and to

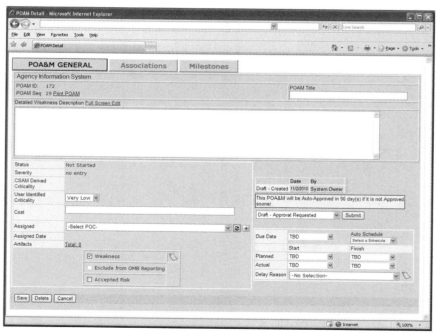

FIGURE 12.4 The Use of Templates or Online Forms For POA&M Creation can Help Ensure Consistency in the Information Entered by POA&M Creators and can Enforce Minimum Data Requirements [19]

determine a schedule of activities and overall duration for completing the POA&M that takes into account resource limitations, competing priorities, and other constraints [6]. Depending on the nature of the weakness, system owners may need to rely on project managers, developers, security officers, or other subject matter experts in order to accurately estimate the scope of remediation actions. Resource requirements are an important input to decision making about choosing to accept or to remediate risks associated with identified weaknesses and deficiencies, so system owners should try to ensure that estimates are well informed. The availability of resources needed to perform corrective actions often drives POA&M timelines, but system owners also need to be aware of applicable policies, directives, regulations, or guidance that influences the timeframe in which particular weaknesses need to be addressed. For example, in the wake of the high-profile theft in 2006 of a government laptop containing personal information on 26.5 million veterans, the Office of Management and Budget directed agencies to implement encryption on all laptop computers and other mobile devices, and asked that the new controls be in place within 45 days [20].

Oversight of POA&M Creation

System owners and common control providers are obligated to create POA&Ms for any unremediated weaknesses and deficiencies identified in security assessment reports. This requirement includes giving primary responsibility to system owners to determine and select the appropriate corrective actions and document those as POA&Ms [6]. Depending on security governance and oversight processes, POA&Ms created by system owners may be subject to approval before remediation can begin. Subjecting POA&Ms to review before their actions are initiated can add administrative steps to the process, but also offers organizations the opportunity to identify actions planned for one system that may help address similar weaknesses in others. Such opportunities are particularly likely when POA&Ms are created in response to weaknesses or issues raised from external sources, such as vulnerability announcements related to commercial software products, notifications provided by agency incident response or security monitoring teams, or government-wide advisories from organizations like the United States Computer Emergency Readiness Team (US-CERT).

WEAKNESSES AND DEFICIENCIES

To determine the appropriate corrective actions (if any) for security control weaknesses and deficiencies, system owners must assess the risk faced by the organization due to the presence of each weakness or vulnerability [21]. Weakness and corrective action information in security assessment reports generally focuses on the vulnerability that might exist, but not on the threats, exploit likelihood, or impact to the organization associated with each weakness. These additional aspects need to be assessed to transform a weakness or deficiency into an estimation of risk that can be used to validate or reset weakness criticality and severity attributes, and to drive

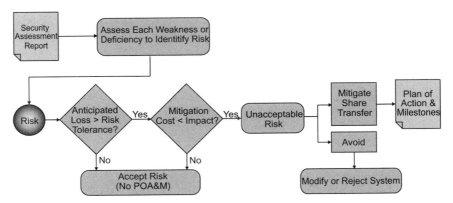

FIGURE 12.5 Weaknesses Must First be Evaluated in Terms of Their Associated Risk, and Those with Unacceptable Levels of Risk May Result in the Creation of POA&M Describing Corrective Actions for Risk Remediation [24]

decisions about risks that the organization can accept (and therefore weaknesses that can be left unremediated), and those that are unacceptable and must be addressed through mitigation or other responses. Risk determination and risk acceptance are core activities in the information system authorization process in step 5 of the RMF [22], while formal risk assessment procedures are provided in Special Publication 800-30 [23]. The combined process of assessing risks due to identified weaknesses and responding to those risks is illustrated in Figure 12.5.

As noted in the previous chapter, RMF guidance sets the expectation that every weakness or deficiency identified during security control assessments will be documented in the security assessment report, and the reporting templates and procedures used by many agencies presume that a POA&M will be created for every other-than-satisfied assessment finding unless an explicit risk-based decision is made by the system owner to accept the risk [6,25]. This guidance should not be interpreted to imply that only insignificant other-than-satisfied findings may result in risk acceptance. Instead, risk-based decision criteria are used to balance the magnitude of any risks against the cost of remediation and the risk tolerance of the organization [21]. As Figure 12.5 indicates, if the cost to an attacker to exploit a weakness exceeds the potential gain, a decision to accept the risk may be justified. Similarly, if the anticipated loss to the organization is at or below the level the organization is willing to tolerate, or if the cost to remediate the weakness exceeds the anticipated loss, the organization may choose to accept the risk and leave the weakness unaddressed [21].

Risk Assessments

According to standard methodologies such as the one described in Special Publication 800-30, to estimate risk, system owners and other risk assessors need to consider not only the vulnerabilities that may be exposed by security control weaknesses, but also the threats that might exploit those vulnerabilities, the likelihood of such an event occurring, and the impact to the organization that would result [23]. Risk assessment is inherently subjective, particularly when estimating the likelihood of occurrence for specific security events. Organizations often employ qualitative rating scales for risk that are similar to the categories used to assign impact levels to systems (low, moderate, or high) [26]. Special Publication 800-30 emphasizes the use of such ratings both for the likelihood that a vulnerability will be exploited by known threats and for the relative impact to the organization should an exploit succeed. By assigning numeric values to each rating level, overall risk estimates can be calculated by taking the product of likelihood and impact, and the estimates can be ordered according to the risk scores. Organizations can then apply their own policies and risk tolerances to determine which risks are sufficiently critical to warrant corrective action [22,27].

Risk Responses

Risk assessments for identified weaknesses may be formal or informal, and are conducted as needed to help system owners and common control providers characterize risk and determine what response to that risk is most appropriate [22]. It is not necessary to conduct a full risk assessment for every weakness, but in order to select the appropriate responses to risk, system owners, authorizing officials, and organizations need to have a good understanding of the nature and magnitude of the risk. Risk assessments can provide this perspective. System owners generally receive initial information regarding the significance of identified weaknesses in the contents of the security assessment report, but this information may or may not be sufficient to enable a decision about corrective actions that should be taken. Appropriate responses to risk may be determined by the system owner, alone or in consultation with others, but the response chosen is often subject to review and approval by the authorizing official or other personnel with information security management responsibility.

Responses to risk generally fall into five distinct categories: accept, avoid, mitigate, share, or transfer the risk [28]. Choices to mitigate, share, or transfer risk all involve some action that serves to reduce risk faced by the organization, the specifics of which can and should be captured in the plan of action and milestones. Risk mitigation includes any actions undertaken by the organization to bring risk down to a level that falls within the organizational tolerance. Sharing and transferring risk are choices

---

TIP

The risk assessment methodology prescribed in Special Publication 800-30 is both detailed and robust, and it is intended to be used to assess any or all vulnerabilities, threats, and resulting risk associated with an information system and the organization that owns, operates, or manages the system [23]. It is not practical to try to conduct a formal risk assessment using this methodology for risk from a single weakness or deficiency. Instead, system owners should use the weaknesses and deficiencies included in the security assessment report as a source of vulnerability information to be included in a risk assessment covering the entire information system authorization boundary.

> **NOTE**
>
> The goal of information security is not to mitigate *all* risk, but to bring risk to a level acceptable to the organization. A decision to authorize a system to operate is a decision to accept the residual risk that remains even after all appropriate security controls are implemented [2], and is a tacit acknowledgment that risk cannot be completely eliminated. The identification of a weakness in information security controls is not an obligation to correct the weakness, unless corrective action is found to be warranted based on organizationally determined criteria. System owners should also consider what risk is posed by vulnerabilities or other weaknesses discovered through automated scanning processes, to evaluate whether a viable threat-source exists that could exploit the vulnerability. For example, many Web-based applications are vulnerable to cross-site scripting or other attacks that exploit poor input validation; the technical mitigation for such vulnerabilities is to code or configure them in such as way that all input is properly validated [30]. System owners running a Web-based application accessible only to internal agency users—such as one available on an agency intranet—may not face the same threats as they would if the applications were publicly available over the Internet, so they may be less willing to incur the costs to fix input validation weaknesses. Many organizations impose a substantial burden on system owners to provide detailed justifications in order to accept risk, providing an incentive to avoid risk-accepting decisions based on administrative requirements rather than actual risk factors. It is both reasonable and expected that some weaknesses will not be corrected, and as long as decisions to accept risk are based on sound analysis, system owners should not be reluctant to make those decisions.

that do nothing to change the magnitude, likelihood, or impact of risk, but shift some or all of the liability associated with the risk to another party. NIST distinguishes between risk sharing and risk transference in that sharing shifts only part of the liability, while transference shifts responsibility for the entire liability to another organization [29]. Both acceptance and avoidance mean that no corrective action will be taken to address the risk in question, but these two responses have very different implications for an information system. A decision to accept represents a risk-based determination that the organization is willing to expose whatever vulnerability the weakness or deficiency entails. In contrast, a decision to avoid risk is an acknowledgment by the organization that the risk is too high to be reduced, and that the organization will instead choose not to operate the system (or to operate the system with reduced capabilities that might make the deficient controls irrelevant) rather than exposing itself to risk.

Sources of Weaknesses

The Risk Management Framework focuses almost exclusively on security control assessments—both for newly authorized systems and operational systems under continuous monitoring—as sources of weaknesses or deficiencies that result in POA&M items [6]. Specifically, information system owners address security assessment report findings of other-than-satisfied control assessment objectives in their plans of action and milestones. System owners and common control providers should also be aware of many other potential sources used to identify weaknesses, such as those described in Table 12.3, and include corrective actions taken in response to those weaknesses on the POA&M as well.

Table 12.3 Additional Sources of System Security Weakness and Deficiency Information

Source of Weaknesses	Explanation
Vulnerability and configuration scanning	Many organizations perform routine automated or manual vulnerability scans against operational systems, and many vulnerabilities found in such scans can be associated back to specific system security controls. Federal agencies also conduct scans to validate that minimum security configuration settings are in place for desktop computers and servers
Penetration testing	Penetration testing attempts to overcome or evade existing security safeguards, and often goes well beyond the scope of testing methods used in security control assessments. Penetration tests resulting in successful simulated attacks provide important information about individual or collective weaknesses in security controls [31]
Security monitoring and incident response	Behavior may be observed in security monitoring or events identified by the computer security incident response team that suggest the presence of system vulnerabilities. Information captured about one system may also be useful in evaluating the safeguards of other systems running in the same environment
Internal audits	Information systems are subject to a variety of security audits to check conformance to or compliance with many different regulatory and policy requirements. Also, inspectors general are expected to receive and review remediation of weaknesses included in POA&Ms, and to assess agency performance in continuous monitoring and several other security program areas [12]
External audits	Systems and the agencies that operate them are often audited by the Government Accountability Office or, in cases where agencies are subject to particular regulatory requirements, by outside auditors checking conformance. Independent assessments may also be considered external audits, to the extent that outside contractors or other third parties perform the assessments
Product vulnerability announcements	Product-specific vulnerability information is frequently released by product vendors and by security researchers or others working to identify flaws that must be corrected. Announcements affecting widely-used software products (e.g. Microsoft Internet Explorer) should be evaluated by each system owner for applicability and potential impact
Vulnerability and threat alerts	Several government and private sector sources (e.g. US-CERT, CERT/CC, National Vulnerability Database, Common Vulnerabilities and Exposures) offer alert notifications and other information related to security threats and vulnerabilities. This information can be used by system owners to help understand the severity and criticality of weaknesses
Government directives	Agencies including GAO, NIST, and OMB often produce security-related guidance, instructions, or requirements for action. These directives may identify weaknesses believed to be pervasive, or use the example of a weakness seen in one or a few agencies to make recommendations for security control modification in all agencies

PRODUCING THE PLAN OF ACTION AND MILESTONES

In the system authorization context, the plan of action and milestones is produced as a document provided to authorizing officials or other reviewers along with other authorization package artifacts. For operational systems, the POA&M generally takes the form of a report that includes status information, progress towards achievement of milestones, and other relevant details about system weaknesses and corrective actions. Authorizing officials use the POA&M, along with the security assessment report and system security plan, to evaluate the overall risk associated with an information system, so it is important that the documentation included in the authorization package provides a complete description of the system's security posture. Just as the security assessment report should include details on all security controls implemented for the system, the plan of action and milestones should describe all corrective actions planned to remediate the weaknesses identified [6]. System owners need to ensure that all weaknesses and deficiencies identified in the security assessment report have been addressed, either with the creation of POA&Ms detailing corrective actions to be taken or with the documentation of decisions to accept the risk associated with weaknesses for which no corrective actions are deemed necessary [6]. This means that system owners need to have completed any risk assessment activities for identified weaknesses and have reached appropriate risk response decisions before the POA&M can be finalized.

Timing and Frequency

Development of the plan of action and milestones for a new system seeking authorization to operate takes place during step 5 of the Risk Management Framework process, and is the last of the major authorization package documents to be produced [6]. Once the initial POA&M has been finalized and the system receives authorization to operate, updates to the POA&M are expected to be produced as needed based on the results of continuous monitoring processes, and as remediation actions are completed [32,33]. There is no set schedule for performing these updates, but the expectation for continuous monitoring activities, in accordance with FISMA requirements [34], is that at least a subset of system security controls will be reassessed on an annual basis [35]. As revised security assessment reports are produced reflecting control reassessments, plans of action and milestones should also be updated to address the current set of weaknesses and deficiencies identified for the system.

To satisfy FISMA reporting requirements, summary information on weaknesses and corrective actions contained in POA&Ms must be provided as part of agencies' annual FISMA reports, and is also included in quarterly updates of agency information [5]. Based on guidance from OMB to agencies for annual FISMA reporting, weaknesses and corrective actions are not items that will be included in the monthly data feeds agencies were required to begin submitting in January 2011 [36]. POA&M updates for internal agency purposes may be required or expected at more frequent

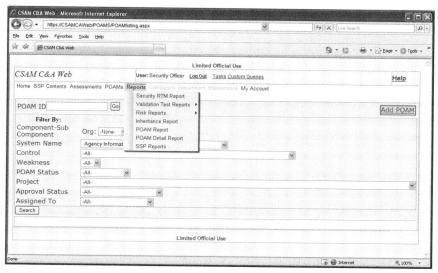

FIGURE 12.6 Agencies Using Automated Systems such to Capture and Manage POA&M Information can Generate POA&M Reports from the System as Needed [19]

intervals, to align with continuous monitoring review cycles or other security management processes. Changes to individual POA&M items occur may occur frequently as milestones are achieved, corrective actions are completed, and POA&Ms are closed. Similarly, new weaknesses may arise at any time, so new POA&M items may be created outside of scheduled updates. Use of an automated tracking system can facilitate the production of POA&Ms as needed, including on-demand, as long as system owners and personnel responsible for completing POA&M actions keep the information in the system up to date. Such tools make it a simple process to create POA&M reports for individual systems, groups of systems under the same authorization authority, or the entire organization. As an example, Figure 12.6 illustrates the option to generate a POA&M report as a standard menu choice in the Cyber Security Assessment and Management (CSAM) tool.

MAINTAINING AND MONITORING THE PLAN OF ACTION AND MILESTONES

The plan of action and milestones has an important operational security role, as it is used by system owners, authorizing officials, and information security program personnel to monitor progress in correcting weaknesses and deficiencies in system security controls. Once the POA&M is approved it becomes a management tool, providing visibility into resource allocations, timelines, and other details associated with addressing weaknesses and remediating risk. Key information in POA&Ms should be updated as milestones are achieved or other progress is made, and when actual progress deviates from expectations set in the plan. Developing, reporting, and maintaining POA&Ms using standard formats and procedures helps authorizing officials monitor corrective actions across multiple systems operating under their authority. Regular monitoring of activities and milestone dates in the POA&M not only helps keep ongoing remediation efforts on track, but also provides indications to authorizing officials or others with risk management responsibility if a system's corrective actions are not implemented according to plan.

Resolving POA&M Items

A POA&M represents a commitment to take explicit action to resolve weaknesses or deficiencies, and to do so within a specified timeframe. System owners and others with responsibility for performing corrective actions are expected to reach the milestones provided in the POA&M, and to complete corrective actions and close out POA&M items. Aside from actually performing the corrective actions specified, resolving POA&M items generally requires documenting the activities that were completed and providing evidence to substantiate completion of the POA&M. Information systems owners also need to re-assess controls once corrective actions have been taken [37]. The level of documentation required and amount or specific type of evidence produced through remediation actions may vary based on the nature and extent of the weakness or deficiency, but in any case should be sufficient to provide security control assessors the justification they need to conduct control reassessments and satisfy assessment objectives. For example, if the remediation of an identified weakness entails a change in system configuration, the assessor may want to see evidence showing that the change occurred, such as change request logs and notification or documentation that requested changes were successfully implemented. If a deficiency exists such as a missing artifact, the likely corrective action is the creation of that artifact, and the assessor will need to see the artifact in order to conclude that the deficiency has been resolved.

RELEVANT SOURCE MATERIAL

Several NIST Special Publications provide guidance, recommendations, and instructions relevant to the preparation and management of plans of action and milestones. OMB also provides guidance for the preparation and submission of agency-level POA&Ms in instructions to agencies on FISMA reporting. The most applicable sources of information include:

- Special Publication 800-37 Revision 1, *Guide for Applying the Risk Management Framework to Federal Information Systems* [37].

- Special Publication 800-53A Revision 1, *Guide for Assessing the Security Controls in Federal Information Systems and Organizations* [38].
- Special Publication 800-30 Revision 1, *Guide for Conducting Risk Assessments* [23].
- Special Publication 800-39, *Managing Information Security Risk: Organization, Mission, and Information System View* [39].
- Special Publication 800-100, *Information Security Handbook: A Guide for Managers* [40].
- OMB Memorandum M-02-01, *Guidance for Preparing and Submitting Security Plans of Action and Milestones* [1].
- OMB Memorandum M-04-25, *FY 2004 Reporting Instructions for the Federal Information Security Management Act* [4].
- OMB Memorandum M-10-15, *FY 2010 Reporting Instructions for the Federal Information Security Management Act and Agency Privacy Management* [5].

NIST Special Publications are available from the NIST Computer Security Division Website, at http://csrc.nist.gov/publications/PubsSPs.html. OMB Memoranda are available from the OMB Website at http://www.whitehouse.gov/omb/memoranda_default.

SUMMARY

The plan of action and milestones specifies the steps to be taken to correct weaknesses or deficiencies in information system security, including weaknesses identified through the security control assessment process, continuous monitoring, vulnerability scanning, or other activities and sources. System owners and common control providers first assess the risk associated with weaknesses and deficiencies, and then select (and document in the POA&M) the appropriate corrective actions to remediate risk to a level acceptable to the organization. POA&Ms are developed and managed both at the system level and at the organization level, so the use of standard procedures, minimum data requirements, and consistent levels of detail for system-level POA&Ms can facilitate the aggregation of POA&M information into organization-level reports. The POA&M provides information that is essential to the system authorization process, as it allows authorizing officials to accept risk on a temporary, conditional basis, and to monitor the completion of corrective actions. Creating POA&M items is also a key aspect of continuous monitoring activities, to describe and track responses to risk associated with weaknesses and deficiencies discovered in operational systems. This chapter described the preparation and delivery of POA&Ms to both internal and external audiences, and summarized the minimum information needed to satisfy FISMA reporting requirements. It also described the use of the POA&M as a management tool that allows authorizing officials and security program managers to monitor the timely completion of corrective actions.

REFERENCES

[1] Daniels ME. Guidance for preparing and submitting security plans of action and milestones. Washington, DC: Office of Management and Budget; October 17, 2001. Memorandum M-02-01.

[2] Guide for applying the risk management framework to federal information systems. Gaithersburg, MD: National Institute of Standards and Technology, Computer Security Division; February 2010. Special Publication 800-37 revision 1. p. 36.

[3] Guide for applying the risk management framework to federal information systems. Gaithersburg, MD: National Institute of Standards and Technology, Computer Security Division; February 2010. Special Publication 800-37 revision 1.

[4] Bolten JB. FY 2004 reporting instructions for the Federal Information Security Management Act. Washington, DC: Office of Management and Budget; August 23, 2004.. Memorandum M-04-25.

[5] Zients J, Kundra V, Schmidt HA. FY 2010 reporting instructions for the Federal Information Security Management Act and agency privacy management. Washington, DC: Office of Management and Budget; April 21, 2010. Memorandum M-10-15.

[6] Guide for applying the risk management framework to federal information systems. Gaithersburg, MD: National Institute of Standards and Technology, Computer Security Division; February 2010. Special Publication 800-37 revision 1. p. 34.

[7] Guide for assessing the security controls in federal information systems and organizations. Gaithersburg, MD: National Institute of Standards and Technology, Computer Security Division; June 2010. Special Publication 800-53A revision 1. See for example control assessment objectives for AC-1 (Access Control Policy and Procedures), MA-1 (System Maintenance Policy and Procedures), CP-2 (Contingency Plan), and IR-8 (Incident Response Plan).

[8] Federal Information Security Management Act of 2002, Pub. L. No. 107-347, 116 Stat. 2952. §301, codified at §3544(c)(3).

[9] Government Information Security Reform Act of 2000, Pub. L. No. 106-398, 114 Stat. 1654A-270. §1061, codified at §3534(c)(2).

[10] Daniels ME. Guidance on implementing the Government Information Security Reform Act. Washington, DC: Office of Management and Budget; January 16, 2001. Memorandum M-01-08.

[11] Lew JJ. Reporting instructions for the Government Information Security Reform Act. Washington, DC: Office of Management and Budget; June 22, 2001. Memorandum M-01-24.

[12] Zients J, Kundra V, Schmidt HA. FY 2010 reporting instructions for the Federal Information Security Management Act and agency privacy management. Washington, DC: Office of Management and Budget; April 21, 2010. Memorandum M-10-15. p. 13.

[13] Bolten JB. FY 2004 reporting instructions for the Federal Information Security Management Act. Washington, DC: Office of Management and Budget; August 23, 2004.. Memorandum M-04-25. p. 14.

[14] Bolten JB. FY 2004 reporting instructions for the Federal Information Security Management Act. Washington, DC: Office of Management and Budget; August 23, 2004. Memorandum M-04-25. p. 19.

[15] Bolten JB. FY 2004 reporting instructions for the Federal Information Security Management Act. Washington, DC: Office of Management and Budget; August 23, 2004.. Memorandum M-04-25. p. 22.

[16] Zients J, Kundra V, Schmidt HA. FY 2010 reporting instructions for the Federal Information Security Management Act and agency privacy management. Washington, DC: Office of Management and Budget; April 21, 2010. Memorandum M-10-15. p. 2.

[17] Preparation, submission, and execution of the budget. Washington, DC: Office of Management and Budget; August 2011. Circular No. A-11, Revised (Transmittal Memorandum No. 85). See section 53.

[18] Preparation, submission, and execution of the budget. Washington (DC): Office of Management and Budget; August 2011. Circular No. A-11, Revised (Transmittal Memorandum No. 85). See sections 53 and 300.

[19] Cyber Security Assessment & Management (CSAM) [computer program]. Version 2.1.5.2. Washington, DC: Department of Justice; 2010.

[20] Johnson C. Protection of sensitive agency information. Washington, DC: Office of Management and Budget; June 23, 2006. Memorandum M-06-16.

[21] Information security handbook: a guide for managers. Gaithersburg, MD: National Institute of Standards and Technology, Computer Security Division; October 2006. Special Publication 800-100. p. 92.

[22] Guide for applying the risk management framework to federal information systems. Gaithersburg, MD: National Institute of Standards and Technology, Computer Security Division; February 2010. Special Publication 800-37 revision 1. p. 35.

[23] Guide for conducting risk assessments. Gaithersburg, MD: National Institute of Standards and Technology, Computer Security Division; September 2011. Special Publication 800-30 revision 1. Initial Public Draft.

[24] Adapted from Information security handbook: a guide for managers. Gaithersburg, MD: National Institute of Standards and Technology, Computer Security Division; October 2006. Special Publication 800-100; Managing information security risk: organization, mission, and information system view. Gaithersburg, MD: National Institute of Standards and Technology, Computer Security Division; March 2011. Special Publication 800-39.

[25] Guide for assessing the security controls in federal information systems and organizations. Gaithersburg, MD: National Institute of Standards and Technology, Computer Security Division; June 2010. Special Publication 800-53A revision 1. p. 23.

[26] Standards for security categorization of federal information and information systems. Gaithersburg, MD: National Institute of Standards and Technology, Computer Security Division; December 2003. Federal Information Processing Standards Publication 199.

[27] Guide for assessing the security controls in federal information systems and organizations. Gaithersburg, MD: National Institute of Standards and Technology, Computer Security Division; June 2010. Special Publication 800-53A revision 1. p. 24.

[28] Managing information security risk: organization, mission, and information system view. Gaithersburg, MD: National Institute of Standards and Technology, Computer Security Division; March 2011. Special Publication 800-39. p. 26.

[29] Managing information security risk: organization, mission, and information system view. Gaithersburg, MD: National Institute of Standards and Technology, Computer Security Division; March 2011. Special Publication 800-39. p. H-2.

[30] Cross-Site Scripting (XSS) [Internet]. Columbia, MD: Open Web Application Security Project [created April 20, 2010; updated October 18, 2010; cited January 30, 2011]. <http://www.owasp.org/index.php/Top_10_2010-A2-Cross-Site_Scripting_(XSS)>.

[31] Guide for assessing the security controls in federal information systems and organizations. Gaithersburg, MD: National Institute of Standards and Technology, Computer Security Division; June 2010. Special Publication 800-53A revision 1. p. E-1.

[32] Guide for applying the risk management framework to federal information systems. Gaithersburg, MD: National Institute of Standards and Technology, Computer Security Division; February 2010. Special Publication 800-37 revision 1. p. 39.

[33] Dempsey K, Chawla N, Johnson A, Johnson R, Jones A, Orebaugh A, et al. Information security continuous monitoring for federal information systems and organizations. Gaithersburg, MD: National Institute of Standards and Technology, Computer Security Division; September 2011.. Special Publication 800-137. p. 34.

[34] Federal Information Security Management Act of 2002, Pub. L. No. 107-347, 116 Stat. 2946. §301, codified at §3544 (b)(5).

[35] Guide for applying the risk management framework to federal information systems. Gaithersburg, MD: National Institute of Standards and Technology, Computer Security Division; February 2010. Special Publication 800-37 revision 1. p. 38.

[36] Zients J, Kundra V, Schmidt HA. FY 2010 reporting instructions for the Federal Information Security Management Act and agency privacy management. Washington, DC: Office of Management and Budget; April 21, 2010.. Memorandum M-10-15. p. 2.

[37] Guide for applying the risk management framework to federal information systems. Gaithersburg, MD: National Institute of Standards and Technology, Computer Security Division; February 2010. Special Publication 800-37 revision 1. p. 33.

[38] Guide for assessing the security controls in federal information systems and organizations. Gaithersburg, MD: National Institute of Standards and Technology, Computer Security Division; June 2010. Special Publication 800-53A revision 1.

[39] Managing information security risk: organization, mission, and information system view. Gaithersburg, MD: National Institute of Standards and Technology, Computer Security Division; March 2011. Special Publication 800-39.

[40] Information security handbook: a guide for managers. Gaithersburg, MD: National Institute of Standards and Technology, Computer Security Division; October 2006. Special Publication 800-100.

Risk Management

INFORMATION IN THIS CHAPTER:

- Fundamentals of Risk Management
- Enterprise Risk Management and the Risk Management Framework
- Risk Management as an Input to Decision Making
- Managing Risk Associated with Information and Information Systems
- Performing Risk Assessments on Information Systems

RISK MANAGEMENT

The Federal Information Security Management Act defines *information security* as "the protection of information and information systems from unauthorized access, use, disclosure, disruption, modification, or destruction" in order to safeguard their confidentiality, integrity, and availability [1]. No organization can provide perfect information security that fully assures the protection of information and information systems, so there is always some chance of loss or harm due to the occurrence of adverse events. This chance is risk, typically characterized as a function of the severity or extent of the impact to an organization due to an adverse event and the likelihood of that event occurring [2]. Organizations identify, assess, and respond to risk using the discipline of risk management. Information security represents one way to reduce risk, and in the broader context of risk management, information security management is concerned with reducing information system-related risk to a level acceptable to the organization. Legislation addressing federal information resources management consistently directs government agencies to follow risk-based decision-making practices when investing in, operating, and securing their information systems, obligating agencies to establish risk management as part of their IT governance [3]. Effective information resources management requires understanding and awareness of types of risk from a variety of sources. Although initial NIST guidance on risk management published prior to FISMA's enactment emphasized addressing risk at the individual information system level [4], the NIST Risk Management Framework and guidance on managing risk in Special Publication 800-39 now position information security risk as an integral component of enterprise risk management practiced at organization, mission and business, and information system tiers, as illustrated in Figure 13.1.

Despite the acknowledged importance of enterprise risk management, NIST explicitly limits the intended use of Special Publication 800-39 to "the management of information security-related risk derived from or associated with the operation and use of information systems or the environments in which those systems operate" [5]. System owners and agency risk managers should not use this narrow scope to treat information security risk in isolation from other types of risk. Depending on the circumstances faced by an organization, the sources of information security risk may impact other enterprise risk areas, potentially including mission, financial, performance, legal, political, and reputation forms of risk. For instance, a government agency victimized by a cyber attack may suffer monetary losses from allocating resources necessary to respond to the incident and may also experience reduced mission delivery capability that results in a loss of public confidence. Enterprise risk management practices need to incorporate information security risk to develop a complete picture of the risk environment for the organization. Similarly, organizational perspectives on enterprise risk—particularly including determinations of risk tolerance—may drive or constrain system-specific decisions about functionality, security control implementation, continuous monitoring, and initial and ongoing system authorization.

Information security risk management may look somewhat different from organization to organization, even among organizations like federal government agencies that often follow the same risk management guidance. The historical pattern of inconsistent

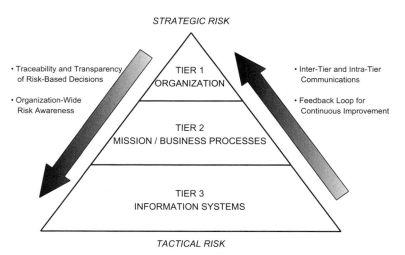

FIGURE 13.1 Information Security Risk Management Must Occur At and Between All Levels of the Organization to Enable Pervasive Risk Awareness and to Help Ensure Consistent Risk-Based Decision Making Throughout the Organization [6]

risk management practices among and even within agencies led NIST to reframe much of its information security management guidance in the context of risk management as defined in Special Publication 800-39, a new document published in 2011 that offers an organizational perspective on managing risk associated with the operation and use of information systems [7]. Special Publication 800-39 defines and describes at a high level an overarching four-phase process for information security risk management, depicted in Figure 13.2, and directs those implementing the process to additional publications for more detailed guidance on risk assessment [8] and risk monitoring [9]. In its guidance, NIST reiterates the essential role of information technology to enable the successful achievement of mission outcomes and ascribes similar importance to recognizing and managing information security risk as a prerequisite to attaining organizational goals and objectives. NIST envisions agency risk management programs characterized by [10]:

- Senior leaders that recognize the importance of managing information security risk and establish appropriate governance structures for managing such risk.
- Effective execution of risk management processes across organization, mission and business, and information systems tiers.

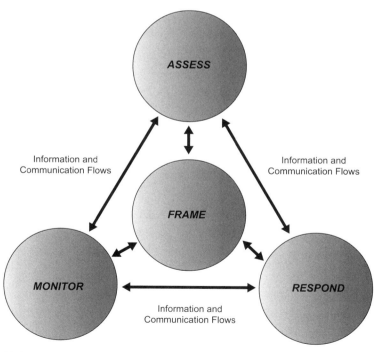

FIGURE 13.2 NIST Defines an Integrated, Iterative Four-Step Risk Management Process That Establishes Organizational, Mission and Business, and Information System-Level Roles and Responsibilities, Activities, and Communication Flows [11]

- An organizational climate where information security risk is considered within the context of mission and business process design, enterprise architecture definition, and system development life cycle processes.
- Better understanding among individuals with responsibilities for information system implementation or operation of how information security risk associated with their systems translates into organization-wide risk that may ultimately affect mission success.

Managing information security risk at an organizational level represents a potential change in governance practices for federal agencies and demands an executive-level commitment both to assign risk management responsibilities to senior leaders and to hold those leaders accountable for their risk management decisions and for implementing organizational risk management programs. The organizational perspective also requires sufficient understanding on the part of senior management to recognize information security risks to the agency, establish organizational risk tolerance levels, and communicate information about risk and risk tolerance throughout the organization for use in decision making at all levels.

Key Risk Management Concepts

Federal risk management guidance relies on a core set of concepts and definitions that all organizational personnel involved in risk management should understand. Risk management is a subjective process, and many of the elements used in risk determination activities are susceptible to different interpretations. NIST provided explicit examples, taxonomies, constructs, and scales in its latest guidance on conducting risk assessments [12] that may encourage more consistent application of core risk management concepts, but ultimately each organization is responsible for establishing and clearly communicating any organization-wide definitions or usage expectations. To the extent that organizational risk managers can standardize and enforce common definitions and risk rating levels, the organization may be able to facilitate the necessary step of prioritizing risk across the organization that stems from multiple sources and systems. NIST guidance adopts definitions of *threat*, *vulnerability*, and *risk* from the Committee on National Security Systems (CNSS) *National Information Assurance Glossary* [13], and uses tailored connotations of the terms *likelihood* and *impact* applied to risk management in general and risk assessment in particular [14].

Threats

A threat is "any circumstance or event with the potential to adversely impact organizational operations (including mission, functions, image, or reputation), organizational assets, individuals, other organizations, or the Nation through an information system via unauthorized access, destruction, disclosure, modification of information, and/or denial of service." NIST guidance distinguishes between threat sources—causal agents with the capability to exploit a vulnerability to cause harm—and threat events: situations or circumstances with adverse impact caused by threat sources [15]. Risk managers need to consider a wide variety of threat sources and potentially relevant threat events, drawing upon organizational knowledge and characteristics of information systems and their operating environments as well as external sources of threat information. In its revised draft of Special Publication 800-30, NIST categorizes threat sources into four primary categories—adversarial, accidental, structural, and environmental—and provides an extensive (though not comprehensive) list of over 70 threat events [16].

Vulnerabilities

A vulnerability is a "weakness in an information system, system security procedures, internal controls, or implementation that could be exploited by a threat source." Information system vulnerabilities often stem from missing or incorrectly configured security controls (as described in detail in Chapters 8 and 11 in the context of the security control assessment process) and also can arise in organizational governance structures, business processes, enterprise architecture, information security architecture, facilities, equipment, system development life cycle processes, supply chain activities, and relationships with external service providers [17]. Identifying, evaluating, and remediating vulnerabilities are core elements of several information security processes supporting risk management, including security control selection, implementation, and assessment as well as continuous monitoring. Vulnerability awareness is important at all levels of the organization, particularly when considering vulnerabilities due to predisposing conditions—such as geographic location—that increase the likelihood or severity of adverse events but cannot easily be addressed at the information system level. Special Publication 800-39 highlights differences in risk management activities related to vulnerabilities at organization, mission and business, and information system levels, summarized in the Three-Tiered Approach section later in this chapter.

Likelihood

Likelihood in a risk management context is an estimate of the chance that an event will occur resulting in an adverse impact to the organization. Quantitative risk analysis sometimes uses formal statistical methods, patterns of historical observations, or predictive models to measure the probability of occurrence for a given event and determine its likelihood. In qualitative or semi-quantitative risk analysis approaches such as the method prescribed in Special Publication 800-30, likelihood determinations focus less on statistical probability and more often reflect relative characterizations of factors such as a threat source's intent and capability and the visibility or attractiveness of the organization as a target [6]. For emergent vulnerabilities, security personnel may consider factors such as the public availability of code, scripts, or other exploit methods or the susceptibility of systems to remote exploit attempts to help determine the range of potential threat agents that might try to capitalize on a vulnerability and to better estimate the likelihood that such attempts could occur. Risk assessors use these factors, in combination with past experience, anecdotal evidence, and expert judgment when available, to assign likelihood scores that allow comparison among multiple threats and adverse impacts and—if organizations implement consistent scoring methods—support meaningful comparisons across different information systems, business processes, and mission functions.

Impact

Impact is a measure of the magnitude of harm that could result from the occurrence of an adverse event. While positive or negative impacts are theoretically possible, even from a single event, risk management tends to focus only on adverse impacts, driven in part by federal standards on categorizing information systems according to risk levels defined in terms of adverse impact. FIPS 199 distinguishes among low, moderate, and high potential impacts corresponding to "limited," "serious," and "severe or catastrophic" adverse effects, respectively [18]. Current NIST guidance on risk assessments expands the qualitative impact levels to five from three, adding very low for "negligible" adverse effects and very high for "multiple severe or catastrophic" adverse effects. This guidance also proposes a similar five-level rating scale for the range or scope of adverse effects due to threat events, and provides examples of adverse impacts in five categories based on the subject harmed: operations, assets, individuals, other organizations, and the nation [19]. Impact ratings significantly influence overall risk level determinations and can—depending on internal and external policies, regulatory mandates, and other drivers—produce specific security requirements that agencies and system owners must satisfy through the effective implementation of security controls.

Risk

Risk is "a measure of the extent to which an entity is threatened by a potential circumstance or event" typically represented as a function of adverse impact due to an event and the likelihood of the event occurring. Risk in a general sense comprises many different sources and types that organizations address through enterprise risk management [20]. FISMA and associated NIST guidance focus on information security risk, with particular emphasis on information system-related risks arising from the

---

WARNING

The use of standardized rating scales for the severity of threats and vulnerabilities, likelihood of occurrence, impact levels, and risk offers enormous value to organizations seeking consistent application of risk management practices, but the subjective nature of the definitions corresponding to numeric rating scores can produce a false sense of consistency. Risk executives operating at the organization tier need to establish clear rating guidelines and organization-specific interpretations of relative terms such as "limited" and "severe" to help ensure that the ratings are applied in the same way across the organization.

loss of confidentiality, integrity, or availability of information or information systems. The range of potential adverse impacts to organizations from information security risk include those affecting operations, organizational assets, individuals, other organizations, and the nation. Organizations express risk in different ways and with different scope depending on which level of the organization is involved—information system owners typically identify and rate risk from multiple threat sources applicable to their systems, while mission and business and organizational characterizations of risk may seek to rank or prioritize different risk ratings across the organization or aggregate multiple risk ratings to provide an enterprise risk perspective. Risk is the primary input to organizational risk management, providing the basic unit of analysis for risk assessment and monitoring and the core information used to determine appropriate risk responses and any needed strategic or tactical adjustments to risk management strategy [21].

THREE-TIERED APPROACH

Effective risk management integrates processes and activities conducted at the organization, mission and business process, and information system levels so that all parts of the organization can access and understand risk information produced at each level. This integrated approach supports organizational objectives such as real-time risk awareness, continuous improvement of management practices, and properly informed risk-based decision making, but depends on the establishment of effective communication channels among all risk management participants. Since the formation of the Joint Task Force Transformation Initiative Interagency Working Group in 2009, NIST guidance issued in support of FISMA provisions reflects a focus on organization-wide information security and risk management that expands the historical emphasis on information system security. The Risk Management Framework defined in Special Publication 800-37 Revision 1 and risk management practices described in Special Publication 800-39 and 800-30 Revision 1 employ a three-tiered approach, illustrated in Figure 13.1, that specifies activities, roles, responsibilities, and areas of emphasis for risk management at organizational, mission and business, and information system levels. Special Publication 800-39 offers a detailed description of risk management from the perspective of each tier in the organization, and highlights aspects of risk management common to all tiers.

Organizational Perspective

In organizations implementing enterprise risk management, the key focus at the organizational level is establishing the governance structure and context for all risk management decisions and activities, significantly including determining the level of risk the organization will tolerate from its information systems. Depending on the organizational governance model, the organizational perspective may set the mission and business priorities that determine investment strategies carried out at lower levels of the organization, including resource allocation for information systems and their protection. To the extent these priorities address primary mission essential functions, the organizational perspective also drives information security contingency planning and continuity of operations planning, described in more detail in Chapter 15.

Governance

Governance in any context identifies the individuals or groups responsible for organizational decision making in pursuit of strategic goals and objectives and the scope of decisions those parties can make. Risk management governance centers on the designated risk executive (whether that role is vested in an individual, a group, or an organizational function) and other senior leaders who determine the types of risk management decisions subject to governance at different tiers and the extent to which risk-based decisions are delegated to mission and business process owners, investment owners, system owners, or other subordinate roles in the organization. Organizational governance should also specify when and how risk management decisions will be communicated within and across the tiers of the organization and ensure that appropriate communication channels are maintained.

Special Publication 800-39 identifies five intended outcomes for organizational risk management [22]:

- Strategic alignment of risk management decisions with mission and business functions consistent with organizational goals and objectives.
- Execution of risk management processes to frame, assess, respond to, and monitor risk.
- Effective and efficient allocation of risk management resources.
- Measurement, monitoring, and reporting of risk management metrics to ensure that organizational goals and objectives are achieved.
- Optimization of risk management investments in support of organizational objectives.

Risk Executive

Because effective enterprise risk management requires the sponsorship of and commitment from the executive leadership in an organization, current federal risk management guidance specifies a risk executive role and associated responsibilities. NIST formalized the risk executive role in 2009 with the release of Special Publication 800-37 Revision 1, and unlike other aspects of its risk management guidance, the functional role envisioned by NIST for the risk executive is not limited to information security risk, but instead provides senior management and oversight of all types of risk faced by the organization [22]. Recent NIST Special Publications incorporate the same risk executive roles and responsibilities [23]:

- Establish risk management roles and responsibilities.
- Develop and implement an organization-wide risk management strategy that guides and informs organizational risk decisions.
- Establish organization-wide forums to consider all types and sources of risk.
- Manage threat and vulnerability information with regard to organizational information systems and the environments in which the systems operate.
- Determine organizational risk based on the aggregated risk from the operation and use of information systems and the respective environments of operation.
- Provide oversight for the risk management activities carried out by the organization to ensure consistent and effective risk-based decisions.
- Develop a greater understanding of risk with regard to the strategic view of the organization and its integrated operations;
- Establish effective vehicles and serve as a focal point for communicating and sharing risk-related information among key internal and external stakeholders.
- Specify the degree of autonomy for subordinate organizations permitted by the parent organization.
- Promote cooperation and collaboration among authorizing officials including security authorization actions requiring shared responsibility.
- Ensure that security authorization decisions consider all factors necessary for mission and business success.
- Ensure shared responsibility for supporting organizational missions and business functions using external providers receives the needed visibility and is elevated to appropriate decision-making authorities.

Risk Management Strategy

The risk management strategy is one of the key outputs of the risk framing component of the NIST risk management process. Typically developed at the organization level, the risk management strategy specifies procedures and methodologies with which mission and business and information system risk managers perform risk assessment, risk response, and risk monitoring activities. As illustrated in

---

NOTE

The establishment of a risk executive function within executive agencies is a NIST recommendation, not a legal or regulatory requirement, and the approach to executive risk management varies widely across agencies. Some organizations maintain enterprise risk management responsibility within the secretary, director, administrator, or other head-of-agency role, while others distribute risk management responsibilities among functional leadership roles, often assigning information security risk management to chief information officers or senior information security officers. Relatively few agencies have designated individual risk executive positions comparable to the chief risk officer often seen in commercial sector organizations, despite repeated recommendations from government oversight and advisory groups [24].

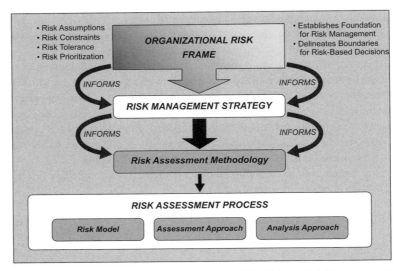

FIGURE 13.3 By Framing Organizational Risk Elements That Inform Risk Management Strategy and Drive Risk Assessment Processes Executed At Mission and Business and Information System Levels, the Organizational Perspective Sets The Context and Establishes the Foundation for All Risk Management Activities [26]

Figure 13.3, the risk management strategy reflects organizational governance decisions in terms of risk assumptions, risk constraints, risk priorities, risk tolerance, and risk acceptance criteria and may—particularly under centralized governance models—also prescribe risk assessment, response, and monitoring practices and methodologies to be used at mission and business and information system tiers. Determining and communicating organizational risk tolerance is one of the most important elements in risk management strategy, as tolerance levels influence all risk management components [25]. Risk tolerance is also a fundamental input to information security management activities conducted throughout the steps in the Risk Management Framework, affecting security control selection, security control assessment, contingency planning, continuous monitoring, and system authorization decisions.

Investment Strategy

Organization-wide risk management also shapes investment strategies, particularly including capital planning and investment control (CPIC) processes and priorities for information technology. Because the organizational perspective reflects the mission and business functions performed across the enterprise and the business and information resource management strategic goals and objectives of the organization, risk management decisions made at the organization tier influence budgetary decisions about developing or acquiring information systems and allocating resources to secure those systems. Federal agencies are required to assess and manage risks associated with their information technology as part of formal CPIC processes, and to measure such risks to enable them to be included as decision criteria in investment strategies [27]. Information technology investment strategies need to balance the organizational needs to support mission execution with the anticipated resources needed to effectively respond to risk. Government agencies face budgetary pressures that constrain IT investment and funding available to implement controls needed to manage risk from information systems to a level acceptable to the organization. Agencies have to prioritize their investments to ensure that limited resources are allocated appropriately. Investment strategies in the context of risk management prioritize strategic and tactical information security investments, and specify possible courses of action to respond to risk in situations where the organization is unable to provide sufficient information security resources to manage risk to acceptable levels [28]. Depending on the risk tolerance of the organization, such responses might include deferring the deployment of information systems until relevant security requirements can be addressed, reducing the functional scope of the system to avoid exposing the organization to risk, or transferring the risk to another organization through insuring against potential losses.

Organizational Culture

Organizational culture pervades all levels of the organization and influences many aspects of risk management. Organizational leaders contribute to the development of organizational culture, but they are not solely responsible for creating, modifying, or responding to cultural factors. Risk management at the organizational level must consider the ways in which organizational culture affects elements of risk framing such as risk tolerance, risk acceptance criteria, and risk management strategy. Senior executives with risk management responsibilities should also be aware of cultural aspects tied to organizational governance models and operating norms, to understand how culture might facilitate or constrain the successful implementation and execution of risk management practices [29]. Cultural awareness at the organizational level can also help to identify and address issues related to cultural differences between organizations, including different bureaus or operating divisions within the same agency. These inter-organizational cultural considerations are increasingly relevant for organizational risk management as agencies seek to expand the use of common controls, shared services, and cross-agency information sharing that require established and authorized interconnection security agreements.

Mission and Business Perspective

Risk management at the mission and business process tier draws on activities performed at both the organization and information system levels to ensure that mission functions executed by the organization incorporate assumptions, constraints, priorities and risk tolerance levels defined in the risk management strategy and accurately reflect information security risk identified at the system level.

The mission and business perspective considers and manages risk in the context of the enterprise architecture and security architecture of the organization, specifying risk-aware business processes that implement mission requirements and effectively support organizational goals and objectives and investment strategies. This perspective also influences risk management at the information system tier by providing common controls, security management oversight, and risk response strategies and by linking organizational policies, procedures, and guidelines for risk assessment and risk monitoring to practices performed for individual information systems.

Mission and Business Processes

Enterprise risk management considers risk associated with all operational aspects of an organization. At the mission and business process level, risk managers evaluate the risk to the organization that could result from implementing business processes; NIST designates processes designed and operated with such risk in mind as "risk-aware." Organizations need to understand business process risk to ensure risk management practices are consistent with organizational risk management strategy and to be able to develop and execute processes sufficiently resilient to perform as intended in the face of potential threats. Risk determination at the information system level may be extended or aggregated to the business process level when processes rely on specific information systems. Federal standards and guidance—including the security categorization approach in FIPS 199—address information and information systems, but not the processes supported by information systems. The specification of risk-aware business processes logically extends the sort of analysis performed for information systems, potentially even leveraging the high-water mark categorization approach used to relate information to information systems. Risk awareness at this level requires senior leadership and business process owners to identify and understand the kinds of threats that can adversely affect their ability to perform mission and business functions, the nature and severity of adverse impacts that could occur due to information security risk, and the expected resilience to such impacts feasible for a given process definition [30]. Risk-aware business processes and resilience requirements also help determine the set of viable risk responses for risk identified at the mission and business tier.

Enterprise Architecture

Enterprise architecture (EA) is an information resources management discipline that links strategic goals, objectives, and performance measures to programs and business processes implemented to realize the organization's strategy and to the information technology and other resources allocated in support of that strategy. Among other provisions, the Clinger-Cohen Act requires federal agencies to develop and maintain an "integrated information technology architecture" [31], a requirement satisfied through the establishment of enterprise architecture programs at virtually all federal agencies. OMB developed a set of reference models, practice guidance, and an enterprise architecture assessment framework under its Federal Enterprise Architecture program. None of these materials devotes much attention to information security management or risk management, although the reference models acknowledge risk management and mitigation as agency management functions [32]. Current NIST guidance emphasizes the importance of integrating security architecture and security management processes and activities prescribed in the Risk Management Framework with enterprise architecture. Enterprise architecture informs risk management by defining mission and business functional segments of the organization and identifying information systems and other resources that support those segments. By thoroughly and accurately documenting its technical environment, an organization can help ensure that it considers all relevant sources of threats and vulnerabilities, reducing the potential risk due to uncertainty about the organization's information resources. Documenting and analyzing technical information at an enterprise-wide level also helps identify areas of redundancy and single points of failure, both of which are relevant inputs to risk management processes [33].

Information Security Architecture

The information security architecture represents the portion of the enterprise architecture that specifically addresses information system resilience and provides architectural information for the implementation of capabilities to meet security requirements. The information security architecture seeks to ensure that information systems and their operating environments consistently and cost-effectively satisfy mission and business process-driven security requirements, consistent with the organizational risk management strategy and sound system and security engineering principles. Agencies can address risk management considerations at the mission and business tier by [34]:

- Developing an information security segment architecture linked to the strategic goals and objectives, well-defined mission and business functions, and associated processes.
- Identifying where effective risk response is a critical element in the success of organizational mission and business functions.
- Defining the appropriate architectural information security requirements based on the organization's risk management strategy.
- Incorporating an information security architecture that implements architectural information security requirements within and across information systems.
- Translating architectural information security requirements into specific security controls for information systems and environments of operation.
- Allocating management, operational, and technical security controls to information systems and environments of operation as defined by the information security architecture.
- Documenting risk management decisions at all levels of the enterprise architecture.

TIP

While almost every federal agency can be expected to have an enterprise architecture—in most cases reflecting a common architecture framework such as the Federal Enterprise Architecture Framework (FEAF) or Department of Defense Architecture Framework (DoDAF)—there is much greater variation among agencies in the existence and structure of formally documented security architectures. NIST considers information security architecture to be an integrated part of enterprise architecture, but conventional security architecture and control frameworks such as ISO 27001, NIST Special Publication 800-53, and the Sherwood Applied Business Security Architecture (SABSA) have structures that do not align directly to the layers typical in enterprise architectures. Where EA frameworks distinguish among separate logical layers such as business, data, application, and technology, security architecture often reflects structural layers such as physical, network, platform, application, and user. In agencies with collaborative working relationships between enterprise architecture and information security programs (both of which commonly reside within the office of the chief information officer), integrating enterprise and security architectures may present little difficulty, but agencies without such close relationships may experience significant challenges harmonizing EA and security architecture perspectives.

Information System Perspective

The primary focus of risk management at the information system tier is executing many of the risk management practices defined at the organizational and mission and business process levels. Particular emphasis centers on implementing the Risk Management Framework and successfully conducting risk assessment, response, and monitoring activities in support of initial and ongoing system authorization requirements, and on integrating risk management into the system development life cycle [35]. Special Publication 800-37 provides detailed guidance and a structured process for applying the RMF to federal information systems, including identifying key risk management activities at each SDLC phase [36]. Special Publication 800-39 also identifies risk-related activities occurring in each SDLC phase, as summarized in Table 13.1.

Table 13.1 Risk Management Activities in the System Development Lifecycle [35]

SDLC Phase	Activity	RMF Step
Initiation	Security requirements definition	Categorize information systems; select security controls
Development/acquisition	Risk assessment	Select security controls; implement security controls
Implementation	Risk assessment Security control assessment	Implement security controls; assess security controls
Operations and Maintenance	Risk monitoring	Monitor security controls
Disposal	Risk assessment	Monitor security controls

The emphasis in NIST guidance on integrating information security requirements and risk management practices early in the system development life cycle targets two separate but related outcomes for organizational risk management. First, early integration of security requirements in the SDLC is an effective way to enforce information system-level implementation of organizational risk management strategy and identify and budget for resources needed to satisfy requirements. Second, linking risk management to other activities conducted as part of the SDLC helps ensure that information system owners do not perform risk management processes in isolation. Achievement of these outcomes also helps to justify system certification and accreditation and related activities in the RMF as processes that enable effective risk management at all levels of the organization [37].

Trust and Trustworthiness

Among the many considerations affecting risk management decisions, NIST places special emphasis on trust and trustworthiness with respect to individuals, organizations, and information systems, and describes several trust models that may apply in different organizations [38]. The relative confidence organizations have that individuals, organizations, or systems will behave as expected influences the risk perceived from those entities, and represents an important input to risk acceptance or other response decisions. NIST guidance acknowledges that trust is subjective, much like risk, but that decisions to rely on trust relationships in internal or inter-organizational contexts can incorporate objective evidence of trustworthiness (or lack thereof) in addition to subjective factors. Decisions to trust are expressions of willingness to take risk—specifically, the risk that the object of trust will behave in a manner contrary to expectations to the detriment of the trusting party [39]. To the extent that security controls can provide assurance that individuals, organizations, or systems will act as expected, information security can reduce risk and facilitate risk management decisions.

> **NOTE**
>
> The references in Special Publication 800-39 to trust and trustworthiness apply these concepts to information systems, in the sense of trusting technology components and assessing the trustworthiness of information systems. Although this usage is common in management literature, most formal definitions of trust and trustworthiness incorporate some assessment of another entity's intent or motivation in addition to expectations of behavior and competence or ability of the entity whose trustworthiness is at issue [40]. Where information systems are concerned, the concept of trust described in Special Publication 800-39 is more accurately labeled "confidence" or "level of assurance," while trustworthiness of information technology can realistically only consider factors such as functional and technical capability, reliability, and consistent performance. These are measurable attributes of trustworthiness subject to formal testing, evaluation, and certification standards such as the Common Criteria for Information Technology Security Evaluation [41]. Comprehensive determinations of an information system's trustworthiness cannot be made without considering how and by whom the system is developed, implemented, operated, and secured.

COMPONENTS OF RISK MANAGEMENT

As shown in Figure 13.2, enterprise risk management comprises four interdependent processes: risk framing, risk assessment, risk response, and risk monitoring. With the exception of risk framing, responsibility for which resides primarily in the organization tier, risk management applies to all levels of the organization and the overall success of the risk management program depends on effective cooperation and information and communication flows across all three tiers. This section describes the activities performed in each part of the risk management process and identifies the key relationships and dependencies among the four components. The information presented here follows the order and structured approach used in Special Publication 800-39, although despite the logical sequence implied, in practice the steps in the risk management process may be executed in different orders depending on the circumstances, organizational risk management governance structure, and level of the organization conducting risk management activities. Table 13.2 provides a summary of the major activities performed in each risk management component and the expected inputs and outputs of those activities.

Frame

Risk framing provides the foundation and establishes the operational parameters for risk management throughout the organization. Risk framing activities define the context for how the organization thinks about risk, including identifying key sources of risk applicable to mission and business processes and information systems. The risk framing step produces the risk management strategy, which documents assumptions, constraints, and priorities; declares organizational risk tolerance levels; and often specifies methods and procedures to be used for risk assessment, response, and monitoring. Risk executives and other senior leaders define the risk frame at the organization tier, and managers at lower levels use the organizational risk frame to guide their own risk management activities. The extent to which organizational strategy dictates risk management across the organization depends in part on the risk governance model, particularly in federal government contexts where multiple bureaus or operating divisions may fall under the supervision of a department or similar top-level organizational structure. The risk framing activities specified in Special Publication 800-39 require careful consideration of internal and external factors that influence the way the organization approaches risk management in general and determine how the organization assesses, monitors, and responds to risk.

Risk Assumptions

To identify assumptions affecting risk management, organizations perform many of the same identification and analysis exercises seen in risk assessment procedures, including identifying and characterizing threat sources, vulnerabilities, impacts, and likelihood determinations and providing representative examples of risk facing the organization [43]. Many mission functions, business processes, and information

Table 13.2 Activities, Inputs, and Outputs in the Risk Management Process [42]

Component	Activities	Inputs	Outputs
Frame	• Risk assumptions • Risk constraints • Risk tolerance • Risk prioritization	• Laws, policies, directives, regulations, contracts, budgets, and governance structures • Feedback from assessment, response, and monitoring activities	• Risk management strategy • Risk management policies, procedures, standards, and guidelines
Assess	• Threat and vulnerability identification • Risk determination	• Risk management strategy • Risk monitoring results • Acceptable assessment methodologies • Assessment expectations and requirements	• Risk assessment report • Risk ratings, priorities, and recommendations
Respond	• Risk response identification • Evaluation of alternatives • Risk response decision • Risk response implementation	• Threats and vulnerabilities from risk assessment or risk monitoring activities • Risk determinations • Risk management strategy	• Implementation of chosen courses of action • Updated plan of action and milestones
Monitor	• Risk monitoring strategy • Risk monitoring	• Risk management strategy • Risk assessment results • Risk remediation strategies	• Risk monitoring information • Changes to information systems and environments

systems face their own specific risks, but identifying and documenting common risk elements applicable to all levels of the organization enables lower-level risk managers to focus their attention on unique or particularly relevant risk factors. Organizations can document broadly applicable risk factors in risk management guidelines and risk assessment templates to help ensure risk management activities use a consistent scope appropriate for each level of the organization. Organizations may also make assumptions about specific risk assessment and risk monitoring methodologies, centrally provisioned tools or services that support risk management processes, and appropriate responses to different types of risk.

Risk Constraints

Because risk managers at all levels of the organization often look to risk management strategy for guidance on performing risk assessment and monitoring, the risk framing process identifies factors that facilitate or constrain risk management and documents those factors in the risk management strategy. Many organizations specify legislative drivers and compliance requirements for risk management activities, but it is also important to identify potential constraints on performing risk assessment, risk response, or risk monitoring, including those that pose challenges to compliance. NIST guidance identifies possible sources of constraints including limits to budgets or available resources; dependencies on legacy information systems; legal, regulatory, or contractual requirements; organizational culture; and governance structures [44]. Risk managers should be aware that the existence of constraints typically does not obviate the need to perform risk management, so constraints often represent additional challenges to be overcome rather than justifications for scaling back risk-related activities.

Risk Tolerance

Every organization has its own mission, strategic goals and objectives, and operating characteristics, and each organization may view risk differently depending on the mission and business functions it performs and the information systems it uses. Organizations facing similar threats and vulnerabilities, similar impacts from adverse events, and similar risk determinations may respond to risk in very different ways. Risk tolerance is the level of risk an organization is willing to accept, from information security-related sources or other types. Risk tolerance varies among organizations and potentially within organizations as well, especially when risk is considered against mission and business objectives or evaluated in specific circumstances. Risk tolerance is one of the most significant factors influencing risk-based decision making, so a clear determination of risk tolerance, effectively communicated throughout the organization, is essential to ensure consistent responses to risk. In organizations with decentralized governance structures, different parts of the organization may have different tolerances for risk that need to be harmonized or adjusted to meet organizational guidelines. Identifying risk tolerance within the risk framing process should also consider what authority, if any, risk managers in different organizational units have to determine—and more importantly, to act on—their own risk tolerance levels.

> **NOTE**
>
> One of the challenges with establishing effective risk-based security management practices across the government is that agency governance is largely decentralized. While the Office of Management and Budget has general responsibility for overseeing and monitoring the implementation of FISMA and other legislative and regulatory requirements, each agency makes its own risk determinations and decides what level of risk it is willing to accept. Agency-level discretion is readily apparent in information system authorization decisions, as federal agencies are self-accrediting and accreditation decisions are rarely subject to outside approval. This characteristic of organizational risk management makes it difficult to develop government-wide risk standards or to apply risk determinations made in one agency to other organizations. Special Publication 800-39 and other sources of risk management guidance specify processes and mechanisms that all agencies should use—such as developing a risk management strategy—and identify types of information that should be addressed, but leaves the implementation details to each agency.

Risk Prioritization

Organizations face many different kinds of risk. Risk exists at different levels of the organization, from different sources, in different timeframes, and with differing levels of severity or magnitude of impact. Given budgetary and other resource constraints, it is rarely feasible to respond fully to all risk at the same time, so organizations need to prioritize their risk management activities. The risk management strategy developed during risk framing should provide guidance on organizational priorities and prioritization criteria used to allocate resources for risk response or other risk management activities. Organizations typically prioritize risk in ways that align with mission priorities and strategic goals and objectives, but the specific factors used in prioritization may vary among organizations according to risk assumptions and constraints, risk tolerance levels, organizational culture, or other factors [45]. Time is an important consideration when making risk management trade-offs, as one approach to risk response (as noted in Chapter 12 on the plan of action and milestones) is to defer immediate corrective action but plan to allocate risk-mitigation resources by some specified point in the future.

Assess

The risk assessment process identifies, characterizes, and estimates risk to the organization. Under FISMA, all executive agencies must perform "periodic assessments of the risk and magnitude of the harm that could result from the unauthorized access, use, disclosure, disruption, modification, or destruction of information and information systems that support the operations and assets of the agency" [46]. To assist agency information security programs in meeting this requirement, NIST provides general guidance on risk assessment in Special Publication 800-39, and offers a detailed methodology for conducting risk assessments in Special Publication 800-30. The original version of Special Publication 800-30 addressed risk assessment of information systems [4]; the revised version expands the scope to include mission and business and organizational risk assessment as well [8]. Performing risk assessments at all levels of the organization supports enterprise risk management by aggregating and prioritizing risk from lower levels, and also facilitates risk assessment within the mission and business and information system tiers by identifying threat sources and vulnerabilities and determining risk sources that affect all parts of the organization.

The risk management strategy produced during risk framing often recommends or specifies risk assessment methodologies that should be used within the organization. Even where no single organizational standard is specified, the assumptions, constraints, priorities, risk tolerance, and governance information in the risk management strategy inform the selection of risk assessment methodologies, as shown in Figure 13.3. Special Publication 800-39 implies but does not mandate the use of the NIST risk assessment methodology in Special Publication 800-30. Many alternative methodologies are available, such as the Software Engineering Institute's OCTAVE method [47] or the risk assessment approach in ISO/IEC 31010 [48]. These methodologies share many common features and prescribed tasks, including identification of the organizational assets subject to risk, threat and vulnerability analysis, and determination of risk [49]. The choice of methodology is often less important in an organization than the consistent use of whatever methodology is preferred—using different methods can frustrate organizational efforts to aggregate or compare risk assessment results, particularly if the methods use different analysis approaches or risk rating scales.

Threat and Vulnerability Identification

Threats and vulnerabilities are the primary sources of risk, and both must be present for material risk to exist. Before assessing risk—to an information system, mission function or business process, or organization—organizations need to identify risk, beginning with the identification of threats facing the organization and the vulnerabilities that those threats could exploit to cause loss or harm. As noted previously in this chapter, NIST guidance distinguishes between threat sources and threat events, separating the entity or actor that might cause harm from the specific types of incidents that might occur. Special Publication 800-30 provides numerous examples of both threat sources and threat events [50]; risk managers should be aware that some threat events can only be caused by certain sources, and that different risk models apply to different types of threat sources. The threat and vulnerability identification activity in risk assessment parallels a similar task in risk framing, where consideration of organization-level threats and vulnerabilities contributes to risk assumptions. In organizations that take the time to document and distribute information about organizational threats and vulnerabilities, risk assessment at the mission and business and information system levels can focus on process-specific or system-specific threats and vulnerabilities and combine information gathered at all levels to support risk determination and response prioritization activities.

Risk Determination

Risk determination assesses threats and vulnerabilities to consider the likelihood that known threat sources will be able to exploit identified vulnerabilities to cause one or more adverse events and the consequences if such events occur. Depending on the type of threat under analysis and the nature of the risk assessment being performed, likelihood and impact may be determined using relative ratings or quantitative estimates. Many factors contribute to likelihood, including some that are difficult to measure accurately, such as ease of exploitation, skill level or sophistication of adversaries, visibility of the organization, and attractiveness of the organization or its assets to attack [51]. Accurate quantitative risk determination requires sufficient historical observations or other evidence to support calculation of probabilities, and also requires impact to be expressed in numeric terms, such as dollar values. Organizations may characterize the nature and severity of adverse impacts according to what aspect of security is impacted, the extent of disruption to operations, the resources lost, or the consequences to mission execution or organizational stakeholders. Whether stated in absolute or relative terms, determinations of risk enable risk managers to compare and prioritize risk—within a specific information system or operational context or across the organization—and represent key inputs to risk response decisions.

Respond

Once the organization determines the nature, significance, and priority of risk, system owners, business owners, and risk mangers consider possible responses to risk and choose the most appropriate course of action. NIST guidance recognizes five primary responses to risk: acceptance, avoidance, mitigation, sharing, or transference [52]. Courses of action for risk response may include more than one type of response, potentially authorized and executed at multiple levels of the organization. While system owners often recommend responses to risk identified at the information system level, analysis of alternative courses of action and selection of risk response consider impacts at all levels of the organization, so typically require decision-making at mission and business or organizational levels. Depending on the governance structure and approach to enterprise risk management used in an organization, the risk management strategy developed during risk framing may include organizational policies or standards regarding risk response alternatives that provide guidance to risk managers on preferred or default courses of action. The appropriate level at which risk response decisions are made also depends in part on the scope of the response measures being considered. Risk-mitigating changes to enterprise infrastructure, operating environments, or common controls affecting the entire organization should be approved at the organizational level. Similarly, decisions to accept risk at lower levels of the organization should be consistent with organizational risk tolerance, so may require review or approval at the organizational level.

Risk Response Identification

For any risk identified and evaluated in the risk management process, risk managers need to consider potential responses to risk, alone or in combination, and identify the possible courses of action. The exact number and variety of alternatives considered for a risk response may be constrained by policies or guidance in the risk management strategy, but candidate responses typically include the following [53]:

- *Acceptance.* When the risk determination falls within the organizational risk tolerance, accepting the risk may be justified. When risk tolerance includes cost-benefit considerations, risk acceptance may also be warranted when the cost of mitigation exceeds the anticipated loss to the organization if the risk is realized.
- *Mitigation.* Risk mitigation includes remedial or corrective action taken to reduce the level of risk to the organization, with the goal of bringing the risk level within organizational risk tolerance so that any residual risk can be accepted. Mitigating actions chosen for a given risk may be implemented at multiple levels of the organization.
- *Sharing.* Risk sharing occurs when responsibility for risk borne by one organization can be shared with another, in a manner that may not reduce the total risk, but reduces the risk faced by each sharing organization to an acceptable level. Organizations with different risk tolerance levels may be able to use risk sharing to align responsibility for different types of risk with commensurate risk tolerance levels, and to assign responsibility for specific types of risk to organizations with the appropriate expertise or resources to address them.
- *Transference.* Organizations unwilling or unable to accept, mitigate, or share risk may choose to transfer the risk by shifting responsibility or liability for the consequences of an adverse event to another organization, such as by purchasing insurance against loss or harm. Risk transference does not reduce the likelihood, harm, or risk associated with an event, but typically compensates the organization for losses.
- *Avoidance.* Risks determined to be unacceptable to the organization and infeasible to mitigate, share, or transfer may warrant changes to information systems or processes implemented by the organization to avoid incurring the risk associated with them. Avoiding information system-level risk often requires reducing the scope or functional capability to reduce the threats or vulnerabilities applicable to systems or business processes. Examples of risk avoidance methods include foregoing system interconnections in favor of manual processes or integration methods, or choosing to limit web-based access methods to intranet or VPN-based connections rather than allowing Internet connections.

Alternative courses of action to respond to risk may involve multiple steps or discrete actions taken at one or more levels of the organization. Risk managers at mission and business or organization tiers may evaluate multiple risk response decisions together to determine appropriate organizational responses, particularly when similar risk is identified in multiple risk assessments.

> **WARNING**
>
> NIST guidance omits an additional response to risk that risk management practitioners may encounter: denial. Risk denial is a refusal to acknowledge a risk produced in an assessment, essentially making an assertion that the risk does not apply to the organization. Risk denial should not occur in organizations with accepted, established risk management procedures, and instances of risk denial often indicate a lack of awareness among risk management decision makers or poor communication between decision makers and business owners or system owners responsible for conducting risk assessments.

Evaluation of Alternatives

In situations where more than one course of action is identified to respond to risk, risk managers must evaluate each alternative to determine the preferred approach. The criteria used in evaluating alternative risk responses may be specified in the risk management strategy or be determined on a case-by-case basis for each risk or type of risk. Typical evaluation factors include costs that will be incurred or other resources that must be allocated to implement each course of action; the feasibility of each response given potential time pressures, necessary technical expertise, or other organizational constraints; and the anticipated effectiveness of each course of action in achieving the desired result. Risk responses in information security contexts usually involve trade-offs between increased assurance levels (and corresponding reductions in risk) and operational capabilities. Risk responses with the potential to reduce operational effectiveness should consider the relative priority of impacted mission functions and business processes, using risk prioritization information contained in the risk management strategy.

Risk Response Decision

The evaluation of risk response alternatives typically results in a recommended course of action. Formal decisions to adopt recommended courses of action often employ many of the same criteria used in the evaluation of alternatives, including the economic impact on the organization and the effect of the risk response on mission and business functions. Organizations face many risks at any point in time, so risk response decisions rely on organizational risk priorities to determine the most appropriate allocation of resources, generally devoting more resources to areas of greater risk, or prioritizing responses with the greatest potential effect in reducing overall risk to the organization. Risk response decisions reflect the organizational goal of consistently managing risk to levels within the organization's risk tolerance. Risk responses do not eliminate risk, but instead reduce or manage risk exposure so that residual risk—risk that remains after responses are implemented—is acceptable to the organization.

Risk Response Implementation

Selected courses of action must be implemented to achieve the results sought from risk response. The time required to fully implement a given course of action varies according to factors such as the complexity of the response, size of the organization, characteristics of its operating environment, and the number of internal or external organizational units that need to be involved. In its risk management strategy, an organization may specify different risk response strategies to guide responses to various types of risk, as well as an overall approach to selecting appropriate responses. NIST provides general guidance on risk response strategies in Special Publication 800-39. Such strategies specify roles within the organization responsible for different risk response types; existing or anticipated dependencies among selected risk response measures or on other factors; implementation timelines for risk responses; procedures and requirements for monitoring risk response effectiveness; triggers invoking risk monitoring or renewed assessment activities; and the availability of any interim risk response measures [54].

Monitor

Organizations are constantly at risk from a variety of sources, and the risk they face changes over time. Risk monitoring helps organizations maintain ongoing risk awareness and provides information about changes to information systems, operating environments, or threats and vulnerabilities relevant to the organization. As defined in current NIST guidance, risk monitoring is a component of continuous monitoring processes and activities that all agencies must implement as part of their security management programs. As described in detail in Chapter 14, continuous monitoring provides organizations with information not only about changes that may alter the risk profile of the organization, but also information used to verify compliance with relevant policies, legislation, regulations, standards, and requirements and to determine the effectiveness of security controls and security management processes. Within the broader context of continuous monitoring, organizations use risk monitoring to measure implemented risk response measures to ensure they achieve their intended effects and to identify events or circumstances posing new or increased information security risk to the organization.

Risk Monitoring Strategy

Organizations develop risk monitoring strategies to establish expectations, policies, and procedures for risk monitoring activities at all levels. Risk monitoring strategies may be developed on their own, specified in the organization risk management strategy, or incorporated in information security continuous monitoring (ISCM) strategy documentation. Like the ISCM strategy described in Chapter 14, the risk monitoring strategy describes the purpose and rationale for monitoring, types of monitoring to be performed, monitoring frequency, security controls or other monitoring targets, and where applicable, the use of automated monitoring tools and techniques. The primary purposes for risk monitoring identified in Special Publication 800-39 include verifying compliance with applicable requirements, measuring the effectiveness of risk response measures and security controls, and identifying changes to information systems and operating environments that may affect the information security risk to the organization.

Risk Monitoring

Risk monitoring activities implement the risk monitoring strategy by gathering information through automated or manual means, alerting or reporting on information relevant to intended purposes for risk monitoring, and providing inputs to ongoing risk assessment and response processes. Depending on risk assumptions, constraints, priorities, and tolerance levels, the set of risk monitoring practices actually implemented at any one time may differ from what is documented in the risk monitoring strategy. NIST guidance recommends that organizations consider risk monitoring from an organizational perspective and coordinate monitoring practices across all three tiers to support the achievement of overall risk management goals and avoid potential duplication of implemented monitoring activities [55].

INFORMATION SYSTEM RISK ASSESSMENTS

Enterprise risk management relies on effective risk assessments. With the number and diversity of threats organizations face, risk managers need to use thorough, consistent methods to evaluate known and emerging threats and vulnerabilities, to consider the impact of changes affecting information systems and their operating environments, and to provide information to guide decisions about appropriate risk responses. Risk assessment is a core function supporting a variety of security management processes, including system certification and accreditation, incident response, contingency planning, and continuous monitoring. In addition to supporting information security management, risk assessments also provide inputs to other information resources management activities such as IT strategic planning, capital planning and investment control, enterprise architecture, program management, and execution of system development life cycle phases. NIST considers risk assessment significant enough to warrant specialized guidance on conducting risk assessments for information systems, mission functions and business processes, and organizations [8]. The expansion in scope for Special Publication 800-30 Revision 1 to apply risk assessment processes to all tiers of the organization reflects a similar shift in focus from information system-specific guidance to enterprise guidance seen in other updated NIST Special Publications [56].

Risk assessment is most often associated with initial system authorization activities or required periodic (usually annual) assessments of operational systems. Organizations can, however, apply the same fundamental risk assessment process at different levels of granularity and with broad or narrow scope. Organizations conduct risk assessments in three primary contexts:

1. Comprehensive assessments performed to implement the Assess step in the risk management process, whether at the information system, mission and business process, or organization level.
2. Focused assessments of specific threats, vulnerabilities, or weaknesses identified during security control assessments or continuous monitoring activities.
3. E-authentication risk assessments required under OMB regulations for information systems providing remote authentication of users.

Organizations need to assess risk on an ongoing basis and whenever new threats or vulnerabilities arise or circumstances change that could impact overall risk levels or otherwise warrant a response. The nature and points of emphasis for information system risk assessments vary depending on which phase in the system development life cycle the system is in and on the types of risk factors that need to be assessed. The results of risk assessments are typically documented in risk assessment reports or incorporated in other security management artifacts such as security assessment reports. As shown in Figure 13.4, risk assessment results provide key information to multiple steps in the Risk Management Framework. Initial risk assessment activities often precede initiation of the RMF and supply key information to system categorization and security control selection. NIST provides guidance to agencies in Special Publication 800-30 Revision 1 applicable to conducting risk assessments of any size or scope. In addition to Special Publication 800-30, primary sources of guidance for conducting e-authentication risk assessments include OMB Memoranda M-04-04 [57] and M-00-10 [58], Special Publication 800-63 [59], and the e-authentication e-RA tool and associated guidance for agencies available from the federal Identity, Credential, and Access Management (ICAM) Subcommittee [60].

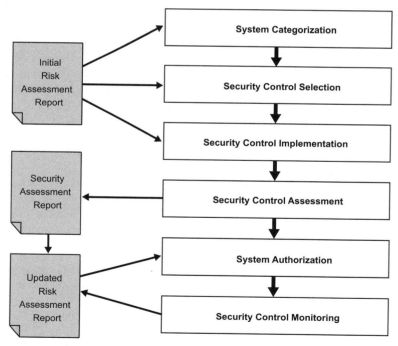

FIGURE 13.4 Information System Risk Assessments Follow an Iterative Development Approach Initiated Before the Beginning of the RMF Process, Informed by Security Control Assessment Results and Other Outputs of RMF Activities, and Updated in Support of Initial and Ongoing System Authorization

Risk Models

There are many risk assessment tools and techniques available for use in analyzing risk components and making risk determinations. Risk modeling is one approach recommended in Special Publication 800-30 to identify all the elements necessary to perform risk analysis for different types of threats. Risk models specify the factors needed to assess risk and the relationship among those factors, producing a sort of template for risk assessors to use in their assessments. By defining required risk elements in a standard way, risk models help ensure that risk assessors consider all relevant factors, encourage consistent assessment procedures for different types of risk, and highlight potential information gaps that may hamper efforts to make accurate risk determinations. Figures 13.5 and 13.6 provide sample risk models for

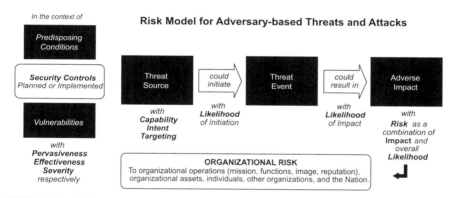

FIGURE 13.5 A Risk Model for Adversarial Threats Includes Related Information About Vulnerabilities, Likelihood, and Impact That Collectively Help Determine the Risk Posed By Each Threat [61]

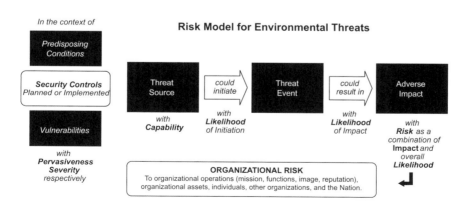

FIGURE 13.6 A Risk Model for Environmental Threats Includes the Same Core Related Factors Such As Vulnerabilities, Likelihood, and Impact, But Omits Factors Related to Threat Source Motivation Or Skills That Would Be Relevant for Adversarial Or Accidental Types of Threats

adversarial and environmental threats, respectively, that identify the set of risk factors that should be included in risk assessments. As these two examples illustrate, different attributes apply to different types of risk—for example, consideration of intent and organizational targeting in the adversary-based model is irrelevant for environmental threats such as natural disasters. When risk assessors can fully populate a risk model for a specific threat with information to address all the factors in the model, the complete model instance provide a risk scenario that can be used to describe in detail the way a threat might materialize and how it would affect the organization.

Assessment Methods

Despite the number and variety of risk assessment methods, approaches to risk assessment typically belong to one of three categories: quantitative, qualitative, or hybrid [62]. Quantitative risk assessment incorporates numeric values produced via direct measurement or observation or obtained through empirical evidence to enable use of mathematical and statistical analysis methods. Quantitative assessments express asset valuation and impact in dollars, time, or other continuous values, and use probability calculations or estimates to determine likelihood. Where objective, accurate measures are available, quantitative risk assessments produce risk determinations easily compared to each other and well suited to cost-benefit analysis. Quantitative assessments facilitate risk ranking and prioritization activities, but their validity depends on the ability of risk assessors to accurately determine values used in risk calculations. The emphasis on numeric scoring can give the impression of clear differences among risk ratings where no significant differences actually exist.

Qualitative assessments measure risk factors using categorical or ordinal ratings, often relying on the knowledge and expertise of risk assessors to correctly apply subjective and relative values. NIST information security standards and guidelines often use qualitative assessment scales, such as the low/moderate/high ratings used in security categorization. Qualitative analysis can be easier to apply than quantitative alternatives, particularly in public sector contexts where operational performance is not often measured in quantitative terms such as revenue or profit. Challenges associated with qualitative assessments include the inherent subjectivity associated with assigning ratings to risk factors and the difficulty in making meaningful differentiations and prioritizing among risk determinations with similar assigned values.

Hybrid assessment methods—often called "semi-quantitative" or "pseudo-quantitative"—add numerical scales to ordinal rating levels to support statistical analysis and facilitate better differentiation among assessed values and risk determinations than in purely qualitative approaches. The guidance on conducting risk assessments in Special Publication 800-30 Revision 1 uses this type of approach, defining five ordinal rating values (very low, low, moderate, high, and very high) for assessing threat sources, vulnerabilities, likelihood, impact, and risk, and assigning numeric rating scales to each value (0–4, 5–20, 21–79, 80–95, and 96–100, respectively) [63].

Analysis Approaches

Regardless of the risk assessment method selected, different organizations may apply different analytical approaches when conducting their assessments. NIST distinguishes approaches by the primary elements on which the analysis focuses, the level of detail and rigor required in the analysis, and the extent to which standard or common risk models are used across the organization to analyze similar threats. The NIST risk assessment process is equally well suited to threat-oriented, vulnerability-oriented, or asset-oriented analysis approaches [64]. Current federal guidance recognizes a variety of possible risk assessment triggers, including new threats or vulnerabilities identified through continuous monitoring, weaknesses identified in security control assessments, and changes to information systems, operating environments, or organizational mission and business priorities. When developing the risk management strategy during risk framing, organizations can identify or recommend specific analytical approaches for use in different risk assessment contexts as well as approved assessment methodologies, striking an appropriate balance between mandated standards that ensure consistency and the flexibility to apply the most effective approaches to different risk assessment needs.

As part of the changes in guidance proposed in Revision 1 to Special Publication 800-30, NIST adopted a structured process defining major assessment steps and tasks performed within each step, mirroring the description of the Risk Management Framework in Special Publication 800-37. Although NIST guidance presumes the use of its risk assessment approach, federal agencies are free to employ other risk assessment methodologies if they wish, and many alternatives to Special Publication 800-30 are available [65]. For consistency with the material presented throughout this book, this chapter describes the NIST process, illustrated in Figure 13.7, which includes preparation and maintenance activities, but emphasizes a sequenced set of tasks for consistently conducting risk assessments.

Prepare

The preparation step establishes the scope and parameters of the risk assessment to be performed. Given the potential volume of information required, resources involved,

---

WARNING

The use of numeric rating scales with qualitative assessment values does not change the subjectivity inherent in the rating process. Organizations hoping to improve their ability to compare and rank risk using semi-qualitative ratings must provide clear guidance and rating criteria to risk assessors to ensure that assessment ratings are used consistently.

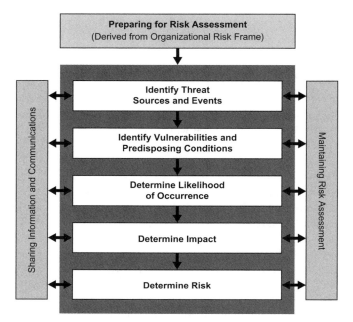

FIGURE 13.7 NIST Guidance for Conducting Risk Assessments Prescribes a Structured Sequence of Tasks That Helps Risk Managers Identify and Evaluate Sources of Risk and Make Consistent Determinations of Risk to Information Systems, Mission Functions and Business Processes, and Organizations [66]

and methods that may be applied, successful completion of the assessment may depend on effective preparation. Risk assessment context may be derived from organizational risk management strategy, with assessment-specific tailoring as needed depending on the level at which the assessment will be conducted and the objectives it is intended to achieve. Risk assessment preparation includes identifying the purpose and scope of the assessment; identifying assumptions and constraints; identifying information requirements and sources; and developing, selecting, or refining the risk model [67]. The risk management strategy may be instrumental in facilitating the completion of these tasks, complemented by information in continuous monitoring strategies, system security plans, and risk assessment policies, procedures, guidelines, and templates.

Risk assessment preparation also includes determining the level of the organization at which risk assessments should be conducted, often depending on the nature and scope of the threat or vulnerability that serves as the catalyst for the assessment. In cases where a threat or vulnerability is identified for a particular information system, organizations should consider whether the risk factor's applicability is limited to that system or applies more broadly to other systems or business processes, or organization-wide. For example, a web application vulnerability found in one information system might also be present in others, and a threat event such as a denial of service attack is likely to threaten any systems sharing the same operating environment or network infrastructure. Some threats are by nature applicable to entire organizations—such as the sort of sophisticated, organized, and ongoing attacks that characterize the advanced persistent threat—and corresponding risk from these threats should be assessed at the organizational level.

Conduct

As explained previously in the description of the Assess component in the risk management process, conducting a risk assessment involves identifying and characterizing the threats and vulnerabilities relevant to the subject of the assessment (such as an information system, business process, or entire organization), estimating the likelihood that threat events will occur and the resulting adverse impact to the organization, and making a risk determination as a function of likelihood and expected impact. NIST guidance organizes its risk assessment tasks in an ordered sequence, as seen in the center of Figure 13.7, but acknowledges that completing the tasks in a different order or choosing to iterate some tasks multiple times before moving to subsequent tasks may be necessary and appropriate [68]. Special Publication 800-30 offers risk assessors extensive supplemental information on threat sources, threat events, vulnerabilities and predisposing conditions that may be relevant to government agencies. The risk factors NIST presents are not intended to be exhaustive or prescriptive, but can provide a foundation for considering and categorizing different types of risk in different organizations and help risk assessors avoid examining too narrow a set of risk inputs. Special Publication 800-30 also provides five-level rating scales and rating level descriptions for likelihood, impact, and risk determinations, which organizations can adapt to their own risk management strategies.

Maintain

Comprehensive risk assessments, like security control assessments, are relatively large-scale efforts requiring significant time and resources to complete. Many organizations conduct risk assessments on an annual basis or at other infrequent intervals, although the current government emphasis on continuous monitoring (including risk monitoring) may encourage a shift to more frequent, smaller-scale assessments. Regardless of scope, risk assessments should reflect current risk to the organization, and therefore need to be maintained and updated to ensure the information produced from risk assessments is relevant, accurate, and up to date. Maintaining a risk assessment requires risk monitoring to identify changes in risk factors or overall risk addressed in the assessment, and revising and updating assessment information, including reassessment of risk elements where necessary.

This aspect of the risk assessment process leverages the risk monitoring strategy and capabilities implemented at organizational, mission and business process, and information system levels. Key risk assessment maintenance activities include documenting the risk factors to be monitored and the monitoring frequency; validating the contextual details of the assessment such as purpose, scope, assumptions, and constraints; performing appropriate risk assessment tasks; and updating risk assessment results and communicating those results to risk managers or other stakeholders [69].

RELEVANT SOURCE MATERIAL

Several NIST Special Publications and Federal Information Processing Standards provide guidance, recommendations, and instructions relevant to the performing risk management processes and activities and the role of risk management in organizational decision making. The most applicable sources of information include:

- Special Publication 800-39, *Managing Information Security Risk: Organization, Mission, and Information System View* [70].
- Special Publication 800-37 Revision 1, *Guide for Applying the Risk Management Framework to Federal Information Systems* [36].
- Special Publication 800-30 Revision 1, *Guide for Conducting Risk Assessments* (Initial public draft) [8].

These and other NIST Special Publications are available from the NIST Computer Security Division website, at http://csrc.nist.gov/publications/PubsSPs.html.

SUMMARY

Effective risk management is the primary goal of information security, which by safeguarding the confidentiality, integrity, and availability of information and information systems reduces the risk associated with operating information systems to a level acceptable to the organization. This chapter described the core concepts of enterprise risk management including implementing and adopting the principles and processes in NIST guidance on managing information security risk, the Risk Management Framework, and related documentation. This chapter also explained the processes for framing risk, conducting risk assessments, responding to risk, and monitoring risk from information systems, and highlighted points of integration with other key information security management processes including system authorization, security control assessment, and continuous monitoring.

REFERENCES

[1] Federal Information Security Management Act of 2002, Pub. L. No. 107-347, 116 Stat. 2946. §301, codified at §3542(b)(1).

[2] NIST adopts the definition of risk in CNSS Instruction No. 4009: national information assurance glossary. Fort Meade, MD: Committee on National Security Systems; April 2009.

[3] In addition to FISMA, see for example the Paperwork Reduction Act of 1995, Pub. L. No. 104-13, 109 Stat. 1643; Information Technology Management Reform Act of 1996, Pub. L. No. 104-106, 110 Stat. 679; and Computer Security Act of 1987, Pub. L. No 100-235, 101 Stat. 1724.

[4] Stoneburner S, Goguen A, Feringa A. Risk management guide for information technology systems. Gaithersburg, MD: National Institute of Standards and Technology, Computer Security Division; July 2002. Special Publication 800-30.

[5] Managing information security risk: organization, mission, and information system view. Gaithersburg, MD: National Institute of Standards and Technology, Computer Security Division; March 2011. Special Publication 800-39. p. vii.

[6] Managing information security risk: organization, mission, and information system view. Gaithersburg, MD: National Institute of Standards and Technology, Computer Security Division; March 2011. Special Publication 800-39. p. 9.

[7] Managing information security risk: organization, mission, and information system view. Gaithersburg, MD: National Institute of Standards and Technology, Computer Security Division; March 2011. Special Publication 800-39. p. 3.

[8] Guide for conducting risk assessments. Gaithersburg, MD: National Institute of Standards and Technology, Computer Security Division; September 2011. Special Publication 800-30 revision 1. Initial Public Draft.

[9] Dempsey K, Chawla N, Johnson A, Johnson R, Jones A, Orebaugh A, et al. Information security continuous monitoring for federal information systems and organizations. Gaithersburg, MD: National Institute of Standards and Technology, Computer Security Division; September 2011. Special Publication 800-137.

[10] Managing information security risk: organization, mission, and information system view. Gaithersburg, MD: National Institute of Standards and Technology, Computer Security Division; March 2011. Special Publication 800-39. p. 2.

[11] Managing information security risk: organization, mission, and information system view. Gaithersburg, MD: National Institute of Standards and Technology, Computer Security Division; March 2011. Special Publication 800-39. p. 8.

[12] Guide for conducting risk assessments. Gaithersburg, MD: National Institute of Standards and Technology, Computer Security Division; September 2011. Special Publication 800-30 revision 1. Initial Public Draft. See Appendices D, E, F, G, H, and I.

[13] National information assurance glossary. Fort Meade, MD: Committee on National Security Systems; April 2009. CNSS Instruction No. 4009.

[14] Guide for conducting risk assessments. Gaithersburg, MD: National Institute of Standards and Technology, Computer Security Division; September 2011. Special Publication 800-30 revision 1. Initial Public Draft. p. 9.

[15] Guide for conducting risk assessments. Gaithersburg, MD: National Institute of Standards and Technology, Computer Security Division; September 2011. Special Publication 800-30 revision 1. Initial Public Draft. p. 7–8.

[16] Guide for conducting risk assessments. Gaithersburg, MD: National Institute of Standards and Technology, Computer Security Division; September 2011. Special Publication 800-30 revision 1. Initial Public Draft. p. D-2 (threat sources) and Appendix E (threat events).

[17] Guide for conducting risk assessments. Gaithersburg (MD): National Institute of Standards and Technology, Computer Security Division; September 2011. Special Publication 800-30 revision 1. Initial Public Draft. p. 8.

[18] Standards for security categorization of federal information and information systems. Gaithersburg, MD: National Institute of Standards and Technology, Computer Security Division; December 2003. Federal Information Processing Standards Publication 199. p. 2–3.

[19] Guide for conducting risk assessments. Gaithersburg, MD: National Institute of Standards and Technology, Computer Security Division; September 2011. Special Publication 800-30 revision 1. Initial Public Draft. Appendix H.

[20] See for example Crouhy M, Galai D, Mark R. The essentials of risk management. New York: McGraw-Hill; 2006. p. 26

[21] Managing information security risk: organization, mission, and information system view. Gaithersburg, MD: National Institute of Standards and Technology, Computer Security Division; March 2011. Special Publication 800-39. p. 6.

[22] Managing information security risk: organization, mission, and information system view. Gaithersburg, MD: National Institute of Standards and Technology, Computer Security Division; March 2011. Special Publication 800-39. p. 12.

[23] Managing information security risk: organization, mission, and information system view. Gaithersburg, MD: National Institute of Standards and Technology, Computer Security Division; March 2011. Special Publication 800-39. p. 12–13.

[24] See for example the written testimony of Norman J. Rabkin. Strengthening the use of risk management principles in homeland security. Washington, DC: Government Accountability Office; June 25, 2008; Risk management approaches to protection. Washington, DC: National Infrastructure Advisory Council; October 11, 2005.

[25] Managing information security risk: organization, mission, and information system view. Gaithersburg, MD: National Institute of Standards and Technology, Computer Security Division; March 2011. Special Publication 800-39. p. 14.

[26] Guide for conducting risk assessments. Gaithersburg, MD: National Institute of Standards and Technology, Computer Security Division; September 2011. Special Publication 800-30 revision 1. Initial Public Draft. p. 13.

[27] Information Technology Management Reform Act of 1996, Pub. L. No. 104-106, 110 Stat. 679; §5122.

[28] Managing information security risk: organization, mission, and information system view. Gaithersburg, MD: National Institute of Standards and Technology, Computer Security Division; March 2011. Special Publication 800-39. p. 16.

[29] Managing information security risk: organization, mission, and information system view. Gaithersburg, MD: National Institute of Standards and Technology, Computer Security Division; March 2011. Special Publication 800-39. p. 28.

[30] Managing information security risk: organization, mission, and information system view. Gaithersburg, MD: National Institute of Standards and Technology, Computer Security Division; March 2011. Special Publication 800-39. p. 17.

[31] Information Technology Management Reform Act of 1996, Pub. L. No. 104-106, 110 Stat. 679; §5125(b)(2).

[32] FEA consolidated reference model version 2.3. Washington, DC: Office of Management and Budget; October 2007. p. 40.

[33] Managing information security risk: organization, mission, and information system view. Gaithersburg, MD: National Institute of Standards and Technology, Computer Security Division; March 2011. Special Publication 800-39. p. 18.

[34] Managing information security risk: organization, mission, and information system view. Gaithersburg, MD: National Institute of Standards and Technology, Computer Security Division; March 2011. Special Publication 800-39. p. 20–21.

[35] Managing information security risk: organization, mission, and information system view. Gaithersburg, MD: National Institute of Standards and Technology, Computer Security Division; March 2011. Special Publication 800-39. p. 22–23.

[36] Guide for applying the risk management framework to federal information systems. Gaithersburg, MD: National Institute of Standards and Technology, Computer Security Division; February 2010. Special Publication 800-37 revision 1.

[37] Managing information security risk: organization, mission, and information system view. Gaithersburg, MD: National Institute of Standards and Technology, Computer Security Division; March 2011. Special Publication 800-39. p. 23.

[38] Managing information security risk: organization, mission, and information system view. Gaithersburg, MD: National Institute of Standards and Technology, Computer Security Division; March 2011. Special Publication 800-39. Appendix G.

[39] Hardin R. Trust and trustworthiness. New York: Russell Sage Foundation; 2004.

[40] Mayer RC, Davis JH, Schoorman, FD. An integrative model of organizational trust. Acad Mgmt Rev; 20:709–34. http://dx.doi.org/10.2307/258792.

[41] The common criteria framework is defined as an international standard: ISO/IEC 15408:2009. Information technology – security techniques – evaluation criteria for IT security.

[42] Managing information security risk: organization, mission, and information system view. Gaithersburg, MD: National Institute of Standards and Technology, Computer Security Division; March 2011. Special Publication 800-39. p. 34–48.

[43] Managing information security risk: organization, mission, and information system view. Gaithersburg, MD: National Institute of Standards and Technology, Computer Security Division; March 2011. Special Publication 800-39. p. 34.

[44] Managing information security risk: organization, mission, and information system view. Gaithersburg, MD: National Institute of Standards and Technology, Computer Security Division; March 2011. Special Publication 800-39. p. 36.

[45] Managing information security risk: organization, mission, and information system view. Gaithersburg, MD: National Institute of Standards and Technology, Computer Security Division; March 2011. Special Publication 800-39. p. 37.

[46] Federal Information Security Management Act of 2002, Pub. L. No. 107-347, 116 Stat. 2946. §3544(b)(1).

[47] Alberts C, Dorofee A. Operationally critical threat, asset, and vulnerability evaluation (OCTAVE) method implementation guide, v2.0. Pittsburgh, PA: Carnegie Mellon University, Software Engineering Institute; 2001.

[48] ISO/IEC 31010:2009. Risk management – risk assessment techniques.

[49] Landoll D. The security risk assessment handbook. Boca Raton, FL: Auerbach; 2006.

[50] Guide for conducting risk assessments. Gaithersburg, MD: National Institute of Standards and Technology, Computer Security Division; September 2011. Special Publication 800-30 revision 1. Initial Public Draft. Appendices D (threat sources) and E (threat events).

[51] Managing information security risk: organization, mission, and information system view. Gaithersburg, MD: National Institute of Standards and Technology, Computer Security Division; March 2011. Special Publication 800-39. p. 40.

[52] Managing information security risk: organization, mission, and information system view. Gaithersburg, MD: National Institute of Standards and Technology, Computer Security Division; March 2011. Special Publication 800-39. p. 42.

[53] Managing information security risk: organization, mission, and information system view. Gaithersburg, MD: National Institute of Standards and Technology, Computer Security Division; March 2011. Special Publication 800-39. p. 42–3.

[54] Managing information security risk: organization, mission, and information system view. Gaithersburg, MD: National Institute of Standards and Technology, Computer Security Division; March 2011. Special Publication 800-39. Appendix H.

[55] Managing information security risk: organization, mission, and information system view. Gaithersburg, MD: National Institute of Standards and Technology, Computer Security Division; March 2011. Special Publication 800-39. p. 48.

[56] Most notably including Special Publications 800-39 (on risk management), 800-37 Revision 1 (on the Risk Management Framework), and 800-137 (on continuous monitoring).

[57] Bolten JB. E-authentication guidance for federal agencies. Washington, DC: Office of Management and Budget; 2003. December 16. Memorandum M-04-04.

[58] Lew JJ. Implementation of the government paperwork elimination act. Washington, DC: Office of Management and Budget; April 25, 2000. Memorandum M-00-10.

[59] Burr WE, Dodson DF, Newton EM, Perlner RA, Polk WT, Gupta S, et al. Electronic authentication guideline. Gaithersburg, MD: National Institute of Standards and Technology, Computer Security Division; December 2011. Special Publication 800-63 revision 1.

[60] The Microsoft Access-based E-Authentication e-RA tool and associated activity guide are available from ICAM at <http://www.idmanagement.gov/>.

[61] Guide for conducting risk assessments. Gaithersburg, MD: National Institute of Standards and Technology, Computer Security Division; September 2011. Special Publication 800-30 revision 1. Initial Public Draft. p. 7.

[62] Guide for conducting risk assessments. Gaithersburg, MD: National Institute of Standards and Technology, Computer Security Division; September 2011. Special Publication 800-30 revision 1. Initial Public Draft. p. 11. Note that NIST adopts terminology used by the Department of Homeland Security to call its hybrid assessment approach "semi-quantitative."

[63] Guide for conducting risk assessments. Gaithersburg, MD: National Institute of Standards and Technology, Computer Security Division; September 2011. Special Publication 800-30 revision 1. Initial Public Draft. Appendices D, F, G, H, and I.

[64] This general risk assessment process applicability is also true for many alternative processes from standards development organizations, academic institutions, or industry groups.

[65] Well-known risk assessment methodologies include ISO/IEC 31010, the Software Engineering Institute's OCTAVE, ISACA's Risk IT Framework, and Risk Management Insight's Factor Analysis of Information Risk (FAIR).

[66] Guide for conducting risk assessments. Gaithersburg, MD: National Institute of Standards and Technology, Computer Security Division; September 2011. Special Publication 800-30 revision 1. Initial Public Draft. p. 19.

[67] Guide for conducting risk assessments. Gaithersburg, MD: National Institute of Standards and Technology, Computer Security Division; September 2011. Special Publication 800-30 revision 1. Initial Public Draft. p. 20.

[68] Guide for conducting risk assessments. Gaithersburg, MD: National Institute of Standards and Technology, Computer Security Division; September 2011. Special Publication 800-30 revision 1. Initial Public Draft. p. 24.

[69] Guide for conducting risk assessments. Gaithersburg, MD: National Institute of Standards and Technology, Computer Security Division; September 2011. Special Publication 800-30 revision 1. Initial Public Draft. p. 32.

[70] Managing information security risk: organization, mission, and information system view. Gaithersburg, MD: National Institute of Standards and Technology, Computer Security Division; March 2011. Special Publication 800-39.

Continuous Monitoring

INFORMATION IN THIS CHAPTER:

- The Role of Continuous Monitoring in Security Management
- Continuous Monitoring and the Risk Management Framework
- Developing a Continuous Monitoring Strategy
- Agency and System Level Perspectives on Continuous Monitoring
- Approaches, Tools, and Techniques for Continuous Monitoring

Information system security focuses on two fundamental activities: implementing and correctly configuring security controls to reduce risk to an acceptable level, and—recognizing that this first activity is difficult or impossible to do perfectly—testing and monitoring the system and its environment to understand whether the controls are providing the intended level of protection [1]. Once systems are put into production, successful risk management requires system owners and agencies to evaluate the effectiveness of their implemented controls in the face of ever-changing threats, new vulnerabilities, and planned and unplanned changes to the system and its operating environment. Until information systems achieve authorization to operate, certification and accreditation and other security management activities in the Risk Management Framework emphasize selecting, implementing, and properly configuring an appropriate risk-based set of security controls. No matter how thoroughly agencies identify and address information system security requirements or how rigorously they follow the certification and accreditation steps described in the Risk Management Framework, the information and documentation upon which system authorization decisions are based reflect security at a single point in time. Information security, however, is not static, and effective security management for operational systems requires identification of and response to circumstances that alter security requirements. *Continuous monitoring* is the process of evaluating a system or organizational levels of security protection, using a set of detective and corrective procedures and tools that complement the preventive measures put in place to safeguard the system and the information it contains.

Agencies have long been required to perform post-authorization review and analysis of security controls for their information systems, but regulatory requirements regarding such reviews gave system owners wide latitude in how frequently they conducted monitoring and re-assessment activities. These requirements direct system owners to review their implemented security controls at a frequency "commensurate with the acceptable level of risk for the system" and when significant modifications occur to the system, or at least every three years regardless of whether the system or its environment has changed [2]. The initial system certification and accreditation guidance NIST published to support FISMA requirements prescribed three continuous monitoring program requirements for agencies: configuration management and configuration control processes; security impact analyses of any changes to the system; and assessment of a selected subset of security controls with assessment results reported to agency officials [3]. Under the revised certification and accreditation process using the Risk Management Framework, the focus of security control monitoring activities in step 6 of the RMF is on security impact analysis and control re-assessment prompted by planned changes to information systems or their environments. Updated guidance also emphasizes the need for organizations to develop agency-level and system-specific monitoring strategies to support near real-time risk management [4], but the lack of specificity regarding the expected scope of monitoring activities and appropriate monitoring methods and tools leads different agencies to adopt widely varying monitoring practices. In September 2011 NIST released the final version of Special Publication 800-137, *Information Security Continuous Monitoring for Federal Information Systems and Organizations* [5], which clarifies expectations for information security continuous monitoring (ISCM), defines a standard six-phase continuous monitoring process (described later in this chapter in the Continuous Monitoring Process section), and provides information on technologies and approaches to automate some aspects of continuous monitoring. With the rapid increase in the number and sophistication of threats to federal information systems, simple validation of system-specific controls is insufficient to address the wide range of changes affecting agency computing environments, networks, and supporting infrastructure. Continuous monitoring as currently envisioned is intended to produce more consistent, timely, and comprehensive information about systems and their operating environments, to provide agencies and system owners with a level of situational awareness that enables them to manage risk effectively on an ongoing basis. As the primary focus of security management in the operations and maintenance phase of the system development life cycle, continuous monitoring complements and depends on activities in earlier phases, and offers opportunities for system owners to enhance or refine protective measures for their systems. OMB offered an additional incentive to agencies to implement effective continuous monitoring programs in its fiscal year 2011 guidance to agencies on FISMA reporting, which eliminates the every-three-year system re-authorization requirement for agencies performing continuous monitoring [6].

This chapter explains the importance of continuous monitoring in information security management and describes key activities, methods, and tools organizations use to perform continuous monitoring. As conducted by federal agencies in accordance with NIST guidance, the process includes evaluating security controls and assessing their effectiveness on an ongoing basis, using detective and corrective controls, and following manual and automated monitoring procedures that assess the security posture of individual information systems and contribute to organization-wide situational awareness. This chapter describes the ISCM process defined in Special Publication 800-137 and incorporates sources of technical guidance for agencies implementing continuous monitoring programs, including a continuous monitoring technical reference model based on the Continuous Asset Evaluation, Situational Awareness, and Risk Scoring (CAESARS) architecture developed by the Department of Homeland Security [7, 8].

THE ROLE OF CONTINUOUS MONITORING IN THE RISK MANAGEMENT FRAMEWORK

As explained in Chapter 9, step 6 of the Risk Management Framework prescribes an integrated set of tasks and activities for monitoring the security controls implemented or inherited by federal information systems [9]. As Figure 14.1 illustrates, continuous

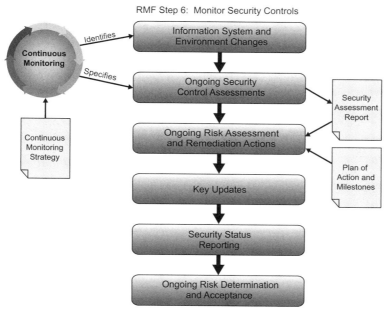

FIGURE 14.1 Continuous Monitoring Supports Security Control Monitoring Activities by Detecting and Communicating Information About Changes to Systems or Operating Environments that Increase the Risk to Organizations from their Information Systems

> **NOTE**
>
> Every system may have functional characteristics or security requirements that lead to system-specific continuous monitoring requirements, but system owners are rarely responsible for developing a full set of ISCM processes and program capabilities for their own systems. System-specific continuous monitoring may be justified for large-scale general support systems such as data centers or agency networks—where the ISCM strategy represents an important source of operational monitoring requirements that might be satisfied by the security operation center or equivalent administrative function—but most systems will leverage organizational ISCM program functions and technologies for some or all of their monitoring needs.

monitoring supports many of these tasks by identifying changes to systems and their operating environments and providing information that can be used in ongoing security control assessments. While the execution of a system's continuous monitoring strategy largely occurs after system authorization, information gathered or produced during tasks performed in earlier RMF steps influences the development of the continuous monitoring strategy. Key activities with implications for continuous monitoring strategy include system categorization, security control selection and implementation, and security control assessment—particularly including the testing methods chosen for assessing security controls and enhancements. Security assessment reports and plans of action and milestones also identify key aspects of information systems that may warrant monitoring or oversight, especially during operational periods where identified weaknesses or deficiencies have not yet been addressed. Current guidance on continuous monitoring requires continuous monitoring activities for each information system, but also acknowledges the clear organization-level responsibility for establishing, implementing, and maintaining information security continuous monitoring (ISCM). System owners need to identify continuous monitoring requirements and implement practices that address those requirements, but should incorporate organizational policies, procedures, expectations, and ISCM program capabilities where possible.

In addition to existing agency obligations to review security controls for information systems when significant modifications are made to those systems, FISMA requires periodic testing and evaluation of security controls to validate effective implementation [10]. Agencies typically meet this requirement with ongoing security control assessments, which focus on a selected subset of system-specific and common controls used by each system. Guidance on continuous monitoring in the first version of Special Publication 800-37 recommended this approach, based in part on an assumption that comprehensive security control monitoring is infeasible [3]. Many organizations conduct annual security control assessments, dividing the total controls each year so that all controls are re-assessed at least once during the typical three-year authorization cycle. By the time NIST published Revision 1 of Special Publication 800-37, continuous monitoring expectations extended to all the security controls implemented or inherited by the system [4], a change necessitated by the increased diversity of threats to federal information systems and enabled by advances in the technical capabilities of automated monitoring tools. NIST guidance gives agencies the discretion to develop their own monitoring strategies and to determine the appropriate frequency for conducting ongoing control assessments [11]. Agencies have many reasons to try to perform monitoring activities more often, including the increase in the number of security incidents at many agencies and instructions from OMB increasing the frequency and level of automation required for agency reports about information system security [12]. One way for agencies to interpret this guidance is to perform the same sort of security control assessments currently used for initial system certification and accreditation and periodic control effectiveness evaluations, but to do so at more frequent intervals. Agencies following this strategy rely on the testing methods and procedures described in Special Publication 800-53A [13]. An alternative approach emphasizes the use of automated scanning and validation tools to produce regularly updated views of organizational security posture based on maintaining correct configurations, allowing organizations to compare day-to-day security status and corresponding changes in risk levels [14]. Wide variation remains among agency approaches to security control monitoring, partly as a result of the latitude FISMA and related NIST guidance gives to agencies to establish their own testing and evaluation programs for determining security control effectiveness. Special Publication 800-137 is intended in part to provide more explicit guidance to agencies on the set of processes and technical capabilities that constitute continuous monitoring, and on aligning continuous monitoring activities at organizational, mission and business process, and information system levels, consistent with the tiered approach to risk management reflected in the Risk Management Framework.

As shown in Figure 14.2, continuous monitoring is an organizational capability with responsibilities spread across all levels of the organization. Organization-level continuous monitoring policy, strategy, and governance and oversight influence the set of information collection, correlation, analysis, and reporting processes needed to support mission and business operations. These in turn drive manual and automated continuous monitoring activities for the information systems that support mission and business processes. Information gathered in the course of system monitoring and other operational security management activities can be reviewed and assessed at mission and business or organizational levels to provide consistent oversight of all information systems and ensure that systems are operating in ways that fit within the organization's level of risk tolerance. In the case of security events that invoke incident response, disaster recovery, or contingency planning processes, continuous monitoring enables more effective response and appropriate activation of needed organizational resources, which in turn can reduce the impact and overall risk to the organization posed by such events. The three-tiered approach to continuous monitoring mirrors the structure of the Risk Management Framework as defined in Special Publication 800-39, which explicitly addresses information security risk from organization, mission, and information system perspectives [15]. Compared to other steps in the RMF, however, security control monitoring is unusual in the presumed reliance by system owners on an ISCM program managed at the organization level. NIST guidance on continuous monitoring consistently distinguishes between the ISCM

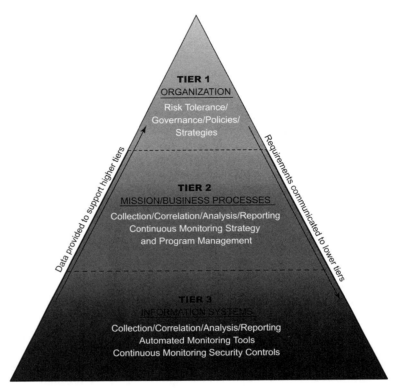

FIGURE 14.2 Information Security Continuous Monitoring Involves All Tiers of the Organization, as Monitoring Strategy and Program Management at the Organization Level Drive System-Level Monitoring Activities, and Aggregated Information Collected at the System Level Provides Organizational Visibility About Changes or Other Factors Impacting Risk [17]

program designed and implemented at the organization level and the ISCM *strategy* developed and implemented at the mission and business process and information system tiers as well as at the organizational level [16]. The ISCM program implements the organizational monitoring strategy and specifies requirements for information system-level monitoring. Different mission functions and business processes may have specific monitoring needs that are reflected in mission and business monitoring strategies. The system owner develops the monitoring strategy for each information system, taking ISCM program expectations and requirements into consideration as well as mission and business drivers, and implements the strategy when the system receives authorization and moves into the operational phase.

Special Publication 800-137 covers ISCM activities at all tiers of the organization, but emphasizes the organization-level process and provision of common controls and automated monitoring capabilities shared among multiple information systems.

In contrast, Special Publication 800-37 describes aspects of information system-level monitoring and related activities performed during the certification and accreditation process before and after systems receive authorization to operate.

Monitoring Strategy

Monitoring strategies for information systems incorporate policies and procedures associated with the organizational ISCM strategy, and leverage monitoring capabilities provided through the organization's ISCM program. Each phase in the system development life cycle contributes to the development of the system continuous monitoring strategy, with requirements and implementation details produced during tasks in each step in the Risk Management Framework. The ISCM strategy developed throughout the initiation, planning, and development (or acquisition) phases of the SDLC is implemented in the operations and maintenance phase. Whether conducted at an information system, mission and business process, or organizational level, effective continuous monitoring allows agencies and their system owners to track the security status of an information system on an ongoing basis, potentially in near real-time depending on the monitoring tools in use. Monitoring also helps maintain system security authorization over time, even in dynamic operating environments subject to frequent or rapidly changing threats, vulnerabilities, functional and technical capabilities, and mission function and business process support needs. True continuous monitoring—providing near real-time visibility into the state of a system's security— represents a significant change from conventional security management and oversight of authorized systems. Such changes often depend on the introduction and effective use of automated monitoring tools to help perform ongoing security control assessment tests and gather and analyze information about the system and its environment. Near real-time risk management—a goal assumed for at least some agencies implementing the RMF—requires real-time or near real-time monitoring, which in turn requires the use of automated tools for at least some key monitoring processes [18].

Not all systems have the same monitoring needs, so ISCM strategies for information systems should specify not only what security controls or other attributes of the system require monitoring, but also whether the timeliness needed for such monitoring differs from organizational standards. Following guidance in Special Publication 800-37, elements of an effective continuous monitoring strategy addressed at the information system level include [18]:

- Configuration management and control processes.
- Security impact analyses on proposed or actual changes to the information system and its operating environment.
- Assessment of selected security controls based on the organizational continuous monitoring strategy, policy, or requirements.
- Security status reporting to appropriate officials.
- Active involvement by authorizing officials in the ongoing management of information system-related security risks.

The first task in step 6 of the RMF prescribes identifying and documenting proposed or actual changes to the information system and its operating environment and determining the impact of those changes on the overall security state of the system. Given the frequency with which changes can occur, documenting information system changes and assessing their potential impact are essential aspects of continuous monitoring, providing support for maintaining the current authorization and evidence for system reauthorization decisions when appropriate.

Selecting Security Controls for Continuous Monitoring

The process of selecting security controls and control enhancements for information systems, described in detail in Chapters 7 and 10, coincides with initial development of the continuous monitoring strategy, including determining which controls will be monitored and the appropriate monitoring frequency [19]. Different organizations may apply different criteria when selecting security controls for monitoring, determining the type and level of monitoring activity to be performed, and prioritizing monitoring resources. Where the ISCM program provides monitoring capabilities shared across multiple systems, organizations can specify standard criteria to encourage consistent security control monitoring decisions and help ensure that resources allocated to monitoring activities reflect organizational priorities. NIST guidance emphasizes security control volatility—a measure of how frequently a control's implementation is likely to change—as well as control criticality to the organization's protection strategy and inclusion in the plan of action and milestones as key prioritization criteria for security control monitoring [20]. Identifying system and environment changes is a core task in security control monitoring, so controls more likely to change over time are also likely to demand closer monitoring attention. Security controls identified in the plan of action and milestones have known weaknesses or deficiencies that the system owner intends to remedy; in addition, some persistent weaknesses may remain if the system owner and authorizing official choose to accept the corresponding risk rather than commit resources to mitigate them. While unremediated weaknesses exist, systems expose vulnerabilities that increase the risk of exploitation, making monitoring for such controls a high priority. The priority associated with implemented security controls may also change as new threats and vulnerabilities emerge, whether discovered internally by the organization or brought to the organization's attention by vendor, industry, or governmental notifications such as the alerts issued by the United States Computer Emergency Readiness Team (US-CERT).

System owners document the monitoring strategy for selected controls in the system security plan and in the security assessment plan, where assessment methods often include tools, tests, or capabilities used in continuous monitoring. Depending on the scope of the information system continuous monitoring strategy, system owners may choose to document their monitoring strategies separately from the system security plan. NIST guidance specifies only that system owners should document their monitoring strategies, but given the dependencies between the ISCM strategy and key security management documents such as the system security plan, security assessment plan, and plan of action and milestones, system owners may find it more efficient to create and maintain a separate monitoring strategy document and incorporate its information by reference in other artifacts.

Integrating Continuous Monitoring with Security Management

Continuous monitoring represents an important operational security capability on its own, but it is also an essential contributing function to ongoing information system security management. Continuous monitoring supports key RMF tasks conducted after system authorization, including ongoing risk assessment, updates to security plans and other documentation, and security status reporting. System owners and authorizing officials consider information provided through ISCM activities to determine necessary changes in implemented system-specific and common controls and to inform risk management practices and decisions. As ongoing security control assessments and continuous monitoring activities proceed, security assessment reports should be updated to reflect assessment findings produced by assessors and any changes to security controls need to be updated in system security plans of systems implementing those controls. Updates to plans of action and milestones occur as needed as corrective actions are completed or as new actions and milestones are added to address vulnerabilities discovered during monitoring or control assessments. System owners, authorizing officials, and others with responsibility for organizational security management and oversight receive status reports that include the results of ISCM activities. Security control monitoring, as an integral part of the operations and maintenance phase of the system development life cycle, continues throughout the operational life of the system [22].

Roles and Responsibilities

Because information security continuous monitoring spans organizational and mission and business levels of the organization as well as individual information systems, agency ISCM programs require the involvement of participants with many different roles and responsibilities. Special Publication 800-137 identifies typical ISCM participants and describes their roles and responsibilities across all levels of mission, risk, and information security management, as summarized in Table 14.1. Special Publication 800-137 focuses on participants with roles in ISCM strategy and program

Table 14.1 Roles and Responsibilities for Continuous Monitoring [23]

Participant	Roles
Head of Agency	Participates in the context of organizational risk management as part of the risk executive function
Risk Executive	Oversees organizational ISCM strategy; reviews ISCM status reports as an input to information security risk posture and risk tolerance decisions; provides input on ISCM program requirements; promotes collaboration and cooperation among organizational entities; facilitates security-related information sharing; enables organization-wide consideration of all sources of risk; and ensures that risk information is applied to continuous monitoring decisions
Chief Information Officer (CIO)	Leads the organizational ISCM program; ensures that an effective ISCM program is established by setting expectations and requirements for the organization; works closely with authorizing officials to provide funding, personnel, and other resources to support ISCM; and maintains communications and working relationships among organizational entities
Senior Information Security Officer	Establishes, implements, and maintains the organizational ISCM program; develops continuous monitoring policies, procedures, and guidelines for the security program and information systems; develops configuration management guidance; consolidates and analyzes POA&Ms to determine organizational security weaknesses and deficiencies; acquires or develops and maintains automated tools to support ISCM and ongoing authorizations; provides training on the ISCM program and processes; and provides support to information system owners and common control providers on how to implement ISCM capabilities
Authorizing Official	Assumes responsibility for ensuring the ISCM program is applied to individual information systems; ensures the maintenance of the information system security posture; reviews security status reports and critical security documents and determines if the risk to the organization from operation of the information system remains acceptable; and determines whether significant information system changes require reauthorization
Information System Owner	Establishes processes and procedures in support of system-level implementation of the organizational ISCM program; develops and documents ISCM strategy for the information system; participates in the configuration management process; establishes and maintains an inventory of components associated with the information system; conducts security impact analyses on changes to the information system; conducts or ensures conduct of security control assessments; prepares and submits security status reports; conducts remediation activities as necessary to maintain system authorization; revises the system-level security control monitoring process as required; reviews ISCM reports from common control providers to verify that common controls continue to provide adequate protection for the information system; and updates critical security documents based on the results of ISCM activities

Table 14.1 Roles and Responsibilities for Continuous Monitoring [23] (*Continued*)

Participant	Roles
Common Control Provider	Establishes processes and procedures in support of ongoing monitoring of common controls; develops and documents an ISCM strategy for assigned common controls; participates in the configuration management process; establishes and maintains an inventory of components associated with the common controls; conducts security impact analyses on changes that affect the common controls; ensures assessment of security controls; prepares and submits security status reports for common controls; conducts remediation activities as necessary to maintain common control authorization; revises the common security control monitoring process as required; updates critical security documents as changes occur; and distributes critical security documents to information system owners whose systems implement common controls
Information System Security Officer	Supports the ISCM program by assisting the information system owner in completing ISCM responsibilities and by participating in the configuration management process.
Security Control Assessor	Provides input into the types of security-related information gathered as part of ISCM; assesses information system or program management security controls for the ISCM program; develops the security assessment plan; submits the security assessment plan for approval prior to conducting assessments; conducts security control assessments as defined in the security assessment plan; updates the security assessment report as changes occur; and updates the security assessment plan as needed

design, management, oversight, and evaluation; many additional types of personnel are usually responsible for performing continuous monitoring, including network and security operations staff, security analysts, system administrators, and users of technical tools supporting continuous monitoring. As should be apparent from the number and types of participants with key ISCM roles, agencies need to ensure that the ISCM program includes well-defined mechanisms for collaboration and communication to support efficient and effective continuous monitoring throughout the organization.

CONTINUOUS MONITORING PROCESS

Current NIST guidance envisions the information security continuous monitoring process as a distinct organizational function, with ISCM program activities tightly integrated with other aspects of information security management and with general information resources management. As FISMA reporting requirements progress towards more frequent and more automated collection and transmission of security-related data, the establishment of a robust continuous monitoring program offers federal agencies the opportunity to facilitate compliance with reporting requirements while simultaneously enabling more effective risk management. Current FISMA reporting instructions encourage agencies to leverage continuous monitoring to support submission of security information to OMB, and look to continuous monitoring to enable further evolution of security reporting metrics and capabilities, suggesting future expansion in the nature and timeliness of data reported by agencies [24]. Virtually all agencies have some level of monitoring capabilities in place, but the detailed guidance in Special Publication 800-137 on planning, establishing, and operating ISCM programs should help agencies develop more robust continuous monitoring in a manner consistent with government-wide efforts to improve the quality and effectiveness of agency security management programs. This section describes the six steps in the ISCM process that, when implemented with appropriate automated and manual monitoring capabilities and enabling technologies, supports ongoing information system security management and contributes key information to organizational risk management. The ISCM process, illustrated graphically in Figure 14.3, includes the following steps [25]:

- Define ISCM strategy at all tiers of the organization consistent with risk tolerance levels and designed to provide the situational awareness necessary to identify and respond appropriately to threats, vulnerabilities, and system and environmental changes that impact information system operations and mission functions and business processes.
- Establish an ISCM program for the organization that specifies performance metrics, status monitoring and control assessment frequencies, monitoring processes and tools, and technical architecture.
- Implement the ISCM program to perform monitoring activities, collect security-related information from monitoring tools and processes, provide

FIGURE 14.3 Information Security Continuous Monitoring in Federal Agencies Follows an Iterative Six-Step Process that Addresses Activities at All Levels of the Organization and Integrates with Ongoing SDLC and Security Management Phases [26]

monitoring information for use in security control assessments and reporting, and measure program performance.

* Analyze the data collected from monitoring activities and report findings, ideally in a format and level of detail that supports the process of determining the appropriate response.
* Respond to findings by taking corrective action to mitigate risk to the organization or by accepting, avoiding, sharing, or transferring risk.
* Review and update the monitoring program, refining ISCM strategy as needed to enhance information system security and organizational resilience and evolving performance metrics to as program maturity increases.

Although all tiers of the organization contribute to ISCM, Special Publication 800-137 distinguishes process roles and responsibilities by tier that emphasize the differences between monitoring activities intended to support system-level security management vs. organizational risk management. Many of the core activities in the ISCM process include roles and responsibilities at both organizational and system-specific levels, as highlighted in Table 14.2. ISCM strategy establishes policies,

Table 14.2 Contributions by Tier to Continuous Monitoring Functions [26]

Function	ISCM Step	Tier 1/2	Tier 3
Provide input to development and implementation of the organizational ISCM strategy	Define	Yes	Yes
Develop system-level ISCM strategy	Define	No	Yes
Plan and implement security controls and automation tools	Implement	No	Yes
Assess ongoing security control effectiveness	Implement	No	Yes
Determine security impact of changes to systems and operating environments	Analyze/Report	Yes	Yes
Review monitoring results and report on security status	Analyze/Report	Yes	Yes
Determine if current risk is within risk tolerance levels	Analyze/Report	Yes	Yes
Include monitoring results as input to SSP, SAR, and POA&M	Respond	No	Yes
Update relevant organizational security documentation	Respond	Yes	No
Respond to risk as needed based on monitoring results and risk assessment	Respond	Yes	Yes
Review new or modified legislation, directives, and policies for changes to security requirements	Review/Update	Yes	No
Determine if organizational plans and policies should be updated	Review/Update	Yes	No
Review monitoring results to identify new information on vulnerabilities	Review/Update	Yes	No
Review information on emerging threats	Review/Update	Yes	No

procedures, and standards that support collection and correlation of information gathered at the system level. Development and implementation of organizational ISCM strategy is an activity shared among tiers, but system owners have additional implementation responsibilities such as selecting system security controls and the tools and processes used to monitor those controls.

Define ISCM Strategy

ISCM strategy development occurs at all levels of the organization, as each tier typically has its own monitoring objectives and needs some level of performance measurement and assessment of control effectiveness. Continuous monitoring strategy at the information system level addresses requirements specified for individual systems, while mission and business and organizational strategy typical spans multiple systems to provide visibility into overall security status. At all levels, ISCM strategy reflects organizational risk management objectives, particularly including risk tolerance, so that agencies can structure their monitoring programs and supporting activities to deliver the information necessary to manage risk to acceptable levels on an ongoing basis. As reflected in Special Publications 800-137 and 800-39 and other federal guidance risk tolerance drives continuous monitoring strategy, and determining organizational risk tolerance is an executive responsibility [27,28]. Organization-wide monitoring strategy may be developed at either organization or mission and business tiers; depending on the size and structure of the organization, there may be overlap rather than clear separation between tier 1 and tier 2 roles for various aspects of ISCM strategy definition. Information system-level ISCM strategy depends in part on organizational strategy, which defines monitoring objectives, reporting requirements, and policies and procedures related to monitoring activities. At the organizational level, ISCM strategy specifies or incorporates policies and procedures including [28]:

- Definition and determination of security metrics.
- Maintenance and update or revision of the monitoring strategy.
- Assessment of security control effectiveness.
- Security status monitoring and reporting.
- Risk assessment and security impact analysis.
- Configuration management.
- Implementation and use of standard monitoring tools.
- Establishment of monitoring frequencies.
- Specification of measurement methods, including sampling where applicable.
- Training personnel in ISCM roles.

ISCM strategy should follow applicable organizational policies and procedures and address any system-specific or security control-specific information gathering needs to enable ongoing determinations of security status and security control effectiveness. Where system monitoring uses consistent processes and tools and data obtained from monitoring is produced in a consistent format, system-level continuous monitoring information can be combined and compared to present an aggregate

> **WARNING**
>
> Development of information system-level continuous monitoring strategy should be an integral part of the system authorization process, leveraging the analysis that goes into security control selection and control assessment and enabling an efficient transition from strategy to execution when the system receives authorization. System certification and accreditation activities in many organizations emphasize the achievement of system authorization at the expense of planning for post-authorization activities. Similarly, system owners may perceive less need to develop system-level monitoring strategies when organization-level ISCM strategy, policy, and program management are in place. Organizations with well-defined continuous monitoring programs can reduce the risk of system owners devoting insufficient attention to planning for ongoing security operations by ensuring that authorizing officials, senior information security officers, and ISCM program managers engage in information-system level planning and strategy development, and by making system ISCM strategy documentation a prerequisite for successful system authorization.

view of security. System-level ISCM strategy may extend organizational strategy where needed to support ongoing authorization or satisfy operational security requirements driven by the technical architecture of the system or the functions the system performs.

Continuous monitoring of all security controls implemented for an information system is rarely feasible from the standpoint of technical capabilities or cost justification. The ISCM strategy defines expectations about how many and what types of controls will be monitored and standard or recommended monitoring methods. System-level strategies that call for selective monitoring typically involve a choice to monitor a subset of controls all the time, or all of the controls on a periodic basis, in accordance with organizational policies and procedures on monitoring frequency. Similar choices need to be made at the organization level, where agencies may choose to monitor a representative subset of their total inventory of systems or to monitor all systems but do so on a non-continuous basis. Agencies can leverage many of the control assessment methods and procedures in Special Publication 800-53A to help determine the most appropriate types of monitoring to implement. Several considerations influence whether using sample populations will provide sufficient information to support risk management decisions, including what metrics monitoring data supports, the level of information already known about the systems and controls subject to monitoring, variability (or consistency) among system-specific control implementations, and the cost and practicality of performing assessment tests or procedures [29].

Establish ISCM Program

The ISCM program implements the ISCM strategy, allocating resources and deploying manual and automated monitoring capabilities that will provide the security-related information needed to maintain awareness of system and organizational security status and to inform risk-based management decisions. The ISCM program defines monitoring performance metrics, assessment criteria and monitoring frequencies, and technical architecture characteristics for the tools, technologies, and processes using in continuous monitoring. While information system owners leverage and, as necessary, modify or extend ISCM program elements, responsibility for establishing the program rests in the mission and business tier, driven by organizational ISCM strategy, policies, procedures, and standards [30]. NIST guidance suggests that senior IT or security leadership—such as the chief information officer or senior information security officer—should assume responsibility for managing and overseeing the ISCM program, either as a dedicated initiative or as part of a broader operations and maintenance capability for information resources management. The primary information system-level role in ISCM program operations is performing monitoring activities and reporting security-related information to support ISCM program objectives for measurement, analysis, and response.

Performance Metrics

Organizations use system-specific and aggregate measures of continuous monitoring information to evaluate security status on an ongoing basis and to inform risk management decision making. Some monitoring data can also be used to support internal and external reporting requirements, particularly as FISMA reporting evolves towards more frequent and more automated data feeds produced as a byproduct of routine operational monitoring activities. The ISCM program defines continuous monitoring metrics and, working with system owners, determines appropriate monitoring tools and methods to produce the data needed to support selected metrics. Agencies have wide latitude in choosing performance metrics for continuous monitoring, with reporting requirements and decision-support needs often driving the choice of specific metrics. Many of the technical tools available to support continuous monitoring offer pre-defined metrics and monitoring reports, so agencies evaluating such tools

---

NOTE

The guidance to agencies NIST provides in Special Publication 800-55 on information security performance measurement distinguishes among three types of measures: implementation, efficiency and effectiveness, and impact [31]. These categories correspond to relative levels of maturity, with implementation measures on the low end and impact measures reflecting more mature security programs and processes. Implementation metrics focus on the use and proper configuration of security controls, and enable system owners and agencies to determine which and how many of their systems comply with organizational or federal standards. Efficiency and effectiveness measures address how well system owners and agencies are using their implemented security controls and help gauge whether the organization is seeing the results it expected from its security controls. Implementation and efficiency and effectiveness measures are commonly used in continuous monitoring. Impact measures assess how information security affects mission and business operations, and are only feasible when the organization achieves consistent and correct implementation of its security controls.

should consider their ability to provide built-in measurement capabilities that satisfy some or all ISCM program needs. Metrics may use information gathered from continuous monitoring activities, security control assessments, specific security controls, or network or environmental operations. Organizations with newly established ISCM programs may focus first on metrics that help define a security baseline for the organization and answer basic questions about system-specific and agency-level compliance with security policies, procedures, and standards, particularly including secure configuration standards. As the ISCM program matures and the organization gains more experience working with monitoring data, its metrics may evolve toward indicators of security control and security program effectiveness and results demonstrating improved organizational security.

Monitoring Frequency

Continuous monitoring represents a significant shift in practice for system owners and agencies accustomed to annual security control re-assessments or point-in-time periodic evaluations of security control effectiveness traditionally associated with FISMA and ongoing system authorization requirements. Continuous monitoring must address all or a representative subset of security controls with sufficient frequency to provide meaningful insight into organizational security status. The appropriate frequency for continuous monitoring metrics and security control assessments varies among organizations based on a wide range of factors. Special Publication 800-137 identifies the following considerations relevant to determining monitoring frequency [32]:

- Security control volatility—higher volatility demands more frequent monitoring.
- System security categorization and impact levels—controls implemented by higher-impact systems warrant more frequent monitoring.
- Security control support for critical functions—controls providing critical security functionality or supporting mission essential functions receive more frequent monitoring.
- Security controls with identified weaknesses—until system owners remediate weaknesses identified in security assessment reports and reflected in plans of action and milestones, controls having weaknesses or deficiencies should be monitored more frequently.
- Organizational risk tolerance—the lower the tolerance for risk, the more frequently monitoring activities should be performed.
- Current threat information—new, emerging, or unmitigated threats to the organization may result in at least a temporary increase in monitoring frequency until organizations identify and execute appropriate corrective actions.
- Current vulnerability information—known vulnerabilities in hardware, software, or security controls used by information systems may warrant increased monitoring until vulnerabilities can be mitigated or to coincide with anticipated changes or updates to systems that may expose vulnerabilities.

> **WARNING**
>
> Continuous monitoring is resource intensive and too frequent use of automated processes such as vulnerability or network scanning may negatively impact the performance of the operating environment or the systems that run within it. Monitoring intended to detect intrusions, malicious actions, or other anomalous behavior may justify continuous, even real-time, operation, but in general organizations need to balance the value of information produced through monitoring activities with the possible unintended effects of those activities, potentially including reducing confidentiality, integrity, or availability of information in monitored systems. Automated vulnerability scanners, intrusion detection systems, and other types of monitoring tools often produce substantial volumes of data, so implementing monitoring without plans and procedures in place to review and, where necessary, respond to monitoring data may limit the effectiveness of an organization's monitoring program.

- Risk assessment results—changing the monitoring frequency is one possible response to mitigate risk identified in assessments.
- ISCM strategy as defined, reviewed, and updated—policies articulated in ISCM strategy and updated to reflect reviews of monitoring findings may require changes in monitoring frequency to provide security information at desired levels of detail and currency.
- Reporting requirements—increased monitoring frequency may be needed to satisfy internally and externally driven security reporting requirements, including data transmitted to OMB for FISMA reporting.

Before agencies can determine potential needs to increase monitoring frequency, the ISCM program should specify a baseline frequency applicable to all controls, with the expectation that more frequent monitoring may be implemented based on organizational factors such as those listed above or on system-specific characteristics or requirements. System owners and agencies also may need to alter continuous monitoring practices to respond to significant security events such as intrusions or data breaches; procedures for activating this sort of ad-hoc monitoring are often described in incident response plans.

ISCM Architecture

An ISCM architecture documents continuous monitoring processes, information needs, functional and technical requirements, and supporting tools and technologies, either alone or as an element of agency enterprise, solution, or security architectures. The architecture provides a consistent point of reference across all levels of the organization for implementing continuous monitoring capabilities, and documents services, technologies, processes, and tools available as common controls to information systems. Federal guidance does not mandate a standard ISCM architecture, but NIST cites the Department of Homeland Security's Continuous Asset Evaluation, Situational Awareness, and Risk Scoring (CAESARS) [7] as an example and has proposed an extension to the CAESARS framework potentially applicable to all federal agencies as a technical reference architecture for continuous monitoring [33]. Any purpose-specific technical architecture should integrate with broader agency security architecture and enterprise architecture models, especially to link technical monitoring capabilities to enterprise risk management and other mission and business functions that monitoring supports.

Implement ISCM Program

Once an organization designs and establishes its ISCM program—including allocating resources and putting the appropriate mechanisms in place to execute the activities specified in the program—it implements the continuous monitoring program. An implemented ISCM program is one that is actively producing and delivering security-relevant information for analysis and response. System owners and ISCM program personnel share responsibility for implementing continuous monitoring and ensuring that data gathering, reporting, and analysis activities proceed as intended. As a prerequisite to program implementation, agencies and system owners assign staff to perform manual and automated monitoring processes and deploy associated tools and technologies. Personnel with responsibility for monitoring activities also need appropriate training and sufficient technical competency to use monitoring tools effectively and help ensure the validity of the data collected. Program implementation focuses on operational monitoring activities, relying on key contributions from system owners, security control assessors, common control providers, security officers, and technical staff [34].

Analyze Data and Report Findings

Depending on the source and nature of the monitoring data collected, ISCM analysis may include processes such as aggregation and event correlation, descriptive statistics and heuristics, security impact analysis, or risk analysis. The forms of data analysis applied to monitoring information also depending on the type of reports the ISCM program intended to produce and the analytical outcomes it seeks. For instance, status reporting requires a different sort of analysis than FISMA reporting. Monitoring results requiring security impact analysis might include information that indicates system misconfiguration, attempted or actual exploits of vulnerabilities, or events invoking incident response procedures. Formal risk analysis, following a process such as the one described in Chapter 13, would be used to develop risk management recommendations to respond to newly identified threats or security control weaknesses discovered through ongoing assessments. Results of data analysis and reports of continuous monitoring findings are key inputs to organizational evaluations of security control effectiveness, determinations of return on security-related investment, and risk-based decisions to mitigate the impact of system and environment changes on mission functions and business processes. Security control assessments are a valuable data source, whether presented in updated security assessment reports covering all implemented controls or in automated or manual reports

> **NOTE**
>
> Continuous monitoring data analysis often focuses on different objectives when performed at the system level vs. the organization level. System owners look to monitoring to identify changes that may impact the system or vulnerabilities or security events that might compromise the confidentiality, integrity, or availability of the system. Organizational monitoring looks to identify weaknesses and report findings that pose risk to the organization, but is also concerned with monitoring to confirm continued satisfactory operation of the systems across the organization. Aggregate findings suggesting normal operational status or continued compliance—and therefore not associated with increased risk—represent important security status monitoring results reported to organizational officials.

of control-specific information produced as a part of routine system operations. Just as with initial security control assessments conducted during the certification and accreditation process, weaknesses or deficiencies found in ongoing security control assessments need to be analyzed for risk by the system owner. Risk responses to security control weaknesses should be reflected in the updated system security plan and, when the response is to mitigate the weakness, planned corrective actions and their scheduled completion dates should be captured in the plan of action and milestones [35].

Respond to Findings

Findings produced through the analysis of continuous monitoring information may warrant a response from the organization, particularly when they indicate increased risk levels. As noted above, not all findings are negative, or even significant, and in cases where results reported by the ISCM program suggest overall risk remains within organizational risk tolerance levels, no responsive action may be necessary. Responses to risk identified through continuous monitoring activities include accepting, avoiding, mitigating, sharing, or transferring risk, consistent with the description of the Risk Management Framework's *respond* component in Special Publication 800-39 [36]. System owners and common control providers share responsibility for responding to findings with risk managers at the organization and mission and business level. Decisions about changes to policy, processes and procedures, or security requirements made at the upper tiers of the organization correspond to changes in security control implementation or other corrective actions at the information system level. System owners also document mitigation strategies intended to address ISCM findings in the plan of action and milestones. All levels of the organization need to cooperate to respond appropriately to findings, recognizing that numerous potential constraints may exist that influence the choice of response. These include internal governance structure and policies, mission performance requirements, resource availability, and technical knowledge, capabilities, and infrastructure [37]. Communication and cooperation across organizational tiers is also important to provide a complete understanding of monitoring data and its potential impact on the organization; individual system owners or personnel in operational monitoring roles may not have access to all information necessary to support an organizational perspective.

Review and Update ISCM Program and Strategy

Continuous monitoring is an essential security management function because information systems and their operating environments change over time, and system owners and IT and organizational managers need to review the impact of such changes and make necessary updates to security requirements, implemented security controls, and plans and other documentation. Changes to the organization, its security status, or internal or external drivers for continuous monitoring may require updates to ISCM strategy and program structure and operations. The results of continuous monitoring activities and evaluations of the effectiveness of those activities often prompt a review of the ISCM program to assess the extent to which it meets the organization's needs and provides data and metrics sufficient to support risk management. Monitoring strategies should be reviewed periodically regardless of specific findings, to try to find ways to maintain or improve the quality of security information reported from continuous monitoring and its usefulness in determining the organization's security posture, informing risk management decisions, and improving the ability to respond to known and emerging threats. Agencies also need to reassess their monitoring strategies as technologies change and evolve over time, to make sure that monitoring capabilities adequately cover the systems and security controls they are intended to monitor and that the agency is able to leverage new or more effective monitoring tools or functionality. Many types of potential changes to the organization can trigger review the ISCM strategy, including [38]:

- Changes to core mission functions or business processes.
- Significant changes in the enterprise architecture.
- Changes in organizational risk tolerance.
- Changes in threat or vulnerability information relevant to the organization.
- Changes to information systems, including security categorization or impact level.
- Changes in the number of POA&M items identified for the system.
- Results of security information analysis or status reports.
- Changes in federal legislative or regulatory requirements.
- Changes to reporting requirements.

At the organization level, aggregated monitoring information may identify common weaknesses or pervasive vulnerabilities that can most efficiently be addressed through controls implemented at the mission and business or organization tier and inherited by multiple information systems.

The ISCM strategy also typically changes as the program matures and its monitoring capabilities improve. Mature ISCM programs exhibit a high degree of standardization in monitoring activities, use automated tools, conduct performance measurement using efficiency and effectiveness or impact metrics, and integrate continuous monitoring with organization risk management functions.

TECHNICAL SOLUTIONS FOR CONTINUOUS MONITORING

Consistent with other federal guidance on information security management, NIST's recommendations to agencies on continuous monitoring describe what organizations should do to establish and implement ISCM programs, but do not prescribe the scope of monitoring activities to be performed or the methods and mechanisms that provide monitoring capabilities. Recognizing the value of technologies and tools that offer the potential to automate some aspects of continuous monitoring, Special Publication 800-137 includes a description of enabling technologies that agencies can use to support ISCM information gathering and other program tasks. Technologies used to implement ISCM help system owners and agencies provide more efficient ongoing security control assessment, security status reporting, security impact analysis, compliance monitoring, and other risk management activities [39]. NIST organizes enabling technologies into three functional categories—data gathering, aggregation and analysis, and automation and reference data sources—and suggests that agencies can facilitate the implementation of an integrated set of technologies by following a standard reference architecture such as the CAESARS Framework Extension [33]. The CAESARS reference architecture separates continuous monitoring functions and supporting technology into four interrelated subsystems—sensor, repository, analysis, and presentation [7]—that align closely with the data gathering and aggregation and analysis categories used in Special Publication 800-137.

Manual vs. Automated Monitoring

To implement a comprehensive monitoring capability that covers all implemented security controls and provides visibility into externally and internally driven sources of changes to information systems and their security posture, agencies cannot rely on automation alone. While automated tools offer agencies the capability to perform monitoring more frequently and more efficiently than would be possible using only manual processes, many administrative and operational controls are non-technical in nature and may not be suitable for automated monitoring. System owners adhering to the methods and security control assessment procedures in the current version of Special Publication 800-53A understand that the set of appropriate assessment methods include examining specifications, mechanisms, and activities associated with implemented controls and interviewing personnel responsible for operating, managing, or overseeing those controls [40]. Only a subset of all security controls can be assessed using testing methods, limiting the applicability of automated testing to some controls and making it infeasible to fully automate security control assessment processes. Automation is a viable option for many of the controls and security procedures that are most likely to require continuous monitoring, including those controls

FIGURE 14.4 Available Technologies can Help Agencies Automate Continuous Monitoring Across Eleven Security Domains Corresponding to Functions that Most Organizations Perform [43]

corresponding to the eleven domains identified in Special Publication 800-137 [41] and shown in Figure 14.4. Data gathering processes, analysis and reporting procedures, and data sources used for continuous monitoring need to accommodate manual as well as automated processing. The CAESARS Framework Extension under development in NIST Interagency Report 7756 is intended to address monitoring of all security controls, whether using manual or automated monitoring [42]. Whether agencies adopt the CAESARS extended reference architecture or another continuous monitoring model, the ISCM program should cover as broad a set of implemented security controls as possible, to ensure that inputs to risk management decisions offer complete and accurate representations of the organization's security status.

Data Gathering

Federal continuous monitoring guidance emphasizes technologies and automated processes that collect security-relevant information about security controls, threats and vulnerabilities, system configuration, operating environments, and network traffic and user activity. Agencies typically implement data gathering technologies at the information system level to support security control monitoring, and at operating environment or organization-wide levels to enable status monitoring and measurement of performance metrics. The ISCM strategy drives the implementation of system-specific and agency-level data gathering mechanisms that provide the information needed for analysis and reporting and enable monitoring at a frequency sufficient to satisfy requirements specified during the *establish* step of the ISCM process. Data gathering for continuous monitoring encompasses manual and automated methods, with opportunities for agencies to employ security automation in support of each of the eleven domains shown in Figure 14.4.

The eleven security automation domains described in Special Publication 800-137 all rely on data gathering technologies and techniques to enable system owners and agencies to effectively implement and execute different continuous monitoring and security management functions. Each of these domains is described briefly below.

Vulnerability Management

A vulnerability is any weakness in an information system, security control, or system configuration that could be exploited to cause harm. Failure to implement a security control, or to implement a control correctly, can expose a vulnerability. Vulnerability management is the process of identifying, assessing, and remediating vulnerabilities, with or without the use of automated tools. Vulnerability management typically involves automated activities such as vulnerability scanning and semi-automated or manual processes such as checking for new vulnerabilities in externally managed databases or alerts issued by government or non-government organizations. Outside sources of vulnerability information include the Common Vulnerabilities and Exposures (CVE) database and National Vulnerability Database and alerts from the Department of Homeland Security United States Computer Emergency Readiness Team (US-CERT) and the Software Engineering Institute's Computer Emergency Response Team Coordination Center (CERT/CC) at Carnegie Mellon University [44]. Vulnerability scanning is a security control (RA-5) required for all federal agency information systems [45], leading many agencies to implement vulnerability scanning as a common control, or as a hybrid control when system-specific characteristics require specialized scanning.

Patch Management

Patching is one common method for remediating vulnerabilities in software, where system administrators make revisions or updates to software deployed in information systems. Patch management is a systematic process of identifying or receiving notice of patches available to reduce or eliminate known vulnerabilities, and testing, installing, and verifying patches to production systems. Because patch management focuses on remediating vulnerabilities by implementing changes to software, it is closely linked to vulnerability management and configuration management. Many tools are available to automate patch management, although agencies need to use caution when enabling automation and test patches sufficiently prior to implementation to ensure that systems are not adversely affected by software patches.

Event Management

Security events are occurrences or incidents affecting an information system. Event management is the process of monitoring security events, making determinations about which events are significant and require a response, and responding as necessary to events. In the course of routine system operations, both benign and potentially harmful events may occur, so agencies implement automated event management tools to collect event data and assess the nature and severity of observed events. Depending on the type of technology used, security event management tools may aggregate data from multiple controls or other data sources and perform event correlation to identify patterns of events that may indicate malicious behavior or other activity that warrants attention. The scope of event management overlaps with incident management and several kinds of monitoring activities; event management considers all events, while incident management focuses on the subset of events that potentially pose harm to information systems [46]. Event management tools receive data from a variety of sources, potentially including logs, intrusion detection systems, and network sensors. Some event management tools provide analytical capabilities in addition to gathering, aggregating, and correlating event data.

Incident Management

Incidents are events that may negatively impact the confidentiality, integrity, or availability of an information system or the information the system stores, processes, or makes available for access. Incident management is the process of monitoring security events for the occurrence of incidents and providing notification about and responding to incidents once they are detected. In this respect incident management is closely related to incident response, and is often implemented as part of system-level or agency incident response capabilities. Incident monitoring, reporting, and handling are all security controls (IR-5, IR-6, and IR-4, respectively) required for information systems at all security categorization levels [47]. In conjunction with manual monitoring processes, intrusion detection and prevention systems represent a key class of technology often used in incident management, particularly for monitoring. Agencies may also rely on incident management technologies to help satisfy external reporting requirements for various types of incidents, some of which necessitate notifying US-CERT within as little as one hour from the time the incident is discovered [48].

Malware Detection

Among the more familiar forms of automated monitoring technologies, malware detection comprises mechanisms to identify and protect against harm from viruses, worms, Trojan horses, spyware, and other forms of malicious code. Malware

---

WARNING

Many automated tools available for vulnerability scanning, intrusion detection, malware prevention, and event monitoring are signature-based, meaning they work by comparing observed network traffic, data flows, computing actions, and system responses to known patterns of malicious activity or misuse and produce alerts such patterns are matched. Signature-based tools can be prone to false positives (traffic or behavior that triggers an alert but is not actually an occurrence of the event corresponding to the signature), so agencies implementing these tools typically cannot rely on automation alone, but must also require perform manual checks and verifications of the monitoring data generated by the tools.

detection and prevention technologies are widely available for servers, gateways, user workstations, and mobile devices, with some tools offering the capability to centrally monitor malware detection software installed on multiple systems or computers. Malware detection tools typically run continuously and provide automated updates of detection signatures or other reference information used to identify malicious code.

Asset Management

Asset management technology is intended to maintain awareness of hardware, software, and information assets deployed within an organization, and to monitor for changes in the number, location, or configuration of assets under management. Agencies implementing typical asset management tools populate asset inventory information to establish a current status or baseline, and then use manual or automated processes to add and subtract assets from the inventory as necessary and to identify unregistered or unmanaged assets deployed in the operating environment. To the extent that asset management technologies gather configuration information as part of monitoring activities, their use complements configuration management tools that not only monitor changes in configuration, but also compare actual configurations to known standards or requirements.

Configuration Management

Configuration management in the system development life cycle context usually refers to the process of carefully controlling planned changes to information systems to prevent unauthorized or improper changes that might negatively affect the operation of the system. In security automation, configuration management focuses on scanning systems to gather information about their current configuration, and compare that information to configuration standards or checklists established for the system. Agencies implementing configuration management technologies to validate system configurations need to develop or choose correct security configuration baselines so that scanning tools have a reference to compare against actual configurations. Many sources of standard configuration information are available to system owners, including specifications and checklists offered by NIST formatted using security content automation protocol (SCAP) specifications [49], security technical implementation guides (STIGs) [50]. published by the Defense Information Systems Agency (DISA), and the government-wide repository of security configuration information maintained under the National Checklist Program [51]. Many of these sources of configuration information provide details about the extent to which automated monitoring tools support each checklist. The long-term objective for checklists maintained by government organizations is to conform to SCAP so that monitoring tools that implement SCAP can validate as large a proportion of system configurations as possible. Agencies and outside organizations developing their own configuration checklists may be able to use them with automated monitoring technologies if they follow recommendations for checklist development in NIST Special Publication 800-70 [52]. Commercially available configuration management and continuous monitoring tools increasingly offer support for SCAP checklists, including those that include manual data collection in addition to automated scanning, making SCAP an important enabler of continuous monitoring of system configuration information.

Network Management

Network management technologies comprise a wide range of tools and protocols that facilitate operational monitoring of network devices, communication flows, and inbound and outbound network traffic. Automated network management tools are often used at the environment or agency level to collect information about the availability, status, and performance of network components, but they can also be used to detect new hardware, software, or devices connected to the network. Specific actions and events monitored with network management tools vary according to organizational policies and monitoring objectives. Potential uses include monitoring network-connected devices for compliance with technical standards, policies, and configuration specifications; managing network access control; and detecting unauthorized devices introduced into the network environment.

License Management

Most organizations implement software applications or systems subject to license agreements. Continuous monitoring activities may include tracking organizational compliance with license terms, license usage levels, and deployment of licensed software, all of which support the implementation of software usage restrictions, a security control (SA-6) required for all federal information systems [53]. License management capabilities may be integrated with asset management, particularly when agencies include licensed software among the items in their asset inventories.

Information Management

Protecting the confidentiality, integrity, and availability of information held by an organization requires visibility into where and how information is stored, accessed, used, and transmitted. Information management technologies enable organizations to track information in a manner similar to any other asset, and to monitor the flow of information within and outside the organization in accordance with security control requirements (such as SI-12) applicable to information systems at all security categorization levels [54]. One current emphasis in information management is protection against unintentional loss or disclosure of information and preventing unauthorized transmission of information outside the organization. Product categories and marketing terms for commercially available tools used for this type of information monitoring and management include data loss prevention, content filtering, and data extrusion (or data exfiltration) prevention. In contrast to intrusion detection systems that often focus on information coming into the organization, many information management technologies are intended to monitor data originating inside the organization to ensure it remains under the organization's control and to comply with privacy and security requirements for safeguarding personally identifiable information.

Software Assurance

Software assurance is similar conceptually to vulnerability management and configuration management, but focuses on the functional operation of software and information systems to verify that they perform as intended [55]. Software assurance monitoring may be employed throughout the system development life cycle to identify weaknesses in design or development that may expose vulnerabilities once the system is put into production. Specialized software assurance tools—often installed alongside the systems they monitor with functionality tailored to specific applications or types of software code—can provide a deeper level of inspection than vulnerability scanners, including analysis of software code and design patterns and tracing functionality to requirements, but they also scan applications for known vulnerabilities. Current research and development on automated technologies for software assurance—including NIST's Software Assurance Metrics and Tools Evaluation (SAMATE) project [56]—emphasize the application of security engineering principles and effective secure design techniques during the software development process.

Aggregation and Analysis

With the wide range of technologies potentially used to gather data to support continuous monitoring efforts, agencies need an effective way to bring together data from different monitoring sources and perform analysis on that data. Aggregation and analysis technologies take monitoring data as inputs and combine, correlate, and present information to support analysis and reporting requirements. With the expansion in the number and variety of data sources used for continuous monitoring, many agencies focus their attention on effective aggregation of monitoring data into centralized management and analysis tools. Common market designations for this class of technologies include security information and event management (SIEM) and event correlation. The functionality typically provided by these technologies includes the ability to read security log files, configuration settings, and output from intrusion detection, firewall, and network devices; associate events from different sources; and prioritize events based on their significance and need for responsive action [57]. Security analysts use SIEM tools to produce summary findings, security impact analyses, and recommended responses to security-related information collected through continuous monitoring activities.

Aggregation and analysis technologies enable more efficient execution of activities in the analysis and reporting step of the ISCM process. The results of security analyses need to be reported in a timely manner to those within the organization responsible for determining responses to findings and making other risk management decisions. Data reported to decision makers needs to be provided in a form and at a level of detail appropriate for the intended use of the information. Automated data reporting and presentation technologies such as information visualization tools and management dashboards allow organizations to deliver consolidated, actionable information to security management stakeholders on a regularly scheduled or as-needed basis. Many reporting tools enable data to be presented in different ways to different audiences, offering the flexibility to tailor dashboards and other representations of security-relevant data to the roles and responsibilities of the recipient.

Automation and Reference Data Sources

Contemporary organizations have too many systems, security controls, and processes in place to make continuous monitoring feasible without some level of automation. Although many technologies are available to automate monitoring for specific types of security controls or to assimilate log files, the lack of consistent standards for security-relevant data and limited interoperability among tools constrain agency efforts to provide comprehensive continuous monitoring and timely analysis, reporting, and response [58]. Federal government efforts to address these problems center on the development of standard formats and data stream definitions for communicating information about security configuration, weaknesses or vulnerabilities in software or security controls, and other source data used in continuous monitoring. The Security Content Automation Protocol (SCAP) is a set of specifications that provide standard data formats, naming conventions, and development approaches for structuring source data intended to facilitate automated monitoring [59]. Technologies supporting SCAP can process security-relevant data transmitted in standard formats and produce reports conforming to relevant specifications, enabling greater automation of data collection and integration of security information from multiple sources. Vendors of products used to implement security controls may choose to implement SCAP formats in their tools to perform data collection and analysis, regardless of the technologies used to perform those tasks. Similarly, agencies selecting SCAP-conforming technologies may require less effort to integrate new data sources into monitoring solutions, and reduce dependence on specific vendors and proprietary data formats. To implement SCAP, agencies choose SCAP-compliant data collection and analysis tools and select security configuration checklists defined using SCAP. Although current SCAP representations are not available for all systems and platforms, using SCAP facilitates at least the partial automation of security control monitoring and configuration management. As noted above in the description of Configuration Management technologies, NIST offers a wide range of security configuration checklists and vulnerability data described using SCAP specifications, and provides guidance for the creation of new SCAP-compliant checklists [52].

RELEVANT SOURCE MATERIAL

Several NIST Special Publications provide guidance, recommendations, and instructions relevant to the continuous monitoring activities and expectations for federal agencies. The most applicable sources of information include:

- Special Publication 800-137, *Information Security Continuous Monitoring for Federal Information Systems and Organizations* [5].
- Special Publication 800-37 Revision 1, *Guide for Applying the Risk Management Framework to Federal Information Systems* [9].
- Special Publication 800-39, *Managing Information Security Risk: Organization, Mission, and Information System View* [15].

- Special Publication 800-53 Revision 3, *Recommended Security Controls for Federal Information Systems and Organizations* [60].
- Special Publication 800-53A Revision 1, *Guide for Assessing the Security Controls in Federal Information Systems and Organizations* [61].

These and other NIST Special Publications are available from the NIST Computer Security Division website, at http://csrc.nist.gov/publications/PubsSPs.html. Much of the current government-wide work on continuous monitoring leverages the Continuous Asset Evaluation, Situational Awareness, and Risk Scoring (CAE-SARS) reference architecture developed by the Department of Homeland Security and incorporated into several NIST Interagency reports. Relevant documentation on CAESARS includes:

- NIST IR 7756, *CAESARS Framework Extension: An Enterprise Continuous Monitoring Technical Reference Model* [8].
- NIST IR 7799, *Continuous Monitoring Reference Model Workflow, Subsystem, and Interface Specifications* [62].
- DHS Document No. MP100146, *Continuous Asset Evaluation, Situational Awareness, and Risk Scoring Reference Architecture Report* [7].

SUMMARY

Continuous monitoring is a core security management function performed during the post-authorization, operations and maintenance phase of the system development life cycle. It provides information about security control effectiveness, software and system configuration, and security status for individual information systems and the organization as a whole.

This chapter described the processes and activities associated with providing continuous monitoring of information system security controls and agency information security in general. It explained the process of establishing and operating an information security continuous monitoring program and highlighted the classes of technology available to help automate and perform monitoring activities more effectively. This chapter also summarized key expectations and requirements for information system owners contained in federal guidance to agencies on developing and implementing continuous monitoring strategies and operational capabilities.

REFERENCES

[1] Northcutt S. Network security: the basics. CSO [Online edition]. April 29, 2008 [cited April 2, 2012]. <http://www.csoonline.com/article/print/342820>.
[2] Appendix III, Security of federal automated information resources. Washington, DC: Office of Management and Budget; November 2000. Circular No. A-130, Revised [Transmittal Memorandum No. 4].

[3] Ross R, Swanson M, Stoneburner G, Katzke S, Johnson A. Guide for the security certification and accreditation of federal information systems. Gaithersburg, MD: National Institute of Standards and Technology, Computer Security Division; May 2004. Special Publication 800-37.

[4] Guide for applying the risk management framework to federal information systems. Gaithersburg, MD: National Institute of Standards and Technology, Computer Security Division; February 2010. Special Publication 800-37 revision 1. p. G-1.

[5] Dempsey K, Chawla N, Johnson A, Johnson R, Jones A, Orebaugh A, et al. Information security continuous monitoring for federal information systems and organizations. Gaithersburg, MD: National Institute of Standards and Technology, Computer Security Division; September 2011. Special Publication 800-137.

[6] Lew JJ. FY 2011 reporting instructions for the Federal Information Security Management Act and agency privacy management. Washington, DC: Office of Management and Budget; September 2011. Memorandum M-11-33. p. 10.

[7] Continuous asset evaluation, situational awareness, and risk scoring reference architecture report. Washington, DC: Department of Homeland Security, Federal Network Security Branch; September 2010.

[8] Mell P, Waltermire D, Feldman L, Booth H, Ouyang A, Ragland Z, et al. CAESARS framework extension: an enterprise continuous monitoring technical reference model. Gaithersburg, MD: National Institute of Standards and Technology, Computer Security Division; January 2012. NIST Interagency Report 7756 Second Public Draft.

[9] Guide for applying the risk management framework to federal information systems. Gaithersburg, MD: National Institute of Standards and Technology, Computer Security Division; February 2010. Special Publication 800-37 revision 1.

[10] Federal Information Security Management Act of 2002, Pub. L. No. 107-347, 116 Stat. 2949. §3544(a)(2)(D).

[11] Guide for applying the risk management framework to federal information systems. Gaithersburg, MD: National Institute of Standards and Technology, Computer Security Division; February 2010. Special Publication 800-37 revision 1. p. 39.

[12] Zients J, Kundra V, Schmidt HA. FY 2010 reporting instructions for the Federal Information Security Management Act and agency privacy management. Washington, DC: Office of Management and Budget; April 21, 2010. Memorandum M-10-15.

[13] Guide for assessing the security controls in federal information systems and organizations. Gaithersburg, MD: National Institute of Standards and Technology, Computer Security Division; June 2010. Special Publication 800-53A revision 1. Appendices D, E, and F.

[14] The Department of State was an early advocate of this type of automated monitoring and risk scoring approach; see for example Streufert J. Testimony before the Subcommittee on Government Management, Organization, and Procurement of the Committee on Oversight and Government Reform, US House of Representatives; March 24, 2010.

[15] Managing information security risk: organization, mission, and information system view. Gaithersburg, MD: National Institute of Standards and Technology, Computer Security Division; March 2011. Special Publication 800-39.

[16] Dempsey K, Chawla N, Johnson A, Johnson R, Jones A, Orebaugh A, Scholl M, Stine K. Information security continuous monitoring for federal information systems and organizations. Gaithersburg, MD: National Institute of Standards and Technology, Computer Security Division; September 2011. Special Publication 800-137. p. 5.

[17] Dempsey K, Chawla N, Johnson A, Johnson R, Jones A, Orebaugh A, Scholl M, Stine K. Information security continuous monitoring for federal information systems and organizations.

Gaithersburg, MD: National Institute of Standards and Technology, Computer Security Division; September 2011. Special Publication 800-137. p. 8.

[18] Guide for applying the risk management framework to federal information systems. Gaithersburg, MD: National Institute of Standards and Technology, Computer Security Division; February 2010. Special Publication 800-37 revision 1. p. G-2.

[19] Guide for applying the risk management framework to federal information systems. Gaithersburg, MD: National Institute of Standards and Technology, Computer Security Division; February 2010. Special Publication 800-37 revision 1. p. 25.

[20] Guide for applying the risk management framework to federal information systems. Gaithersburg, MD: National Institute of Standards and Technology, Computer Security Division; February 2010. Special Publication 800-37 revision 1. p. 26.

[21] Risk Management Framework (RMF) – Step 6: Monitor [Internet]; October 4, 2011 [cited January 13, 2012]. <http://csrc.nist.gov/groups/SMA/fisma/Risk-Management-Framework/monitor/index.html>.

[22] Guide for applying the risk management framework to federal information systems. Gaithersburg, MD: National Institute of Standards and Technology, Computer Security Division; February 2010. Special Publication 800-37 revision 1. p. G-3.

[23] Dempsey K, Chawla N, Johnson A, Johnson R, Jones A, Orebaugh A, et al. Information security continuous monitoring for federal information systems and organizations. Gaithersburg, MD: National Institute of Standards and Technology, Computer Security Division; September 2011. Special Publication 800-137. p. 13–5.

[24] Lew JJ. FY 2011 reporting instructions for the Federal Information Security Management Act and agency privacy management. Washington, DC: Office of Management and Budget; September 2011. Memorandum M-11-33.

[25] Dempsey K, Chawla N, Johnson A, Johnson R, Jones A, Orebaugh A, et al. Information security continuous monitoring for federal information systems and organizations. Gaithersburg, MD: National Institute of Standards and Technology, Computer Security Division; September 2011. Special Publication 800-137. p.16.

[26] Dempsey K, Chawla N, Johnson A, Johnson R, Jones A, Orebaugh A, et al. Information security continuous monitoring for federal information systems and organizations. Gaithersburg, MD: National Institute of Standards and Technology, Computer Security Division; September 2011. Special Publication 800-137. p.17.

[27] Managing information security risk: Organization, mission, and information system view. Gaithersburg, MD: National Institute of Standards and Technology, Computer Security Division; March 2011. Special Publication 800-39. p. 14.

[28] Dempsey K, Chawla N, Johnson A, Johnson R, Jones A, Orebaugh A, et al. Information security continuous monitoring for federal information systems and organizations. Gaithersburg, MD: National Institute of Standards and Technology, Computer Security Division; September 2011. Special Publication 800-137. p. 18.

[29] Dempsey K, Chawla N, Johnson A, Johnson R, Jones A, Orebaugh A, et al. Information security continuous monitoring for federal information systems and organizations. Gaithersburg, MD: National Institute of Standards and Technology, Computer Security Division; September 2011. Special Publication 800-137. p. 23.

[30] Dempsey K, Chawla N, Johnson A, Johnson R, Jones A, Orebaugh A, et al. Information security continuous monitoring for federal information systems and organizations. Gaithersburg, MD: National Institute of Standards and Technology, Computer Security Division; September 2011. Special Publication 800-137. p. 28.

[31] Chew E, Swanson M, Stine K, Bartol N, Brown A, Robinson W. Performance measurement guide for information security. Gaithersburg, MD: National Institute of Standards and Technology, Computer Security Division; July 2008. Special Publication 800-55 revision 1.

[32] Dempsey K, Chawla N, Johnson A, Johnson R, Jones A, Orebaugh A, et al. Information security continuous monitoring for federal information systems and organizations. Gaithersburg, MD: National Institute of Standards and Technology, Computer Security Division; September 2011. Special Publication 800-137. p. 25–7.

[33] Mell P, Waltermire D, Feldman L, Booth H, Ouyang A, Ragland Z, et al. CAESARS framework extension: an enterprise continuous monitoring technical reference model. Gaithersburg, MD: National Institute of Standards and Technology, Computer Security Division; January 2012. NIST Interagency Report 7756 Second Public Draft. p. 7.

[34] Dempsey K, Chawla N, Johnson A, Johnson R, Jones A, Orebaugh A, et al. Information security continuous monitoring for federal information systems and organizations. Gaithersburg, MD: National Institute of Standards and Technology, Computer Security Division; September 2011. Special Publication 800-137. p. 30.

[35] Guide for applying the risk management framework to federal information systems. Gaithersburg, MD: National Institute of Standards and Technology, Computer Security Division; February 2010. Special Publication 800-37 revision 1. p. 39.

[36] Managing information security risk: Organization, mission, and information system view. Gaithersburg, MD: National Institute of Standards and Technology, Computer Security Division; March 2011. Special Publication 800-39. p. 7.

[37] Dempsey K, Chawla N, Johnson A, Johnson R, Jones A, Orebaugh A, et al. Information security continuous monitoring for federal information systems and organizations. Gaithersburg, MD: National Institute of Standards and Technology, Computer Security Division; September 2011. Special Publication 800-137. p. 33.

[38] Dempsey K, Chawla N, Johnson A, Johnson R, Jones A, Orebaugh A, et al. Information security continuous monitoring for federal information systems and organizations. Gaithersburg, MD: National Institute of Standards and Technology, Computer Security Division; September 2011. Special Publication 800-137. p. 34.

[39] Dempsey K, Chawla N, Johnson A, Johnson R, Jones A, Orebaugh A, et al. Information security continuous monitoring for federal information systems and organizations. Gaithersburg, MD: National Institute of Standards and Technology, Computer Security Division; September 2011. Special Publication 800-137. Appendix D.

[40] Guide for assessing the security controls in federal information systems and organizations. Gaithersburg, MD: National Institute of Standards and Technology, Computer Security Division; June 2010. Special Publication 800-53A revision 1. Appendix D describes methods; Appendix F provides a catalog of control assessment procedures.

[41] Dempsey K, Chawla N, Johnson A, Johnson R, Jones A, Orebaugh A, et al. Information security continuous monitoring for federal information systems and organizations. Gaithersburg, MD: National Institute of Standards and Technology, Computer Security Division; September 2011. Special Publication 800-137. p. D-3.

[42] Mell P, Waltermire D, Feldman L, Booth H, Ouyang A, Ragland Z, et al. CAESARS framework extension: an enterprise continuous monitoring technical reference model. Gaithersburg, MD: National Institute of Standards and Technology, Computer Security Division; 2012. NIST Interagency Report 7756 Second Public Draft. p. 12.

[43] Dempsey K, Chawla N, Johnson A, Johnson R, Jones A, Orebaugh A, et al. Information security continuous monitoring for federal information systems and organizations.

Gaithersburg, MD: National Institute of Standards and Technology, Computer Security Division; September 2011. Special Publication 800-137. p. D-4.

[44] See <http://cve.mitre.org>, <http://nvd.nist.gov>, <http://www.us-cert.gov>, and <http://www.cert.org>, respectively.

[45] Recommended security controls for federal information systems and organizations. Gaithersburg, MD: National Institute of Standards and Technology, Computer Security Division; August 2009. Special Publication 800-53 revision 3. p. F-94.

[46] Dempsey K, Chawla N, Johnson A, Johnson R, Jones A, Orebaugh A, et al. Information security continuous monitoring for federal information systems and organizations. Gaithersburg, MD: National Institute of Standards and Technology, Computer Security Division; September 2011. Special Publication 800-137. p. D-5.

[47] Recommended security controls for federal information systems and organizations. Gaithersburg, MD: National Institute of Standards and Technology, Computer Security Division; August 2009. Special Publication 800-53 revision 3. p. F-62–3.

[48] Johnson C. Safeguarding against and responding to the breach of personally identifiable information. Washington, DC: Office of Management and Budget; May 22, 2007. Memorandum M-07-16. p. 10.

[49] The Security Content Automation Protocol [Internet]. Gaithersburg, MD: National Institute of Standards and Technology, Information Technology Laboratory; May 12, 2009 [updated March 30, 2011; cited February 11, 2012]. <http://scap.nist.gov>.

[50] Security Technical Implementation Guides [Internet]. Defense Information Systems Agency, Information Assurance Support Environment [updated February 14, 2011; cited February 18, 2012]. <http://iase.disa.mil/stigs/index.html>.

[51] National Vulnerability Database National Checklist Program Repository [Internet]. Washington, DC: Department of Homeland Security, National Cyber Security Division [updated February 17, 2012; cited February 18, 2012]. <http://checklists.nist.gov>.

[52] Quinn S, Souppaya M, Cook M, Scarfone K. National checklist program for IT products—guidelines for checklist users and developers. Gaithersburg, MD: National Institute of Standards and Technology, Computer Security Division; February 2011. Special Publication 800-70 revision 2.

[53] Recommended security controls for federal information systems and organizations. Gaithersburg, MD: National Institute of Standards and Technology, Computer Security Division; August 2009. Special Publication 800-53 revision 3. p. F-99.

[54] Recommended security controls for federal information systems and organizations. Gaithersburg, MD: National Institute of Standards and Technology, Computer Security Division; August 2009. Special Publication 800-53 revision 3. p. 131.

[55] Dempsey K, Chawla N, Johnson A, Johnson R, Jones A, Orebaugh A, et al. Information security continuous monitoring for federal information systems and organizations. Gaithersburg, MD: National Institute of Standards and Technology, Computer Security Division; September 2011. Special Publication 800-137. p. D-10.

[56] SAMATE—Software Assurance Metrics and Tools Evaluation [Internet]. Gaithersburg, MD: National Institute of Standards and Technology, Information Technology Laboratory [cited February 14 2012]. <http://samate.nist.gov>.

[57] Dempsey K, Chawla N, Johnson A, Johnson R, Jones A, Orebaugh A, et al. Information security continuous monitoring for federal information systems and organizations. Gaithersburg, MD: National Institute of Standards and Technology, Computer Security Division; September 2011. Special Publication 800-137. p. D-11.

[58] Dempsey K, Chawla N, Johnson A, Johnson R, Jones A, Orebaugh A, et al. Information security continuous monitoring for federal information systems and organizations. Gaithersburg, MD: National Institute of Standards and Technology, Computer Security Division; September 2011. Special Publication 800-137. p. D-12.

[59] Waltermire D, Quinn S, Scarfone K, Halbardier A. The technical specification for the security content automation protocol [SCAP]. Gaithersburg, MD: National Institute of Standards and Technology, Computer Security Division; September 2011. Special Publication 800-126 revision 2.

[60] Recommended security controls for federal information systems and organizations. Gaithersburg, MD: National Institute of Standards and Technology, Computer Security Division; August 2009. Special Publication 800-53 revision 3.

[61] Guide for assessing the security controls in federal information systems and organizations. Gaithersburg, MD: National Institute of Standards and Technology, Computer Security Division; June 2010. Special Publication 800-53A revision 1.

[62] Mell P, Waltermire D, Halbardier A, Feldman L. Continuous monitoring reference model workflow, subsystem, and interface specifications. Gaithersburg, MD: National Institute of Standards and Technology, Computer Security Division; January 2012.

Contingency Planning

INTRODUCTION TO CONTINGENCY PLANNING

Mission execution in federal agencies relies on information systems and related technology to support mission and business functions, provide and maintain key information, and improve the effectiveness and efficiency of programs, initiatives, and operational processes. The fundamental role played by information systems in supporting agency operations makes it essential for agencies and their system owners to establish plans and implement procedures and mechanisms to keep systems operating without prolonged interruption. *Contingency planning* addresses these requirements for each information system by specifying policies, procedures, and guidelines and implementing controls intended to minimize system disruptions where possible, and to recover from system outages or other disruptions as quickly and effectively as possible. The discipline of information security protects the confidentiality, integrity, and availability of information and information systems; contingency planning is a central element in security management and IT and business strategy to ensure the availability of information systems and the business processes and functions they support. Contingency planning is mandated under several federal laws, directives, and policies, requiring agencies to perform a variety of planning activities and to implement preventive and corrective controls to safeguard their information systems. This chapter describes the drivers, obligations, and considerations system owners should understand in order to conduct effective contingency planning. The material presented in this chapter incorporates contingency planning guidance for federal information systems provided by NIST in Special Publication 800-34 [1] and other agency-level and government-wide policies and regulations. This chapter also explains the distinction between *information system contingency planning* applicable to all federal information systems, agency-level efforts in support of continuity of operations planning, and government-wide policies, procedures, and requirements for continuity of government and coordinated and cooperative efforts to respond to events with a national impact.

Information system owners have primary responsibility for the development and maintenance of information system contingency plans and related activities, as contingency planning encompasses a subset of required minimum security controls under NIST Special Publication 800-53 [2] and the information system contingency plan (ISCP) is included as part of the system authorization package, typically as an appendix to the system security plan [3]. NIST defines information system contingency planning as "a coordinated strategy involving plans, procedures, and technical measures that enable the recovery of information systems, operations, and data after a disruption" [4]. Under this general strategy, contingency planning includes specific capabilities and supporting plans, processes, and procedures to restore information systems after a disruption, including restoring operations at an alternate processing site; using alternate mechanisms to perform all or a subset of business processes affected by a system disruption; and implementing preventive and corrective security controls commensurate with each system's assigned impact level [4]. Agencies must develop individual information system contingency plans for all their major applications and general support systems [5], although it is common for at least some of the contingency planning controls implemented for a system to be shared among multiple systems or even delivered as common controls for agency-wide use. The contingency planning process is integral to the system certification and accreditation process defined in the Risk Management Framework, with system-specific security requirements serving as an input to contingency planning activities and contingency plans, processes, and capabilities providing the implementation of an entire family of system security controls.

Contingency Planning Drivers

While system owners are right to focus on the operational security needs of the systems for which they are responsible, developing thorough contingency plans and processes and providing for effective contingent operations requires awareness and understanding of many factors that influence the information system contingency plan. These planning drivers include regulations and guidance focused on information technology management in general and information security management in particular, including provisions in OMB Circular A-130 explaining federal legislative requirements for information resources management [5] and standards and guidance published by NIST pursuant to the authority delegated by FISMA [6]. As indicated in Figure 15.1, agency and government-wide requirements for

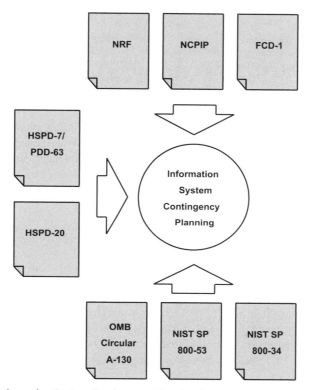

FIGURE 15.1 Information System Contingency Planning is Influenced by a Large Number of Internal Agency and Government-Wide Mission and Business Drivers in Addition to Technical Considerations

continuity planning, critical infrastructure protection, and disaster or emergency response also affect information system contingency planning. Federal continuity policies, directives, and requirements specify planning activities that apply to individual agencies or involve cross-agency coordination or collaboration, so agencies may find that these external drivers apply consistently across some or all of their information systems. System owners responsible for information system contingency planning should look to leaders designated as agency or departmental continuity coordinators for information about the relationship between their information systems and the agency's continuity program and planning activities and obligations [7]. Understanding the requirements dictated by federal continuity policy and agency continuity program management helps ensure that information system contingency planning reflects the appropriate scope, processes, and security controls not only to satisfy requirements associated with the system's security categorization but also its role supporting mission essential functions of the agency.

NIST Special Publication 800-34 provides detailed guidance to system owners on the contingency planning process, contingency planning expectations and obligations, content elements to be included in the information system contingency plan, and templates and instructions for creating the ISCP and related contingency planning documentation [1]. Special Publication 800-34 focuses explicitly on contingency planning for information systems, distinct from facility, mission, or agency perspectives. Within this scope, the drivers most relevant for information system contingency planning are the legislative and regulatory requirements addressing the security of federal information systems and information technology management. Consistent with standards and guidance issued to implement several provisions in FISMA, the core requirements for information system contingency planning come from the Contingency Planning family of operational controls in NIST Special Publication 800-53 [2].

Contingency Planning Controls

The security control framework defined in Special Publication 800-53 includes nine contingency planning security controls, all of which are required as minimum controls in the security control baselines for moderate- and high-impact level systems (six of the nine are required for low-impact systems). For systems categorized as moderate or high impact, the security control baselines require additional control enhancements, including 13 for moderate-impact systems and 25 for high-impact systems [8]. Many of the additional control enhancements correspond to practices and mechanisms designed to ensure that information system recovery minimizes disruption to mission essential functions, including establishing and maintaining active alternate site storage, processing, and telecommunications services to take over operations quickly if the primary environment suffers an outage. The number and scope of required controls and enhancements—coupled with the need to coordinate with other system owners, facility owners, common control providers, and organizational elements responsible for managing and executing related plans—means that contingency planning often demands a substantial commitment of time and resources. System owners need to recognize the importance of selecting and implementing appropriate contingency planning controls and of developing the ISCP as a prerequisite to completing the security authorization package. Special Publication 800-34 addresses contingency planning processes and considerations applicable for all information systems, but does not provide the sort of detailed guidance system owners need to determine the right way to implement contingency planning processes and controls for their systems. To make those determinations, system owners instead look to the detailed security control descriptions and recommendations in the Special Publication 800-53 security control catalog [9]. The ISCP describes implementation details for each of the contingency planning controls and control enhancements selected for the system, including system-specific requirements or contingency parameters that may differ from agency policy.

Contingency Planning Policies and Procedures

Control CP-1 directs federal agencies to develop, disseminate, and periodically review and update as necessary formally documented policies and procedures that address contingency planning purpose, scope, roles and responsibilities, and intra- and inter-organizational coordination and describe and facilitate the implementation of appropriate contingency planning controls. These policies and procedures are expected to incorporate relevant provisions of drivers external to the agency and otherwise comply with applicable federal laws, directives, and requirements. The CP-1 control applies to information systems at all security impact levels. Unlike other contingency planning controls with system-specific expectations, NIST guidance suggests that contingency planning policies and procedures developed at the organizational unit or agency level may satisfy the needs for information systems within the agency, making system-specific policies and procedures unnecessary [10]. Many agencies implement policies and procedures (which appear as the first control in all control families) as common controls; with respect to contingency planning, system owners need to consider the security requirements for their systems and evaluate the extent to which agency-level policies and procedures adequately address those requirements to determine whether system-specific augmentation is required.

Contingency Plan

Information system owners implement control CP-2 by developing, maintaining, and disseminating information system contingency plans for each information system, and by coordinating contingency planning activities with incident response and other related functions and capabilities. System owners must also perform periodic updates of their contingency plans; previous versions of Special Publication 800-53 separately required contingency plan updates as control CP-5, but Revision 3 consolidated the update requirement into CP-2. Satisfying this control is the primary focus of Special Publication 800-34, and the language and instructions in that document are consistent with the guidance in Special Publication 800-53. Information system contingency plans are required for systems at all security impact levels, but additional expectations apply to moderate- and high-impact systems, specifically to ensure that system owners coordinate their ISCP development with others in the organization responsible for related functions, including incident response, disaster recovery, business continuity, and continuity of operations [11].

Contingency Training

Information system contingency plans identify individuals with roles and responsibilities for maintaining systems during contingent operations and for executing the processes and procedures described in the plan. To implement control CP-3, agencies and their system owners need to train these people to make sure they understand their roles and responsibilities and know what they need to do when the contingency plan is activated. Contingency planning personnel need to receive periodic refresher training as well; NIST guidance leaves the frequency of refresher training up to each agency, but it is common to require annual training, separately or combined with security awareness training, as part of an agency's continuous monitoring strategy. Control CP-3 is required for information systems at all impact levels, and the use of simulated events as part of contingency training is required in addition for high-impact systems [11].

Contingency Plan Testing and Exercises

Control CP-4, also required for all information systems, directs agencies and system owners to test processes and procedures included in the contingency plan to assess the plan's effectiveness and the organization's readiness to execute it, and to review the results of contingency plan testing or exercises and take corrective actions where needed. Both the testing frequency and the parameters of tests or exercises used to evaluate contingency plans are left to the discretion of each agency. In many organizations testing and exercise requirements are specified according to security impact level in agency policies and procedures, but the responsibility for conducting the tests or exercises and documenting and analyzing the results is the responsibility of each system owner. As with contingency training, the rationale for contingency plan testing and exercises is to increase the likelihood that the contingency plan will be executed successfully when and if it is activated. For moderate- and high-impact systems, contingency plan testing should be coordinated with testing for related functions, including incident response, disaster recovery, business continuity, and continuity of operations [12]. Acceptable methods for contingency plan testing range from reviews of documented checklists, tabletop exercises, and event simulations to full system recovery and reconstitution at an alternate processing site; actual (as opposed to simulated) recovery and reconstitution is only required for high-impact systems.

Alternate Storage Site

Incidents or outages affecting information systems often preclude the use of the primary operating location for system recovery. In such circumstances contingency operations teams perform system recovery activities at an alternate site, until the primary facility is again operational or a permanent replacement is chosen. To facilitate alternate site recovery and reconstitution, control CP-6 requires agencies to establish an alternate storage site for its moderate- and high-impact systems, and to put in place the agreements necessary to permit storage of and access to backup information to support recovery phase processes. Alternate storage sites also must be located far enough away from the primary storage site that the alternate site is not likely to be affected by the same hazards that might disrupt the primary site. Interpretations of what constitutes a sufficient geographic distance vary among organizations, but when selecting alternate sites, agencies must also identify potential issues (and describe actions to mitigate those issues) for accessing the alternate storage site in the event of a widespread outage or disaster [13]. Because all moderate- and high-impact systems share this requirement, agencies often designate one or more standard alternate storage sites to be used to support multiple systems; in such cases system owners or common control providers are responsible for implementing control mechanisms to transport system backups and other recovery information to the alternate storage site.

Alternate Processing Site

For the same reasons underlying alternate storage, control CP-7 requires agencies to establish an alternate processing site for moderate- and high-impact systems that enables resumption of system operations in the event of a primary site outage, within a recovery timeframe specified by the organization or defined according to system-specific requirements. All necessary agreements must be in place to support system recovery at the alternate processing site, and appropriate equipment and supplies needed to resume system operation must either be in place at the alternate site or be able to be delivered to the site in time to satisfy resumption timeframe requirements. As described in more detail in the section later in this chapter on creating contingency strategies, alternate processing sites offer different capabilities to support the recovery timeframes that may be required for different systems, including "hot" sites providing fully redundant hardware and software to enable system failover with little or no interruption in system operation [14]. Alternate processing sites must be located far enough away from the primary storage site that the alternate site is not likely to be affected by the same hazards that might disrupt the primary site. As with alternate storage requirements, agencies must identify potential issues with accessing the alternate processing site during contingent operations, and explain actions to mitigate those issues. Because agencies often use the same alternate processing site for recovering multiple information systems, the agreements in place for the site and the system-specific alternate processing requirements need to include priority-of-service provisions that dictate which systems get recovered first, in

---

NOTE

Although Special Publication 800-53 security control baselines for moderate- and high-impact systems require an alternate processing site, not all systems categorized at these levels implement alternate processing capabilities. Control applicability is based on the FIPS 199 security categorization, but a system containing information categorized as moderate or high for confidentiality or integrity may still be assigned a low category for availability. Where agencies or system owners determine that availability requirements are insufficient to warrant alternate site processing (or assign a low priority-of-service that in practice means the system will not be included in the set of systems to be recovered at the alternate processing site), both the information system contingency plan and system security plan should document the decision and provide any explanatory details necessary to justify acceptance of the associated risk. As an additional consideration, systems supporting primary mission essential functions subject to continuity of operations planning typically require alternate processing sites, but systems that do not support these functions may still implement alternate processing sites if needed to meet system security requirements.

accordance with the availability requirements for each system. To support recovery of high-impact information systems, agencies need to configure the alternate processing site in advance to ensure it is ready to support essential missions and business functions, including provisioning sufficient space and resources to support the personnel deployed to the alternate site to manage recovery operations. Agencies also must ensure that alternate processing sites provide information security measures equivalent to that of the primary site [15]. Neither alternate storage nor alternate processing sites are required for systems categorized as low-impact, with the assumption that if the loss of availability of a system or its information has only a limited adverse effect on the organization, allocating the often substantial resources required to provide alternate site capabilities is not justified.

Telecommunications Services

Control CP-8 addresses telecommunications services in much the same way as CP-6 and CP-7 do for storage and processing, respectively. It requires agencies to establish alternate telecommunications services that allow the resumption of information system operations for moderate- and high-impact systems when primary telecommunications capabilities are unavailable. Agencies implementing alternate telecommunications services need to have appropriate agreements in place that enable service resumption within the timeframe specified to meet agency or system-specific requirements, and that contain priority-of-service provisions reflecting the organization's availability requirements for its systems. Where a common carrier provides alternate telecommunications services, agencies also must request priority service for telecommunications services used for national security emergency preparedness. Consistent with provisions in CP-6 and CP-7 regarding geographic separation of primary and alternate sites, CP-8 directs agencies to consider ways to avoid or reduce the chance that alternate telecommunications services share a single point of failure with primary services. With respect to high-impact systems, agencies must choose alternate service providers separated from primary service providers and require their telecommunications service providers to have contingency plans [16].

Information System Backup

Effective recovery and restoration of information systems depends on proactive measures that create backup copies of key information and store and protect backups in a manner that ensures they are available for use in system recovery. Control CP-9 requires agencies to conduct backups of information system documentation and user-level and system-level information contained in each system, and to implement measures to protect the confidentiality and integrity of backup information. Backup procedures are required for information systems at all impact levels. Backup requirements are often specified in agency-level policies and procedures, but responsibility rests with system owners to ensure backups are performed in accordance with agency and system-specific requirements. Agencies must periodically test backup procedures implemented for moderate- and high-impact systems, and backup information for high-impact systems is subject to additional protection requirements including offsite storage in a facility separate from the primary operational site and the use of sample backup information in system restoration activities performed as part of contingency plan testing [17].

Information System Recovery and Reconstitution

Recovery and reconstitution are fundamental elements in contingency planning. Control CP-10 requires recovery and reconstitution of information systems to a known state after a disruption, compromise, or failure. Recovery and reconstitution apply to information systems at all impact levels, although the timeframes specified for achieving system recovery vary across impact levels and potentially even among systems categorized at the same level. Additional requirements apply to systems categorized as moderate or high impact, including the implementation of transaction recovery for transaction-based systems and provision of compensating controls for anticipated circumstances that can inhibit system recovery and reconstitution.[17]

CONTINGENCY PLANNING AND CONTINUITY OF OPERATIONS

All executive branch federal agencies are subject to government-wide requirements for continuity planning, comprising continuity of operations (COOP) at the individual agency or department level, and continuity of government (COG) efforts coordinated among agencies to ensure the continuous performance of national essential functions [18]. While many system owners have little direct COOP management responsibility, it is important for system owners to be fully aware of the continuity expectations for their agencies and corresponding contingency planning requirements applicable to their systems. Specific contingency performance requirements apply to systems that provide support for primary mission essential functions (PMEFs), critical infrastructure, or emergency response, so system owners need to consider the mission operations that depend on their systems and structure contingency plans and procedures accordingly. The primary authoritative sources of guidance for federal agencies on continuity planning include the National Continuity Policy Implementation Plan [19] and Federal Continuity Directive 1 [20], both of which describe continuity program expectations and COOP requirements for executive branch agencies pursuant to the National Continuity Policy declared in Homeland Security Presidential Directive 20 (HSPD-20) [18].This guidance prescribes an integrated approach to continuity planning in which individual agency and cross-agency efforts explicitly overlap to provide a level of redundancy similar in concept to the information security model of defense in depth. Information system contingency planning is a key element of continuity planning, falling within the communications and technology "pillar" of the federal continuity program, as illustrated in Figure 15.2 [21], and considered as part of the personnel, physical, and information security elements that support continuity programs [22].

Federal Requirements for Continuity of Operations Planning

Under federal continuity policy, agencies must incorporate continuity planning into their daily operations, with particular emphasis on activities designated as one of three categories of *essential functions*: mission essential functions (MEFs), primary mission essential functions (PMEFs), and national essential functions (NEFs). The National Continuity Policy in HSPD-20 explicitly defines eight national essential functions that "represent the overarching responsibilities of the Federal Government to lead and sustain the Nation during a crisis" [18]. Primary mission essential functions are those "that need to be continuously performed during an event or resumed within 12 h of an event, and that need to be maintained for up to 30 days after an event or until normal operations can be resumed," while mission essential functions include PMEFs as well as those "that enable an organization to provide vital services, exercise civil authority, maintain the safety of the public, and sustain the industrial/ economic base during disruption of normal operations" [23].

In contrast to the government-wide NEFs, agencies must identify their own mission essential functions and determine which of those functions directly support one

FIGURE 15.2 Contingency Planning Supports Agency Continuity of Operations Planning and Operational Processes, Particularly Where Information Systems Provide Communications or Technology that Enable Primary Mission Essential Functions

or more NEFs and require uninterrupted operation. Mission essential functions meeting both of these criteria are categorized as primary mission essential functions [24]. Agency continuity planning policy focuses on the preservation of primary mission essential functions, with a set of requirements that directly impact the implementation of controls for contingency planning: [18]

- The continuation of the performance of PMEFs during any emergency must be for a period up to 30 days or until normal operations can be resumed, and the capability to be fully operational at alternate sites as soon as possible after the occurrence of an emergency, but not later than 12 h after COOP activation;
- Succession orders and pre-planned devolution of authorities that ensure the emergency delegation of authority must be planned and documented in advance in accordance with applicable law;
- Vital resources, facilities, and records must be safeguarded, and official access to them must be provided;
- Provision must be made for the acquisition of the resources necessary for continuity operations on an emergency basis;
- Provision must be made for the availability and redundancy of critical communications capabilities at alternate sites in order to support connectivity between and among key government leadership, internal elements, other executive departments and agencies, critical partners, and the public;
- Provision must be made for reconstitution capabilities that allow for recovery from a catastrophic emergency and resumption of normal operations; and
- Provision must be made for the identification, training, and preparedness of personnel capable of relocating to alternate facilities to support the continuation of the performance of PMEFs.

Recovery requirements specified for PMEFs—such as the capability to maintain operations at an alternate site for up to 30 days and to perform recovery within 12 h—represent important drivers for contingency planning for information systems that support PMEFs, affecting control implementation decisions such as the selection and configuration of alternate processing sites. System owners must understand the purpose and function of their systems in sufficient detail to recognize when their systems support primary mission essential functions so information system contingency plans and processes satisfy the appropriate requirements.

Distinguishing Contingency Planning from Continuity of Operations Planning

Both *contingency planning* and *continuity planning* provide key contributions to government efforts to ensure uninterrupted operation of essential functions, and both terms incorporate multiple related (and sometimes overlapping) processes, procedures, and planning activities. The key differences between contingency planning and continuity planning are the scope and level of responsibility associated with each function. Contingency planning applies to individual information systems and

NOTE

Federal continuity policy applies to all agencies and the systems they operate. There are additional obligations and functional requirements that influence contingency planning for systems in agencies with emergency or disaster response roles and responsibilities specified in the National Response Framework [25], or for protecting critical infrastructure as detailed in HSPD-7 [26]. Federal guidance on continuity planning also assigns agencies to one of four categories (I though IV) according to their roles and responsibilities during emergency operations. All cabinet-level departments fall within categories I and II; members of category I include the Departments of Defense, State, the Treasury, Justice, Health and Human Services, Transportation, Energy, and Homeland Security, the Office of the Director of National Intelligence, and the Central Intelligence Agency. Many smaller executive agencies in category III; category IV includes all agencies not explicitly assigned to one of the other three categories [27]. System owners need to understand the set of mission and business functions their systems support and incorporate any requirements applicable to those functions into their information system contingency plans. System owners should also consult with their agency continuity coordinators or emergency response leads to make sure they are aware of the agency's roles and responsibilities in continuity of government, critical infrastructure protection, and emergency response and recognize the extent to which their systems support those responsibilities.

is the responsibility of the system owner, while continuity planning applies to the agency and is the responsibility of the continuity coordinator or other designated agency official. Special Publication 800-34 makes a further distinction based on the primary focus of each activity: continuity planning "concerns the ability to continue critical functions and processes during and after an emergency event" and contingency planning "provides the steps needed to recover the operation of all or part of designated information systems at an existing or new location in an emergency [28]." Continuity planning comprises an interrelated set of plans and associated procedures that describe the actions taken by the organization in response to an emergency situation with the potential to disrupt government operations. These typically include the continuity of operations plan, crisis communications plan, occupant emergency plan, and—to the extent the organization manages key components and resources of the national infrastructure—critical infrastructure protection plan.

Contingency Planning Components and Processes

Like continuity planning, contingency planning also encompasses multiple related plans and procedures, some or all of which may be invoked in response to an information system outage or other incident. Information system owners are directly responsible for the information system contingency plan, but may contribute to and leverage other plans related to their systems, including those for business continuity, disaster recovery, and incident response. Where these plans and corresponding capabilities are developed and maintained at a facility, organizational unit, or agency level, information systems may inherit some or all of the controls provided, or implement them as hybrid controls with system-specific provisions put in place to supplement or more effectively execute plans and processes managed by others within the organization.

Information System Contingency Plan

As described in more detail in subsequent sections of this chapter, the information system contingency plan (ISCP) defines procedures for activating contingent operations based on the severity of an event disrupting the system and for the recovery and reconstitution of the system to support business continuity objectives. The ISCP provides key information needed for system recovery, including roles and responsibilities, outage assessment procedures, hardware and software inventory, results of business impact analysis, and detailed recovery and reconstitution procedures, including testing and validation. The ISCP may invoke disaster recovery procedures if an outage occurs to the system's primary operating environment, as indicated in Figure 15.3.

Business Continuity Plan

The business continuity plan (BCP) focuses on sustaining a mission capabilities or business processes during and after a disruption, typically activated at the time of disruption and remaining in effect until normal business operations are restored. A BCP differs from a continuity of operations plan in that the scope of the BCP may be limited to a single mission function or set of related business processes, while the COOP plan addresses continuity of all essential functions. Because mission functions and business processes rely on information systems, business continuity planners and

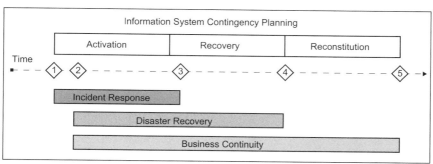

1. Event occurs impacting system; incident response begins
2. If primary operating capability is lost, disaster recovery and business continuity begin
3. Incident resolution deactivates incident response
4. Successful alternate site recovery deactivates disaster recovery
5. Restoration of normal operations deactivates business continuity

FIGURE 15.3 Effective Contingency Plan Execution Often Depends on Related Plans and Procedures—Defined in Incident Response, Disaster Recovery, and Business Continuity Plans—That May Be Invoked When an Event Occurs That Involves a Disruption to Information System Operations

information system owners need to coordinate to ensure the alignment of provisions and expectations in the BCP and ISCP, and to accurately identify the information system capabilities needed to effectively support the relevant mission functions or business processes. This requirement applies equally to systems, services, and infrastructure owned or operated by external service providers on behalf of the government; agencies need to evaluate the business continuity capabilities of external service providers to ensure contingency operations will satisfy agency objectives.

Disaster Recovery Plan

The disaster recovery plan (DRP) covers major outages or disruptions in service that prevent the use of primary operating facilities or infrastructure for an extended period. A DRP describes the use of an alternate processing site for recovery and temporary restoration of system operations; it is only invoked for disruptions that require system relocation [29]. A disaster recovery plan may address a single system—such as a major application—or multiple systems in the case of DRPs for general support systems such as data centers or other hosting facilities supporting the operation of multiple applications. Similarly, a single DRP may be referenced by one or more information system contingency plans; when multiple systems leverage a common DRP and corresponding facility, disaster recovery operations rely on priority-of-service levels designated for each system to determine the order in which systems will be recovered.

Incident Response Plan

The incident response plan (IRP) establishes procedures to address adverse events affecting one or more information systems, regardless of the source of such events or whether they are intentional attacks or inadvertent disruptions. Procedures in the IRP enable security personnel such as incident response teams to identify, mitigate, and recover from incidents. Depending on the nature and severity of the incident, the IRP may call for the activation of business continuity and disaster recovery plans, as indicated in Figure 15.3.

WARNING

The increasing prevalence of the modifier "cyber" in information security contexts introduces the potential for confusion when consulting NIST Special Publications and other federal guidance addressing incident response. The most recent revision of Special Publication 800-34, published in May 2010, uses the term *cyber incident response plan* [29] to refer to an artifact that Special Publication 800-53 calls simply *incident response plan* [30], the latter use matching NIST's authoritative guidance on security incident handling in Special Publication 800-61, which prescribes the development of the incident response plan [31]. In addition, cyber incidents on a national scale are addressed separately in the Cyber Incident Annex to the National Response Framework [32]. Agencies and system owners choosing to refer to their incident response plans using the *cyber* label need to indicate clearly whether the scope of such plans is individual information systems or agency incident response capabilities, and whether the plans are limited to computer-based incidents.

INFORMATION SYSTEM CONTINGENCY PLANNING

NIST's *Contingency Planning Guide for Federal Information Systems* (Special Publication 800-34 revision 1) establishes a seven-step process for information system contingency planning, illustrated in Figure 15.4, that is executed by system owners and other agency personnel with contingency planning responsibilities. The contingency planning process is designed to be integrated into key activities in the system certification and accreditation process defined as part of the Risk Management Framework in Special Publication 800-37 [3], and with standard systems development life cycle phases such as those specified in Special Publication 800-64 [33]. Ideally, some contingency planning activities, such as the development of contingency planning policy and completion of the business impact analysis, occur during the initiation phase of the SDLC, before the system security categorization that begins step 1 of the RMF [34]. Contingency planning activities are involved in all SDLC phases, and with the exception of plan maintenance typically must be completed before a system receives authorization to operate. Once the system is operational, contingency planning becomes an integral part of continuous monitoring and other ongoing security management activities.

Develop Contingency Planning Policy

Contingency planning policy is typically developed at the agency level, rather than the individual information system level, often as a component of organizational policies for continuity of operations. System owners should consider the functional, technical, and security needs of their own systems in the context of agency contingency planning policy, to determine whether any system-specific policy statements are required to extend or differ from agency policy. Contingency planning policy

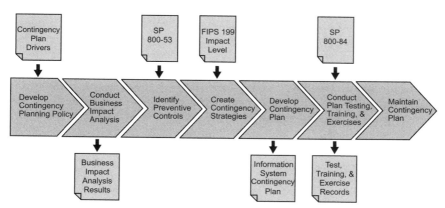

FIGURE 15.4 The Contingency Planning Process Represents a Series of Interrelated Processes and Activities Initially Performed During System Authorization and Repeated Periodically for Operational Systems

defines the agency's contingency objectives, identifies contingency and continuity planning drivers applicable to the agency, and establishes expectations and responsibilities for system owners and others with roles in the contingency planning process. Contingency planning policies should specify agency requirements and standards for systems categorized at different FIPS 199 impact levels, and identify obligations for systems that support mission essential and primary mission essential functions. Special Publication 800-34 specifies the following elements contingency planning policies should address: [35]

- Roles and responsibilities.
- Scope as applies to common platform types and organization functions subject to contingency planning.
- Resource requirements.
- Training requirements.
- Exercise and testing schedules.
- Plan maintenance schedule.
- Minimum frequency of backups and storage of backup media.

As the key system-specific artifact produced in the contingency planning process, the information system contingency plan should reflect organizational policies for contingency planning and for related functions, including information and physical security, system operations and maintenance, and emergency preparedness and response. Agencies do not develop contingency planning policies or contingency plans in isolation, but instead should recognize the interdependencies between contingency planning and subordinate processes like disaster recovery planning, as well as with information system security planning and continuity of operations planning.

Conduct Business Impact Analysis

The business impact analysis (BIA) assesses the potential adverse consequences to the agency's mission functions and business processes should an outage occur to the information system. The severity of the impact as determined through the BIA process is a key input to the FIPS 199 system categorization, which assigns categories based on the relative impact of a loss of confidentiality, integrity, or availability of an information system or the information it contains [36]. The security categorization in turn determines the set of minimum security controls required for the system, so the BIA directly affects the selection and implementation of contingency planning controls as well as those in other control families. Special Publication 800-34 describes business impact analysis as a three-step process: [37]

1. Determine mission/business processes and recovery criticality. System owners must first identify the mission functions and related business processes supported by the system and assess the impact of an outage or other system disruption to those processes. The nature and operational requirements of the functions and processes identified—including such factors and PMEF

designation and tolerance for system downtime and recovery time objectives—help determine the recovery criticality for the system and drive the selection and implementation of contingency planning controls.

2. Identify resource requirements. Performing recovery operations commensurate with the criticality level of the system may require significant allocation of resources, including facilities, personnel, equipment, software, data files, system components, and vital records. Accurate estimation of resource requirements is an essential input to contingency strategy creation and contingency plan development, and helps ensure that contingency operations perform as intended when the contingency plan is activated.

3. Identify recovery priorities for system resources. Federal information systems do not operate in isolation and particularly in the context of system recovery many information systems share or even compete for the same organizational resources. System owners and agency contingency planning coordinators need to first establish recovery criticality for each system and then determine the relative priority of each system compared to others that share contingency resources such as alternate processing sites, communications infrastructure, or recovery personnel. Priority levels help agencies align contingency resources with critical mission functions and business processes and determine the appropriate sequencing for recovery activities and resource allocation.

The results of the business impact analysis influence all subsequent activities in the contingency planning process and, when the BIA is conducted properly, help ensure that information system contingency plans, procedures, and other controls satisfy system-specific security objectives and continuity of operations requirements.

Identify Preventive Controls

The identification of preventive controls within the contingency planning process is closely aligned with the security control selection task in step 2 of the Risk Management Framework. The magnitude of potential business impacts due to system outages identified in the BIA can often be reduced through the use of effective preventive and corrective security controls. Preventive controls often represent more cost-effective alternatives to corrective controls to lessen the impact

---

TIP

Information system contingency planning and continuity of operations planning both involve business impact analysis, although COOP focuses on analyzing processes, while contingency planning analysis is system-focused. Business impact analysis is a common element of many commercial and public sector risk management functions, so detailed guidance on performing and documenting the results of a BIA is widely available. In a federal government context, BIA resources include a process-based BIA template required for federal continuity planning in Federal Continuity Directive 2 [38] and a recommended system-based BIA template provided as an appendix to Special Publication 800-34 [39].

of incidents affecting information systems [40], particularly when preventive controls avoid the need to execute resource-intensive recovery procedures such as restoring systems at alternate processing sites. The security control framework defined in Special Publication 800-53 includes a variety of preventive controls relevant to contingency planning, including many categorized within the Physical and Environmental Protection, System and Communications Protection, and System and Information Integrity control families [2]. In contrast to these preventive controls, most of the controls within the Contingency Planning family, described earlier in this chapter, address preparation for and response to events that disrupt information systems. Contingency planning controls help reduce the impact to the organization when outages or disruptive events occur, but do not reduce the likelihood of such events or avert disruptions in the way that preventive controls can. System owners need to consider the broader set of possible security controls when identifying and implementing preventive controls to support contingency planning.

Create Contingency Strategies

System owners conduct contingency planning to address potential business impacts resulting from the loss of system availability. Adverse impacts to an organization due to anticipated or unanticipated events and the likelihood of those events occurring are key components of the risk faced by the organization [41]. As described in detail in Chapter 13, once system owners identify risk through the risk assessment process, they must implement security controls or choose other courses of action to respond accordingly and mitigate risk to a level acceptable to the system owner and the information system's authorizing official. Implementing preventive and corrective contingency planning controls is an important contingency strategy, but the use of controls is not the only strategy available to system owners and their agencies. System owners select and implement contingency planning security controls as part of the broader security control selection process described in step 2 of the RMF. System owners create contingency strategies to mitigate risk associated with system outages and to address the processes and procedures necessary to execute the activation, recovery, and reconstitution phases of the contingency plan as well as ongoing contingency planning activities such as training, testing, and maintenance. Contingency planning strategies specify approaches the organization or system owner will use to conduct contingency-related functions such as backup and storage, recovery, alternate site configuration, and hardware and software replacement. Where multiple alternative strategies are available, system owners and contingency planning personnel should evaluate the resource requirements and costs associated with each strategy to ensure that the requirements for any selected strategy do not exceed the resources budgeted for contingency planning. System owners must designate personnel with roles and responsibilities for contingency planning strategies and document those roles and responsibilities in the ISCP.

Key decision points for system owners addressed in contingency strategies include the type and frequency of backup methods to be used for the system, the nature of the alternate processing site supporting recovery of the system following an outage, and the approach for replacing equipment damaged, destroyed, or otherwise unavailable. Contingency strategies created for a given information system typically differ according to the security categorization, with cost, recovery criticality, and system priority as additional influential factors. Table 15.1 summarizes typical differences in contingency strategy for systems categorized at each impact level.

Table 15.1 Contingency Strategy Elements by Impact Level [42].

Strategy Element	FIPS 199 Impact Level		
	Low	Moderate	High
Backup Medium	Tape	Optical	Mirrored disk
Alternate Site	Cold	Warm	Hot
Equipment Replacement	Procure	Activate	Fully redundant

NOTE

Alternate processing sites referenced in contingency planning are categorized according to their level of readiness to assume operations as "cold," "warm," or "hot" sites. Cold sites offer physical facilities with power and basic infrastructure but no equipment or telecommunications capabilities in place. Recovery in a cold site requires first relocating or procuring the equipment and hardware necessary to support the system and installing it in the environment before data and software backups can be loaded. Cold sites are less expensive to maintain, but require the longest time to recover systems. Warm sites are facilities with infrastructure, telecommunications, computing hardware, and other operating environment capabilities in place to support recovery, but do not have system-specific components or software installed or running in advance of contingency plan activation. Recovery in a warm site leverages the existing operational environment to load data and software from backup media more quickly than is possible in a cold site. The greater level of operational readiness comes with greater cost, as agencies must invest in equipment, hardware, and telecommunications capabilities that are essentially held in reserve until needed to support recovery operations. Hot sites have all the infrastructure and technical capabilities of warm sites, but also have system-specific software installed and operational and copies of current data backups loaded, enabling hot sites to take over system operations in very short timeframes after the primary site becomes unavailable. Running redundant environments provides recovery with minimal disruption, but also requires the greatest agency investment. Some agencies choose to share production processing between two or more sites instead of reserving hot sites purely for contingency operations; in such cases agencies respond to outages affecting one site by using the other sites to assume the processing load for the impacted site [14].

Develop Contingency Plan

The development of the information system contingency plan (ISCP) is both a discrete step in the contingency planning process and an integral part of each of the other contingency planning activities. The ISCP references contingency planning policy, includes the results of business impact analysis, and documents contingency strategies, security controls selected and implemented for contingency planning, testing and training information, and ongoing contingency plan maintenance procedures. The content and structure Special Publication 800-34 specifies for the ISCP are described in the following section of this chapter. The ISCP defines roles, responsibilities, teams, and contingency procedures associated with restoring an information system following a disruption. The ISCP also documents technical characteristics of the system and its operating environment designed to support contingency operations, including system-specific and common controls. The information provided in contingency plans should offer sufficient detail to enable contingency teams to execute all necessary processes and activities when the ISCP is activated. Special Publication 800-34 notes that contingency plans need to balance detail with flexibility, as more detailed plans with greater levels of specificity may be less versatile, scalable, or adaptable to different types of events leading to outages [43].

Conduct Plan Testing, Training, and Exercises

All personnel with roles and responsibilities for executing contingency planning processes need training to ensure they understand whom to contact and what and when to do upon contingency plan activation. Processes and procedures specified in the contingency plan must also be tested to ensure that the content in the plan is valid, accurate, current, and sufficiently complete to support successful plan execution. Contingency plan exercises include specific testing methods, such as tabletop exercises and functional exercises defined in federal guidance on testing, training, and exercise programs [44]. Contingency plan testing is also part of the security control assessment process (described in Chapter 11) to evaluate the effectiveness of the ISCP and other required contingency planning security controls. The system security categorization drives the scope of contingency planning testing or exercises—tabletop exercises or recovery simulations suffice for low- or moderate-impact systems, while the security control requirements associated with high-impact levels include full recovery and reconstitution at an alternate processing site. Following guidance in Special Publication 800-53 Revision 3, agencies define their own frequencies for contingency plan testing, training, and exercises [45], a change from prior versions of the control catalog that specified annual testing at a minimum. Federal agencies often align testing, training, and exercises with annual security control re-assessment activities, although high-impact systems or those supporting mission-critical operations may warrant specification of more frequent intervals. Testing, training, and exercises for the ISCP should be conducted initially as part of the security authorization process, and periodically repeated in accordance with system or agency continuous monitoring or ongoing control assessment activities.

Training

Training for personnel with contingency plan roles and responsibilities focuses on ensuring all personnel understand their contingency roles and, where necessary, on teaching them the skills necessary to perform those roles as expected. The primary intent of contingency plan training is to help ensure personnel are prepared to participate in testing and exercises as well as actual outage events. Training should be provided to all personnel new to the organization or newly assigned to contingency planning roles, and refreshed at least annually. The ISCP is an important point of reference for contingency planning personnel, but one goal for training is to obviate the need for the ISCP itself by sufficiently training personnel to execute their roles and responsibilities without the aid of the ISCP document. Training for recovery personnel should cover ISCP elements including: [46]

- Purpose of the plan and the function of the system it addresses.
- Cross-team coordination and communication expectations.
- Reporting procedures, including points of contact with decision making authority.
- Security requirements.
- Team-specific processes, including those designed for the information system.
- Individual responsibilities for each of the contingency phases.

Testing

Contingency plan testing is a critical element of an effective contingency capability, to identify and address plan deficiencies and to confirm the viability of the plan to support recovery operations. System owners can use different forms of testing to evaluate contingency plans depending on the environment in which the system operates, its impact level, or the objectives sought from testing. Information system components, system interconnections, and supporting infrastructure should be tested separately to confirm the accuracy of individual recovery procedures and together to assess end-to-end contingency procedures. Contingency plan tests should address applicable procedures and elements, including: [47]

- Notification procedures.
- System recovery on an alternate platform from backup media.
- Internal and external connectivity.
- System performance using alternate equipment.
- Restoration of normal operations.
- Testing in conjunction with other plans (e.g. COOP, incident response, disaster recovery).

Contingency plan testing should follow an explicit test plan designed to evaluate specific functional or technical capabilities and to examine the plan elements against test objectives and success criteria. The test plan should clearly define scope, scenarios to be tested, and logistics, as well as detailing the time frame for each test and test participants.

Maintain Plan

Contingency planning is not a static process, and the ISCP should be periodically reviewed and updated as necessary to validate the processes and procedures it describes and ensure the plan accurately reflects current system requirements, organizational structure, and policies and procedures. For systems in the operations and maintenance phase of the SDLC, changes may occur to the system, its functional or technical capabilities, its operating environment, or the support it provides to mission functions and business processes. Changes in agency or government policy, directives, or regulations also can result in changes to an information system or the contingency planning requirements applicable to the system. Contingency plan maintenance can be coordinated with routine review and update procedures for system security plans or other artifacts and incorporated into continuous monitoring strategies within step 6 of the RMF. Changes made to contingency plans, strategies, and policies should be coordinated through the system owner and personnel responsible for related plans and processes, so that changes in the ISCP are accurately reflected in dependent plans or processes that reference it [48].

As with the system security plan or other key security documents, the contingency plan should be reviewed on a routinely scheduled basis and whenever significant changes occur to any element of the plan, the system, or its role or use within the organization. Because the ISCP contains potentially sensitive operational and personnel information as well as detailed technical information about the system, distribution of the plan or access to the information it contains should be controlled to limit access to personnel with a legitimate need to know. Copies of the ISCP are typically stored at the primary and alternate processing sites, and with backup media that will be used to support recovery.

DEVELOPING THE INFORMATION SYSTEM CONTINGENCY PLAN

The information system contingency plan contains the primary contingency planning documentation, including information produced during each activity in the contingency planning process. The ISCP, typically delivered in the system authorization package as an appendix to the system security plan, identifies personnel involved in contingency operations, defines individual and organizational roles and responsibilities associated with contingency plan execution, and presents detailed processes and procedures to be followed in each contingency operation phase. The content and structure of an ISCP should reflect organizational policy and requirements and facilitate the effective use of the plan to prepare for and respond to events that trigger plan activation. Many agencies provide standard templates for their system owners to use when developing the various plans and supporting documentation needed for the system authorization package, including contingency plans. System owners and contingency planners working without an agency-standard format may choose to utilize one of the sample ISCP templates included with Special Publication 800-34. This guidance document provides three separate versions reflecting typical content for low-, moderate-, and high-impact systems [49], which system owners can modify as necessary to accommodate agency requirements or system-specific considerations. The rest of this section describes the typical components of an information system contingency plan, shown in Figure 15.5, structured according to the guidance in Special Publication 800-34.

ISCP Introduction and Supporting Information

The introductory section of the ISCP describes the context and purpose for the contingency plan, including system-specific and agency-level contingency planning drivers and requirements and other reasons for developing the plan. The introduction provides background information about the system relevant to the contingency plan,

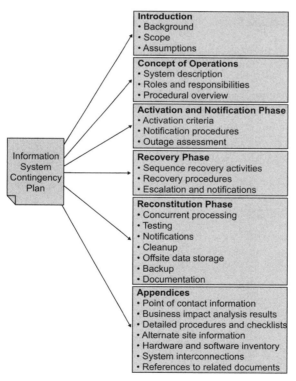

FIGURE 15.5 Federal Guidance on Information System Contingency Plans Prescribes a Standard Format Structured Around the Three Core Phases of Activation, Recovery, and Reconstitution

including summary findings from the business impact analysis and other contingency planning activities preceding the development of the ISCP. Depending on the approach the agency takes to standardizing contingency planning policy and procedures for its systems, some introductory information may be common across all systems and pre-populated in the ISCP template to ensure consistency in contingency plan documents. Supporting information in the introduction gives system owners the opportunity to explain the rationale for and intended use of contingency planning controls and procedures specified in the ISCP and applicability of agency-level or federal guidance. The introduction also describes the structure and highlights the key content included in the plan.

Even where agency-level contingency planning policies and procedures apply to all information systems, each system is different and the ISCP for each system should reflect system-specific attributes and security management decisions that influence the controls and procedures selected for the system. Many factors affect the scope of the contingency plan, notably including results of the business impact analysis, the nature and mission criticality of functions and business processes supported by the system, and the system security categorization. The introduction also specifies key implications and scoping details such as alternate storage, processing, and telecommunications needs, recovery time objectives and minimum acceptable outage thresholds, recovery criticality, and system priority levels. Lastly, the introduction lists contingency planning assumptions for the system, including expectations about organizational responsibilities for managing contingency planning activities, dependencies on other processes or functional areas, and reliance on common controls for contingency plan execution. Assumptions about the provision of common controls leveraged by the system are particularly relevant where preventive and corrective controls are provided by government or contractor-operated data centers or other general support systems or by external service providers.

Concept of Operations

In addition to the contingency planning context established in the introduction, the ISCP includes a detailed system description, including functional and technical characteristics relevant to the contingency planning requirements for the system. As noted in chapter 10, the system security plan typically describes the system purpose, concept of operations, and technical components, potentially including architecture diagrams and system interconnections. To the extent this information is documented already in the system security plan, system owners may replicate or reference the system description information in the SSP for the ISCP [50]. The concept of operations section in the ISCP provides an overview of the key contingency phases addressed in the plan: activation, recovery, and reconstitution. This overview gives contingency plan readers a concise summary of the end-to-end contingency process and explains the objectives and intent of each phase and the relationship and dependencies among those phases.

The ISCP defines all individual and organizational roles and responsibilities necessary to successfully execute system recovery and other key activities described in the plan. Roles and responsibilities in the ISCP should include the composition of contingency teams and any reporting relationships, hierarchical structure, and coordination mechanisms among team members, both prior to activation and during contingency plan execution [50]. This information—along with the detailed procedural information about the contingency phases—provides the basis for contingency plan training delivered to personnel with contingency responsibilities.

Activation and Notification

The activation and notification phase includes initial actions that should be taken and procedures to be followed when an outage or other system disruption occurs that invokes the contingency plan. Depending on the nature of the event or incident causing the outage, contingency plan activation may take place in anticipation of an outage or once the outage occurs. This phase includes all activities performed from the time the ISCP is activated until recovery operations begin. Key activities in the activation and notification phase include the initial determination to activate the ISCP, notification of contingency personnel when activation occurs, and assessment of the nature of the outage and severity of the disruption to the system. The decision to activate the contingency plan should be based on explicit criteria specified at the agency or system level, such as the impact level assigned to the system, criticality of the mission functions and business processes it supports, extent of damage to the system, expected duration of the outage, and likelihood of resumption of normal operations without intervention. Given the commitment of resources that usually accompanies contingency plan execution, organizations may limit the individuals or functional positions with the authority to activate contingency operations. The specific individual or individuals given contingency plan activation authority varies among agencies, but Special Publication 800-34 recommends that such authority be assigned to a single authoritative role for each system, with overall contingency operations falling under the authority of the CIO or other senior manager [51]. Contingency plan activation may also occur as the result of outcomes or determinations made as part of related processes performed by the agency, such as incident response or emergency response.

When the ISCP is activated, notification must be provided to contingency planning personnel so that they can initiate appropriate actions as specified in the plan, and to system administrators and users if possible to minimize the potential disruption to mission and business activities. Advance notification is preferred where feasible—such as when outages are anticipated due to weather, explicit threats, or patterns of activity—to avoid the loss of data or other adverse impacts that may occur with unexpected outages and to invoke standard or emergency change management processes where applicable. The ISCP documents notification procedures for both anticipated and unanticipated outages, clearly delineating who is responsible for providing notification, the messaging and communication channels used for notification, and the timeframe and relative priority for notifying contingency teams, system personnel, users, and others affected by the system outage. Such procedures often include automated and manual notification methods and may entail notification using multiple channels to increase the likelihood that notifications reach their intended recipients. The content provided in notifications may vary depending on the nature and severity of the outage and what response or other action, if any, the notified party is asked to take. Notification information may include: [52]

- Nature of the outage or disruption that has occurred or is impending.
- Any known outage estimates.
- Response and recovery details.
- Where and when to convene for briefing or further instructions;
- Instructions to prepare for relocation for estimated time period (if applicable).
- Instructions to communicate the notification to others, such as by using a call tree.

Recovery procedures to be followed depend to some extent on the nature of the event leading to contingency plan activation and the severity of the impact to the organization due to system outage or other consequence of the event. Members of the contingency team should perform an outage assessment as quickly as possible to determine the severity of the outage and prepare for and execute the appropriate recovery procedures. Specific outage assessment procedures vary across agencies and among different systems, but Special Publication 800-34 suggests assessments at a minimum address: [52]

- Cause of the outage or disruption.
- Potential for additional disruptions or damage.
- Status of physical infrastructure.
- Inventory and functional status of system.
- Type of damage to system equipment or.
- Items to be replaced (e.g. hardware, software, firmware, supporting materials).
- Estimated time to restore normal services.

The results of the outage assessment influence the execution of recovery phase procedures, so assessment findings should be communicated to contingency operations personnel with responsibility for recovery, with additional notification provided to appropriate agency authorities and system personnel identified in the ISCP.

Recovery

The recovery phase comprises the activities most commonly associated with contingency operations, including the core procedures necessary to restore an information system to an operational state following an outage. The primary objective of the recovery phase is to resume system operations—potentially at a reduced level of functionality and using alternate processing capabilities where necessary—to enable continuity of operations for the mission functions and business processes the system supports. Many prerequisites must be met before recovery operations can begin, typically including contingency plan activation, notification of recovery team personnel, retrieval of backup media, preparation of the alternate processing site, and physical or remote access to the site so that recovery personnel can perform restoration activities. The ISCP specifies the sequence of recovery activities to be performed, including indicating whether other systems, technical infrastructure, and communications capabilities must also be recovered in order to restore the information system. The ISCP should reflect the recovery criticality and relative priority of the system so recovery team personnel understand which systems or components must be recovered first [53]. The ISCP should describe recovery activities in sufficient detail to ensure that contingency personnel can validate that all necessary steps are taken, in the appropriate order, and that all needed materials and technical components are transferred to the recovery site, already in place, or procured. The sequence of recovery activities and the description of individual recovery procedures may be supplemented by more detailed guidance that provides explicit step-by-step instructions for recovery tasks such as installing and configuring software components, restoring data from backup media, and testing recovered systems to validate proper operation before putting them into production. Detailed instructions for such recovery procedures are typically included as appendices to the ISCP.

While recovery activities tend to be similar across systems, the specific procedures required to fully restore a particular information system depend on a variety of system-specific factors and technical considerations. System owners using ISCP templates such as the ones NIST provides need to confirm which of the typical recovery procedures apply to their information systems, and augment general recovery activity information with system-specific procedures, including specifying which recovery team members have responsibility for each procedure. Common recovery activities include: [54]

- Obtaining authorization to access damaged facilities or areas.
- Notifying internal and external business partners associated with the system.
- Obtaining and securing access to necessary recovery facilities and materials.
- Obtaining and installing necessary hardware components.
- Obtaining and loading backup media.
- Restoring critical operating system and application software.
- Restoring system data to a known state.
- Testing system functionality, including security controls.
- Establishing network connectivity and necessary system interconnections.
- Confirming successful operation of alternate equipment.

Agencies typically want disrupted system operations restored as expediently as possible, subject to recovery criticality requirements, recovery time objectives, system priority levels, and situational constraints. The ISCP includes escalation and notification procedures to be followed in circumstances where recovery activities do not proceed as planned. These procedures should define performance thresholds, time delays, or other issues that trigger escalation, and identify points of contact to whom escalation requests should be directed. In many cases, recovery escalation entails actions above and beyond the procedures specified in the ISCP that require additional personnel, funding, or other resources. Depending on the circumstances, the criticality of the system, and applicable agency policy, recovery teams may need to request and receive approval before committing additional resources or taking additional recovery action. The escalation and notification procedures in the ISCP should clearly explain the authority given to the recovery team to make decisions and take actions it deems necessary, and indicate when agency approval is required before taking such actions.

Reconstitution

System reconstitution is the process of resuming normal system operation and completing contingency plan activities. Depending on the nature of the outage to the system, "normal" system operations may involve putting the information system back into production at the original primary processing site, or establishing a new permanent primary processing site if the original site was damaged beyond the point of restoration [55]. Reconstitution phase activities emphasize testing and validation of system functionality and, once the system successfully passes those steps, closing out contingency operations including stand-down of temporary recovery facilities and infrastructure, documenting completed contingency activities, and restoring contingency planning resources and capabilities to their pre-activation state of readiness. Recovery validation activities conducted during the reconstitution phase typically include concurrent processing and validation testing procedures for both data and system functionality.

Concurrent processing means operating the information system at two separate locations—such as the alternate site and primary site—concurrently for a specified period of time or until there is sufficient confidence that the recovered system is operating as intended, allowing operation at the secondary location to be suspended. For systems whose impact level and mission criticality are sufficient to warrant high availability measures such as redundant processing, real-time failover, and hot-site alternate processing locations, concurrent processing may be continuous rather than temporary. None of the Special Publication 800-53 security control baselines requires concurrent processing, although there are optional control enhancements that, if implemented, provide redundant processing facilities and recovery and reconstitution capabilities that enable system recovery at alternate processing sites with little or no interruption in operations [56].

Validation data testing is the process of testing and validating recovered data to ensure that files, databases, or other data used by the information system are complete and current at least to the last available backup at the time the system outage occurred. Validation functionality testing focuses on system functionality, to ensure that the reconstituted system performs as intended and that the system is able to resume normal operations [55]. Information system owners, information owners, and other personnel responsible for normal business operations of the system and with detailed knowledge of its proper functions may need to participate in validation testing. Following successful completion of data and functional testing and validation, the system owner or other designated agency authority makes a formal recovery declaration, indicating the end of recovery efforts and the return of the system to normal business operations. The ISCP should describe the criteria for reaching a recovery declaration and the procedures and responsibility for providing notification of the recovery declaration to users and other applicable personnel.

With the information system restored to normal operations, the final activities in the reconstitution phase involve performing procedures necessary to return all contingency planning assets and personnel to their pre-activation readiness states and documenting contingency operations that have occurred. This includes the stand-down of the alternate processing site, re-provisioning of materials, supplies, or equipment used during recovery operations, return of any temporarily relocated assets, documentation, and other resources, and physical facility cleanup in accordance with ISCP procedures or agreements for alternate site usage. Even at the point of contingency plan deactivation, system and data backups represent an essential control to support future contingency needs. Backup media used in system recovery should be returned to its designated storage location, and a full backup of the reconstituted system should be performed at the next scheduled period or within an alternate timeframe specified in the ISCP. Events occurring and actions taken throughout the contingency phases should be documented, noting any problems or issues, responses to problems, and decisions, requests, and approvals made during contingency operations. Information about parts of the process that worked as intended or failed to meet expectations can offer practical feedback on the ISCP and serve as the basis for updates or improvements to the plan. At the conclusion of activities specified in the ISCP, the system owner or other agency authority formally deactivates the contingency plan and provides notification to contingency personnel and other business and technical points of contact designated in the plan.

Appendices and Supplemental Information

The core content in the ISCP describes the operational procedures to be performed in each phase of contingency plan execution. Successfully performing these activities depends on a great deal of system-specific and organization-specific information that is too detailed or too voluminous to be included in the procedural descriptions. The ISCP typically includes several appendices that provide supplemental information and link the contingency plan to other relevant sources of guidance and information that contingency team personnel may need to perform their duties. Information included in appendices to the ISCP may include: [57]

- Contact information for contingency planning team personnel.
- Contact information for vendors, including those providing offsite storage and alternate processing sites, where applicable.

- Detailed recovery procedures.
- Alternate processing procedures.
- Validation testing plans, procedures, and checklists.
- Hardware, software, and equipment inventory and system requirements.
- System architecture and input/output diagrams.
- System interconnections;
- Alternate storage, site, and telecommunications information;
- Service level agreements, reciprocal agreements, or other contract terms with other organizations.
- ISCP testing and maintenance schedule and procedures.
- References to associated plans and procedures or other documentation.
- Business impact analysis results;
- Record of changes or version history for the ISCP.

The set of supplemental information included with the ISCP may differ for systems at different impact levels, due to system-specific requirements or considerations or applicable agency policies or standards.

OPERATIONAL REQUIREMENTS FOR CONTINGENCY PLANNING

With the structure and content expectations for contingency planning processes and the ISCP in mind, system owners need to determine appropriate and effective contingency planning requirements for their information systems. In addition to the system's security categorization level, recovery criticality, and role in supporting primary mission essential functions, several source of technical drivers and considerations influence contingency planning details. These contingency planning factors also influence system development life cycle activities including design and implementation decisions about the information system, the environment in which it is deployed, and interconnections established to other systems inside and outside the agency.

System Development and Engineering

Agencies have many sources of guidance on system development life cycle methodologies and associated processes and standards, many of which explicitly address contingency planning in the context of secure system engineering or security requirements associated with life cycle processes, inputs, and outputs. Special Publication 800-64 addresses security considerations across SDLC phases commonly found in most methodologies: initiation, development or acquisition, implementation and assessment, operations and maintenance, and disposal [33]. This guidance identifies elements of SDLC activities that influence contingency planning, disaster recovery, continuity of operations, and related functions, as well as the contribution contingency planning processes and artifacts such as the business impact analysis make to the SDLC. NIST also offers a set of engineering principles for securing information technology systems [58], building on previously published security principles and practices directed at organization-level security programs [59]. These SDLC-centric perspectives emphasize the importance of contingency planning to support agency continuity of operations and integrate planning activities and expectations into broader information technology processes and activities. Contingency planning represents one of the 33 engineering principles for IT security enumerated in Special Publication 800-27: "Develop and exercise contingency or disaster recovery procedures to ensure appropriate availability" [60]. The description of this principle notes the supporting role contingency planning serves in initiation, development, and implementation phases, and considers contingency planning key to successful execution of operations and maintenance. Special Publication 800-34 incorporates relevant security principles addressing systems engineering and development, but the perspectives and recommendations in other guidance may be useful to system owners driven by agency or government SDLC methodologies.

System Interconnections

When agencies establish interconnections between their information systems and other systems, they introduce dependencies in one or both directions that are likely to be affected by outages to either interconnected system. Guidance to federal agencies on planning, establishing, and maintaining system interconnections recommends coordination of contingency planning activities between the individuals and organizations responsible for each system [61]. Contingency plans for systems with established interconnections should describe the nature and purpose of each interconnection and include procedures for restoring, recovering, or replacing system interconnections in the event that the connected system becomes unavailable. The ISCP should address interconnected system owners or other personnel within the plan's notification procedures and specify any roles and responsibilities assigned to personnel in either organization to support contingency operations. System interconnections should be reflected with all other system components in analysis and decisions about preventive controls, alternate processing capabilities, recovery requirements, and redundant operations. Contingency plan training, testing, and exercises should also be coordinated between teams supporting interconnected systems [62].

Technical Contingency Planning Considerations

Agencies use technical solutions to implement the contingency planning strategies, controls, and procedures documented in the ISCP. Many factors influence the choice of appropriate contingency solutions, including the type of information system and its operational environment as well as its security categorization, recovery criticality, and security requirements. Special Publication 800-34 addresses common considerations applicable to all systems as well as platform-specific considerations for client/server systems, telecommunications systems, and mainframe systems. In light of the federal "cloud first" policy issued in late 2010 requiring agencies to adopt cloud computing platforms for their IT solutions whenever feasible [63], system owners should also incorporate contingency planning considerations for cloud computing platforms. Common considerations for all information systems include use of the business impact analysis to help determine effective technical solutions; maintenance of system data and software security and integrity by performing regular backups and protecting backup media; protection of system resources through the implementation of physical and environmental controls; adherence to required contingency planning controls and control enhancements; identification and selection of alternate storage and processing facilities; and use of redundancy and failover processes to enable high availability [64]. System owners applying the same set of common considerations will still select different contingency planning solutions for their information systems, reflecting each system's unique set of mission and business needs and functional, technical, and security requirements. By ensuring, however, that contingency planning for all systems addresses the same set of considerations and decision criteria, agencies can improve the consistency of technical solution selection processes and facilitate the selection of the right solutions for each system.

Client/Server Systems

Client/server systems often store data and perform processing on both the server and the client, meaning contingency planning for this type of system needs to address potential disruptions to the server, clients, and the connectivity between clients and server components of the system. Contingency strategies for client/server systems that system owners should consider include: [65]

- Using results of the business impact analysis to determine contingency requirements for mitigating possible impacts.
- Storing backups for all data and both client and server software components offsite or at an alternate site.
- Standardizing hardware, software, and peripherals to facilitate recovery of multiple clients following and outage.
- Documenting system configuration information and vendor contact information for hardware, software, and other system components to assist in system recovery or procurement of replacement components.
- Aligning contingency solutions with security policies and system security controls, including coordinating security provisions between primary and alternate sites.
- Minimizing the amount of data stored on client computers such as user workstations by recommending or requiring data storage on the server or centralized storage technologies.
- Automating system and data backups for server and client computers and configuring computers in a manner that facilitates centralized backup, such as

by ensuring that computers remain powered up overnight or during scheduled backup windows.

- Coordinating contingency solutions with cyber incident response procedures to limit the impact to the system from security incidents and ensure that no compromise of data confidentiality or integrity occurs during contingent operations.

Key decision points for selecting client/server contingency solutions include the choice of backup procedures, media, and hardware and software and of encryption technologies and cryptographic modules to provide sufficiently strong protection for removable media as well as data stored on client and server computers.

Telecommunications Systems

Telecommunications systems include wired and wireless local and wide area networks and hardware and software providing the capabilities for systems to communicate with each other or with users. The set of telecommunications systems supporting most federal government agencies includes network infrastructure and other technical solution components owned by commercial telecommunications service providers and managed on behalf of the government. Dependencies on telecommunications systems vendors raise special contingency planning issues for system owners that the ISCP should address, such as whether the same or a separate vendor will be responsible for providing alternate telecommunications services if the primary service becomes unavailable. Contingency planning strategies for telecommunications systems include: [66]

- Using results of the business impact analysis to determine contingency requirements for maintaining or restoring telecommunications services.
- Documenting telecommunications infrastructure and services with physical and logical network or architectural diagrams.
- Documenting system configuration information, names and contact information of telecommunications providers, and service level agreements for contingency operations.
- Aligning contingency solutions to network security policies and security controls to provide adequate safeguards against network outages or other disruptions.

Contingency planning for telecommunications systems should seek to avoid single points of failure by implementing redundant communication linkages, network devices, and even service providers. In addition to network and provider redundancy, capabilities provided by telecommunications systems for normal operations may provide contingency solutions when primary processing sites or supporting infrastructure components are unavailable. Such capabilities include remote access services for system administrators and other authorized personnel and wireless networking technology as an alternative or backup communication mechanism during a disruption affecting the LAN or other wired network components.

Mainframe Systems

Mainframe systems perform processing and data storage operations in a single centralized location. In contrast to client/server systems, client workstations accessing mainframe systems often have little or no processing capabilities of their own, putting the emphasis for contingency planning almost entirely on the mainframe itself as the primary component of the system. Even where conventional workstations offer access to mainframes, the system's processing all takes place on the mainframe platform. Mainframe systems tend to be larger and more expensive than other types of servers, limiting the number of alternative processing sites that may be able to accommodate a mainframe system recovery. Contingency planning strategies for mainframe systems include: [67]

- Using results from the business impact analysis to assess the criticality of the mainframe system and the mission functions and business processes it supports, particularly where redundant processing capabilities are recommended.
- Storing backup media offsite, such as at alternate storage or processing site.
- Documenting system configurations and vendors already under contingency agreement or otherwise able to provide essential hardware and software necessary to recovery the mainframe system.
- Aligning contingency planning controls with organizational security policy and mainframe system security requirements, potentially including duplication of system interfaces and telecommunications infrastructure.

Contingency solutions for mainframe systems emphasize redundant data storage and processing capabilities where feasible. Mainframe systems rely on centralized technical architecture and purpose-specific configuration, increasing the difficulty of system restoration from newly provisioned hardware and software. One possible mainframe contingency solution is to establish a replacement system at a warm or hot alternate processing site capable of providing primary system failover. The significant acquisition and maintenance costs associated with mainframes may constrain the ability of a single agency to provide redundant system capabilities, although some IT management and outsourcing vendors do offer mainframe processing, support, and recovery services.

Cloud Computing

Cloud computing provides organizations access to infrastructure, platform, and application services running in centralized or distributed environments that allow system owners to use operating capacity, processing, and data storage offered by the cloud provider, at a cost determined by the amount of resources the system actually uses or requires. Because cloud services are often managed outside an agency's own IT infrastructure, contingency planning for cloud computing relies on the capabilities, procedures, and solutions offered by the cloud provider and on outside personnel to perform contingency operations and activities. Service level agreements established with cloud computing providers typically specify availability targets and other performance measures, but the potential for outages affecting cloud computing services certainly exists. Agencies and their system owners need to assess the service resilience and contingency capabilities of their service providers and determine whether those capabilities are sufficient to meet contingency requirements for the information system. Considerations relevant to cloud computing services include the anticipated frequency and duration of outages and expected recovery times and the alternate processing capabilities or other contingency solutions are available to cloud computing subscribers in the event of prolonged outages [68]. Current guidelines on security for public cloud computing suggest that agencies cannot rely solely on cloud providers to ensure availability levels sufficient to support mission essential functions. Where cloud computing is used, the ISCP should define contingency strategies for prolonged and permanent system disruptions that support continuity of operations objectives, including the possibility of restoring essential functions at an alternate external location or using internal infrastructure or contingency resources [69].

RELEVANT SOURCE MATERIAL

Several NIST Special Publications, OMB requirements, and other federal directives provide guidance, recommendations, and instructions relevant to contingency planning for federal information systems. Applicable sources of information include:

- Special Publication 800-34 Revision 1, *Contingency Planning Guide for Federal Information Systems* [1].
- Special Publication 800-53 Revision 3, *Recommended Security Controls for Federal Information Systems and Organizations* [2].
- Special Publication 800-84, Guide to Test, *Training, and Exercise Programs for IT Plans and Capabilities* [44].
- Special Publication 800-47, *Security Guide for Interconnecting Information Technology Systems* [61].
- Special Publication 800-64, Revision 2, *Security Considerations in the System Development Life Cycle* [33].

These and other NIST Special Publications are available from the NIST Computer Security Division website, at http://csrc.nist.gov/publications/PubsSPs.html.

Federal agency requirements for contingency planning in support of continuity of operations (COOP) efforts are contained in source material including:

- Homeland Security Presidential Directive 20 (HSPD-20): *National Continuity Policy* [18].
- Federal Continuity Directive 1 (FCD 1): *Federal Executive Branch National Continuity Program and Requirements* [20].
- Federal Continuity Directive 2 (FCD 2): *Federal Executive Branch Mission Essential Function and Primary Mission Essential Function Identification and Submission Process* [70].
- The Homeland Security Council's *National Continuity Policy Implementation Plan* [19].

SUMMARY

Contingency planning is a core activity in the effective implementation and operation of federal information systems, and the information system contingency plan is an essential artifact in the system authorization package. This chapter described the core principles of contingency planning and related concepts falling under continuity of operations in government agencies, particularly including the close relationship between business continuity, disaster recovery, and incident response and system-level considerations for developing contingency plans. This chapter emphasized the process of developing the information system contingency plan and explained its role in the broader contingency planning process. It addresses key factors system owners need to consider to determine the appropriate contingent operational requirements for their systems, and the corresponding implication for the contingency planning family of security controls selected for implementation.

REFERENCES

[1] Swanson M, Bowen P, Philips A, Gallup D, Lynes D. Contingency planning guide for federal information systems. Gaithersburg, MD: National Institute of Standards and Technology, Computer Security Division; May 2010. Special Publication 800-34 revision 1.

[2] Recommended security controls for federal information systems and organizations. Gaithersburg, MD: National Institute of Standards and Technology, Computer Security Division; August 2009. Special Publication 800-53 revision 3.

[3] Guide for applying the risk management framework to federal information systems. Gaithersburg, MD: National Institute of Standards and Technology, Computer Security Division; February 2010. Special Publication 800-37 revision 1.

[4] Swanson M, Bowen P, Philips A, Gallup D, Lynes D. Contingency planning guide for federal information systems. Gaithersburg, MD: National Institute of Standards and Technology, Computer Security Division; May 2010. Special Publication 800-34 revision 1 p. 1.

[5] Appendix III, Security of federal automated information resources. Washington (DC): Office of Management and Budget; November 2000. Circular No. A-130, Revised [Transmittal, Memorandum No. 4].

[6] Federal Information Security Management Act of 2002, §303, Pub. L. No. 107–347, 116 Stat. 2957: December 17, 2002.

[7] Federal executive branch national continuity program and requirements. Washington, DC: Department of Homeland Security, Federal Emergency Management Agency; February 2008. Federal Continuity Directive 1. p. 20.

[8] Recommended security controls for federal information systems and organizations. Gaithersburg, MD: National Institute of Standards and Technology, Computer Security Division; August 2009. Special Publication 800-53 revision 3. p. D-3-D-4.

[9] Recommended security controls for federal information systems and organizations. Gaithersburg, MD: National Institute of Standards and Technology, Computer Security Division; August 2009. Special Publication 800-53 revision 3. Appendix F.

[10] Recommended security controls for federal information systems and organizations. Gaithersburg, MD: National Institute of Standards and Technology, Computer Security Division; August 2009. Special Publication 800-53 revision 3. p. F-47.

[11] Recommended security controls for federal information systems and organizations. Gaithersburg, MD: National Institute of Standards and Technology, Computer Security Division; August 2009. Special Publication 800-53 revision 3. p. F-48.

[12] Recommended security controls for federal information systems and organizations. Gaithersburg, MD: National Institute of Standards and Technology, Computer Security Division; August 2009. Special Publication 800-53 revision 3. p. F-49.

[13] Recommended security controls for federal information systems and organizations. Gaithersburg, MD: National Institute of Standards and Technology, Computer Security Division; August 2009 . Special Publication 800-53 revision 3. p. F-50.

[14] Swanson M, Bowen P, Philips A, Gallup D, Lynes D. Contingency planning guide for federal information systems. Gaithersburg, MD: National Institute of Standards and Technology, Computer Security Division; May 2010. Special Publication 800-34 revision 1. p. 47.

[15] Recommended security controls for federal information systems and organizations. Gaithersburg, MD: National Institute of Standards and Technology, Computer Security Division; August 2009. Special Publication 800–53 revision 3. p. F-50.

[16] Recommended security controls for federal information systems and organizations. Gaithersburg, MD: National Institute of Standards and Technology, Computer Security Division; August 2009. Special Publication 800–53 revision 3. p. F-51.

[17] Recommended security controls for federal information systems and organizations. Gaithersburg, MD: National Institute of Standards and Technology, Computer Security Division; August 2009. Special Publication 800–53 revision 3. p. F-52.

[18] National continuity policy. Washington, DC: Department of Homeland Security; May 2007; Homeland Security Presidential Directive 20.

[19] National continuity policy implementation plan. Washington, DC: Homeland Security Council; August 2007.

[20] Federal executive branch national continuity program and requirements. Washington, DC: Department of Homeland Security, Federal Emergency Management Agency; February2008. Federal Continuity Directive 1.

[21] National continuity policy implementation plan. Washington, DC: Homeland Security Council; August 2007. p. 5–6.

[22] National continuity policy implementation plan. Washington, DC: Homeland Security Council; August 2007. p. 9.

[23] Federal executive branch national continuity program and requirements. Washington, DC: Department of Homeland Security, Federal Emergency Management Agency; February 2008. Federal Continuity Directive 1. p. 7.

[24] National continuity policy implementation plan. Washington, DC: Homeland Security Council; August 2007. p. 18–20.

[25] National response framework. Washington, DC: Department of Homeland, Security; January 2008.

[26] Critical infrastructure identification, prioritization, and protection. Washington, DC: Department of Homeland Security; December 2003. Homeland Security Presidential Directive 7.

[27] National continuity policy implementation plan. Washington, DC: Homeland Security Council; August 2007. Appendix B. p. 56.

[28] Swanson M, Bowen P, Philips A, Gallup D, Lynes D. Contingency planning guide for federal information systems. Gaithersburg, MD: National Institute of Standards and Technology, Computer Security Division; May 2010. Special Publication 800-34 revision 1. p. 7.

[29] Swanson M, Bowen P, Philips A, Gallup D, Lynes D. Contingency planning guide for federal information systems. Gaithersburg, MD: National Institute of Standards and Technology, Computer Security Division; May 2010. Special Publication 800-34 revision 1. p. 10.

[30] Recommended security controls for federal information systems and organizations. Gaithersburg, MD: National Institute of Standards and Technology, Computer Security Division; August 2009. Special Publication 800–53 revision 3. p. F-64.

[31] Scarfone K, Grance T, Masone K. Computer security incident handling guide. Gaithersburg, MD: National Institute of Standards and Technology, Computer Security Division; March 2008. Special Publication 800–61 revision 1.

[32] National response plan cyber incident annex. Washington, DC: Department of Homeland, Security; December 2004.

[33] Kissel R, Stine K, Scholl M, Rossman H, Fahlsing J, Gulick J. Security considerations in the system development life cycle. Gaithersburg, MD: National Institute of Standards and Technology, Computer Security Division; October 2008. Special Publication 800-64 revision 2.

[34] Swanson M, Bowen P, Philips A, Gallup D, Lynes D. Contingency planning guide for federal information systems. Gaithersburg, MD: National Institute of Standards and Technology, Computer Security Division; May 2010. Special Publication 800-34 revision 1. p. 13.

[35] Swanson M, Bowen P, Philips A, Gallup D, Lynes D. Contingency planning guide for federal information systems. Gaithersburg, MD: National Institute of Standards and Technology, Computer Security Division; May 2010. Special Publication 800-34 revision 1. p. 14.

[36] Standards for security categorization of federal information and information systems. Gaithersburg, MD: National Institute of Standards and Technology, Computer Security Division; December 2003. Federal Information Processing Standards Publication 199.

[37] Swanson M, Bowen P, Philips A, Gallup D, Lynes D. Contingency planning guide for federal information systems. Gaithersburg, MD: National Institute of Standards and Technology, Computer Security Division; May 2010.. Special Publication 800-34 revision 1. p. 15–6.

[38] Federal executive branch mission essential function and primary mission essential function identification and submission process. Washington, DC: Department of Homeland Security, Federal Emergency Management Agency; February 2008. Federal Continuity Directive 2. Attachment A.

[39] Swanson M, Bowen P, Philips A, Gallup D, Lynes D. Contingency planning guide for federal information systems. Gaithersburg, MD: National Institute of Standards and Technology, Computer Security Division; May 2010. Special Publication 800-34 revision 1. Appendix B.

[40] Swanson M, Bowen P, Philips A, Gallup D, Lynes D. Contingency planning guide for federal information systems. Gaithersburg, MD: National Institute of Standards and Technology, Computer Security Division; May 2010. Special Publication 800-34 revision 1. p. 19.

[41] Guide for conducting risk assessments. Gaithersburg, MD: National Institute of Standards and Technology, Computer Security Division; September 2011. Special Publication 800–30 revision 1, initial public draft.

[42] Swanson M, Bowen P, Philips A, Gallup D, Lynes D. Contingency planning guide for federal information systems. Gaithersburg, MD: National Institute of Standards and Technology, Computer Security Division; May 2010. Special Publication 800-34 revision 1. p. 20–5.

[43] Swanson M, Bowen P, Philips A, Gallup D, Lynes D. Contingency planning guide for federal information systems. Gaithersburg, MD: National Institute of Standards and Technology, Computer Security Division; May 2010. Special Publication 800-34 revision 1. p. 34.

[44] Grance T, Nolan T, Burke K, Dudley R, White G, Good T. Guide to test, training, and exercise programs for IT plans and capabilities. Gaithersburg, MD: National Institute of Standards and Technology, Computer Security Division; September 2006. Special, Publication 800–84.

[45] Recommended security controls for federal information systems and organizations. Gaithersburg, MD: National Institute of Standards and Technology, Computer Security Division; August 2009. Special Publication 800–53 revision 3. p. F-49.

[46] Swanson M, Bowen P, Philips A, Gallup D, Lynes D. Contingency planning guide for federal information systems. Gaithersburg, MD: National Institute of Standards and Technology, Computer Security Division; May 2010. Special Publication 800-34 revision 1. p. 28.

[47] Swanson M, Bowen P, Philips A, Gallup D, Lynes D. Contingency planning guide for federal information systems. Gaithersburg, MD: National Institute of Standards and Technology, Computer Security Division; May 2010. Special Publication 800-34 revision 1. p. 27.

[48] Swanson M, Bowen P, Philips A, Gallup D, Lynes D. Contingency planning guide for federal information systems. Gaithersburg, MD: National Institute of Standards and Technology, Computer Security Division; May 2010. Special Publication 800-34 revision 1.p. 31–2.

[49] Swanson M, Bowen P, Philips A, Gallup D, Lynes D. Contingency planning guide for federal information systems. Gaithersburg, MD: National Institute of Standards and Technology, Computer Security Division; May 2010. Special Publication 800-34 revision 1. Appendix A.

[50] Swanson M, Bowen P, Philips A, Gallup D, Lynes D. Contingency planning guide for federal information systems. Gaithersburg, MD: National Institute of Standards and Technology, Computer Security Division; May 2010. Special Publication 800-34 revision 1. p. 35.

[51] Swanson M, Bowen P, Philips A, Gallup D, Lynes D. Contingency planning guide for federal information systems. Gaithersburg, MD: National Institute of Standards and Technology, Computer Security Division; May 2010. Special Publication 800-34 revision 1. p. 36.

[52] Swanson M, Bowen P, Philips A, Gallup D, Lynes D. Contingency planning guide for federal information systems. Gaithersburg, MD: National Institute of Standards and Technology, Computer Security Division; May 2010. Special Publication 800-34 revision 1. p. 38.

[53] Swanson M, Bowen P, Philips A, Gallup D, Lynes D. Contingency planning guide for federal information systems. Gaithersburg, MD: National Institute of Standards

and Technology, Computer Security Division; May 2010. Special Publication 800-34 revision 1. p. 39.

[54] Swanson M, Bowen P, Philips A, Gallup D, Lynes D. Contingency planning guide for federal information systems. Gaithersburg, MD: National Institute of Standards and Technology, Computer Security Division; May 2010. Special Publication 800-34 revision 1. p. 40.

[55] Swanson M, Bowen P, Philips A, Gallup D, Lynes D. Contingency planning guide for federal information systems. Gaithersburg, MD: National Institute of Standards and Technology, Computer Security Division; May 2010. Special Publication 800-34 revision 1. p. 41.

[56] See contingency planning control enhancements CP-2(5), CP-2(6), CP-7(4), and CP-10(5) in Recommended security controls for federal information systems and organizations. Gaithersburg, MD: National Institute of Standards and Technology, Computer Security Division; August 2009. Special Publication 800–53 revision 3. p. F-48-F-52.

[57] Swanson M, Bowen P, Philips A, Gallup D, Lynes D. Contingency planning guide for federal information systems. Gaithersburg, MD: National Institute of Standards and Technology, Computer Security Division; May 2010. Special Publication 800-34 revision 1. p. 42.

[58] Stoneburner G, Hayden C, Feringa A. Engineering principles for information technology security. Gaithersburg, MD: National Institute of Standards and Technology, Computer Security Division; June 2004. Special Publication 800–27 revision A.

[59] Swanson M, Guttman B. Generally accepted principles and practices for securing information technology systems. Gaithersburg, MD: National Institute of Standards and Technology, Computer Security Division; September 1996. Special, Publication 800–14.

[60] Stoneburner G, Hayden C, Feringa A. Engineering principles for information technology security. Gaithersburg, MD: National Institute of Standards and Technology, Computer Security Division; June 2004. Special Publication 800–27 revision A. p. 16.

[61] Grance T, Hash J, Peck S, Smith J, Korow-Diks K. Security guide for interconnecting information technology systems. Gaithersburg, MD: National Institute of Standards and Technology, Computer Security Division; August 2002. Special, Publication 800–47.

[62] Grance T, Hash J, Peck S, Smith J, Korow-Diks K. Security guide for interconnecting information technology systems. Gaithersburg, MD: National Institute of Standards and Technology, Computer Security Division; August 2002. Special, Publication 800–47. p. 3–4.

[63] Kundra V. 25 point implementation plan to reform federal information technology management. Washington, DC: Office of Management and Budget; 2010.

[64] Swanson M, Bowen P, Philips A, Gallup D, Lynes D. Contingency planning guide for federal information systems. Gaithersburg, MD: National Institute of Standards and Technology, Computer Security Division; May 2010. Special Publication 800-34 revision 1. p. 43.

[65] Swanson M, Bowen P, Philips A, Gallup D, Lynes D. Contingency planning guide for federal information systems. Gaithersburg, MD: National Institute of Standards and Technology, Computer Security Division; May 2010. Special Publication 800-34 revision 1. p. 49–50.

[66] Swanson M, Bowen P, Philips A, Gallup D, Lynes D. Contingency planning guide for federal information systems. Gaithersburg, MD: National Institute of Standards

and Technology, Computer Security Division; May 2010. Special Publication 800-34 revision 1. p. 53–4.

[67] Swanson M, Bowen P, Philips A, Gallup D, Lynes D. Contingency planning guide for federal information systems. Gaithersburg, MD: National Institute of Standards and Technology, Computer Security Division; May 2010. Special Publication 800-34 revision 1. p. 56.

[68] Badger L, Grance T, Patt-Corner R, Voas J. Cloud computing synopsis and recommendations. Gaithersburg, MD: National Institute of Standards and Technology, Computer Security Division; May 2011. Draft Special Publication 800-146. p. 8-3.

[69] Jansen W, Grance T. Guidelines on security and privacy in public cloud computing. Gaithersburg, MD: National Institute of Standards and Technology, Computer Security Division; December 2011. Special, Publication 800–144. p. 32.

[70] Federal executive branch mission essential function and primary mission essential function identification and submission process. Washington, DC: Department of Homeland Security, Federal Emergency Management Agency; February 2008. Federal Continuity Directive 2.

Privacy

INFORMATION IN THIS CHAPTER:

- Privacy Requirements for Federal Agencies under FISMA and the E-Government Act
- Federal Agency Requirements Under the Privacy Act
- Privacy Impact Assessments
- Protecting Personally Identifiable Information (PII)
- Other Legal and Regulatory Sources of Privacy Requirements

Information systems store and process many types of data. In many systems, some of that data includes personal details about individuals, the collection, use, and disclosure of which is protected by a variety of laws and regulations. In government contexts the official term for this sort of data is *personally identifiable information* [1], and most of the legal and regulatory requirements currently in effect are intended to protect the privacy of or otherwise safeguard personally identifiable information (PII). Such information includes names, social security numbers or other unique identification numbers, contact information, demographics, photographs, biometric data, or other descriptive characteristics that can be linked to or used to identify an individual. The field of information privacy focuses on how personal information is handled, including the implementation of appropriate safeguards against misuse, loss, theft, or unauthorized disclosure of that information. Information security and information privacy are closely interrelated, and often mentioned together, but they are quite distinct subjects. Information security controls are needed to safeguard data in a way that protects and maintains privacy, but effective security controls do not necessarily result in effective privacy protections. In the context of federal agency operations, a different emphasis is placed on information privacy than on information security. Security is about managing risk. Intrusions upon or violations of privacy are one source of risk, with impacts that range from negative publicity, to civil or criminal penalties, to actual harm caused to individuals whose privacy is compromised, to an erosion of trust between government agencies and the citizens they serve. Security controls implemented to protect privacy should be selected in a risk-based manner just as any other controls. Privacy protection in federal agencies focuses more on complying with legal and regulatory requirements and securing personal information against misuse or unauthorized disclosure and less about managing the risk of compromising the privacy information of individuals.

The Federal Information Security Management Act (FISMA) is primarily focused on information security, not on privacy, and FISMA does not impose privacy requirements on federal agencies [2]. There were, however, privacy protection requirements stipulated in the E-Government Act of 2002 [3] (of which FISMA was enacted as Title III) that are commonly addressed together with the information security requirements under FISMA, especially when it comes to FISMA reporting to the Office of Management and Budget (OMB) by federal agencies [4]. Federal agencies are also subject to the provisions of the Privacy Act of 1974 [5], which constrains the way in which agencies collect, manage, and disclose information about individuals, and to numerous other legal requirements and regulatory guidance on privacy. This chapter summarizes the privacy requirements with which agencies must comply, and describes specific practices that must be followed when implementing privacy protections for information contained in federal information systems. It also explains the relationship between information privacy and information security, highlighting dependencies and identifying activities within the Risk Management Framework where privacy concerns are particularly relevant.

PRIVACY REQUIREMENTS FOR FEDERAL AGENCIES UNDER FISMA AND THE E-GOVERNMENT ACT

In the four years prior to the passage of the E-Government Act of 2002, federal government attention to privacy focused on agency web sites, which were increasingly used for both information dissemination and information collection. The E-Government Act served to codify rules issued as executive memoranda to federal agencies that emphasized compliance with various provisions in the Privacy Act, giving particular attention to reviewing agency systems of records [6], and established requirements for creating and posting privacy policies on federal web sites [7].

At the executive level, responsibility for information privacy protections in federal government agencies rests with chief information officers [8], and with designated senior agency officials for privacy [9] (in some agencies the CIO also serves as the senior agency official for privacy). OMB first directed agencies to designate a senior official for privacy policy in 1999 [6], and beginning in 2005 annual FISMA reporting requirements were expanded to include a section with a set of questions to be answered by the senior agency official for privacy [9]. These questions cover a variety of privacy practices and activities that agencies are obligated to conduct, making annual FISMA reporting on privacy a sort of consolidated overview of agency compliance with requirements that aren't actually specified in FISMA. For practical purposes, privacy reporting under FISMA comprises the privacy provisions contained in Section 208 of the E-Government Act of 2002 [3] and the privacy practices addressed in instructions to agencies for annual FISMA reporting [10]. This section addresses those privacy provisions and required activities.

> **NOTE**
>
> By adding privacy reporting requirements to information security program reporting, OMB placed some agency privacy practices under the same governance and oversight structure used for FISMA. This created an association between FISMA and privacy that is not found in the text of the legislation, but that in practice makes a great deal of sense in most agencies, given the close relationship between privacy and security practices and their shared executive authority. The majority of the annual FISMA reporting requirements about privacy [10] come not from FISMA but from the E-Government Act, the Privacy Act, or guidance issued to agencies by OMB in the form of circulars or memoranda.

Privacy Provisions in the E-Government Act of 2002

Section 208 of the E-Government Act stipulates two key privacy provisions for federal executive agencies: the requirement for agencies to conduct privacy impact assessments (PIAs) "before developing or procuring information technology that collects, maintains, or disseminates information that is in an identifiable form" [11],

> **TIP**
>
> Federal agencies are required both to make their privacy impact assessments publicly available, and to report to OMB the uniform resource locator (URL) of the web page where links to PIAs are listed [10]. Many agencies also include prominent links to privacy information on other parts of their web sites, so locating PIA documents is often a straightforward process. The privacy impact assessment URLs for the 15 cabinet-level agencies are listed here:
>
> * Department of Agriculture: http://www.usda.gov/wps/portal/usda/usdahome?navid=PRIVACY_POLICY_ES.
> * Department of Commerce: http://ocio.os.doc.gov/ITPolicyandPrograms/IT_Privacy/dev01_003746.
> * Department of Defense: http://dodcio.defense.gov/Home/Issuances/DoDCIOPrivacyImpactAssessmentsPIAs.aspx.
> * Department of Education: http://www2.ed.gov/notices/pia/index.html.
> * Department of Energy: http://energy.gov/cio/office-chief-information-officer/services/guidance/privacy/impact-assessments.
> * Department of Health and Human Services: http://www.hhs.gov/pia/.
> * Department of Homeland Security: http://www.dhs.gov/files/publications/editorial_0511.shtm.
> * Department of Housing and Urban Development: http://www.hud.gov/offices/cio/privacy/pia/pia.cfm.
> * Department of the Interior: http://www.doi.gov/ocio/privacy/pia.htm.
> * Department of Justice: http://www.justice.gov/opcl/pia.htm.
> * Department of Labor: http://www.dol.gov/cio/programs/pia/mainpia.htm.
> * Department of State: http://www.state.gov/m/a/ips/c24223.htm.
> * Department of Transportation: http://www.dot.gov/pia.html.
> * Department of the Treasury: http://www.treasury.gov/SitePolicies/Pages/pia.aspx.
> * Department of Veterans Affairs: http://www.privacy.va.gov/Privacy_Impact_Assessment.asp.

and to implement privacy protections on federal agency web sites [12]. More specifically, agencies must identify systems that contain personally identifiable information, perform privacy impact assessments on those systems, and, depending on the results of those assessments, publish information describing the systems, the types of personally identifiable information they hold, and the specific purposes for which the agency collects and intends to use the information [13]. Agencies are also required to make their privacy impact assessments publicly available, whether or not the assessment results for a given system obligate the agency to provide additional public notice about the system [13]. Separate from performing privacy impact assessments, agencies are required to post privacy policies on all websites used by the public, with policy details published in both human-readable and machine-readable formats [13].

The procedures for conducting privacy impact assessments are described in detail later in this chapter. Before focusing on the PIA process system owners—working in collaboration with information owners, information security officers, and privacy officers—must first determine whether an assessment is needed. The process for making this determination is illustrated in Figure 16.1. The primary determining factor

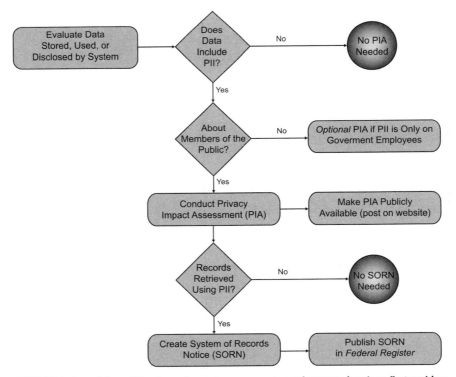

FIGURE 16.1 Complying with privacy impact assessment requirements involves first making a determination whether a PIA is required and, if so, conducting the assessment and publishing the results and associated notices [13]

is the nature of the data collected or used by the system—§208 of the E-Government Act requires a PIA if that data includes "information in identifiable form," which the Act defines as "any representation of information that permits the identity of an individual to whom the information applies to be reasonably inferred by either direct or indirect means" [14]. The term "information in identifiable form" has been superseded by "personally identifiable information," which as defined by OMB "refers to information which can be used to distinguish or trace an individual's identity, such as their name, social security number, biometric records, etc. alone, or when combined with other personal or identifying information which is linked or linkable to a specific individual" [1]. Significantly, these definitions obligate agencies to evaluate the data contained in their information systems not only for the presence of obviously personal details such as unique identifiers, but also for combinations of data elements or potential usage patterns that would enable the identification of individuals through inference. Due to the difficulty in performing this sort of data analysis on many modern systems, some agencies may choose to require privacy impact assessments for all systems, unless system owners can credibly assert that no identification of individuals is possible based on the data in the system. Although the provisions of the E-Government Act apply to all US citizens and legally resident aliens, federal agencies are not required to perform privacy impact assessments for systems containing personally identifiable information if that PII is only about government employees or contractors [13,15].

Privacy Protections on Agency Web Sites

The second general requirement for federal agencies under §208 of the E-Government Act is to develop and publish privacy notices—formally termed "privacy policies"—on agency web sites used by the public [12]. These policies are intended to explain the data collection and information handling practices of the agency, particularly with respect to information covered by the Privacy Act. Agencies are also required to refer to their notices of information handling practices as "privacy policies" and to label them clearly and make them easy to find for visitors to agency web sites [7]. The visible result on many federal agency web sites is a "Privacy Policy" link accessible from the home page and most, if not all, web pages on the site. Minimum contents of agency privacy policies are specified in §208 of the E-Government Act, derived from provisions in the Privacy Act, and include the following elements [16]:

i. what information is to be collected;
ii. why the information is being collected;
iii. the intended use of the agency of the information;
iv. with whom the information will be shared;
v. what notice or opportunities for consent would be provided to individuals regarding what information is collected and how that information is shared;
vi. how the information will be secured; and
vii. the rights of the individual under the Privacy Act, and other laws relevant to the protection of the privacy of an individual.

These required elements were updated in 2010 to reflect the increasing use by federal agencies of third-party web sites and applications, the privacy practices of which typically fall outside the control of the agencies that use them. In addition to providing links to the privacy policies of third parties, agencies were instructed to update their privacy policies to explain their use of third-party sites and applications, including addressing the following items [17]:

i. the specific purpose of the agency's use of the third-party websites or applications;
ii. how the agency will use PII that becomes available through the use of the third-party websites or applications;
iii. who at the agency will have access to PII;
iv. with whom PII will be shared outside the agency;
v. whether and how the agency will maintain PII, and for how long;
vi. how the agency will secure PII that it uses or maintains; and
vii. what other privacy risks exist and how the agency will mitigate those risks.

Guidance to federal agencies on privacy policies offered by OMB after the passage of the E-Government Act [13] referenced a set of instructions issued four years earlier that included sample language for agencies to use when developing their privacy policies [18]. The use of consistent structure and contents for agency privacy policies not only helps members of the public to locate and understand policy information that may be important to them, but also facilitates the representation of privacy policies in machine-readable formats. Although the law does not stipulate a particular format to use, agencies must publish a machine-readable version of their privacy policies. Guidance to agencies on reporting about machine-readability of privacy policies cites as an example the Platform for Privacy Preferences Project (P3P) developed by the World Wide Web consortium [19] and supported by Microsoft's Internet Explorer, Mozilla's Firefox, and other web browsers. In contrast to privacy impact assessments and system authorization activities required for agency information systems, the rules on privacy policies apply to agencies overall. This means that individual system owners ordinarily do not create privacy policies, but for systems with public-facing interfaces, system owners should be aware of the contents of their agency's privacy policies and ensure that their systems conform to the data handling practices declared in those policies.

Reporting on Privacy Practices

In the guidance to agencies on implementing the E-Government Act requirements on privacy impact assessments and federal web site privacy policies, OMB established annual reporting on agency compliance with these privacy provisions [13]. The reporting rules apply to "all agencies that use information technology systems and conduct electronic information collection activities" and required the following information to be submitted [13]:

- A listing of information technology systems for which PIAs were conducted, with information about when and how each PIA was made publicly available.
- Whether the agency uses persistent tracking technology such as cookies, which were banned for federal web sites beginning in 2000 [20] until a change of administration policy in 2010 [21]. Agencies no longer need to provide detailed justifications for the use of such tracking technology, but they are required to give clear notice of any use and give members of the public the opportunity to opt out of any collection of information using web measurement and customization technologies [21].
- Progress towards and achievement of agency goals for machine-readability of privacy policies, including compatibility with relevant privacy protection technology.
- Contact information for the designated individual or individuals serving as the agency's primary point of contact for web site and related information technology matters, and the senior agency official for privacy or other individual with responsibility for agency privacy policies.

Annual compliance reporting for the privacy provisions in the E-Government Act was combined with FISMA reporting requirements beginning in 2005 [9], and senior agency officials for privacy are currently instructed to submit documentation on agency privacy practices via OMB's CyberScope electronic reporting tool as part of updated FISMA reporting instructions [22].

Privacy and Minimum Security Controls

The minimum security control baselines defined in Special Publication 800-53 require some controls related to privacy, such as need to perform a privacy impact assessment (PL-5) and various control enhancements specifying the use of encryption to safeguard confidentiality of data in transit (SC-9) or at rest (SC-28) [23]. With the release of the draft of Special Publication Revision 4, NIST added a separate set of 26 privacy controls arranged into eight control families [24]:

- *Authority and Purpose (AP):*
  - AP-1 Authority to Collect.
  - AP-2 Purpose Specification.

- *Accountability, Audit, and Risk Management (AR):*
  - AR-1 Governance and Privacy Program.
  - AR-2 Privacy Impact and Risk Assessment.
  - AR-3 Privacy Requirements for Contractors and Service Providers.
  - AR-4 Privacy Monitoring and Auditing.
  - AR-5 Privacy Awareness and Training.
  - AR-6 Privacy Reporting.
  - AR-7 Privacy-Enhanced System Design and Development.
  - AR-8 Accounting of Disclosures.

- *Data Quality and Integrity (DI):*
  - DI-1 Data Quality.
  - DI-2 Data Integrity and Data Integrity Board.
- *Data Minimization and Retention (DM):*
  - DM-1 Minimization of Personally Identifiable Information.
  - DM-2 Data Retention and Disposal.
  - DM-3 Minimization of PII Used in Testing, Training, and Research.
- *Individual Participation and Redress (IP):*
  - IP-1 Consent.
  - IP-2 Individual Access.
  - IP-3 Redress.
  - IP-4 Complaint Management.
- *Security (SE):*
  - SE-1 Inventory of Personally Identifiable Information.
  - SE-2 Privacy Incident Response.
- *Transparency (TR):*
  - TR-1 Privacy Notice.
  - TR-2 System of Records, Notices and Privacy Act Statements.
  - TR-3 Dissemination of Privacy Program Information.
- *Use Limitation (UL):*
  - UL-1 Internal Use.
  - UL-2 Information Sharing with Third Parties.

NIST included the proposed privacy control catalog as an appendix, rather than integrating the privacy controls into the main security control catalog, but the addition of the privacy controls reflects a continued government focus on improving privacy protections for data in federal information systems and suggests tighter integration between privacy and security practices in future guidance.

Privacy in FISMA Reporting

Since 2005, when annual FISMA reporting requirements were amended to include questions to be answered by senior agency officials for privacy, agencies have been obligated to report the same core information about privacy, but additional requirements have been added by OMB in response to new technological developments with potential privacy impacts, to the emergence of new or increased threats to privacy, and to high-profile security incidents that threatened to compromise the privacy of personal information held by federal government agencies. In particular, increased attention given by the government to issues such as identity theft and breaches of personally identifiable information resulted in new requirements for agency privacy practices [1] and corresponding requirements to report on those practices [22]. The categories of privacy information sought in annual FISMA reports and key details to be provided by senior agency officials for privacy are summarized in Table 16.1.

In addition to the information listed in Table 16.1, beginning in 2008 OMB directed agencies to submit documentation about their practices and activities related to preventing and responding to breaches of personally identifiable information [25]. These additional reporting requirements include the following items, which senior agency officials for privacy are expected to submit via CyberScope [28]:

- Breach notification policy if it has changed significantly since last year's report;
- Progress update on eliminating unnecessary use of Social Security Numbers; and
- Progress update on review and reduction of holdings of personally identifiable information.

Table 16.1 FISMA Report Questions for Senior Agency Officials for Privacy [25,10]

Privacy Topic	Questions for Senior Agency Officials for Privacy
Inventory of Systems with Information in Identifiable Form	Number of agency and contractor systems: • Containing information in identifiable form • Requiring a privacy impact assessment • Covered by an existing privacy impact assessment • Requiring a system of records notice (SORN) • For which a current SORN has been published
Links to Privacy Impact Assessments and System of Record Notices	Uniform resource locators for the page on the agency web site where links are provided to privacy impact assessments and system of record notices
Senior Agency Official for Privacy Responsibilities	Whether the agency can demonstrate through documentation that its privacy official participates in: • All information privacy compliance activities • Evaluating the privacy ramifications of legislative, regulatory, and other policy proposals • Assessing the impact of technology on the privacy of personal information
Privacy Training and Awareness	Whether the agency has a policy in place to ensure that personnel are familiar with privacy legal and regulatory requirements, and a program for providing job-specific privacy training for all personnel involved in administering personally identifiable information, information technology systems, or information security
Policies Complying with E-Government Act Provisions	Whether the agency has appropriate policies in place for the PIA and web site privacy notice requirements in §208 of the E-Government Act

Table 16.1 FISMA Report Questions for Senior Agency Officials for Privacy [25,10] (*continued*)

Privacy Topic	Questions for Senior Agency Officials for Privacy
Mandatory Privacy Reviews	Which of the reviews required under the Privacy Act [5], E-Government Act [26], or Federal Data Mining Reporting Act [27] were conducted in the previous year
Privacy Complaints	Number of complaints received by type: process and procedural, redress, operational, and referral
Policy Compliance	Whether the agency can provide documentation showing: • Review of privacy compliance • Planned, in progress, or completed corrective actions for compliance deficiencies • Use of technologies for continuous auditing of privacy compliance • Coordination with agency Inspector General on privacy program oversight
Advice Provided by Senior Agency Officials for Privacy	Whether formal written advice been provided on: • Agency handling of personally identifiable information • Interagency or non-federal written agreements • Reviews or feedback on budgetary or program planning • Privacy training
Use of Persistent Tracking Technology (requirement likely to change due to change in policy restricting use)	Whether the agency uses persistent tracking technology, and if so, is that use reviewed, justified, and approved, and does the privacy policy inform web site visitors about the tracking technology
Contact Information	Name, telephone number, and email address for: • Agency Head • Chief Information Officer • Inspector General • Chief Information Security Officer • Senior Agency Official for Privacy • Chief Privacy Officer • Privacy Advocate • Privacy Act Officer • Reviewing Official for PIAs • Point of contact for PIA and SORN URLs

FISMA Incident Reporting and Handling

The provisions in FISMA requiring agencies to detect, report, and respond to security incidents [29] do not explicitly mention privacy, but are nevertheless applicable to agency practices to protect the privacy of personally identifiable information. The text of the law requires agency information security programs to implement "procedures for detecting, reporting, and responding to security incidents" that include providing notification of incidents when they occur to the designated federal information security incident center, law enforcement authorities, and other agencies as appropriate [29]. OMB gave more explicit instructions to agencies in 2006 [30] that specified the name of the federal information security incident center to which incidents must be reported—the US Computer Emergency Readiness Team (US-CERT) [31], managed by the Department of Homeland Security—and revised reporting requirements in FISMA to require agencies to report all incidents involving personally identifiable information to US-CERT within one hour of discovering the incident" [30]. Subsequent guidance directed agencies to develop and implement policies for breach notification, to address considerations including whether breach notification is required; timeliness, source, and contents of any required notification; the means of providing notification; and to whom the notification is provided [1]. In addition to mandatory notification to US-CERT and other government authorities, agency breach notification policies detail the subjective aspects of disclosing incidents involving personally identifiable information, such as the determination of actual or potential harm to the individuals whose personal information is disclosed, and whether notifications to the public are appropriate [1]. Agencies also need to be aware of several additional data breach notification requirements that apply to specific types of data; these requirements are described later in this chapter in the section on Other Legal and Regulatory Sources of Privacy Requirements.

FEDERAL AGENCY REQUIREMENTS UNDER THE PRIVACY ACT

The seminal privacy legislation for federal agencies is the Privacy Act of 1974 [5], which focused on government records containing information about individuals (defined to be US citizens and legal resident aliens). Many provisions in FISMA and the E-Government Act reference the Privacy Act, and FISMA explicitly affirms the statutory authority of the Privacy Act for matters relating to the use and disclosure of personal information, including privacy protections [32]. The Privacy Act applies to all federal agencies, stipulating that "No agency shall disclose any record which is contained in a system of records by any means of communication to any person, or to another agency, except pursuant to a written request by, or with the prior written consent of, the individual to whom the record pertains, unless disclosure of the record" falls under one of 12 permitted types [5]. Perhaps the most important of these exceptions is for disclosure as part of "routine use," which is use that falls within the purpose for which the data was originally collected [33]. The Privacy Act provides authoritative rules for information maintained by federal agencies on individuals, including the conditions of disclosure for that information, accounting of disclosures, providing individuals access to records about themselves, agency requirements for maintaining systems of records and publishing rules describing agency policies and procedures for maintaining systems, and civil and criminal penalties for violation of the terms in the law [33].

The Privacy Act's provisions focus on federal agency handling of *records* and *systems of records*. A record is any information an agency maintains about an individual that also contains identifying information about the individual, such as a name, number, fingerprint, photograph, or other information or characteristic that can be used to uniquely identify the individual [34]. A system of records is a collection of records under the control of an agency that uses identifying attributes of the individual to retrieve information [35]. While personally identifiable information is subject to a variety of legal and regulatory requirements, many provisions of the Privacy Act apply only to information in systems of records. Thus, when evaluating the privacy requirements that apply to a particular information system, system owners and organizations need first to determine whether the system contains personally identifiable information, and whether that personally identifiable information is used in a way that satisfies the definition of a system of record under the Privacy Act. The legislation itself offers little guidance on identifying personally identifiable information, but agencies trying to make this determination can leverage guidance from OMB on implementing the privacy provisions of the E-Government Act [13] and from NIST on protecting personally identifiable information [36].

Fair Information Practices

The Privacy Act codifies a set of fair information practices originally issued by the US Department of Health, Education, and Welfare in 1973 [37]. These practices provide the basis for a variety of privacy principles and requirements found in other laws, including the ability for individuals to prevent the use of their personal information for purposes other than which it was originally collected. The original code of fair information practices articulated five core privacy principles [37]:

1. There must be no personal-data record-keeping systems whose very existence is secret.
2. There must be a way for an individual to find out what information about him is in a record and how it is used.
3. There must be a way for an individual to prevent information about him obtained for one purpose from being used or made available for other purposes without his consent.
4. There must be a way for an individual to correct or amend a record of identifiable information about him.
5. Any organization creating, maintaining, using, or disseminating records of identifiable personal data must assure the reliability of the data for their

intended use and must take reasonable precautions to prevent misuse of the data.

These principles were incorporated by Congressional legislators and, during the process of drafting the Privacy Act, were expanded to eight and associated with descriptive labels [38], as shown in Table 16.2. The provisions of the Privacy Act are followed by some state government agencies and other non-federal government authorities, and in other cases privacy principles or guidelines that may be used by non-federal entities can be traced to the same fair information practices. For example, these practices provided the basis for the *OECD Guidelines on the Protection of Privacy and Transborder Flows of Personal Data* [39], which are used by some non-federal government agencies and many public and private sector organizations, especially outside the US.

Table 16.2 Principles Reflected in the Provisions of the Privacy Act of 1974 [38]

Name	Principle
Openness	There shall be no personal-data record-keeping system whose very existence is secret and there shall be a policy of openness about an organization's personal-data record-keeping policies, practices, and systems.
Individual Access	An individual about whom information is maintained by a record-keeping organization in individually identifiable form shall have a right to see and copy that information.
Individual Participation	An individual about whom information is maintained by a record-keeping organization shall have a right to correct or amend the substance of that information.
Collection Limitation	There shall be limits on the types of information an organization may collect about an individual, as well as certain requirements with respect to the manner in which it collects such information.
Use Limitation	There shall be limits on the internal uses of information about an individual within a record-keeping organization.
Disclosure Limitation	There shall be limits on the external disclosures of information about an individual a record-keeping organization may make.
Information Management	A record-keeping organization shall bear an affirmative responsibility for establishing reasonable and proper information management policies and practices which assure that its collection, maintenance, use, and dissemination of information about an individual is necessary and lawful and the information itself is current and accurate.
Accountability	A record-keeping organization shall be accountable for its personal-data record-keeping policies, practices, and systems.

The principles in Table 16.2 are reflected, separately or in combination, in key provisions of the Privacy Act. Several of these principles—particularly including information management and accountability—have a direct impact on information system security, in the form of requirements to implement appropriate safeguards (i.e. security controls) to secure the confidentiality, integrity, and availability of information contained in systems of records [40]. Most of the privacy provisions in the Privacy Act influence security at least indirectly, as systems of records should be designed with functional and technical characteristics (and selected security controls) that facilitate compliance with Privacy Act requirements.

Restrictions on Collection, Use, and Disclosure

The Privacy Act established requirements—applicable to all executive-branch federal government agencies—that constrain the ways in which agencies collect personal information from citizens, use that information once collected, and disclose that information to anyone outside the agency that maintains the information, including to the individuals themselves [40]. These constraints center on why the agency collecting the information wants it, as the Privacy Act requires agencies to first explain the purpose or purposes for which the information will be used, and also to limit the amount of personal information collected to the minimum necessary to accomplish the intended purpose [41].

The Privacy Act begins with a broad prohibition on disclosure of personal information contained in agency systems of records, unless the individual to whom the information pertains has requested the disclosure, or has given written consent allowing the disclosure. There are, however, 12 enumerated exceptions to the restriction on disclosure, any one of which permits an agency to disclose information in records without consent. Disclosure is allowed [42]:

1. To employees of the agency maintaining the information, if the information is needed to perform their duties;
2. If it is required under other regulations governing public information, agency rules, opinions, orders, records, and proceedings [43]:
3. For routine use of the information for its intended purpose;
4. To the Census Bureau in support of planning or conducting a census or related activity;
5. For research or reporting, if the information is in a form that is not individually identifiable;
6. To the National Archives and Records Administration if the value of the record warrants its preservation;
7. To another agency or government entity for use in civil or criminal law enforcement;
8. If circumstances exist where the health or safety of an individual is at risk (notification of disclosure after the fact is still required);
9. To either house of Congress or any committee or subcommittee with jurisdiction over the information;

10. To the Comptroller General or other authorized personnel representing the General Accountability Office;

11. Pursuant to a valid court order; or

12. To a consumer reporting agency where the information in the record establishes that a person is responsible for a claim of the government [44].

Information owners and system owners should evaluate information systems not only to determine if the systems contain PII, but also to understand the purposes for which that information is being or will be used. Developing a clear understanding of the anticipated information usage patterns for a system will help clarify the need to prevent inappropriate disclosures of personal information, and to choose relevant security controls, including providing awareness and training for users accessing the system and operational procedures to maintain compliance with provisions in the Privacy Act.

Accounting of Disclosures

Agencies are also required under the Privacy Act to maintain a record of the disclosures it makes, and to maintain this record (called an "accounting of disclosures") for at least five years after it discloses the information. So for each instance in which personal information is disclosed—even for cases where individual consent has been obtained in advance—an agency needs to capture the date of disclosure, the type of disclosure, the reason for making the disclosure, and the name and address of the recipient of the disclosed information [45]. This requirement applies generally to personal information in agency records of all types, but accounting of disclosure requirements are often associated with health care, since HIPAA-covered entities and business associates are required to maintain accountings of disclosures of protected health information under provisions of the HIPAA Privacy Rule [46], which was to be revised by the Health Information Technology for Economic and Clinical Health (HITECH) Act to require more types of disclosure to be included [47]. The ability to produce accountings of disclosures aligns functionally with audit and accountability security controls used for federal information systems [23].

Access, Review, and Correction of Records by Individuals

System owners responsible for information systems containing personally identifiable information are obligated under the Privacy Act to provide access to the individuals whose information is in the records. This access includes a right for individuals to review the information stored about them by an agency, and to receive a copy of the record upon request [48]. Agencies also must allow individuals to request correction or amendment of inaccurate, incomplete, or out of date information in records about them. When such requests are received, agencies must either make the changes as requested or, if the request is refused, provide a reason for refusing and explain the process by which the individual may appeal the refusal and add a note to the record stating why the individual disagrees with the agency's position [48].

Openness, Notice, and Transparency

One of the goals of the Privacy Act was to ensure that the government does not engage in secret information gathering about members of the public, but instead makes public its intention to collect personal information and to store and maintain that information in a system of records. This goal embodies the fair information principle of openness [38], and is satisfied by a requirement in the Privacy Act that agencies publish a notice declaring the existence and characteristics of any systems of records it maintains or plans to implement [49]. Since information systems containing personal information about individuals are termed systems of records within the Privacy Act, the public notification is known as a *system of records notice* (SORN) [13]. These notices must be published in the *Federal Register*—the official daily publication of rules, notices, and federal agency and executive actions produced by the Office of the Federal Register under the authority of the National Archives and Records Administration (NARA)—both when a system of records is first deployed and upon any subsequent changes to the details about the system described in the SORN. The creation and publication of system of record notices for systems that require them is not explicitly addressed in the Risk Management Framework, but agencies are required as part of FISMA reporting to provide the number of systems for which a SORN is needed and the number of notices that have actually been published [10].

Information Management

The Privacy Act requires agencies to safeguard personally identifiable information contained in systems of record against threats to confidentiality and integrity. The law refers generally to "appropriate administrative, technical, and physical safeguards" [40], all of which can be addressed using the reference set of security controls contained in Special Publication 800-53 [23]. With respect to the integrity of PII contained in agency systems of records, the language in the Privacy Act focuses on the correctness or validity of the information, which should be accurate, complete, current, and relevant to the purposes for which the information was collected and will be used [51]. It is important for system owners and information system security officers to identify and incorporate privacy protection requirements and objectives during the process of selecting appropriate security controls for the

---

NOTE

A quick search of notices published in the *Federal Register* yield many examples of systems of records notices, such as this summary disclosure provided by the Social Security Administration for its e-Authentication File:"In accordance with the Privacy Act (5 U.S.C. 552a(e)(4) and (e)(11)), we are issuing public notice of our intent to establish a system of records, the *Central Repository of Electronic Authentication Data Master File* (hereinafter referred to as the *e-Authentication File*) and its applicable routine uses. The *e-Authentication File* will maintain personally identifiable information (PII) we collect and use to verify the identity of persons using our electronic services" [50].

system, as agencies can be held accountable for failing to comply with the provisions of the Privacy Act due to insufficient or ineffective security controls to protect privacy [52].

PRIVACY IMPACT ASSESSMENTS

While the Privacy Act includes numerous provisions intended to protect personal information held by government agencies about individuals, the law was enacted in 1974, and therefore was not written in a way that considered the pervasive use of computers and computer-based interaction between government and the public that occurs today. Recognizing the transformation in the nature of interactions between the government and citizens brought about by expanded use of computers, the Internet, and related technologies, with the E-Government Act of 2002 Congress saw the need to require agencies to protect privacy of personal information about citizens collected and used by electronic government services [26]. As noted previously in this chapter in the section "Privacy Requirements for Federal Agencies under FISMA and the E-Government Act," the primary protective mechanism required of agencies is the privacy impact assessment (PIA). As defined by OMB, a privacy impact assessment is "an analysis of how information is handled: (i) to ensure handling conforms to applicable legal, regulatory, and policy requirements regarding privacy, (ii) to determine the risks and effects of collecting, maintaining and disseminating information in identifiable form in an electronic information system, and (iii) to examine and evaluate protections and alternative processes" [13]. This section describes the criteria with which agencies determine whether privacy impact assessments are necessary for their information systems, the process of performing assessments and publishing PIAs and related notices and documentation, and the content required to be included in that documentation. The authoritative guidance for privacy impact assessments is OMB Memorandum M-03-22, *Guidance for Implementing the Privacy Provisions of the E-Government Act of 2002* [13].

NOTE

Both the Privacy Act and the privacy provisions of the E-Government Act obligate agencies to consider the privacy implications of information systems and data collection activities before they are implemented, but the privacy impact assessment is the only formal privacy requirement that applies to systems under development [53]. Privacy requirements addressed in this chapter other than the PIA apply to operational systems and aspects of agency information privacy and security programs, but are only a part of the system development lifecycle in the sense that organizations and system owners should plan to comply with relevant privacy requirements once their systems are authorized to operate and in production.

Applicability of Privacy Impact Assessments

Under §208 of the E-Government Act, agencies are required to conduct privacy impact assessments when they acquire or develop information technology systems that will collect, store, or distribute information in identifiable form about members of the public, or whenever they intend to collect information in identifiable form electronically from at least 10 people [54]. Both of these scenarios apply to new collections of information, but agencies are also required to perform PIAs when new privacy risks are identified due to any of a number of potential changes in an existing information system, including [13]:

- Converting paper-based records to electronic systems;
- Changing anonymous information into information in identifiable form;
- Adding new uses of an existing IT system, including application of new technologies, that significantly change how information in identifiable form is managed in the system;
- Merging, centralizing, or matching databases with information in identifiable form with other databases;
- Applying new user authentication technology to an electronic information system accessed by members of the public;
- Systematically incorporating commercial or public data sources of information in identifiable form into existing information systems;
- Adding new interagency uses or exchanges of information in identifiable form;
- Altering a business process that results in significant new uses or disclosures of information or incorporation into the system of additional items of information in identifiable form; or
- Altering the character of data in a way that adds new information in identifiable form, raising the risks to personal privacy.

The key determining factor driving the need to perform a PIA for a given system is whether system collects, maintains, retrieves, or disseminates information that can be used to identify an individual, directly or indirectly. Generally, if a system does not process personally identifiable information, then a PIA is not required. Agencies often include initial questions about PII in PIA templates or guidelines used by system owners [55–57], so that cases where a PIA is not required can be identified before expending unnecessary additional effort. The results of these questions are included in system description information such as that found in system security plans or in summary information screens displayed in FISMA reporting tools such as the Cyber Security Assessment & Management application (see Figure 16.2). It is common practice in the context of system certification and accreditation procedures to require formal documentation regarding PIAs for all systems—if a PIA is needed, then this documentation would be the PIA itself; if no PIA needs to be conducted, then a statement explaining the reason why no PIA is necessary would be provided instead.

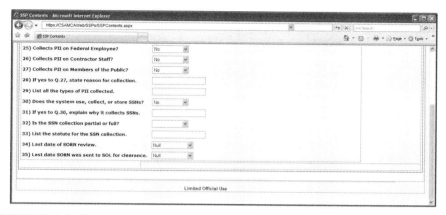

FIGURE 16.2 As Illustrated in the 11 Questions Shown Here in the Cyber Security Assessment and Management Tool, Privacy Details are Among the General Descriptive Information Collected for FISMA systems [58]

Conducting Privacy Impact Assessments

Once a system owner determines that a PIA is required, the process of performing the assessment involves first describing the system and the personally identifiable information it will collect, use, or disseminate, and then analyzing the nature of the data, the way it will be used, threats to privacy faced by the system, and any measures put in place to secure PII in the system or otherwise protect the privacy of that information [13]. The descriptive information in the PIA should include [13]:

i. what information is to be collected;
ii. why the information is being collected;
iii. intended use or uses of the information;
iv. with whom the information will be shared;
v. what opportunities individuals have to decline to provide information or to consent to particular uses of the information, and how individuals can give consent;
vi. how the information will be secured (e.g. security controls to be implemented); and
vii. whether a system of records is being created under the Privacy Act.

The final item in this list is an important consideration for system owners, because if the system in question is a system of records, then the agency will need to prepare and publish a *system of records notice* (SORN) to make the public aware of the existence of the system and the data it will collect, use, or disseminate [49].

Based on the information to be collected and maintained in the system, the PIA should also analyze the threats to the privacy of personally identifiable information, and the potential impact to individuals should that privacy be breached. In addition to describing the specific data collection and handling approach the system will use, the PIA should address the benefits and potential weaknesses of that approach, identify any alternative approaches considered for the system, and provide an explanation of why the adopted approach was chosen [13]. The PIA should also describe security controls or other mechanisms that will be used to mitigate the risk to privacy associated with the system, based on the threats and potential vulnerabilities identified. OMB's guidance to agencies notes that approaches for handling PII in a system may vary depending on the system's stage of development and on the phase of the information life cycle (e.g. information handling practices during collection may differ from those during processing or destruction) [13]. Agencies are advised to approach PIA development as a collaborative effort combining program or system knowledge with expertise in information technology, security, privacy, and records management [13].

The process of assessing information systems for potential privacy implications is not complicated, but it needs to be thorough. System owners—working with information owners, information system security officers, privacy officers and others with relevant knowledge and expertise about the sensitivity of the data to be maintained in the system and its intended use—need to identify all PII in the system, determine who will have access to that PII, and understand (and document) whether that PII is used as the basis for retrieving records [13]. Agencies have detailed guidance available on identifying PII and evaluating its sensitivity in Special Publication 800-122, *Guide to Protecting the Confidentiality of Personally Identifiable Information* [36], which was released in April 2010. The requirements for system owners are that this information be documented, reviewed, and made publicly available. Agencies are delegated the responsibility of determining (and instructing their system owners) what additional security controls or risk mitigating actions should be taken to address the findings in the PIA.

Documenting and Publishing PIA Results

PIAs have intended audiences both inside and outside the agency that performs them. Once completed, PIA documentation should be reviewed and approved by an appropriate agency official, such as the agency CIO, senior agency official for privacy, or other designated official separate from personnel procuring or developing the system and those who conducted the PIA [13].

PIAs (including statements explaining why no PIA is required for relevant systems) are typically included as appendices or attachments to system security plans prepared and submitted to authorizing officials during the system certification and accreditation process. While agencies were once instructed to submit PIA documents to OMB in addition to making them publicly available [13], this process has been superseded by current guidance that instead requires agencies to make PIAs available online on agency websites, and report only the URL where links to the PIAs can be found [10]. The final step in the PIA process is to publish the PIA on the agency website (see the list of major agency URLs earlier in this chapter).

Agencies are permitted to redact portions of their PIAs or not to publish a given PIA document at all, if doing so would present security risks or result in classified or sensitive information being revealed [13]. System owners should be mindful of the fact that a PIA describes the personally identifiable information associated with an information system, but should not include any PII in the assessment documentation [13].

System of Records Notices

Agencies must prepare and publish a system of records notice (SORN) for any information system that meets the Privacy Act definition of a system of record: "a group of any records under the control of any agency from which information is retrieved by the name of the individual or by some identifying number, symbol, or other identifying particular assigned to the individual [35]." The Privacy Act also stipulates the minimum content to be included in a SORN [49]:

- Name and location of the system;
- Categories of individuals on whom records are maintained in the system;
- Categories or types of records maintained in the system;
- Routine uses of the records contained in the system, including the categories of users and the purpose for use;
- Agency policies and practices regarding storage, retrievability, access controls, retention, and disposal of the records;
- Contact information for the agency official who is responsible for the system of records;
- Agency procedures whereby an individual can be notified upon request if the system of records contains a record pertaining to the individual;
- Agency procedures whereby an individual can gain access to any record pertaining to the individual contained in the system of records, and can contest its content; and
- Categories of sources of records in the system.

Once prepared, agencies satisfy the publication requirement by publishing SORNs in the *Federal Register*. When changes to systems occur that cause system owners to update or revise privacy impact assessments, agencies should evaluate current system of record notices to ensure they accurately reflect the system, and revise and re-publish SORNs if necessary [13].

Updates to Privacy Impact Assessments for Third-Party Sources

As government systems have become more integrated with non-government data sources and applications, the potential has grown for agencies to gain access to personally identifiable information from third parties. OMB issued updated guidance to agencies in June 2010 with new requirements for agencies to conduct and make publicly available an "adapted PIA" when the use of a third-party website or other data source makes personally identifiable information available [17]. Adapted PIA content is similar to that of ordinary PIAs, and includes [59]:

 i. the specific purpose of the agency's use of the third-party website or application;
 ii. any PII that is likely to become available to the agency through public use of the third-party website or application;
 iii. the agency's intended or expected use of PII;
 iv. with whom the agency will share PII;
 v. whether and how the agency will maintain PII, and for how long;
 vi. how the agency will secure PII that it uses or maintains;
 vii. what other privacy risks exist and how the agency will mitigate those risks; and
 viii. whether the agency's activities will create or modify a system of records under the Privacy Act.

Adapted PIAs for third-party websites and applications differ from typical PIAs in that their scope is defined by the external source of PII, not by the agency system that accesses it. This means that the use of third-party sources of PII is covered in a separate PIA, rather than being addressed within the scope of a system-specific PIA [60].

Privacy Impact Assessments within the Risk Management Framework

Conducting a privacy impact assessment (and where appropriate, publishing the results) is the only explicit privacy activity performed during the process of certifying and accrediting a system to obtain authorization to operate [53]. The sensitivity of information maintained in federal information systems is one among many factors influencing the security categorization of those systems and the corresponding security controls selected [61], meaning initial PIAs should be performed during step 1 of the RMF, so its results can inform both system categorization and security control selection activities (see Figure 16.3) [53].

PROTECTING PERSONALLY IDENTIFIABLE INFORMATION (PII)

As explained throughout this chapter, federal privacy requirements applicable to government agencies and their information systems are intended to protect personally identifiable information held by the agencies about individual members of the public. Current rules and guidance in effect for federal government agencies about safeguarding personally identifiable information reflect a three-part approach, in which agencies are directed to reduce the amount of PII they maintain [1], to implement additional or more effective security controls to protect the PII they have [62], and to

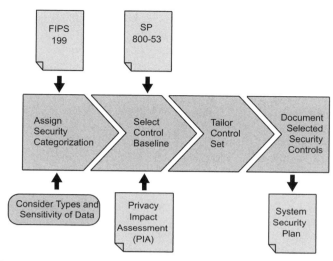

FIGURE 16.3 The Identification of PII for a System and the Information in Subsequent Privacy Impact Assessment Documentation are Important Influences on the System Security Categorization and the Security Control Selection Activities Described in the Risk Management Framework [53]

establish and adhere to formal breach notification policies for incidents involving PII [30,1]. System owners need to be aware of requirements related to protecting privacy in order to select appropriate security controls for their information systems before they are authorized to operate, and to follow appropriate operational procedures for their systems after they are authorized and in production.

While the E-Government Act emphasized the need for agencies to assess their use of systems of records and ensure the public is notified about those systems, the government's attention shifted to protective measures to prevent identity theft [63]. Beginning in 2007, OMB began requiring agencies to periodically review the personally identifiable information they held and reduce PII holdings to the minimum necessary to perform whatever function the information is intended to support [64]. Agencies are already obligated under the Privacy Act to maintain "only such information about an individual as is relevant and necessary to accomplish a purpose of the agency required to be accomplished by statute or by Executive order" [65]. The purpose of implementing regular reviews is to confirm that agencies are not holding on to more PII than necessary, and therefore not accepting more risk than can be justified by actual business needs. Stemming from a key recommendation of the President's Identity Theft Task Force [66], agencies are also instructed to reduce their use of social security numbers in agency information systems, both by identifying current uses that may be unnecessary and by seeking alternative personal identifiers [67]. These requirements should be considered by system owners as a factor constraining system design and, in particular, the set of personally identifiable data elements to be included in the system. Where agencies identify the use of social security numbers in an information system—whether during the privacy impact assessment process or other periodic review or evaluation—using alternative personal identifiers should be considered as a means of reducing the privacy risk exposed by the system [67].

Privacy protections in federal information systems can often be increased by adding or enhancing security controls, particularly controls intended to safeguard confidentiality, and Special Publication 800-122 offers examples of specific controls and the ways they can be used to protect PII [36]. Usage of these controls in privacy-enhancing ways is recommended for system owners responsible for information systems that handle PII, but the decision of which specific controls or control enhancements to implement is made by system owners and other agency officials involved in system authorization. Other security measures specified for the protection of sensitive information are mandatory. For instance, in the wake of the widely-reported theft of a laptop containing personal information on millions of US veterans, OMB directed all agencies to implement a set security measures (or verify they had already been implemented) including data encryption on laptop computers and other mobile devices; two-factor authentication for remote access to agency information systems containing sensitive data; automated time-out for remote access to require re-authentication after periods of inactivity; logging extracts of sensitive data from agency systems; and making sure authorized users with access to PII are aware of their responsibilities for safeguarding that information [62]. In this instance, agencies were given explicit guidance for determining what protections of mobile or remotely accessed information are needed, and for specific security controls and control assessment procedures to ensure the effective implementation of protective measures [62].

Notification Requirements for Breaches of Personally Identifiable Information

Although FISMA included a provision requiring agencies to report security incidents to designated federal authorities [29], subsequent guidance to agencies issued by OMB clarified expectations and procedures for reporting security incidents involving personally identifiable information. Specifically, in the event of a suspected or confirmed incident involving PII, agencies are required to notify US-CERT within one hour [30], and depending on the nature of the breach, may be required to provide external notification as well [1], as shown in Figure 16.4. These reporting requirements escalate the relative importance of a breach of PII to a level commensurate with US-CERT's Category 1—the highest level category, ordinarily associated with unauthorized access to federal agency networks, systems, or data [31].

When an agency suffers a breach of personally identifiable information, there are several factors that help determine whether external notification is required. Under current rules applicable to PII breaches in general, the key consideration is whether the breach is likely to cause harm [1]. For example, in situations where data disclosed

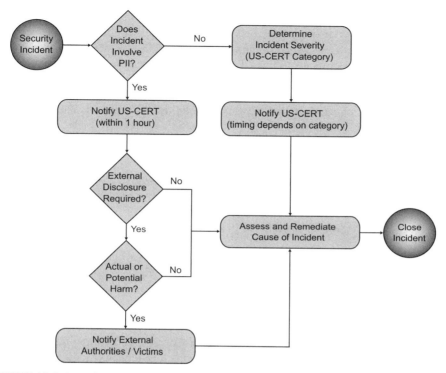

FIGURE 16.4 Agencies Experiencing Suspected or Confirmed Security Breaches Are Required to Notify US-CERT, and Depending on the Nature of the Breach and the Information Exposed, Also May Need to Report the Incident to Other Authorities, Breach Victims, or the Public [1]

in a breach is encrypted or in another form rendering it unreadable or unusable, external notification may not be warranted. The harm-based exemption from external breach notification requirements is incorporated in some federal rules governing specific types of data, such as the rule covering notification for breaches of unsecured protected health information [68], promulgated under the authority of the Health Information Technology for Economic and Clinical Health Act [69]. Determining the risk of harm due to a breach of PII is a subjective process, but guidance to agencies provided by OMB lists five factors that should be taken into consideration when making such a determination [70]:

1. Nature of the data elements breached.
2. Number of individuals affected.
3. Likelihood the information is accessible and usable.
4. Likelihood the breach may lead to harm.
5. Ability of the agency to mitigate the risk of harm.

Where external notification is deemed necessary, agencies are advised to provide notification "without unreasonable delay," which generally allows delays needed to support law enforcement efforts, to protect national security incidents, or to give the agency time to correct vulnerabilities that may have enabled the breach to occur [71]. While public disclosure of the occurrence of the breach may be provided through the media, online, direct communication, or other channels, written notification is expected for individuals whose PII was disclosed due to a breach. The content of such notifications includes [72]:

- a brief description of what happened, including the date(s) of the breach and of its discovery;
- a description of the types of personal information involved in the breach;
- a statement whether the information was encrypted or protected by other means;
- what steps individuals should take to protect themselves from potential harm, if any;
- what the agency is doing, if anything, to investigate the breach, to mitigate losses, and to protect against any further breaches; and
- who affected individuals should contact at the agency for more information, including a toll-free telephone number, e-mail address, and postal address.

Tracking agency compliance with these requirements remains a priority for OMB, as current FISMA reporting requirements for privacy information emphasize updates and progress reports on mandatory actions to safeguard personally identifiable information [22].

OTHER LEGAL AND REGULATORY SOURCES OF PRIVACY REQUIREMENTS

Protecting privacy within FISMA-mandated agency information security activities emphasizes identifying personally identifiable information stored in information systems and implementing security controls appropriate to safeguard that information. The set of privacy requirements applicable to federal agencies is much broader than the context of FISMA compliance, so chief information officers and other senior agency officials responsible for privacy must focus their attention beyond privacy impact assessments. Table 16.3 summarizes major legislation that includes privacy requirements applicable to federal agencies.

Privacy Requirements Potentially Applicable to Agencies

The privacy provisions in the Privacy Act of 1974 and the E-Government Act of 2002 apply generally to all executive agencies and any type of personally identifiable information held by those agencies on members of the public. There are

Table 16.3 Key Privacy Legislation Applicable to US Federal Agencies

Legislation	What it Covers	Who it Applies To
Privacy Act of 1974 [5]	Records on individuals	All federal agencies
Family Educational Rights and Privacy Act of 1974 (FERPA) [73]	Student records	Educational institutions and agencies handling student records
Electronic Communications Privacy Act of 1986 (ECPA) [74]	Wired and wireless telephone and network communications	All federal agencies and most non-government entities
Health Insurance Portability and Accountability Act of 1996 (HIPAA) [75]	Protected health information (personal information in health records)	Health care providers, plans, and clearinghouses and their business associates
Children's Online Privacy Protection Act of 1998 (COPPA) [76]	Personal information about individuals younger than 13	All federal agencies and non-federal entities
Financial Services Modernization Act of 1999 (Graham-Leach-Bliley or GLBA) [77]	Non-public personal information about consumers	All financial institutions, including government agencies conducting relevant activities
E-Government Act of 2002 [26]	Personally identifiable information on individuals	All federal agencies and contractors operating systems on their behalf
Health Information Technology for Economic and Clinical Health Act of 2009 (HITECH) [78]	Protected health information	Extends HIPAA coverage to business associates and non-HIPAA-covered entities offering personal health records
Code of Federal Regulations, Title 42, Part 2 (42 CFR Part 2)	Information in medical records relating to alcohol or substance abuse treatment	All federal agencies and non-federal entities
US Code, Title 38, §5701, §5726, and §7332	Information on claims and medical records on veterans and members of the armed forces	All federal agencies and non-federal entities

numerous other legal privacy protections that apply to specific types of information or that cover specific categories of individuals. System owners in federal agencies at a minimum should be aware of the rules that apply to their data, systems, and operations. This section summarizes the key privacy provisions in domain-specific federal legislation. System owners and agency officials should give particularly attention to the applicability of the laws and regulations described in this section when evaluating the nature and types of information used in their information systems.

Family Educational Rights and Privacy Act of 1974

The Family Educational Rights and Privacy Act (FERPA) affords privacy protections to information contained in student educational records. Generally, it limits the ability of educational institutions or other holders of student records to disclose the contents of those records without the permission of either the student to whom the record pertains, or of the parent of the student if the student is a minor [73]. While the law was primarily intended to give explicit privacy rights to students and their parents with respect to the way schools handle the information in student records, the privacy provisions in the law are relevant for any organization seeking access to student records (such as a human resources officer trying to validate the educational credentials of a job applicant), and also may constrain the redisclosure of student records after they are legally obtained from the institution that maintains them [79].

Health Information Portability and Accountability Act of 1996

The legislative requirements for privacy and security contained in HIPAA were implemented as federal regulations known as the HIPAA Privacy Rule and the HIPAA Security Rule, which took effect in 2003 and 2005, respectively. HIPAA's privacy and security requirements apply to *protected health information*, which is any information transmitted or maintained electronically or in any other medium "created or received by a health care provider, health plan, public health authority, employer, life insurer, school or university, or health care clearinghouse" about the current, former, or future health of an individual, health care provided to an individual, or payment for health care provided to an individual [80]. The Office for Civil Rights within the Department of Health and Human services, which is responsible for enforcing HIPAA compliance, provides a consolidated set of information on provisions of the HIPAA legislation, as an alternative to consulting the Code of Federal Regulations directly [80]. This administrative simplification defines key terms relevant to HIPAA—such as "covered entities" and "business associates" to which the regulations apply—and provides a comprehensive listing of all the statutory provisions associated with the law. HIPAA rules apply to government and non-government organizations that are involved in providing, paying for, and administering health care. The privacy requirements in HIPAA, as codified in federal regulations at 45 CFR §164 Subpart E, prohibit the use or disclosure of personal health information by covered entities without explicit authorization from the individuals to whom the information pertains, except for specifically enumerated permitted uses. The primary permitted uses for health information *without* consent are treatment, payment, and health care operations, unless the health care operation in question is marketing, for which explicit authorization (consent) is required [81]. The same regulations also address specific uses of personal information which are permitted as long as the individual is given an opportunity in advance to opt out and a list of uses and disclosures permitted without the need for consent, mostly related to public health, public safety, and legal and administrative proceedings [82]. System owners working with protected health information need to take HIPAA privacy and security requirements into account, both when conducting privacy impact assessments and when selecting security controls to implement.

Health Information Technology for Economic and Clinical Health Act of 2009

Enacted as Title XIII of the American Recovery and Reinvestment Act of 2009 [83], the HITECH Act strengthened many of the regulations implemented due to HIPAA, including changes to enforcement guidelines and increases in the civil and criminal penalties that may be imposed on entities found to be in violation of HIPAA security and privacy rules [84]. HITECH also mandated new privacy practices for federal agencies that collect, store, or disseminate protected health information, including rules requiring notification and public disclosure of breaches of protected health information that went into effect in September 2009 [68].

Code of Federal Regulations, Title 42, Part 2

There is a portion of the federal regulations on health care that generally prohibit any disclosure, without patient consent, of information in medical records relating to diagnosis of or treatment for substance abuse. When patient consent is sought, any consent granted applies only to disclosure to the specific individual or organization making the request for disclosure. Any subsequent intent to re-disclose or use medical record data by the same entity for a different purpose requires a separate consent [85]. These rules apply not only to health care providers who administer such treatment, but also to any information about substance abuse treatment that might be contained in employee records, so agencies should be aware of these privacy rules when considering security controls for any systems that might use this type of information.

Financial Services Modernization Act of 1999

More commonly known as the Graham-Leach-Bliley Act (GLBA), the Financial Services Modernization Act of 1999 included provisions intended to protect "nonpublic personal information" held by financial institutions about their customers [86]. GLBA requires institutions to provide notices to their customers regarding their privacy policies and practices for disclosing personal information to third parties and for protecting their customers' personal information, and to give customers an opportunity to opt out of such disclosures [87]. While the primary focus of the law was commercial financial institutions, its provisions apply to any organization engaged in "activities that are financial in nature," defined to include a broad range of services including lending or investing money, providing insurance, providing financial advisory services, issuing or underwriting securities, and engaging in other banking activities [88]. Under this broad definition, many government agencies are subject to GLBA, and need to implement appropriate privacy policy notification procedures and safeguards to protect the confidentiality of information in customer records against unauthorized access or other threats to those records [86].

Electronic Communications Privacy Act of 1986

Government and non-government organizations alike are subject to restrictions on intercepting or recording telephone communications with other parties; the Electronic Communications Privacy Act (ECPA) extended such restrictions to cover electronic data transmissions, and the law puts strict constraints on the ability of government agencies to access the contents of electronic communications [74]. Under ECPA, federal agencies who provide electronic communications services to the public must safeguard the privacy of the contents of any communications, both while in transit and while stored by the agency, and must not disclose the contents of such communications without the consent of the sender (subject to several exceptions, such as when the disclosure is previously authorized, directed to the recipient, incidental to the provision of the service, or for law enforcement purposes) [89]. Collectively, the provisions in ECPA are largely intended to protect individuals from unlawful or unreasonable intrusions on their privacy by the government, but the applicability of the law to specific technologies that were not in pervasive use at the time it was enacted—such as email, text messaging, cellular telephones, and global positioning systems—makes it particularly challenging for agencies to follow the letter and spirit of the law [90]. Program managers, system owners, and others responsible for ensuring compliance with privacy regulations should be aware not only of the statutory provisions stemming from ECPA, but also of the evolving legal standards and policy changes related to collecting, storing, and disclosing information in electronic communications.

Children's Online Privacy Protection Act of 1998

Federal agencies and commercial organizations alike are required under the terms of the Children's Online Privacy Protection Act (COPPA) to adhere to specific rules when collecting personal information from individuals under age 13. Organizations that collect such information must include details about data collection and handling practices for information about children in their privacy policies, and must obtain parental consent in advance for any collection, use, or disclosure of personal information about children [76].

US Code, Title 38 §5701, §5726, and §7332

Several sections of the US Code of Federal Regulations provide privacy protections for certain types of personal information concerning current or former members of the armed forces. Any information related to a claim for benefits (such as disability) by active service members, veterans, or dependents is confidential, and can be disclosed only in specific situations or under explicit conditions [91]. While HIPAA includes privacy and security provisions for individually identifiable health information about individuals in general, and medical records related to substance abuse are afforded special protection under 42 CFR Part 2, there are additional privacy regulations protecting the confidentiality of certain medical records on US veterans. These regulations apply to medical records containing diagnosis and treatment information about substance abuse, human immunodeficiency virus, or sickle

> **WARNING**
>
> Achieving and maintaining compliance with the array of federal information privacy requirements can be a daunting task for any organization, but federal requirements are not the only consideration. Many states have enacted privacy legislation or regulations with requirements that may exceed or even conflict with federal rules. The US Constitution does not declare an explicit right to privacy, but 10 states have included such rights in their own constitutions [94], and the objective of upholding individual privacy rights sometimes leads states to put additional constraints on personal data collection, use, and disclosure beyond what federal laws provide. Similarly, with respect to notifications for breaches of personally identifiable information, 46 states have enacted legislation [95] with provisions about notifications required when such security breaches occur.

cell anemia [92]. Breaches of sensitive personal information about current members of the armed forces or about veterans is also subject to special notification requirements, as any such breach determined to be significant must be reported to the appropriate oversight committees in both the Senate and the House of Representatives [93]. These requirements apply primarily to the Department of Veterans Affairs and the Department of Defense, but are specific to the status of the individual, so can be relevant for any agency in possession of records about current or former service members.

RELEVANT SOURCE MATERIAL

The primary source for agency requirements regarding privacy is the Office of Management and Budget, which has issued detailed guidance to agencies on implementing and complying with legislative and regulatory privacy requirements, and on adopting additional practices and security controls to more effectively safeguard personally identifiable information. Some NIST Special Publications also provide guidance on protecting PII and taking privacy requirements into account when categorizing information systems and selecting appropriate security controls. The most applicable sources of information include:

- OMB Memorandum M-00-13, *Privacy Policies and Data Collection on Federal Web Sites* [20].
- OMB Memorandum M-03-22, *OMB Guidance for Implementing the Privacy Provisions of the E-Government Act of 2002* [13].
- OMB Memorandum M-06-16, *Protection of Sensitive Agency Information* [62].
- OMB Memorandum M-06-19, *Reporting Incidents Involving Personally Identifiable Information and Incorporating the Cost for Security in Agency Information Technology Investments* [30].
- OMB Memorandum M-07-16, *Safeguarding Against and Responding to the Breach of Personally Identifiable Information* [1].
- OMB Memorandum M-10-23, *Guidance for Agency Use of Third-Party Websites and Applications* [17].

- Special Publication 800-122, *Guide to Protecting the Confidentiality of Personally Identifiable Information (PII)* [36].
- Special Publication 800-37 Revision 1, *Guide for Applying the Risk Management Framework to Federal Information Systems* [53].

NIST Special Publications are available from the NIST Computer Security Division website, at http://csrc.nist.gov/publications/PubsSPs.html. OMB Memoranda are available from the OMB website at http://www.whitehouse.gov/omb/memoranda_default.

SUMMARY

Federal government agencies and the information systems they operate are subject to a wide range of legislative, regulatory, and policy-driven privacy requirements, collectively intended to ensure appropriate procedural and technical safeguards are in place to protect personally identifiable information collected and maintained by agencies. Under provisions of the Privacy Act and the E-Government Act, agencies must provide public notice about any planned or implemented systems that collect, use, or disseminate personally identifiable information about members of the public. System owners must perform privacy impact assessments on these systems to evaluate the potential impact due to loss, theft, or unauthorized disclosure of PII, and select and implement appropriate security controls to mitigate the risk of such incidents occurring. As the number of security incidents experienced by agencies has increased and breaches of personal information have been publicized, additional requirements have been added obligating agencies to try to limit the amount of PII they hold, reduce the use of social security numbers and other sensitive personal identifiers, and develop and follow formal notification policies and procedures to report incidents involving PII. While the majority of these privacy requirements are not specified in FISMA or in NIST's Risk Management Framework, information on privacy practices is included within the scope of agency reporting required under FISMA, with the result that privacy and security are often addressed together. The implementation of system security controls in key areas—particularly those intended to maintain confidentiality such as access control and encryption—have an essential role in safeguarding privacy, so effective information security is a prerequisite to protecting privacy. System owners and other agency stakeholders with information system security responsibilities need to be aware of privacy protection requirements as one of many considerations driving risk management activities such as system security categorization, security control selection, security planning, and continuous monitoring.

REFERENCES

[1] Johnson C. Safeguarding against and responding to the breach of personally identifiable information. Washington, DC: Office of Management and Budget; May 22, 2007. Memorandum M-07-16.

[2] Federal Information Security Management Act of 2002, Pub. L. No. 107–347, 116 Stat. 2946.

[3] E-Government Act of 2002, Pub. L. No. 107–347, 116 Stat. 2899. §208.

[4] See, for exampleZients JG, Kundra V. FY 2009 reporting instructions for the Federal Information Security Management Act and agency privacy management. Washington, DC: Office of Management and Budget; August 20, 2009. Memorandum M-09-29.

[5] Privacy Act of 1974, Pub. L. No. 93–579, 88 Stat. 1896.

[6] Lew JJ. Instructions on complying with President's Memorandum of May 14, 1998, "Privacy and Personal Information in Federal Records". Washington, DC: Office of Management and Budget; January 7, 1999. Memorandum M-99-05.

[7] Lew JJ. Privacy policies on federal web sites. Washington, DC: Office of Management and Budget; Jun 2, 1999. Memorandum M-99-18.

[8] Management of federal information resources. Washington, DC: Office of Management and Budget; November 2000. Circular No. A-130, Revised (Transmittal, Memorandum No. 4).

[9] Johnson C. FY 2005 reporting instructions for the Federal Security Management Act and agency privacy management. Washington, DC: Office of Management and Budget; June 13, 2005. Memorandum M-05-15.

[10] Annual FISMA reporting: Senior Agency Official for Privacy (SAOP) questions, attachment to Zients JG, Kundra V. FY 2009 reporting instructions for the Federal Information Security Management Act and agency privacy management. Washington, DC: Office of Management and Budget; August 20, 2009. Memorandum M-09-29.

[11] E-Government Act of 2002, Pub. L. No. 107–347, 116 Stat. 2899. §208(b)(1)(A)(i).

[12] E-Government Act of 2002, Pub. L. No. 107–347, 116 Stat. 2899. §208(c).

[13] Bolten JB. OMB Guidance for implementing the privacy provisions of the E-Government Act of 2002. Washington, DC: Office of Management and Budget; September 26, 2003. Memorandum M-03-22.

[14] E-Government Act of 2002, Pub. L. No. 107–347, 116 Stat. 2899. §208(d).

[15] Zients J, Kundra V, Schmidt HA. FY 2010 reporting instructions for the Federal Information Security Management Act and agency privacy management. Washington, DC: Office of Management and Budget; April 21, 2010. Memorandum M-10-15. p. 18.

[16] E-Government Act of 2002, Pub. L. No. 107–347, 116 Stat. 2899. §208(c)(1)(B).

[17] Orszag PR. Guidance for agency use of third-party websites and applications. Washington, DC: Office of Management and Budget; June 25, 2010. Memorandum M-10-23.

[18] Lew JJ. Guidance and model language for federal web site privacy policies, attachment to Privacy policies on federal web sites. Washington, DC: Office of Management and Budget; June 2, 1999. Memorandum M-99-18.

[19] Platform for Privacy Preferences Project. Cambridge (MA): World Wide Web Consortium; [updated November 20, 2007; cited 2011 Jan 14]. <http://www.w3.org/P3P/>.

[20] Lew JJ. Privacy policies and data collection on federal web sites. Washington, DC: Office of Management and Budget; June 22, 2000. Memorandum M-00-13.

[21] Orszag PR. Guidance for online use of web measurement and customization technologies. Washington, DC: Office of Management and Budget; June 25, 2010. Memorandum M-10-22.

[22] Zients J, Kundra V, Schmidt HA. FY 2010 reporting instructions for the Federal Information Security Management Act and agency privacy management. Washington, DC: Office of Management and Budget; April 21, 2010. Memorandum M-10-15.

[23] Recommended security controls for federal information systems and organizations. Gaithersburg (MD): National Institute of Standards and Technology, Computer Security Division; August 2009. Special Publication 800–53 revision 3.

[24] Security and privacy controls for federal information systems and organizations. Gaithersburg (MD): National Institute of Standards and Technology, Computer Security Division; February 2012. Special Publication 800–53 revision 4. Initial Public Draft.

[25] Johnson C. FY 2008 reporting instructions for the Federal Information Security Management Act and agency privacy management. Washington, DC: Office of Management and Budget; July 14, 2008. Memorandum M-08-21.

[26] E-Government Act of 2002, Pub. L. No. 107–347, 116 Stat. 2899.

[27] Federal Agency Data Mining Reporting Act of 2007, Pub. L. No. 110–53, 121 Stat. 362.

[28] Zients J, Kundra V, Schmidt HA. FY 2010 reporting instructions for the Federal Information Security Management Act and agency privacy management. Washington, DC: Office of Management and Budget; April 21, 2010. Memorandum M-10-15. p. 4.

[29] Federal Information Security Management Act of 2002, Pub. L. No. 107–347, 116 Stat. 2946. §301, codified at §3544(b)(7).

[30] Evans KS. Reporting incidents involving personally identifiable information and incorporating the cost for security in agency information technology investments. Washington, DC: Office of Management and Budget; July 12, 2006. Memorandum M-06-19.

[31] Incident reporting guidelines [Internet]. Washington, DC: United States Computer Emergency Readiness Team [cited January 15, 2011]. <http://www.us-cert.gov/federal/reportingRequirements.html>.

[32] Federal Information Security Management Act of 2002, Pub. L. No. 107–347, 116 Stat. 2946. §301, codified at §3549.

[33] Privacy Act of 1974, Pub. L. No. 93-579, 88 Stat. 1896. See 5 U.S.C. §522a(b)(3).

[34] Privacy Act of 1974, Pub. L. No. 93-579, 88 Stat. 1896. See 5 U.S.C. §522a(a)(4).

[35] Privacy Act of 1974, Pub. L. No. 93-579, 88 Stat. 1896. See 5 U.S.C. §522a(a)(5).

[36] McCallister E, Grance T, Scarfone K. Guide to protecting the confidentiality of personally identifiable information (PII). Gaithersburg, MD: National Institute of Standards and Technology, Computer Security Division; April 2010. Special, Publication 800–122.

[37] The code of fair information practices. Washington, DC: Department of Health, Education and Welfare, Secretary's Advisory Committee on Automated Personal Data Systems, Records, computers, and the Rights of Citizens; 1973.

[38] The relationship between citizen and government: the Privacy Act of 1974. In: Personal privacy in an information society: the report of the privacy protection study commission. Washington, DC: Privacy Protection Study Commission; 1977.

[39] OECD guidelines on the protection of privacy and transborder flows of personal data. Paris (France): Organization for Economic Cooperation and, Development; September 23, 1980.

[40] Privacy Act of 1974, Pub. L. No. 93–579, 88 Stat. 1896. See 5 U.S.C. §522a(e)(10).

[41] Privacy Act of 1974, Pub. L. No. 93–579, 88 Stat. 1896. See 5 U.S.C. §522a(e).

[42] Privacy Act of 1974, Pub. L. No. 93–579, 88 Stat. 1896. See 5 U.S.C. §522a(b).

[43] Public information; agency rules, opinions, orders, records, and proceedings. 5 U.S.C. §552. 2010.

[44] Collection and compromise. 31 U.S.C. §3711(e). 2010.

[45] Privacy Act of 1974, Pub. L. No. 93–579, 88 Stat. 1896. See 5 U.S.C. §522a(c).

[46] Privacy of individually identifiable health information. 45 C.F.R. §164.528. 2011.

[47] Health Information for Economic and Clinical Health Act, Pub. L. No. 111–5, 123 Stat. 226. §13405(c).

[48] Privacy Act of 1974, Pub. L. No. 93–579, 88 Stat. 1896. See 5 U.S.C. §522a(d).

[49] Privacy Act of 1974, Pub. L. No. 93–579, 88 Stat. 1896. See 5 U.S.C. §522a(e)(4).

[50] Privacy Act of 1974, as amended; Proposed system of records and routine use disclosures. 75 Fed. Reg. 79065; December 17, 2010.

[51] Privacy Act of 1974, Pub. L. No. 93–579, 88 Stat. 1896. See 5 U.S.C. §522a(e)(5).

[52] Privacy Act of 1974, Pub. L. No. 93–579, 88 Stat. 1896. See §522a(g).

[53] Guide for applying the risk management framework to federal information systems. Gaithersburg, MD: National Institute of Standards and Technology, Computer Security Division; Febraury 2010. Special Publication 800–37 revision 1.

[54] E-Government Act of 2002, Pub. L. No. 107–347, 116 Stat. 2899. §208(b).

[55] See for example Privacy impact assessment. Washington, DC: Department of Defense; November 2008. DD Form 2930.

[56] See for example DOJ privacy impact assessment template. Washington, DC: Department of Justice; 2006. <http://www.justice.gov/jmd/pia/preliminary_pia.pdf>.

[57] See for example, Privacy impact assessment guide. Alexandria (VA): Securities and Exchange Commission, Office of Information Technology; January 2007. <http://www.sec.gov/about/privacy/piaguide.pdf>.

[58] Cyber Security Assessment & Management (CSAM) [computer program]. Version 2.1.5.2. Washington, DC: Department of Justice; 2010.

[59] Orszag PR. Guidance for agency use of third-party websites and applications. Washington, DC: Office of Management and Budget; June 25, 2010. Memorandum M-10-23. p. 4.

[60] Orszag PR. Guidance for agency use of third-party websites and applications. Washington, DC: Office of Management and Budget; June 25, 2010. Memorandum M-10-23. p. 5.

[61] Standards for security categorization of federal information and information systems. Gaithersburg (MD): National Institute of Standards and Technology, Computer Security Division; December 2003. Federal Information Processing Standards Publication 199.

[62] Johnson C. Protection of sensitive agency information. Washington, DC: Office of Management and Budget; June 23, 2006. Memorandum M-06-16.

[63] Bush GW. Strengthening federal efforts to protect against identity theft. 71 Fed. Reg. 27945; May 10, 2006. Executive, Order 13402.

[64] Bush GW. Strengthening federal efforts to protect against identity theft. 71 Fed. Reg. 27945; May 10, 2006. Executive, Order 13402. p. 6.

[65] Privacy Act of 1974, Pub. L. No. 93–579, 88 Stat. 1896. See 5 U.S.C. §522a(e)(1).

[66] Combating identity theft: a strategic plan. Washington, DC: President's Identity Theft Task Force; April 2007.

[67] Johnson C. Safeguarding against and responding to the breach of personally identifiable information. Washington, DC: Office of Management and Budget; May 22, 2007. Memorandum M-07-16. p. 7.

[68] Breach notification for unsecured protected health information; interim final rule. 74 Fed. Reg. 42740; August 24, 2009.

[69] Health Information Technology for Economic and Clinical Health Act of 2009, Pub. L. No. 111–5, 123 Stat. 226. §13402.

[70] Johnson C. Safeguarding against and responding to the breach of personally identifiable information. Washington, DC: Office of Management and Budget; May 22, 2007. Memorandum M-07-16. p. 14–5.

[71] Johnson C. Safeguarding against and responding to the breach of personally identifiable information. Washington, DC: Office of Management and Budget; May 22, 2007. Memorandum M-07-16. p. 16.

[72] Johnson C. Safeguarding against and responding to the breach of personally identifiable information. Washington, DC: Office of Management and Budget; May 22, 2007. Memorandum M-07-16. p. 16–7.

[73] Family Educational Rights and Privacy Act of 1974, Pub. L. No. 93–380, 88 Stat. 574.

[74] Electronic Communications Privacy Act of 1986, Pub. L. No. 99–508, 100 Stat. 1848.

[75] Health Insurance Portability and Accountability Act of 1996, Pub. L. No. 104–191, 110 Stat. 1936.

[76] Children's Online Privacy Protection Act of 1998, Pub. L. No. 105–277, 112 Stat. 2581.

[77] Financial Services Modernization Act of 1999, Pub. L. No. 106–102, 113 Stat. 1338.

[78] Health Information Technology for Economic and Clinical Health Act of 2009, Pub. L. No. 111–5, 123 Stat. 226.

[79] Family educational and privacy rights. 20 U.S.C. §1232g (b)(4)(B).

[80] HIPAA administrative simplification. Washington, DC: Department of Health and Human Services, Office for Civil Rights; 2006.

[81] Privacy of individually identifiable health information, 45 C.F.R. §164.508; 2011.

[82] Privacy of individually identifiable health information, 45 C.F.R. §§164.510-512; 2011.

[83] American Recovery and Reinvestment Act of 2009, Pub. L. No. 111–5, 123 Stat. 115.

[84] Health Information Technology for Economic and Clinical Health Act of 2009, Pub. L. No. 111–5, 123 Stat. 226. See §13410.

[85] Confidentiality of Alcohol and Drug Abuse Patient Records, 42 C.F.R. Part 2; 2002. See §§2.32-2.35.

[86] Financial Services Modernization Act of 1999, Pub. L. No. 106–102, 113 Stat. 1338. §501.

[87] Financial Services Modernization Act of 1999, Pub. L. No. 106–102, 113 Stat. 1338. §§502-503.

[88] Activities that are financial in nature, 12 U.S.C. §1843(k)(4).

[89] Electronic Communications Privacy Act of 1986, Pub. L. No. 99-508, 100 Stat. 1848. See §201, amending Title 18 of the U.S. Code.

[90] The Electronic Communications Privacy Act: promoting security and protecting privacy in the digital age. Hearing before the Senate Judiciary Committee, 111th Cong., 2nd Sess; September 22, 2010.

[91] Confidential Nature of Claims, 38 U.S.C. §5701; 2007.

[92] Confidentiality of certain medical records, 38 U.S.C. §7332; 2007.

[93] Reports and notice to Congress on data breaches, 38 U.S.C. §5726; 2007.

[94] Privacy protections in state constitutions [Internet]. Denver (CO): National Conference of State Legislatures [cited April 15, 2012]. <http://www.ncsl.org/issues-research/telecom/privacy-protections-in-state-constitutions.aspx>.

[95] Security breach notification laws [Internet]. Denver (CO): National Conference of State Legislatures [updated Febraury 6, 2012; cited April 15, 2012]. <http://www.ncsl.org/issues-research/telecom/security-breach-notification-laws.aspx>.

Federal Initiatives

17

INFORMATION IN THIS CHAPTER:

- Network Security-Related Initiatives
- Government-wide Application Security Initiatives
- Identity and Access Management Initiatives
- Executive Branch Programs, Directives, and Requirements
- Information Resources Management Initiatives

Although FISMA and associated implementation guidance specify a wide array of requirements for federal agencies, the scope of information security management in government organizations extends well beyond FISMA. Federal agencies are subject to a variety of security-related regulations, policy directives, and other sources of requirements driven by government-wide programs, priorities, and initiatives that information system owners, security officers, risk managers, and other agency personnel need to consider when operating their security management programs. This chapter identifies and briefly describes major federal initiatives, programs, and policies that influence or impose requirements on agency information security management practices and summarizes the key implications of these drivers on information security risk management at all levels of government organizations. The material in this chapter emphasizes the relevance of federal initiatives to agency information security management and identifies authoritative sources of requirements and guidance that assist agencies in achieving compliance with applicable mandates and policy directives.

NETWORK SECURITY

Recognizing the common needs of agencies with respect to telecommunications and network services, Congress established government-wide contract programs for the acquisition of such services that require agencies to procure and utilize the services offered by specified telecommunications vendors. Use of these contracts—beginning with the Federal Telecommunications System 2000 (FTS2000) contract awarded in 1988 and continuing with FTS2001 and Networx contracts, the last of which was awarded in 2007—is mandatory for all executive agencies unless they can justify an exemption to the General Services Administration [1], which manages the government-wide telecommunications contracts. All agencies were directed in 2008 to establish plans and initiate the process of transitioning from FTS2001 to Networx for information technology services provided under the contract [2], including Internet Protocol-based network services. The mandatory use of Networx means that all agencies will rely to some extent on commercial telecommunications providers [3] for their network infrastructure and business owners and system owners responsible for securing information systems that use network services need to be aware of the characteristics and set of services their agency's vendors offer. It also means that system owners are rarely responsible (or authorized) for provisioning their own network infrastructure and services unless their systems outsource relevant infrastructure, such as with systems using conventional third-party hosting or cloud computing services. Most federal agencies manage one or more network environments as general support systems that provide internal or external-facing network connectivity, telecommunications services, and security controls.

The common network infrastructure used by most federal agencies [4] facilitates the development and rollout of network-centric government initiatives intended to augment the security provisions put in place by individual agencies and support cyber security and critical infrastructure protection efforts on a national scale. Telecommunications networks and other IT infrastructure are among the elements the government considers critical infrastructure and therefore subject to federal policy and agency requirements for critical infrastructure identification, prioritization, and protection specified in Homeland Security Presidential Directive 7 [5]. HSPD-7 requires all federal agencies to develop plans for protecting critical infrastructure components and associated resources under their control, including physical facilities and IT assets. Government-wide critical infrastructure protection is coordinated and overseen by the Department of Homeland Security (DHS). This department, working in coordination with OMB from a governance perspective and the National Security Agency for operational and technical expertise, established several key programs and capabilities focused on monitoring and securing network infrastructure across the federal government.

US-CERT

FISMA includes a provision for the operation of a federal information security incident center that collects information about threats, vulnerabilities, and events posing risk to federal agencies and information systems and provides assistance to agencies on detecting and handling security incidents and remediating identified vulnerabilities [6]. Following enactment of the Homeland Security Act, the Federal Computer Incident Response Center, originally created by NIST and managed by the General

Services Administration (GSA), moved under the authority of the Department of Homeland Security [7], which reestablished the center as the United States Computer Emergency Response Team (US-CERT). US-CERT is an importance source of threat and vulnerability information for agencies to use in their own incident monitoring and response, risk assessment, and continuous monitoring activities. Agencies are also required to report security incidents to US-CERT within a time interval that corresponds to the severity categorization of each incident, in cases involving unauthorized access to agency information or information systems, including breaches of personally identifiable information, agencies must report the incident within one hour [8].

Comprehensive National Cybersecurity Initiative

Persistent concerns about the relative security of the government's network infrastructure, and in particular its vulnerability or resilience to cyber attacks, have increased the attention focused on protecting information and telecommunications infrastructure. In Homeland Security Presidential Directive 23 [9], the government proposed a series of measures to improve the defensive posture of government networks as part of a Comprehensive National Cybersecurity Initiative (CNCI). While the full contents of HSPD-23 are classified, publicly released details of the program identify 12 initiatives [10]:

1. Manage the Federal Enterprise Network as a single network enterprise with Trusted Internet Connections.
2. Deploy an intrusion detection system of sensors across the Federal enterprise.
3. Pursue deployment of intrusion prevention systems across the Federal enterprise.
4. Coordinate and redirect research and development (R&D) efforts.
5. Connect current cyber operations centers to enhance situational awareness.
6. Develop and implement a government-wide cyber counterintelligence plan.
7. Increase the security of classified networks.
8. Expand cyber education.
9. Define and develop enduring "leap-ahead" technology, strategies, and programs.
10. Define and develop enduring deterrence strategies and programs.
11. Develop a multi-pronged approach for global supply chain risk management.
12. Define the Federal role for extending cybersecurity into critical infrastructure domains.

While many of these initiatives are focused on government-wide management and operation, individual agencies are expected to contribute to their execution and, in the case of initiatives such as Trusted Internet Connections and intrusion detection and prevention in government networks, the CNCI both drives and constrains some of the network security choices agencies make to protect their own environments and systems.

Trusted Internet Connections

OMB and DHS jointly manage the Trusted Internet Connections (TIC) initiative, an effort announced in 2007 that seeks to consolidate network services across the federal government and reduce the total number of Internet points-of-presence from over 4000 to fewer than 100 [11]. During 2008, federal agencies were obligated to develop and submit plans for reducing external network connections and to complete capability statements that included self-assessments of each agency's ability to serve as access providers for trusted Internet connections, either for their own internal needs or potentially as service providers to other agencies as well. The General Services Administration also modified the scope of services provided by Networx contract vendors to enable agencies to satisfy TIC requirements by procuring network services through Networx. A limited number of agencies received authorization from OMB to operate their own external network connections, while all other agencies are expected to provision managed trusted IP services (MTIPS) from Networx contractors [12], with a deadline originally set for January 31, 2011 [13]. The TIC initiative not only supports the government's broad goal of consolidating network and telecommunications services with a common approach, but also facilitates network security monitoring by reducing the physical number of connections to be monitored. Decisions about choosing and establishing external network connections and associated services are typically made at the agency level, so the capabilities provided to agency information systems typically represent shared services and common controls. Depending on the scope of a system and the environment in which it operates, secure network services, including those required under the TIC initiative, may also be relevant for interconnection security agreements.

EINSTEIN

The Department of Homeland Security launched the EINSTEIN program in 2003 to help achieve government objectives to collect, analyze, and share security information, subsequently expanding and enhancing the program to provide intrusion detection and prevention capabilities to protect federal networks. As originally implemented, US-CERT operated EINSTEIN as an automated set of processes for collecting and analyzing computer security information voluntarily provided by federal civilian agencies. In 2008, DHS updated the program to include the implementation of network intrusion detection sensors to monitor federal agency network traffic and report potential malicious activity to US-CERT. The enhanced program, dubbed EINSTEIN 2, is intended to augment individual agency network security controls and monitoring practices and enable more insightful analysis of information flowing into and out of federal government networks [14]. EINSTEIN 2 will leverage agencies' trusted Internet connections by implementing intrusion detection sensors within the infrastructure provided by Networx MTIPS contractors. Further planned enhancements to the program would add intrusion prevention capabilities to the passive intrusion detection monitoring provided under EINSTEIN 2. Specifically, the next-generation EINSTEIN 3 program will leverage commercial security technology and analytical capabilities developed by the National Security Agency to perform deeper inspection of network traffic and to enable active response to detected malicious activity, including blocking network traffic determined to pose a threat to government agencies, systems, or infrastructure [15]. Initial EINSTEIN 3 pilot exercises suggest that the deployment model for the program, like that for EINSTEIN 2, will involve implementing new technical components within the network infrastructure of commercial telecommunications service providers. This approach may optimize the efficiency of information gathering and analysis performed by the NSA, US-CERT, and other program participants, but would also effectively remove individual agencies and their system owners and risk managers from meaningful interaction with the program.

CLOUD COMPUTING

Legislation and federal policy aimed at improving the efficiency and effectiveness of government IT management practices have long encouraged agencies to consider using private sector organizations to develop and operate information systems and perform IT-related services in support of mission functions and business processes. Agency decisions about application hosting, information system development, and the provision of shared government services often focus on cost and performance criteria, comparing the capabilities of government agencies with private sector organizations to determine whether systems and IT services should be outsourced to third-party organizations [16]. In recent years discussions about IT outsourcing shifted to include the use of *cloud computing*, a service-based IT delivery model in which organizations deploy their applications or use infrastructure and services offered by external providers, paying only for the capacity and services they use. Cloud computing promises substantial potential benefits for public sector and commercial organizations, including more efficient capacity utilization, reduction in IT capital expenditures, flexibility to scale capacity and usage up or down as demand changes, and more rapid deployment of applications and services than in traditional internal agency deployments. Cloud computing is similar in many respects to conventional application hosting, but is distinguished from other types of hosting by characteristics including on-demand service provision, ubiquitous network access, resource pooling, elastic capabilities and services, and measured usage and associated billing and payment models [17]. Many private sector organizations have been quick to embrace cloud computing. Federal government agencies seek many of the same benefits in terms of cost-efficiency, flexibility, and speed that led OMB to issue a "cloud first" policy for new IT deployments [18], but the new service delivery model also raises issues about information security, data stewardship, privacy, governance, and change management. Several government-wide initiatives have been established to address these concerns and help agencies realize the benefits of cloud computing, with key guidance to agencies issued by OMB, NIST, and GSA to help agencies understand the new IT service paradigm and properly evaluate its use to support agency operations.

Given the FISMA security requirements that apply to any operating environment used for federal information systems and NIST's statutory authority for developing information security standards and guidelines for agency use, NIST took on the task of producing the common government definition of cloud computing [19]. This definition identifies three service models—infrastructure as a service, platform as a service, and software as a service—and distinguishes among different potential deployment models for cloud services, including public, private, community, and hybrid models. Private and community cloud models use infrastructure and capabilities dedicated to a specific agency or group of agencies, while public and hybrid clouds offer infrastructure and capabilities open to multiple organizations, potentially including government and non-government users. Regardless of the type of organization that owns or manages a cloud environment, for a federal government agency to use cloud computing the cloud environment must satisfy relevant security standards and requirements. In private cloud deployments the agency using cloud services is often in a position to exert a strong influence over the way the environment is operated—including the selection and implementation of security controls—just as it would in a conventional data center or managed hosting environment. In contrast, agencies considering public cloud environments typically have less control over the specific security controls and configuration the environment provides, so agencies considering public cloud deployments must evaluate the security and privacy protections offered by public cloud providers against the agency's own requirements [20].

While many agencies conduct their own evaluations of cloud computing alternatives and deploy private cloud solutions, at a government-wide level the General Services Administration coordinates efforts among federal agencies to identify and evaluate third-party providers of cloud computing services, consistent with the approach the government uses for procuring network and telecommunications services. These efforts include working with commercial vendors to approve cloud-provisioned services and make them available through government-wide acquisition contracts, awarding contracts to cloud computing service providers, and overseeing agency-specific and government-wide programs to evaluate cloud service providers, including assessing their security and privacy capabilities. As federal agencies learn more about cloud computing and its benefits and risks, additional issues beyond security emerge that agencies and their business owners, information system owners, and risk managers need to consider. NIST describes and provides initial recommendations relating to many of these issues in Special Publication 800-146, *Cloud Computing Synopsis and Recommendations* [21], which addresses performance, reliability, economic factors, and compliance in addition to information security.

FedRAMP

Recognizing the value of cloud computing to the federal government and the need to appropriately address agency and government-wide concerns about security, interoperability, portability, reliability, and resiliency, in late 2011 OMB issued new federal policy directing agencies to use the requirements, security assessment procedures, and cloud service authorization packages developed under the Federal Risk and Authorization Management Program (FedRAMP) [22]. FedRAMP is a multi-agency collaborative effort managed by GSA that provides a standard process for assessing cloud service providers against FISMA requirements and the security control framework specified in Special Publication 800-53. Using this process, cloud service providers seeking to do business with government agencies hire approved third-party assessment organizations to conduct independent reviews of their security and to produce system security plans, security assessment reports, and other Risk Management Framework documentation that can be used by the FedRAMP Joint Authorization Board [23] to decide whether to authorize the cloud service providers for use by government agencies. This approach essentially establishes pre-authorized cloud computing providers so that individual agencies can avoid incurring the time and resource costs ordinarily required to perform an agency-specific assessment. Even where agencies have specific requirements that may not be fully addressed by FedRAMP authorization packages, the use of RMF artifacts and Special Publication 800-53 controls should help agencies align FedRAMP authorization documentation to their own internal requirements and identify gaps that cloud service providers need to address.

FedRAMP represents something of a departure from standard federal acquisition practices, as cloud service providers will apply directly to the FedRAMP program when seeking authorization, potentially allowing them to first complete authorization and then compete for government agency contracts for cloud services. In contrast, when GSA awarded the first federal cloud computing contracts in 2010 (to 11 companies to provide infrastructure as a service offered through Apps.gov), all of the service providers receiving prime contracts still needed to demonstrate FISMA compliance and achieve authorization to operate [24]. Under current federal policy, agencies must include FedRAMP authorization requirements in acquisition contract language used to procure cloud computing services [22], so cloud service providers that have already achieved authorization should have a significant competitive advantage in the federal market.

When using cloud computing services, agencies and information system owners will need to adapt their information security management practices to incorporate security control assessment information produced under the FedRAMP third-party authorization process, in a manner analogous to their current use of common control providers. Agencies also need to include the operational and security monitoring capabilities of their cloud service providers in their information security continuous monitoring strategies and ensure that cloud computing environments comply with agency and system-specific business continuity and disaster recovery requirements specified in continuity plans.

APPLICATION SECURITY

Under current federal information resources management policy, agencies are required to acquire commercially available software unless they can demonstrate the cost effectiveness of custom development or other alternatives [25]. Before implementing commercial information technology products, tools, or components in federal information systems, system owners must identify and evaluate the security implications, including potential vulnerabilities associated with acquired applications and the security capabilities provided or security requirements associated with the technology that must be addressed with security controls. Independent testing and security evaluation of commercially available software can facilitate information technology acquisition by offering agencies certifications or other evidence of different products' relative security and compliance with applicable standards. Federal security standards and acquisition policies mandate product certification for some types of technology, and individual agencies may require security certifications for commercial products as a prerequisite to their implementation in government operating environments. In cases where security testing or certification is available, but not required, system owners may be able to use product certification as a criterion in selection procedures for information technology. Different standards and initiatives address security capabilities and secure configuration for applications, application components, operating systems, and software product categories.

Tested Security Technologies

Various security testing programs exist to evaluate hardware and software products in the marketplace, including evaluations performed by non-government testing and certification providers. NIST manages a National Voluntary Laboratory Accreditation Program (NVLAP) that accredits third-party organizations to conduct specific types of evaluations in support of federal rules requiring the use of standard or certified products, processes, or facilities. The NVLAP program covers organizations that provide testing on a broad range of products, industry domains, and technologies, including information security testing programs for software and other computer-related products, cryptographic modules used to provide encryption, and health information technology software applications and modules [26]. Vendors offering information technology products subject to certification can in some cases work directly with accredited testing organizations to have their products evaluated and certified. NIST develops and maintains security-related standards and specifications for vendors to incorporate in their technology products and also oversees product certification using standards and processes developed by other government agencies or standards organizations.

Federal Information Processing Standards

NIST issues Federal Information Processing Standards (FIPS) publications to specify mandatory requirements for federal information systems. Notable FIPS publications relevant to application security include those addressing encryption and cryptography, including: [27]

- FIPS 140-2, *Security Requirements for Cryptographic Modules*
- FIPS 197, *Advanced Encryption Standard*

- FIPS 186-3, *Digital Signature Standard*
- FIPS 180-4, *Secure Hash Standard*

System owners developing or acquiring information technology for use in agency information systems need to ensure that the products or technical components implemented by their systems comply with applicable standards. Vendors whose products have received certification often market that fact, but NIST also maintains publicly available inventories of validated technologies under its Cryptologic Module Validation Program (CMVP) [28], so system owners and security officers have an authoritative source of information to confirm whether the products or technologies they use comply with federal security standards.

Common Criteria

The Common Criteria for Information Technology Security Evaluation is an international standard used to evaluate, assert, and certify the relative security assurance levels of hardware and software products [29]. Although developed outside the federal government, the Department of Defense adopted Common Criteria beginning in 1999 as a replacement for its own Trusted Computer System Evaluation Criteria (TCSEC). At roughly the same time, NIST and the NSA established the National Information Assurance Partnership (NIAP) to evaluate IT products for conformance to Common Criteria. Under the Common Criteria Evaluation and Validation Scheme for IT Security (CCEVS), NIAP approves third-party organizations to perform Common Criteria certification testing, provides oversight of these independent testing organizations, and manages collaborative research and development activities to specify protection profiles for various types of technologies and security functions [30]. Once certified, products evaluated against Common Criteria standards are listed on a publicly available website, providing the assurance level achieved, date of certification, and full security report details for each product [31]. System owners, security officers, IT managers, acquisition officials, and other agency personnel involved in the selection of information technology use certification information to confirm that the products they implement satisfy applicable security requirements, standards, and policies.

Secure Configuration Checklists

Secure configuration of information systems and supporting hardware and software is an essential element of effective implementation of security controls. System owners and security officers are responsible for properly implementing the controls they select for their systems, and for validating secure configuration in initial and ongoing security control assessments and continuous monitoring activities. For many types of system components and computer operating systems, NIST or other government organizations have produced standard security configuration checklists that provide instructions for configuring products and technologies for secure operation in agency environments. With respect to desktop operating systems, OMB issued guidance in 2007 requiring all federal agencies to adopt NIST-developed secure configurations when deploying Windows operating systems [32]. These requirements, formalized as the NIST Federal Desktop Core Configuration (FDCC) and revised and updated as the United States Government Configuration Baseline (USGCB), apply to government agency use of operating systems, Web browsers, and other computer workstation features. NIST applies a similar approach to many other types of products and technologies through the National Checklist Repository, a publicly available set of secure configuration guidelines managed as part of the National Vulnerability Database [33]. In its guidance to agencies on using secure configuration checklists, NIST directs system owners to prioritize NIST-developed checklists if they exist, and to next look to security technical implementation guides from the Defense Information Systems Agency (DISA) or checklists from NSA or other agencies [34]. For many products, NIST directs system owners to secure configuration information produced by the product vendors or other trusted third parties, providing information through the checklist repository about the source of each checklist and sponsoring agency, if any. Wherever possible NIST represents secure configuration checklists as technical specifications defined using the Security Content Automation Protocol (SCAP), to facilitate scanning and configuration validation of IT products using automated tools. Information system owners should identify security checklists for the products or system components they deploy to ensure that their systems are implemented with secure configuration settings. To the extent that applicable secure configuration checklists are available, system owners can also align their security control assessment and continuous monitoring strategies to leverage checklist specifications.

IDENTITY AND ACCESS MANAGEMENT

Agencies and their system owners typically need to address a large number of security controls and information system considerations related to access control, including identification and authentication, user authorization, and system and communications protection [35]. Many of these functions, services, and controls are addressed collectively through federal programs and initiatives for identity and access management, so system owners need to be aware of these initiatives and the obligations some of them impose on agency decisions about the use of identity and access management capabilities, controls, and technologies. Federal identity and access management activities across the government are coordinated under the authority of the Federal Chief Information Officers Council, with consolidated information available online through the IDManagement.gov Website. From a national perspective, the release by the Obama administration of the National Strategy for Trusted Identities in Cyberspace (NSTIC) [36] focused greater attention on identity and access management capabilities necessary to realize the vision of an "identity ecosystem" providing secure and interoperable online access to services. This strategy and associated initiatives call for large-scale collaboration among private sector and public sector organizations to improve the privacy, security, and convenience of online transactions. By enhancing public confidence in the security and privacy of online services, government agencies (and commercial organizations) could offer more services online, potentially reducing the cost of service delivery while also increasing access to and quality of those services. As of early 2012, the identity ecosystem envisioned in the NSTIC was still in the conceptual phase, but many ongoing federal agency-level and government-wide identity and access management initiatives could have key roles if the vision is realized.

Identity, Credential, and Access Management (ICAM)

The federal government's Identity, Credential, and Access Management (ICAM) program began in 2008, when the CIO Council chartered a subcommittee to develop government-wide policies, define an ICAM segment architecture [37], and provide implementation guidance to agencies on the processes, technologies, and other considerations necessary to create and manage digital identities and associated credentials. The ICAM program addresses the distinct but interrelated areas of identity management, credential management, and access management, driven by federal regulations and standards for electronic authentication, personal identity verification, public key infrastructure, and user and entity authorization to access government information and information systems. The ICAM transition plan specifies a series of government-wide and agency-specific implementation initiatives, listed in Table 17.1, necessary to achieve the key goals of the program. The ICAM goals include achieving compliance with applicable laws and regulations, streamlining access to electronic government services, improving online security across the government, enabling trust and interoperability, and reducing costs and increasing efficiency associated with identity, credential, and access management functions [38].

The long-term strategy for federal identity, credential, and access management, consistent with the policy articulated in HSPD-12, is for all government agencies to use standard forms of identification and credentials issued to all federal employees and contractors, and to leverage those standards to enable consistent and interoperable physical and logical access control capabilities for all federal facilities and information systems [40]. Agencies implementing identity, credential, and access management to satisfy their own information system and business process requirements also need to incorporate government-wide standards to ensure that agency-specific technologies and solutions conform to requirements and specifications needed to implement interoperable federated identity management.

Personal Identity Verification

Prompted by concerns over the risk to federal government facilities due to variation in the types of identification used by different agencies, the administration mandated a government-wide standard for forms of government identification in Homeland

Table 17.1 Federal ICAM Transition Roadmap Initiatives and Implications for Agencies [39]

Government-wide Initiatives	Implications
Augment policy and implementation guidance to agencies	Agencies are expected to adhere to policy and execute implementation guidance in their own programs and initiatives
Establish a federated identity framework for the Federal Government	Agencies are expected to implement the government-wide framework when it is available, meaning agency systems and services will need to be planned and designed for interoperability at the federal level
Enhance performance measurement and accountability within ICAM initiatives	Agency compliance will be measured and enforced to ensure that ICAM programs and services are implemented and operated consistently
Provide government-wide services for common ICAM requirements	Agencies may be able (and might be required) to leverage common services rather than implementing or deploying their own
Agency-level Initiatives	Implications
Streamline collection and sharing of digital identity data	Agencies need to assess their data management practices related to identity and consolidate or otherwise eliminate potential redundancies in identity data
Fully leverage Personal Identity Verification and PIV-I credentials	In accordance with HSPD-12 and subsequent guidance from OMB, agencies need to continue to mature their use of personal identity verification credentials, including accepting compliant externally issued credentials as well as their own
Modernize physical access control systems (PACS) infrastructure	With broader use of PIV credentials, agencies need to update physical security processes and technologies to accommodate PIV-enabled physical access control mechanisms
Modernize logical access control systems (LACS) infrastructure	Agencies need to update logical access control processes and capabilities to allow PIV-enabled access control to information systems and leverage the stronger security that PIV credentials offer
Implement federated identity capability	Agencies are expected to implement federated identity management services and standards to ensure interoperability of their own identity, credential, and access management services with those of other federal agencies and leverage common government services where appropriate

Security Presidential Directive 12. Forms of identification satisfying the security and reliability objectives in HSPD-12 must be issued only after verifying an individual's identity, resist fraud, tampering, counterfeiting, and exploitation, support electronic authentication, and be issued only by providers whose credentialing systems have been formally certified and accredited [41]. The standard HSPD-12 calls for is defined in FIPS 201, *Personal Identity Verification (PIV) of Federal Employees and Contractors*, which provides technical specifications for identity credentials issued by government agencies and interoperability specifications intended to ensure that federal credentials, when issued, can be consistently and reliably used by agencies to control physical and logical access [42]. The standard addresses the physical, technical, and functional characteristics of the actual credentials issued by agencies to their employees and contractors and specifies requirements for the processes of identity proofing individuals, issuing, registering, and maintaining PIV credentials, and authenticating holders of PIV credentials for physical access to facilities and logical access to information resources.

More than 5.1 million credentials have been issued to federal employees and contractors as a result of HSPD-12 and FIPS 201, representing the vast majority of personnel covered under federal policy [43]. Federal agencies are required to use PIV credentials for authenticated access to both physical facilities and logical information resources such as networks and information systems. The initial focus in most agencies was updating physical access control systems to support PIV credentials, although OMB reported in 2011 a steady upward trend in agency logical access control, with almost two-thirds of government users' access to agency information systems requiring PIV-based authentication (although some agencies reported little or no capabilities implemented to support PIV credentials for logical access) [44]. In early 2011 OMB issued direction to agencies mandating that all newly developed information systems be enabled for PIV credential-based access and requiring agencies to upgrade their physical and logical access controls to support PIV credentials before using IT funding for other development, modernization, or enhancement activities [40]. Agencies are also obligated to accept and be able to electronically verify credentials issued by other agencies—an interoperability requirement long envisioned under HSPD-12 but realized by few federal agencies, even among bureaus or operating divisions of the same department. For agencies and their system owners, these collective requirements directly impact the technical design and security control selection and implementation decisions made for individual information systems, and also position agency user identification and authentication functions as processes that should be implemented as common controls provided to all agency information systems.

Electronic Authentication

One benefit to agencies from implementing identification and authentication mechanisms that satisfy HSPD-12 requirements is the support that PIV credentials provide for electronic authentication. Under guidance from OMB issued to agencies in 2003, electronic authentication (or *e-authentication*) to all Web-based, externally facing federal information resources occurs at one of four levels of assurance, where the designated assurance level corresponds to the confidence the agency requires that a user credential presented for identification is valid [45]. The scope of e-authentication guidance and subsequent technical guidelines on implementing electronic authentication mechanisms only addresses individual user authentication to government information systems, so it represents a subset of identity, credential, and access management functions and associated security controls for identification and authentication and access control. E-authentication guidance for federal information systems does require system owners to conduct a specific type of risk assessment—distinct from broader information system, mission and business process, or organizational risk assessments described in Chapter 13—to determine the appropriate e-authentication assurance level for each system. The overall e-authentication assurance process prescribed for federal information systems involves five steps [45]:

1. Conduct a risk assessment of the system.
2. Map identified risks to the required assurance level.
3. Select technology based on e-authentication technical guidance.
4. After implementation, validate that the implemented system has achieved the required assurance level.
5. Periodically reassess the information system to determine technology refresh requirements.

The e-authentication risk assessment process follows an approach similar to the initial steps of the Risk Management Framework, and if conducted concurrent with RMF activities the e-authentication risk assessment can leverage some of the key outputs of RMF tasks, particularly security categorization and common control identification. System owners conducting stand-alone risk assessments can use the e-RA tool (shown in Figure 17.1) and associated guidance for agencies available from the ICAM program [46]. The e-authentication risk assessment addresses risk due only to authorization errors, considering the relative impact to the agency from "inconvenience, distress, or damage to standing or reputation; financial loss or agency liability; harm to agency programs or public interests; unauthorized release of sensitive information; personal safety; and civil or criminal violations" [45]. System owners compare the level of impact for each category to the maximum impact allowed at each assurance level to determine the appropriate overall e-authentication assurance level. Once assigned, the assurance level corresponds to minimum technical identity proofing and authentication requirements that must be implemented for the system, described in detail in Special Publication 800-63. Each assurance level is associated with protocols for validating user identity and implementing authentication tokens and processes. A summary of the four e-authentication levels and associated technical requirements appears in Table 17.2.

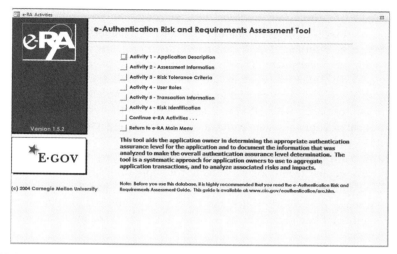

FIGURE 17.1 The Stand-alone e-RA Risk and Requirements Assessment Tool Provides Step-by-Step Data Entry Forms to Support System Owners in Gathering and Evaluating the Information Necessary to Determine the Appropriate E-Authentication Assurance Level

Table 17.2 E-Authentication Assurance Levels and Associated Technical Requirements [47]

E-Authentication Assurance Level	Requirements
Level 1: Little or no confidence in the asserted identity's validity	• No identity proofing required • Any token type permitted • Any secure protocol permitted
Level 2: Some confidence in the asserted identity's validity	• Users must present identifying materials or information • Memorized secret, pre-registered knowledge, look-up secret, out-of-band, and one-time password tokens permitted • Single-factor authentication permitted
Level 3: High confidence in the asserted identity's validity	• Systems must validate user-presented identifying materials or information • Soft or hard cryptographic tokens permitted • Multi-factor authentication required with cryptographic proof of key possession
Level 4: Very high confidence in the asserted identity's validity	• In-person identity proofing required • Hard cryptographic tokens only • Multi-factor authentication required with cryptographic proof of key possession

For federal information systems accessed by non-government personnel, including employees of commercial organizations or members of the public, higher e-authentication assurance levels can have a significant impact on the way users interact with the government. This is especially true at assurance Level 4, which requires in-person identity proofing and therefore precludes fully online interactions. With respect to government employees and contractors, PIV credentials issued in conformance with HSPD-12 satisfy all e-authentication assurance levels, as credential applicants must appear at least once in person before the issuing agency [48] and the storage of X.509 certificate-based keys on PIV credentials satisfies the hard token and multi-factor authentication requirements [49]. Agencies typically deploy technologies suitable for supporting higher e-authentication assurance requirements at an organizational level rather than for individual information systems, particularly when the tokens and authentication methods used involve significant key management or other functions associated with public key infrastructures.

Federal PKI

The use of public key infrastructure (PKI) in the federal government is coordinated by the Federal PKI Policy Authority—an interagency group established by the CIO Council—and managed by the General Services Administration as the designated Federal PKI Management Authority. Under the governance of these authorities, the Federal Public Key Infrastructure (FPKI) specifies policies, processes, and standards for public key cryptography in the government, offers PKI services to agencies, and maintains a Federal Bridge Certification Authority (FBCA) that cross-certifies individual agency PKIs to ensure their interoperability with each other and with federal PKI policies and standards. Federal agencies generally are not required to use PKI, but if they choose to do so, they must follow policies and guidance issued by the Federal PKI Policy Authority [50]. Agencies wanting to implement PKI have the option of standing up their own infrastructures (and getting them cross-certified with the FBCA), joining PKI systems already deployed in other agencies, or leveraging third-party services provided by government or commercial entities certified by the Federal PKI Management Authority. The technical requirements for setting up and managing a public key infrastructure go beyond the scope of this book, but with respect to the generic certificate issuance process shown in Figure 17.2, agencies may choose to perform or to outsource each of the key functions associated with issuing credentials suitable for use with PKI. Because PIV credentials issued to employees and contractors include digital certificates that conform to Federal PKI common policy [51], the primary focus for agencies and system owners seeking to leverage PKI authentication capabilities is implementing or configuring PKI-enabled authentication technologies for their systems. System owners also need to be aware of their agencies' plans to comply with government-wide requirements to enable their information systems to control access using PIV credentials.

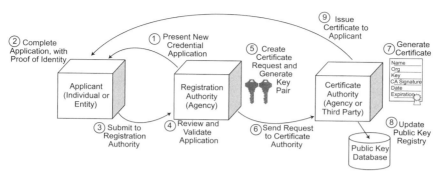

FIGURE 17.2 Agencies Implementing PKI Typically Perform the Function of the Registration Authority When Issuing PKI-Enabled Credentials to Employees and Contractors, They May Also Serve As the Certificate Authority or Leverage Third Party Services—Including Those Offered By GSA and the Federal PKI Management Authority—to Generate the Digital Certificates Bound to Approved User Identities

OTHER FEDERAL SECURITY MANAGEMENT REQUIREMENTS

Most federal information security management requirements, including the provisions in FISMA, give agencies substantial flexibility to achieve compliance using whatever practices and technologies they choose. With the exception of Federal Information Processing Standards, which are mandatory for all agencies, it is up to each agency (and in some cases each system owner) to adopt security procedures and tailor security controls to their own requirements and risk tolerance levels. NIST is responsible for developing standards and guidelines associated with the requirements in the law but does not have the authority to set new requirements. When new threats or risks emerge that demand government-wide response, OMB issues official guidance, direction, and requirements, typically through formal memoranda. In 2010, OMB clarified agency responsibilities in the sphere of federal information security management, delegating to the Department of Homeland Security primary responsibility for "operational aspects of Federal agency cybersecurity with respect to the Federal information systems that fall within FISMA" [52]. While OMB continues to provide budgetary oversight and to deliver annual progress reports to Congress on FISMA compliance, DHS oversees agency implementation of security requirements, information security programs, and operational performance in such areas as incident response and the provision of adequate, cost-effective security measures. With existing responsibility for running US-CERT, DHS is well-positioned to identify and assess new threats or incidents encountered by federal agencies. In recent years, OMB has specified new requirements for federal agency reporting and oversight processes, revised the security metrics, report content, and frequency of agency information submissions for FISMA reporting, and mandated new technical and procedural requirements to provide more effective protection of personally identifiable information [53].

Personally Identifiable Information Protection

Changes in federal security policy and requirements sometimes occur due to the occurrence of specific threat events with significant impact to one or more federal agencies. Federal regulations for safeguarding personally identifiable information (PII) maintained by agencies date back at least to the Privacy Act of 1974, but current requirements reflect policy changes partly in response to specific security incidents. The well-publicized theft in 2006 of a government laptop computer from the home of an employee of the Department of Veterans Affairs led to a mandatory requirement that agencies encrypt data on all mobile devices, including computers as well as removable devices such as flash drives [54]. One week after that incident occurred, President Bush issued an executive order [55] intended to strengthen government protections against identity theft and creating an identity theft task force that developed a set of recommendations released the following year. Some of those recommendations became mandatory requirements for agencies, including the need to implement data breach notification policies and procedures and elevating all incidents involving breaches of PII to category 1 on US-CERT's scale of federal agency incident categories, requiring agencies to report such incidents within one hour of discovery [56]. In each of these cases OMB specified deadlines by which agencies had to implement the mandatory requirements—45 days for mobile device data encryption and 120 days for implementing breach notification policies. The relative unpredictability of new requirements and short timeframe for agency compliance make it imperative for agencies to stay abreast of changes in federal security policy and to operate their information security programs in a way that affords sufficient agility to respond to new requirements in a timely manner.

OMB Memoranda

Guidance from OMB bears close scrutiny by agencies for reasons beyond staying aware of policy changes or new management, operational, or technical requirements. In many cases the provisions stated in OMB memoranda are the authoritative source of policy direction and requirements for agencies, even if they are not formally codified or published as official rules. For instance, the change in information system authorization policy allowing agencies to forego system reauthorization every three years—as stipulated in OMB Circular A-130—if they implement continuous monitoring programs appeared not as stand-alone guidance but as a response in the frequently asked questions section of OMB's 2011 FISMA reporting instructions [57]. Agencies cannot rely on NIST guidance or federal rulemaking processes to address all policies and requirements applicable to information security management, so system owners, security officers, and risk management personnel should routinely review and analyze memoranda and other information and guidance from OMB and DHS as well as reports on security incidents, networks and information system operating environments, and information resources management.

Information Resources Management

Federal agencies are subject to a variety of information resources management policies, regulations, and guidance that influence information security management practices. Many information management requirements stem from policies articulated in OMB Circular A-130, guidance that reflects provisions in multiple pieces of federal legislation, including the Paperwork Reduction Act, the Information Technology Management Reform Act, the Privacy Act, the Chief Financial Officers Act, the Federal Property and Administrative Services Act, the Budget and Accounting Act, the Government Performance and Results Act, and the Government Paperwork Elimination Act as well as precursor legislation to FISMA [25]. In addition to the explicit information security requirements in Appendix III, Circular A-130 establishes policy and prescriptive guidance for information management, information collection, records management, information dissemination, information systems and technology management, capital planning and investment control, enterprise architecture, technology acquisition, and information system security. Agencies must integrate information security into all other information resources management processes, giving security officers and risk managers an essential role in budgeting, IT investment management, enterprise architecture, and the system development life cycle. In many government agencies, management responsibility for each of these areas—including information security—falls under the authority of the Chief Information Officer, but having a peer relationship and common reporting structure in the organization chart is not sufficient to ensure the level of cooperation necessary to successfully incorporate security in all relevant information resources management functions. System owners and security officers often emphasize technical management activities associated with system development and operation, but also need to establish and maintain communication across functional domains that have roles and responsibilities in ensuring effective information resources management. NIST information security risk management guidance to agencies emphasizes a similar need for effective communication among stakeholders within and between different levels of the organization [58].

Federal Enterprise Architecture

Although NIST guidance on risk management refers to enterprise architecture (EA) in the context of mission and business process perspectives on risk [59], enterprise architecture is a core information resources management program in most federal agencies, driven in part by provisions in the Clinger-Cohen Act and subsequent guidance that require each agency to develop and maintain an enterprise architecture [60]. Concurrent with the establishment of many individual agency EA programs, the CIO Council developed a Federal Enterprise Architecture Framework, released in 1999, that provided the foundation for the Federal Enterprise Architecture (FEA) program, managed within the OMB Office of E-Government and Information Technology. The FEA is defined in a series of reference models that use a common vocabulary and serve as a government-wide definition of mission and business functions, performance measurement categories, service components, types of technologies, and data used and exchanged by agencies [61]. Agencies use the FEA reference models to show the alignment of their IT investments to mission areas, common business functions, or enterprise services. The use of a common taxonomy for all agencies allows government-wide analysis of IT investments and information resources allocated for different purposes. The FEA includes many elements related to information security and risk management, providing investment owners the ability to align some security-related activities to correlated business processes, performance measures, data exchanges, services, and technologies specified in agency enterprise architectures. Recognizing a gap between organization-level activities on which EA often focuses and system-level security and privacy, the CIO Council sponsored the development of a Security and Privacy Profile to link the FEA reference models and NIST security standards and guidance and to help identify organizational security and privacy requirements. The most recent version of the Security and Privacy Profile, published in 2010, reflects the NIST Risk Management Framework and the multi-tier perspective on managing risk presented in Special Publication 800-39 to apply the RMF process to agency enterprise, segment, and solution architectures, as illustrated in Figure 17.3. Agencies can

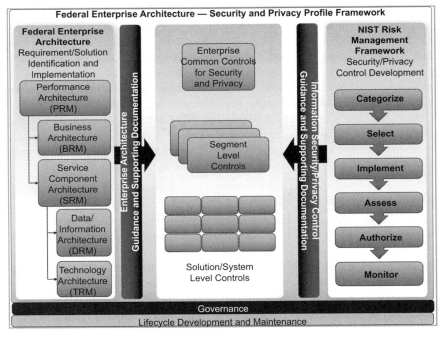

FIGURE 17.3 Using the Security and Privacy Profile, Federal Agencies Apply Risk Management Framework Security Controls and Processes to the Appropriate Enterprise Architecture Elements at Organization-Wide, Segment, and Solution or System Levels [62]

use this voluntary guidance to facilitate the integration of security architecture and enterprise architecture and to support the development of mission and business process and organizational perspectives on information security risk management.

Open Government

The trend towards greater transparency and more open government, formalized as government-wide policy in 2009 obligating agencies to increase the amount and quality of information published online, [63] can alter expectations for the use and dissemination of information in federal information systems. Open government policy makes clear that favoring openness and public information dissemination should not abrogate security or privacy concerns that limit information disclosure to protect confidentiality or for other valid reasons. The expectation that agencies will make more information available online—even non-sensitive information—opens government programs and activities to greater public scrutiny, giving agency personnel addition incentive to ensure that their actions reflect effective practices and legal and regulatory compliance and the information documenting their activities is accurate. To date little of the information published by agencies in association with open government initiative is related to information security, and key security performance metrics included in annual reports to Congress on FISMA emphasize aggregate agency results rather than providing individual agency program details. Many agencies make their annual FISMA compliance assessments, inspector general findings, and other audit reports to OMB publicly available, but there is no central dashboard or other publicly available location for reviewing agency information security management information. Agency inspectors general assess their agencies' information security programs in 127 attributes across eleven performance areas specified by OMB: risk management, configuration management, incident response and reporting, security training, plans of actions and milestones, remote access management, identity and access management, continuous monitoring management, contingency planning, contractor systems, and security capital planning [64]. The use of consistent program assessment metrics facilitates cross-agency comparisons and government-wide aggregation of security performance information by OMB and, where inspector general reports are made public, enables similar analysis by anyone interested in examining federal agency information security program performance.

RELEVANT SOURCE MATERIAL

In contrast to FISMA implementation standards and guidance produced by NIST, there is no single primary source of information for government-wide programs and initiatives related to information security management. As noted throughout this chapter, many government agencies and cross-agency governance bodies are involved in establishing and overseeing federal initiatives, including the Office of Management and Budget, the General Services Administration, the Department of

Homeland Security, and the Chief Information Officers Council. Background information, policies, directives, and technical information regarding government-wide and agency expectations for federal initiatives are largely available online. The most applicable sources of information include:

- OMB Memoranda: http://www.whitehouse.gov/omb/memoranda_default
- NIST Special Publications: http://csrc.nist.gov/publications/PubsSPs.html
- Federal Information Processing Standards: http://csrc.nist.gov/publications/PubsFIPS.html
- Federal CIO Council: http://www.cio.gov/
- Federal ICAM, PKI, and Personal Identity Verification: http://idmanagement.gov/
- GSA Areas of Interest: http://www.gsa.gov/portal/category/21023
- Homeland Security Presidential Directives: http://www.fas.org/irp/offdocs/nspd/

SUMMARY

Although FISMA drives many aspects of information security management in government organizations, agency personnel with risk management and information security responsibilities are influenced by a wide array of government initiatives beyond FISMA with significant security management implications. Agencies continue to have broad authority to determine their own security requirements and structure information security programs and practices in whatever manner they find most effective, but policy directives, technical standards, and other government-wide obligations may constrain agency and system owner decisions and courses of action. Common services or security technologies available to agencies may provide opportunities for agencies to make cost-effective improvements to security operations, provision new or enhanced capabilities, or achieve interoperability with other government organizations. This chapter identified and briefly described a variety of federal initiatives relevant to agency security management, explaining key expectations for agencies and system owners and noting points of intersection or overlap between federal initiatives and agency practices under the Risk Management Framework.

REFERENCES

[1] Treasury, Postal Service and General Government Appropriations Act of 1989, Pub. L. No. 100-440, 102 Stat. 1721. §627.
[2] Evans KS. Transition from FTS2001 to Networx. Washington, DC: Office of Management and Budget; August 28, 2008. Memorandum M-08-26.
[3] The five prime contract holders for Networx Enterprise, which offers IP network services, are AT&T, Century Link (Qwest), Level 3 Communications, Sprint Nextel, and

Verizon Business (MCI). AT&T, Century Link, and Verizon Business are also the three prime contractors for Networx Universal.

[4] The Department of Defense maintains two private networks, and the intelligence community also uses secure private networks provisioned separately from Networx.

[5] Critical infrastructure identification, prioritization, and protection. Washington, DC: Department of Homeland Security; December 2003. Homeland Security Presidential Directive 7.

[6] Federal Information Security Management Act of 2002, Pub. L. No. 107-347, 116 Stat. 2946. §301.

[7] Homeland Security Act of 2002, Pub. L. 107-296, 116 Stat. 2135. §201.

[8] Johnson C. Safeguarding against and responding to the breach of personally identifiable information. Washington, DC: Office of Management and Budget; May 22, 2007. Memorandum M-07-16. p. 10.

[9] Cyber security and monitoring. Washington, DC: Department of Homeland Security; December 2003. Homeland Security Presidential Directive 23.

[10] The Comprehensive National Cybersecurity Initiative. Washington, DC: National Security Council; March 2010.

[11] Johnson C. Implementation of Trusted Internet Connections (TIC). Washington, DC: Office of Management and Budget; November 20, 2007.. Memorandum M-08-05

[12] Kundra V. Update on the Trusted Internet Connections initiative. Washington, DC: Office of Management and Budget; September 17, 2009. Memorandum M-09-32.

[13] Howell M. Networx managed trusted IP service (MTIPS) deadlines [email memorandum]. Washington, DC: Office of Management and Budget; May 12, 2010.

[14] Privacy impact assessment for EINSTEIN 2. Washington, DC: Department of Homeland Security; May 19, 2009.

[15] Privacy impact assessment for the initiative three exercise. Washington, DC: Department of Homeland Security; March 18, 2010.

[16] Among other legislative drivers, the Clinger-Cohen Act directs agencies to make such performance- and results-based IT management decisions. Information Technology Management Reform Act of 1996, Pub. L. No. 104-106, 110 Stat. 679. §5113.

[17] Mell P, Grance T. The NIST definition of cloud computing. Gaithersburg, MD: National Institute of Standards and Technology, Computer Security Division; September 2011. Special Publication 800-145. p. 2.

[18] Kundra V. 25 point implementation plan to reform federal information technology management. Washington, DC: Office of Management and Budget; December 2010.

[19] Mell P, Grance T. The NIST definition of cloud computing. Gaithersburg, MD: National Institute of Standards and Technology, Computer Security Division; September 2011. Special Publication 800-145.

[20] Jansen W, Grance T. Guidelines on security and privacy in public cloud computing. Gaithersburg, MD: National Institute of Standards and Technology, Computer Security Division; December, 2011. Special Publication 800-144.

[21] Badger L, Grance T, Patt-Corner R, Voas J. Cloud computing synopsis and recommendations. Gaithersburg, MD: National Institute of Standards and Technology, Computer Security Division; May 2011. Draft Special Publication 800-146.

[22] VanRoekel S. Security authorization of information systems in cloud computing environments. Washington, DC: Office of Management and Budget; December 8, 2011.

[23] The FedRAMP Joint Authorization Board includes CIOs from the Department of Homeland Security, the Department of Defense, and the General Services Administration.

[24] Cloud-based infrastructure as a service comes to government [press release]. Washington, DC: General Services Administration; October 19, 2010.

[25] Management of federal information resources. Washington, DC: Office of Management and Budget; November 2000. Circular No. A-130, Revised (Transmittal Memorandum No. 4).

[26] NVLAP Accreditation Programs [Internet]. Gaithersburg, MD: National Institute of Standards and Technology; [created February 1, 2010; updated March 14, 2012 cited March 24, 2012]. <http://www.nist.gov/nvlap/nvlap-fields.cfm>.

[27] FIPS Publications [Internet]. Gaithersburg, MD: National Institute of Standards and Technology; [created July 3, 2007 updated March 6, 2012 cited March 24, 2012]. <http://csrc.nist.gov/publications/PubsFIPS.html>.

[28] Cryptologic Module Validation Program (CMVP) [Internet]. Gaithersburg, MD: National Institute of Standards and Technology; [created January 28, 1996 updated February 16, 2012 cited March 24, 2012]. <http://csrc.nist.gov/groups/STM/cmvp/index.html>.

[29] ISO/IEC 15408:2009. Information technology—Security techniques—Evaluation criteria for IT security.

[30] US Government Approved Protection Profiles [Internet]. Ft. Meade, MD: National Information Assurance Partnership; [cited March 24, 2012]. <http://www.niap-ccevs.org/pp/>.

[31] Certified Products: The Common Criteria Portal [Internet]. Cheltenham, UK: Communications-Electronics Security Group [cited March 24, 2012]. <http://www.commoncriteriaportal.org/products/>.

[32] Johnson C. Implementation of commonly accepted security configurations for Windows operating systems. Washington, DC: Office of Management and Budget; March 22, 2007. Memorandum M-07-11.

[33] National Vulnerability Database National Checklist Program Repository [Internet]. Gaithersburg, MD: National Institute of Standards and Technology [cited 2012 March 24, 2012]. <http://web.nvd.nist.gov/view/ncp/repository>.

[34] Quinn SD, Souppaya M, Cook M, Scarfone K. National checklist program for IT products—guidelines for checklist users and developers. Gaithersburg, MD: National Institute of Standards and Technology, Computer Security Division; February 2011. Special Publication 800-70 revision 2.

[35] Recommended security controls for federal information systems and organizations. Gaithersburg, MD: National Institute of Standards and Technology, Computer Security Division; August 2009. Special Publication 800-53 revision 3.

[36] National strategy for trusted identities in cyberspace. Washington, DC: The White House; April 2011.

[37] The term "segment architecture" comes from OMB's Federal Enterprise Architecture guidance, in which a segment is a single core mission area, business service, or enterprise service that represents a portion of the enterprise architecture. See FEA practice guidance. Washington, DC: Office of Management and Budget, Federal Enterprise Architecture Program Management Office; November 2007.

[38] Federal identity, credential, and access management (FICAM) roadmap and implementation guidance (version 2.0). Washington, DC: Federal Chief Information Officers Council; December 2, 2011. p. 14–8.

[39] Federal identity, credential, and access management (FICAM) roadmap and implementation guidance (version 2.0). Washington, DC: Federal Chief Information Officers Council; December 2, 2011. p. 144–7.

[40] Lew JJ. Continued implementation of Homeland Security Presidential Directive (HSPD) 12—policy for a common identification standard for federal employees and contractors. Washington, DC: Office of Management and Budget; February 3, 2011. Memorandum M-11-11.

[41] Policy for a common identification standard for federal employees and contractors. Washington, DC: Department of Homeland Security; August 2004. Homeland Security Presidential Directive 12.

[42] Personal identity verification (PIV) of federal employees and contractors. Gaithersburg, MD: National Institute of Standards and Technology, Computer Security Division; March 2006. Federal Information Processing Standards Publication 201-1.

[43] Current Status—HSPD-12 [Internet]. Washington, DC: IDManagement.gov. <http://www.idmanagement.gov/presentations/HSPD12_Current_Status.pdf>.

[44] Fiscal year 2011 report to Congress on the implementation of the Federal Information Security Management Act of 2002. Washington, DC: Office of Management and Budget; March 2012. p. 22.

[45] Bolten JB. E-authentication guidance for federal agencies. Washington, DC: Office of Management and Budget; December 16, 2003. Memorandum M-04-04.

[46] The Microsoft Access-based E-Authentication e-RA tool and associated activity guide are available from ICAM at <http://www.idmanagement.gov/>.

[47] Burr WE, Dodson DF, Newton EM, Perlner RA, Polk WT, Gupta S, Nabbus EA. Electronic authentication guideline. Gaithersburg, MD: National Institute of Standards and Technology, Computer Security Division; December 2011. Special Publication 800-63 revision 1.

[48] Personal identity verification (PIV) of federal employees and contractors. Gaithersburg, MD: National Institute of Standards and Technology, Computer Security Division; March 2006. Federal Information Processing Standards Publication 201-1. p. 6.

[49] Burr WE, Dodson DF, Newton EM, Perlner RA, Polk WT, Gupta S, Nabbus EA. Electronic authentication guideline. Gaithersburg, MD: National Institute of Standards and Technology, Computer Security Division; December 2011. Special Publication 800-63 revision 1. p. viii.

[50] X.509 certificate policy for the U.S. Federal PKI common policy framework. Washington, DC: Federal Public Key Infrastructure Policy Authority; December 9, 2011. p. 3.

[51] Personal identity verification (PIV) of federal employees and contractors. Gaithersburg, MD: National Institute of Standards and Technology, Computer Security Division; March 2006. Federal Information Processing Standards Publication 201-1. p. 41.

[52] Orszag PR. Clarifying cybersecurity responsibilities and activities of the Executive Office of the President and the Department of Homeland Security (DHS). Washington, DC: Office of Management and Budget; July 6, 2010. Memorandum M-10-28.

[53] See OMB Memoranda M-11-33 on reporting and oversight; M-10-15 on FISMA report submissions; and M-07-16 on safeguards for personally identifiable information.

[54] Johnson C. Protection of sensitive agency information. Washington, DC: Office of Management and Budget; June 23, 2006. Memorandum M-06-16.

[55] Bush G. Strengthening federal efforts to protect against identity theft. Washington, DC: The White House; May 10, 2006. Executive Order 13402.

[56] Johnson C. Safeguarding against and responding to the breach of personally identifiable information. Washington, DC: Office of Management and Budge; May 22, 2007. Memorandum M-07-16.

[57] Lew JJ. Reporting instructions for the Federal Information Security Management Act and agency privacy management. Washington, DC: Office of Management and Budget; September 14, 2011. Memorandum M-11-33. Question 28.

[58] Managing information security risk: Organization, mission, and information system view. Gaithersburg, MD: National Institute of Standards and Technology, Computer Security Division; March 2011. Special Publication 800-39. p. 9.

[59] Managing information security risk: Organization, mission, and information system view. Gaithersburg, MD: National Institute of Standards and Technology, Computer Security Division; March 2011. Special Publication 800-39. p. 17–9.

[60] Information Technology Management Reform Act of 1996, Pub. L. No. 104-106, 110 Stat. 679. §5125(b)(2). The text of the law refers to "information technology architecture" but as implemented by agencies and referenced in guidance from OMB the term "enterprise architecture" is used.

[61] FEA consolidated reference model document (version 2.3). Washington, DC: Office of Management and Budget; October 2007.

[62] Federal Enterprise Architecture Security and Privacy Profile (version 3.0). Washington, DC: Federal Chief Information Officers Council; September 2010. p. 33.

[63] Orszag PR. Open government directive. Washington, DC: Office of Management and Budget; December 8, 2009. Memorandum M-10-06.

[64] Fiscal year 2011 report to Congress on the implementation of the Federal Information Security Management Act of 2002. Washington, DC: Office of Management and Budget; March 2012. Appendix 1, p. i.

References

REFERENCES

Legislation and Statutes

[1] American Recovery and Reinvestment Act of 2009, Pub. L. No. 111-5, 123 Stat. 115.

[2] Brooks Act of 1965, Pub. L. No. 89-306, 79 Stat. 1127.

[3] Children's Online Privacy Protection Act of 1998, Pub. L. No. 105-277, 112 Stat. 2581.

[4] Collection and compromise. 31 U.S.C. §3711.

[5] Computer Fraud and Abuse Act of 1986, Pub. L. No. 99-474, 100 Stat. 1213.

[6] Computer Security Act of 1987, Pub. L. 100-235, 101 Stat. 1724.

[7] Confidential nature of claims, 38 USC §5701.

[8] Confidentiality of alcohol and drug abuse patient records, 42 C.F.R. Part 2.

[9] Confidentiality of certain medical records, 38 USC §7332.

[10] Coordination of federal information policy. 44 U.S.C. §§3501–3549.

[11] Cybersecurity Act of 2012, S. 2105, 112th Cong.; 2012.

[12] E-Government Act of 2002, Pub. L. No. 107-347, 116 Stat. 2899.

[13] Electronic Communications Privacy Act of 1986, Pub. L. No. 99-508, 100 Stat. 1848.

[14] Electronic Freedom of Information Act Amendments of 1996, Pub. L. No. 104-231, 110 Stat. 3048.

[15] Family Educational Rights and Privacy Act of 1974, Pub. L. No. 93-380, 88 Stat. 484.

[16] Federal Agency Data Mining Reporting Act of 2007, Pub. L. No. 110-53, 121 Stat. 362.

[17] Federal Information Security Amendments Act of 2012, H.R. 4257, 112th Cong. 2012.

[18] Federal Information Security Management Act of 2002, Pub. L. No. 107-347, 116 Stat. 2946.

[19] Federal Property and Administrative Services Act of 1949, Pub. L. No. 81-152, 63 Stat. 377.

[20] Financial Services Modernization Act of 1999, Pub. L. No. 106-102, 113 Stat. 1338.

[21] General Services Administration Acquisition Regulation; implementation of information technology security provision; final rule. 77 Fed. Reg. 749; 2012.

[22] Government Information Security Reform Act of 2000, Pub. L. 106-398, 114 Stat. 1654A.

[23] Government Paperwork Elimination Act of 1998, Pub. L. 105-277, 112 Stat. 2681.

[24] Government Performance and Results Act of 1993, Pub. L. 103-62, 107 Stat. 285.

[25] Health Insurance Portability and Accountability Act of 1996, Pub. L. No. 104-191, 110 Stat. 1936.

[26] Health Information Technology for Economic and Clinical Health Act of 2009, Pub. L. No. 111-5, 123 Stat. 226.

[27] HIPAA administrative simplification. Washington, DC: Department of Health and Human Services, Office for Civil Rights; 2006.

[28] Homeland Security Act of 2002, Pub. L. No. 107-296, 116 Stat. 2135.

[29] Information Technology Management Reform Act of 1996, Pub. L. No. 104-106, 110 Stat. 679.

[30] Intelligence Reform and Terrorism Prevention Act of 2004, Pub. L. No. 108-458, 118 Stat. 3638.

[31] Paperwork Reduction Act of 1980, Pub. L. No. 96-511, 94 Stat. 2812.

[32] Paperwork Reduction Act of 1995, Pub. L. No. 104-13, 109 Stat. 1643.

[33] Privacy Act of 1974, Pub. L. No. 93-579, 88 Stat. 1896.

[34] Privacy of individually identifiable health information. 45 C.F.R. §§160 and 164.

[35] Reports and notice to Congress on data breaches, 38 USC §5726.

[36] Strengthening and Enhancing Cybersecurity by using Research, Education, Information, and Technology Act of 2012, H.R. 4263; S.2151, 112th Cong. 2012.

[37] Treasury, Postal Service and General Government Appropriations Act of 1989, Pub. L. No. 100-440, 102 Stat. 1721. §627.

[38] Uniting and Strengthening America by Providing Appropriate Tools Required to Intercept and Obstruct Terrorism (USA PATRIOT ACT) Act of 2001, Pub. L. 107-56, 115 Stat. 272.

Policies, Directives, and Memoranda

[1] Appendix III, Security of federal automated information resources. Washington, DC: Office of Management and Budget; 2000 November Circular No. A-130, Revised (Transmittal Memorandum No. 4).

[2] Bolten JB. E-authentication guidance for federal agencies. Washington, DC: Office of Management and Budget; December 16, 2003. Memorandum M-04-04.

[3] Bolten JB. FY 2004 reporting instructions for the Federal Information Security Management Act. Washington, DC: Office of Management and Budget; August 23, 2004. Memorandum M-04-25.

[4] Bolten JB. OMB Guidance for implementing the privacy provisions of the E-Government Act of 2002. Washington, DC: Office of Management and Budget; September 26, 2003. Memorandum M-03-22.

[5] Bush GW. Strengthening federal efforts to protect against identity theft. Washington, DC: The White House; May 10, 2006. Executive Order No. 13402.

[6] Capital programming guide version 3.0. Supplement to OMB Circular A-11: Preparation, submission, and execution of the budget. Washington, DC: Office of Management and Budget; August 2011.

[7] Clinton WJ. Classified national security information. Washington, DC: The White House; April 17, 1995. Executive Order No. 12958.

[8] Critical infrastructure identification, prioritization, and protection. Washington, DC: Department of Homeland Security; December 2003; Homeland Security Presidential Directive 7.

[9] Cyber security and monitoring. Washington, DC: Department of Homeland Security; December 2003; Homeland Security Presidential Directive 23.

[10] Daniels ME. Guidance for preparing and submitting security plans of action and milestones. Washington, DC: Office of Management and Budget; October 17, 2001. Memorandum M-02-01.

[11] Daniels ME. Guidance on implementing the Government Information Security Reform Act. Washington, DC: Office of Management and Budget; January 16, 2001. Memorandum M-01-08.

[12] Evans KS. Reporting incidents involving personally identifiable information and incorporating the cost for security in agency information technology investments. Washington, DC: Office of Management and Budget; July 12, 2006. Memorandum M-06-19.

[13] Evans KS. Transition from FTS2001 to Networx. Washington, DC: Office of Management and Budget; August 28, 2008. Memorandum M-08-26.

[14] Federal executive branch mission essential function and primary mission essential function identification and submission process. Washington, DC: Department of Homeland Security, Federal Emergency Management Agency; February 2008. Federal Continuity Directive 2.

[15] Federal executive branch national continuity program and requirements. Washington, DC: Department of Homeland Security, Federal Emergency Management Agency; February 2008. Federal Continuity Directive 1.

[16] Howell M. Networx managed trusted IP service (MTIPS) deadlines [email memorandum]. Washington, DC: Office of Management and Budget; May 12, 2010.

[17] Johnson C. FY 2005 reporting instructions for the Federal Information Security Management Act and agency privacy management. Washington, DC: Office of Management and Budget; June 13, 2005. Memorandum M-05-15.

[18] Johnson C. FY 2008 reporting instructions for the Federal Information Security Management Act and agency privacy management. Washington, DC: Office of Management and Budget; July 14, 2008. Memorandum M-08-21.

[19] Johnson C. Implementation of commonly accepted security configurations for Windows operating systems. Washington, DC: Office of Management and Budget; March 22; 2007. Memorandum M-07-11.

[20] Johnson C. Implementation of Trusted Internet Connections (TIC). Washington, DC: Office of Management and Budget; November 20, 2007. Memorandum M-08-05.

[21] Johnson C. New FISMA privacy reporting requirements for FY 2008. Washington, DC: Office of Management and Budget; January 18, 2008. Memorandum M-08-09.

[22] Johnson C. Protection of sensitive agency information. Washington, DC: Office of Management and Budget; June 23, 2006. Memorandum M-06-16.

[23] Johnson C. Safeguarding against and responding to the breach of personally identifiable information. Washington, DC: Office of Management and Budget; May 22, 2007. Memorandum M-07-16.

[24] Kundra V. 25 point implementation plan to reform federal information technology management. Washington, DC: Office of Management and Budget; December 2010.

[25] Kundra V. Update on the Trusted Internet Connections initiative. Washington, DC: Office of Management and Budget; September 17, 2009. Memorandum M-09-32.

[26] Lew JJ. Continued implementation of Homeland Security Presidential Directive (HSPD) 12 – policy for a common identification standard for federal employees and contractors. Washington, DC: Office of Management and Budget; February 3, 2011. Memorandum M-11-11.

[27] Lew JJ. Implementation of the Government Paperwork Elimination Act. Washington, DC: Office of Management and Budget; April 25, 2000. Memorandum M-00-10.

[28] Lew JJ. Instructions on complying with President's Memorandum of May 14, 1998, "Privacy and Personal Information in Federal Records." Washington, DC: Office of Management and Budget; January 7, 1999. Memorandum M-99-05.

[29] Lew JJ. Privacy policies and data collection on federal web sites. Washington, DC: Office of Management and Budget; June 22, 2000. Memorandum M-00-13.

[30] Lew JJ. Privacy policies on federal web sites. Washington, DC: Office of Management and Budget; June 2, 1999. Memorandum M-99-18.

[31] Lew JJ. Reporting instructions for the Federal Information Security Management Act and agency privacy management. Washington, DC: Office of Management and Budget; September 14, 2011. Memorandum M-11-33.

[32] Lew JJ. Reporting instructions for the Government Information Security Reform Act. Washington, DC: Office of Management and Budget; June 22, 2001. Memorandum M-01-24.

[33] Management of federal information resources. Washington, DC: Office of Management and Budget; November 2000. Circular No. A-130, Revised (Transmittal Memorandum No. 4).

[34] National continuity policy. Washington, DC: Department of Homeland Security; May 2007. Homeland Security Presidential Directive 20.

[35] National policy for the security of national security telecommunications and information systems. Washington, DC: The White House; July 5, 1990. National Security Directive 42.

[36] National policy on certification and accreditation of national security systems. Fort Meade, MD: Committee on National Security Systems; October 2005.

[37] National policy on telecommunications and automated information systems security. Washington, DC: The White House; September 17, 1984. National Security Decision Directive 145.

[38] Obama B. Controlled unclassified information. Washington, DC: The White House; November 4, 2010. Executive Order 13556.

[39] Orszag PR. Clarifying cybersecurity responsibilities and activities of the Executive Office of the President and the Department of Homeland Security (DHS). Washington, DC: Office of Management and Budget; July 6, 2010. Memorandum M-10-28.

[40] Orszag PR. Guidance for agency use of third-party websites and applications. Washington, DC: Office of Management and Budget; June 25, 2010. Memorandum M-10-23.

[41] Orszag PR. Guidance for online use of web measurement and customization technologies. Washington, DC: Office of Management and Budget; June 25, 2010. Memorandum M-10-22.

[42] Orszag PR. Open government directive. Washington, DC: Office of Management and Budget; December 8, 2009. Memorandum M-10-06.

[43] Policy for a common identification standard for federal employees and contractors. Washington, DC: Department of Homeland Security; August 2004. Homeland Security Presidential Directive 12.

[44] Policy on information assurance risk management for national security systems. Fort Meade, MD: Committee on National Security Systems; January 2012. CNSS Policy No. 22.

[45] Preparation, submission, and execution of the budget. Washington, DC: Office of Management and Budget; July 2010. Circular No. A-11, Revised (Transmittal Memorandum No. 84).

[46] Preparation, submission, and execution of the budget. Washington, DC: Office of Management and Budget; August 2011. Circular No. A-11, Revised (Transmittal Memorandum No. 85).

[47] Schaffer G. FY 2012 reporting instructions for the Federal Information Security Management Act and agency privacy management. Arlington, VA: Department of Homeland Security, National Protection and Programs Directorate; February 2012. Federal Information Security Memorandum 12-02.

[48] Security of federal automated information systems. Washington, DC: Office of Management and Budget; July 27, 1978. Circular No. A-71 (Transmittal Memorandum No. 1).

[49] VanRoekel S. Security authorization of information systems in cloud computing environments. Washington, DC: Office of Management and Budget; December 8, 2011.

[50] X.509 certificate policy for the US Federal PKI common policy framework. Washington, DC: Federal Public Key Infrastructure Policy Authority; December 9, 2011.

[51] Zients JG, Kundra V. FY 2009 reporting instructions for the Federal Information Security Management Act and agency privacy management. Washington, DC: Office of Management and Budget; August 20, 2009. Memorandum M-09-29.

[52] Zients J, Kundra V, Schmidt HA. FY 2010 reporting instructions for the Federal Information Security Management Act and agency privacy management. Washington, DC: Office of Management and Budget; April 21, 2010. Memorandum M-10-15.

Instructions and Guidance

[1] Badger L, Grance T, Patt-Corner R, Voas J. Cloud computing synopsis and recommendations. Gaithersburg, MD: National Institute of Standards and Technology, Computer Security Division; May 2011. Draft Special Publication 800-146.

[2] Barker E, Roginsky A. Transitions: recommendation for transitioning the use of cryptographic algorithms and key lengths. Gaithersburg, MD: National Institute of Standards and Technology, Computer Security Division; January 2011. Special Publication 800-131A.

[3] Barker WC. Guideline for identifying an information system as a national security system. Gaithersburg, MD: National Institute of Standards and Technology, Computer Security Division; August 2003. Special Publication 800-59.

[4] Bowen P, Hash J, Wilson M. Information security handbook: a guide for managers. Gaithersburg, MD: National Institute of Standards and Technology, Computer Security Division; October 2006. Special Publication 800-100.

[5] Bowen P, Kissel R, Scholl M, Robinson W, Stansfield J, Voldish L. Recommendations for integrating information security into the capital planning and investment control process. Gaithersburg, MD: National Institute of Standards and Technology, Computer Security Division; July 2009. Draft Special Publication 800-65 revision 1.

[6] Burr WE, Dodson DF, Newton EM, Perlner RA, Polk WT, Gupta S, et al. Electronic authentication guideline. Gaithersburg, MD: National Institute of Standards and Technology, Computer Security Division; December 2011. Special Publication 800-63 revision 1.

[7] Chew E, Swanson M, Stine K, Bartol N, Brown A, Robinson W. Performance measurement guide for information security. Gaithersburg, MD: National Institute of Standards and Technology, Computer Security Division; July 2008. Special Publication 800-55 revision 1.

[8] The comprehensive national cybersecurity initiative. Washington, DC: National Security Council; March 2010.

[9] Defense acquisition guidebook. Washington, DC: Department of Defense; January 10, 2012.

[10] Dempsey K, Chawla N, Johnson A, Johnson R, Jones A, Orebaugh A, et al. Information security continuous monitoring for federal information systems and organizations. Gaithersburg, MD: National Institute of Standards and Technology, Computer Security Division; September 2011. Special Publication 800-137.

[11] DoD architecture framework version 2.0. Washington, DC: Department of Defense; May 28, 2009.

[12] DoD information assurance certification and accreditation process (DIACAP). Washington, DC: Department of Defense; November 28, 2007. DoD Instruction 8510.01.

[13] DoD information technology security certification and accreditation process (DITSCAP). Washington, DC: Department of Defense; December 30, 1997. DoD Instruction 5200.40.

[14] FEA consolidated reference model version 2.3. Washington, DC: Office of Management and Budget; October 2007.

[15] FEA practice guidance. Washington, DC: Office of Management and Budget, Federal Enterprise Architecture Program Management Office; November 2007.

[16] Federal enterprise architecture framework version 1.1. Washington, DC: Chief Information Officers Council; September 1999.

[17] Federal enterprise architecture security and privacy profile (version 3.0). Washington, DC: Federal Chief Information Officers Council; September 2010.

[18] Federal identity, credential, and access management (FICAM) roadmap and implementation guidance (version 2.0). Washington, DC: Federal Chief Information Officers Council; December 2, 2011.

[19] Federal information system controls audit manual (FISCAM). Washington, DC: Government Accountability Office; February 2009.

[20] Grance T, Hash J, Peck S, Smith J, Korow-Diks K. Security guide for interconnecting information technology systems. Gaithersburg, MD: National Institute of Standards and Technology, Computer Security Division; August 2002. Special Publication 800-47.

[21] Grance T, Nolan T, Burke K, Dudley R, White G, Good T. Guide to test, training, and exercise programs for IT plans and capabilities. Gaithersburg, MD: National Institute of Standards and Technology, Computer Security Division; September 2006. Special Publication 800-84.

[22] Guide for applying the risk management framework to federal information systems. Gaithersburg, MD: National Institute of Standards and Technology, Computer Security Division; February 2010. Special Publication 800-37 revision 1.

[23] Guide for assessing the security controls in federal information systems and organizations. Gaithersburg, MD: National Institute of Standards and Technology, Computer Security Division; June 2010. Special Publication 800-53A revision 1.

[24] Guide for conducting risk assessments. Gaithersburg, MD: National Institute of Standards and Technology, Computer Security Division; September 2011. Special Publication 800-30 revision 1. Initial Public Draft.

[25] Information assurance (IA). Washington, DC: Department of Defense; April 23, 2007. DoD Instruction 8500.01E.

[26] Information assurance (IA) implementation. Washington, DC: Department of Defense; February 6, 2003. DoD Instruction 8500.02.

[27] Information assurance technical framework (release 3.0). Washington, DC: National Security Agency; September 2000.

[28] Information security program. Washington, DC: Department of Defense; February 24, 2012. DoD Manual 5200.01.

[29] Jansen W, Grance T. Guidelines on security and privacy in public cloud computing. Gaithersburg, MD: National Institute of Standards and Technology, Computer Security Division; December 2011. Special Publication 800-144.

[30] Kissel R, Stine K, Scholl M, Rossman H, Fahlsing J, Gulick J. Security considerations in the system development life cycle. Gaithersburg, MD: National Institute of Standards and Technology, Computer Security Division; October 2008. Special Publication 800-64 revision 2.

[31] Managing information security risk: organization, mission, and information system view. Gaithersburg, MD: National Institute of Standards and Technology, Computer Security Division; March 2011. Special Publication 800-39.

[32] McCallister E, Grance T, Scarfone K. Guide to protecting the confidentiality of personally identifiable information (PII). Gaithersburg, MD: National Institute of Standards and Technology, Computer Security Division; April 2010. Special Publication 800-122.

[33] Mell P, Grance T. The NIST definition of cloud computing. Gaithersburg, MD: National Institute of Standards and Technology, Computer Security Division; September 2011. Special Publication 800-145.

[34] National information assurance certification and accreditation process (NIACAP). Fort Meade, MD: National Security Telecommunications and Information Systems Security Committee; April 2000. NSTISS Instruction No. 1000.

[35] National continuity policy implementation plan. Washington, DC: Homeland Security Council; August 2007.

[36] National information assurance glossary. Fort Meade, MD: Committee on National Security Systems; April 2009. CNSS Instruction No. 4009.

[37] National response framework. Washington, DC: Department of Homeland Security; January 2008.

[38] National response plan cyber incident annex. Washington, DC: Department of Homeland Security; December 2004.

[39] National strategy for trusted identities in cyberspace. Washington, DC: The White House; April 2011.

[40] National training standard for information systems security (INFOSEC) professionals. Fort Meade, MD: National Security Telecommunications and Information Systems Security Committee; June 20, 1994. NSTISS Instruction No. 4011.

[41] OECD guidelines on the protection of privacy and transborder flows of personal data. Paris, France: Organisation for Economic Cooperation and Development; September 23, 1980.

[42] Quinn S, Scarfone K, Barrett M, Johnson C. Guide to adopting and using the Security Content Automation Protocol (SCAP). Gaithersburg, MD: National Institute of Standards and Technology, Computer Security Division; July 2010. Special Publication 800-117.

[43] Quinn SD, Souppaya M, Cook M, Scarfone K. National checklist program for IT products – guidelines for checklist users and developers. Gaithersburg, MD: National Institute of Standards and Technology, Computer Security Division; February 2011. Special Publication 800-70 revision 2.

[44] Recommended security controls for federal information systems. Gaithersburg, MD: National Institute of Standards and Technology, Computer Security Division; December 2006. Special Publication 800-53 revision 1.

[45] Recommended security controls for federal information systems. Gaithersburg, MD: National Institute of Standards and Technology, Computer Security Division; December 2007. Special Publication 800-53 revision 2.

[46] Recommended security controls for federal information systems and organizations. Gaithersburg, MD: National Institute of Standards and Technology, Computer Security Division; August 2009. Special Publication 800-53 revision 3.

[47] Redwine ST, editor. Software assurance: a curriculum guide to the common body of knowledge to produce, acquire and sustain secure software. Washington, DC: Department of Homeland Security, Software Assurance Workforce Education and Training Working Group; October 2007.

[48] Roback EA. Guidelines to federal organizations on security assurance and acquisition/use of tested/evaluated products. Gaithersburg, MD: National Institute of Standards and Technology, Computer Security Division; August 2000. Special Publication 800-23.

[49] Ross R, Katzke S, Johnson A, Swanson M, Stoneburner G, Rogers G, et al. Recommended security controls for federal information systems. Gaithersburg, MD: National Institute of Standards and Technology, Computer Security Division; February 2005. Special Publication 800-53.

[50] Ross R, Swanson M, Stoneburner G, Katzke S, Johnson A. Guide for the security certification and accreditation of federal information systems. Gaithersburg, MD: National Institute of Standards and Technology, Computer Security Division; May 2004. Special Publication 800-37.

[51] Ruthbert ZG, Neugent W. Overview of computer security certification and accreditation. Washington, DC: Government Printing Office; April 1984. Special Publication 500-109.

[52] Scarfone K, Grance T, Masone K. Computer security incident handling guide. Gaithersburg, MD: National Institute of Standards and Technology, Computer Security Division; March 2008. Special Publication 800-61 revision 1.

[53] Security and privacy controls for federal information systems and organizations. Gaithersburg, MD: National Institute of Standards and Technology, Computer Security Division; February 2012. Special Publication 800-53 revision 4. Initial Public Draft.

[54] Security categorization and control selection for national security systems. Fort Meade, MD: Committee on National Security Systems; October 2009. CNSS Instruction 1253.

[55] Stine K, Kissel R, Barker W, Fahlsing J, Gulick J. Guide for mapping types of information and information systems to security categories, vol. I. Gaithersburg, MD: National Institute of Standards and Technology, Computer Security Division; Augugst 2008. Special Publication 800-60 revision 1.

[56] Stine K, Kissel R, Barker W, Fahlsing J, Gulick J. Appendices to guide for mapping types of information and information systems to security categories, vol. II. Gaithersburg, MD: National Institute of Standards and Technology, Computer Security Division; August 2008. Special Publication 800-60 revision 1.

[57] Stoneburner S, Goguen A, Feringa A. Risk management guide for information technology systems. Gaithersburg, MD: National Institute of Standards and Technology, Computer Security Division; July 2002. Special Publication 800-30.

[58] Stoneburner G, Hayden C, Feringa A. Engineering principles for information technology security. Gaithersburg, MD: National Institute of Standards and Technology, Computer Security Division; June 2004. Special Publication 800-27 revision A.

[59] Swanson, M. Security self-assessment guide for information technology systems. Gaithersburg, MD: National Institute of Standards and Technology, Computer Security Division; November 2001. Special Publication 800-26.

[60] Swanson M, Bowen P, Philips A, Gallup D, Lynes D. Contingency planning guide for federal information systems. Gaithersburg, MD: National Institute of Standards and Technology, Computer Security Division; May 2010. Special Publication 800-34 revision 1.

[61] Swanson M, Guttman B. Generally accepted principles and practices for securing information technology systems. Gaithersburg, MD: National Institute of Standards and Technology, Computer Security Division; September 1996. Special Publication 800-14.

[62] Swanson M, Hash J, Bowen P. Guide for developing security plans for federal information systems. Gaithersburg, MD: National Institute of Standards and Technology, Computer Security Division; February 2006. Special Publication 800-18 revision 1.

[63] Waltermire D, Quinn S, Scarfone K, Halbardier A. The technical specification for the security content automation protocol (SCAP). Gaithersburg, MD: National Institute of Standards and Technology, Computer Security Division; September 2011. Special Publication 800-126 revision 2.

Articles and Reports

[1] Alberts C, Dorofee A. Operationally critical threat, asset, and vulnerability evaluation (OCTAVE) method implementation guide, v2.0. Pittsburgh, PA: Carnegie Mellon University, Software Engineering Institute; 2001.

[2] Association of Insurance and Risk Managers, Public Risk Management Association, Institute of Risk Management. A structured approach to enterprise risk management and the requirements of ISO 31000. London, UK: Institute of Risk Management; 2010.

[3] Bell DE, LaPadula LJ. Secure computer system: unified exposition and multics interpretation. Bedford, MA: The MITRE Corporation; 1976. MITRE Technical Report 2997.

[4] Biba KJ. Integrity considerations for secure computer systems. Bedford, MA: The MITRE Corporation; 1975. MITRE Report MTR-3153.

[5] Boyens JM, Paulsen C, Bartol N, Moorthy RS, Shankles SA. Notional supply chain risk management for federal information systems. Gaithersburg, MD: National Institute of Standards and Technology, Computer Security Division; March 2012. Interagency Report 7622 Second Public Draft.

[6] Clark DD, Wilson DR. A comparison of commercial and military computer security policies. In: IEEE symposium on security and privacy; April 1987. pp. 184–94.

[7] Cloud-based infrastructure as a service comes to government [press release]. Washington, DC: General Services Administration; October 19, 2010.

[8] The code of fair information practices. Washington, DC: Department of Health, Education and Welfare, Secretary's Advisory Committee on Automated Personal Data Systems, Records, computers, and the Rights of Citizens; 1973.

[9] Combating identity theft: a strategic plan. Washington, DC: President's Identity Theft Task Force; April 2007.

[10] Committee of Sponsoring Organizations of the Treadway Commission. Enterprise risk management – integrated framework. Durham, NC: American Institute of Certified Public Accountants; 2004.

[11] Continuous asset evaluation, situational awareness, and risk scoring reference architecture report. Washington, DC: Department of Homeland Security, Federal Network Security Branch; September 2010.

[12] Fiscal year 2009 report to Congress on the implementation of the Federal Information Security Management Act of 2002. Washington, DC: Office of Management and Budget; March 2010.

[13] Fiscal year 2010 report to Congress on the implementation of the Federal Information Security Management Act of 2002. Washington, DC: Office of Management and Budget; March 2011.

[14] Fiscal year 2011 report to Congress on the implementation of the Federal Information Security Management Act of 2002. Washington, DC: Office of Management and Budget; March 2012.

[15] FY 2012 inspector general Federal Information Security Management Act reporting metrics. Washington, DC: Department of Homeland Security, National Cyber Security Division; March 2012.

[16] Goertezl KM, Winograd T, McKinley HL, Oh L, Colon M, McGibbon T, et al. Software security assurance: a state-of-the-art report. Herndon, VA: Information Assurance Technology Analysis Center; July 2007.

[17] Information security weaknesses continue amid new federal efforts to implement requirements. Washington, DC: Government Accountability Office; October 2011. Report GAO-12-137.

[18] Intelligence community classification guidance findings and recommendations report. Washington, DC: Office of the Director of National Intelligence; January 2008.

[19] Johnson A, Toth P. Security assessment provider requirements and customer responsibilities: building a security assessment credentialing program for federal information systems. Gaithersburg, MD: National Institute of Standards and Technology, Computer Security Division; September 2007. Interagency Report 7328 Initial Public Draft.

[20] Jones, JA. An introduction to factor analysis of information risk (FAIR). Columbus, OH: Risk Management Insight; 2005. <http://riskmanagementinsight.com/media/documents/FAIR_Introduction.pdf>.

[21] Kohn LT, Ragland S. Completion of comprehensive risk management program essential to effective oversight. Report to the Ranking Member, Committee on Finance, US Senate. Washington, DC: Government Accountability Office; September 2009. GAO-09-687.

[22] Mayer RC, Davis JH, Schoorman FD. An integrative model of organizational trust. Acad Mgmt Rev 1995;20:709–34.. doi:10.2307/25879.

[23] Mell P, Waltermire D, Feldman L, Booth H, Ouyang A, Ragland Z, et al. CAESARS framework extension: an enterprise continuous monitoring technical reference

model. Gaithersburg, MD: National Institute of Standards and Technology, Computer Security Division; January 2012. NIST Interagency Report 7756 Second Public Draft.

[24] Mell P, Waltermire D, Halbardier A, Feldman L. Continuous monitoring reference model workflow, subsystem, and interface specifications. Gaithersburg, MD: National Institute of Standards and Technology, Computer Security Division; January 2012. Draft NIST Interagency Report 7799.

[25] Nissenbaum H. Will security enhance trust online, or supplant it?. In: Kramer RM, Cook KS, editors Trust and distrust in organizations. New York: Russell Sage Foundation; 2004. pp. 155–88.

[26] Northcutt S. Network security: the basics. CSO; April 29, 2008 [online edition, cited December 20, 2011]. <http://www.csoonline.com/article/print/342820>.

[27] Personal privacy in an information society: the report of the privacy protection study commission. Washington, DC: Privacy Protection Study Commission; 1977.

[28] Privacy impact assessment for EINSTEIN 2. Washington, DC: Department of Homeland Security; May 19, 2009.

[29] Privacy impact assessment for the initiative three exercise. Washington, DC: Department of Homeland Security; March 18, 2010.

[30] Ring PS, Van de Ven AH. Structuring cooperative relationships between organizations. Strat Mgmt J 1992;13:483–98.. doi:10.1002/smj.4250130702.

[31] The risk IT framework. Rolling Meadows, IL: ISACA; 2009.

[32] Simon HA. A behavioral model of rational choice. Qtrly J Econ 1955;59:99–118.. doi:10.2307/1884852.

[33] Sitkin SB, Pablo AL. Reconceptualizing the determinants of risk behavior. Acad Mgmt Rev 1992;17:9–38. doi:10.2307/258646.

[34] Ware WH. Security controls for computer systems: report of defense science board task force on computer security. Santa Monica, CA: Rand Corporation; February 1970 (declassified October 1975; reissued October 1979). RAND Report R-609-1.

[35] Wrightson MT, Caldwell SL. Further refinements needed to assess risks and prioritize protective measures at ports and other critical infrastructure. Report to Congressional Requesters. Washington, DC: Government Accountability Office; December 2005. GAO-06-91.

Standards

[1] Guidelines for computer security certification and accreditation. Gaithersburg, MD: National Bureau of Standards; September 1983. Federal Information Processing Standards Publication 102.

[2] IEEE 610.12-1990. IEEE Standard Glossary of Software Engineering Terminology. New York: Institute of Electrical and Electronics Engineers; 1990.

[3] IEEE P1074-2006. Developing a software project life cycle process. New York: Institute of Electrical and Electronics Engineers; 2006.

[4] ISO Guide 73:2009. Risk management – vocabulary.

[5] ISO/IEC 15026:2011. Systems and software engineering – systems and software assurance.

[6] ISO/IEC 15408:2009. Information technology – security techniques – evaluation criteria for IT security.

[7] ISO/IEC 27000:2009. Information technology – overview and vocabulary.

[8] ISO/IEC 27001:2005. Information – security techniques – information security management systems – requirements.

[9] ISO/IEC 27002:2005. Information technology – security techniques – code of practice for information security management.

[10] ISO/IEC 31000:2009. Risk management – principles and guidelines.

[11] ISO/IEC 31010:2009. Risk management – risk assessment techniques.

[12] Minimum security requirements for federal information and information systems. Gaithersburg, MD: National Institute of Standards and Technology, Computer Security Division; March 2006. Federal Information Processing Standards Publication 200.

[13] Personal identity verification (PIV) of federal employees and contractors.

[14] Gaithersburg, MD: National Institute of Standards and Technology, Computer Security Division; March 2006. Federal Information Processing Standards Publication 201-1.

[15] Standards for security categorization of federal information and information systems. Gaithersburg, MD: National Institute of Standards and Technology, Computer Security Division; December 2003. Federal Information Processing Standards Publication 199.

Books

[1] Abran A, Moore JW, editors. Guide to the software engineering body of knowledge. Los Alamitos, CA: Institute of Electrical and Electronics Engineers; 2004.

[2] Barber B. Logic and the limits of trust. New Brunswick, NJ: Rutgers University Press; 1983.

[3] Crouhy M, Galai D, Mark R. The essentials of risk management. New York: McGraw-Hill; 2006.

[4] Grady RB, Caswell DL. Software metrics: establishing a company-wide program. Upper Saddle River, NJ: Prentice Hall; 1987.

[5] Grembi J. Secure software development: a security programmer's guide. Boston: Course Technology, Cengage Learning; 2008.

[6] Hardin R. Trust and trustworthiness. New York: Russell Sage Foundation; 2004.

[7] Hurley RF. The decision to trust: how leaders create high-trust organizations. San Francisco: Jossey-Bass; 2012.

[8] Landoll D. The security risk assessment handbook. Boca Raton, FL: Auerbach; 2006.

[9] Luhman N. Risk: a sociological theory. New Brunswick, NJ: Transaction Publishers; 1993.

[10] March J, Simon H. Organizations. 2nd ed. Cambridge, MA: Blackwell; 1993.

[11] McCumber J. Assessing and managing security risk in IT systems: a structured methodology. Boca Raton, FL: Auerbach; 2005.

[12] McGraw G. Software security: building security in. Upper Saddle River, NJ: Addison-Wesley; 2006.

[13] Moore MH. Creating public value: strategic management in government. Cambridge, MA: Harvard University Press; 1995.

[14] Nye JS, Zelikow PD, King DC, editors. Why people don't trust government. Cambridge, MA: Harvard University Press; 1997.

[15] Parker DB. Fighting computer crime: a new framework for protecting information. New York: Wiley; 1998.

[16] Pfleeger CP, Pfleeger SL. Security in computing. 4th ed. Upper Saddle River, NJ: Prentice Hall; 2006.

[17] Project Management Institute . A guide to the project management body of knowledge. 4th ed. Newtown Square, PA: Project Management Institute; 2008.

[18] Reina DS, Reina ML. Trust and betrayal in the workplace. 2nd ed.. San Francisco: Berrett-Koehler; 2006.

[19] Solove DJ. Understanding privacy. Cambridge, MA: Harvard University Press; 2008.

[20] Whitman ME, Mattord HJ. Principles of information security. 3rd ed. Boston: Course Technology, Cengage Learning; 2009.

Online Sources

[1] Arguing security – creating security assurance cases. Washington, DC: Department of Homeland Security, National Cyber Security Division [Internet, created January 4, 2007; updated June 21, 2012; cited July 11, 2012]. <https://buildsecurityin.us-cert.gov/bsi/articles/knowledge/assurance/643-BSI.html>.

[2] Assessment cases download page. Gaithersburg, MD: National Institute of Standards and Technology, Computer Security Division [Internet, created August 7, 2008; updated February 12, 2012; cited May 11, 2012]. <http://csrc.nist.gov/groups/SMA/fisma/assessment-cases.html>.

[3] Certified products: the common criteria portal. Cheltenham, UK: Communications-Electronics Security Group [Internet, cited March 24, 2012]. <http://www.commoncriteriaportal.org/products/>.

[4] Committee on national security systems. Fort Meade, MD: National Computer Security Center [Internet, cited March 27, 2012]. <http://www.cnss.gov/>.

[5] Cryptologic module validation program (CMVP). Gaithersburg, MD: National Institute of Standards and Technology [Internet, created January 28, 1996; updated February 16, 2012; cited March 24, 2012]. <http://csrc.nist.gov/groups/STM/cmvp/index.html>.

[6] Cyber Security Assessment and Management (CSAM) [computer program]. Version 2.1.5.2. Washington, DC: Department of Justice; 2010.

[7] DoD issuances [Internet]. Fort Belvoir, VA: Defense Technical Information Center [cited March 27, 2012]. <http://www.dtic.mil/whs/directives/index.html>.

[8] Federal Agency Security Practices (FASP) [Internet]. Gaithersburg, MD: National Institute of Standards and Technology, Computer Security Division [updated October 24, 2010; cited December 9, 2011]. <http://csrc.nist.gov/groups/SMA/fasp/index.html>.

[9] Federal IT Dashboard [Internet]. Washington, DC: Office of Management and Budget [cited May 2012]. <http://www.itdashboard.gov/>.

[10] FIPS Publications [Internet]. Gaithersburg, MD: National Institute of Standards and Technology [created July 3, 2007; updated March 6, 2012; cited March 24, 2012]. <http://csrc.nist.gov/publications/PubsFIPS.html>.

[11] Incident reporting guidelines [Internet]. Washington, DC: United States Computer Emergency Readiness Team [cited January 15, 2011]. <http://www.us-cert.gov/federal/reportingRequirements.html>.

[12] National vulnerability database national checklist program repository [Internet]. Washington, DC: Department of Homeland Security, National Cyber Security Division [updated February 17, 2012; cited February 18, 2012]. <http://checklists.nist.gov>.

[13] NVLAP Accreditation Programs [Internet]. Gaithersburg, MD: National Institute of Standards and Technology [created February 1, 2010; updated March 14, 2012; cited March 24, 2012]. <http://www.nist.gov/nvlap/nvlap-fields.cfm>.

[14] Platform for privacy preferences project [Internet]. Cambridge, MA: World Wide Web Consortium [updated November 20, 2007; cited January 14, 2011]. <http://www.w3.org/P3P/>.

[15] Privacy protections in state constitutions [Internet]. Denver, CO: National Conference of State Legislatures [cited April 15, 2012]. <http://www.ncsl.org/default.aspx?tabid=13467>.

[16] Risk management framework (RMF) overview [Internet]. Gaithersburg, MD: National Institute of Standards and Technology, Computer Security Division [created October 24, 2002; updated June 8, 2010; cited January 13, 2012]. <http://csrc.nist.gov/groups/SMA/fisma/framework.html>.

[17] SAMATE – Software Assurance Metrics and Tools Evaluation [Internet]. Gaithersburg, MD: National Institute of Standards and Technology, Information Technology Laboratory [cited February 14, 2012]. <http://samate.nist.gov>.

[18] Security breach notification laws [Internet]. Denver, CO: National Conference of State Legislatures [cited April 15, 2012]. <http://www.ncsl.org/Default.aspx?TabId=13489>.

[19] Security content automation protocol validated products [Internet]. Washington, DC: Department of Homeland Security, National Cyber Security Division; [cited May 17, 2012]. <http://nvd.nist.gov/scapproducts.cfm>.

[20] The security content automation protocol [Internet]. Gaithersburg, MD: National Institute of Standards and Technology, Information Technology Laboratory; May 12, 2009 [updated March 30, 2011; cited February 11, 2012]. <http://scap.nist.gov>.

[21] Security technical implementation guides [Internet]. Defense information systems agency, information assurance support environment [updated February 14, 2011; cited February 18, 2012]. <http://iase.disa.mil/stigs/index.html>.

[22] Special Publications [Internet]. Gaithersburg, MD: National Institute of Standards and Technology [created July 3, 2007; updated February 28, 2012; cited April 24, 2012]. <http://csrc.nist.gov/publications/PubsSPs.html>.

[23] US-CERT – United States Computer Emergency Readiness Team [Internet]. Washington, DC: Department of Homeland Security [cited January 15, 2012]. <http://www.us-cert.gov>.

[24] US Government Approved Protection Profiles [Internet]. Fort Meade, MD: National Information Assurance Partnership [cited March 24, 2012]. <http://www.niap-ccevs.org/pp/>.

Acronyms

ACRONYMS AND ABBREVIATIONS

ADP	Automatic Data Processing
AO	Authorizing Official
APT	Advanced Persistent Threat
ATO	Authority (or Approval or Authorization) to Operate
BCP	Business Continuity Plan
BIA	Business Impact Analysis
BRM	Business Reference Model
C&A	Certification and Accreditation
CAESARS	Continuous Asset Evaluation, Situational Awareness, and Risk Scoring
CAP	Certified Authorization Professional
CC	Common Criteria
CCA	Clinger-Cohen Act
CCEVS	Common Criteria Evaluation and Validation Scheme
CDC	Centers for Disease Control and Prevention
CERT	Computer Emergency Response Team
CFO	Chief Financial Officer
CFR	Code of Federal Regulations
CIA	Confidentiality, Integrity, Availability
CIO	Chief Information Officer
CISA	Certified Information Systems Auditor
CISO	Chief Information Security Officer
CISSP	Certified Information Systems Security Professional
CM	Configuration Management
CMS	Centers for Medicare and Medicaid Services
CMVP	Cryptologic Module Validation Program

CNCI	Comprehensive National Cybersecurity Initiative
CNSS	Committee on National Security Systems
CNSSI	Committee on National Security Systems Instruction
CONOPS	Concept of Operations
COOP	Continuity of Operations
COPPA	Children's Online Privacy Protection Act
COSO	Committee of Sponsoring Organizations of the Treadway Commission
COTS	Commercial Off-the-Shelf
CP	Contingency Plan
CPIC	Capital Planning and Investment Control
CSAM	Cyber Security Assessment and Management
CSIRT	Computer Security Incident Response Team
CUI	Controlled Unclassified Information
CVE	Common Vulnerabilities and Exposures
DIACAP	DoD Information Assurance Certification and Accreditation Process
DIARMF	DoD Information Assurance Risk Management Framework
DISA	Defense Information Systems Agency
DITSCAP	DoD Information Technology Security Certification and Accreditation Process
DHS	Department of Homeland Security
DoD	Department of Defense
DoDI	Department of Defense Instruction
DoDM	Department of Defense Manual
DoDAF	Department of Defense Architecture Framework
DR	Disaster Recovery
DRM	Data Reference Model
EA	Enterprise Architecture
ECPA	Electronic Communications Privacy Act
EDP	Electronic Data Processing
EO	Executive Order
EOP	Executive Office of the President
e-RA	Electronic Risk Assessment
ERM	Enterprise Risk Management
EVM	Earned Value Management
FAIR	Factor Analysis of Information Risk
FBCA	Federal Bridge Certification Authority
FCD	Federal Continuity Directive
FDIC	Federal Deposit Insurance Corporation
FDCC	Federal Desktop Core Configuration
FEA	Federal Enterprise Architecture

FEAF	Federal Enterprise Architecture Framework
FedCIRC	Federal Computer Incident Response Capability
FedRAMP	Federal Risk and Authorization Management Program
FERPA	Family Educational Rights and Privacy Act
FIPS	Federal Information Processing Standards
FISMA	Federal Information Security Management Act
FPKI	Federal Public Key Infrastructure
FTS	Federal Telecommunications System
FURPS	Functionality, Usability, Reliability, Performance, Supportability
GAO	Government Accountability Office
GISRA	Government Information Security Reform Act
GLBA	Graham-Leach-Bliley Act
GPEA	Government Paperwork Elimination Act
GPRA	Government Performance and Results Act
GSA	General Services Administration
GSS	General Support System
HHS	Department of Health and Human Services
HIPAA	Health Insurance Portability and Accountability Act
HITECH	Health Information Technology for Economic and Clinical Health Act
HSPD	Homeland Security Presidential Directive
HUD	Department of Housing and Urban Development
IA	Information Assurance
IaaS	Infrastructure as a Service
IATAC	Information Assurance Technology Analysis Center
IATF	Information Assurance Technical Framework
IAVA	Information Assurance Vulnerability Alert
IC	Intelligence Community
ICAM	Identity, Credential, and Access Management
IDS	Intrusion Detection System
IEC	International Electrotechnical Commission
IEEE	Institute of Electrical and Electronics Engineers
INFOSEC	Information Security
IP	Internet Protocol
IPsec	Internet Protocol Security
IPS	Intrusion Prevention System
IPv6	Internet Protocol Version 6
IR	Incident Response
IRM	Information Resources Management
ISCM	Information Security Continuous Monitoring
ISCP	Information Security Contingency Plan
ISA	Interconnection Security Agreement

ISACA	Information Systems Audit and Control Association
ISMS	Information Security Management System
ISO	International Organization for Standardization
ISSO	Information System Security Officer
IT	Information Technology
MEF	Mission Essential Function
MOU	Memorandum of Understanding
MTIPS	Managed Trusted Internet Protocol Services
NARA	National Archives and Records Administration
NASA	National Aeronautics and Space Administration
NBS	National Bureau of Standards
NIACAP	National Information Assurance Certification and Accreditation Process
NIAP	National Information Assurance Partnership
NIST	National Institute of Standards and Technology
NSA	National Security Agency
NSD	National Security Directive
NSPD	National Security Presidential Directive
NSS	National Security System
NSTIC	National Strategy for Trusted Identities in Cyberspace
NSTISSC	National Security Telecommunications and Information Systems Security Committee
NVD	National Vulnerability Database
NVLAP	National Voluntary Laboratory Accreditation Program
OCR	Office for Civil Rights
OCTAVE	Operationally Critical Threat, Asset, and Vulnerability Evaluation
ODNI	Office of the Director of National Intelligence
OECD	Organisation for Economic Cooperation and Development
OMB	Office of Management and Budget
PaaS	Platform as a Service
PHI	Protected Health Information
PIA	Privacy Impact Assessment
PII	Personally Identifiable Information
PIV	Personal Identity Verification
PKI	Public Key Infrastructure
PMBOK	Project Management Body of Knowledge
PMEF	Primary Mission Essential Function
POA&M	Plan of Action and Milestones

PRA	Paperwork Reduction Act
PRM	Performance Reference Model
RA	Risk Assessment
RFID	Radio Frequency Identification
ROB	Rules of Behavior
RMF	Risk Management Framework
RTM	Requirements Traceability Matrix
SaaS	Software as a Service
SANS	SysAdmin, Audit, Network, Security
SAISO	Senior Agency Information Security Officer
SAOP	Senior Agency Official for Privacy
SAR	Security Assessment Report
SBU	Sensitive But Unclassified
SCA	Security Control Assessment
SCAP	Security Content Automation Protocol
SDLC	System Development Life Cycle
SIEM	Security Information and Event Management
SISO	Senior Information Security Officer
SORN	System of Records Notice
SP	Special Publication
SPP	Security and Privacy Profile
SRM	Service Component Reference Model
SSAA	System Security Authorization Agreement
SSL	Secure Sockets Layer
SSP	System Security Plan
STIG	Security Technical Implementation Guide
TCSEC	Trusted Computer System Evaluation Criteria
TIC	Trusted Internet Connections
TLS	Transport Layer Security
TRM	Technical Reference Model
UII	Unique Investment Identifier
UPI	Unique Project Identifier
URL	Uniform Resource Locator
USC	United States Code
US-CERT	United States Computer Emergency Response Team
USGCB	United States Government Configuration Baseline
VA	Department of Veterans Affairs
VPN	Virtual Private Network
WBS	Work Breakdown Structure
WiMAX	Worldwide Interoperability for Microwave Access
XML	Extensible Markup Language

Glossary

GLOSSARY

This appendix provides definitions for common terms used in this book. Wherever possible, the definitions presented here match those in authoritative government sources, including applicable sections of the United States Code, official guidance issued by NIST and OMB, and the CNSS *National Information Assurance Glossary* (CNSS Instruction 4009). Where applicable, the source appears in brackets following each definition.

Term	Definition [Source]
Access Control	The process of granting or denying specific requests for obtaining and using information and related information processing services and to enter specific physical facilities [CNSS]
Accountability	Principle that an individual is entrusted to safeguard and control equipment, keying material, and information and is answerable to proper authority for the loss or misuse of that equipment or information [CNSS]
Adequate Security	Security commensurate with the risk and magnitude of harm resulting from the loss, misuse, or unauthorized access to or modification of information [OMB]
Advanced Persistent Threat	An adversary that possesses sophisticated levels of expertise and significant resources which allow it to create opportunities to achieve its objectives by using multiple attack vectors (e.g. cyber, physical, and deception) [NIST]
Application	The use of information resources (information and information technology) to satisfy a specific set of user requirements [OMB]
	A software program hosted by an information system [NIST]

Term	Definition [Source]
Assessment Findings	Assessment results produced by the application of an assessment procedure to a security control or control enhancement to achieve an assessment objective; the execution of a determination statement within an assessment procedure by an assessor that results in either a *satisfied* or *other than satisfied* condition [NIST]
Assessment Method	One of three types of actions (examine, interview, test) taken by assessors in obtaining evidence during a security control assessment [NIST]
Assessment Object	The item (specifications, mechanisms, activities, individuals) upon which an assessment method is applied [NIST]
Assessment Objective	A set of determination statements that expresses the desired outcome for the assessment of a security control or control enhancement [NIST]
Assessment Procedure	A set of assessment objectives and an associated set of assessment methods and assessment objects [NIST]
Asset	A major application, general support system, high impact program, physical plant, mission critical system, personnel, equipment, or a logically related group of systems [CNSS]
Assurance	Measure of confidence that the security features, practices, procedures, and architecture of an information system accurately mediates and enforces the security policy [CNSS]
	Grounds for confidence that the set of intended security controls in an information system are effective in their application [NIST]
Authentication	Verifying the identity of a user, process, or device, often as a prerequisite to allowing access to resources in an information system [NIST]
Authenticity	The property of being genuine and being able to be verified and trusted; confidence in the validity of a transmission, message, or message originator [NIST]
Authorization to Operate	The official management decision given by a senior organizational official to authorize operation of an information system and to explicitly accept the risk to organizational operations (including mission, functions, image, or reputation), organizational assets, individuals, other organizations, and the Nation based on the implementation of an agreed-upon set of security controls [NIST]
Authorization Boundary	Comprises all components of an information system to be authorized for operation by an authorizing official and excludes separately authorized systems to which the information system is connected [NIST]

Term	Definition [Source]
	All components of an information system to be authorized for operation by an authorizing official and excludes separately authorized systems, to which the information system is connected [CNSS]
Authorizing Official	A senior (federal) official or executive with the authority to formally assume responsibility for operating an information system at an acceptable level of risk to organizational operations (including mission, functions, image, or reputation), organizational assets, individuals, other organizations, and the Nation [NIST]
Authorizing Official Designated Representative	An organizational official acting on behalf of an authorizing official in carrying out and coordinating the required activities associated with security authorization [NIST]
Authorization Package	Collected information about a system used by authorizing officials to make authorization decisions; typically defined to include the System Security Plan, Security Assessment Report, and Plan of Action and Milestones [NIST]
Availability	Ensuring timely and reliable access to and use of information [44 U.S.C. §3542]
Business Continuity Plan	The documentation of a predetermined set of instructions or procedures that describe how an organization's mission/business processes will be sustained during and after a significant disruption [NIST]
Business Impact Analysis	An analysis of an information system's requirements, functions, and interdependencies used to characterize system contingency requirements and priorities in the event of a significant disruption [NIST]
Capital Planning and Investment Control	Management process integrating the planning, acquisition, and management of capital assets and the management and operation of those assets through their usable life after initial acquisition [OMB]
Chief Information Officer	Agency official responsible for: (i) providing advice and other assistance to the head of the executive agency and other senior management personnel of the agency to ensure that information technology is acquired and information resources are managed in a manner that is consistent with laws, Executive Orders, directives, policies, regulations, and priorities established by the head of the agency; (ii) developing, maintaining, and facilitating the implementation of a sound and integrated information technology architecture for the agency; and (iii) promoting the effective and efficient design and operation of all major information resources management processes for the agency, including improvements to work processes of the agency [40 U.S.C. §11315]

Term	Definition [Source]
Classified Information	Information that has been determined: (i) pursuant to Executive Order 12958 as amended by Executive Order 13292, or any predecessor Order, to be classified national security information; or (ii) pursuant to the Atomic Energy Act of 1954, as amended, to be Restricted Data (RD) [NIST]
Cloud Computing	A model for enabling ubiquitous, convenient, on-demand network access to a shared pool of configurable computing resources (e.g. networks, servers, storage, applications, and services) that can be rapidly provisioned and released with minimal management effort or service provider interaction [NIST]
Common Control	A security control that is inherited by one or more organizational information systems [NIST]
Common Control Provider	An organizational official responsible for the development, implementation, assessment, and monitoring of common controls [NIST]
Compensating Security Control	A management, operational, and/or technical control employed by an organization in lieu of a recommended security control in the low, moderate, or high baselines that provides equivalent or comparable protection for an information system [CNSS]
Computer Security Incident Response Team	A capability set up for the purpose of assisting in responding to computer security-related incidents; also called a Computer Incident Response Team (CIRT) or a Computer Incident Response Center (CIRC) [NIST]
Concept of Operations	A description of an information system, its operational policies, classes of users, interactions between the system and its users, and the system's contribution to the operational mission [CNSS]
Confidentiality	Preserving authorized restrictions on information access and disclosure, including means for protecting personal privacy and proprietary information [44 U.S.C. §3542]
Continuity of Operations Plan	A predetermined set of instructions or procedures that describe how an organization's mission essential functions will be sustained within 12 hr and for up to 30 days as a result of a disaster event before returning to normal operations [NIST]
Continuous Monitoring	Maintaining ongoing awareness to support organizational risk decisions [NIST]
	The process implemented to maintain a current security status for one or more information systems or for the entire suite of information systems on which the operational mission of the enterprise depends [CNSS]

Term	Definition [Source]
Controlled Unclassified Information	A categorical designation that refers to unclassified information that does not meet the standards for National Security Classification under Executive Order 12958, as amended, but is (i) pertinent to the national interests of the United States or to the important interests of entities outside the federal government, and (ii) under law or policy requires protection from unauthorized disclosure, special handling safeguards, or prescribed limits on exchange or dissemination [NIST]
Countermeasure	Action, device, procedure, technique, or other measure that reduces the vulnerability of an information system. Synonymous with *security control* and *safeguard* [CNSS]
Coverage	An attribute associated with an assessment method that addresses the scope or breadth of the assessment objects included in the assessment. The values for the coverage attribute are basic, focused, and comprehensive [NIST]
Critical Infrastructure	System and assets, whether physical or virtual, so vital to the US that the incapacity or destruction of such systems and assets would have a debilitating impact on security, national economic security, national public health or safety, or any combination of those matters [CNSS]
Cyber Security	The ability to protect or defend the use of cyberspace from attack [CNSS]
Cyberspace	A global domain within the information environment consisting of the interdependent network of information systems infrastructures including the Internet, telecommunications networks, computer systems, and embedded processors and controllers [CNSS]
Defense-in-Depth	Information security strategy integrating people, technology, and operations capabilities to establish variable barriers across multiple layers and missions of the organization [CNSS]
Depth	An attribute associated with an assessment method that addresses the rigor and level of detail associated with the application of the method. The values for the depth attribute are basic, focused, and comprehensive [NIST]
Disaster Recovery Plan	A written plan for recovering one or more information systems at an alternate facility in response to a major hardware or software failure or destruction of facilities [NIST]

Term	Definition [Source]
Dynamic Subsystem	A component of an information system that becomes part of an organizational information system at various points in time throughout the life cycle of the system [NIST]
Electronic Authentication	The process of establishing confidence in user identities electronically presented to an information system [CNSS]
Enterprise	An organization with a defined mission/goal and a defined boundary, using information systems to execute that mission, and with responsibility for managing its own risks and performance. An enterprise may consist of all or some of the following business aspects: acquisition, program management, financial management (e.g. budgets), human resources, security, and information systems, information and mission management [CNSS]
Enterprise Architecture	A management practice for aligning resources to improve business performance and help agencies better execute their core missions. An EA describes the current and future state of the agency, and lays out a plan for transitioning from the current state to the desired future state [OMB]
	The description of an enterprise's entire set of information systems: how they are configured, how they are integrated, how they interface to the external environment at the enterprise's boundary, how they are operated to support the enterprise mission, and how they contribute to the enterprise's overall security posture [CNSS]
Executive Agency	An executive department specified in 5 U.S.C. §101; a military department specified in 5 U.S.C. §102; an independent establishment as defined in 5 U.S.C. §104(1); or a wholly owned Government corporation fully subject to the provisions of 31 U.S.C. Chapter 91 [41 U.S.C. §403]
External Information System	An information system or component of an information system that is outside of the authorization boundary established by the organization and for which the organization typically has no direct control over the application of required security controls or the assessment of security control effectiveness [NIST]
External Subsystem	A component of an information system outside of the direct control of the organization that owns the information system and authorizes its operation [NIST]

Term	Definition [Source]
Failover	The capability to switch over automatically (typically without human intervention or warning) to a redundant or standby information system upon the failure or abnormal termination of the previously active system [NIST]
Federal Bridge Certification Authority	A collection of Public Key Infrastructure components (Certificate Authorities, Directories, Certificate Policies, and Certificate Practice Statements) that are used to provide peer-to- peer interoperability among agency principal certification authorities [CNSS]
Federal Enterprise Architecture	A business-based framework for government wide improvement developed by the Office of Management and Budget that is intended to facilitate efforts to transform the federal government to one that is citizen-centered, results-oriented, and market-based [OMB]
Federal Information Processing Standard	A standard for adoption and use by Federal agencies that has been developed within the Information Technology Laboratory and published by the National Institute of Standards and Technology [CNSS]
Federal Information System	An information system used or operated by an executive agency, by a contractor of an executive agency, or by another organization on behalf of an executive agency [40 U.S.C. §11331]
General Support System	An interconnected set of information resources under the same direct management control which shares common functionality [OMB]
High-Impact System	An information system in which at least one security objective (i.e. confidentiality, integrity, or availability) is assigned a potential impact value of high [CNSS]
Hybrid Control	A security control that is implemented in an information system in part as a common control and in part as a system-specific control [NIST]
Identification	An act or process that presents an identifier to a system so that the system can recognize a system entity (e.g. user, process, or device) and distinguish that entity from all others [CNSS]
Identity	The set of attribute values by which an entity is recognizable and that, within the scope of an identity manager's responsibility, is sufficient to distinguish that entity from any other entity [CNSS]
Impact	The adverse effect on organizational operations, organizational assets, or individuals resulting from a loss of confidentiality, integrity, or availability [NIST]

Term	Definition [Source]
Impact Level	The magnitude of harm that can be expected to result from the consequences of unauthorized disclosure of information, unauthorized modification of information, unauthorized destruction of information, or loss of information or information system availability [CNSS]
Incident	An assessed occurrence that actually or potentially jeopardizes the confidentiality, integrity, or availability of an information system; or the information the system processes, stores, or transmits; or that constitutes a violation or imminent threat of violation of security policies, security procedures, or acceptable use policies [CNSS]
Incident Response Plan	The documentation of a predetermined set of instructions or procedures to detect, respond to, and limit consequences of a malicious cyber attacks against an organization's information system(s) [NIST]
Information	Any communication or representation of knowledge such as facts, data, or opinions in any medium or form, including textual, numerical, graphic, cartographic, narrative, or audiovisual [CNSS]
	An instance of an information type [NIST]
Information Assurance	Measures that protect and defend information and information systems by ensuring their availability, integrity, authentication, confidentiality, and non- repudiation. These measures include providing for restoration of information systems by incorporating protection, detection, and reaction capabilities [CNSS]
Information Management	The planning, budgeting, manipulating, and controlling of information through its life cycle [CNSS]
Information Owner	Official with statutory or operational authority for specified information and responsibility for establishing the controls for its generation, classification, collection, processing, dissemination, and disposal [CNSS]
Information Resources	Information and related resources, such as personnel, equipment, funds, and information technology [44 U.S.C. §3502]
Information Security	The protection of information and information systems from unauthorized access, use, disclosure, disruption, modification, or destruction in order to provide confidentiality, integrity, and availability [44 U.S.C. §3542]

Term	Definition [Source]
Information Security Architect	An individual, group, or organization responsible for ensuring that the information security requirements necessary to protect the organization's core missions and business processes are adequately addressed in all aspects of enterprise architecture including reference models, segment and solution architectures, and the resulting information systems supporting those missions and business processes [NIST]
Information Security Architecture	An embedded, integral part of the enterprise architecture that describes the structure and behavior for an enterprise's security processes, information security systems, personnel and organizational sub-units, showing their alignment with the enterprise's mission and strategic plans [NIST]
Information Security Policy	Aggregate of directives, regulations, rules, and practices that prescribe how an organization manages, protects, and distributes information [CNSS]
Information Security Program Plan	Formal document that provides an overview of the security requirements for an organization-wide information security program and describes the program management controls and common controls in place or planned for meeting those requirements [NIST]
Information Steward	An agency official with statutory or operational authority for specified information and responsibility for establishing the controls for its generation, collection, processing, dissemination, and disposal [CNSS]
Information System	A discrete set of information resources organized for the collection, processing, maintenance, use, sharing, dissemination, or disposition of information [44 U.S.C. §3502]
Information System Contingency Plan	Management policy and procedures designed to maintain or restore business operations, including computer operations, possibly at an alternate location, in the event of emergencies, system failures, or disasters [NIST]
Information System Owner	Official responsible for the overall procurement, development, integration, modification, or operation and maintenance of an information system [NIST]
Information System Resilience	The ability of an information system to continue to: (i) operate under adverse conditions or stress, even if in a degraded or debilitated state, while maintaining essential operational capabilities; and (ii) recover to an effective operational posture in a time frame consistent with mission needs [NIST]

Term	Definition [Source]
Information System Security Engineer	An individual, group, or organization responsible for conducting information system security engineering activities, including capturing and refining information security requirements and ensuring that the requirements are effectively integrated into information technology component products and information systems through purposeful security architecting, design, development, and configuration [NIST]
Information System Security Officer	Individual assigned responsibility by the senior agency information security officer, authorizing official, management official, or information system owner for maintaining the appropriate operational security posture for an information system or program [NIST]
Information Security Risk	The risk to organizational operations (including mission, functions, image, reputation), organizational assets, individuals, other organizations, and the Nation due to the potential for unauthorized access, use, disclosure, disruption, modification, or destruction of information and/or information systems [NIST]
Information System-Related Security Risk	Risk that arises through the loss of confidentiality, integrity, or availability of information or information systems and consider impacts to the organization (including assets, mission, functions, image, or reputation), individuals, other organizations, and the Nation [NIST]
Information Technology	Any equipment or interconnected system or subsystem of equipment that is used in the automatic acquisition, storage, manipulation, management, movement, control, display, switching, interchange, transmission, or reception of data or information by the executive agency. The term information technology includes computers, ancillary equipment, software, firmware, and similar procedures, services (including support services), and related resources [40 U.S.C. §1401]
Information Type	A specific category of information (e.g. privacy, medical, proprietary, financial, investigative, contractor sensitive, security management) defined by an organization or in some instances, by a specific law, Executive Order, directive, policy, or regulation [NIST]
Integrity	Guarding against improper information modification or destruction, and includes ensuring information non- repudiation and authenticity [44 U.S.C. §3542]

Term	Definition [Source]
Low-Impact System	An information system in which all three security objectives (i.e. confidentiality, integrity, or availability) are assigned a potential impact value of low [CNSS]
Management Controls	The security controls for an information system that focus on the management of risk and the management of information system security [NIST]
Major Application	An application that requires special attention to security due to the risk and magnitude of the harm resulting from the loss, misuse, or unauthorized access to or modification of the information in the application [OMB]
Moderate-Impact System	An information system in which at least one security objective (i.e. confidentiality, integrity, or availability) is assigned a potential impact value of moderate and no security objectives are assigned a potential impact value of high [CNSS]
National Information Assurance Partnership	A US government initiative established to promote the use of evaluated information systems products and champion the development and use of national and international standards for information technology security [CNSS]
National Security System	Any information system (including any telecommunications system) used or operated by an agency or by a contractor of an agency, or other organization on behalf of an agency (i) the function, operation, or use of which involves intelligence activities; involves cryptologic activities related to national security; involves command and control of military forces; involves equipment that is an integral part of a weapon or weapons system; or is critical to the direct fulfillment of military or intelligence missions (excluding a system that is to be used for routine administrative and business applications, for example, payroll, finance, logistics, and personnel management applications); or (ii) is protected at all times by procedures established for information that have been specifically authorized under criteria established by an Executive Order or an Act of Congress to be kept classified in the interest of national defense or foreign policy [44 U.S.C. §3542]
National Vulnerability Database	The US government repository of standards-based vulnerability management data, enabling automation of vulnerability management, security measurement, and compliance [CNSS]

Term	Definition [Source]
Non-Repudiation	Assurance that the sender of information is provided with proof of delivery and the recipient is provided with proof of the sender's identity, so neither can later deny having processed the information [CNSS]
	Protection against an individual falsely denying having performed a particular action [NIST]
Operating Environment	The physical surroundings in which an information system processes, stores, and transmits information [NIST]
Operational Controls	The security controls for an information system that are primarily implemented and executed by people (as opposed to systems) [NIST]
Organization	An entity of any size, complexity, or positioning within an organizational structure (e.g. a federal agency or, as appropriate, any of its operational elements) [NIST]
Patch Management	The systematic notification, identification, deployment, installation, and verification of operating system and application software code revisions [CNSS]
Penetration Testing	A test methodology in which assessors, typically working under specific constraints, attempt to circumvent or defeat the security features of an information system [CNSS]
Personally Identifiable Information	Any information about an individual maintained by an agency, including (1) any information that can be used to distinguish or trace an individual's identity, such as name, social security number, date and place of birth, mother's maiden name, or biometric records; and (2) any other information that is linked or linkable to an individual, such as medical, educational, financial, and employment information [GAO]
Personal Identity Verification	The process of creating and using a government-wide secure and reliable form of identification for Federal employees and contractors, in support of HSPD 12, *Policy for a Common Identification Standard for Federal Employees and Contractors* [CNSS]
Plan of Action and Milestones	A document that identifies tasks needing to be accomplished. It details resources required to accomplish the elements of the plan, any milestones in meeting the tasks, and scheduled completion dates for the milestones [OMB]

Term	Definition [Source]
Privacy Impact Assessment	An analysis of how information is handled that ensures handling conforms to applicable legal, regulatory, and policy requirements regarding privacy; determines the risks and effects of collecting, maintaining and disseminating information in identifiable form in an electronic information system; and examines and evaluates protections and alternative processes for handling information to mitigate potential privacy risks [OMB]
Protection Profile	Common Criteria specification that represents an implementation-independent set of security requirements for a category of Target of Evaluations (TOE) that meets specific consumer needs [CNSS]
Public Key Infrastructure	The framework and services that provide for the generation, production, distribution, control, accounting and destruction of public key certificates. Components include the personnel, policies, processes, server platforms, software, and workstations used for the purpose of administering certificates and public-private key pairs, including the ability to issue, maintain, recover, and revoke public key certificates [CNSS]
Reciprocity	Mutual agreement among participating organizations to accept each other's security assessments in order to reuse information system resources and/or to accept each other's assessed security posture in order to share information [NIST]
Recovery Procedures	Actions necessary to restore data files of an information system and computational capability after a system failure [CNSS]
Remediation	The act of mitigating a vulnerability or a threat [CNSS]
Remote Access	Access to an organization's nonpublic information system by an authorized user (or an information system) communicating through an external, non-organization-controlled network [CNSS]
Residual Risk	Portion of risk remaining after security measures have been applied [CNSS]
Risk	A measure of the extent to which an entity is threatened by a potential circumstance or event, and typically a function of: (i) the adverse impacts that would arise if the circumstance or event occurs; and (ii) the likelihood of occurrence [NIST]

Term	Definition [Source]
Risk Assessment	The process of identifying risks to organizational operations (including mission, functions, image, reputation), organizational assets, individuals, other organizations, and the Nation, resulting from the operation of an information system. Part of risk management, incorporates threat and vulnerability analyses, and considers mitigations provided by security controls planned or in place. Synonymous with risk analysis [NIST]
Risk Executive	An individual or group within an organization that helps to ensure that: (i) security risk-related considerations for individual information systems, to include the authorization decisions for those systems, are viewed from an organization-wide perspective with regard to the overall strategic goals and objectives of the organization in carrying out its missions and business functions; and (ii) managing risk from individual information systems is consistent across the organization, reflects organizational risk tolerance, and is considered along with other organizational risks affecting mission/business success [NIST]
Risk Management	The program and supporting processes to manage information security risk to organizational operations (including mission, functions, image, reputation), organizational assets, individuals, other organizations, and the Nation, and includes: (i) establishing the context for risk-related activities; (ii) assessing risk; (iii) responding to risk once determined; and (iv) monitoring risk over time [NIST]
Risk Mitigation	Prioritizing, evaluating, and implementing the appropriate risk-reducing controls/countermeasures recommended from the risk management process [CNSS]
Risk Monitoring	Maintaining ongoing awareness of an organization's risk environment, risk management program, and associated activities to support risk decisions [NIST]
Risk Response	Accepting, avoiding, mitigating, sharing, or transferring risk to organizational operations (i.e. mission, functions, image, or reputation), organizational assets, individuals, other organizations, or the Nation [NIST]
Risk Response Measure	A specific action taken to respond to an identified risk [NIST]
Risk Tolerance	The level of risk or degree of uncertainty that is acceptable to the organization [NIST]

Term	Definition [Source]
Root Cause Analysis	A principle-based, systems approach for the identification of underlying causes associated with a particular set of risks [NIST]
Safeguard	Protective measure prescribed to meet the security requirements (i.e. confidentiality, integrity, and availability) specified for an information system. Synonymous with *security control* [CNSS]
Scoping Guidance	Specific factors related to technology, infrastructure, public access, scalability, common security controls, and risk that can be considered by organizations in the applicability and implementation of individual security controls in the security control baseline [CNSS]
Security	A condition that results from the establishment and maintenance of protective measures that enable an enterprise to perform its mission or critical functions despite risks posed by threats to its use of information systems [CNSS]
Security Assessment Report	Document describing the findings and recommendations resulting from the security control assessment process [NIST]
Security Categorization	The process of determining the security category for information or an information system based on the potential impact on an organization should certain events occur which jeopardize the information and information systems needed by the organization to accomplish its assigned mission, protect its assets, fulfill its legal responsibilities, maintain its day-to-day functions, and protect individuals [NIST]
Security Control Assessment	The testing and/or evaluation of the management, operational, and technical security controls to determine the extent to which the controls are implemented correctly, operating as intended, and producing the desired outcome with respect to meeting the security requirements for an information system or organization [NIST]
Security Control Assessor	The individual, group, or organization responsible for conducting a security control assessment [NIST]
Security Control Baseline	The set of minimum security controls defined for a low- impact, moderate-impact, or high-impact information system [CNSS]
Security Control Enhancement	Statement of security capability to: (i) build in additional, but related, functionality to a basic control; and/or (ii) increase the strength of a basic control [NIST]

Term	Definition [Source]
Security Control Inheritance	A situation in which an information system or application receives protection from security controls (or portions of security controls) that are developed, implemented, assessed, authorized, and monitored by entities other than those responsible for the system or application; entities either internal or external to the organization where the system or application resides [CNSS]
Security Controls	The management, operational, and technical controls prescribed for an information system to protect the confidentiality, integrity, and availability of the system and its information [NIST]
Security Engineering	An interdisciplinary approach and means to enable the realization of secure systems that focuses on defining customer needs, security protection requirements, and required functionality early in the systems development lifecycle, documenting requirements, and then proceeding with design, synthesis, and system validation while considering the complete problem [CNSS]
Security Functions	The hardware, software, and/or firmware of the information system responsible for enforcing the system security policy and supporting the isolation of code and data on which the protection is based [NIST]
Security Impact Analysis	The analysis conducted by an organizational official to determine the extent to which changes to the information system have affected the security state of the system [NIST]
Security Objective	Confidentiality, integrity, or availability [NIST]
Security Policy	A set of criteria for the provision of security services [CNSS]
Security Posture	The security status of an enterprise's networks, information, and systems based on IA resources (e.g. people, hardware, software, policies) and capabilities in place to manage the defense of the enterprise and to react as the situation changes [CNSS]
Security Requirements	Requirements levied on an information system that are derived from applicable laws, Executive Orders, directives, policies, standards, instructions, regulations, procedures, or organizational mission/business case needs to ensure the confidentiality, integrity, and availability of the information being processed, stored, or transmitted [NIST]

Term	Definition [Source]
Security-Relevant Information	Any information within the information system that can potentially impact the operation of security functions in a manner that could result in failure to enforce the system security policy or maintain isolation of code and data [NIST]
Senior Agency Information Security Officer	Official responsible for carrying out the Chief Information Officer responsibilities under FISMA and serving as the Chief Information Officer's primary liaison to the agency's authorizing officials, information system owners, and information system security officers [44 U.S.C. §3544]
Sensitive Information	Information, the loss, misuse, or unauthorized access to or modification of, that could adversely affect the national interest or the conduct of federal programs, or the privacy to which individuals are entitled under 5 U.S.C. §552a, but that has not been specifically authorized under criteria established by an Executive Order or an Act of Congress to be kept classified in the interest of national defense or foreign policy [CNSS]
Sensitivity	A measure of the importance assigned to information by its owner, for the purpose of denoting its need for protection [CNSS]
Service Level Agreement	Defines the specific responsibilities of the service provider and sets the customer expectations [CNSS]
Situational Awareness	With a volume of time and space, the perception of an enterprise's security posture and its threat environment; the comprehension or meaning of both taken together (risk); and the projection of their status into the near future [CNSS]
Software	Computer programs and associated data that may be dynamically written or modified during execution [CNSS]
Software Assurance	Level of confidence that software is free from vulnerabilities, either intentionally designed into the software or accidentally inserted at any time during its lifecycle and that the software functions in the intended manner [CNSS]
Subsystem	A major subdivision or component of an information system consisting of information, information technology, and personnel that performs one or more specific functions [NIST]
Supplementation	The process of adding security controls or control enhancements to a security control baseline in order to adequately meet the organization's risk management needs [NIST]

Term	Definition [Source]
Strong Authentication	The requirement to use multiple factors for authentication and advanced technology, such as dynamic passwords or digital certificates, to verify an entity's identity
System	Any organized assembly of resources and procedures united and regulated by interaction or interdependence to accomplish a set of specific functions [CNSS]
System Development Life Cycle	The scope of activities associated with a system, encompassing the system's initiation, development and acquisition, implementation, operation and maintenance, and ultimately its disposal that instigates another system initiation [CNSS]
System Interconnection	The direct connection of two or more information systems for the purpose of sharing data and other information resources [CNSS]
System of Records	A group of any records under the control of any agency from which information is retrieved by the name of the individual or by some identifying number, symbol, or other identifying particular assigned to the individual [5 U.S.C. §552a(a)(5)]
System Owner	Person or organization having responsibility for the development, procurement, integration, modification, operation and maintenance, and/or final disposition of an information system [CNSS]
System Security Plan	Formal document that provides an overview of the security requirements for an information system or an information security program and describes the security controls in place or planned for meeting those requirements [NIST]
System-Specific Control	A security control for an information system that has not been designated as a common control or the portion of a hybrid control that is to be implemented within an information system [NIST]
Tailoring	The process by which a security control baseline is modified based on: (i) the application of scoping guidance; (ii) the specification of compensating security controls, if needed; and (iii) the specification of organization-defined parameters in the security controls via explicit assignment and selection statements [NIST]
Tailored Security Control Baseline	A set of security controls resulting from the application of tailoring guidance to the security control baseline [NIST]
Technical Controls	Security controls for an information system that are primarily implemented and executed by the information system through mechanisms contained in the hardware, software, or firmware components of the system [NIST]

Term	Definition [Source]
Threat	Any circumstance or event with the potential to adversely impact organizational operations (including mission, functions, image, or reputation), organizational assets, individuals, other organizations, or the Nation through an information system via unauthorized access, destruction, disclosure, modification of information, and/or denial of service [CNSS]
Threat Assessment	Process of formally evaluating the degree of threat to an information system or enterprise and describing the nature of the threat [CNSS]
Threat Monitoring	Analysis, assessment, and review of audit trails and other information collected for the purpose of searching out system events that may constitute violations of system security [CNSS]
Threat Source	The intent and method targeted at the intentional exploitation of a vulnerability or a situation and method that may accidentally exploit a vulnerability [CNSS]
Trusted Computer System	A system that employs sufficient hardware and software assurance measures to allow its use for processing simultaneously a range of sensitive or classified information [CNSS]
Trustworthiness	The attribute of a person or enterprise that provides confidence to others of the qualifications, capabilities, and reliability of that entity to perform specific tasks and fulfill assigned responsibilities [CNSS]
US-CERT	A partnership between the Department of Homeland Security and the public and private sectors, established to protect the nation's internet infrastructure, that coordinates defense against and responses to cyber attacks across the nation [CNSS]
Vulnerability	Weakness in an information system, system security procedures, internal controls, or implementation that could be exploited by a threat source [CNSS]
Vulnerability Assessment	Systematic examination of an information system or product to determine the adequacy of security measures, identify security deficiencies, provide data from which to predict the effectiveness of proposed security measures, and confirm the adequacy of such measures after implementation [CNSS]

Index

Note: Page numbers followed by "f" and "t" indicate figures and tables respectively